# FEDERAL FURNITURE

I

# AMERICAN FURNITURE

## *The Federal Period*

in the Henry Francis du Pont Winterthur Museum

A Winterthur Book
by *Charles F. Montgomery*

Foreword by *Henry Francis du Pont*

With photographs by *Gilbert Ask*

BONANZA BOOKS
New York

*To Joseph Downs*

*who, through his writing, exhibitions,*
*and collecting from 1929 through 1954, was*
*the fountainhead of information for all students*
*of American furniture.*

Copyright MCMLXXVIII in all countries
of the International Copyright Union
by The Henry Francis du Pont
Winterthur Museum, Inc.

Library of Congress Catalog Card Number: 66-19411
All rights reserved.
This edition is published by Bonanza Books,
a division of Crown Publishers, Inc.,
by arrangement with The Viking Press, Inc.
a  b  c  d  e  f  g  h
Bonanza 1978 Printing

# Contents

# Foreword

In January of 1949 Joseph Downs and Charles Montgomery began the preparation of a series of books on the furniture in my collection. Already there had been many requests for information about particular pieces; and, because books had been so helpful to me in my collecting, I wanted to make my collection available to others through them. This seemed especially important since many collectors might never get to Winterthur, and besides one needs books for study in his own home.

When I decided in 1950 to establish and open the Winterthur Museum as soon as possible, it delayed the work on the books. Nevertheless, in 1952 *American Furniture of the Queen Anne and Chippendale Periods* was completed by Mr. Downs and published. It was scholarly and it went beyond anything attempted previously in a furniture book. Mr. Downs set forth clearly for the first time the regional characteristics of American furniture of the two periods, and every piece was illustrated. Mr. Downs began work immediately on the second furniture book, but there were many demands on his time as curator of the Museum, and progress was slow. It came to a halt with his untimely death in 1954. Mr. Montgomery, as executive secretary of the Museum and after Mr. Downs' death as director, was busily engaged in the day-to-day operation of the Museum and teaching in the Winterthur Program in Early American Culture.

Following ill health in 1959, Mr. Montgomery asked to be relieved of his duties as director to devote his time to writing and teaching. His successor, Mr. Edgar P. Richardson, formerly director of the Detroit Institute of Arts, has taken many steps to strengthen and speed up the Museum's publication program, for he feels as I do that an important part of a museum's role as an educational institution is the regular publication of books.

Furniture of the Federal period has always interested me greatly. In 1929 I had the good fortune to acquire ten pieces of furniture made in 1807 for William Bayard of New York, together with their original bill from Duncan Phyfe. In the following year, I got the labeled desk by John Seymour & Son which is the frontispiece of this book. The Phyfe chairs and the desk pleased me especially because they were not only fine furniture; they were identified. I particularly like small pieces with good lines. They may sometimes lack inlay and carving, but in their simplicity they often achieve greatness.

Over the years, I have bought many pieces of American furniture in the Hepplewhite and Sheraton styles for the furnishing of rooms, and I am pleased to see them brought together in this book, which ought to set a new standard for furniture books in 1966 just as Mr. Downs' book did in 1952. In the past ten years, great advances have been made to assist the scholar, curator, and writer. At Winterthur the library of printed books has been built up with great effort. There are now probably more original records and copies of records dealing with cabinetmaking in the manuscript collection established in Joseph Downs' memory than he had a chance to use in his lifetime. Photographs of documented objects in other collections are being gathered and indexed. Microscopic analyses of woods is another great help, as are the increasing number of good articles being written and published each year on individual cabinetmakers. Mr. Montgomery has used all these resources to assign a given piece to a city or maker.

Often he lets the words of people who were there in the early 1800's tell the story. Sometimes their old words like "lolling chair" are better than our new ones. Such fresh discoveries from old information are included in the five introductory chapters, the twenty articles summarizing each of the furniture forms, and the captions for the 491 pieces of Winterthur furniture—many published here for the first time. Especially interesting to me are the charts of woods and the handsome colored illustrations of inlays and room settings. I find them fascinating. These make this book really an encyclopaedia of the furniture of the early years of the United States.

HENRY FRANCIS DU PONT

# Acknowledgments

Joseph Downs, Winterthur's first curator, knew more about the broad field of American arts than any other man of his time. Scholar at heart, with a love of and respect for learning, he was careful in observation, exact in statement, and he wrote out of long experience. I learned a great deal from him.

Before his death in 1954, Joseph Downs had written tentative drafts for some two hundred captions of pieces included here. When I began the preparation of this book in 1961, these helped me greatly. But, alas, I could not bring them to completion for publication. Mr. Downs's observations were based on his experience, and I did not have the specific information on which he based his comments. Also, in the intervening seven years and those that have followed, new resources provided information not available in 1954: microscopic identification of woods; furniture exhibitions with new discoveries; new publications; and increased library holdings of manuscripts and books, among them, hitherto unknown cabinet-makers' price books. I began anew, following an approach that had been largely shaped by my experience in teaching in the Winterthur Program at the Winterthur Museum and the University of Delaware. Because all too often I could not find the "why" for statements I found in furniture books, I determined to include not only when, where, what, who, and how, but why—with a generous number of footnotes citing the sources of information.

For support and patience in this undertaking, I thank the Board of Trustees of the Henry Francis du Pont Winterthur Museum. For their confidence in my ability to write this book, I am grateful to Lammot du Pont Copeland, president of the Museum, and to Dr. Edgar P. Richardson, its director.

Many, many people from the staff at Winterthur and others from all over the country have helped me. Among those who ought to be singled out are: Gordon K. Saltar, for perseverance in analyzing thousands of wood samples; Florence M. Montgomery, for her chapter on "Upholstery and Furnishing Fabrics," and for assistance in textile identification; Charles F. Hummel, for reading much of the manuscript and for endless checking of facts; Jonathan L. Fairbanks, who made the colored drawings of stringing and the layouts for the color plates of inlays; Nancy A. Goyne, who was a feminine Sherlock Holmes in finding needed information; Ian M. G. Quimby and his assistant, Mrs. Carl Schlatter, for their unfailing good humor and cooperation in supplying information from Museum records; Mrs. Gail Belden for information about billiards and the billiard table; John A. H. Sweeney, curator, for a thousand courtesies and for reading a part of the manuscript.

I can never repay the members of the Winterthur library staff: especially Helen R. Belknap, librarian of printed books; Mrs. Charles B. Wood, III, librarian of the Joseph Downs Manuscript and Microfilm Collection; and Mr. and Mrs. John J. Evans, Jr., of the Decorative Arts Photographic Collection. This group and others, under the direction of Dr. Frank H. Sommer, have created resources upon which I was highly dependent. Of good heart and with enthusiasm, they brought things to my attention about which I would not otherwise have known. Two former members of the library staff sought answers from old records and correspondence: M. Elinor Betts as the first librarian of the Joseph Downs Manuscript and Microfilm Collection, and as editorial assistant, was like a right hand in the early stages of research. A. Chapin Rogers was always patient with my requests. The assistance of Miss Ruth P. McCollum and Mrs. Henry H. Skomorucha of Mr. du Pont's office was invaluable.

Several Winterthur Fellows have supplied information or assisted in specific research while students, or immediately following graduation: Robert F. Brown, Joseph T. Butler, Mr. and Mrs. Cary Carson, Anne Castrodale, Martha Gandy Fales, John C. Freeman, Wendell D. Garrett, John H. Hill, Marilynn A. Johnson, Edward F. LaFond,

Jr., G. Carroll Lindsay, Milo M. Naeve, Rodris Roth, David B. Warren, Richard J. Webster.

I am grateful to scholars in other institutions who have come to my assistance on numerous occasions: specifically to Kathryn C. Buhler, Museum of Fine Arts, Boston; E. Milby Burton, Charleston Museum; Mrs. Florence R. Calderwood, Patten Free Library; Clarkson A. Collins, 3rd, and Mrs. Clifford P. Monahon, Rhode Island Historical Society; Edward H. Feltus, III, Monmouth County Historical Society; Catherine Fennelly, Old Sturbridge Village; Mary Glaze and Frances Gruber, Metropolitan Museum of Art; Thompson R. Harlow, Connecticut Historical Society; Walter J. Heacock and Norman B. Wilkinson, Hagley Museum; Ralph Hill, Shelburne Museum; J. W. Joyce, Schenectady Historical Society; J. Barry Lord, New Brunswick Museum, Canada; Susan Parsons, Boston Athenaeum; Norman S. Rice, Albany Institute of History and Art; Margaret Stearns and V. Isabelle Miller, Museum of the City of New York; Charles C. Wall, Mount Vernon; Edwin P. Wolf, II, The Library Company, Philadelphia. For special information and invaluable aid, I am indebted to Houghton Bulkeley, Mrs. Albert H. Chase, Wendell Hilt, Charles N. Mellowes, John C. Mogridge, M. Jean O'Connell, Charles S. Parsons, Helen McKearin Powers, Mrs. Cecil Rowland, E. Weyhe, and A. E. Wooderson.

The following dealers have brought unusual pieces to my attention and supplied photographs which have been extremely useful for comparative purposes: Harry Arons, George and Ben Arons, Edgar Bingham, Philip Bradley, George Considine, Mr. and Mrs. Rockwell Gardiner, O. D. Garland, Mr. and Mrs. Carl Jacobs, Miss Katrina Kipper, Mr. and Mrs. Edgar Sittig, and John S. Walton. Especially, I appreciate the interest and help of Benjamin Ginsburg, John E. Walton, Joseph Lionetti, Albert Sack, and David Stockwell. Each, a student at heart, spent many hours discussing specific problems and searching out information and photographs to help me in making attributions.

For reading parts of the manuscript, I am indebted to Dean A. Fales, Jr., John J. Evans, Jr., Dr. E. McClung Fleming, Albert Sack, David Stockwell, Robert Robinson, and Charles F. Mont-gomery, Jr. The latter was also a mainstay in the preparation of the sections on clocks and fancy furniture.

Gilbert Ask made more than five hundred black-and-white photographs and color transparencies of individual objects and room settings used for illustrations. It gives me pleasure to record the invaluable assistance of two others: Geoffrey Clements photographed most of the carved details and labels. By means of infrared films, he skillfully made discolored labels readable. Both Mr. Clements and Joan M. Kriszat, who prepared the index, cheerfully worked long hours to meet deadlines.

Two people who have worked with me daily for the past three years have been stalwart. I thank them: Catherine A. Hull, my secretary, for bringing this manuscript through five drafts, from penned scrawl to legible typescript; and Mrs. Robert L. Kroll, my editorial assistant, for painstaking and never-ceasing alertness against error and blunder.

The chasm between the "last draft" with photographs and a beautifully printed book is immense. No writer has ever been more privileged than I in having sympathetic, dedicated, talented editors and designers. This publication has benefitted greatly from the gifted editorial hand of John D. Morse, head of the National Extension Program at Winterthur and general editor of Winterthur publications. My warm thanks go to the following members of Chanticleer Press: Milton Rugoff, editor, for wisdom and "know-how"; to Ulrich Ruchti for the sheer brilliance of the book's overall design; and to Susan Grafman for unending patience on a thousand details and for a blue pencil with a sharp point. The printers, Conzett and Huber, set type with their minds as well as their hands. On proofs that were works of art, the mistakes were mine not theirs.

Would that my words were better able to capture the spirit of the furniture here brought together in the image of Henry Francis du Pont. In his many-sidedness, he is a Renaissance man: agriculture, nature, and the arts are his domain. For five years, his furniture has been my world—a hard one for my wife, a happy one for me.

CHARLES F. MONTGOMERY

# Introduction

Sweeping changes in American cabinetmaking and furniture styles closely parallel the emergence and coalescence of the thirteen American colonies into one nation. As self-reliant individuals and as craftsmen able to turn their hands to any task, some cabinetmakers, such as Stephen Badlam, held important posts as leaders in the Revolutionary Army; others, including David Evans, made tents and a hundred other necessities for the American forces. After the peace, and during the forty years now generally called the Federal era (variously described by historians as "The Completion of Independence" (Dixon Ryan Fox), "The Nation Takes Shape" (Marcus Cunliffe), and "The Federal Age" (Keith Berwick), the United States, still primarily an agricultural country, became increasingly concerned with manufacturing, commerce, and trade. American cabinetmakers were quick to take advantage of the opportunities in this time of growth and expansion as new markets for new products were created.

The first intimation of the stylistic changes which were about to occur in American furniture is found in the small desk upon which Thomas Jefferson wrote the Declaration of Independence in 1776. The line inlay in this small writing box (now in the Smithsonian Institution) made by Benjamin Randolph in Philadelphia was a harbinger of the neoclassical styles that became current almost immediately after the adoption of the Federal Constitution in 1788. The new nation was receptive to new ideas. Chippendale furniture was now old fashioned in London (still the fashion capital for America) as clearly set forth by Archibald Alison in his *Essays on the Nature and Principles of Taste* (1790):

"...Strong and Massy Furniture is everywhere vulgar and unpleasing.

"Some years ago every article of furniture was made in what was called the Chinese Taste.... To this succeeded the Gothic Taste.... The Taste which now reigns is that of the Antique. Everything we now use, is made in imitation of those models which have been lately discovered in Italy."

This was the result of the revolution in taste set in motion in the 1760's by Robert Adam and his brothers whose innovations and designs incorporating classical ornament and emphasizing linear relationships had a profound effect upon architecture and every art and craft in England after about 1770. Although old forms lingered on, new patterns appeared each year thereafter in London cabinet shops. Usually these were known in the trade by the name of their craftsmen inventors, viz. "Buckley's pattern," "Curwen's pattern," et al. Although to the public in this country and apparently in London the styles were anonymous, they were summarized and illustrated in *The London Cabinet-Makers' Book of Prices* (for workmanship) and Hepplewhite's *The Cabinet-Maker and Upholsterer's Guide*. Both were published in 1788! These two books and those of Thomas Sheraton published slightly later gave currency to the new styles in the United States. The book of prices which appears to have been widely used listed rates of pay for making all standard furniture forms with innumerable optional details. They thus provided the basics of form and ornament with wide latitude for individual interpretation. When in the 1790's American price books incorporating demands for higher rates were published, the idea of Federal strength through union was not forgotten by the workmen. Imbued with the idea of freedom, the journeymen's societies, really unions, appealed to their fellows in other cities and other crafts for support. In New York they even modeled their plea on the Declaration of Independence!

It is not easy to find a satisfactory name for these anonymous fashions in furniture which evolved for the most part in the shops of the cabinetmakers. As a result of the publications associated with the names of George and Alice Hepplewhite and Thomas Sheraton, the name of Hepplewhite has often been applied to the delicate inlaid and carved furniture with essentially linear forms of the 1780's and the early 1790's, and the name of Sheraton has been used to designate furniture first made about 1790, often employing turned or reeded supports and frequently with bowed (eliptic) and/or hollowed façades. However, these names are confusing because there is considerable overlap in the styles associated with the two men— as would be expected since their books were issued at approximately the same time, and if, as I strongly suspect, both men were primarily reporters rather than creators of original styles. Unquestionably their books played an important part in the "broadcasting" and dissemination of London fashions, but I doubt that many of them were original to either Hepplewhite or Sheraton. This is a question that deserves a great deal of further study.

In the catalogue I have used whenever possible the names actually used by the cabinetmakers themselves, and have attempted to approximate the actual dates of manufacture for each piece. I believe that the term "Federal furniture" is appropriate for these pieces. In Philadelphia, and perhaps elsewhere, furniture was made by "The Federal Society of Cabinetmakers," and many pieces of the period were carved or inlaid with the American eagle, symbol of the Federal union. Also appropriately for furniture with ornament and sometimes forms derived from Greek and Roman sources, the term Federal seems to have embodied more than a little of classical idea and ideal in a country where the study of the classics and a knowledge of Greek and Latin were basic ingredients of higher education and where the "Grand Federal Edifice" in the Philadelphia Federal Procession was conceived as a domed temple supported by thirteen Corinthian columns.

It might be assumed that American furniture, having been modeled on English furniture, is like English furniture. It is not. Many facets of American government are modeled on English institutions. Few would say they are imitations. They are indeed new syntheses. This is also true of American furniture; the differences are subtle. Many of the parts are similar, but they are combined in different ways and often in different proportions.

American furniture has stood the test of time. Thousands of pieces have survived in American families, and much more probably exists scattered unrecognized over the face of the globe. This study is based on about one thousand pieces in the Winterthur collection, 491 of which are included and illustrated in the catalogue. To understand any one of these pieces of furniture, one must understand the organization of the crafts which produced it, the materials employed, local preferences for ornament and decoration, and other information not readily available. Over the last one hundred and fifty years, many original names for furniture forms have been lost, and the functions which they were to serve obscured. My findings on these subjects have been summarized in five introductory chapters, and in twenty short introductory essays on the various forms. The 127 details of colored inlays (colorplates 2–7), the details of carving, and the two charts showing local use of woods are an initial attempt to plot regional preferences and practice.

As I have indicated in the Acknowledgments, this study encompasses the work of many people, but in its final form it has been my responsibility. Necessarily, every page involves value judgments. Some, like the furniture, may stand the test of time; others may be revised, for it must be remembered that although the study of American arts is in its infancy, it is in a healthy state. Like architecture, furniture is a universal; and, as such, it deserves much further study. The furniture in this book stands not only as an affirmation of the taste and connoisseurship of Henry Francis du Pont, it attests to the validity of Hector St. John de Crevecœur's observation on the American people in the early years of their independence: "They will habitually prefer the useful to the beautiful, and they will require that the beautiful should be useful."

# The Business of Cabinetmaking

The remarkable fact about cabinetmaking in America is that each native workman learned his trade through an apprenticeship supervised not by a guild but under the general surveillance of civil authorities. Basic attitudes toward the responsibilities and capabilities of craftsmen as "artists in their trade," as being able "to take charge of others for government and manual instruction in their occupations," as being responsible citizens, and as contributing to the welfare of their communities are revealed in an edict of a Boston Town Meeting in 1660.

> Whereas it is found by sad experience that many youths in this Town, being put forth Apprentices to several manufactures and sciences, for but 3 or 4 years time, contrary to the Customs of all well governed places, whence they are uncapable of being Artists in their trade, besides their unmeetness at the expiration of their Apprenticeship to take charge of others for government and manual instruction in their occupations, which, if not timely amended, threatens the welfare of this Town, it is therefore ordered that no person shall henceforth open a shop in this Town, nor occupy any manufacture or science, till he hath completed 21 years of age, nor except he hath served seven years Apprentice-ship, by testimony under the hands of sufficient witnesses. And that all Indentures made between any master and servant shall be brought in and enrolled in the Town's Records within one month after the contract made, on penalty of ten shillings to be paid by the master at the time of the Apprentices being made free.[1]

Such views continued to be held throughout the eighteenth and well into the nineteenth century, with apprenticeship indentures regarded as legal contracts, required by law to be registered with the local government.

However, it has been conclusively shown that the period of apprenticeship in Philadelphia (and probably elsewhere) became progressively shorter toward the end of the eighteenth century.[2] The shortening of the training period, coupled with larger shops and more apprentices in training, increased the number of journeymen available for furniture production. But the market for furniture was also expanding in a new nation—rapidly growing in population as well as in wealth. Cabinetmakers flocked here from England, Ireland, Scotland; after 1800, a number came from France.

In the seventeenth and early eighteenth century, the joiner—that is, one skilled in the craft of joining wood—not only made furniture but worked on the construction and finishing of dwellings. He made doors, sash, interior woodwork, and sometimes framed buildings. Despite the fact that, as early as 1714, Samuel Sewall refers to "Howell the cabinetmaker [who] takes down the closet that stands in the corner to make way for the window," the term joiner continued to be used to some extent, especially in rural areas throughout the eighteenth century in America: and it is significant that in the tax rolls prepared in 1772 by the Philadelphia cabinetmaker William Savery all cabinetmakers are listed as joiners.[3]

The work of the cabinetmaker, like the work of the joiner, was many-sided. It included the making and repairing of furniture, and a great variety of odd jobs of a service nature such as the putting up and taking down of beds and the hanging of looking glasses. Often in cabinetmakers' account books, especially those of rural craftsmen, there are as many or more entries for repairs than for new pieces of furniture. Repairs were also a part of the normal work of the larger shops located in the cities. It appears, for instance, that while 120 new pieces were made in the shop of Samuel Ashton of Philadelphia in the year 1801, repairs were made to seventy pieces of old furniture.[4]

One cabinetmaker might, and in rural areas apparently did, make and finish with his own hands chairs, tables, chests of drawers, and a variety of other forms. However, in the larger cities several distinct craft divisions emerged during the eighteenth century. It is, of course, conceivable that journeymen cabinetmakers, chairmakers, turners, upholsterers, inlay makers, and carvers and gilders might have worked together all under one roof as was apparently the case of the New York cabinet shop of Duncan Phyfe in the nineteenth century; here, it is said, more than one hundred men were at times employed.[5] But actually most of these operations seem to have been carried on in independent shops frequently located near one another. After 1790 the major craft divisions were:

*Cabinet- and chairmakers* usually worked together in one establishment. Occasionally the individual journeyman specialized in a particular activity such as the making of chairs or case pieces.

*Inlay makers,* were specialists of whom little is known as yet, but in Boston, New York, Philadelphia, and Baltimore there were men with substantial stocks of inlays for sale, some of which they made and some of which may have been imported.

*Carvers and gilders* made frames for prints and pictures and some looking glasses. They also did carving and gilding for others, and after 1790 they produced much composition work and many more looking glasses than previously.

*Turners* frequently specialized in the making of turned slat-back, Windsor, and fancy chairs, and turned wood, metal, and ivory for others.

*Upholsterers* sometimes made their own chair frames and bedsteads. More often they bought them to be upholstered and sold in their warerooms. Custom work for cabinet- and chairmakers was also done by them.

Such specialization was always greatest in the cities. Although it began in England in the seventeenth century, for several reasons it was slower to develop and was never as rigid in America. Because of the lack of guilds supervising individual crafts, because of the great shortage of highly skilled artisans, and perhaps because of their desire to accumulate the capital necessary to move upward into the merchant class, many craftsmen practiced related trades and participated in trading "adventures" of various kinds. Hence, more often than not, they probably did their own turning, carving, and, on occasion, upholstering and gilding, prior to the middle of the eighteenth century. About that time several factors operated to increase specialization among craftsmen. The rapidly increasing population created new demands for furniture at home, and expanding sea trade offered new markets all up and down the coast, particularly in the South and West Indies. These opportunities

were seized by the larger shops staffed by both native and immigrant journeymen.

Although the pattern of development is clear, sufficient records have not as yet come to the attention of the writer to document completely the growth and specialization of the earlier period; but several books have touched upon cabinetmaking in the American colonies prior to the Revolution; notably, Joseph Downs' *American Furniture of the Queen-Anne and Chippendale Periods* and William MacPherson Hornor's *Blue Book of Philadelphia Furniture.* But to date no writer has produced a study in depth of the organization and conduct of the woodworking crafts in colonial America.[6] Too little is known of the working methods of the earlier cabinetmakers to enable one to chart exactly the changes as they took place, but it seems reasonable to suppose that in such large city shops as those of Thomas Affleck, Benjamin Randolph, Thomas Tuffts, and William Savery in Philadelphia, of the Burlings in New York City, and in such family enterprises as those of the Townsends and Goddards in Newport specialization began.

Important information on the business of cabinetmaking in Charleston, South Carolina, is provided by the account book of Thomas Elfe for the years 1768 to 1775. Though covering only eight years of Elfe's work, it contains a vital part of his records and shows that, in addition to his four slave sawyers and five slave joiners and cabinetmakers, he occasionally employed other journeymen and cabinetmakers to produce some 1,502 pieces of furniture during this period. As early as 1751, Elfe advertised that "having now a very good upholsterer from London," [he, Elfe,]

> does all kinds of upholsterer's work, in the best and newest manner, and at the most reasonable rates, viz: tapestry, damask, stuff, chints, or paper hangings for rooms; beds after the newest fashion, and so they may be taken off to be washed without inconvenience or damage; all sorts of festoons and window curtains to draw up, and pully rod curtains; chairs stuff covered, tight or loose cases for ditto; All kinds of Machine Chairs are likewise made, stuffed and covered for sickly or weak people, and all sorts of cabinet work done in the best manner, by the said Thomas Elfe.

And in 1756 Elfe seems to have had a turner in his shop; he and his partner, Thomas Hutchinson, made some of the balusters to be used on the steeple of St. Michael's Church.[7] Elfe's shop may not have been the first of the larger and more diversified cabinetmaking establishments, but it anticipated what was to become a pattern for the East Coast cabinetmaking trade in the late eighteenth century—large-scale production that spread inland with the growth of the country to Cincinnati, Pittsburgh, Albany, and probably to many other cities by the third and fourth decades of the nineteenth century. After 1783 cabinetmaking grew rapidly, and by 1820 the craft became a business.

This trend from craft to business began earlier. To name but two of many such instances: the Philadelphia chair- and cabinetmaker, Solomon Fussell, master of William Savery, gravitated to merchandising after many years as a craftsman; Joshua Delaplaine engaged in shipping adventures frequently during his fifty years of activity as a cabinetmaker in New York City, and at his death in 1771 he was listed as a merchant. The reason for this trend is not hard to find if one studies the nature of the enterprise and the position of the master cabinetmaker. Both Fussell and Delaplaine maintained close relationships with apprentices and journeymen after these men had left their employ. Reference after reference in their accounts indicate that they furnished tools, lumber, hardware, and other supplies to men who were formerly associated with them. From former employees and others they received payment in money, in kind, and in labor to work off debts. On occasion Delaplaine sold the furniture of others, including that of the Quaker cabinetmaker Christopher Townsend of Newport, Rhode Island. His shipping ventures brought profit both in cash and goods to be sold. Entrepreneurship seems to have been a part of the spirit of the times in that it offered ample opportunity for the accumulation of wealth and rise in status. As has been well shown by Louis Wright[8] and others, the natural trend in this open American society was for rising craftsmen to aspire and gravitate toward the aristocracy of the merchant class.

The work cycle of a cabinetmaker normally started with apprenticeship at the age of fourteen to sixteen. Upon its termination at twenty-one, or sometimes earlier, the former apprentice went to work as a journeyman on piecework and/or wages. After that he may have worked for many shops in the course of a few years. When he had accumulated enough money to set up in business on his own as a cabinetmaker, he may have worked by himself for a short time or entered into a partnership with another cabinetmaker or an upholsterer; but in all likelihood he soon took an apprentice.

Many newspaper notices by cabinetmakers announce the formation or dissolution of partnerships. Often their advertisements end: "An apprentice wanted." His apprentice worked six days a week. He received his woods from another cabinetmaker, a lumber yard, or a sawmill on credit or open account. He fashioned furniture and did his own stringing, inlaying, veneering, and finishing. In a larger city, he may often have purchased his inlays ready-made from a specialist such as Thomas Barrett of Baltimore,[9] who apparently had an extremely large business with the furniture-making trade, for among his thirty debtors, fifteen can be identified as cabinetmakers. Some stringing and ornamental inlays were probably imported. Richard Wevill, "Upholsterer, opposite Congress Hall, in Chesnut street," Philadelphia, advertised in 1799 "an assortment of Stringing, &c. for Cabinet-makers" along with "fine Sattin-wood, tulip wood, and purple wood Veneers." In the same advertisement, he asserts that "having conducted the above business [upholsterer] in two of the principal houses in that line in London, for near twenty years, [he] flatters himself he is capable of giving satisfaction" and offers "Window Cornices manufactured in the newest taste, gilt or painted, to suit the furniture; brass and iron rods and staples for stairs, carpeting, Venetian blinds, &c." Although he intimates that those items were made by him, he does state that he has "Just imported in the Active, from London, and for sale at his house, No. 32, south Fifth street, a quanity of Hair Seating, Gold Leaf, Composition, Glass Paper, Sattin Wood and Mahogany Knife Cases."[10]

The beginning cabinetmaker probably worked part of the time on a piecework basis for other shops when he did not have orders for furniture from householders; but, as he prospered and his business grew, he hired a journeyman to work for him. The records of the Philadelphia cabinetmaker, Samuel Ashton, for 1795–1803, give a good picture of the organization of one shop.

The cabinetmaker near the coast or a waterway used mahogany as his principal wood. If inland, as at Pittsburgh in the 1790's or early 1800's, he used instead the local walnut, a wood so popular in Pennsylvania that as late as 1786 Benjamin Lehman's survey[11] of the prices charged by Philadelphia cabinetmakers lists the selling price for each furniture form in both mahogany and walnut. The wood of the wild cherry tree was popular everywhere and especially so in Connecticut and the Connecticut River Valley, where it vied with mahogany as the principal wood for cabinetwork.

He probably sent his upholstery work, turning, and carving out for others to do. He could easily make mahogany or walnut frames for looking glasses without gilt, carved, or composition ornaments. If such ornaments were needed, he could acquire them on open account from the looking-glass maker, who specialized in carving and gilding. In return the cabinetmaker supplied mahogany frames, swingers, or dressing glasses to be ornamented and fitted with glass.

Tools and hardware, including nails, screws, hinges, locks, and furniture brasses, often came from a larger cabinetmaker or hardware merchant who, in most cases, had imported them from England. As yet, not much is known about manufacture of hardware in this country. Unquestionably some hardware was made here, but local metal craftsmen probably could not supply ten per cent of the needs.[12]

As the business in a shop grew, the owner-cabinetmaker became more and more of a businessman. He bought the lumber—mahogany, cherry, maple, pine, and other secondary woods—the veneers, the furniture mounts, the stains and varnishes, and dealt with the customers. He placed advertisements in the newspapers, he paid the help, and kept the books, and on occasion took a "flyer" at sending out a cargo of venture furniture. He was responsible for the standard set by his shop, and in the words of one famous cabinetmaker concerning his "Useful and Ornamental Cabinet Furniture," it was "all made by, or under the immediate inspection of THOMAS SEYMOUR."[13] The shop owner's name was on the label that was glued to the furniture that went out of his shop regardless of whether he had made it personally or of how many men may have worked on it in his shop or in the shops of others. In a sense, the label on a piece of furniture was and is like a brand name on an article today.

From typical early and mid-eighteenth-century American cabinetmakers' advertisements, one may gain the impression that furniture was only made to order to fill the needs of a particular buyer, since advertisements often read, "makes and sells all kinds of cabinetwork, etc..." or "Manufactures all kinds of Cabinet-Work in the neatest manner and on the most moderate terms"[14] or "Notice is hereby given that all Persons may be supplied with all sorts of Joyner's and Cabinet-Maker's Work, as Desk and Book Cases, with Arch'd Pediment and O.G. Heads..."[15] But there are enough notices such as those that follow that are so specific as to show that some ready-made furniture was available in many shops throughout the eighteenth century. "George Miller, Joiner, In Chestnut-Street next Door to the Dolphin, Gives Notice, that he is about to leave off his Trade, and has a Quantity of Joiners Work, as Chairs, Tables, Desks, Chests of Drawers, &c. [Philadelphia, 1737]."[16]

George Houghton next to the Coffeehouse in Front Street, Philadelphia, gave notice that "...as he is going to decline the Cabinet Making business, he is determined to sell all his ready made Joiners Work on very low terms, or will exchange for other goods [Philadelphia, 1778]."[17]

This practice of stocking furniture reached a climax in the early nineteenth century with the rise of the furniture warehouse or warerooms. Such enterprises often made their own furniture, but apparently they frequently bought from cabinetmakers just as furniture stores do today. The stocking of furniture enabled the customer to fill his needs on the spot and the master cabinetmaker to keep his men busy through slack seasons. Typical of many advertisements is the following:

> Bankson & Lawson, in Light-Street [Baltimore, 1788], nearly opposite Mr. D. Grant's Fountain-Inn, continue to manufacture and sell every Article in the Line of their Business, in the most fashionable manner, and on moderate Terms. Their Ware-Room now contain a Variety of elegant and useful Furniture, *viz:* Mahogany Chairs of the most approved Patterns; Circular, Pier, and Card Tables, highly ornamented, and plain Ditto; Pembroke, or Breakfast Tables; complete Sets of Dining-Tables; Ward-robes ornamented and plain; Desks and Book Cases; Dressing Drawers; Commode and plain Side-Board Tables; Wine-coolers ornamented, and plain Ditto; Cabriole and plain Sofas; Easy Chairs, Bedsteads of various Prices, etc, etc.[18]

Many such advertisements end: "All orders, from town and country, will be thankfully received, and diligently attended to."[19] Others note: "Orders from the West-Indies, or any part of the Continent, will be thankfully attended to." On the banner carried by the "Windsor and Rush Chair Makers" in the New York Federal Procession of 1788 was shown "...a view of the river, several vessels bound to different parts" and the motto, "Free Trade. The Federal States in union bound, O'er all the world our chairs are found."[20] Exportation was a sales outlet that many shops relied upon. The Sandersons of Salem formed a combine which regularly entrusted furniture to ships' captains for sale wherever they could vend it to the best advantage—often by auction in Charleston, Savannah, or the West Indies. A famous example of such distribution is the secretary desk (No. 181) labeled by Nehemiah Adams of Salem. Found by Mr. du Pont in Capetown, South Africa, it apparently had been there since the early 1800's.

Other outlets, especially for beds and seating furniture, were the shops of upholsterers. Sometimes they employed their own woodworking journeyman and were in competition with cabinetmakers, but more often they seem to have bought frames to be upholstered and bedsteads to be fitted out with sacking bottoms or ropes, mattresses, and hangings.

The role of the upholsterer in America is one about which little is known. And the mystery will continue until upholsterers' accounts and records come to light. An intriguing Charleston advertisement of 1792 indicates the interrelationship of the two crafts and offers some evidence of interior decorating.

> Bradford, T., Clements, Henry.—Ladies and Gentlemen—T. Bradford, late of Church street, Upholsterer, and Henry Clements, Cabinet and Chair Maker, sensible how essentially necessary both branches are to be together to render either compleat, have entered into co-partnership, and most respectfully take this method to inform them they will undertake to furnish houses, in the most elegant and fashionable manner, and on far more reasonable terms than usual; and as they have a compleat knowledge of their separate branches, flatter themselves they will be able to give general satisfaction. Orders for sofas or chairs will be well and neatly executed; also all kinds of Cabinet furniture, on the shortest notice; second hand sofas or chairs restuffed and covered; all kinds of upholstery furniture made up, or old altered. Paper Hanging done in the neatest manner. Funerals Furnished, King street nearly opposite Price's alley.[21]

For a century or more joiners and cabinetmakers had been making coffins, but references to their conducting funerals seem to start about 1750 and increase in number with the passage of time. The above notice intimates that Bradford and Clements were prepared to conduct a business not unlike that of the English firm of Gillow and Company which was located in Lancaster, England, some two hundred miles out from London. This firm combined cabinetmaking, upholstering, and interior decorating; and its incomparable records covering almost two hundred years of activity from 1731 to well into the 1900's illuminate many aspects of the craft organization and practice for which no comparable American records are known. Of great interest is the fact that so many practices of this firm parallel those known to have been followed in America. Gillow's had warerooms, where they stocked ready-made furniture. They entrusted large quantities of furniture to ships' captains as venture cargo and often consigned shipments to merchants in other parts of England, in Teneriffe, and in Jamaica. They endured the same problems of collecting their bills that plagued their American colleagues. Their methods of doing business with distant customers and the role of this firm as interior decorators are fascinating. Occasionally, they furnished whole houses with furniture, window curtains, and carpets. Several sketches of various kinds of chairs, tables, chests, and other forms were submitted to the customer for each room with comments on what was new and fashionable both in furniture and fabrics.[22] That this practice was not unknown in America is indicated by these words in the advertisement of the Charleston cabinetmaker Peter Hall from London: "Gentlemen and ladies that please to favour him with commands, will be waited on with patterns of different kinds, and may depend on having their work finished and ornamented in the neatest and most satisfactory manner."[23]

These records also reveal their shop practice and methods of paying their employees. Theirs was a diversified shop with specialists—men who made more chairs or case pieces than other forms. Nevertheless some turning was sent out to other firms, and some carved parts of looking glasses were sent up from London ready for assembly with parts made in Lancaster. Their men were largely paid on a piecework basis. In fact, there is strong evidence that as early as the 1760's they had a working agreement with their journeymen as to the price to be paid for standard forms. In 1785, three years before the first *London Book of Prices* was published, they spelled out in great detail the prices to be paid journeymen for making each piece of furniture, with additional amounts for extras of various kinds including a wide variety of ornament.

In the Gillow account books covering payments to journeymen, there are repeated references to chair patterns such as Buckley's, Clifton's, Curwen's, Denison's, Edward's, Joseph's, Lloyd's, Lowther's, Montgomery's, St. Clair's, Stewarts's,

Suddell's, Warwick's, Whitby's, and Williams's pattern. Were these taken from the names of designers or cabinetmakers who introduced them, or from names of customers for whom the patterns were first made? Other names of a topical nature were easier to explain. These include Bonaparte, Herculaneum, Trafalgar, Wellington (with cannonball legs), and honeysuckle chairs (with an anthemion in the back).

As is noted at the beginning of the chapter on Unusual and Specialized Furniture, cabinetmakers occasionally made odd and special pieces to fill unusual requirements of their customers. But it is indeed difficult to ascertain what direct influence the taste of the customer generally had in shaping the designs and ornamentation of the furniture he bought. How often did he have furniture designed and ornamented to suit his taste? How often did the customer simply leave it to the cabinetmaker to supply furniture of the "newest fashion"? The following letter from Oakley Philpotts of Richmond, Virginia, to Samuel Payson, a cabinetmaker of Boston, not only documents three instances of furniture made in Boston for Virginia use but also the method used by one customer to describe his wants. For the most part, Mr. Philpotts asks for furniture such as he or his neighbor has had before. But one sentence is an enigma. What does he mean by "One Bureau Such as I[saac] W[hite] Bot of you, Say the front to be Veeneard with Sattin Wood with Same Kind Knobs." Does he want a bureau exactly like Isaac White's? Or does he want one of the size and shape of White's but veneered with satinwood? If the latter interpretation is correct, it is an example of the taste of the customer exerting itself.

Richmond March 28    1806

M.r Samuel Payson

D.r Sir being in Want of Some Firneture I take the Liberty to Request you to foward by first Vesele for this place the articles as p.r memo below--------that is to say
One Bed Stead of the Same make of Isaac Whites    One Bureau Such as I.W. Bot of you Say the front to be Veeneard with Sattin Wood with Same Kind Knobs    One p.r Card Tables Such a I had of you, one Wash Stand, one p.r Dining Tables Common Size    the Side Board you can Send also as p.r agreement--------Should you not have those articles on hand you may purchase them your Self or hand this to M.r Thomas White & Request him to purchase them for me    I shall allow either of you to Draw on me for the am.t at 60 Days Sight or pay you in flour at the 60 Day price as you please

which Shall be shiped p.r the Vesell that you Ship the firneture in
Please to Send them as Low as possible & make the freight before they are Shiped    please present my Compliments to M.r T.White and family
Yours with Respect
OAKLEY PHILPOTTS

P.S. You will oblige me by Letting me hear from [you] by the first mail.
O.P.

Although the exportation of furniture from New England, especially to the South, is well known, little has been published on the substantial shipments of furniture to Baltimore, Virginia, the Carolinas, and Georgia from New York and Philadelphia. And, virtually unexplored are the fashions associated with particular centers. A tantalizing advertisement in *The Federal Gazette and Baltimore Advertiser* (June 28, 1817) by the Baltimore Carpet, Furniture and Looking Glass Ware House offers "Sideboards of Boston, New York and Baltimore style." It is evident that most cabinetmakers were well aware of current London fashions, and at least one instance of private ownership of a book of patterns (probably English) is known. In the letters of Eliza Southgate Bowne (*A Girl's Life Eighty Years Ago,* 1887, p. 203), mention is made of choosing articles to be made after patterns "in our own furniture book."

As will be shown in the chapter on Price Books, there existed in the late eighteenth and early nineteenth centuries a "language of workmanship" among cabinetmakers throughout the English-speaking world. This common understanding of forms and methods of fabrication (codified in the price books) made piecework possible.

The piecework system may have been partly responsible for the comparatively short terms of employment of most journeymen cabinetmakers. They seem to have moved from shop to shop and city to city, working for other or setting up for themselves as opportunity offered. This moving about spread new styles rapidly. To name but a few of many instances, Oliver Pomroy, then of Northampton, Massachusetts, advertised that "as he has worked two or three years in the city of Philadelphia, and is acquainted with the newest fashion ... he flatters himself that he shall give satisfaction to all those who favor him with their custom." [24] Edward Johnson, cabinetmaker, late from Philadelphia, advertised in the *Charleston Gazette* in 1796 that "he has opened a Ware-Room in Meeting-street [Charleston, South Carolina] where he has for sale, A General Assortment of

Modern and Elegant Cabinet Work, finished in a style of Elegance and Neatness that surpasses anything of the kind, hitherto offered for Sale in this City."[25] In Hanover, New Hampshire, Samuel Cutter advertised on March 8, 1815, in the *Dartmouth Gazette* that "Being lately from Salem, he will endeavor to make furniture of the newest fashion [for] those who will please to favor him with their custom with any kind of Cabinet-Work of Mahogany, or wood the produce of this Country."

The publication in rapid succession in the late eighteenth century of cabinetmakers' books of prices with illustrations, George Hepplewhite's *The Cabinet-Maker and Upholsterer's Drawing Book*, Thomas Sheraton's *The Cabinet-Maker and Upholsterer's Drawing Book*, and George Smith's *Collection of Designs for Household Furniture and Interior Decoration*, provided cabinetmakers outside of London with reports of London fashions. For the most part, it seems that each of these books must have performed somewhat the same service for the furniture maker and buyer as do *Vogue, Harper's Bazaar, Town and Country* and other fashion magazines in keeping the New York garment manufacturer and the American woman *au courant* with Paris fashions today. They reported what was in vogue and what was to be seen in the shops.[26] High-style furniture with much ornament was illustrated, but there was often a note in the text indicating possibilities of simplification. Of a sofa with carved tablet and flanking scrolls above the rail, Sheraton suggests, "If the top rail be thought to have too much work, it can be finished in a straight rail."[27] Although one can find innumerable early reference to price books, the writer has been unable to locate more than a brief occasional mention of ownership of the works of Hepplewhite, Sheraton, and Smith.

Wide ownership of price books which offer almost unlimited opportunity for innovation because of the number of extras or options listed for each form was undoubtedly a contributing factor to the variety of furniture forms and ornament. As an example is the fact that for any given chair there were listed several types of back which might be left plain or carved or inlaid, combined with a round, bell-shaped, swelled, or square seat frame, either straight or hollowed (dipped), and upholstered over all the frame, half the frame, or with slip seat. The upholstery could be ornamented with large-headed brass nails set in straight lines or arranged in swags. The legs could be straight, tapered, turned, or outflaring, either plain, molded in various patterns, carved, pattern veneered, in-

laid with one, two, or three lines of stringing in panels, or otherwise, and with or without dependent inlaid decoration. The permutations and combinations possible were almost as numerous as there are words in Webster's unabridged dictionary. Although for any given time in any given place possibilities were manifold and the vocabulary large, the usage was limited—in part by preference of the public and what it was willing to pay, especially for ornament—in part perhaps by the enthusiasm of a cabinetmaker for a form or style and by the skills of workmen and variety of materials available to him (exotic woods for veneers and inlays, stylish fabrics for upholstery, fancy brass tacks, furniture mounts, etc.). All of these seem to have been factors in the emergence of regional preferences of styles and the rise of local cabinetmaking schools.

In studying old furniture, it is of prime importance to remember that basic forms continued to be made for long periods. A succession of new forms and fashions were rapidly introduced between 1780 and 1825 but old ones lingered on for twenty, thirty, forty, or fifty years. Proof of this is to be seen in the new and revised editions of the price books. As late as the 1830's and 1840's, and even into the 1860's, price books printed in London continued to illustrate and state the amounts to be paid journeymen for making furniture in what are known as the Hepplewhite or Sheraton styles. However, the writer believes this may have been primarily for the benefit of workmen in the country where styles were slower to change. There the simplicity and rectangularity of late eighteenth-century forms were admirably suited to the abilities of workmen (often with less skill) and to the conservatism of their customers. Inasmuch as most of the furniture included in this book is believed to have been made in urban centers, and in fact a substantial number of pieces are labeled or documented as to maker and locale, it is possible to assign fairly narrow date ranges for its manufacture.

Although certain factors which underlie or made possible the Industrial Revolution were present in the cabinetmaking trade during the last half of the eighteenth century (the use of interchangeable parts for Windsor and other chairs, drawer fronts, and legs), the impulse of the Revolution was not to make itself felt until after about 1800, and even then, the development was slow. The most remarkable instances were the mass production of clock parts by Eli Terry in Connecticut and chair parts by Lambert Hitchcock in Connecticut, the harnessing of water power for the sawing of lumber and veneers, and increased specialization of work-men in the production of individual parts. The most notable early example of the latter probably occurred in the shop of Duncan Phyfe, where there were a larger number of workmen under one roof than in any other establishment prior to 1825. But it was not really until the 1830's and 1840's that the use of power machines and large establish-ments became the norm. Even then the production of fine furniture largely utilized handcraft proc-esses. For the period from 1780 to 1825, cabinet-making remained as it had been for almost one hundred years—a craft based on skills learned through apprenticeship and dependent upon the skill and artistry of the cabinetmaker.

## FOOTNOTES

1 Quoted in Kathryn C. Buhler's *Colonial Silversmiths, Masters and Apprentices* (Boston: Museum of Fine Arts, 1956), p. 17. The spelling is modernized here.

2 Ian M. G. Quimby, "Apprenticeship in Colonial Phila-delphia." See fn. 6.

3 A Transcript of the Fifteenth Eighteen Penny Provin-cial Tax... 1772, for the City and County of Philadelphia. "Chestnut Ward—William Savery, Assessor," pp. 67–73. Manuscript in the Historical Society of Pennsylvania.

4 Morrison H. Heckscher, "The Organization and Prac-tice of Philadelphia Cabinetmaking Establishments, 1790–1820," p. 48. See fn. 6.

5 Nancy McClelland, *Duncan Phyfe and The English Regency, 1795–1830* (New York: William R. Scott, Inc., 1939), p. 123.

6 Admirable research on individual furniture crafts-men or area studies for limited periods have been done as Masters Theses (unpublished) in the Winterthur Pro-gram of Early American Culture at the University of Delaware. These I have drawn upon for general informa-tion. For example the information about Joshua Dela-plaine is from the thesis of J. Stewart Johnson, "New York Cabinetmaking Prior to the Revolution." These theses are listed by author under "Monographs..." in the bibliography at the end of the book. See Castro-dale, Anne; Clark, Raymond B., Jr.; Goyne, Nancy Ann; Heckscher, Morrison H.; Hummel, Charles F.; Hunter, Dard, Jr.; Johnson, J. Stewart; Johnson, Marilynn Ann; LaFond, Edward F., Jr.; Leibundguth, Arthur W.; Pearce, Lorraine Waxman; Quimby, Ian M. G.; Rippe, Peter M. The forthcoming study by Charles Hummel of the activities of the cabinetmaking Dominy family of East Hampton, Long Island, will greatly increase the fund of information about rural artisans of the second half of the eighteenth century.

7 Milby Burton, "Thomas Elfe, Charleston Cabinet-Maker," *Museum Leaflet No. 25* (Charleston, South Caro-lina: The Charleston Museum, 1952), pp. 6, 7, 15. In this excellent study on Elfe and in the same author's book, *Charleston Furniture*, is to be found valuable information on the furniture of Charleston.

8 Louis B. Wright, *The Cultural Life of the American Colonies, 1607–1763* (New York: Harper, 1957), pp. 23–44.

9 Inventory of Thomas Barrett, Baltimore County In-ventories, Maryland Hall of Records, Annapolis, Mary-land. The Joseph Downs Manuscript and Microfilm Collection (hereafter referred to as DMMC), No. M-10.

10 *Federal Gazette* (Philadelphia), November 16, 1779, as quoted in Alfred Coxe Prime (comp.), *The Arts and Crafts in Philadelphia, Maryland, and South Carolina, 1786–1800*, Vol. II (Topsfield, Massachusetts: Printed for the Wal-pole Society at The Wayside Press, 1932), 229. Hereafter referred to as Prime, II.

11 Harrold E. Gillingham, "Benjamin Lehman, A Ger-mantown Cabinetmaker," *The Pennsylvania Magazine of History and Biography*, LIV (1930), 289–306.

12 Charles F. Hummel, "Samuel Rowland Fisher's Cata-logue of English Hardware," *Winterthur Portfolio I* (Win-terthur, Delaware, 1964).

13 *Columbian Centinel* (Boston), Wednesday, June 3, 1812.

14 *Maryland Gazette or the Baltimore General Advertiser* (Baltimore), November 1, 1785, as quoted in Alfred Coxe Prime (comp.), *The Arts and Crafts in Philadelphia, Maryland, and South Carolina, 1721–1785*, Vol. I (Tops-field, Massachusetts: Printed for the Walpole Society at The Wayside Press, 1929), 162. Hereafter referred to as Prime, I.

15 *South Carolina Gazette*, Mar. 22, 1740. Prime, I, 163.

16 *Pennsylvania Gazette*, Mar. 21, 1737. Prime, I, 177.

17 *Pennsylvania Evening Post*, Mar. 30, 1778. Prime, I, 171.

18 *Maryland Journal*, June 17, 1788. Prime, II, 167.

19 *Baltimore Daily Repository*, May 18, 1793. Prime, II, 180.

20 *The Impartial Gazeteer*, August 9, 1788. Gottesman, *1777–1799*, p. 109, No. 335.

21 *Charleston City Gazette and Advertiser*, Mar. 29, 1762. Prime II, p. 218.

22 Original records of the Gillow Company, now in the possession of Waring & Gillow, Ltd.

23 *South Carolina Gazette*, December 19, 1761. Prime, I, 169.

24 *Hampshire Gazette*, April 8, 1795, as quoted from one of 18,000 cards with Philadelphia, Maryland, and South Carolina newspaper advertisements and notices tran-scribed by Mr. and Mrs. Alfred Coxe Prime, which are now in the Winterthur Library. Information from about 2500 of these was included by them in Prime, I and II. Hereafter referred to as Prime Cards.

25 *South Carolina Gazette*, April 23, 1796. Prime, II, pp. 185–186.

26 Thomas Sheraton, *The Cabinet-Maker and Upholsterer's Drawing Book* (3rd ed. revised. London, 1802). Of his book Sheraton states in the Introduction to Part III: "The design of the Part of this Book is intended to exhibit the present taste of furniture, and at the same time to give the workman some assistance in the manufacturing part of it."

27 Sheraton, *The Cabinet-Maker and Upholsterer's Drawing Book* (London, 1793), p. 388, Pl. 35.

# Price Books

*...And it is further agreed, that this book shall be the standard or start price by which we will regulate the prices of our work...*[1]

Cabinetmakers' and journeymen's price books are manuscripts or printed lists of prices for the making of furniture at rates sought by journeymen or agreed upon by masters.

When viewed in their broadest sense, price books are of great significance. Some give retail prices for furniture. All but two give the wages to be paid the workman on a piecework basis, and from these rates the time necessary for making each piece can be determined. As opposed to the separate books issued in London for *cabinetmakers* and for *chairmakers,* those published in Edinborough, Glasgow, Norwich, and the United States included prices for the two crafts in one book, thus implying less rigid craft separation outside London. Each edition published there also provided designs valued then by the workman and today by the scholar and collector. In so doing, these price books spread a common knowledge of London furniture fashions and ways of working throughout the English-speaking world. But, price books also chart a key development in the emergence of labor from its vassal-like beginnings to its present-day position of power. They mark the organization of labor and document its demands, the acceptance of arbitration, and the reaching of agreements based on a piecework system of remuneration. The very existence of these wage demands and agreements indicates the growth of a spirit of independence and concomitant bargaining strength which was to lead to great strikes in Philadelphia in 1796, and New York in 1802.

Vestiges of the medieval guild systems with feudal overtones are inherent in the very names *masters* and *journeymen.* The latter, said to be a holdover from the practice of apprentices taking a journey on the completion of their apprenticeship, is significant until the end of the eighteenth century in England and America of the insecurity and lack of independence of the craft worker who journeyed from employer to employer and city to city as he sought work or tried to improve his lot. Price books illustrate industry-wide demands and acceptance of a standard wage to be paid for a specific job—a wage basically related to that paid in London, but in 1795 actually fifty per cent higher in Philadelphia and seventy-five per cent higher in Charleston.

Price books demonstrate that there existed in the late eighteenth and early nineteenth centuries in the English-speaking world a "language of workmanship" which was familiar to all cabinetmakers. This language was in essence the "art and mystery" of the craft learned through apprenticeship. It included a knowledge of furniture forms of the time and the methods of fashioning them, the use of tools and ways of working, and a "rule of thumb" understanding of the orders of architecture and the historic principles of geometry. Basically this language like a mother tongue, once learned, enabled a man to participate in the cabinetmaking fraternity and qualify for a job whether he was in London or Belfast, New York, Philadelphia, Boston, or Charleston. Printed proof of the existence of this language of the craft was the publication of *The Cabinet-Makers' London Book of Prices, and Designs of Cabinet Work* of 1788. It apparently codified earlier agreements that had existed only in manuscript. Many subsequent counterparts were modeled almost verbatim upon it, and published in Glasgow, Edinborough, Norwich, New York, Philadelphia, Pittsburgh, Cincinnati, or Indianapolis. Each of these implied a common knowledge of the forms and the methods of making them. It codified for all English and urban American cabinetmakers standards of remuneration on a piecework basis. The prices in these books provided the basis of employer-employee contracts much like union contracts with the steel or motorcar industries today.

Contributing to the widespread knowledge of London furniture forms were the illustrations included in the London price books. From the first, they included engraved designs of complete pieces of furniture and usually details of parts such as "Doors for Libraries, bookcases, etc." In addition, the later London books included patterns for "Pier Table Tops," "Mouldings," "Standards, stretchers of Brackets for Sofa or writing tables," table legs, claws, and many other parts. Sheraton had high praise for these designs. Referring to the "Quarto book of different pieces of furniture [issued] with the Cabinet-makers' London Book of Prices" (1788), he commented, "Considering that it did not make its appearance under the title of a Book of Designs, but only to illustrate the prices, it certainly lays claim to merit and does honour to the publishers" and "it may be observed, with justice, that their designs are more fashionable and useful than his [Hepplewhite's] in proportion to their number."[2] American price books include many references to the plates of the London books but show only a few of them. Several have no illustrations at all, and at most the American versions are sparsely illustrated with such details as bookcase doors, claws, feet, and moldings.

For a long time prior to the first-known printed price book, *The Cabinet-Makers' London Book of Prices, and Designs of Cabinet Work* (also called *The London Cabinet Book of Prices*) of 1788, isolated agreements of one kind or another apparently had existed between masters for prices to be charged and between masters and journeymen for prices to be paid for the making of furniture. Although only a few of the price books known to date include retail prices, even these few instances intimate an effort to avoid price cutting and a trend toward monopolistic and cartel-like tendencies on the part of the masters that cannot be ignored.

The earliest-known "Rule and Price of Joyners Work" is an American manuscript "Agreement of February 19, 1756" involving six cabinetmakers of Providence, Rhode Island. Beneath the heading, "Particular Price of Joinery Work," prices for thirty-five items of furniture are given. These can be recognized as retail prices because at the bottom of the page the rate for "Journeymen's Work for making" two of the pieces are also cited. New prices ranging from ten to forty per cent higher were apparently made necessary by the rapidly diminishing purchasing power of Rhode Island currency (paper money) and were incorporated in a "Revised Agreement of March 24, 1757," on the reverse of the sheet.

The earliest English list known to the writer is one in the early 1780's between the firm of Robert Gillow in Lancaster, England, and its journeymen. In a fiery letter from the head of the company, castigating the workmen for their profligacy and unjust demands, there is evidence that an earlier agreement had existed which was superseded by this one. Prices for the making of chairs are included in the Gillow price list and in the Philadelphia list of 1786, but not in the London printed list of 1788. Not until 1802 was a price list, *The London Chair-Makers' and Carvers' Book of Prices for Workmanship,* to be published for chairmakers.

Another important manuscript list, this time for Philadelphia, dated 1786, is entitled "Prices of Cabinet & Chair work." Because "Binjamin Lehman" appears in handwriting on the first page, it was erroneously thought in 1930 to be the list of prices charged by Benjamin Lehman "A Germantown Cabinetmaker" for furniture which he was prepared to produce.[3] Later, it was shown that Lehman was never more than a lumber dealer and livery-stable keeper, and the thought was expressed that "in conjunction with the buying and selling of lumber the enterprising young man formulated in January, 1786, possibly with the valuable aid of the numerous friendly master artificers, the list of furniture for the benefit of the Cabinet and Chair-making trade, in an effort to establish uniform prices of furniture and remuneration for the employees."[4] The writer believes it is no less than (1) an agreement between Philadelphia masters (employers) on the retail prices for their walnut and mahogany furniture and (2) the rates agreed upon between these masters and their journeymen (employees) for the making of furniture. It seems likely that Lehman simply copied for his own interest one of several lists in the possession of master cabinetmakers and journeymen. The list itself is fascinating. At the late date of 1786, all the furniture forms still appear to be in the Chippendale or Queen Anne styles. In three columns specific prices are given in pounds, shillings, and pence, for "mahogany" and "walnut" furniture forms and for "Journeymen's wages." No less than seven models of desks are listed, with nine variations of bookcases to accompany them. There are equally as many high chests of drawers. One, a highboy, with "scroll pedim' head, Carved-work not to exceed three pounds ten shillings," was to sell for twenty-one pounds. "A table to suit ditto" (a lowboy), was priced at six pounds. Taken as a whole, the list is indeed a sophisticated one, including almost all the Philadelphia Chippendale forms known today and some as yet undiscovered. Among the latter are "horse fire screens with a fret under the stretcher," a "dumb waiter with four tops and plain feet," and "bedsteads with Gothic pillers." With many more forms than the Providence list of thirty years earlier, the Philadelphia list is in accord with a recurrent theme stated in later price books, "The recent improvements in our trade, will evince the necessity of the enlargment of our book of prices, especially as many in our former book, were not clear enough to prevent different constructions being put upon them by employers and journeymen, which has been the cause of frequent disputes between them."[5] It seems doubtful that this is the first such agreement in effect in Philadelphia, but there is no way of knowing at present whether price-fixing agreements for either wages or retail prices evolved there as early as in Providence (1756).

On August 1, 1792, the first-known printed American price book appeared in Hartford. In the six pages that survive, there are only a few prices and the resolutions agreed on by the "Cabinet Makers" of that city. It is obviously a retail price agreement of a group "who have formed ourselves into a Society for the purposes of regulating the prices of our work; on the principle of dealing in CASH, and of establishing a uniformity in our trade for the general interest of ourselves and customers: ...Resolved, That we will strictly conform to the prices which are or shall be affixed to our work; a deviation therefrom, shall be deemed a forfeiture of *word* and *honour*."[6]

In 1794 the first major volume of American cabinet-making prices for workmanship, entitled *The Philadelphia Cabinet and Chair-Makers' Book of Prices,* was published in Philadelphia. No copy is known, but its contents may be guessed on the basis of the "second edition, corrected and enlarged" which appeared in 1795. The first edition is recorded in a newspaper notice by Samuel Caldwell, Clerk of the District of Pennsylvania, to the effect that on "the thirteenth day of April, 1794, Thomas Timmings, Christopher Appleton, and John Gregory, have deposited in this office the title of a book, the right whereof they claim for themselves, and for and on behalf of the Federal Society of Chair Makers, as authors and proprietors, in the words following to wit, 'The Philadelphia Cabinet and Chair Makers' Book of Prices'."[7] The publication of this book by the journeymen marked the beginning of a two-year battle between employer and employee. Who was the aggressor is now unknown, but the masters had not waited for the journeymen to fire the first shot. Two days before the copyrighting of the first edition, a committee of masters

advertised as follows: "Wanted, From Thirty to Forty Journeymen Cabinet-Makers, to whom the best prices will be given. Apply to the subscribers, who are a committee appointed by the Master Cabinet Makers. Samuel Claphamson, Jacob Wayne, John Douglass, John Aitken, Henry Ingle, Jacob Schreiner." The masters were obviously eager to replace the troublemakers.[8]

Whether the next year was one of uneasy peace and cold war is not known, but the publication by the employees of the second edition of *The Journeymen Cabinet and Chair-Makers Philadelphia Book of Prices* in 1795 was apparently tantamount to waving a red flag in the faces of the masters. They published a handbill, yet to be found; but its implications are clear from the employees' rebuttal. In the reply, the journeymen advertised in effect—we will not work now until the employers agree to our proposals nor will we work hereafter with any journeyman who doesn't abide by our rules. Their adamant notice read:

> At a meeting of the Federal Society of Journeymen Cabinet and Chair Makers of the City and Liberties of Philadelphia, July 18th, 1795—convened in consequence of a hand-bill being published by a certain number of the employers, in which it was mentioned, they would not employ any journeymen cabinetmakers as society men, but as individuals—
>
> It was therefore unanimously resolved, That we will not work for any of the employers who have propagated the same, either as society men, or as individuals, until they agree to the last proposals of our committee to theirs, which we are conscious are fair and equitable.
>
> 2dly. That we will not hereafter work with any journeyman who is, or may be employed by any of the above employers, contrary to our rules.
>
> Signed by order and in behalf of the Society.
>
> THOMAS NOBLE
> JOHN LINDSAY
> THOMAS TIMINGS.[9]

These were strong words, but not nearly so demanding in those early years of American labor strife as were to be written into the "Constitution and Bye-Laws of the United Society of Journeymen Cabinet and Chair-Makers of the city of Baltimore" in 1817. That society then demanded what was in effect a closed shop. It proclaimed in articles II and III that every "Cabinet-maker, having worked at the business at least one year, and free from all indentures of apprenticeship... shall become a member of this society within the terms of six weeks after working as Journeymen in Baltimore...." True, it gave the noncomplying journeyman what appears to be an easy alternative. "In case of non compliance," the fine levied for every month "he neglects to do so" was "the sum of twenty five cents," exactly twice the dues of members and equal to approximately two hours' wages. The society also ruled in Section VIII of its "Bye-Laws": "No member or members shall be permitted to work any other way than by the Book of Prices now established, provided the work can be made out thereby."

Automatic expulsion from the Society followed the failure of a member to pay his dues for three months. As will be shown later, the Societies of Masters were not limited to one city, nor were those of journeymen. "Every person admitted a member" of the Baltimore Society was required "at his initiation [to] pay the sum of one dollar (unless such person present a *certificate from any one of our correspondent societies*)..." Although the italics are the writer's, this is proof enough of intercity relationships of this early cabinetmakers' union. The first appeal for "union of the respective mechanical branches in ... [one] City, and throughout America" was that of the Federal Society of Philadelphia Cabinet Makers when they advertised in the *Argus* of New York on March 4, 1796:

> From the working Cabinet Makers of Philadelphia, to their mechanical Fellow Citizens...
> We hope and entreat that an union of the respective mechanical branches in this City, and throughout America, will immediately take place, in order to repel any attack that has or may be made on societies of this description.... Hasten then, fellow citizens, to declare yourselves ready at any time to assist one another, in a cause which will determine the independence of so useful a body as the working Citizens of America.... George Wilson, President. John Lindsay, Secretary.[10]

Their next newspaper broadside was fired a month later on April 7, 1796. In their "Appeal to the Public," they began

> ...In consequence of the rapid advance of price in every article of life, we found it necessary to our receiving even a bare support, to raise the price of our work. Accordingly with all that respect which is due from man to man, we submitted our New Book of Rates to our Employers for their perusal and approbation.

But as they explained in a long and fascinating statement, their demands being rejected, they had now opened "a Ware-Room in Market Street" for the sale of furniture to be made by themselves. A parallel action today would be for the United Auto Workers Union to establish their own fac-

tory and salesrooms while on strike. As will be noted in the concluding paragraph of their appeal, the cabinetmakers had the support of some other craft societies but sought to "digest a plan of union" of all such societies.

> We ... return our most grateful thanks to those Societies who have assisted us at this crisis; in particular the respectable and independent Societies of Hatters and Shoemakers whose generous assistance has enabled us to answer the most extensive demands of the Public. The Committees from these and other Mechanical Societies, Viz., House-Carpenters, Tailors, Goldsmiths, Sadlers, Coopers, Painters, Printers, &c &c. are requested to meet at Myer's Tavern, 5th and Race streets, on the first Monday of May next, at 2 o'clock, P.M. in order to digest a plan of union, for the protection of their mutual independence.
> The Federal Society of Philadelphia Cabinet and Chair-Makers.
> Signed by order, CHARLES CHRISTIAN, PRES'T.
> WILLIAM CALVERT, SEC.
> No. 96, Market-street.[11]

However, not all printers sided with the journeymen. Six weeks later on May 21, 1796, Richard Folwell received from Daniel Trotter, "Thirty dollars, in full for Printing Lists of the Prices of Cabinetwork."[12] Exactly why Trotter, and undoubtedly other masters, had *The Philadelphia Cabinet and Chair-Makers Book of Prices* published is not now clear. Like Lehman's manuscript list of 1786, it gives what are apparently the retail prices of Philadelphia-made furniture; but unlike the earlier list, there is no mention of wages to be paid journeymen. Was this book possibly for general circulation to acquaint the public with standard rates and to combat the journeymen's efforts in their "Ware-Room" enterprise? Its purpose is not known but its usefulness is manifold; it gives a retail price for some seventy different furniture forms in both walnut and mahogany being offered for sale in Philadelphia in May of 1796.

Details of the struggle which continued for several months are also lacking, but the outcome was written into the "Introduction" and the rates stipulated in *The Cabinet-Makers' Philadelphia and London Book of Prices* advertised as "lately published" on September 3, 1796. Because of its importance, the 1796 agreement incorporated in the "Introduction" is reproduced on page 24.

The escalator clause for cost-of-living increases (or decreases) written into the wage contract between the auto workers' union and the motorcar industry in the late 1950's was considered revolutionary, but the idea was actually more than one hundred and fifty years old. The cabinetmaking employers agreed in 1796 that "...whenever the necessaries of life, house-rent, &c. shall rise above what they are at present, the Employers agree to advance the percentum to what shall be agreed on: And in like manner, the Workmen do agree to reduce the prices in the same proportion as the said necessaries lower, which shall be agreed on by the Committee of both parties."

In the "agreement entered into by the Employers and workmen," it was determined to take as a regulation the London book of prices lately published (1793) with this stipulation, "that all work done and executed to the satisfaction of the Employer, should be paid at the rate of 50 per cent advance; and any work not executed to please, to be valued and paid for, as shall be agreed on by the Committee appointed by both parties." Perhaps to give the appearance of victory for the employers, the fifty per cent increases are not actually printed in the compromise book, *The Cabinet-Makers' Philadelphia and London Book of Prices.* The rates are exactly reprinted from the 1793 "London Book." But, as will be noticed under the heading *Advertisement* (see illustration on page 25), is the legend: "The Prices throughout the following work are stated in sterling money. It is proposed to make an advance of 50 per cent; which, when reduced to currency, will give the established prices."

Comparison of these prices with those in the 1795 edition of *The Journeymen Cabinet and Chair-Makers Philadelphia Book of Prices* which incorporated the workmen's demands shows that they won their case. The differences between demands and settlement are minor despite the complaint of the employers in the "Introduction" of the later book that the workmen had sought to fix prices "which on examination, were found not to regulate the work in such manner as to make all parts alike beneficial to the employer."

Although the settlement of this first great strike of American craftsmen written into *The Cabinet-Makers' Philadelphia and London Book of Prices* was an important victory for the workmen, it should be observed that the standard work week was six days with "Day-men to work eleven hours" and that the average pay was seven shillings, six pence—one dollar a day. This was still the rule in 1828 with the "employer to find candles"; but, by that time, the average wage for day work had increased from one dollar to "not less than $1.33⅓ per day."

To bring all employers "into line," William

Cock of the journeymen's society advertised that jobs were readily available at fifty per cent above the prices "in the London book" and there was no need to work for "employers who do not give this price."[13]

Thus ended the Philadelphia cabinetmakers strike of 1796. A similar struggle, equally acrimonious, was repeated in New York in 1802 and 1803. While it is unnecessary to detail the events of that strike since they parallel closely what had already taken place in Philadelphia, these strikes were indeed early declarations of independence on the part of labor. In fact in advertising their grievances, these journeymen modeled their statement on "The American Declaration" of 1776, a fact that was not lost on the masters. They ended their rejoinder, "The Journeymen's Grievances Answered," with "We have in the above not been studious to adorn it by an imitation of the Declaration of Independence, but have confined ourselves to plain and correct narrative."[14]

In their statement of grievances, the journeymen of New York proclaim, "...there has existed in this city, for many years past, a Book of Prices, in which is specified the precise sum to be paid by the master cabinet-maker to his journeymen, for every particular piece of workmanship in that line."[15]

To show the relationship between labor costs and retail furniture prices, the following 1796 prices are revealing:

| Form | Piecework Price (Labor)[16] | Masters' Retail prices |
|---|---|---|
| Mahogany | | |
| Dining Table 4 × 5 ft. | $8.08 | $16.05 |
| Pembroke Table | 3.50 | 14.00 |
| Square Card Table | 3.22 | 14.00 |
| Cradle | 2.67 | 9.33 |
| Splatt Back Chair honeysuckle pattern | 1.93 | 7.67 |
| Heart Back Chair | 2.09 | 7.67 |
| Circular Bureau | 9.45 | 30.00 |
| A Clock Case | 8.00 | 30.00 |

If one applies the rule of thumb stated earlier that the labor cost in dollars approximates the number of days necessary to make a particular piece of furniture, one finds that a dining table (labor, $8.08) required eight days for making and a pembroke table (labor, $3.50) only about three and a half days. In addition to labor, the masters paid for materials, rent, heat, candles, and other overhead. These costs with profit increased the retail price to an average of three and one half times the labor cost. Hence it follows that if one

# INTRODUCTION.

As a great deal of trouble has been occafioned between the Employers and Workmen, on account of the many late improvements in our trade; and a part of the Workmen having, without our confent, thought proper to fix the prices at which they would bind us to pay them; and which, on examination, were found not to regulate the work in fuch manner as to make all parts alike beneficial to the Employer, and therefore liable to new caufe of complaint: in confequence of an agreement entered into by the Employers and Workmen, it was determined to take, as a regulation, the London Book of Prices lately publifhed, with this ftipulation, " that all work done and executed to the fatisfaction of the Employer, fhould be paid at the rate of 50 per cent. advance; and any work not executed to pleafe, to be valued and paid for, as fhall be agreed on by the Committee appointed by both parties. And it is further agreed, that this book fhall be the ftandard or ftart price by which we will regulate the prices of our work; and whenever the neceffaries of life, houfe-rent, &c. fhall rife above what they are at prefent, the Employers agree to advance the per centum to what fhall be agreed on: And in like manner, the Workmen do agree to reduce the prices in the fame proportion as the faid neceffaries lower, which fhall be agreed on by the Committee of both parties."

The prices of Chairs, &c. &c. have been fixed by us, mutually.—Day-men to work eleven hours; and any difputes arifing between the parties to be fettled by the Committee appointed as aforefaid, and their award to be final.

Signed,     JOHN AITKEN,
              JOHN DOUGLAS,     } Employers.
              JOHN ALEXANDER.

Signed,     WILLIAM COCKS,
              THOMAS JANVIER,     } Workmen.
              GEORGE HOG.

# ADVERTISEMENT.

*T*HE *prices throughout the following work are stated in sterling money.
It is proposed to make an advance of* 50 *per cent ; which, when reduced to currency, will give the established prices.*

## E X A M P L E.

A DRESSING CHEST or BU-
REAU,

THREE feet long, four drawers in ditto, cock beaded,
astragal or stone moulding
on the edge of the top, the
edge veneer'd, and a
string in the upper corner,
fast plinth or common
brackets, - - - - -

| | £. | s. | d. |
|---|---|---|---|
| fast plinth or common brackets, | 0 | 18 | 0 |
| 6 inches extra in length, at 6d. | 0 | 3 | 0 |
| 5 inches extra in height at 4d. | 0 | 1 | 8 |
| Veneering drawer fronts, each 6d. | 0 | 2 | 0 |
| Colouring and polishing in-side of drawer front, each 1d. | 0 | 0 | 4 |
| Oiling and polishing, - - | 0 | 0 | 8 |

| | £.1 | 5 | 8 |
|---|---|---|---|
| 50 *per cent.* advance, | 0 | 12 | 10 |

| Sterling money, | £.1 | 18 | 6 |
|---|---|---|---|
| | | | 5 |

| | 3)9 | 12 | 6 |
|---|---|---|---|

| | 3 | 4. | 2 |
|---|---|---|---|

8 feet 9 inches veneer saw-
ing, at 6d. per foot, -    0    4    4½

Currency,    £.3    8    6½

BUREAU or DESK,

Two feet eight inches long,
four drawers in ditto,
cock beaded, six small
drawers and six letter
holes inside, on plinth or
common brackets,

| | £. | s. | d. |
|---|---|---|---|
| common brackets, | 1 | 12 | 0 |
| 10 inches extra in length, at 9d. | 0 | 7 | 6 |
| Veneering drawer front, each 6d. | 0 | 2 | 0 |
| 2 extra small drawers, | 0 | 0 | 2 |
| 2 extra letter holes, - | 0 | 0 | 9 |
| 8 plain arches, - - | 0 | 1 | 0 |
| A plain prospect door, - | 0 | 1 | 6 |
| Oiling and polishing, | 0 | 0 | 11 |

| | £.2 | 7 | 8 |
|---|---|---|---|
| 50 *per cent.* advance, | 1 | 3 | 10 |

| Sterling money, | £.3 | 11 | 6 |
|---|---|---|---|
| | | | 5 |

| | 3)17 | 17 | 6 |
|---|---|---|---|

| | 5 | 19 | 2 |
|---|---|---|---|

7 feet 6 inches of veneer
sawing, at 6d. per foot,    0    3    9

Currency,    £.6    2    11

The illustrations above and on the facing page from *The Cabinet-Makers' Philadelphia
and London Book of Prices* show how price books were actually used. This one served
both as a contract and as a detailed listing of piecework wages to be paid. The
examples cited indicate how each extra added to the cost of manufacture.

In addition to citing "the precise sum ... for every particular piece of workmanship," price books also give the present-day student an accurate list of each form
commonly made and the many variations of ornament or parts that were optional.
Besides that, they offer another extraordinary piece of information for the collector,
economist, and scholar—by deduction, the approximate length of time required to
make any piece of furniture can be determined! Conveniently, the prevailing
journeyman cabinetmaker wage scale of seven shillings, six pence (in both New York
and Philadelphia, 1795–1810) figures out to one dollar a day.[17] By extension, any
piecework rate from a price book when converted to dollars is equivalent to the
number of days required to make that piece of furniture.

knows the retail price of a piece of furniture just before or after 1800 he can approximate the time required for making it by converting the retail price to dollars and dividing by three and a half.

This formula is useful for such a case as that cited in No. 66 where Duncan Phyfe charged $15.00 each for making the chairs. By dividing fifteen by 3½, one finds that it took approximately four days to make each chair.

Through the 1830's, revisions of earlier price books were printed in New York and Philadelphia, and new ones usually modeled on one or another of the editions of these cities were published in Buffalo, Cincinnati, and Pittsburgh. The last-known price book was printed in 1878 in Indianapolis. All editions of cabinetmakers' price books of the English-speaking world presently known by the writer are included in the bibliography at the end of this book. Others unquestionably exist, and any word about them will be welcomed.

## FOOTNOTES

1 *The Cabinet-Makers' Philadelphia and London Book of Prices* (Philadelphia, 1796), in the "Introduction."

2 Sheraton, *The Cabinet-Maker and Upholsterer's Drawing Book* (London, 1793), p. 11.

3 Gillingham, op. cit.

4 W. M. Hornor, Jr., "Correspondence and Comment," *The Antiquarian*, XV (November, 1930), 76, 108, 112.

5 *The Journeymen Cabinet and Chair-Makers Philadelphia Book of Prices* (2d ed.; Philadelphia, 1795), in the "Introduction."

6 Irving W. Lyon, *The Colonial Furniture of New England* (Boston and New York: Houghton, Mifflin Company, 1924), p. 267.

7 *Pennsylvania Gazette*, May 28, 1794. Prime Cards.

8 *Federal Gazette* (Philadelphia), April 11, 1794.

9 *Pennsylvania Packet, Dunlap and Claypoole's American Daily Advertiser* (Philadelphia), July 16, 1795. Prime Cards.

10 *The Argus* (New York), March 4, 1796. Gottesman, *1777–1799*, p. 131, No. 412.

11 *Aurora* (Philadelphia), April 7, 1796.

12 Receipt Book of Daniel Trotter owned by Theodore T. Newbold. Microfilm copy. DMMC.

13 *Federal Gazette* (Philadelphia), September 3, 1796.

14 *American Citizen* (New York), December 31, 1802. Gottesman, *1800–1804*, p. 146, No. 351.

15 *American Citizen* (New York), December 8, 1802. Gottesman, *1800–1804*, p. 145, No. 350.

16 The piecework prices cited are from *The Cabinet-Makers' Philadelphia and London Book of Prices* of 1796 and the retail prices from *The Philadelphia Cabinet and Chair-Makers'* Book of Prices of the same year. For simplicity, pounds, shillings, and pence have been converted into dollars according to the table given in *The Journeymen Cabinet and Chair-Makers Philadelphia Book of Prices* (1795) equating one pound Pennsylvania currency to $2.66⅔.

17 Despite the claim of the New York masters (1802) that "an industrious man may earn from twelve to fourteen shillings a day" on piecework (see fn. 14) it appears, from study and comparison of cabinetmakers' accounts and price books, that the earnings of journeymen were about the same whether they worked on day rates or piecework. One can assume, however, they had much more freedom to come and go as they liked when on the latter basis. The account books and allied papers (DMMC 62.60.1–.351) of Samuel and Isaac Ashton, cabinetmakers of Philadelphia from the 1780's through 1832 contain several agreements and many payments to journeymen both on day work and piecework.

# Woods Used in American Furniture 1790–1825

Historically, each furniture style has dictated or at least influenced the major woods used by the cabinetmaker.[1] For strength and appearance, he chose hard woods for the main parts. For economy and ease of working, he used soft woods for interior parts which didn't show. Sometimes, he made inexpensive "common" furniture (such as pine kitchen tables) completely of soft woods which he often concealed with paint. For the principal or the primary wood, mahogany served extremely well for furniture of the Federal period as it had in the Chippendale era; it was the principal wood used in most cabinetmaking centers.

## IDENTIFICATION

Identification by eye alone of the woods used in old furniture, especially those discolored by age, dirt, or varnish, is always difficult, and usually inconclusive. For a more exact method, one need not look far. Long before the widespread publicity given to the identification by experts of the wood in the ladder used in the Lindburgh kidnapping, the microscope had been employed by botanists and wood technologists—chiefly to identify woods used commercially. To learn if minute samples would provide positive identification of species and geographical origin, experimentation was begun at Winterthur in 1953 by Gordon K. Saltar, with the help and encouragement of William N. Watkins, then curator of Crafts and Industries of the Smithsonian Institution, and Dr. Rutherford J. Gettens of the Freer Gallery of Art. Over the years, B. J. Rendle of the Forest Products Research Laboratory (England) has helped tremendously with advice and has provided Winterthur with many botanically identified European specimens. It was the goal of the project to identify as accurately as possible the woods in the furniture of the Winterthur collection. The answers sought were new ones—the problems different from those faced daily in the United States Forest Products Laboratory. The curator not only wishes to establish the identity of each kind of wood in a piece of furniture, but he also wishes to know where it grew. He cannot offer large samples for testing, since this would of course ruin the piece. For many years it had been supposed that the secondary woods in American furniture were those that grew in the region where the furniture was made. Consequently it was supposed that if one could identify the woods one would have a valuable tool for identifying the origin of the furniture. The Winterthur study confirms this theory.

Fortunately, most secondary woods are out of sight; and small samples, usually ranging between the size of a grain of wheat and a small pea, can be taken without defacing the furniture. Samples of primary woods are taken from the bottom of the feet or the inside of the frame, so as not to leave a visible blemish. In some cases the identification was easy, but in others the problems were fantastic. The woods tested were from 150 to 300 years old and from all over the world. The writer estimates that Mr. Saltar has made at least ten thousand analyses in the course of gathering the information necessary for the captions accompanying the pieces of furniture in this book and for the charts on page 37.

In any such investigation, the greater the number of samples tested, the surer the results. Much more sampling and testing is needed, especially of woods used in southern furniture. But, from Winterthur's investigation of woods, it seems conclusive that microscopic identification offers a valuable tool for arriving at the regional origin of American furniture.

An additional advantage of this exact identification of secondary woods is that it offers evidence for the separation of American and European furniture, since most woods that grew on the American East Coast can be differentiated from those that grew in Europe. It is true that some American and European pines, particularly those used in looking glasses, cannot be separated and that definite answers cannot always be given as to where beeches and white oaks grew. It is also true that the English cabinetmaker, and perhaps some on the Continent, increasingly used imported American woods after 1790. However, at least one similar investigation of European furniture is now being carried on; as the findings are compared with those being gathered on American furniture, a much clearer picture will emerge as to which woods were employed by European cabinetmakers as compared with those used by Americans.[2]

### PRIMARY WOODS

Mahogany was the universal favorite with American cabinetmakers as the primary, or principal, wood for fine furniture between 1790 and 1825. While it is true that stylish and fashionable chairs of native woods were increasingly painted and japanned during this era and that cherry, maple, walnut, and other primary woods were also used, most of the best furniture was made of mahogany. One writer summed up the reason for the preference as follows: "The exquisite beauty of the finer kinds of mahogany, the incomparable lustre of which it is susceptible, exempt also from the depredations of worms, hard, durable, warping and shrinking very little, it is preeminently calculated to suit the work of the cabinet-maker. Accordingly, these admirable properties, added to its abundance, and the largeness of its dimensions, have occasioned it to be manufactured into every description of furniture."[3]

Some pieces of cherry furniture will be found listed among the sales in virtually every cabinetmaker's account book from Massachusetts to Pennsylvania; but, while advertisers often mentioned cherry in Connecticut, western Massachusetts, and Albany, one seldom finds it included in the newspaper notices of Salem, Boston, New York, and Philadelphia. The cabinetmakers in these cities used it on occasion but not so frequently as in nonurban areas. Seldom does one see in the seaboard cities such advertisements as that of Amos Broad of Albany in 1799: "...a large and general assortment of Mahogany and Cherry Furniture, Sideboards, Secretaries, Desks, Book-Cases, Mahogany and cherry Tables of all kinds."[4]

For less expensive furniture, city cabinetmakers as well as those in the country also employed birch and maple which when stained resembled mahogany. Although these woods were more often used in New England, Thomas Timpson of 25 John Street, New York, advertised in 1803 "mahogany, birch and maple bedsteads, [and] dining tables with ends."[5] High and low bedsteads, sometimes with turned posts and sometimes with "pencil

posts," were painted green or red throughout the United States. Those of New York and northward were usually of birch or maple; southward they were often of buttonwood or tulip.

In Pennsylvania and southern New Jersey, walnut had been a favorite from the end of the seventeenth century; and, as late as 1796, its use in Philadelphia was extensive enough for prices to be publicly quoted for all furniture forms in walnut as well as mahogany.[6] Rural Pennsylvania craftsmen continued to employ this rich brown wood throughout the nineteenth century.

In summary it appears that as much as seventy-five per cent of the best furniture (with the exception of chairs) made in the seaboard cities between 1790 and 1825 was of mahogany or was finished with mahogany veneers. The mahogany was of two principal kinds, Honduras and San Domingo. The latter, sometimes called Spanish wood, included Cuba wood and Jamaica mahogany. San Domingo is hard, dark, and with little figure; Cuba wood, not quite so hard, often has more figure but is less "flashy" than Honduras, or Bay wood, which is softer and redder. Certain cuts of Cuban mahogany show a fine figure sometimes called crotch, or branch, mahogany. And, as noted above, it is darker and heavier in weight than that of Honduras with its more open grain.

Henry Fearon, the diarist, observed:

> ...Mahogany yards [in New York] are generally separate concerns....Honduras mahogany is five-pence halfpenny to seven-pence farthing the superficial foot; and St. Domingo, nine-pence three farthing to seventeen-pence half penny. Mahogany is used for cupboards, doors, and banisters, and for all kinds of cabinet work...Veneer is in general in demand, and is cut by machinery. Chests of drawers are chiefly made of St. Domingo mahogany...shaded veneer and curl maple are also used for this purpose. I would remark, that the cabinet work executed in this city is light and elegant, superior indeed, I am inclined to believe, to English workmanship. I have seen some with cut glass, instead of brass ornaments, which had a beautiful effect.[7]

Mahogany was an important article of commerce. Traders and ships' captains bought it in the Caribbean islands and brought it to the principal coastal cities. It was sold not only by lumber yards but by cabinetmakers as well. Cabinetmaker Charles Watts engaged heavily in the trade, importing thousands of feet to Charleston and New York, where the list of his customers—headed by Duncan Phyfe, William Burling, and Michael Allison—for mahogany and hardware reads like the New York Social Register of cabinetmakers.

The sale of wood by cabinetmakers was not restricted to mahogany. James Hallet, Jr., was but one of many who advertised "all kinds of Mahogany [including a few logs of choice St. Domingo Mahogany], Cherry, Bilsted Whitewood Boards and Joice."[8] Earlier, country cabinetmakers more often used native woods, but after 1800 they increasingly employed mahogany. Their source of supply is not always clear, but the following from the *Journal* (1845) of Edward Carpenter, an apprentice of Miles & Lyons, cabinetmakers in Greenfield, Massachusetts, is revealing and may be typical: "Miles started this noon for Hartford to buy hardware and mahogany, he went down on the *Telegraph*" (the fast stage line which operated up and down the river). Later, Carpenter noted, "Miles reported on his return that he had to send to New York for veneers for there were none in Hartford that were good for anything." Elsewhere in his journal, Carpenter wrote: "Lyons went to Colrain [Massachusetts] today to see about some lumber... This forenoon, Miles went over to Montague City & got about 300 feet of the best up river pine that I ever saw; it is so good that I am afraid that I shan't have the pleasure of working much of it."[9]

Furniture of excellent quality made of curled or bird's-eye maple is sometimes found. Such pieces, often striking in appearance, are highly prized by collectors. Much rarer are a few American pieces of solid satinwood, among them a desk made by the Seymours and three or four kidney-shaped work tables from Philadelphia (Nos. 426 and 427).

## SECONDARY WOODS

Secondary woods are those that do not show on a piece of furniture. They include structural woods used for internal bracing or for backboards and shelving and those upon which mahogany and other veneers are glued. In America, native woods were employed for these purposes. Before the Revolution, the cabinetmaker used secondary woods which grew in his vicinity. He acquired them by barter or purchase from individuals with timber lots or sawmills. Later, in 1790, William Harris, Jr., of New London sought "Whitewood Plank" (herein called tulip) through the *Connecticut Gazette*. He wanted it immediately, "suitable for making Windsor Chairs."[10] Ten years later Joshua Pen-

ninman, cabinetmaker, of the same city, advertised "for Maple or ash Joist and Half inch Whitewood."[11] Even as early as 1750, occasional references were made in Philadelphia to the use by carpenters of white pine imported from New England. But in general, cabinetmakers do not seem to have employed to any great extent woods imported from other areas until about 1790. After that time, one may expect to find white pine in furniture produced all up and down the Atlantic Coast and even occasionally in English furniture.

## VENEERS

Although practised by the ancients, the use of veneers and inlays is seldom if ever found in American furniture made before the beginning of the eighteenth century. Burled walnut and ash veneers, much used on chests and high chests in the William and Mary style, are found, but less often, in furniture of the Queen Anne style. Mahogany veneers are found only rarely in the finest American case pieces in the Chippendale mode, because veneers like inlays were little used by American cabinetmakers between about 1760 and 1790. But after 1790 veneers and ornamental inlays of many kinds became one of the principal methods of ornamenting furniture. Crotch mahogany was most often used for veneers. To provide points of interest and contrast these were sometimes inset with pictorial inlays such as shells, flowers, or eagles. Light and dark inlaid lines were more commonly used. Sometimes these were patterned.

Patterned stringing or banding composed of small pieces of wood of different colors, often intricately arranged to form geometrical patterned narrow bands, was widely used in New England and to some extent elsewhere (Plates II and III). It corresponds to one kind of marquetry which is described in *The Encyclopaedia of Domestic Economy* of 1845 (p. 208) as follows: "Marquetry is in wood what mosaic is in stone; pieces of various woods, or those which have been stained for the purpose, being put together.... Marquetry is sometimes confined to simple forms, as squares, lozenges, etc."

*The following color plates represent the first attempt ever made to set forth the regional use of inlays in American furniture. They reveal that these tiny pieces of wood intricately worked into colorful pictures and abstract designs not only beautify furniture, but are an invaluable tool in determining the place of its manufacture. They even provide clues to the shop in which a particular piece of furniture was made.*

# Stringing and Banding

*Coastal Massachusetts, New Hampshire, and Rhode Island*

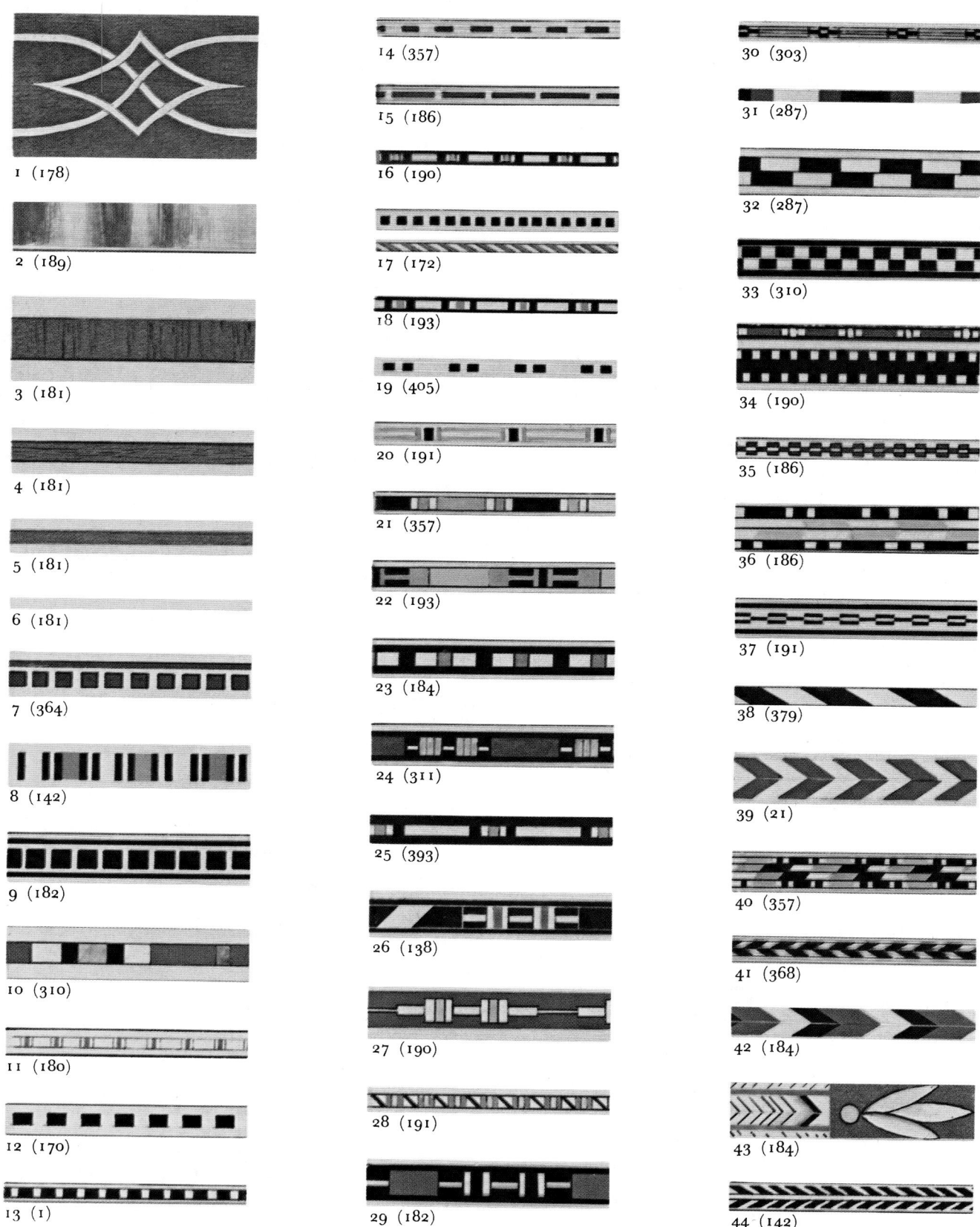

1 (178)

2 (189)

3 (181)

4 (181)

5 (181)

6 (181)

7 (364)

8 (142)

9 (182)

10 (310)

11 (180)

12 (170)

13 (1)

14 (357)

15 (186)

16 (190)

17 (172)

18 (193)

19 (405)

20 (191)

21 (357)

22 (193)

23 (184)

24 (311)

25 (393)

26 (138)

27 (190)

28 (191)

29 (182)

30 (303)

31 (287)

32 (287)

33 (310)

34 (190)

35 (186)

36 (186)

37 (191)

38 (379)

39 (21)

40 (357)

41 (368)

42 (184)

43 (184)

44 (142)

II

*Drawings by Jonathan L. Fairbanks*

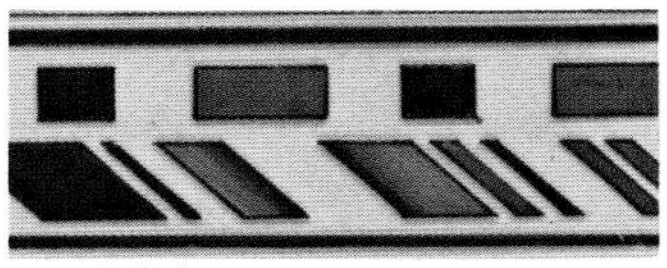

45 (364)

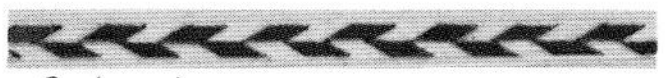

46 (310)

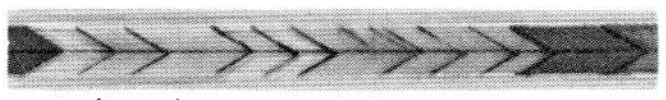

47 (253)

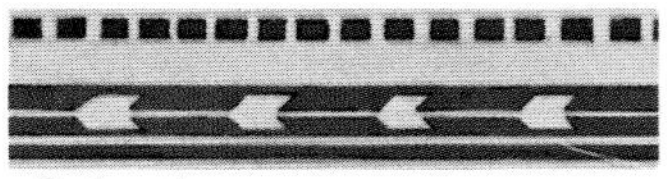

48 (357)

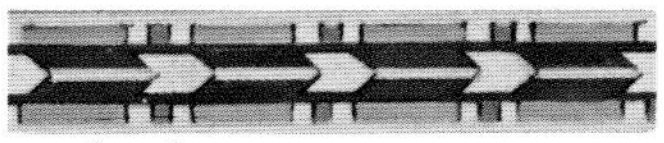

49 (303)

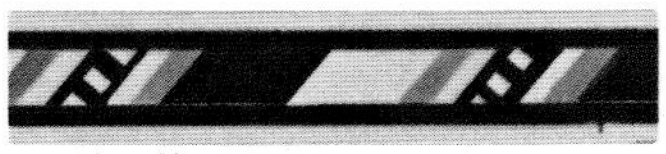

50 (138)

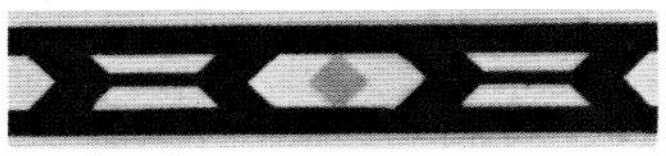

51 (115)

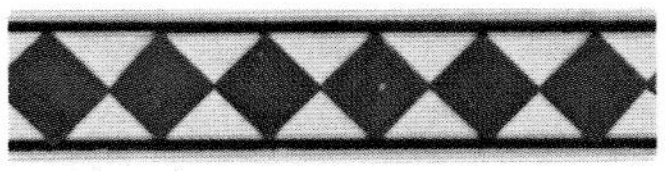

52 (294)

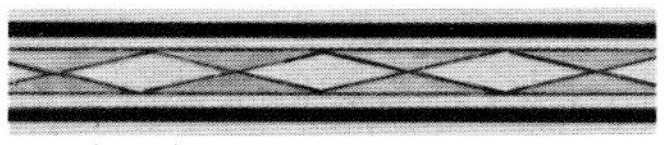

53 (191)

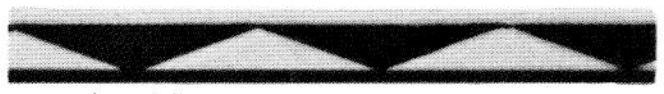

54 (393)

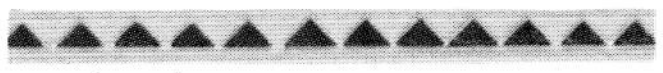

55 (172)

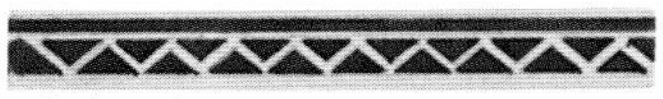

56 (303)

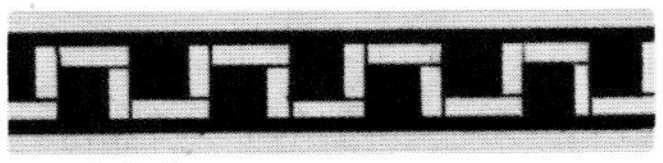

57 (182)

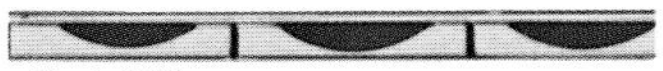

58 (186)

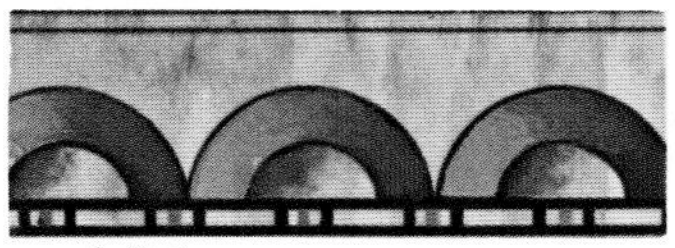

59 (365)

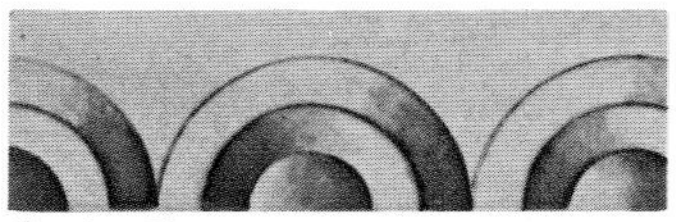

60 (338)

### *Connecticut and Connecticut Valley*

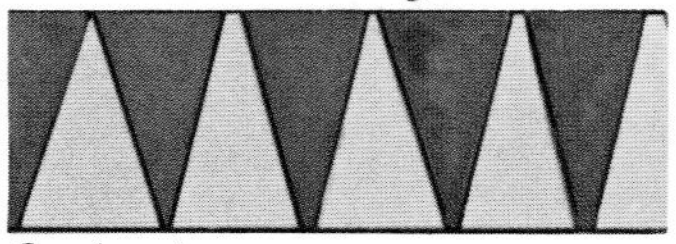

61 (323)

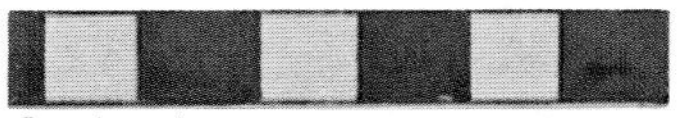

62 (323)

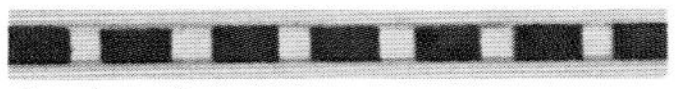

63 (295)

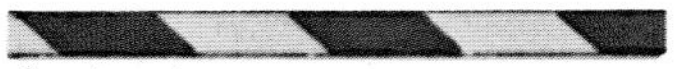

64 (177)

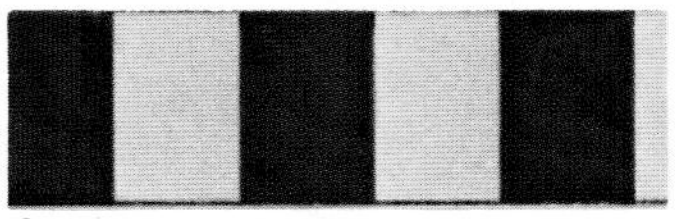

65 (177)

### *New York and New Jersey*

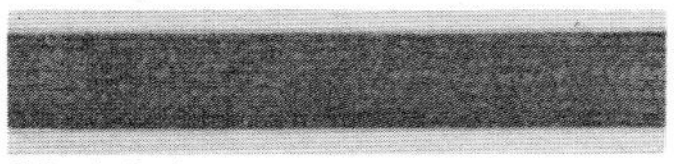

66 (183)

67 (297)

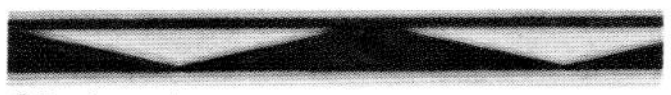

68 (297)

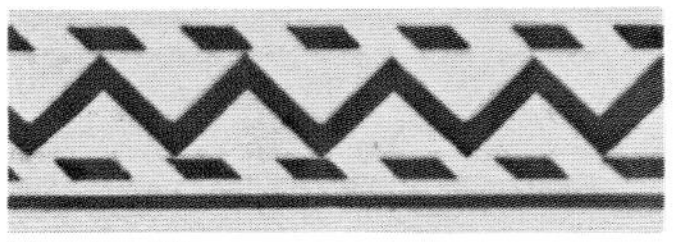

69 (448)

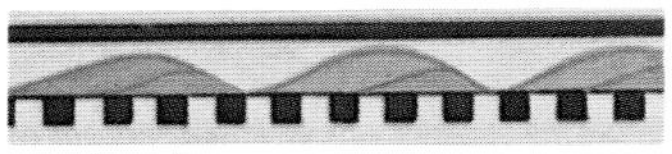

70 (450)

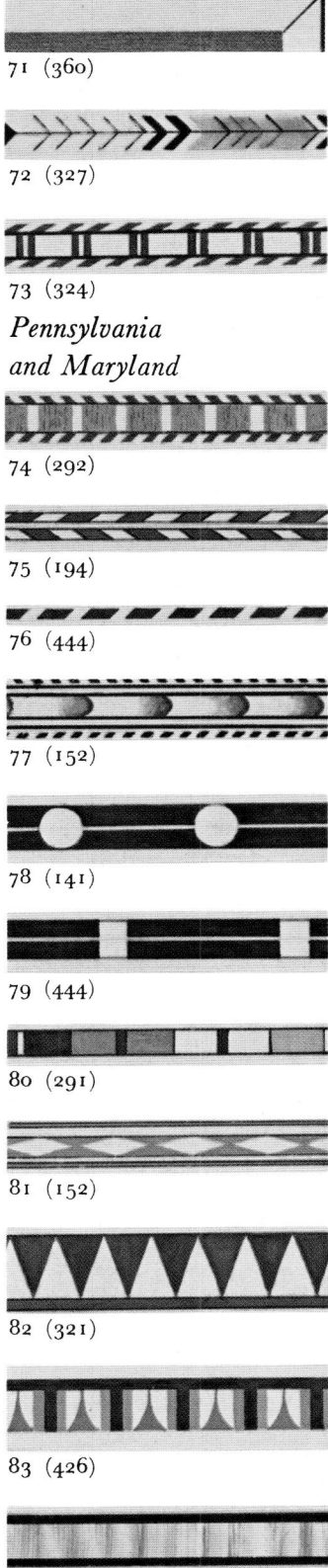

71 (360)

72 (327)

73 (324)

### *Pennsylvania and Maryland*

74 (292)

75 (194)

76 (444)

77 (152)

78 (141)

79 (444)

80 (291)

81 (152)

82 (321)

83 (426)

84 (293)

III

Occasionally very excellent accounts of the art of veneering, banding, and inlaying appear in English and American "books of the trades" and encyclopedias after 1800. Descriptions from these books sometimes sound old-fashioned, but they offer excellent explanations of the processes involved. One writer began thus: "Owing to the unceasing demand for ornamental furniture, and the limited supply of valuable wood, originated the practice of veneering. Veneers are thin surfaces, not much thicker than card-board, of fine or handsomely-grained wood. These, when firmly united to a commoner material, impart to the whole a solid appearance, and thus a great saving is effected. Objections are sometimes taken to veneered articles, on the ground that they are not what they pretend to be."[12]

Another writer, in *The Great Industries of the United States* (p. 214), published in Chicago and Cincinnati in 1872, says:

> The principal woods used for veneering are the American bird's-eye maple, ebony, mahogany, rose-wood, king-wood, satin-wood, sandal-wood, sycamore, kiabocca or (amboyna), zebra-wood, tulip-wood, and a few others. From these woods sections can be selected which present knots, gnarls, or other excrescences, which, when sawn in strips, present surfaces showing beautiful and variform figures. In parts of the trunk where limbs have protruded, the veneers will give elliptical figures, sometimes two or three feet in length, by from four to six inches in breadth. In such parts of the tree the fibres not only assume a vast variety of twists and shapes, but they acquire deeper colors, and, by interlacing the texture, the wood becomes denser and more compact. Other parts of the same wood exhibit a wavy and grotesque appearance, or that mottled surface seen in the bird's-eye maple, and the similar, though far more beautiful and costly, kiabocca. These dots or "eyes" are incipient or partially formed knots. The knots and excrescences turned into veneers furnish the endless and pleasing varieties of shapes seen in finished furniture and cabinet work, and what in nature is in reality a deformity becomes beauty of a high order in art.

An 1825 Philadelphia notice is illuminating.

> Steam Saw Mill and Mahogany Yard, Richardson & Co. Having recently put in operation their Improved Patent Rotatory Veneer Cutters, propelled by steam power, are pre-

pared to cut Veneers of any given dimension.... They also Saw Boards, Plank &c. in the best manner, with an improved VERTICAL SAW.... Fine Veneers, cut to convenient sizes, can be supplied for shipping, on the shortest notice ... [to] any part of the United States.[13]

The circular saw came into general use in the United States during the first half of the nineteenth century, and Edwin T. Freedly in *Philadelphia and its Manfuacturers* (p. 272) noted "About this time [1840] Circular Saws, some of which were seven to eight feet in diameter were introduced, and gradually improvements were made, so that at the present time [1857] it is not uncommon to produce sixteen Veneers to the inch. Mahogany, Rosewood, Walnut, and all the finer woods, are now used in Veneering with such skill, that elliptic, ogees, or oval surfaces of common wood, are covered with a thin coating of fine wood, thus reducing the consumption, comparatively, of the finer woods."

The methods of applying veneers were thus described by another writer:

> Veneers are laid either by means of a tool called a veneering-hammer, or by cauls. In veneering with the hammer, the ground should by warmed at the fire, and the outside of the veneer being wetted with warm water, or thin glue, with a sponge, and the side to be laid covered with a coat of thin glue, and warmed at a fire, the veneer is to be quickly laid on the ground and worked by the hammer, and commencing at one end, work from the middle to each side till neither air nor glue will come out.
>
> Veneering with the hammer answers very well, when veneers are tolerably straight and even; but this is rarely the case with finely-figured woods, hence it is necessary to employ another method called veneering with a caul.
>
> A caul is made out of solid wood, shaped to the surface to be veneered, and, being well heated, and afterwards oiled and greased, it is screwed down upon the veneer, and by the pressure and its heat sends out the glue, causing the veneer to bed close to the ground.... Various opinions are held regarding the use of cauls, but where the veneer is of a nature to admit of being laid by the hammer, we would prefer it.[14]

It is stipulated in *The Cabinet-Makers' Philadelphia and London Book of Prices* that "molds and cauls are to be provided for the workman, or paid for according to time."

Satinwood veneers were sometimes used on furniture made in American coastal cities to provide contrasting panels against dark mahogany. But figured birch, long mistaken for satinwood, was much more frequently used—especially on the fronts of card tables, chests of drawers, and other furniture made in Boston, Salem, and surrounding areas of New England. Honey-colored like satinwood but with a strong veining of darker coloring, these veneers are now identified by microscopic analysis to be birch. In the Gillow records "birchen veneers" appears repeatedly on drawings showing feathery light woods. A mid-nineteenth century writer confirmed that "paper birch, Betula papyracea ... is valuable for its timber.... Furniture is made from it in Canada and the United States, and elegant cabinet-wood from the feathered and variegated portions taken from the regions of the trunk whence the branches spring."[15]

Banding was described in 1837 as follows:

Banding is a term applied to a narrow strip of veneer used as a border, or part of a border, either to a large veneer, or to solid wood; in the latter case, a rebate is sunk for the banding. Banding is of three kinds: it is called *Straight-banding* when the wood is cut lengthwise of the grain; *Cross-banding* when the wood is cut across the grain; and *Feather-banding,* when cut at an angle between the two.... The chief object of banding is to increase the beauty of a plane surface by forming a species of border to it; and it requires considerable skill to give the desired effect....[16]

*STRINGING*

The inlaying of lines of light or dark wood was called stringing. It was much used in most cabinet-making centers. Sometimes a single string was used (see Inlay Figure 6 in the Plates that follow) and sometimes several of alternating colors (Inlay Figure 5), usually black and white, with occasionally as many as five being used as a band. Legs, drawers, bookcase doors, and other parts were often outlined, but inlaid lines (stringing) were also frequently used to form panels. Usually, price books include "A Table of Paneling with String, etc." with prices given for "oval panel with a single string 4 inches long and under," "a square panel with a hollow or round top and bottom," "ditto with an astragal top and bottom. etc., etc."

The woods used in stringing and inlays are usually identified in this book only as light or dark woods because of the difficulty of obtaining samples for microscopic analysis without spoiling the inlays. It is safe to say, however, that in urban centers holly was the wood most widely used for stringing. In its natural state it is white, but it can readily be dyed black in imitation of ebony. Satinwood, boxwood, and ebony were also used in city shops. In the country, maple and birch were often substituted. A little before 1800 in England the inlaying of brass and even silver strings followed a practice much favored by the French. There are early references to furniture in the United States with silver inlays, and one unique and superb sideboard (believed to have been made in Baltimore) in the collections of the Metropolitan Museum of Art has inlays of Sheffield plate. Brass inlays are also occasionally found in American furniture, especially in New York and Philadelphia, but their use was not widespread or frequent.

Inasmuch as the light woods employed in inlays were so frequently shaded by scorching, it is of some interest to have an early writer's version of the method used "to produce that shady brown edge, on works inlaid with white holly, and which, when well executed, has a very pleasing and ornamental effect." The method is as follows:

Into a shallow iron or tin-pot, put a sufficient quantity of fine dry sand, to be level with the top edge of it; place it on the fire till it is quite hot, then having your veneer cut out to the required pattern, dip the edges into the hot sand, and let them remain till the heat has made them quite brown; but be careful not to burn them; it is best to bring them to a proper colour, by repeatedly renewing the operation, than all at once, as you then do not injure the texture of the wood, and by immersing more or less of the edge, you produce a shaded appearance to your satisfaction. I would here recommend the workman, previous to beginning the operation, to have his pattern before him, shaded with umber, or any brown colour, in those parts that the wood is to be stained, as he then will be enabled, as he proceeds, to copy the various shades of the pattern, for the wood when once shaded cannot be altered; and as much of the beauty of this work depends on a proper judgment in placing your shadows, it is best always to have a guide to go by, that we may produce the best possible effect. Sometimes it is requisite to give a shadow in the centre, and not on the edge of your wood; and as this cannot be done by dipping it in

# Pictorial Inlays

*Coastal Areas of Massachusetts, New Hampshire, and Rhode Island*

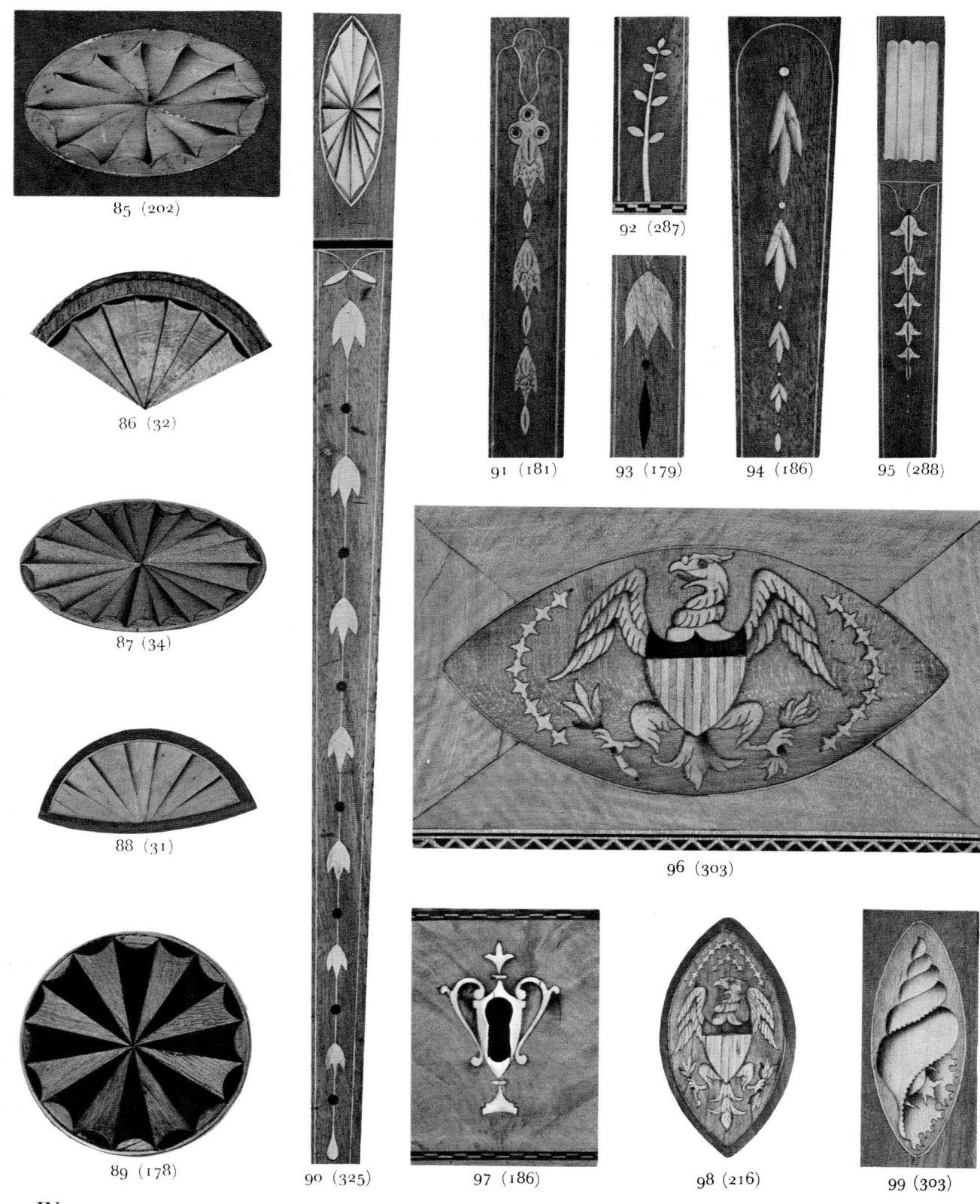

85 (202)

86 (32)

87 (34)

88 (31)

89 (178)

90 (325)

91 (181)

92 (287)

93 (179)

94 (186)

95 (288)

96 (303)

97 (186)

98 (216)

99 (303)

IV

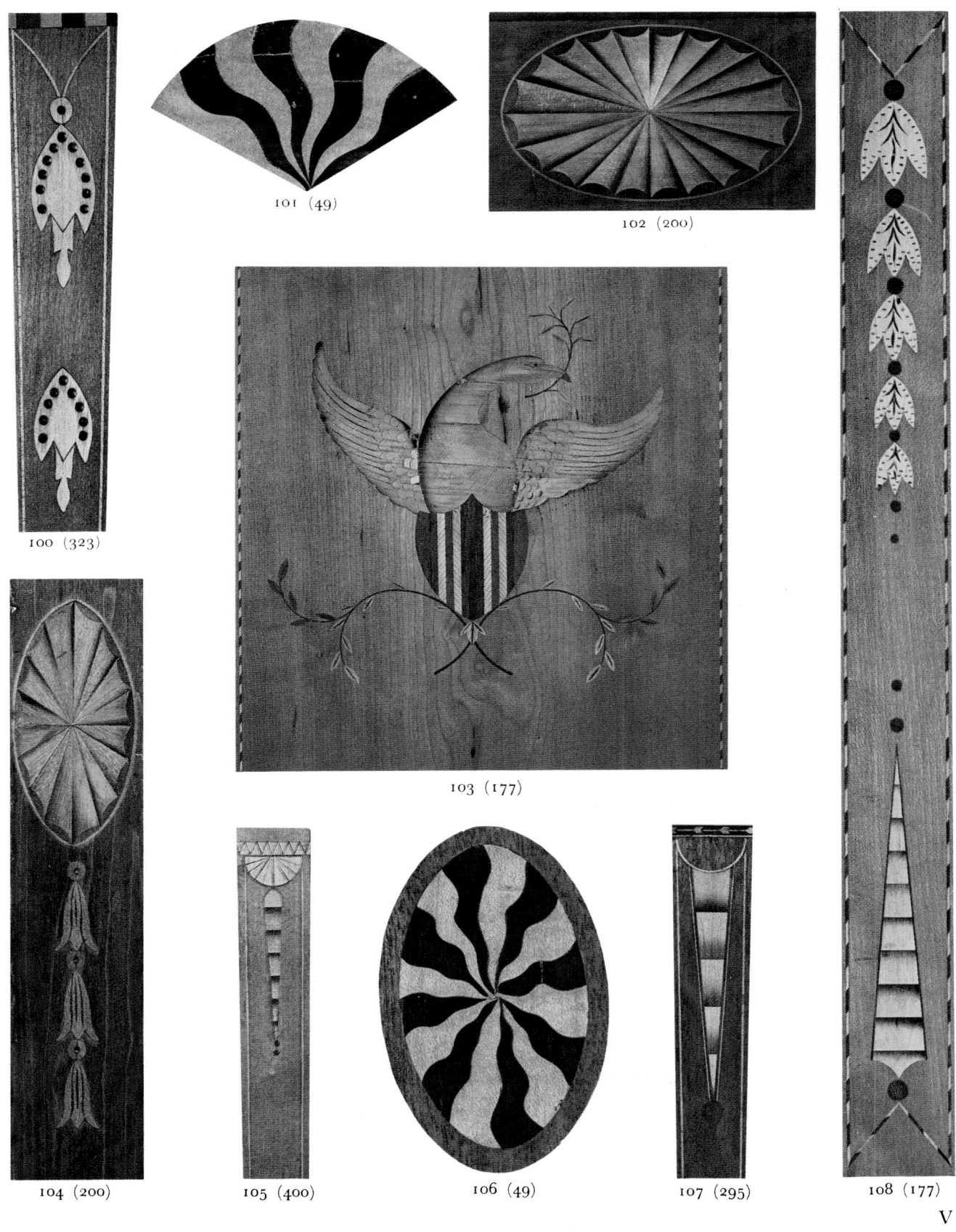

100 (323)

101 (49)

102 (200)

103 (177)

104 (200)

105 (400)

106 (49)

107 (295)

108 (177)

V

the sand, you must do it by taking up a little of the hot sand, and sprinkling it, or heaping it up on those parts required to be darkened, letting it remain a short time, then shaking it off, and, if necessary, apply more where the colour is not deep enough.[17]

## INLAYS

In earlier times the representation of birds, flowers, and other ornamental motifs, such as paterae, came under the heading of marquetry. Today in America this term is seldom used except for the very complicated and complex designs found in Dutch and other European furniture. Instead, the word inlays is used. Perhaps because paterae—oval or round inlays composed of radiates—were so often used, the prices for making inlays and for their application are included in American price books under the heading "Patries." The following transcript is from *The Journeymen Cabinet and Chair Makers' New-York Book of Prices* of 1796 (p. 76):

| | |
|---|---|
| For an oval patrie, two and a half inches long, with twelve strait points, fill'd up at the end with different wood, and a single string round ditto | £ 0 1 3 |
| Letting in each patrie, | 0 0 3 |
| Making a husk and drop, | 0 0 2 |
| Letting in ditto, | 0 0 2 |
| Making a half circular shade eight inches long, and under | 0 2 6 |
| Letting in ditto | 0 1 0 |
| Each quarter fan from one to two inches, with six strait points | 0 0 9 |

In the illustrations that follow, the reader will immediately recognize the "husk and drop" as the bellflower found inlaid in table, desk, and chair legs; "the half circular shade" as the fan- and shell-like ornaments inlaid on Baltimore table tops and chests of drawers; and "the quarter fan" as that commonly found in the corners of many New York sideboards and New England clocks, to name but two of many instances of its use. In no price book seen by the writer is there mention of either shells or the American eagle.

That inlays were sometimes imported is shown by a 1796 advertisement in *The Argus* (New York City) which reads "Shells for Cabinet Work—To Cabinet Makers. A Gentleman has just arrived from London with an Assortment of Shells for Cabinet work, which he will dispose of on reasonable terms, for cash. Enquire of C. Brenneysen No. 263 Broadway."[18]

Though less exact, it seems probable that the "fine satin-wood, tulip wood and purple wood Veneers, and an assortment of Stringing, &c for cabinet-makers" offered for sale by Richard Weevill in Philadelphia in 1799 were also from London. Noted as being "also for Sale," their position in his advertisement is just after goods "Just imported in the *Active*, from London."[19]

It is clear, though, that there were craftsmen in American cities who specialized in making inlays.

(continued on page 40)

## FURNITURE WOODS—REGIONAL USAGE

The following chart based in large part on about one thousand pieces of furniture in the Winterthur collection (but also including woods listed in cabinetmakers' accounts and shop inventories) represents an attempt to summarize the general use of both primary and secondary woods in American furniture. The reader must be warned that almost any secondary wood might have been used in an isolated instance anywhere. In the past, pieces of furniture which have included bilsted, or gumwood, have been automatically attributed to New York workmanship because that wood was so prevalently used in that area. However, substantial quantities of gumwood have been found in the accounts of one Providence cabinetmaker and in the inventories of Chester County, Pennsylvania, cabinetmakers and, surprisingly, in that of William Camp, one of the most prominent early nineteenth-century Baltimore cabinetmakers. The following symbols are used in the wood charts on the facing page.

* Cannot be separated with certainty by microscope from comparable European woods
√ Used but frequency undetermined
1 Used but not often
2 Used quite commonly
3 Used often
CF Chair Frames
DS Drawer Sides and Bottoms
F Fancy Furniture
I Inlays and Stringing
TF Table Frames and Flying Rails
U Common Painted Furniture
V Veneers

Note: "CF 2," for example, on the same line as *Ash* (left-hand column) and beneath *N.E.Mass.* (printed at the top of the page) means that ash was quite commonly used for chair frames in northeastern Massachusetts. Similarly, "TF 3" on the same line as *Oak, white* and under *E. Maryland* means that white oak was often used for table frames or their "flying rails" in eastern Maryland.

| PRIMARY WOODS—REGIONAL USAGE | N.E. MASS. S.N.H. | CONN. VALLEY | R.I. & E. CONN. | N.Y., L.I., N.N.J., HUDSON VALLEY | E. PENNA. & ADJACENT N.J. | E. MARYLAND | W. PENNA. & W. MD. | VA., GA., N.C. | CHARLESTON AREA | CANADA |
|---|---|---|---|---|---|---|---|---|---|---|
| BEECH (Fagus grandifolia) | F√ | | | | | | | | | |
| BIRCH (*Betula lenta, etc.) | 2 V3 | √ | √ V√ | √ | | | | | | |
| CHERRY (Prunus serotina, etc.) | 1 | 3 | 2 | 2 | 2 | √ | √ | √ | | |
| CYPRESS (Taxodium distichum) | | | | | | | | | U√ | |
| HOLLY (*Ilex opaca) | I3 | I2 | I3 | I3 | I3 | I3 | | | I√ | |
| MAHOGANY (St. Domingo, etc., Swietenia mahogani; Honduras, Swietenia macrophylla) | 3 | 2 | 3 | 3 | 3 | 3 | 2 | 3 | 3 | √ |
| MAPLE (*hard group, Acer saccharum, etc.; soft group, Acer saccharinum, etc.) | 2 F2 | 2 F2 | 2 F2 | √ F2 | √ | F3 | | | | √ |
| PINE (southern, Pinus—taeda group) | | | | | | | U2 | U3 | | |
| (*red, Pinus resinosa) | | | | | | | | | | |
| (white, Pinus strobus) | U3 | U3 | U3 | U2 | | | | | | U3 |
| RED GUM (Liquidamber styraciflua) | | | | U√ | | | | | | |
| SATINWOOD (East Indian, Chloroxylon swietenia; West Indian, Zanthoxylum flavum) | V3 | √ | √ | √ | √ | √ | | | √ | |
| TULIP (poplar or whitewood, Liriodendron tulipifera) | | | | U2 | U2 | √ | U2 | √ | √ | |
| WALNUT (Juglans nigra) | | | | | 3 | √ | 3 | 3 | | |

SECONDARY WOODS

| | N.E. MASS. S.N.H. | CONN. VALLEY | R.I. & E. CONN. | N.Y., L.I., N.N.J., HUDSON VALLEY | E. PENNA. & ADJACENT N.J. | E. MARYLAND | W. PENNA. & W. MD. | VA., GA., N.C. | CHARLESTON AREA | CANADA |
|---|---|---|---|---|---|---|---|---|---|---|
| ASH (*white, Fraxinus americana; black, F. nigra; red, F. pennsylvanica) | CF2 | | CF1 | CF3 | CF2 | | | | | |
| BASSWOOD (*Tilia) | 1 | | | | | | | | | |
| BEECH (Fagus grandifolia) | √ | F√ | | √ | | | | | | |
| BIRCH (*Betula lenta, etc.) | 3 | 2 | 2 | 1 | | | | | | |
| CEDAR (red, Juniperus virginiana) | DS1 | | DS1 | | | | | | | |
| (white, North—arbor vitae—Thuja occidentalis) | | | | √ | | | | | | |
| (white, South, Chamaecyparis thyoides) | | | DS2 | √ | DS3 | DS2 | | | | |
| CHERRY (Prunus serotina, etc.) | √ | CF2 | | 2 | 1 | | | | | |
| CHESTNUT (*Castanea dentata) | | | 3 | | | | | | | |
| CYPRESS (Taxodium distichum) | | | | | | | | | 3 | |
| HICKORY (Carya ovata, etc.) | | | | F√ | | | | | | |
| MAHOGANY (St. Domingo, etc., Swietenia mahogani; Honduras, Swietenia macrophylla) | DS1 | | DS1 | DS1 | DS1 | | | | DS1 | |
| MAPLE (*hard group, Acer saccharum, etc.) | 2 | 2 | | CF2 | | | | | | √ |
| (soft group, Acer saccharinum, etc.) | 2 | 2 | | | | | | | | √ |
| OAK (red group, Quercus borealis, etc.) | | | | | TF3 | TF3 | | | | |
| (white group, Quercus alba, etc.) | | | | | CF2, TF3 | CF2, TF3 | | | | |
| PINE (southern, Pinus—taeda group) | | | | | 3 | 3 | 3 | | 3 | |
| (*red, Pinus resinosa) | | | | | | | | | | |
| (white, Pinus strobus) | 3 | 3 | 2 | 2 | √ | | | | √ | √ |
| RED GUM (Liquidamber styraciflua) | | | √ | 2 | √ | √ | | | | |
| TULIP (poplar or whitewood, Liriodendron tulipifera) | | | 2 | 3 | 3 | 3 | 3 | √ | √ | |
| WALNUT (Juglans nigra) | √ | | √ | √ | √ | √ | √ | √ | | |

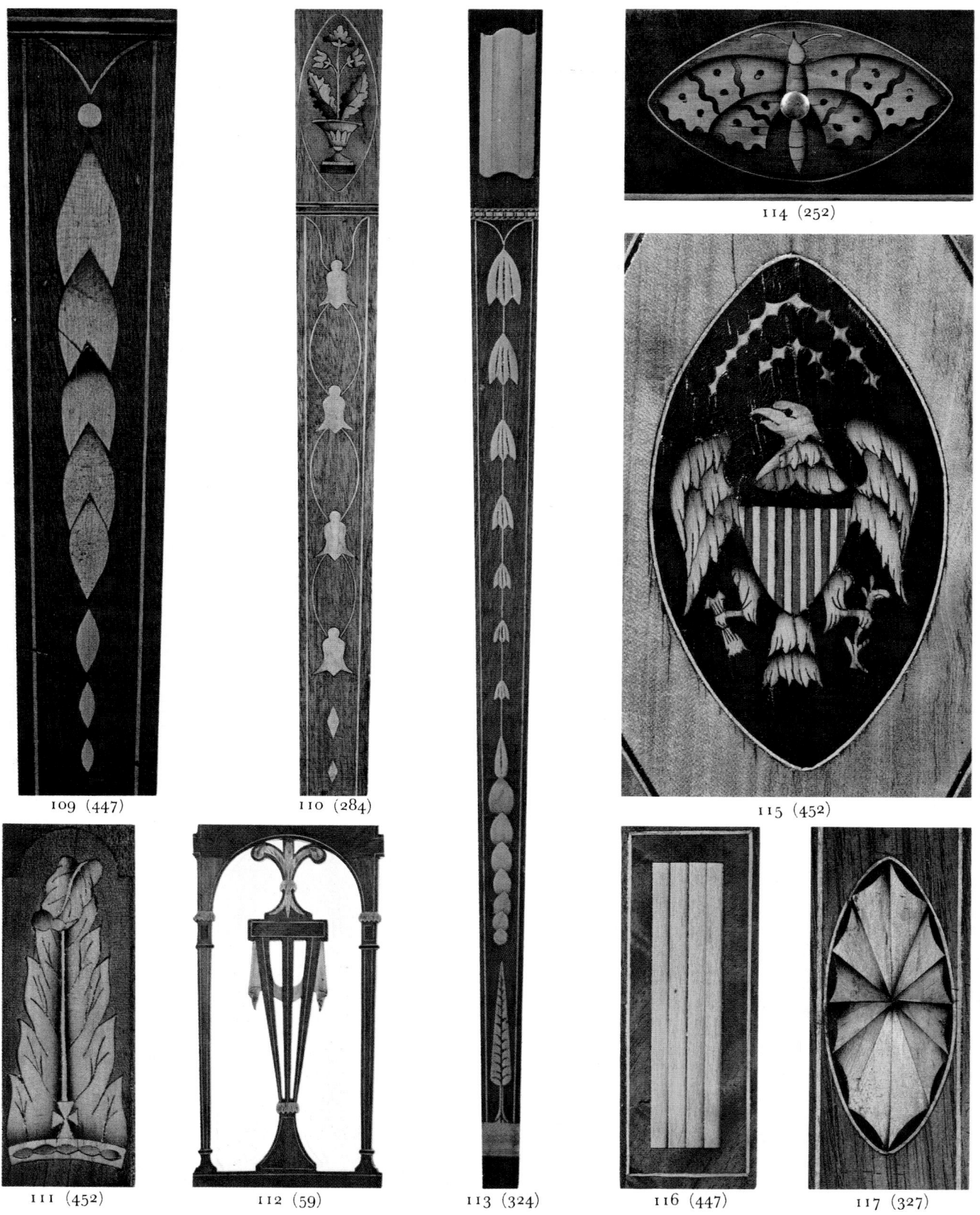

109 (447)     110 (284)                                                 115 (452)

                                                              114 (252)

111 (452)          112 (59)          113 (324)          116 (447)          117 (327)

VI

38

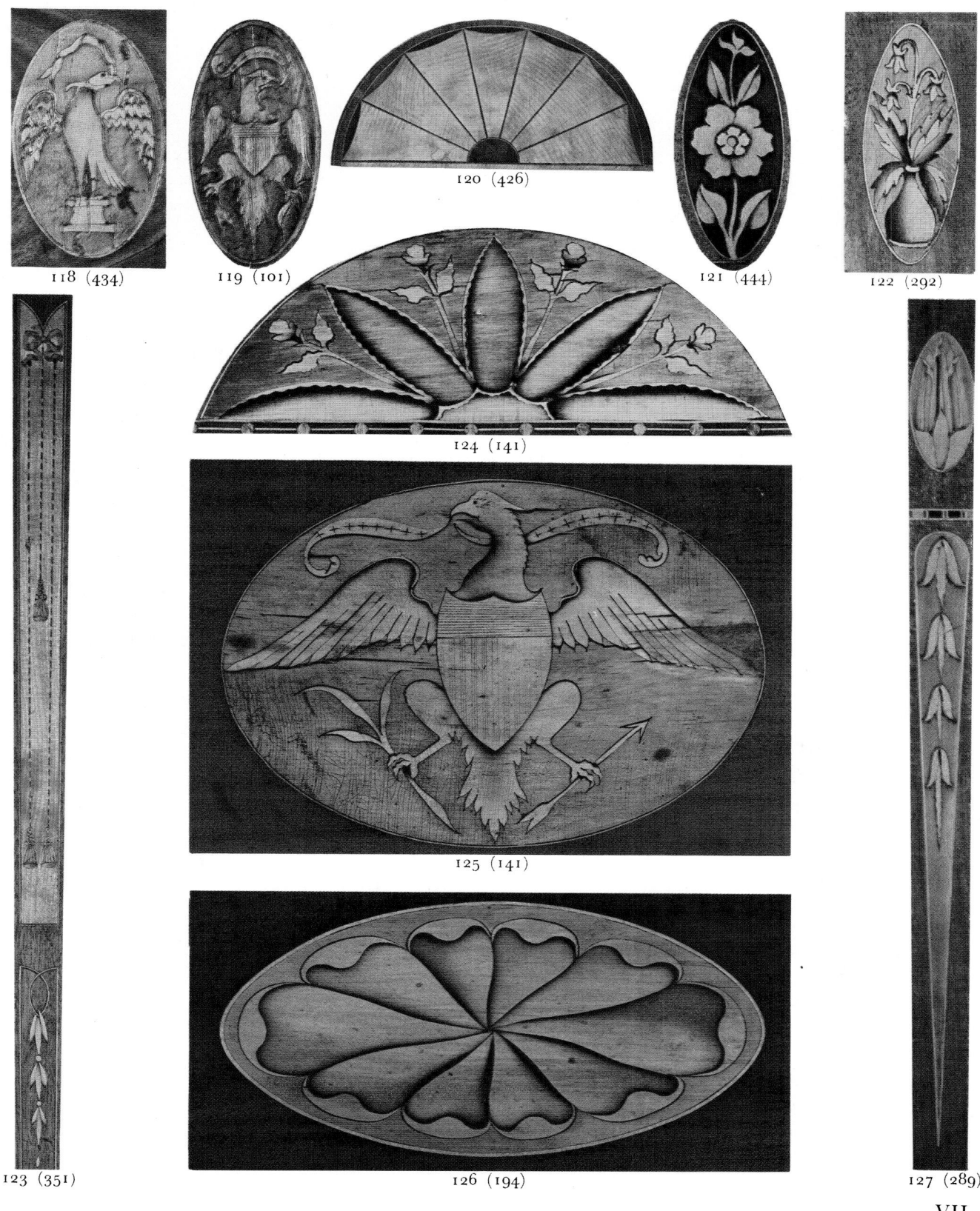

118 (434)    119 (101)    120 (426)    121 (444)    122 (292)

124 (141)

123 (351)    125 (141)    126 (194)    127 (289)

VII

John Dewhurst is listed in the Boston Directory for 1809 as "banding and stringing maker."[20] And an extraordinary record of an inlay-maker's stock is included in the inventory of Thomas Barrett of Baltimore. Listed in the *Baltimore Directory* as "ebiniste," his inventory made on November 8, 1800, lists the debts of at least fifteen Baltimore cabinetmakers: "1 sett of tools compleat for Manufactory work—$50.00"; 1316 "shells for inlaying in furniture" appraised at from 7 to 25 cents each; "36 yards of band    12½ cents, 9 ditto    8 cents, and 31 ditto    5 cents."[21] The number of debtor-cabinetmakers gives a clue to the scope of his business. The size of this stock proves he could have supplied all the "shells" used in Baltimore furniture of the time.

Although the known records of inlay suppliers and inlay makers are sparse, it is clear from those quoted that there was a substantial traffic in these charming vignettes and ornamental framing devices; and there seems little doubt that a large proportion of the inlays used in the city shops were bought ready-made. On the other hand, some rural cabinetmakers made their own inlays. Comparison of these with those found in city-made furniture show that they are large in scale and usually cruder in execution.

The significance of the supposition that city cabinetmakers obtained their inlays locally from a common source is that it accounts for the similarity in the inlays in the furniture of each urban center. Unquestionably in each shop there were preferences for particular kinds of inlays, but that does not mean that all inlays of one kind were exclusive to one shop. For example, the "thumbprint" inlays favored by the Seymours were unquestionably used by others.[22] In Plates II through VII an attempt has been made to group the principal kinds of inlays and bandings used in each of the cabinetmaking areas. There is much patterned stringing to be found in New England, especially in the Boston, Salem, Newburyport, Portsmouth, and Providence centers. Plain stringing, crossbanding, and inlaid eagles and shells are often found in New York work. Philadelphia appears also to have relied heavily on stringing and crossbanding. Baltimore cabinetmakers utilized patterned stringing; but, as will be observed, except for "rope" and chevron stringing, it was very different from that used in New England. Many three-part husks, or bellflowers; inlaid shells; eagles; and floral-and-leaf motifs are also found on what is believed to be Baltimore work. Similar inlays have been found in Philadelphia work, and

the writer suspects more were used there than is now recognized. In Charleston, elliptical paterae, floral motifs, and husks were widely used.

## FOOTNOTES

1 F. Lewis Hinckley, *Directory of The Historic Cabinet Woods* (New York: Crown Publishers, Inc., 1960) is by all odds the best study of the use of woods in American and English furniture.

2 Professor Pal Greguss at the University of Szeged is carrying out similar investigations in Hungary and has published on the subject. See *Holzanatomie der Europäischen Laubhölzer und Sträucher* (Budapest: Akadémiai Kiadó, 1959).

3 James Smith, *The Panorama of Science and Art*, I (Liverpool: Nuttall, Fisher, and Dixon [c. 1816–1830]), 91.

4 *Albany Register*, March 8, 1799. Gottesman, *1777–1799*, p. 110, No. 340.

5 *Republican Watch-Tower*, April 2, 1803. Gottesman, *1800–1804*, p. 153, No. 373.

6 *The Philadelphia Cabinet and Chair-Makers' Book of Prices*, 1796.

7 Henry Bradshaw Fearon, *Sketches of America, A Narrative of a Journey* (2d ed.; London: Longman, Hurst, Rees, Orme, and Brown, 1818), p. 23.

8 *New-York Daily Gazette*, March 26, 1794. Gottesman, *1777–1799*, p. 120, No. 373.

9 Winifred C. Gates, "Journal of a Cabinet Maker's Apprentice," *The Chronicle of Early American Industries Association, Inc.*, XV, No. 3 (September, 1962), 35.

10 *Connecticut Gazette* (New London), March 19, 1790.

11 *The Bee* (New London), December 24, 1800.

12 *The Book of Trades* (London, [after 1851]), pp. 50–51.

13 *Poulson's Daily Advertiser*, August 10, 1825.

14 *Practical Carpentry, Joinery, and Cabinet-Making* (London: Thomas Kelly, 1837), p. 19.

15 Charles Tomlinson (ed.), *Cyclopaedia of Useful Arts & Manufactures* (London and New York: George Virtue, [probably late 1850's]), p. 1019.

16 Kelly, op. cit., pp. 19–20.

17 J. Stokes, *The Complete Cabinet Maker and Upholsterer's Guide* (London: Dean & Monday, [1829]), pp. 47–48.

18 *The Argus*, February 17, 1796. Gottesman, *1777–1799*, p. 136, No. 432.

19 *Federal Gazette* (Philadelphia), November 16, 1799. Prime, II, pp. 229–230.

20 An excellent discussion of the pitfalls to be encountered in the identification of furniture on the basis of inlays and stylistic attributes appears in Richard H. Randall, Jr., "Works of Boston Cabinetmakers, 1795–1825: Part II," *Antiques*, LXXXI (April, 1962), 412–415.

21 Inventory of Thomas Barrett, Baltimore County Inventories, Maryland Hall of Records, Annapolis, Maryland. DMMC, No. M-10.

22 Randall, op. cit., pp. 412–415.

# Upholstery and Furnishing Fabrics

Conclusions concerning the various materials used for upholstery on early American furniture and the reasons for their suitability and use can be drawn from several kinds of evidence. The first kind is to be found in published books of English designers whose works are known to have been used in American urban centers. American paintings, especially portraits, provide visual evidence to support such usage. Both manuscript and printed American records such as upholstery bills, inventories, advertisements, and room descriptions contain many clues. Lastly, examples of original upholstery have survived.

Haircloth was by far the commonest material and was offered in various grades and patterns; leather has often survived as original upholstery on furniture of the early Federal period. At that time, leather was tanned thinner and with a finer-grained surface than was the custom earlier in the century. It was dyed in red, blue, green, or black.

Undoubtedly many woolen or combination fabrics stronger than silk, but susceptible to moths, have been completely lost. Sky-blue silk and worsted damask covered "a sofa, twelve chairs, and three window curtains" offered for sale in New York in 1784.[1] Crimson mohair with white woven designs in the Empire style, made with a matching border, was used by Duncan Phyfe in 1837.[2] Several examples of American furniture upholstered in wool velvet have survived. Among them are an Empire sofa and matching chairs, with their original cut and stamped burgundy-colored coverings, in the American Wing at the Metropolitan Museum of Art. In the study collection of textiles at Winterthur several pieces in bright yellow, or gold, and green with stylized Empire medallions have been preserved.

It has been indicated elsewhere that the design books of George Hepplewhite, Thomas Sheraton, George Smith, and other English designers were used by American cabinetmakers and upholsterers, as well as by Englishmen, to create furniture in the new classical taste. These writers comment on the general appearance of rooms, and specify materials which will give a stylish effect when used for hangings and upholstery. One must remember that they were suggesting materials in the richest and most fashionable taste for wealthy patrons.

Thomas Sheraton defined the drawing room as "the chief apartment of a noble, or genteel house, to which it is usual for company to draw to after dinner, and in which formal visits are paid." It "should possess all the elegance embellishments can give." Of furniture for the room, he says it "should always be the produce of studied elegance, though it is extremely difficult to attain to anything really novel." The dictum that the upholstery should be of the same material throughout the room and in general should match or harmonize with the window curtains is stated by all the designers. As an example, George Smith in his *Household Furniture*, of 1808, suggests the following general principles:

> In elegant Drawing Rooms plain coloured satin or figured damask assumes the first rank, as well for use as for richness: lustring and tabarays the next: the latter, however, makes but indifferent drapery. Calico, the next in choice and of so great variety of patterns, should, where good drapery is required, be glazed mellow.
>
> It may be proper here to mention the various sorts of materials used for the different descriptions of Curtains: for Eating Rooms and Libraries, a material of more substance is requisite than for Rooms of a lighter cast; and for such purposes superfine cloth, or cassimere [both woolen goods], will ever be the best; the colours as fancy or taste may direct; yet scarlet and crimson will ever hold the preference:...calico when used should be of one colour, in shades of moroon or scarlet.

Only in the drawing room of the most "elegant" homes was silk or satin recommended. The library and the dining room were draped in heavier materials of more somber colors. Chintz seems to have been used for bedrooms and family rooms for upholstery but more often for cases or slipcovers. Leather was most frequently suggested for chairs as being durable and practical if food might be spilled on them. The Gillow firm pointed out the practicality of black morocco, which would not stain as readily as red or green, and was less expensive.

From the many sources examined, it seems safe to assume that English taste and fashion were the general rule in America in the late eighteenth and early nineteenth centuries. What was available in England was available here. Silk was probably used at most in one or two rooms—and then by people of considerable means or public prominence—in houses of the highest fashion.

Surviving bills for furnishing some of our civil and federal buildings are useful sources of information. In Hartford, Connecticut, very detailed accounts exist for the furnishing of the New State House in 1796. Armchairs for the two speakers, the most important members of the assembly, were covered with crimson silk velvet; the window stools were covered in more durable moreen and the other chairs in red leather:

Jonathan Brights Bill of Upholstery Work for the New State House
To Seating 19 chairs in red Morocco Leather
To do 2 do with Stuffed Backs & Arms exclusive of Velvet
To do 1 ditto with Stuffed Arms exclusive of Morocco Leather
To do 10 Wind^w Stools in Tow Cloth exclusive of Moreen & Brass Nails.[3]

Occasional descriptions and inventories of the furnishing for the White House have survived. The architect Benjamin Latrobe designed furniture for President Madison in the new Greek style in 1808, following closely the designs published by Thomas Hope in *Household Furniture and Interior Decoration*, 1807. In Latrobe's sketches, stylish chairs in the Greek taste with loose red cushions trimmed with tassels are shown.[4] When the White House was burned by the British, the furniture was lost; but Mrs. Madison saved the matching window curtains.

Another handsome set of furniture, ordered in Paris for President Monroe, was upholstered in red silk described as woven with a classic laurel wreath and eagle centered in the back. The upholstery has been changed, but a few pieces of this state furniture may be seen in the Blue Room today.[5] In 1825 an inventory of all the White House furnishings was published. The Green Drawing Room was furnished in silk; the furniture of the Elliptical Drawing Room, judging from the fact that the window curtains were of silk and the furniture gilded, probably was also upholstered in *silk* satin. Some of the items in the inventory are of particular interest:

Green Drawing Room
14 elegant gilt green silk bottomed chairs
2 sets ,, green silk & white dimity window curtains, worn
4 gilt curtains pins & cornice
Elliptical Drawing Room
2 elegant gilt & satin fire screens
2 ,, ,, ,, sofas & pillows
24 ,, ,, ,, chairs
4 ,, ,, ,, settees for recesses
5 ,, ,, ,, foot stools, one broken
3 sets of double silk window curtains
3 elegant gilt eagle cornices
1 Large elliptical French carpet[6]

Of the many extant newspaper advertisements only a few offer pieces of furniture with rich silk coverings. "An elegant drawing room suit, consisting of a set of curtains fitted up with French damask silk of superior quality and in the most modern styles; chairs and sofas to match..." was offered in New York in 1808.[7] "Six elegant French Back Stools, covered with very rich brocade" were for sale in South Carolina in 1798.[8] Henry Wansey's 1794 description of William Bingham's Mansion House in Philadelphia denotes a much greater degree of richness than we might generally expect, but Mr. Bingham was one of the wealthiest men in the country and his house was the gathering place of socially and politically eminent people.[9]

I found a magnificent house and gardens in the best English style, with elegant and even superb furniture. The chairs of the drawing room were from Seddon's in London, of the newest taste; the back in the form of lyre, adorned with festoons of crimson and yellow silk, the curtains of the room a festoon of the same. The carpet one of Moore's most expensive patterns. The room was papered in the French taste, after the style of the Vatican at Rome.[10]

Hepplewhite's *Guide*, in the editions of 1789 and 1794, suggests that "mahogany chairs should have the seats of horse hair, plain, striped, chequered, &c. at pleasure." This very strong material was woven on a cotton, linen, or woolen warp with a weft formed from the long mane and tail hairs of horses. White hair could be dyed various colors, or the warp could be made of colored thread with a weft of black hair. Advertisements in American newspapers afford descriptions of some of the types available here. Jonathan Gostelowe, of Philadelphia, advertised in 1793 "ten neat Mahogany Chairs—fan backs, covered with sattin hair cloth and brass nail'd." [11] "Plain and Satin-Stripe Hair-Cloth Seating," or "a few Pieces of 22 and 19 Inch narrow Stripe Hair-Seating" were also offered at this time. [12] The records of another Philadelphia cabinetmaker, Daniel Trotter, indicate that hair-cloth was used by him more frequently than any other covering. The inventory of the contents of his shop, taken in 1800, shows eighty-five yards of haircloth in several different grades. [13] This material, which is listed frequently in inventories, had the advantage of being patterned like a true textile while having the strength of hair. Although black was unquestionably the most common color for haircloth, other more brilliant colors are known. At least one piece in blue-green with an Empire medallion in gold was known in America and must have made a handsome substitute for the more perishable French satin from which it was undoubtedly copied. [14] Green haircloth woven in an octagonal pattern was the covering on an American Empire sofa made about 1815. Another piece with a small conventional floral pattern in red and white is known. [15] In 1794, John Davis had the following in his upholstery shop in Philadelphia: "7 yd 30 In[ch] plain Sattin hair Cloth, 16 yd Sattin Stripe, 11 yd plain Dᵒ, 4½ yd plain & Stripe, [and] 4 yd narrow." [16]

In the search for practical materials with small woven figures, other strong fabrics were invented. At Winterthur several pieces of furniture are now covered in an antique brown material, with a small leaf figure, resembling haircloth except for being thinner and more pliable. Microscopic analysis of the fibers, however, shows them to be cotton in one case and silk and cotton in another, stiffened with a heavy sizing.

In describing "a saddle check [cheek], or easy chair," Hepplewhite again recommends leather or horsehair for the covering but gives an alternate— "a linen case to fit over the canvas stuffing as is most usual and convenient." Thomas Sheraton defines cushions as "stuffed with hair in a canvas case... [they] are then quilted or tied down, and have loose cases into which they slip." Mahogany chairs with cane bottoms were furnished with cushions covered with the same material as the

curtains. English wood-block printed chintzes for such cases were being produced at this time in an endless variety of patterns, with new fashions appearing each season. [17] Some printed fabrics were commissioned by the most fashionable London linen-drapers (they would be called interior decorators today) and were designed and printed in such a way that the material could be used for draping beds or windows as well as for chair cushions or slipcovers. The patterns included three parts—the "furniture print" for curtains, the so-called "filling," and the chair seat. [18] Sheraton suggests covering a drawing-room chair with this kind of material "which may now be had of various patterns on purpose for chair-seats, together with borders to suit them."

An early nineteenth-century pattern book of printed cottons from the firm of Dudding, now in the possession of the Victoria & Albert Museum in London, shows matching patterns for four borders—narrow and broad running horizontally and the same running vertically. A Greek fret, for instance, is shown not only in these four stripes, but also in several color combinations.

For the housewife sewing at home, a rather more explicit description of the use of chintz for slipcovers is offered in the *Workwoman's Guide*, first published in London and Birmingham in 1838:

> When chairs and sofas are fitted up with damask, merino, stuff, horse hair, or other material that does not wash, they are generally covered with Holland, chintz, or glazed calico, which protects them from dust and dirt, and are easily removed, when required for company. Holland covers are the most durable but look cold; chintz, unless very strong, should be lined with thin glazed calico. The cover should be made exactly to fit the chair or sofa, with or without piping at the edge, and with loops sewed on three of the sides underneath, and a pair of strings on the fourth side; the cover is firmly fastened down by passing one of the strings through the three loops and making it tie.

Not only were the "cases" or "covers" protection against dust and dirt, they were washable, a fact which was clearly recognized by Gillow when he wrote a customer concerning an easy chair upholstered only in canvas: "...we presume it will require some sort of *washing* cover which requires a good deal of nicety to make them fit well to such sort of chairs." (Gillow records, Folio No. 22, page 202)

*An Encyclopaedia of Cottage, Farm, and Villa Archi-*

*tecture...* by J. C. Loudon, first published in 1833, describes loose cushions and mattress covers:

> A very cheap and yet tasteful loose sofa cover may be made of glazed self-coloured calico, with a narrow piece of different coloured calico, or shawl bordering, laid on about a couple of inches from the edge. This kind of cover lasts clean much longer than one of common printed cotton; and when the bordering is carried round the covers of the cushions, bolster, &c., it has a pretty and even elegant effect.

A few of these cases for round, loose cushions have survived, and we know that this practice was followed in America, for on September 22, 1783, George Washington wrote from Rocky Hill to his nephew, Bushrod Washington, in Philadelphia begging him to inquire

> ...of some of the best cabinet-makers at what price, and in what time, two dozen strong neat and plain, but fashionable, Table chairs (I mean chairs for a dining room) could be had; with strong canvas bottoms to receive a loose covering of check or worsted, as I may hereafter choose.[19]

For Lansdowne, the home of John Penn, an undated inventory of the late eighteenth-century lists in the North Bow Room:

> 10 Japanned Chairs
> 10 Canvass Cushions to d° [ditto]
> 2 Sophas with Cushion Seats
> Yellow stormont for two setts of Covers to
>     Chairs & Sophas.[20]

Stormont, a printed chintz with an all-over pin-dotted ground, was also used for window curtains in the room.

A few slipcovers with deep ruffles and tapes to tie around the chair legs have survived. One example at Winterthur is made from an English block-printed cotton of about 1790 in the design of a pillar with roses, perhaps the sort referred to by the Gillow firm as an "architectural print." It matched a set of bed hangings belonging to the forebears of the donor, David McKibbin. They lived in the Cumberland Valley.

However desirable a good, trim fit to slipcovers might be, the evidence of English political prints and illustrations for English novels attests to their rather blousy and ill-fitting appearance. Their purpose was to protect finer materials beneath or to conceal shabby upholstery. A very literal record by an American folk artist is found in the painting by Mr. Freeman (1816) of Mrs. James Fenimore Cooper seated in her house, Otsego Hall. Her son

described the settee in this picture from chapter five of *The Pioneers* as follows: "An enormous settee, or sofa, covered with light chintz, stretched along the walls for near twenty feet on one side of the hall. The material is printed in blue-green on white. The style of the covering is loose with a ruffle to the floor."

Unless specifically designated as furniture chintz, the cotton materials listed in merchants' accounts cannot be distinguished from dress-goods, but there can be no doubt of the following items from several different sources:

> 7 pieces furniture callico
> 1 ps. Super furniture callico
> 6 ps Super green ground callico
> 4 Plain [chintz] Plumb Col^d with Border
> a select and neat collection of purple, red,
>     blue and gold and olive copper-plate
>     Furniture Callicoes

"Nine pieces superfine furniture chintzes, large noble figures" were advertised by William Mooney in 1792.[21] Incontrovertible evidence of the popularity of English chintz for furnishing in this country lies in the large number of examples which have survived. Patterns dating from the second half of the eighteenth throughout the nineteenth century have been preserved in great variety.

Although English designers illustrated opulent pieces of furniture for the richest of customers, they noted that where expense was a factor silk could be replaced by combination fabrics or by wool as well as by cotton. George Smith, for instance, gives the following alternatives:

> The curtains with their draperies are supposed to be made up, either in plain coloured satin or damask, of which there are two kinds; the one being composed of silk altogether, the other being a mixture of silk and worsted;
> ...In addition to these there is another material greatly in use, called Merino Damask, much of which is manufactured at Norwich, and makes up very beautifully, not requiring a lining.

Robert Ackermann in his Repository of *Arts, Literature, Commerce, Manufactures, Fashions and Politics* suggests another inexpensive substitute in cotton velvet: "Manchester coloured velvets, used for furniture and curtains, produce a rich effect." He also speaks of cottons with printed patterns in imitation of the expensive silk damasks: "Should silk become objectionable from its expence, we strongly recommend the use of these new patterns. They need only be seen to become approved, and are particularly calculated for candlelight effect."

Among furnishing materials mentioned in advertisements and furniture design books are several whose names are no longer known to us. Many fabrics were removed from furniture and thrown away because they suffered damage from moths or mildew, became shabby, dirty, worn, or torn. Identification of these unfamiliar fabrics is made difficult for several reasons. Merchants in this country seldom sold furnishing fabrics exclusively, and therefore these materials cannot be distinguished from those meant for clothing. Advertisements list "new" goods, "dry" goods, "latest fashion," "summer" or "winter" goods, "European" and "India" goods, etc. Upholsterers show concern with the quality and high fashion of their workmanship rather than with descriptions of materials which they could supply. Undoubtedly new and fashionable names were given to older fabrics whose manufacture continued with little change except in technology. Other fabric names remained the same, but the character of the material changed over the years. An example of this is *dimity* which is discussed under bed hangings. A few definitions, however, can be established from dictionaries and encyclopedias.

Several names of fabrics fashionable for upholstery in the early nineteenth century stem from the verb *to tabby*, which meant to give a wavy appearance to stuffs with a calender, or to water. Among these was *taberray*, also spelled *tabaret* or *tabouret*, a stout silk with broad alternating stripes of satin and watered material in contrasting colors.[22] A late nineteenth-century dictionary describes it as having "blue, crimson, or green satin stripes... divided by cream-coloured tabby ones."[23] For window stools Hepplewhite says, "the covering should be of taberray or morine, of a pea-green, or other light colour." *Taboreen* or *tabyrean* (a word which combines tabby and morine), another watered material made of silk and worsted, in pink, green, crimson, mulberry, black, and two shades of blue, was listed in the inventory of Joseph Hopkins of New York.[24] *Tabinet* is described as a heavy poplin with a silk warp and a woolen or linen weft, with figures woven on a watered ground.

*Lustring* or *lutestring*, suggested for bed-curtain linings and window curtains, was also fashionable as a dress fabric. This silk was "lustrated," or given a glazed shiny surface, by being stretched and moistened. In the late eighteenth century, fashionable colors in lustrings were plum, pink, cinnamon, lilac, green, garnet, light blue, and brown.[25]

*Cassimere* or *kerseymere*, most often mentioned for men's clothing, was a soft twilled wool recommended by George Smith for dining rooms. In 1827 the Boston *Merchant's Memorandum and Price Book* listed this material in blue, black, brown, drab, green, and "mixed."[26]

*Harateen* was used extensively for upholstery during the eighteenth century, and one frequently comes across the term prior to 1770. Essentially this watered woolen material seems to be indistinguishable from *morine* or *moreen*. In the price book referred to above, it is listed among the worsted and silk-and-worsted goods in red, green, crimson, scarlet, and yellow. Merchants' inventories of New York in 1803 and 1807 list this material, although it is not differentiated as a furnishing fabric. Beck's *Draper's Dictionary* of 1882 describes it as "an imitation of moiré in commoner materials for purposes of upholstery." Examples believed to have been made in the eighteenth century are different in appearance from those of nineteenth-century manufacture. The predominant colors of the former period, when the fabric is found clean and unfaded, are strong red, green, and less frequently, yellow. The red could be called cherry; the green, forest; and the yellow, bright golden. In the nineteenth century, pale blue appears. The red is either a bright orange or a pink which fades to beige. The nineteenth-century watered patterns are generally woven from more evenly spun, although not necessarily finer, yarn. Floral designs, less often found, are more stylized, more uniform, and lack the invention and charm of some of the eighteenth-century patterns.[27] The selvedges are more regular. The cloth, less hairy with higher finish, was often pressed to a glossy smoothness. An American sofa with tapered, molded legs, probably made as late as 1790, was originally covered in green, watered morine. The edges of the seat frame and arms were outlined with large brass tacks nailed tight against one another over a binding or tape the width of the tack heads.

The late eighteenth-century upholsterer, like those of previous periods, employed curled horsehair to provide a thin, neat, but firm foundation held in place by coarse cotton or linen, as muslin is used by upholsterers today. Original upholstery, when found, is invariably characterized by its trim lines and flat, rather than overstuffed, appearance.

Both the engraved plates and the texts in design books show quite specifically how furniture was to be upholstered. In Hepplewhite's *Guide* a sofa termed a *duchesse* is described: "The stuffing may be of the round manner... or low-stuffed, with a loose squab or bordered cushion fitted to each part." Sheraton says of a sofa: "The seat is stuffed up in front about three inches high above the rail, denoted by the figure of the sprig running longways; all above that is a squab, which may be taken off occasionally." This method of upholstery is shown in the armchair probably made by Duncan Phyfe, No. 135. Frederick A. Muhlenberg is seated in such a chair in the painting by Joseph Wright of about 1790.[28] "Three caberoul [cabriole] sophas, square stuffed, French modern fashion, covered with figured sattin, setts of sattin covered chairs to match..." were offered for sale in 1812.[29] Ackermann describes two handsome chairs as having "the seat and back French stuffed and quilted. They may be covered with the best red morocco leather, velvet, or (which is far more elegant) rich damask silk, ornamented with rich Persian fringe, and beautifully bordered *en suite* with the window curtains." The quilting or buttoning [French: *capitonné*] to which he refers did not have the appearance of the exaggerated tufting characteristic of the mid-nineteenth century when furniture looked overstuffed or bloated. This style came in vogue after 1828 when the first patent for springs was issued in England, after which they soon came into general use.

The design books offer two methods of tacking the upholstery to the seat rail by means of brass-headed tacks. They are placed tight against each other in a double row or in scallops. The inventory of John Penn's possessions, published in 1788, included "3 elegant large settees, having hair bottoms, with sattin stripe, a double row of gilt nails and fluted legs." The original haircloth covering of a New York side chair similar to No. 79, which was used in the Banquet Hall at Mount Vernon, was held in place by two rows of brass tacks over narrow horsehair tape at the bottom and top of the seat frame. (Lewis Collection, The National Museum, Smithsonian Institution)

A bill of 1812 from Roxbury, Massachusetts, itemizes "Eight Mahogany Chairs, with hair bottoms covered with Strip'd hair cloth and brass nails festoon fashion – $40."[30] In portraits of the period, artists repeatedly painted such rows of bright tacks; the paintings of Ralph Earl show chairs tacked both in festoons and in double rows. Early in the nineteenth century this use of round-headed brass tacks was supplanted either by a narrow border of tape covering the iron upholstery tacks or a cord of another color to accent the squared edges of the piece. In at least one instance, a thin strip of pewter was found. Wider tapes with conventionalized floral patterns were used decoratively on plain fabrics of a contrasting color. A list of such trimmings, too long to be quoted here, was appended to the following New York advertisement of 1792.

John DeGrushe, Upholsterer, has just opened and for sale at his stores No. 63 Wall-street, and No. 30 Broad-way a very handsome assortment of Upholstery Trimmings, consisting of best white lace, cotton and thread, do. tassels, fringes, cotton and thread, from 1– ½ inch to 4– ½ inches, chintz fringes, tassels, cords and laces of all colours, and the most fashionable figures, all different and superior to any of the kind in this city, viz....[31]

Upholstery work, although not necessarily for the most fashionable chair and settee styles, is included in Benjamin Lehman's 1786 Philadelphia price list for cabinetwork:[32]

|  | Mahog-any | Wall-nut | Jurny-man |
|---|---|---|---|
| Chair with Plain feet & Banister with Leather Bottoms | £1.14.0 | 1.5.0 | 0. 9.0 |
| Arm Do | 2.18.0 | 2.5.0 | .16.0 |
| For Damask Bottoms add 2 shi¹ |  |  |  |
| For Hair 2 s–6 d |  |  |  |
| For any Chair as above Stuffed over the rails & Brass nails add 8 Shillings |  |  |  |
| Setees plain Crooked Legs feet & Banisters without Casters with hair or Damask Bottoms | 6.10.0 | 5.0.0 | 1. 6.0 |

While decorative grills of gilt wire seem not to have been used in the doors of case pieces by cabinetmakers in this country, Sheraton's dictum that green or other colored silk be tacked in the opening to conceal the contents behind glass doors was widely followed. Later Ackermann even suggested a kind of roller shade to hide the contents on the shelves. The glazed doors of American break-front bookcases and especially of secretary bookcases almost all bear telltale tack holes where cloth was once fastened in pleats or flutes.

With regard to other pieces of American furniture which may have had swags of drapery hung beneath a seat, across the back of a sofa, or at the top of a bookcase door in front of the pleated silk, no original examples have been found. Sheraton says of a cylinder desk and bookcase with such drapery: "This design shows green silk fluting behind the glass, and drapery put on at top before the fluting is tacked to, which has a good look when properly managed." American sewing tables seem generally to have been draped in accordance with English precedent. Another decorative finish, also suggested by the English, is fringe of a contrasting color tacked all around the skirt of a chair. Ralph Earl's portrait of Oliver Ellsworth and his wife shows an example.[34] The portrait of Henry Clay painted by George Cooke in 1839 shows a later use of fringe of a much heavier type, probably made of wool rather than silk, placed beneath the arms and skirt of a chair.[35]

In general, during the Federal period in the United States, English materials were used, and English upholstery practices were followed. The availability of English design books, furnishing materials, and, more often than not, upholsterers who had either migrated from England or prided themselves on a familiarity with English fashion support this conclusion.

## FOOTNOTES

1 Richard Kip, *New York Packet and the American Advertiser*, December 13, 1784. Gottesman, *1777–1799*, No. 472.

2 McClelland, op. cit., p. 273, Pls. 260 and 261.

3 Connecticut State Library, Hartford, Conn. Another bill lists the yardage of crimson silk velvet for the two armchairs, the red morocco, and the moreen, together with fringe and brass nails furnished by Jeremiah Halsey. Photostatic copy Ph 1053 a–b in DMMC.

4 Robert L. Raley, "Interior Designs by Benjamin Henry Latrobe for the President's House," *Antiques*, LXXV (1959), 569.

5 White House Historical Association, *The White House, an Historic Guide to the White House* (Washington, D. C., 1962), p. 91. Text by Lorraine Waxman Pearce.

6 *Letter from the Commissioner of the Public Buildings Transmitting an Inventory of the Furniture in the President's House* (1825).

7 Lorraine Waxman [Pearce], "French Influence on American Decorative Arts of the Early Nineteenth Century," p. 48. An advertisement for Porri and Rinaldi in the *New York Gazette*, November 2, 1808, is quoted.

8 Richard Fowler, *South Carolina Gazette*, June 4, 1798. Prime, II, 223.

9 *Dictionary of National Biography*. Entries for both William and Anne Willing Bingham.

10 Henry Wansey, *Excursion to the United States of North America in the Summer of 1794* (2d ed; Salisbury, Easton, 1798), p. 123.

11 Jonathan Gostelowe. *Independent Gazetteer*, May 11, 1793. Prime, II, 180.

12 Bankson & Lawson, *Maryland Journal* (Baltimore), October 25, 1791 and April 17, 1792. Prime, II, 168.

13 Castrodale, "Daniel Trotter, Philadelphia Cabinetmaker," p. 30.

14 "The Editor's Attic," *Antiques*, LVI (July, 1949), 57.

15 Owned by Mrs. Benjamin Ginsberg, N. Y. C.

16 William M. Hornor, Jr., *Blue Book of Philadelphia Furniture* (Philadelphia, 1935), p. 266.

17 For a discussion of styles in English chintz, see the catalogue *English Chintz*, published for the exhibition held at the Victoria & Albert Museum, London, 1960.

18 Peter Floud, "Richard Ovey and the Rise of the London Furniture-Printers," *Connoisseur, 140*, No. 564 (November, 1957), 95.

19 *The Writings of George Washington from Original Sources, 1745–1799, Prepared under the Direction of the United States George Washington Bicentennial Commission and Published by the Authority of Congress*. John C. Fitzpatrick, ed. Vol 27, June 11, 1783–November 28, 1784. Washington, D. C.: United States Government Printing Office, 1938.

20 Inventory of John Penn, Philadelphia, n. d. DMMC 55.513.
See also *The Pennsylvania Magazine of History and Biography, 15* (1891), 374.

21 William Mooney, *The Diary; or Loudon's Register*, March 12, 1792. Gottesman, *1777–1799*, No. 479.

22 *Connoisseur Period Guides: The Early Victorian Period* (New York, Reynal, 1958), p. 120.

23 S. F. A. Caulfield and Blanche, C. Saward, *Dictionary of Needlework* (London: Gill [188–]).

24 Inventory of Joseph Hopkins, New York, 1803. DMMC 54.106.33.

25 Lorraine Waxman [Pearce], op. cit., p. 48. An advertisement for Power and Paxton in the *New York Evening Post*, December 16, 1812, is quoted.

26 Charles P. Forbes, *Merchant's Memorandum and Price Book* (Boston, 1827). The author describes this book as a pocket memorandum for the country trader who could insert quantities of goods needed and prices paid. It was to serve as a key to the almost endless variety of merchandise required for the country trade.

27 Abbott Lowell Cummings, *Bed Hangings* (Boston: The Society for the Preservation New England Antiquities, 1961), Fig. 15. An example of eighteenth-century moreen.

28 Owned by Mrs. Edward K. Tullidge, Philadelphia.

29 Lorraine Waxman [Pearce], op. cit., p. 48. An advertisement for Power and Paxton in the *New York Evening Post*, December 16, 1812, is quoted.

30 Essex Institute Library, Salem, Massachusetts. Bill of Elisha Adams to David Greenough, Roxbury, Mass., March 25, 1812. Photostatic copy 786 in DMMC.

31 *The Diary; or Loudon's Register*, August 15, 1792. Gottesman, No. 470.

32 Gillingham, *The Pennsylvania Magazine of History and Biography*, LIV (1930), 289.

33 Probably wool damask.

34 Wadsworth Atheneum, Hartford, Conn.

35 Destroyed by fire. Reproduced in *Georgia Historical Quarterly, 64*, No. 2 (June, 1960).

# Connoisseurship and Attribution

Connoisseurship involves not only *evaluation* of an object but also its *identification*. Evaluation raises such questions as how good the piece is, how it compares with others made about the same time in terms of workmanship, materials, and condition, and whether it is all original. Identification requires that we decide where and when it was made and who made it. Since connoisseurship is a matter of judgment, and attributions are at best tentative, the connoisseur is like a judge in a courtroom—he must gather all available evidence and then weigh it as objectively as possible. Occasionally, an object still retains some identification put on by the maker, such as an inscription, signature, mark, stamp, or label. Such "marks" as well as the original bill of sale or the history of ownership and acquisition may enable the connoisseur to identify accurately the shop, place of manufacture, or date of an object. In most cases, however, such evidence is not available. Without it, identification can never be positive. That is why most attributions are merely guesses as to when, where, and by whom an object was made.

The connoisseur constantly uses two standards for comparison: documented pieces—those that can be identified as to maker, time and place of manufacture—and masterpieces—those that are recognized as the finest in form, ornament, workmanship, and materials. Let us examine these standards.

Documented pieces bear the mark of the maker or more often the label of the master of the shop in which they were made. Many cabinetmaking shops during the Federal era had a number of journeymen and apprentices working in them and often employed the skills of men outside them for inlays, turning, carving, and upholstering. Thus, the label of Duncan Phyfe on a piece of furniture doesn't mean that he actually made it. Rather, it means that it was made to his standards and in accord with his interpretation of a design. In those instances where several documented pieces from the same shop are known, a high percentage of them seem to be of the same character, although individual details of workmanship are often different. However, one must not assume that a particular form or pattern of chair was made in only one shop. Similar forms were undoubtedly made in many shops. Through comparison of documented pieces in terms of form, ornament, materials used, and craftsmanship, it has been found in general that furniture made in Massachusetts differs sometimes in form and almost always in details from furniture made in New York or Philadelphia. Lolling chairs and tambour writing tables were favorites in the Boston area, square-back chairs with a triangular urn splat and three feathers were a favorite in New York, and square-back chairs with carved and reeded spindles in the back were popular in Philadelphia. As one studies the surviving forms of each area, he detects not only regional preferences but also patterns of workmanship that amount to local idioms. The study of documented pieces thus becomes an important part of a connoisseur's education. Often he must rely on photographs and books for illustrations of forms. But, unfortunately, pictures can never take the place of personal examination, even for over-all form.

What constitutes a masterpiece? In the abstract, this is a hard question to answer; in specific instances, it is easier. The connoisseur looks at each object first from a distance as he tries to get a sensual reaction to it. Sometimes he may look at it with half-closed eyes from various angles to sense the sweep of line and massing of form. He need not ask himself if the lines are clean and the stance one of grace. He knows and reacts instinctively, especially if the piece is sculpturesque in the relationship of masses and voids. In furniture of the Federal era, the harmonies are subtle, some almost abstract in the interrelationships of line and surface pattern. In all great pieces of this style, such as the Seymour desk in the frontispiece, one finds an interplay of geometrical outlines of form, inlays, and veneer patterns that is like point and counterpoint in music. But novelty and movement attained through ornament and form is not enough. There must be unity. The idea of unity is a subtle one—a piece has it, or it doesn't have it; without it, a piece can never be a masterpiece.

Complexity, intricacy, ornament—none of these qualities makes a piece of furniture great. But it must be remembered that whereas a great piece of furniture is a work of art, it also represents the mastery of a problem. The 491 pieces of furniture in this catalogue presented 491 problems to the maker. No two were solved in exactly the same way.

Some problems were bigger ones than others, and their solutions more complex. To make a tripod stand is less difficult than a chair or a secretary and bookcase. Strange as it may seem, although there are many more stands than secretaries, there are probably almost as many "great" secretaries as stands. And, because the initial problem was greater, the "great" secretary will be more highly regarded than the "great" stand.

For any outstanding piece of furniture, the materials and workmanship must be fine and in accord with the lines, proportions, and character of its style. In addition, a masterpiece of the early Federal era must have grace, delicacy, richness and variety of color (sometimes achieved through figure of the woods, sometimes through inlay, sometimes through painted designs), and its parts must be so interrelated as to give it unity. Lastly, it must be in character with the user and appropriate to its function. In other words, a lady's work table or lady's writing table ought not only to fill the needs respectively of a seamstress or a writer, they should also be feminine in character. The requirements for a masterpiece of the later Federal era change in certain respects: the lines, whether curvilinear or rectilinear, are usually more vigorous, the masses heavier, the scale larger, the mien more sober, the wood darker, the effect richer, the colors of the upholstery bolder. The general appearance is frequently more dignified.

To determine the area in which a piece of Federal furniture was made, there are five major factors to be considered: (1) secondary woods; (2) regional preferences for certain forms or patterns; (3) inlays; (4) carved motifs; (5) workmanship.

## SECONDARY WOODS

As already indicated in the charts, cabinetmakers in each area tended to use secondary woods which grew in their locale. These help to some extent in determining the place of manufacture. They also are useful in separating English and European furniture from American. Though the presence of a single American wood is not conclusive, the presence of two or more such woods is substantial assurance of American origin (United States or Canadian). The presence of tulip, often called poplar or tulip poplar, is a reliable sign of American manufacture; the writer has seen no instance of its use north of Rhode Island and Connecticut. The presence of white pine is generally regarded as proof of American origin, but it is sometimes found in English work. Although the presence of oak is often regarded as proof of English workmanship, this supposition is not true. Oak was used for table frames in Pennsylvania and Maryland where the writer has seen a few instances of its use for drawer linings and chair frames.

In summary, for casework, and especially for linings of drawers, in Massachusetts and northward, white pine was normally used; in Rhode Island, white pine, tulip, or chestnut, and occasionally white cedar; in Connecticut, white pine and tulip; in New York, tulip, bilsted or gumwood, and sometimes white pine; in Pennsylvania, white cedar, tulip, and occasionally hard pine; in Maryland, white cedar and hard pine; and in Charleston, cypress, tulip, and white pine. Only one of these woods may be used, but sometimes two are found in the same drawers.

For swing-leg tables, the gates and often the framing are of white pine in New England; tulip in New York; oak in Philadelphia and Maryland. For chair frames, birch and ash were both used in New England; ash and tulip and sometimes cherry in New York; ash, white oak (cherry for easy chairs), and sometimes walnut, in Philadelphia. Oak and tulip have been found in several Maryland chairs.

## FORM

Wide ownership by American cabinetmakers of the London price books, Hepplewhite's *Guide* and Sheraton's *Drawing Book,* and the publications of George Smith and others means that cabinetmakers were familiar with the full range of London furniture patterns; but, for reasons which can only be called regional preferences, certain forms were more popular in one center such as Massachusetts than in another, such as New York or Philadelphia. In an isolated instance, any form may have been made anywhere, but a survey of surviving examples show distinct regional preferences for certain patterns of chairs, desks, or tables, etc. These preferences become abundantly clear in the catalogue.

## INLAYS

In Plates II through VII of inlays, 127 details of inlays are grouped according to regional use. Line inlay or plain stringing was used in all cabinetmaking centers, but heavy outlines of light wood on the extreme edges of drawers and tops is most often found in New York and Philadelphia. Crossbanding was also widely used. But frequently in New York and southward, cross-banding was set between light lines on bookcase doors. Much patterned stringing was used in New England and in Baltimore. In New England the stringing is often more intricate and less professional in execution than that of Baltimore. The writer believes that some very intricate, showy patterned stringing found on pianos and clocks, such as that in Figure 69, was imported from England. This is also unquestionably true of some of the shells and flowers, but for the most part these were probably supplied by inlay specialists working in Boston, New York, Philadelphia, or Baltimore. The presence of identical inlay, even if of an unusual type, on two pieces of furniture suggests a common source for the inlay, but the furniture may have been made in different shops, although probably in the same region. Certain unusual inlays like Figures 26 and 27 seem to have been used only in New England, others like 78 and 79 only in Maryland. When three or four identical inlays are found on two pieces of furniture, the probability is high that both pieces came from the same shop. It should be noted that occasionally one sees an inlaid piece on which the scale of the individual elements in the inlays is larger than usual. This is a characteristic of shop-made, meaning "home-made," inlays, often by rural workmen. Just as old styles often lingered on in the country after their vogue in the city was past, so did the use of inlays. The writer has seen one fine inlaid table whose Plattsburg, New York, label is dated 1823.

## CARVING

A broad survey of carved motifs is very much needed. An attempt has been made in the section on carved details at the back of this book to isolate typical treatments and elements of carved motifs found on chairs made in several cabinetmaking centers. A study of regional preferences will give the connoisseur one more clue to the area of origin.

Salem carving is generally fine in quality; that of New York is usually first rate; that of Philadelphia often scratchy and flat; and Baltimore carving varies widely in quality, some of it being extremely coarse. On splay-leg tripod tables the pointed-leaf carving of New York is so characteristic as to be almost always recognizable. In the past, such carving has often been attributed solely to Phyfe, but many cabinetmakers used it. They may even have employed the same carvers that Phyfe used. Philadelphia carvers favored leaves "squared off" on the ends instead of being pointed, but isolated instances of this kind of carved leaf are known on New York tables made after about 1820.

## WORKMANSHIP

In comparing any two pieces of furniture of the same form and pattern, one soon becomes aware of many idiosyncrasies of workmanship in their structuring—for example in the shape, size, number of dovetails, and the way the bottoms of drawers are fashioned. Sometimes the grain of the wood in the bottom runs lengthwise, sometimes front to back. Sometimes the bottoms are fitted in rabbets, sometimes in grooves. Certain methods of construction may be typical of a single workman or shop but more often they seem to be the idiom of a regional group of workmen.

There is still a great deal to be learned about regional methods of construction, but it may be pointed out that Salem chair frames are often braced with triangular nailed blocks (with the grain horizontal). Boston chairs sometimes have open braces at the inner corners; New York chairs often have long medial braces running from front to back. In early Philadelphia Federal chairs, large quarter-round blocks (grain vertical) are to be expected. Open braces are commonly found on Baltimore chairs. Perhaps fifty per cent of Philadelphia chairs have side rails completely tenoned through the rear legs, showing what are commonly called "open tenons" on the back. But it must be pointed out that a considerable number of Rhode Island and Connecticut chairs were constructed in the same way.

The reader will soon see the importance of the study of documented pieces. These, after all, provide the criteria essential for attribution. For many pieces, determination of regional origin is not difficult; but to determine the exact shop in which a piece of furniture was made is in most cases impossible. Of the thousands of cabinetmakers who made Federal furniture, probably not more than one or two out of each hundred men practicing the craft can be credited with even a single object which he made. For this reason every piece of furniture whose maker is known is doubly precious. It rescues one more American cabinetmaker from oblivion.

## DATING

The dating of furniture is largely guesswork. To make an educated guess, the connoisseur depends not only on the data gained from the preceding observations, but on other factors as well. For example, a knowledge of the first appearance of a form or type of ornament is very helpful. In the past, many pieces of Federal furniture have been dated in the 1780's. As has already been pointed out, the Chippendale style was still in vogue through 1788 (Chippendale furniture continued to be made on occasion until at least 1810); the earliest date that can be assigned with any assurance to a shield-back chair or any other piece in the Federal style is 1790.

The early Federal style, from about 1790 to 1805, is marked by such attributes as delicate proportions, square tapered legs, inlays, and sometimes carving. The square-back chair, turned legs, reeded motifs, and certain other carved elements were introduced in the late 1790's. These forms and motifs were most popular from about 1800–1815. The Grecian chair (Klysmos type, but often with scrolled back) was first introduced about 1805 and became popular after 1810; it was widely made until 1840 or later. The late Federal style, increasingly heavy and bold, was in vogue by 1815 and was continued with ever-increasing novelties through the era covered by this book. The French bed (often called Empire today) was a popular form at this time. Marble-top tables with caryatid and, more commonly, columnar supports came into fashion about 1815. Because of space limitations, it has not been possible to include here several forms of this kind which reached their full development about 1825.

Hardware and fasteners also may offer valuable evidence for dating. Nails are a convenient, though at best a loose, dating aid. Nail-making machines were introduced about 1790; and in most cities cut nails, that is, machine-made nails, were generally available about 1800. Hence, the presence of hand-wrought nails (usually with rose heads) suggests an early date, probably in the 1790's, for Federal furniture, whereas the use of cut nails points to a date of 1800 or later.

Although their purpose was primarily functional, furniture mounts, commonly called brasses, underwent certain ornamental changes during the Federal era. Bails (without backplates) held in place by a post at either end were much used in the late Chippendale and early Federal period (see No. 178). A small oval or round "rosette" (plate) was normally used with each post. Oval or rec-tangular backplates made of thin sheet brass with motifs stamped in relief to give a three-dimensional effect were invented in 1779 and probably in common use by 1795.

Sheffield plate and enameled backplates were sometimes used, as were inlaid ivory and light wood escutcheons. Much emphasis is placed by collectors on the presence of original brass mounts, and rightly so. They played an important part in the over-all effect sought and achieved by the maker of the piece. To give a brilliant appearance, they were usually brightly finished. To give a similar effect today, they should be either lacquered as they often were originally or kept well polished.

About 1810, mahogany knobs held in place by wood screws came into use. Too often today collectors or dealers replace these with brasses. This is unfortunate for they were meant to harmonize with the over-all effect of rich dark wood rather than punctuate it with bright motifs as brass mounts do. Another type of drawer mount used during the Federal era was the glass knob. An early mention of these is Henry Fearon's observation of 1818 (quoted in the chapter on woods): "I have seen some [furniture] with cut glass, instead of brass ornaments, which had a beautiful effect." In the 1820's, pressed glass pulls came into vogue.

Two more observations should be made before the connoisseur faces the culminating question: When between 1788 and the present was the piece of furniture made? For the possibility always exists that it is a reproduction, a copy made after say 1840, or a fake made with intent to deceive. The coloration of interior woods and evidence of natural wear are factors that help determine whether it is a piece of its style period or later. What evidence is there of natural aging and wear? Are interior surfaces colored in the way old wood colors with time—more where exposed, hardly at all where enclosed. Or, is the wood "smudged," dirtied or colored with rotten-stone, shellac, or other agents employed by the faker? Are there natural dents, chips, and softening of edges, contours, and corners? Such signs of wear that come with use are to be expected. The true connoisseur is seldom misled by condition so pristine as to be unnatural. He expects the bottoms of drawer sides to be worn down, a broken toe or a crack here and there. These are some of the signs of antiquity.

At this point in his study of a piece of furniture, the connoisseur is almost ready to assign a date. But before doing so, he asks himself if the parts are all of one period? Dealers occasionally speak of "married pieces"—parts of two or more old pieces that have been assembled to make one complete piece. A common example of this is the adding of a bookcase to a secretary or desk. The connoisseur must then remember that consistency of workmanship is the hallmark of every craftsman!

The congruency or lack of congruency of the parts of a piece of furniture is all-important in determining whether the whole was made by one author or made up at a later date of two or more antique parts. If original, the dovetails in each drawer, and the structure and fashioning of the bottoms ought to be identical. Exceptions demand clear explanation because man is a systematic animal and tends to work in a systematic way.

## ASSIGNMENT OF DATE

Now to sum up the evidence. For an example consider a serpentine chest or chest with "french" front feet. In both upper and lower sections, the dovetails, the drawer bottom construction, the spacing of holes for brasses and the nails are identical for all drawers—except one. The color of the inner woods of each drawer is comparable except for one—the middle drawer of three in the top tier. On this drawer, the dovetails are different from those on the other drawers, and the nails are square headed and cut instead of being rose-head and wrought as in the other drawers. The drawer sides are smudged and a dirty gray instead of the clean olive and green of tulip found in other drawers. The line inlays forming oval panels on the drawer front are slightly finer and the glowing attractive spread eagle on its front (similar to No. 125) is pristine and smooth as glass to the touch. The veneers of its wings and tail have never buckled or bulged up to uneven contours. The varnish on this mahogany drawer seems thinner than the crackled surface on the rest of the piece except for one back bracket foot which doesn't match its counterpart. A printed label on the bottom of the upper middle drawer reads "Made by Benjamin Frothingham, Charlestown, Massachusetts." The label is yellowed and printed on old hand-laid paper. When an edge is gently raised, the wood is the same color underneath. The letters are without serifs.

What is the verdict? Stylistically, the serpentine façade, the line inlays, the "french" feet point to a date between 1790 and 1805 or 1810. The presence of hand-wrought nails throughout the piece except for the one drawer support a date prior to 1800. Apparently one back foot has been broken or lost and replaced—and so has the center drawer. The one who had the repairs made obviously wished to deceive a buyer. He tried not only to cover up his repairs by smudging the new cuts of the old wood he used, but glorified his work with a modern inlaid eagle and added a label printed on old hand-laid paper. But he failed to note that type without serifs did not come into general use until the 1820's or that Benjamin Frothingham's labels were engraved. Nor was the faker aware that tulip was not used as a secondary wood in Massachusetts. Upon ascertaining all of these things, the connoisseur may of course decide that if the price is reasonable, he will buy the piece anyway. It is, after all, a fine Baltimore double chest. He will have the label and inlaid eagle removed and the one drawer front matched to those on either side.

Always the connoisseur must come to grips with the demerit to be attached to wear, tear, and accidents. The older, the rarer, the less obtainable, and the finer the object, the more restoration, repairs, or blemishes he is prepared to accept. Here, each man must be his own judge and set his own criteria.

It should be evident by now that connoisseurship is based on knowledge. It engenders taste but taste that has grown out of study—out of a constant search to learn what makes one thing great and another near great, out of striving to be analytical and objective, out of the study of innumerable objects in museums, shops, books, and magazines. The true connoisseur cultivates habits of objectivity, skepticism, and humility. Remembering that "pride goeth before a fall," he knows that if he parades his knowledge before the seller, he will stop the flow of information that might be had for the asking. He will avoid avarice, and flee like the plague the desire to get a great bargain. In time he approaches the ideal set forth by Jonathan Richardson in his *Two Discourses,* first published in London in 1719: "Those who are connoisseurs have this farther advantage; they will have no occasion to ask, or rely upon the judgment of others; they can judge for themselves."

# CATALOGUE

# Explanations

*Arrangement.* The furniture in the catalogue is numbered in sequence and, generally, with the exception of three sections—"Looking Glasses," "Unusual and Specialized Furniture," and "Fancy Furniture"—is arranged within each section as to geographical origin—from north to south.

*Provenance.* With an instinctive flair for collecting, Henry Francis du Pont personally bought between 1923 and the opening of the Museum in 1951, 383 of the 491 pieces included in this catalogue. Since 1951, as new Museum rooms have been planned and as important pieces have appeared on the market, Mr. du Pont has generously continued to buy furniture as well as other objects for the Museum collections.

Other benefactors have also supported the growth of the Winterthur Museum in numerous ways. Among their gifts have been objects or funds for the purchase of objects. Twenty-two pieces of the furniture illustrated came to the Museum in this way. They add dimension to the collection and several are documented. After "Gift of" the names of donors other than Mr. du Pont are listed under "Provenance," following the names of early owners, if known.

*Inlays.* Carved details and inlays not only add greatly to the character and beauty of Federal furniture, but they are often beautiful in themselves. Inasmuch as they are barely visible in illustrations, even of individual pieces, and since they provide important clues for regional identification, many have been included—often in larger than actual size; 127 details of inlays are reproduced in colorplates II through VII. References to inlays so illustrated will be found after the Accession number at the foot of the caption for the piece of furniture on which the inlay occurs.

*Carved Details.* Forty details of carving and bed posts will be found near the end of the book with the catalogue number of the piece on which each occurs and the origin of that piece.

*Brands, Labels, Stamps, and Inscriptions.* Most of those which appear on the furniture in the catalogue are illustrated in a special section following "Biographies of Cabinetmakers." Like the biographies, these are arranged alphabetically.

*Chair Blocks and Braces.* Although individual cabinetmakers may have favored different types of blocks and braces for chairs, it appears that the different types fall into regional patterns of usage for a large percentage of the chairs in the Winterthur collection. The following six types of blocks and braces were those most frequently noted in the initial study of the collection. The references to them in the captions represent an attempt to characterize one group of structural devices by type. The results are at best tentative, but the writer believes this kind of approach would yield helpful information if carried out on a broad scale.

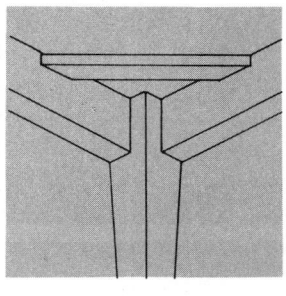
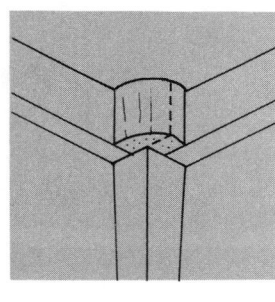
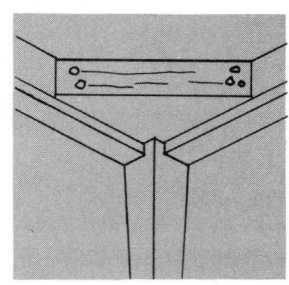
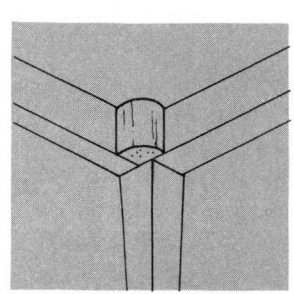
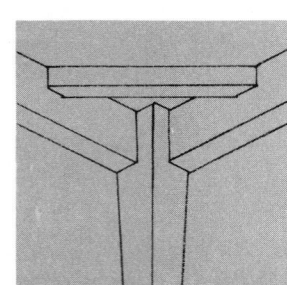
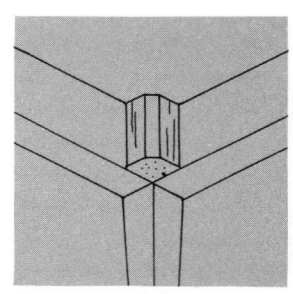

# Beds and
# Bed Hangings

During the Federal period in America, cabinetmakers and upholsterers offered two main types of beds: low-post and high-post. Low-post beds have survived in large numbers. Made of maple or other native woods (no low-post bed of this period in mahogany is known to the author) and usually with turned head and footposts, they were invariably painted. Most families owned one or more high-post beds, sometimes with all four posts of mahogany, though more often than not the headposts were of stained native wood, as were the rails and usually the headboard, all normally covered by the hangings or bedspread. Some surviving "four posters," as they are often called today, are of stained or painted cherry, maple, birch, or tulip, frequently with lathe-turned posts. The finer examples are also carved and, occasionally, inlaid.

The two varieties of high-post beds are those with posts six feet or more in height with straight canopies (No. 7) and another group with shorter posts—variously known as tent, camp, or field beds—with high arched or serpentine canopies (No. 3). Sheraton suggested that these field bedsteads "may be considered for domestic use, and suit for low rooms, either for servants or children to sleep upon; and they receive this name on account of their being similar in size and shape to those really used in camps...." Excellent illustrations of two field beds and a page of stylish sweeps (canopies) for field-bed tops are shown in Hepplewhite's *Guide* (1788 edition), Plates 102, 103, 104. A little before 1810, a new style of bed with curved paneled ends was introduced and became tremendously popular. Today these beds, made to stand with the side instead of the head against the wall, are called "Empire" or "sleigh" beds. Originally they were known as "French" beds, but by about 1820 variants were referred to as "Grecian" beds. At first they were made of mahogany, later of maple and other native woods, and eventually even of cast iron. When first listed in *The New York Price Book* of 1810, a "French Bedstead" was described as follows: "Three feet wide, with scroll ends, one panel in each, to come within five inches of the top of the scroll, all plain, a frame for a sacking bottom." Journeymen were to be paid three pounds, seventeen shillings, six pence, for making one of these beds, whereas they received only a pound for making a mahogany high-post bedstead with "four turned posts, plain teaster lath, pins for bottom, eight screws, and valen laths." It is assumed that a turner had already prepared the posts before the journeyman cabinetmaker started his work.

Both the inventories and accounts of cabinetmakers and upholsterers indicate that the hangings and furnishings of a bed were more costly than the bedstead itself, and contemporary writers, as quoted here, often gave rather explicit information about the furnishings.

> Bed furniture is composed of a top, a back, two head curtains, two foot curtains, one top outer and one top inner valance, one bottom valance, and sometimes extra drapery

laid on the back of the bed. When beds are lined, the lining is put inside the curtains, and within the top and back of the bed... The curtains should just touch the ground, as also should the foot valance. The inner top valance should be half a nail[1] narrower than the outer. In making up, the curtains are bound round, or if lined, sometimes the lining is brought outside to form a hem all round. Lace is often laid on at about one nail from the edge. The valances accord with the rest, having often fringe added to give a greater finish.[2]

Although these directions for the furnishings of a full-sized four-post bed were written in 1838, they may be regarded as a summary of earlier nineteenth-century practice. Most engravings for beds in late eighteenth- and early nineteenth-century design books show long head and foot curtains to enclose or surround the bed entirely. Very few complete sets of original bed hangings exist in America today; but a four-post bed with arched canopy in the Essex Institute, Salem, has its original drapery of furniture chintz printed from wood blocks in England about 1805. This set consists of a full complement of curtains, swags, valances, and tails, much like the above description.

In contrast to this bed, which seems almost smothered in curtains, the beds at Winterthur in their period room settings appear, for several reasons, with a minimum of drapery. The fabrics used, as well as the tassels, cords, and fringes trimming them, are almost without exception antique, and such materials are difficult to find in the large quantities originally used. A bill from Stephen Collins of Philadelphia for furniture cotton for a bed included "56 yd copperplate Furniture-cotton."[3] Not only would such a quantity be almost impossible to find today, the necessary handling of such fabrics soils and musses them and would soon wear out all except the sturdiest. In the interest of conservation, a minimum amount of material has been used at Winterthur and the design of the hangings is only suggestive of the voluminous creations shown in design books. Actually, the beds appear as they might have looked in summer, when the extra curtains were probably removed to allow greater circulation of air.

Sheraton, Hepplewhite, George Smith, and Ackermann suggested fashions to satisfy the taste of wealthy patrons. Perhaps carried away by their own fancies, they offered designs for all kinds of beds—state, canopy, dome, elliptic, and alcove. In a desire to imitate the French, they illustrated duchesses, Polonaises, and French sofa beds. Sheraton states in several places that he has used his fancy in some of his designs to please the upholsterers or to appeal to the taste of a lady, but he assures the reader:

> Upon the whole, though a bed of this kind is not likely to be executed according to this design, except under the munificence of a royal order, yet I am not without hopes that useful ideas may be gathered from it, and applied to beds of a more general kind.[4]

George Hepplewhite's remarks on the subject are more specific:

> Beds are an article of much importance, as well on account of the great expence attending them, as the variety of shapes, and the high degree of elegance which may be shewn in them.
>
> They may be executed of almost every stuff which the loom produces. White dimity, plain or corded, is peculiarly applicable for the furniture, which, with a fringe with a gymp head, produces an effect of elegance and neatness truly agreeable.
>
> The Manchester stuffs [cotton velvets] have been wrought into Bed-furniture with good success. Printed cottons and linens are also very suitable; the elegance and variety of patterns of which, afford as much scope for taste, elegance, and simplicity, as the most capricious fancy can wish....
>
> In state-rooms where a high degree of elegance and grandeur are wanted, beds are frequently made of silk or satin, figured or plain, also of velvet, with gold fringe, &c.[5]

In contrast to these London styles, the *Workwoman's Guide* offers many practical hints to the housewife who might want to make curtains or bed hangings at home.

> The most usual and simple methods alone will be treated of here, all best beds and drapery for sitting-rooms should be put up by regular upholsterers, as it requires much correctness of eye, added to taste and knowledge of the prevailing fashion.
>
> Beds for common use are hung with linen or cotton check, or stripe, print or stuff, but for better purposes, with dimity, fine stuff, moreen, damask, chintz, Turkey twill, and lined with glazed calico or muslin of various colours, and for state rooms, fine silk, satin, or velvet is employed.[6]

In speaking of "stuff, moreen, and damask" the writer unquestionably had woolen fabrics in mind.

Since the moth has taken great toll of woolen fabrics, it is impossible on the basis of surviving examples to gain an idea of the extent of their original use for bed hangings, or to identify the various kinds of cloth employed. Moreen, a woolen cloth with a moiréd appearance, one which was widely used earlier in the eighteenth century, continued to be used until at least 1840, possibly later. A point generally overlooked is that woolen damasks were manufactured as well as silk ones. In the Winterthur collection and elsewhere are late eighteenth-century sample books containing hundreds of examples of woolens produced at that time in Norwich, England. Many of the patterns are identified by contemporary handwritten titles as "Sattins," "Com^n Sattins," "Sattins de Lit," and "Bed Damasks," all referring to woolen damasks, sometimes woven in solid colors and sometimes in two colors. Such references strengthen the likelihood that the many listings of satin and damask "bed furniture" in inventories most often meant handsome, warm, and durable woolen materials of this kind, rather than silks.

The dimity suggested by Hepplewhite and others is a fabric whose character has changed greatly. Three grades, or kinds, of dimity were listed in the *Merchant's Memorandum and Price Book* under cotton goods as "*cambric* dimity, *common* dimity, and *furniture* dimity."[7] As found in old bed hangings, it was a heavy cotton material with raised stripes. Surviving examples look like heavy seersucker, but a swatch of dimity for white beds shown by Ackermann in the November issue of the *Repository* for 1812 is a very finely woven cotton material with a narrow stripe and embossed design which he says is quite new.[8] At Richmond Hill, the home of Aaron Burr in New York, the White Room was completely furnished in this material:

6 Stuffed Back Chairs (dimity covers)
2 ditto with arms
3 Window Curtains (dimity)
1 Bedstead fluted Post (dimity curtains)
1 Cotten Counterpane[9]

In 1806, Thomas Rumsey imported hundreds of yards of furniture dimity along with furniture calico, chintz furniture, bed lace, fringe, and tassels.[10] Window curtains, chair covers, and bedspreads were made on occasion with chintz borders sometimes called "shawl bordering."[11] The practical aspects of dimity, chintz, or muslin curtains are apparent, for as one author says: "The usual material for the hangings of cottage beds, especially for tent beds, is dimity, which has the advantage of being easily washed and may thus be always contrived to have a clean appearance."[12] Considering the number of dimity bed curtains which have survived and the frequency with which the term appears in inventories, this was undoubtedly a very popular material for the purpose. Abraham Rees in his *Cyclopaedia,* published in Philadelphia 1810–1824, considered the material important enough to give the following lengthy definition:

> The distinction between fustian and dimity...seems to be this: that the word fustian is used to express a common tweeled [twilled] cotton cloth of a stout fabric, upon which no ornament is woven in the loom; but which is most frequently dyed after being woven. Dimity is also a stout cotton cloth of a similar fabric; but is ornamented in the loom, either with stripes or fanciful figures, and when woven is seldom dyed, but commonly bleached of a pure white. The striped dimities are the most common, as they require less labour in weaving than the others, and the mounting of the looms being more simple, and consequently less expensive, they can be sold at much lower rates.

Rees further describes the threading of the loom for a striped dimity under the heading "draught and cording of looms" and devotes several illustrations to patterns for it in his volume of plates.

From the records of the Gillow firm of cabinetmakers and upholsterers (Lancaster, England), certain generalizations about furnishing materials can be made which are probably equally applicable to American rooms. In virtually all cases the fabrics used for upholstery, bed hangings, and curtains were matched, unless the more practical choice of haircloth or leather was made for the covering of certain chairs. After 1780, cottons were most fashionable: dimity, calicos (printed cotton from India), chintzes or prints. The latter probably referred to copperplate-printed cottons. In houses completely furnished by the Gillow firm, cottons were suggested and used for six, eight, or ten rooms, and wool—moreen or damask—for one, two, or three rooms. Only the wealthiest afforded themselves silk hangings, and then usually for only one or two rooms out of a dozen or more.

1 One nail equals 2¼ inches, or ¹/₁₆ of a yard.

2 *Workwoman's Guide* (2d ed.; London and Birmingham, 1840), p.193.

3 Goyne, "Furniture Craftsmen in Philadelphia," p.83. The Stephen Collins Papers, Library of Congress, are quoted.

4 Sheraton, *Appendix to the Cabinet-Maker and Upholsterer's Drawing Book,* 1802, p.40.

5 *The Cabinet-Maker and Upholsterer's Guide* [Hepplewhite's Guide]...from Drawings by A.Hepplewhite and Co., Cabinet-Makers (London: I. & J.Taylor, 1789), pp.17–18.

6 *Workwoman's Guide,* p.192.

7 Forbes, op.cit. See No.26 in Upholstery Footnotes.

8 Hazel E.Cummin, "What was Dimity in 1790?" *Antiques,* XXXVIII (July, 1940), 23.

9 New-York Historical Society, "The Furnishings of Richmond Hill in 1797, The Home of Aaron Burr in New York City," *Quarterly Bulletin,* XI (April, 1927), 17.

10 Merchant's Account, Thomas Rumsey, New York, 1806, Joseph Downs Manuscript and Microfilm Collection, 54.83.115.

11 Barbara Morris, "The Indian Taste in English Wood-Block Chintzes," *Connoisseur,* CXLIII (March, 1959), 23. Figs.9 and 10 are "shawl" chintzes.

12 J.C.Loudon, *An Encyclopaedia of Cottage, Farm, and Villa Architecture.* First published in 1833; page 337 in 1839 edition.

# VIII

# Franklin Room

*The Franklin Room, as urbane and cosmopolitan as Benjamin Franklin himself, includes souvenirs of his long and illustrious career as writer, scientist, and statesman. The superb bed (No. 1), the marble-top night table (No. 366), and corner wash stand (No. 362), and the armchair at the right (No. 20), like the other furniture in the room, were probably made in or near Boston, Massachusetts, where Franklin was born in 1706. The square sofa (No. 275) from New York was once owned by Victor du Pont whose father, Pierre Samuel, was a friend of Franklin. Also from New York is the center table (No. 377) which stands on a Khorassan carpet of the early nineteenth century. The armchair in the foreground is from Philadelphia, which Franklin claimed as his home. The window curtains and bed hangings used at other seasons of the year, also commemorate the genius of Franklin. Printed in England about 1785 by copperplate, they show him accompanied by "Liberty" being guided by Minerva to the Temple of Fame.*

## 1 BED

*1800–1810   Probably Boston or Salem, Massachusetts*

Details of this bedstead, one of the most important in the Winterthur collection, are related to the famous Elias Hasket Derby bed of more elaborate design in the Metropolitan Museum of Art.[1] Similar features on the footposts of this bed and the one in the Metropolitan, which has been attributed to the Seymours of Boston, are the short fluted drums (just above the rails) and leaf-carved inverted cups above the vase turnings. The footposts of this bed are handsomely reeded and inlaid with panels of figured birch.

The cornice formed of symbols of Cupid—bow and arrow, quiver and torch, painted gray and ornamented in gold and sepia—suggests that this bed may have been made for a bride.[2] Sheraton's *Cabinet Dictionary*, 1803 (Pl. 43, "French Rod"), illustrates a cornice of this shape, although a laurel wreath substitutes for the quiver and torch.

The curtain swags and short cascaded tails are made of linen and cotton cloth with a small conventionalized floral sprig brocaded in pink silk. A cotton bedspread with scattered flowers in an inner square bordered by large blossoms and undulating vines is representative of those painted in India for the East India Company trade with England and America.

Dimensions: height over-all 100; posts 96; width 55½; length 79.
Materials: footposts, mahogany inlaid with figured birch panels; headposts and rails, birch; headboard and canopy frame, white pine.
Accession: 55.784                    see Inlay Fig. 13

## 2 BED

*About 1800   Northeastern Massachusetts*

Although very few American bedsteads can be documented as to maker, several features of this one relate to other furniture made in Northeastern Massachusetts: the fine reeding on the shapely posts, inlaid rectangles of satinwood, and the ogee outline of the turnings just above the rails on the footposts.

In accord with early usage and the dictum that for bedrooms "the window curtains should always accord with the hangings on the bed, both in colour and materials, as also in shape,"[3] the window curtains and bed hangings are of the same material—a very popular late eighteenth-century English chintz printed in red from copperplates on white cotton cloth. With many allegorical allusions,

it commemorates both General Washington and Benjamin Franklin. Several other subjects of historical and patriotic appeal appear on other copperplate printed textiles. They include "America Presenting at the Altar of Liberty Portraits of Her Illustrious Sons," the "Death of Wolfe," and "William Penn's Treaty with the Indians." A set of hangings owned by John Penn of Lansdowne, a great Philadelphia house, was included in the 1788 inventory of his estate:

> 1 set of hair colour furniture cotton bed curtains, pattern William Penn's Treaty with the Indians.
> 3 window curtains to match ditto, with cord, tassells and screws.[4]

Most of the subjects were adapted from well-known paintings and engravings of the time. Although the place of manufacture for only one of these textiles can be identified, it is presumed that one English factory made a specialty of American historical subjects, capitalizing on their popularity with the citizens of the new Republic. One such textile that shows Washington standing before a pyramid is signed "Henry Gardiner, Wandsworth, Surrey." Related historical textiles were made in France.

Dimensions: height over-all 97; posts 83½; width 55½; length 79.
Materials: mahogany; footposts inlaid with Ceylon satinwood panels.
Accession: 55.785

## 3 FIELD BED

*1800–1810   Northeastern Massachusetts*

For field beds, canopy frames of serpentine outline were more often used during the Federal period than the straight or simple arched frames of earlier times.

A "Mahog. Field Bedsted & Sacking bottoms, green gauze curtains" listed in the inventory of James Mease of Philadelphia[5] may have been similar to this one, which is draped with satin striped curtains of green silk gauze. The words of a Lady of Quality, written in 1774, at Point Pleasant, North Carolina, dramatically illustrate the original function of such hangings:

> The heat daily increases, as do the Musquetoes, the bugs and the ticks. The curtains of our beds are now supplied by Musquetoes' nets. Fanny has got a neat or rather elegant dressing room, the settees of which are canopied over with green gauze, and on these we lie panting for breath and air, dressed in a single muslin petticoat and short gown.[6]

**1**

Delicate sprays and festoons of small flowers are embroidered in colored silks on the white satin spread, probably made in China after French designs. Panels of figured birch veneered on the turned and reeded mahogany footposts relate this bedstead to much north-of-Boston cabinetwork.

Dimensions: height over-all 82; posts 65½; width 56; length 77½.

Materials: footposts, mahogany with inlaid figured birch panels; headposts, beech; headboard, white pine; rails (bed and canopy), birch.

Accession: 55.796

## 4 BED

*About 1800   New York City or Albany*

The footposts of this painted bed are a fine expression of the Hepplewhite style—stop fluted, carved with crisp leaves, and reeded. The white finish enhanced with highlights of gold leaf emphasizes the delicacy and refinement of details.

This handsome bed was originally owned in Albany by Joseph C. and Ann Elizabeth Yates.

Yates was born in Schenectady November 9, 1768. After the deaths of his first two wives, he married Anna Elizabeth De Lancey on December 1, 1800. In recent years this bed, two side chairs (No. 63), settee (No. 64), and looking glass (No. 235) have been known as the furniture of Governor Yates (Joseph C. was elected Governor of New York in 1822) but descendants claim that it was Mrs. Yates's furniture—perhaps a part of her dowry.

Dimensions: height 96½; width 56½; length 77½.

Materials: rails, equipped with flat knobs to hold the roping for the mattress, maple; headposts, birch; footposts and rails, soft maple; headboard, white pine; hangings, green-and-white-striped silk, probably French, about 1800, trimmed with contemporary fringe; bedspread, white satin embroidered in color, French, late eighteenth century.

Provenance: Gov. and Mrs. Joseph C. Yates; Jane Josepha De Lancey Neill; Edward Montandevert Neill; Anna De Lancey Neill Grinnell (Mrs. Edward).

Accession: 55.786

## 5 BED

*1805–1819   New York   Attributed to Charles-Honoré Lannuier (working 1803–1819)*

This handsome bed in the Louis XVI manner is attributed to the French cabinetmaker Charles-

Honoré Lannuier. For fifteen years this skillful *ébeniste* advertised in the New York newspapers "new Fourniture"; his work always kept its French accent.[7] This bed, except for canopy rail of white pine, is constructed of mahogany throughout, as are most of Lannuier's finest pieces. It is finished on all four sides, including quarter-round brass trim around the recessed panels. French in character and related to other work of Lannuier are: the fluted posts carved with acanthus leaves on the lower parts; the high outcurving headboard and footboard; and the canopy rail painted green and gold and mounted with ormolu stars, eagles, and anthemion patterns. The bedstead is as neatly finished within as without. The rails and posts are marked in Continental fashion with notches and Roman numerals, and large cherry-wood casters are mounted under the frame in forged iron to permit easy movement of the bed.

Among du Pont family heirlooms in the Nemours Room are the silk window curtains, bed hangings, and spread, the material for which was brought from France by Eleuthère Irénée du Pont de Nemours from whom it has descended to Henry Francis du Pont. In one repeat of the material are delicate floral swags, ribbons, and bowknots surrounding a garden temple and in another a fountain with *amorini*. Such motifs are characteristic of classical ornament as it was reinterpreted by late eighteenth-century French designers working in the Directoire style.

This bedstead, the night table (No. 361), easy chair (No. 148), and sewing table (No. 408) were all made in New York soon after 1800, about the same date as the French Aubusson-type, tapestry-weave carpet.

The carved and reeded woodwork is from the dining room of Montmorenci, a house built in Shocco Springs near Warrenton, North Carolina, for William Williams in 1822.

Dimensions: height 98½; width 59½; length 80¾.
Materials: mahogany except for canopy frame of white pine; bedspread and hangings, light-blue-and-white silk, French lampas of a type called *camaieu*.
Accession: 55.789

**4**

**5**

**6 BED**

*1800–1810   Philadelphia*

The turned, reeded, and carved posts of this bed are related to No. 7 in their over-all outline, details of leaf carving, and deep chamfering above the rails. Contrary to the practice in New England and New York where headposts were usually left plain, in Philadelphia, headposts as well as footposts frequently received the attention of the turner and carver; here they are both equally well decorated with festoons of husks, paterae, leaves, and reeding.

A molded serpentine cornice painted with red-and-green flowering vines supports hangings made from an English roller-printed chintz. Such striped furniture chintzes, with dark-green stripes alternating with flowers printed in red on a tan ground, were popular about 1825.

Twenty years earlier, Sheraton wrote in his *Dictionary* (p. 181): "Printed cotton furniture or hangings for beds have been varied to almost an infinite number of patterns, and it is difficult to fix upon the most approved or fashionable ones." An olive-green homespun woolen blanket with loose embroidery of colored wools in a large floral pattern harmonizes with the chintz curtains.

The early nineteenth-century woodwork in this bedroom, the Albany Room, is from the Peter P. Breen house, which stood at 249 South Tenth Street in Philadelphia. On the floor is a brilliant Feraghan rug of about 1800. For a long time, such golden-colored and flamelike veneers as those on the trunk (No. 440) have been thought to be satinwood. They can now be identified as figured birch. The corner washstand (No. 361) bears the label of Jacob Forster of Charlestown, Massachusetts, and the serpentine-sided two-drawer stand is richly carved in the style associated with Samuel Field McIntire. Before the window stands a type of chair (No. 75) called Empire or Phyfe today, but which was known in its heyday from 1810 to 1840 as French or Grecian.

Dimensions: height over-all 94½; posts 88; width 56½; length 77.

Materials: posts, mahogany; headboard, stained white pine; rails, tulip; cornice, hard pine.

Accession: 55.795

**7 BED**

*Late eighteenth century   Philadelphia*

Its posts gracefully turned and skillfully carved with reeding, swags, and dependent tassels, this is one of the most beautifully proportioned beds of its time. Although lacking carved ornament on the turned headposts, it bears many similarities to No. 6.

On June 25, 1796, Jacob Wayne billed "Capⁿ Joseph Da Costa" £100.5.6 for nineteen pieces of furniture. Among these were two "high post" bedsteads. According to W. M. Hornor, Jr., all of this furniture passed from father to son for five successive generations to John Chalmers Da Costa, 3rd.[8] This bedstead, sold at auction[9] in 1930, is believed to have been one of the original nineteen pieces from Wayne's shop. However, it must be pointed out that the original bill reads in part:

To 1 high post bedstead 2 post Mahoʸ £6.. ..
To Dᵒ      all Button wood £4..10..

One hundred and sixty years later it is difficult to account for the fact that this bedstead was made entirely of mahogany, including the *four* posts. And it seems significant that the standard charge by Philadelphia cabinetmakers in 1796 for "a plain high post [mahogany] Bedstead with [canopy] rails and facings" was £9.0.0. "Reeding the foot posts"

7

cost £1.10.0 extra, with "any carving according to the expence of it." [10] Did Wayne make a mistake on his bill or is this another bed?

The valance of yellow-and-white-striped silk with a small conventionalized grapevine pattern is trimmed with swags of yellow cord (often called "lace" in inventories) with tassels hanging between. The quilted bedspread is made of bright yellow taffeta.

C. Alder, upholsterer of Philadelphia, advertised in 1797 as follows:

> ... he continues to manufacture every article in his line (whether useful or ornamental) on the newest and most approved principle. Having lately received from Europe the most modern fashions, English and French, and hopes from the advantages he possesses of European experience, and an extensive correspondence in that quarter with the first proficients in his art, will enable him to give the most ample satisfaction to his employers. Fringes, linens and tassels imported and manufactured as usual. [11]

H. Taylor of Philadelphia also prided himself upon being able to supply large assortments of these embellishments:

> He makes up all sorts of Bed and Window Curtains in the neatest fashion. Lines and Tassels for ditto, all Kind of Fringe... [12]

Dimensions: height 92¼; width 56½; length 77.
Materials: all mahogany.
Provenance: John Chalmers Da Costa, 3rd.
Accession: 55.791

## 8 BED

*About 1800   Charleston, South Carolina*

"Any bed with movable headboard and mahogany rails has an excellent chance of Charleston origin." [13] This statement by E. Milby Burton in 1952 is an excellent "rule of thumb" for American bedsteads. In *Charleston Furniture*, Mr. Burton illustrates details of Charleston workmanship, many of which are to be found on this imposing and important example: mahogany rails, notched for slats; movable headboard; footposts, turned above the rails and square-tapered below, terminating in spade feet. The upper turned sections are distinctively carved in Charlestonian fashion with sharp-pointed leaves on the urn and the capitol, and leaves and heads of rice between fine and coarse reeding. Fringed crescents at the base of the reeding are believed to be unique to this area.

**8**

In the late eighteenth century in England and on the Continent, patterns in silks were reduced to small repeating designs. Stripes were favored, as in this pale-blue-and-white-striped silk with small figures. The bedspread is of late eighteenth-century taffeta with festoons and floral sprigs.

Dimensions: height over-all 111¼; posts 93½; width 64½; length 77½.
Materials: posts, rails, and cornice, mahogany with "stringing" and veneers of light wood; headboard, white pine.
Accession: 55.798

## 9 FIELD BED

*1790–1800   New England*

The repetition of the shape of the headboard in the canopy frame and the finesse of the moldings of the posts are the work of a cabinetmaker with an eye for detail. Although this bedstead is hard to date, the thin lines of its extremely delicate posts and the shape of the headboard point to a slightly later date than that of related "pencil post" beds with

permitted the air to circulate freely. As early as 1770, a Boston newspaper carried a notice for "1 Suit Nett Curtains for a Bed,"[14] and occasionally an antique example comes to light today. But unusual indeed is the net tester patterned with large leaves and vines worked into the cotton mesh of coarse thread or string with which this rare child's bed is trimmed. The shape of its cusped headboard suggests an earlier date for the bedstead than do the baluster turnings of its footposts, which are similar to posts illustrated by Hepplewhite. Because of the presence of hard pine, the bedstead is thought to have been made in the Middle Atlantic states, perhaps in Pennsylvania or Maryland.

Dimensions: height over-all 64; posts 54; width 35½; length 58½.

Materials: footposts, tulip; headposts and rails, hard pine; headboard, white pine.

Accession: 55.801

FOOTNOTES

1 Joseph Downs, "Derby and McIntire," *Metropolitan Museum of Art Bulletin*, VI (October, 1947), 79.

hexagonal or octagonal posts, normally thought to have been made prior to the revolution. The woods are those frequently used in New England.

Allegorical subjects with patriotic appeal to Americans were produced for the American market by French, as well as English, textile printers. Jean-Baptiste Huet, the leading artist for Oberkamf's manufactury at Jouy, designed the original cartoon, *L'Hommage de l'Amérique à la France,* for the red copperplate-printed toile of the bedspread and window curtains (not shown) which match.

Dimensions: height over-all 78; posts 62½; width 49⅛; length 79½.

Materials: posts, birch; rails, maple; canopy and headboard, white pine.

Accession: 55.797

## 10 CHILD'S BED
*1780–1800   Middle States*

Lacy net canopies for beds must have served especially well during the summer months since they

2 Mabel M. Swan, "Where Elias Hasket Derby Bought His Furniture," *Antiques*, XX (November, 1931), 280–282. A similar cornice on a bed in the Museum of Fine Arts in Boston, which is believed to have belonged to Elizabeth Derby West, may be dated by an entry in an account book of John Doggett, famous Roxbury, Massachusetts, looking glass and cabinetmaker, who also supplied other furniture and services to Mrs. Derby. On November 23, 1808, Doggett credited William Lemmon as follows:

    to gilding Bed Cornice
    Bows Darts Quivers Arrows    $16

3 *Workwoman's Guide.*
4 Broadside advertising the sale of John Penn, Jr.'s goods, May 22, 1788. DMMC, 55.512. (Hereafter referred to as DMMC.)
5 W. H. Hornor, Jr., *The Blue Book of Philadelphia Furniture* (Philadelphia: 1935), p. 158.
6 Janet Schaw, *Journal of a Lady of Quality* (New Haven: Yale University Press, 1922), p. 182.
7 Cf. documented examples, 305 (card table), and 342, 343 (pier tables). An excellent summary of Lannuier's work and style is to be found in Lorraine W. Pearce's article, "Distinguishing Characteristics of Lannuier's Furniture," *Antiques*, LXXXVI (December, 1964), 712–717.
8 W. H. Hornor, Jr., "Documented Furniture by Jacob Wayne," *International Studio*, CXVI (June, 1930), 40–43, 82. Therein Hornor states emphatically that this furniture "has passed from father to son for five successive generations" but does not name the Da Costa family.
9 *The John Chalmers Da Costa, 3rd, Collection of Documented Early Philadelphia Furniture* (Philadelphia: Wm. D. Morley, Inc., December 15, 1930), Sale Catalogue.
10 *The Philadelphia Cabinet and Chair-Makers' Book of Prices*, 1796, pp. 25–26.
11 C. Alder, *Federal Gazette* (Philadelphia), July 14, 1797. Prime II, p. 215.
12 H. Taylor, *Pennsylvania Packet*, August 10, 1782. Prime I, p. 214.
13 E. Milby Burton, "The Furniture of Charleston," *Antiques*, LXI (January, 1952), 49.
14 *Boston News-Letter*. August 30, 1770. Dow, p. 125.

# New England Chairs

*Side Chairs, Armchairs, and Chair-back Settees*

In London, chairmaking and carving were each distinct branches of cabinetmaking during the late eighteenth century and the first half of the nineteenth century. In the United States, although chairmakers were not as highly organized and specialized as in England, the practice was unquestionably greatly influenced by English custom. The earliest book of prices specifically for chairmakers, *The London Chair-Makers' and Carvers' Book of Prices for Workmanship*, is dated 1802—fourteen years after the first publication of a book of prices for other forms; but it is evident from the shop records of the Gillow firm of Lancaster, England, that carefully stated piecework agreements between masters and journeymen chairmakers were in effect before 1780. Whereas *The Cabinet-Makers' London Book of Prices* (1788) contains no reference to chair work, the second edition of the Norwich (England) book of prices of 1801, entitled *The Cabinet and Chair Makers' Norwich Book of Prices*, contains a separate section of seventy-five pages of text and four pages of tabulation concerned with chair construction.[1]

In American price books, beginning with the first (1792), chairs are included as an integral part of each publication; but the listings are not nearly so complete as in the above-mentioned London publication. In the 1807 London reprint, 108 pages of text and thirteen engraved plates are devoted to the making of chairs and sofas, and twenty-six pages of text and three plates to carving, moldings, and ornament. For chairs, there are more than 250 references in the index to specific forms or operations and about forty in the index for carving. It is estimated by this writer that in this one book there are enough variables listed to produce five thousand chairs, each differing from the other. These include a wide variety of forms and variations thereof, such as square, sweeped, serpentine, oval, and bell-shaped seats as well as many types of legs, arms, banisters, splats, braces, and ornamental details; these are often illustrated. Unfortunately, there are no names for many illustrations such as those of eight types of banisters and sixteen types of spindles for backs. They are referred to only by plate and figure numbers, as are eleven kinds of therms (spade feet) for front legs. Nevertheless, the book provides much information, including the London sources for many chair designs and the names for many parts of chairs and sofas long since forgotten.

In the London price book, there are no specific references to dining, parlor, or chamber chairs; and the standard width of front for square, oval, and vase- (shield-) back chairs—chairs intended for use in any room—is listed as twenty-one inches—one inch wider than the norm cited by Hepplewhite, who gave the general dimension and proportion of chairs as follows: "Width in front 20 inches, depth of the seat 17 inches, height of the seat frame 17 inches; total height about 3 feet 1 inch." However, he remarked that "other dimensions are frequently adapted according to the size of the room, or pleasure of the purchaser."

For the finest homes, there undoubtedly were definite canons of taste which governed choice of chairs and furnishings. Sheraton's attitudes toward the furnishing of rooms as set forth under the heading "Furnish" in his *Dictionary* (p. 218) probably reflect those of his time. He states:

> The dining parlour must be furnished with nothing trifling, or which may seem unnecessary, it being appropriated for the chief repast, and should not be encumbered with any article that would seem to intrude on the accommodation of the guests.

When describing the Prince of Wales's "dining parlour" in Carleton House, Sheraton illustrates side chairs and describes them as having seats covered with red leather. He includes pillars "emblematic of the use we make of these rooms, in which we eat the principal meal for nature's support." He further declares "The furniture without exception is of mahogany, as being the most suitable for such apartments."[2] But in contrast, he also remarks that a drawing room is "of that sort which admits of the highest taste and excellence; in furnishing of which, workmen in every nation exert the utmost efforts of their genius."[3]

The backs, armrests, and seats of sixteen armchairs shown in his illustration of a drawing room (Pl. 61, *Drawing Book*, 1793) appear to be upholstered in silk, and everything else in the room is of the richest sort. Ten years later his ideas had not changed; for, in his *Dictionary*, he states (p. 218): "The drawing-room is to concentrate the elegance of the whole house, and is the highest display of richness of furniture."

Concerning bedrooms or chambers he notes:

> The lodging-room admits of furniture simply necessary, but light in appearance, and should include such pieces as are necessary for the accidental occasions of the night. Here should be a small book shelf with such books as should tend to promote our pious resignation of body and soul to the care of the great author of the universe, and divine superintendant of human happiness. (*Dictionary*, p. 219)

"Hall chairs" with solid backs and wooden seats (with no upholstery to be stained by wet garments) are listed in most English chairmaking price books, and many such English hall chairs survive. But they are not listed in any American price book, nor are American examples known today. The writer believes there was good reason that they were seldom, if ever, made in the United States. Windsor chairs, also with wooden seats, were used instead. Since they were painted, they were impervious to wet and damp and could readily be taken to the porch or garden; thus, being useful for the outdoors as well as inside, they were used in halls instead of the more stylish English kind. In American probate inventories, Windsors are listed time and again as being used in the front hall or entry, even in the finest houses.

In summary, stout, serviceable chairs, probably of the plainer sort with upholstery of leather or horsehair, were deemed appropriate for dining rooms. Simpler ones, perhaps smaller in size, were satisfactory for bedrooms. The most ornamental and richly upholstered chairs were reserved for parlors and drawing rooms.

Sets of chairs seem to have ranged from five side chairs and one armchair, up to ten or more side chairs with two armchairs. Complete sets of six or twelve armchairs were made infrequently and probably only for great houses.

Within the four New England states of Massachusetts, New Hampshire, Rhode Island, and Connecticut, chairs from several principal centers are generally recognizable. However, it must be kept in mind that chairmakers, cabinetmakers, masters, and journeymen moved about from one area to another carrying patterns and personal methods of working with them. Obviously, when a man moved from Salem to East

Windsor, Connecticut, or from Boston to Northampton, Massachusetts, he did not leave behind his methods of joinery, furniture patterns, or stock of inlays. He continued to work in his new shop much as he had at his old stand. But to satisfy local preferences and price standards, he probably modified the type and amount of ornament.

Actually, when one speaks of Salem furniture or Boston furniture, one means furniture bearing the imprint of men who have been trained in or worked under the influence of the Salem or the Boston schools of cabinet- and chairmakers. Within each "school," some men unquestionably had more business, more influence, and more talent than others. This was true of the Sandersons of Salem and of the Seymours of Boston. Through their training of apprentices, employment of journeymen, and purchase of ready-made furniture (made to their specifications) from others, their ideas, standards, and methods inevitably had a great influence and gave impetus to a local "school." This does not mean that all furniture made in the area conformed in every way to one standard. Human nature is too diverse for that; but the main production of a group of men in each area seems to have many characteristics in common.

In terms of style, the earliest chairs made between 1783 and 1825 are the ladder-back, or slat-back, chairs. They seem to have been made in all urban centers and by many country cabinetmakers as well. Numbers 11, 12, and 13 are illustrative of the form as made in Massachusetts, all with molded marlboro legs. Such chairs usually have stretchers, three or four pierced slats, and seats upholstered over the frame.

Beginning about 1790, chairs which are called shield-backs today but were then referred to as vase-backs when pointed at the bottom and as urn-backs when rounded at the bottom, appear to have been the most popular chair form in New England; but, beginning five or ten years later, many square-back chairs were made in Boston, Salem, and Portsmouth. Some of these with plain square backs were reeded, as in No. 28. Also occasionally reeded were those with "elliptic cornered tops" and tablets, as in No. 25. Northern New England backs of the latter type and with "sweep tops," as in No. 26, were more often finished with a bead on the edges than with reeded surfaces.

The filling in the backs of the chairs might be cut from one broad piece of wood, as is the lattice back of No. 27 or the gothic back of No. 20, in which case it was known as a banister. The filling could also be made from several narrower pieces of wood framed separately as spindles as in No. 28, as "upright splats with shoulders" as in Nos. 31 and 32, or with "double shoulders" as in No. 24. Sometimes banisters were fitted into pedestals at the lower ends as in Nos. 40, 41, and 42.

Most New England seat frames are squarish in shape, broader in front than in back, and usually have "plain sweeped side or front rails" (bowed in a gentle curve). Some are serpentine in front; and a few chairs, such as Nos. 11, 30, and 42, have "hollow," or saddle, seats. Every New England chair of this period in the Winterthur collection has a stuffed seat upholstered over the rails, with three exceptions—one with a slip seat (No. 40) and another with a rush seat (No. 13) are essentially old-fashioned chairs. The third exception (No. 38) is upholstered over only half the rail.

Tapered legs braced by stretchers were the norm for New England chairs of the early Federal period, although the legs of the finest were usually carved and without stretchers. About equal numbers of these were left plain or were ornamented with two single strings of light-colored wood running through to the floor or were molded with "two beads and two hollows." Occasionally, one sees a Boston chair with reeded legs;

but these are far less common among surviving examples of that city than of those of Philadelphia or New York. Spade feet, except for the very finest Salem examples with carved legs and appliqués of ebony, are rarely seen on New England chairs. These chairs (Nos. 14, 15, 16) have no stretchers.

Most Salem chairs, whether they had vase, square, or oval backs, have considerable carving and little or no inlay. The predominance of carving over inlay is probably due to the presence there in the late eighteenth century of several excellent carvers, among them the famed Samuel McIntire. Although there is conclusive proof that McIntire carved furniture made by others for the fabulously rich Elias Hasket Derby, there is no evidence that he actually made furniture himself. And it seems highly probable that a man so busily engaged in the building and designing of houses would have had little time for personally carving furniture except for special and important commissions.

One later type of chair made in Boston deserves mention—the scroll-back chair with a roller and tablet in the top (Nos. 37, 38, and 39). Among New England chairs known to the writer, this is the only type to be upholstered over only half of the seat rail. In Northern New England and often found in Portsmouth are many square-back chairs with carved flowers in the corners of the back and with reeded stiles and banisters (Nos. 28, 29).

Too little is known of Rhode Island chairs to generalize broadly, but pedestal-back chairs such as Nos. 41 and 42 were popular there. The latter type and its variant (No. 40) were also commonly made in Connecticut, along with such vase-backs as No. 46. Although the design for the modified square-back with stiles bulging outward to meet a serpentine cresting rail as in Nos. 41 and 42 is illustrated in Plate I of the 1802 and later editions of *The London Chair-Makers' and Carvers' Book of Prices,* it seems not to have been used by American chairmakers except in Rhode Island and Connecticut, and possibly in Albany.

Among the many kinds of arms found on chairs of Massachusetts, Rhode Island, and Connecticut are: rather straight stiff elbows (arms) supported on turned stumps which are a continuation of the front legs (No. 23) and sweeped elbows with ogee supports, set back from the front legs and screwed to the frame (No. 20). Sometimes the juncture of elbow and support is square (No. 20), or rounded (No. 29), and, occasionally, sharply pointed as on the arm of a chair which matches No. 32.[4] Elbows of Rhode Island and Connecticut chairs are usually not so well modeled as Massachusetts examples, and sometimes they extend slightly over the ogee support to form a knob at the front.

1 No existing copy of the first edition is known to the author.
2 Thomas Sheraton, *Drawing Book,* p. 440.
3 *Ibid.,* p. 441.
4 Chair owned by Harry Arons, Bridgeport, Connecticut, April, 1965.

# IX

# Corner of the Montmorenci Stair Hall

*Stylish side chairs (No. 38), a chair-back settee (No. 37), and sewing table (No. 403) are shown in the Montmorenci Stair Hall. All four pieces have been attributed to the English-trained Boston cabinetmaker John Seymour and/or his son Thomas. They were in partnership part, if not all, of the time from 1794 to 1804, when Thomas Seymour opened "Seymour's Boston Furniture Warehouse." John may have supervised the workmen there until 1808, when it closed and Thomas went into a short-lived partnership with James Cogswell.*

*On June 3, 1812, under the heading of "Elegant Furniture," Thomas advertised in the Columbian Centinel [Boston]: "This Day the Ware Room of the Boston Cabinet Manufactury, Congress-Street, will be opened, where will be for sale—Useful and Ornamental Cabinet Furniture, all made by, or under the immediate inspection of Thomas Seymour." The last point is important because it emphasizes the responsibility assumed by the master of a shop.*

**11** SIDE CHAIR with splat back (one of four)[1]
*About 1790    Massachusetts*

Although this style of chair was probably introduced during the Chippendale era, and the straight molded legs and carved round corners of the upper splat found here are Chippendale features, such chairs were highly popular until 1800 or 1810. Today these chairs are called ladder-back or slat-back. The old name was "splatt back" or "slatt back." In *The Journeymen Cabinet and Chair-Makers Philadelphia Book of Prices* for 1795 we find listed a "Splatt back chair with three cross Splatts" as well as a "Splatt back Chair, Honey suckle pattern made for stuffing over the seat rail." The latter name seems to describe this particular chair, a type which is found frequently around Boston and which was apparently popular in Massachusetts as well

as in Pennsylvania. "Hollowed seat" is the old name for such a concave seat.

Dimensions: height 37½; width 21½; depth 17¾.
Materials: mahogany; front and side rails, birch; rear rail, mahogany; no corner blocks originally; upholstery, original black leather and brass nails.
Provenance: Museum Purchase, 1959; Exhibited, *Accessions* 1960; No. 9, in Catalogue.
Accession: 59.123–126

**12** SIDE CHAIR with splat back
*About 1790    Massachusetts    Branded "W. Porter"*

The name "W. Porter" branded on the bottom of the back seat rail has not been identified with certainty. If it is the name of the maker, it may be that of William Porter, who was working in

**11**

**12**

Charlestown, Massachusetts, in the early nineteenth century. Although the seat has a serpentine front instead of being "hollowed," there is one less splat, and the crowned anthemion is pierced in this close variant of the preceding chair (No. 11).

Dimensions: height 37¼; width 21¼; depth 18¼.

Materials: mahogany; seat frame and stretchers, maple; no corner blocks originally; upholstery, green silk damask, probably Italian, early eighteenth century.

Provenance: Museum Purchase, 1962.

Accession: 62.161

**13** SIDE CHAIR with splat back
*About 1790    Massachusetts*

Although the carving of the splats is well executed in this simplified version of the preceding chairs,

**13**

the large overhanging squares of the seat framing, the thinness of the front legs, the prominent placing of the overwide front stretcher between the legs instead of between the side stretchers, and the substitution of maple and rush for mahogany and upholstery suggest that this chair was made in the country.

Dimensions: height 38¼; width 21⅝; depth 17¾.

Materials: entire chair is made of soft maple; rush seat.

Provenance: Museum Purchase, 1960.

Accession: 60.215

**14** SIDE CHAIR with vase back or shield back
*About 1795    Salem    The carving is attributed to Samuel McIntire*

In concept, quality of carving, and general skill of execution, this is one of the finest American chairs. The design, taken from Plate 2 of Hepplewhite's

*Guide,* 1788, has been handsomely enriched with carved beading, grapes and grape leaves at the base of the splat, dependent grape streamers down the front legs, and applied strips of ebony to give shape to the spade feet. These motifs occur frequently on the richest Salem-made furniture and are linked time and again to the name of Samuel McIntire, who did carving and building of all kinds for Elias Hasket Derby and his relatives. Four chairs exactly matching these were Derby family heirlooms.[2]

Dimensions: height 38⅛; width 22; depth 18⅝.

Materials: mahogany and ebony; rear seat rail, maple; side and front rails, ash; corner blocks (type III), white pine; upholstery, flowers painted in colors on cream-colored satin (faded from bright yellow), probably French, late eighteenth century.

Accession: 57.692

**15** SIDE CHAIR with vase back or shield back

*About 1795     Salem     The carving is attributed to Samuel McIntire*

This is one of the finest known chairs of the Salem school and may well be the sixth chair of a set which originally belonged to Elizabeth Derby West, daughter of the great Salem merchant, Elias Hasket Derby.[3] It matches the superb quality of the preceding chair in over-all concept, finesse of detail, arrangement and execution of carving, and the use of ebony appliqués to give form and color to the spade feet.

Dimensions: height 39¼; width 21½; depth 18½.

Materials: mahogany and ebony; rear rail, birch; other rails, ash; front and rear corner blocks (type III), white pine; upholstery, flowers painted in colors on cream-colored satin (faded from yellow), probably French, late eighteenth century.

Accession: 57.693

**16** SIDE CHAIR with oval back (one of four)

*About 1798     Salem     With carving attributed to Samuel McIntire*

Much admired for their quality as well as their rarity, chairs of this set parallel the finest Salem examples in terms of their ample size, incurved rear legs, and grape-carved front supports tipped with spade feet appliquéd in ebony.

Long thought to have been stuffed-back chairs, the discovery of a pristine example still in the possession of a Derby descendant proves the set as originally executed to be a brilliant interpretation of Plate 8 in the 1794 edition of Hepplewhite's

*Guide.*[4] The original carver, in all likelihood Samuel McIntire, enriched Hepplewhite's design by adding a dependent streamer of grapes and grape leaves on each front leg. As illustrated, the three feathers and ribbons of the back have recently been exactly executed to match faithfully the original surviving chair. These chairs may be a part of the eight referred to in Samuel McIntire's bill to Elias Hasket Derby:

[1798]  Feb 17   To Carving 8 Chairs
         @ 10/6 each                    £4:40

The price noted, almost double that usually charged by McIntire or others, would be justified by the amount of the lavish and brilliant carving on these examples.

**16**

Dimensions: height 39⅜; width 21; depth 18¼.

Materials: mahogany and ebony; rear seat rail, birch; other seat rails, ash; front and rear corner blocks (type III), white pine; upholstery, light-blue silk brocaded in several colors, French, third quarter of the eighteenth century.

Accession: 57.799.1–4

### 17 PAINTED SIDE CHAIR with oval back and five plumes
*1796 (?)   Probably Philadelphia*

An occasional painted chair is included in the midst of mahogany chairs in this catalogue to emphasize how fashionable they were at an early date. Hepplewhite asserted that for chairs, "a new and very elegant fashion has arisen within these few years, of finishing them with painted or japanned work, which gives them a rich and splendid appearance."

Among the handsomest of all known American painted chairs, this white chair and the following (No. 18), are a part of a group of some fifteen or twenty extant chairs (no less than nine are owned by the Boston Museum of Fine Arts) which have an intricate history. In brief, pursuant to earlier correspondence on December 13, 1796, Joseph Anthony and Company of Philadelphia billed Elias Hasket Derby for "24 Oval Back Chairs, Stuff'd Seats covered with Hair Cloth, 2 Rows Brass Nails at 34/£40:16:0."[5] Five years later on December 11, 1801, John Stille Jun & Co. (Philadelphia) enclosed the bills of lading and memorandum of cost to John Derby (Elias's brother) for the following:

| | |
|---|---|
| 3 packs cont'g 6 Gold and green chairs | £24:00:0 |
| 3 [packs cont'g] 6 Gold and black [chairs] | £24:00:0 |

Although there is no indication from either the invoice or surviving correspondence that the chairs in the earlier shipment were painted white or that those in the latter shipment were oval-backs, this has been the supposition for many years because many white and a few dark greenish-brown oval-back chairs have come down through successive generations of the Derby family. The gilt decoration on the front legs and frame of the back of this chair were overpainted at one time. This overpainting has been recently removed and the gilt restored.

Dimensions: height 38⅜; width 21½; depth 18½.

Materials: legs, back, and rails, soft maple; corner blocks (type IV), white pine; upholstery, pale-blue silk brocaded in colors, French or English, third quarter of the eighteenth century.

Provenance: Museum Purchase, 1957.

Accession: 57.21.1

### 18 PAINTED SIDE CHAIR with oval back and six plumes
*1801 (?)   Probably Philadelphia*

This chair which is dark brownish-black, with six ostrich feathers and other decoration handsomely painted in several colors, may be one of the chairs received by John Derby from Philadelphia in 1801.

Nevertheless both this example and No. 17 are included in this section because of their Salem association, because of their design (similar to No. 16), and because their incurving rear legs are so like those found on Salem chairs. A possible explanation of the latter circumstance may be that both Salem chairmakers and the Philadelphia maker of these chairs followed the patterns for incurving rear legs illustrated by Hepplewhite. It seems of considerable significance to the writer that a drawing of a chair whose back appears to be almost identical to No. 17 is included among the records of the Gillow Company of Lancaster, England.[6] The Gillows' rate of pay was two shil-

lings, six pence, to one of their workmen, James Ripley, for painting such chairs with five feathers in 1785—four years before Hepplewhite was to publish his design for a carved oval back with only three feathers! It would be interesting to know if Ripley or another Gillow chairmaker-ornamenter migrated to Philadelphia and after arriving there painted these chairs for the Derbys.

Dimensions: height 38½; width 21½; depth 18½.
Materials: soft maple; front seat rail, striped maple; corner blocks (type IV), white pine; upholstery, cream-colored silk brocaded in colors, 1770–1790.
Provenance: Museum Purchase, 1957.
Accession: 57.21.2

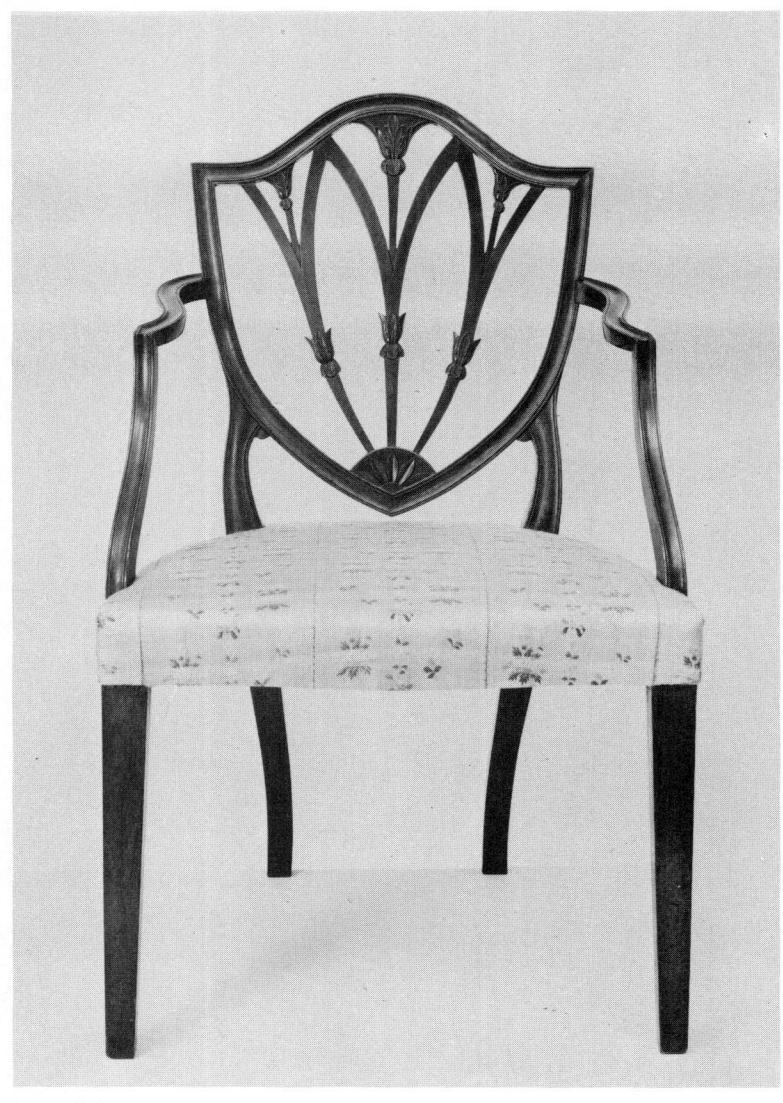

**19** SIDE CHAIR with vase back or shield back
(one of a pair)
*About 1795    Salem*

The history of these chairs supports a Salem attribution. They are a part of a set made for Joseph Waters, whose three-story brick mansion at 114 Derby Street, erected in 1806–1807, is attributed to McIntire's design. This pair of chairs was acquired from a descendant in 1930 at the same time that four others of the set were acquired for the Philadelphia Museum of Art.[7]

The dominant features seen here were all favorites of the Salem cabinetmakers. The pointed shield-shaped back with three splats, each ornamented with flower-carved ovals, springing from a sector of a carved lunette is a Salem earmark, as are the incurving back legs almost always found in the finest Salem chairs, which usually have no stretch-

ers. The carving on the front legs is very similar but not identical to that on chairs owned by Elias Hasket Derby, illustrated as No. 90 in *Eighteenth Century American Arts* by Edwin J. Hipkiss.

Dimensions: height 37¾; width 21½; depth 18¼.
Materials: mahogany; rear rail, birch; front and side rails, ash; front blocks (type III), rear blocks (type IV), white pine; upholstery, tan silk called *droguet* (faded from yellow and mauve) woven in a small floral pattern, French, second half of the eighteenth century.
Provenance: Joseph Waters; Mrs. Edward Waters; Mrs. Marietta Bourne Pillsbury.
Accession: 57.878.1, 2

**20** ARMCHAIR with vase back or shield back
(one of three)[8]
*About 1800    Salem*

Rather more plainly interpreted than Baltimore[9] and Portsmouth (No. 21) chair backs taken from the same design source—Plate 5, Hepplewhite's *Guide*—the backs of these chairs have, nevertheless, considerable grace and the over-all effect is one of beauty. A punched background for the carved clusters of leaves at the top and center of the shield heightens the relief and sharpens the effect of light and shade. The seat has a serpentine front; the upper edges of the curvilinear arms are hollowed and outlined with a bead; and the subtle lines of the shield supports are artfully carried down through the rear legs. The punched background of the carving, the plain unornamented front legs, and the incurving rear legs are features common to other Salem chairs. A pair of side chairs of the same design are shown in an oil painting of the Sargent family of Charlestown, Massachusetts.[10]

Dimensions: height 37½; width 22; depth 17¾.
Materials: mahogany; front and side rails, maple; rear seat rail, birch; front blocks (type IV), mahogany, rear blocks (type III), white pine; upholstery, polychrome lampas with stripes and floral sprigs, French, Louis XVI style, third quarter of the eighteenth century.
Accession: 57.923.1–3

**21** CURVED CHAIR-BACK SETTEE[11]
*About 1800    Probably Portsmouth, New Hampshire though possibly Boston*

"Bar back Sofa" is Hepplewhite's name for a curved chair-back settee illustrated as Plate 26 of his *Cabinet-Maker and Upholsterer's Guide*, first issued in 1788. He pointed out:

Plate 26 is a design for a bar-back sofa: this kind of sofa is of modern invention; and the lightness of its appearance has procured it a favorable reception in the first circles of fashion. The pattern of the back must match the chairs; these also will regulate the sort of frame work and covering.

Derived from Hepplewhite's design but executed with the independence often seen in the work of American artisans, this unique settee is freed of the nervous complexity of the English prototype. Here the tops of the shield have been made straight like that of the New York chair (No. 55) and the square legs tapered sharply at the foot like many seen on New England card tables. Comparison of a similar shield-back from Salem (No. 20) with those of this settee shows a marked difference in approach. The carving on these ribs is incised, rather than modeled, and a fan inlay substitutes for the leaf-carved sector and punctuates each shield. The honey-colored fans, along with the chevron stringing which outlines the shields, bring emphasis, contrast, and over-all unity to the composition.

This settee was made to fit a semicircular alcove at the foot of the spiral staircase in the house built by John Pierce, in 1799, on Haymarket Square, Portsmouth, New Hampshire, where he and his descendants continued to live until recent years.

In 1948 the family sold the settee to Henry Francis du Pont.

Dimensions: height 33½; length 7 feet; depth 16¾; depth of curve 34.

Materials: mahogany with satinwood inlays; seat rails and three curved medial braces, soft maple; corner blocks (type III), white pine; upholstery, brown cotton woven in floral-and-leaf pattern, fibers sized to resemble haircloth, late eighteenth century.

Provenance: John Pierce and descendants.

Accession: 57.1015 see Inlay Fig. 39

## 22 SIDE CHAIR with vase back or shield back
*About 1795 Salem*

At first glance this chair might be mistaken for one from New York inasmuch as this shield-and-drapery pattern was so often used there.[12] The shape of the fattened shield (like No. 14 rather than No. 50), the incurved back legs (like Nos. 14 and 15), and the star-punched background at the base of the shield (like No. 24) are typical of Salem practice. In comparison, the New York chairs (Nos. 50 and 51) of similar design show a surer and bolder handling of the carved drapery, foliated center ornament, and petals at the base of the splat.

Dimensions: height 39¾, width 21; depth 18⅜.

**21**

Materials: mahogany; rails, birch; front and rear blocks
(type III), white pine; upholstery, black haircloth,
probably English, late eighteenth or early nineteenth
century.
Accession: 57.674

### 23 ARMCHAIR with square back
*About 1802   Salem   Probably carved by Samuel McIntire*

This armchair, one of a unique set of twelve, was
made for the parlor of the Peirce-Nichols house in
Federal Street, Salem, and probably dates from
the completion of the room in 1802, when, in preparation for the marriage of his daughter, Jerathmeel
Peirce employed Samuel McIntire to replace the
parlor of 1782 with woodwork in the current
fashion. The classic design of the chimney breast,
cornice, and dado of the room complement perfectly the superb overmantel glass, the window
seats, and the several chairs of this set still there;[13]

and it was McIntire's guiding genius that brought
it all to completion.

The design of the chair is illustrated in Plate 33
(dated 1792) of Sheraton's *Drawing Book*. It shows
two "Parlour Chairs"; that at the right is the pattern for this armchair, which was copied faithfully,
save for minor changes, principally in the turned
legs and the "sweeping" (swelling) of the sides of
the seat to relieve the severity of the original design.
The bowknots and bellflowers have the punched-
snowflake background associated with Salem carving.

Dimensions: height 34½; width 20¾; depth 18.
Materials: mahogany; rails, birch; corner blocks (type
IV), rear, white pine, front, mahogany; upholstery,
yellow-and-white-striped satin, French or English, late
eighteenth century.
Accession: 57.879

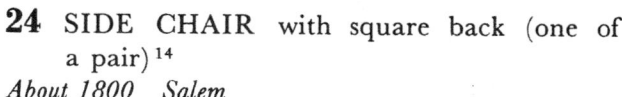

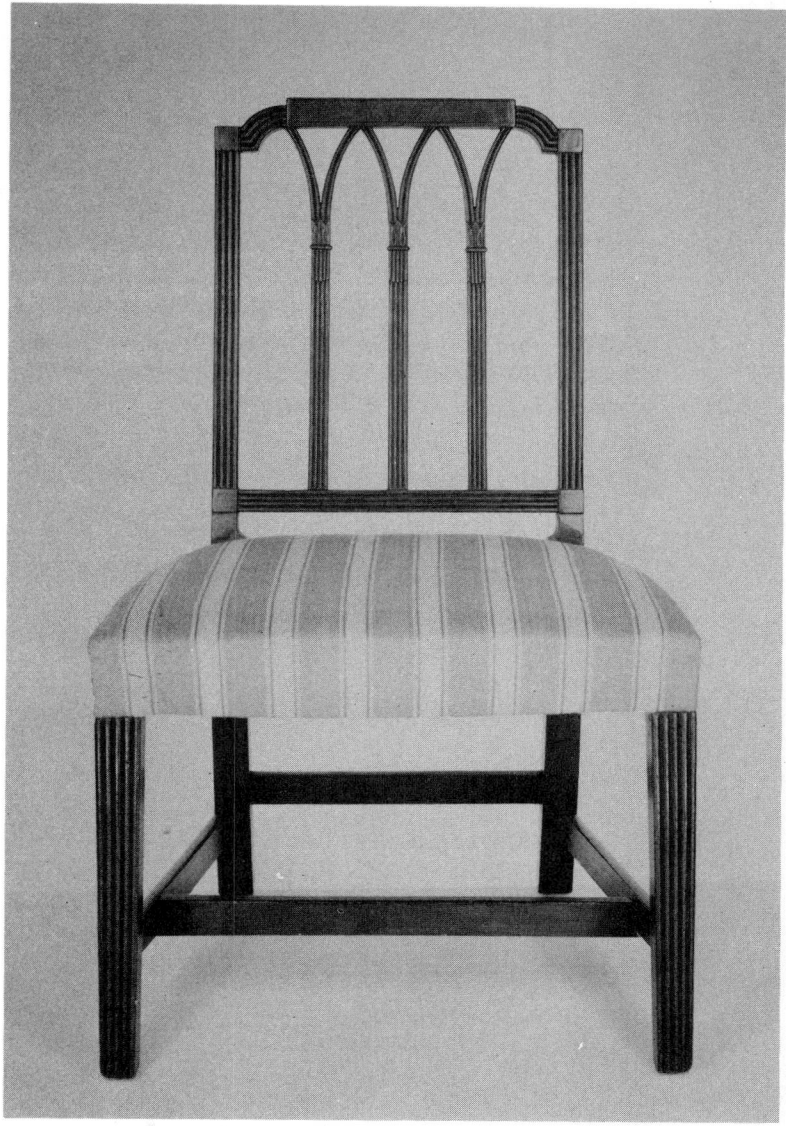

**24** SIDE CHAIR with square back (one of a pair) [14]

*About 1800  Salem*

"A Square Back Chair, with straight top and stay rail, three upright splatts, [and] straight seat made for stuffing over the rails" [15] cost fourteen shillings for labor in Philadelphia in 1795, but this note-worthy small carved chair would have cost a great deal more to make. [16] The "tablet" in the top with carved eagle, the addition of pedestals and carved clusters of leaves to the "splatts," the "sweeping" (swelling) of the sides and front of the seat, and the molding of the stiles and upper and lower rails of the back would have been extras. Although the legs are plain and the snowflake background is not uncommon in Salem carving, only on the very best work does one find such skillfully carved details.

Dimensions: height 35; width 18½; depth 17½.
Materials: mahogany; rails, birch; large triangular nailed corner blocks (type III), tilia (basswood or linden); upholstery, polychrome silk with stripes and floral sprigs, French, Louis XVI style, third quarter of the eighteenth century.
Accession: 57.800.1, 2

**25** SIDE CHAIR with square back (one of four) [17]

*About 1800  Boston*

"Square back chair with elliptic cornered top containing a tablet" partially describes this chair in the words of the 1802 edition of *The London Chair-Makers' and Carvers' Book of Prices for Workmanship*. Whether the initials "BS" branded on the rear rail of each of these four chairs are those of the maker

or an early owner is not known; but the tablet and squares at the corners of the back veneered with satinwood and the skillful reeding of the legs, back, and "Gothic splatts" are features found on other chairs which have been loosely attributed to the hand of the Seymours. However, no strong proof for such an attribution has been presented. Chairs from several sets, all varying but almost matching these admirable expressions of the chairmaker's art, have been found in the Boston area.

Dimensions: height 35¾; width 20¾; depth 17.

Materials: mahogany with satinwood veneers; seat rails, birch; medial stretcher, maple; no corner blocks originally; upholstery, red-green-and-white-striped satin called *imberline* (part silk), French, late eighteenth century.

Accession: 57.518.1–4

**26** SIDE CHAIR with square back
*About 1800    Massachusetts*

The thin angular lines of this side chair (accentuated by the beading on the edges of the back), the reeding on the splats, the veneered panel on the top rail, and especially the stringing which runs through to the floor on the legs suggest Boston workmanship. Although one of two groups of chairs with nearly identical backs in the Museum of Fine Arts in Boston originally belonged to Elizabeth Derby West, of South Danvers, near Salem,[18] it has been well demonstrated by Mabel Munson Swan that Madame Elizabeth Derby West bought furniture in both Boston and Salem, as did her famous father, Elias Hasket Derby,[19] ship owner, merchant, and entrepreneur of Salem.

Materials: mahogany; rear seat rail, birch; front and side rails, maple; no corner blocks originally; upholstery, brown silk woven in rosette and leaf-scroll pattern, fibers sized to resemble haircloth, about 1800.
Provenance: Frank Ladd; Gift of Carl Jacobs, 1954.
Accession: G 54.34.5

**28** SIDE CHAIR with square back
*About 1800–1815  Probably Portsmouth, New Hampshire  Attributed to the shop of Langley Boardman*

By 1800 Langley Boardman was well established in Portsmouth as a cabinetmaker with several journeymen and apprentices. He prospered, and about 1815 built a fine house which remained in the family until 1900. In the house at that time were several pieces of furniture believed by the family to have been made in Boardman's shop for his own home. Among this furniture was a set of chairs.[21] That set and others owned in Portsmouth by descendants of the cabinetmaker's relatives and friends are identical in concept and in several details to this chair and the settee (No. 29) which follows. Although the splats vary, all have square, reeded backs with square rosettes at the corners, tapered molded front legs, sturdy outcurving rear legs, and stretchers.

Dimensions: height 35⅜; width 21¼; depth 17¾.
Materials: mahogany; seat rails, maple; corner blocks (type III), white pine; upholstery, emerald green silk, about 1800.
Accession: 54.34.6

# 29

Dimensions: height 35⅝; width 20½; depth 17⅜.
Materials: mahogany with light wood stringing; rear rail, beech; corner blocks (type III), white pine; upholstery, brown silk woven in rosette and leaf-scroll pattern, fibers sized to resemble haircloth, about 1800.
Accession: 53.169

**27** SIDE CHAIR with square back
*About 1800  Possibly Salem*

Proof seems to be lacking to determine whether this sturdy "square back chair with plain sweep top" originated in Salem, as suggested by one writer, or was made in Boston or Newburyport or Portsmouth.[20]

Dimensions: height 35½; width 20; depth 17.

**29** SETTEE (one of a pair)
*1800–1815   Probably Portsmouth, New Hampshire*

This rare two-chair-back settee is a simplified version of two engraved Plates, 12 and 13, in Hepplewhite's *Guide* of 1794, which show square-backed chairs with vertical ribs, and carved rosettes at the corners. The molded, tapered legs are illustrated on a chair on the first plate of the *Guide*. This pair of settees was published in the *Connoisseur*[22] with the description: "Originally in an 18th-century house in New Castle, N.H." and on the inside rail is inscribed: "Two Settees one in Brockton. (Sheriton) Belonged to Elizabeth Wentworth wife of Joseph Haven, Grandmother Thachers Uncle." A matching side chair formerly in the Francis Hill Bigelow Collection was described in his sale catalogue as being from Portsmouth. When recently upholstered, the pattern for the brass

nailing was copied from a chair on Plate 4 of Hepplewhite's *Guide*.

Dimensions: height 35½; width 37; depth 17¼.
Materials: mahogany; seat rails, birch; curved medial braces, maple; corner blocks (type III), white pine; upholstery, emerald green silk, eighteenth century.
Provenance: Henry A. Hoffman; Museum Purchase, 1952.
Accession: 52.133.1, 2

**30** SIDE CHAIR with vase back or shield back
*About 1795   Dorchester Lower Mills, Massachusetts
Stamped on rear rail "S. Badlam"*

There seems little reason to doubt that the "S. Badlam" stamped by means of a die on the outside of the back seat rail of this chair and on other pieces of well-made mahogany furniture

**30**

**31**

(No. 110) stands for Stephen Badlam,[23] who, after having risen to the rank of major in the Revolutionary Army, suffered a violent fever and resigned his commission. In 1776 or 1777, he set up shop as a cabinetmaker in Dorchester Lower Mills, Massachusetts, where he seems to have flourished until his death in 1815.

A beaded Gothic arch with acorn finial, and the carved husks and ears of wheat give distinction to the back of this fine chair.[24] Although the carving is flat, without the modeling of the best Salem work, it has vitality and grace. The combination of carving and stopped fluting on the legs of Badlam's chairs is almost equivalent to a signature. Stamped inside the rear seat rails are the initials S. F., possibly those of an early owner; but more likely, it is the mark of a journeyman who made the chairs for Badlam. Although variants of this

**32**

design of chair back are familiar in England, no closely related design is to be found in the usual published sources of English cabinetmaking patterns.

Dimensions: height 38; width 21; depth 18.
Materials: mahogany; front seat rail, soft maple; rear seat rail, hard maple; side rails, ash; corner blocks replace original open braces (type I), maple; upholstery, cream-colored silk with stripes and floral sprigs in dark blue and white, English or French, late eighteenth century.
Accession: 52.245

**31** SIDE CHAIR with vase back or shield back
*1792–1796   Boston   Label of [William] Stone and [Samuel?] Alexander (in partnership, 1792–1796)* [25]

The comparatively small size, the tapered front legs with line inlay running through to the floor without benefit of cuffs, the high arc of the shield top, and the tassel-like outline of the splats are features common to this chair and the one following. Perhaps these can be isolated as attributes of one type of Boston-made vase-, or shield-back, side chairs. The incomplete date *179* is printed on the label.[26]

Dimensions: height 38; width 21¼; depth 17¾.
Materials: mahogany with satinwood inlays; seat rails, birch; no corner blocks; upholstery, cream-color silk woven in satin and plain stripes with floral sprigs embroidered in pastel shades, about 1800.
Provenance: Museum Purchase, 1955.
Accession: 55.80.3                              see Inlay Fig. 88

**32** SIDE CHAIR with vase back or shield back
*1795   Charlestown, Massachusetts   Label of Jacob Forster (working 1786–1838)*

Although similar in form to the preceding chair, this one, labeled by Jacob Forster, is given distinction by the individuality of the stringing which highlights the perfectly curved shield and the back supports. Each splat is inlaid with a three-petaled posy and long stem. Similar simplified flowers on gently curving stems (No. 287) are found on several other pieces bearing Forster's labels. The first three numbers, *179,* of the date are printed on the label. The last number, inscribed in ink, appears to be *5.*

Dimensions: height 37; width 20½; depth 17¾.
Materials: mahogany with satinwood and holly inlays; seat rails and open braces in front (type I), American maple; no rear blocks; upholstery, cream-colored silk

woven in satin and plain stripes with floral sprigs embroidered in pastel shades, about 1800.

Provenance: Museum Purchase, 1960.

Accession: 60.349        see Inlay Fig. 86

**33** SIDE CHAIR with vase back or shield back
(one of a pair)
*About 1800   Boston*[27]

The basket-of-fruit motif has long been associated with Salem furniture and architecture. However, as executed and dispersed on the crest rail of this shield-back chair, both basket and trailing vine are crowded, confined, and lifeless in appearance. They lack the freedom expected in the best Salem carving. The brilliance of the inlaid paterae on the

**33**

**34**

splats and lunette at the base of the shield remind one of Boston chair work, as does the line inlay on the front legs, running through to the floor unstopped by cuffs. The inlay, stretchers, and shape of shield are virtually identical to those of a labeled chair by Jacob Forster of Charlestown, Massachusetts (No. 32). This attribution to Boston instead of Salem was confirmed by the discovery that an identical chair in the Museum of Fine Arts, Boston, can now be documented as the work of William Fiske, a cabinetmaker who in 1800 went from Salem to Roxbury, a part of Boston.[28]

Dimensions: height 38; width 21; depth 17⅜.

Materials: mahogany with inlays of satinwood; seat rails,

handsome shield, which frames uncarved splats highlighted by inlaid paterae and fan.

Dimensions: height 38½; width 21; depth 18.

Materials: mahogany with satinwood inlays; left and front seat rails, soft maple; rear rail, birch; no corner blocks used; upholstery, blue-and-white-striped and watered taffeta, late eighteenth century.

Accession: 56.545, 546

**35** SIDE CHAIR with vase back or shield back
   (one of four)
*About 1800   Boston*

The multiple-ribbed shield back with carved basket of fruit and trailing-vine ornament of Salem inspiration is another version of English design commonly used by cabinetmakers of several states,

birch; corner blocks not original; upholstery, cream-colored silk satin (faded from bright yellow) with flowers painted in colors, probably French, late eighteenth century.

Accession: 57.695.1, 2              see Inlay Fig. 87

**34** SIDE CHAIR with vase back or shield back
   (one of a pair)
*About 1800   Boston*

Unity of composition lends importance to this simply executed Massachusetts chair. Molded outer surfaces lead the eye from the tip of the front legs upward through the stiles and around the

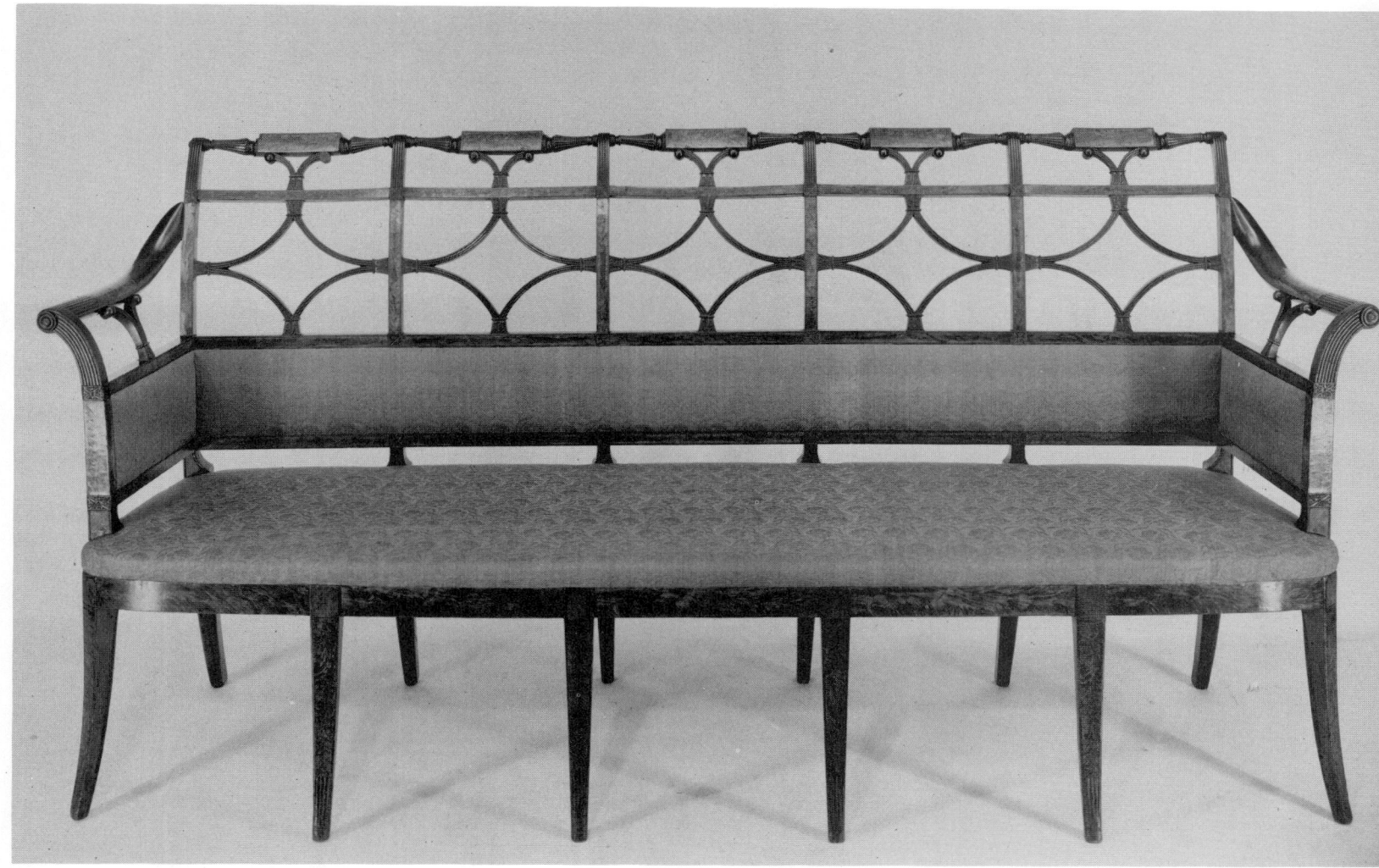

particularly those south of New England (Nos. 87, 88). Here the finely carved cresting rail gives it a local character worthy of McIntire's hand, but the inlaid satinwood fan at the base of the back is not often seen in Salem work.

Inside the back seat rail is die-punched *I\*C*. It is not certain whom these initials represent. Possibly they are those of an early owner; possibly they signify the work of a Salem cabinetmaker, John Chipman, who was born about 1746, married Elizabeth Towzer in January 16, 1802, and whose shop stood at the southeast corner of Liberty Street "passing from Vine to Market." [29] But far more likely, the writer believes, they are the initials of a Boston cabinetmaker who was trained in Salem and later worked for Stephen Badlam. The same die was used to stamp *I.C.* on a fine tall clock bearing Badlam's stamp. [30]

Dimensions: height 38; width 21½; depth 18½.

Materials: mahogany with light wood inlay; front and rear rails and front open corner braces (type I), a soft maple; no rear blocks; left side rail, beech; upholstery, yellow satin with fleurs-de-lis woven in mauve and white, French, Empire style, early nineteenth century. Accession: 57.906.1–4

**36** PAINTED SIDE CHAIR with square back
*About 1800 Boston*

A nineteenth-century label which reads "Made by John Seymour for the Hon. Nathaniel Silsbee about 1790 when he built his house" was found about 1905 pasted on the inside rail of a chair that appears to be almost identical to this one and is now owned by Mr. and Mrs. Bertram K. Little. [31] Although the information on that label, like all remembered family history, must be "taken with a grain of salt," a number of facts make it plausible: the label was discovered before the name John Seymour was meaningful; Mrs. Nathaniel Silsbee was the niece of Elias Hasket Derby who also owned painted and decorated chairs (see Nos. 17

and 18); painted furniture was à la mode in the late eighteenth century; the chairs themselves are exceedingly stylish with caned seats and backs curved in plan (hollowed); both the design and execution are worthy of the talents for which John and Thomas Seymour are famous; and there were a number of ornamental painters working in Boston who, among other things, painted clock dials and glass tablets for the Willards. Indeed it is clock dial ornament which this floral decoration in naturalistic colors most closely resembles. Here, however, the background used is black on a red undercoating to give the appearance of japanning or lacquer work. The design of the back with urn between colonnettes is a variant of No. 1, Plate 36 of Sheraton's *Drawing Book* (1791–1794).

Dimensions: height 35⅛; width 19; depth 15⁵/₁₆.

Materials: birch; no secondary woods.

Provenance: Clarence Wilson Brazer; Esther Stevens Brazer.

Accession: 58.46.5

**37 FIVE-CHAIR-BACK SETTEE** with scroll back

*About 1805   Boston   Attributed to the shop of John and/or Thomas Seymour (see Plate IX)* [32]

Contrasts of light and dark; of plain and richly figured woods; of carved, reeded, and smooth surfaces; and of squares, broad rectangles, thin rectangles, diamonds, quarter ellipses, half ellipses, and scrolled ellipses make this unique piece of seating furniture an aesthetic *tour-de-force*.

Dimensions: height 42½; width 81; depth 22¼.

Materials: mahogany with figured birch inlays; seat rails, birch; three curved medial braces, soft maple; original corner blocks missing; upholstery, green silk called *droguet* woven in stylized leaf-and-fruit pattern, French, second half of the eighteenth century.

Accession: 57.683

**38 SIDE CHAIR** with scroll back (one of a pair)

*About 1805   Boston   Attributed to the shop of John and/or Thomas Seymour*

As early as 1802, in *The London Chair-Makers' and Carvers' Book of Prices for Workmanship* (p. 39), many details for scroll-back chairs are listed: "Framing a square chair (for stuffing over), with scroll upper end back legs...square or turn'd..., straight roller and stayrail (the roller screw'd through the eye of the scrolls), either with or without a veneer, on a straight back rail...." Prices are also listed for

veneering "tablets in tops" of such chairs. The splat in the back of this chair is a variant of one shown on Plate 3, Figure 4, of the same book. The Seymours may have owned it.

Such chairs are among the most sophisticated of early nineteenth-century American chair forms. They have long been attributed to the shop of John and Thomas Seymour because of the type of carving and the lavish use of figured birch veneers which overlie the mahogany on all flat surfaces. [33] Several other chairs with identical or closely related backs are known, both with outturning front legs as shown here and with variant turned and reeded front supports. The inner surfaces of all legs are rounded, and the background of the carving is star punched.

Dimensions: height 35; width 18¾; depth 16¼.

Materials: mahogany with figured birch veneers; seat

**38**

rails, birch; originally no corner blocks; upholstery, green silk called *droguet,* woven in stylized leaf-and-fruit pattern, French, second half of the eighteenth century.

Accession: 57.676.1, 2

## 39  DOUBLE-CHAIR-BACK SETTEE  with scroll back

*About 1805  Boston  Attributed to the shop of John and/or Thomas Seymour*

Doubling of the back design of the preceding chair produces in this settee one of the liveliest and most interesting pieces of seating furniture of the Federal period. The chairs (No. 38), this settee, and that with a five-part back (No. 37) appear to have been made in the same shop and perhaps were originally all part of a set. As noted earlier, they are attributed to the shop of John and Thomas Seymour on the basis of the carving and the unusual veneered panels of figured birch. However, it should be noted that no seating furniture known at the present time can be documented by label or bill as the work of John or Thomas Seymour.

Dimensions: height 33½; width 40½; depth 18⅜.

Materials: mahogany with figured birch veneers; seat

rails, medial seat brace with adjoining blocks, birch; original corner blocks missing; upholstery, green silk damask with stylized-leaf pattern, second half of the eighteenth century.

Accession: 57.682

**40** SIDE CHAIR with pedestal back (one of a pair)

*About 1795   Hartford, Connecticut   Attributed to [Samuel] Kneeland and [Lemuel] Adams (in partnership, 1792–1796)*

One might with justification call this chair a Chippendale chair. It has a pierced central splat resting on a pedestal, marlboro legs, a back with curvilinear crest, and ears like many Chippendale chairs. However, the chair anticipates the new styles. The design of the splat, which is light in appearance, features an Adamesque urn. Marlboro legs were the standard quoted in the price books for most furniture in the new styles in vogue at the end of the eighteenth century. Only the outline of the back is exclusively Chippendale.

Similar chairs were made in Rhode Island and Connecticut and possibly in Massachusetts. It seems likely that the chairs with "urn'd banister for loose seats" specifically noted in the list of prices published on August 1, 1792, by the cabinet-makers of Hartford [34] were of this type. They were priced at one pound nine shillings each. "Seats ... exclusive of covers" cost five shillings each.

A set of chairs almost identical to this pair has been handed down in the family of the first owner and is accompanied by the original bill, which reads:

Hartford Dec. 23, 1793
Mrs. Dickerson Bot
of Kneeland and Adams
6 Parlor chairs finished @ 36    £10..16..0 [35]

On the basis of that set, this pair is also attributed

**40**

**41**

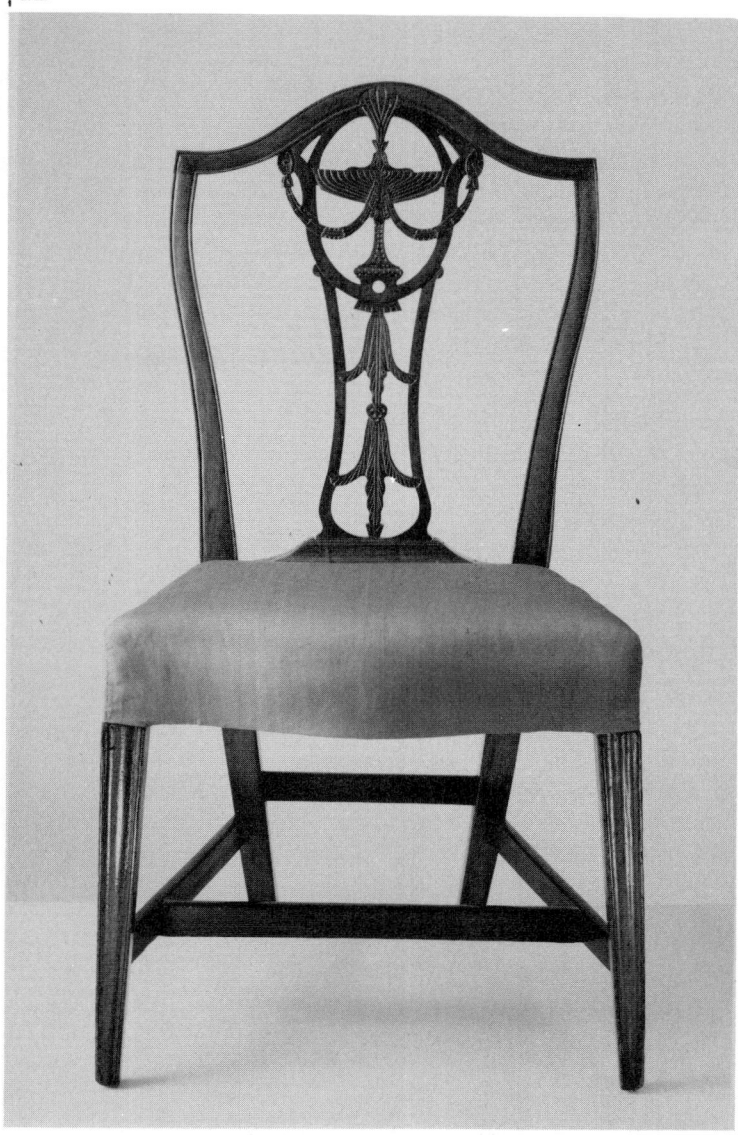

are well known; but, as yet, it is impossible for this writer to set forth characteristics to differentiate clearly between chairs made in one area and those made in the other. Although a chair with an almost identical back to the one illustrated here has a history of having been made by Thomas Goddard of Newport,[36] most chairs with this kind of back made in Providence have rather more graceful, taller, and thinner stiles than those seen here.

Rhode Island chairs seem to have been made most often of mahogany though sometimes of birch and cherry. Inasmuch as most chairs of the latter wood have Connecticut histories plus the fact that the pointed flutes on this urn have no carved indented line between them as is often found on Rhode Island chairs,[37] a Connecticut origin is suggested. The similarity of this carving to that on the six chairs referred to in No. 40 and documented as having been made by Kneeland and Adams of Hartford points to that city as the place of origin for this chair.

**43**

to Kneeland and Adams. The chairs are chisel-marked "V" and "VI" respectively on the seat rails.

Dimensions: height 38½; width 21¼; depth 16⅝.
Materials: cherry; seat rails, cherry; corner blocks (type IV front, II rear), white pine; upholstery, cut, uncut, and voided velvet, dark-blue-and-tan, about 1800.
Provenance: Museum Purchase, 1959.
Accession: 59.104.1, 2

**41** SIDE CHAIR with pedestal back and serpentine top
*About 1795   Hartford*

Serviceable chairs of this type, an interesting variation from the normal shield and urn backs, were popular in both Rhode Island and Connecticut. Examples of mahogany, of birch, and of cherry

Dimensions: height 37¾; width 20⅜; depth 16½.

Materials: mahogany; seat rails, soft maple; front and rear heavy open braces (type I), white pine; upholstery, brown cotton woven in floral-and-leaf pattern, fibers sized to resemble haircloth, late eighteenth century.

Accession: 57.877

**42** SIDE CHAIR with pedestal back or modified square back (one of a pair)

*About 1795   Rhode Island*

Chairs of this silhouette with slightly variant splats are not uncommon in Rhode Island and appear to have been popular there. Such chairs are one step further than No. 40 in the transition from the Chippendale chair to that of the square-backed chair of the Federal period. No closely related counterpart to this design is to be seen in Hepplewhite's or Sheraton's books, but this shape of back

44

is illustrated and called a pedestal-back chair in *The London Chair-Makers' and Carvers' Book of Prices for Workmanship* of 1802. The well-carved central splat, reminiscent of pierced examples in earlier chairs, is supported on a pedestal, or shoe, at the base, as are those common to the older style. The cylix with drapery is similar to No. 45, but the overlarge carved leaves beneath it are out of scale and less successful than the ribbed design of the other chair, which gives the effect of fluting. The seat rails are mortised through the rear legs.

Dimensions: height 39¾; width 19¾; depth 17¾.

Materials: mahogany; seat rails, birch, except rear which is red oak; open braces (type I) missing; upholstery, green silk.

Provenance: Gift of Charles K. Davis, 1956. Companion chair given to the Metropolitan Museum of Art.

Accession: G 56.46.25

**43** SIDE CHAIR with upholstered back, a cabriole chair (one of a pair)

*About 1795   New England   Probably Rhode Island*

In the statement that "chairs with stuffed backs are called cabriole chairs"[38] Hepplewhite gave a new name to upholstered-back chairs that had been termed "French Chairs" by Chippendale and "back stools" and "back stool chairs" by Ince and Mayhew in *The Universal System of Household Furniture* of 1762. The presence of chestnut as a secondary wood supports the Rhode Island attribution as does the fact that the outline of the back is almost identical to that of No. 41, a common Rhode Island type. Why more of such chairs were not made is a mystery since they are both handsome and comfortable. Perhaps many have been lost because of the perishable nature of their upholstery and the fragility of their construction.

Dimensions: height 35¾; width 21½; depth 19.

Materials: mahogany with light wood inlay; seat rails, soft maple; 4 corner blocks (type II), chestnut; upholstery, flowered blue silk moiré, French, late eighteenth century.

Accession: 57.870.1, 2

**44** SIDE CHAIR with upholstered back, a cabriole chair

*About 1795   Probably New England*

The contours of the gracefully curved back are similar to those of chairs in the Chippendale style. Also reminiscent of earlier design are serpentine corner blocks. Birch rails are to be found frequently on New England chairs though occasionally rails of this wood are found in New York and infrequently in Philadelphia examples. However, almost identical chairs—a set of six,[39] and another pair[40]—with New England histories of ownership, have recently come to light, which strengthens the suggestion of that area as the origin for this fine chair. It may well have been used in a bedroom, possibly at a dressing table.

Dimensions: height 36¾; width 21½; depth 14¾.

Materials: mahogany; seat rails, birch; no corner blocks ever; upholstery, white satin with polychrome chain-stitch embroidery in silk and chenille threads, French, third quarter of the eighteenth century.

Accession: 57.951

## 45  SIDE CHAIR with vase back or shield back
*About 1800   Rhode Island*

Chairs featuring a cylix framed in an oval were made in both Massachusetts and Rhode Island. One which bears the inscription "Mr. Benja.ⁿ Frothingham, Charlestown"[41] is typical of the Massachusetts type and appears to be a literal interpretation of a sketch by Samuel McIntire.[42]

On Rhode Island chairs, in contrast to Massachusetts practice, a honeysuckle flower replaces vines on the top rail, festoons of narrow leaves substitute for drapery, and a carved sunburst fills the lunette at the base of the shield. On Massachusetts chairs the lunette is often blank, but sometimes carved with a basket and flowers. A former owner wrote concerning this chair, "When I removed the numerous covers on the seat, an old piece of cloth was signed

    Chas. Burling Stevenson
    Stephens & Satler Co.
    Providence 1810."

At present nothing is known of this firm.

Dimensions: height 38⅝; width 21; depth 19.

Materials: mahogany; front rail, ash; rear rail, soft maple; open braces (type I, front and rear), soft maple; front very small corner blocks, chestnut; upholstery, green silk, eighteenth century.

Provenance: Mrs. Calvin H. Pease; Fort Lauderdale, Florida.

Accession: 52.132

## 46  SIDE CHAIR with vase back or shield back
    (one of a pair)
*About 1800   Hartford, Connecticut*

Several sets of this design, based on Plate 5 of Hepplewhite's *Guide* of 1788, have survived. With both carved and inlaid ornament, they are probably the most ambitious and distinctive of Connecticut chairs. For many years, they have been attributed to Lemuel Adams of Hartford, Connecticut, because approximately three months after the dissolution (March 5, 1796) of his partnership with Samuel Kneeland (see No. 218) he billed the State of Connecticut[43] for twenty armchairs with carved backs of this type and ten window seats for the Senate chamber of the then new State House. Jonathan Bright upholstered the chairs in red morocco and the window seats in moreen. Those chairs, of which many have survived, may now be seen in their original setting, which has recently been restored.

Comparison of this chair with the State House chairs reveals similarities, but also differences. Those armchairs are of mahogany instead of cherry,

**45**

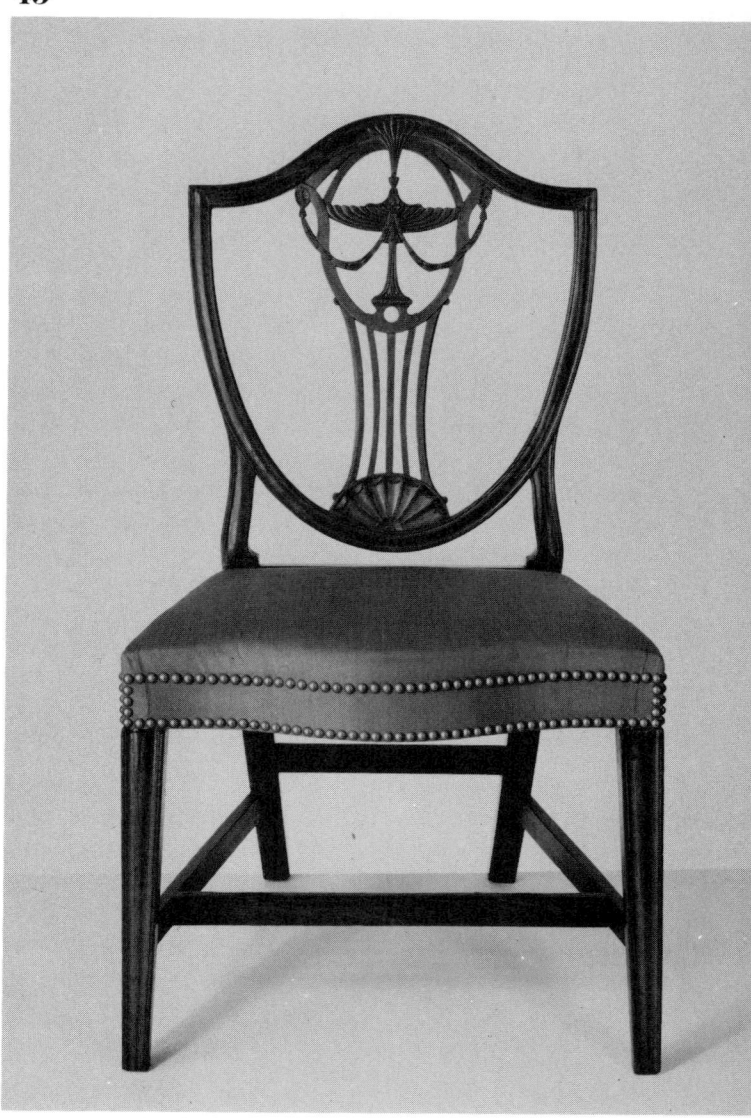

and their side rails are not tenoned through the rear legs as is the case with this example. This practice was more widely followed in Pennsylvania than elsewhere; and, though found occasionally in Connecticut and sometimes in Rhode Island chairs, it was not the normal procedure in either locale. This chair is less well carved than the State House armchairs and the "icicle inlay" lacks the teardrop inlaid on those examples. It seems probable that this design was so popular in Hartford that it may have been made in any one of the shops in operation there in the late eighteenth or early nineteenth century.

Dimensions: height 39⅛; width 19⅞; depth 17½.
Materials: cherry; seat rails, cherry; corner blocks (type IV front, II rear), white pine; upholstery, black hair-cloth, early nineteenth century.
Accession: 52.167.1

**46**

**47** SIDE CHAIR with vase back or shield back
*About 1795    Connecticut*

The question of where this unusual interpretation of a "Vase back chair ... with three distinct sweeps in the top"[44] was made is a difficult one. The in-curved shape of the rear legs and the sturdy, plain-surfaced front legs are like many found on Salem chairs; but this chair and others like it were owned by James Dana, D.D. (1735–1812), who was minister of the Congregational Church in Wallingford, Connecticut, from 1758 to 1789; and the seat rails are of cherry, a wood commonly used in Connecticut chairs and not found in any Salem chairs in the Winterthur collection. Also, since the

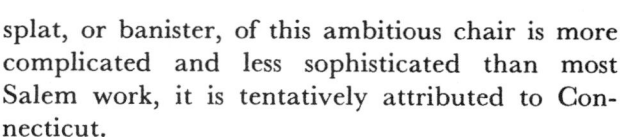

splat, or banister, of this ambitious chair is more complicated and less sophisticated than most Salem work, it is tentatively attributed to Connecticut.

Dimensions: height 40; width 21¼; depth 18½.

Materials: mahogany; corner blocks (front IV, rear II), white pine; front seat rail, hard maple; left and rear seat rails, cherry; upholstery, green silk damask, probably Italian, early eighteenth century.

Provenance: Museum Purchase, 1957.

Accession: 57.40.1

**48** SIDE CHAIR with vase back or shield back
*About 1800   Connecticut*

Such careful attention has been paid to molding the members which outline this chair that one might think they were the frame for a picture. The

front legs and the shield are molded with two beads and two hollows, the back supports channeled, and the rear legs rounded to stumplike contours. In contrast the five back splats are simply cut, without benefit of carving or other ornament, to give full play to the highly effective tulip-like silhouettes, made even more decorative by repeating them in inverted form. Such stump rear legs, seen so often on earlier Philadelphia chairs, are another instance of the Quaker City's apparent influence on Connecticut cabinetmaking practice.

Dimensions: height 36½, width 22; depth 20¼.

Materials: cherry; rear and side rails, cherry; front rail, maple; original corner blocks are missing; upholstery, polychrome silk with stripes and floral sprigs, English or French, Louis XVI style, third quarter of the eighteenth century.

Provenance: Gift of Henry Francis du Pont, 1955.

Accession: G 55.3.1

**49** SIDE CHAIR with vase back or shield back
*About 1800    Probably Connecticut    Possibly Rhode Island*

The writhing fan and patera of contrasting satinwood and ebony here provide centers of interest, but they seem out of character with the plainness of surface apparent throughout the composition. Also, the dominant outlines and complexity of the curved splats tend to create a feeling of disorder, in contrast to the rhythm and harmony achieved in No. 48. Nevertheless the effect is dramatic and the idea unusual.

Dimensions: height 37; width 19¾; depth 17¼.

Materials: mahogany with light and dark wood inlays; front and rear rails, birch; side rails, white oak; no blocks originally; upholstery, black haircloth, English, late eighteenth century.

Accession: 54.34.7                    see Inlay Figs. 101, 106

## FOOTNOTES

1 *Accessions 1960*, Henry Francis du Pont Winterthur Museum, Exhibit No. 9.

2 Edwin J. Hipkiss, *Eighteenth-Century American Arts. The M. and M. Karolik Collection* (Cambridge, Massachusetts: Harvard University Press, 1941), No. 91.

3 Hipkiss, op. cit., No. 92.

4 Fiske Kimball, "Furniture Carvings by Samuel McIntire," *Antiques*, XIX (January, 1931), 30–32, Fig. 1.

5 Quoted from Mabel M. Swan "Where Elias Hasket Derby Bought his Furniture," *Antiques*, XX (November, 1931), 280–282.

6 Gillow Records. ESL-557 (1784–1787) No. 164.

7 Kimball, op. cit., Fig. 4.

8 In the Sale Catalogue of the *Collection of the Late Philip Flayderman* (New York: American Art Association Anderson Galleries, Inc., 1930), Lot 309, six side chairs are listed. From the illustration, they appear to be identical to these.

9 *Baltimore Furniture, 1760–1810* (Baltimore, Maryland: The Baltimore Museum of Art, 1947), Figs. 56, 59.

10 *101 Masterpieces of American Primitive Painting* (New York: American Federation of Arts, 1961), illus. No. 33. This rare and charming group portrait showing a room interior is in the National Gallery of Art, Washington, D.C., the gift of Edgar William and Bernice Chrysler Garbisch.

11 Illustration 1672 in Wallace Nutting's *Furniture Treasury* (1948) shows this settee at the base of the stairs in the John Pierce House; his errors as to the date of the house and details of the settee in the accompanying caption should be noted. Views of the John Pierce House are to be seen in Howells' *The Architectural Heritage of the Piscatugua*, Figs. 28–32.

12 Chairs with this type of back are illustrated in E. Milby Burton's *Charleston Furniture*, Nos. 123, 125, 126, 127. Presumably they were made in Charleston, but they may have been imported from northern cities.

13 One of a pair from the same set, now in the Philadelphia Museum of Art, is illustrated in Fiske Kimball, op. cit., Fig. 5.

14 A similar chair, probably from the same set, is illustrated as Fig. 7 in Fiske Kimball's article.

15 *The Journeymen Cabinet and Chair-Makers Philadelphia Book of Prices* for 1795, p. 81.

16 Similar chairs owned by the late Mrs. Francis B. Crowninshield are now owned by Frederick J. Bradlee. Six others are in the collection of the Essex Institute.

17 Wallace Nutting, *Furniture Treasury*, No. 2387.

18 See Hipkiss, op. cit., No. 114.

19 Mabel M. Swan, "A Revised Estimate of McIntire," *Antiques*, XX (December, 1931), 338–343.

20 No. 109 in Hipkiss which appears to be identical and perhaps from the same set is attributed to "New England, probably Salem."

21 Stephen Decatur, "Langley Boardman, Portsmouth Cabinetmaker," *American Collector*, VI (May, 1937), 4–5.

22 February, 1937, pp. 101–102.

23 Similar chairs, stamped "S. Badlam" and possibly from the same set, are in the collections of the Metropolitan Museum of Art and of Cornelius C. Moore of Newport, Rhode Island. A few chairs with simpler versions of the back design and with plain molded legs and Philadelphia histories are known (William M. Hornor, Jr., "Documented Furniture by Jacob Wayne," *International Studio*, XCVI (June, 1930), Plate 396.

24 Mabel M. Swan, "General Stephen Badlam—Cabinet and Looking Glass Maker," *Antiques*, LXV (May, 1954), 380–383, illus. p. 382.

25 In Mabel M. Swan, "Boston's Carvers and Joiners. Part II. Post-Revolutionary," *Antiques*, LIII (April, 1948), 282–283, a slant-top desk bearing a different label of the firm of Stone and Alexander is illustrated.

26 A pair of side chairs by the same makers, with labels dated 1792, is at the Henry Ford Museum.

27 In Hipkiss, op. cit., No. 93, an identical chair is attributed to Salem; but, for the reasons given here, Boston seems more likely as the place of origin.

28 Information from Richard H. Randall, Jr., December 3, 1964.

29 Henry Wyckoff Belknap, *Artists and Craftsmen of Essex County, Massachusetts* (Salem, Massachusetts: The Essex Institute, 1927), p. 33.

30 Photograph of this clock and stamp in Decorative Arts Photographic Collection at Winterthur, courtesy of John S. Walton, who owned the clock in 1964.

31 See "A Chair Ascribed to the Seymours," an editorial footnote in *Antiques*, XL (September, 1941), 149.

32 Illustrated in Vernon C. Stoneman, *John and Thomas Seymour* (Boston: Special Publications, 1959), No. 224.

33 Vernon C. Stoneman, op. cit., No. 209, illustrates one of a pair of what appear to be identical chairs owned by the Museum of Fine Arts, Boston.

34 The only known copy of the resolutions and prices

agreed upon by the "Cabinet Makers" of Hartford, August 1, 1792, is in the Library of Trinity College (Hartford). Though incomplete, it is the earliest *printed* list of prices for American cabinet work.

35 Photographs of one of these chairs and of the original bill are in the Decorative Arts Photographic Collection at the Winterthur Museum. The chairs with accompanying bill were sold at the sale of the effects of Miss Anna W. Peck, Pittsfield, Massachusetts, about 1960.

36 Mabel M. Swan, "John Goddard's Sons," *Antiques,* LVII (June, 1950), 448–449.

37 Catalogue of *The John Brown House Loan Exhibition of Rhode Island Furniture, May 16 to June 20, 1965* (Providence: The Rhode Island Historical Society, 1965), illustration No. 16, p. 16. For other related chairs see *Colonial Furniture in America* (Lockwood, 1926 edition), p. 111, Fig. 585; *Connecticut Chairs in the Collection of the Connecticut Historical Society,* pp. 48–49; *Fine Points of Furniture,* p. 52; L. Earle Rowe, "John Carlile, Cabinetmaker," *Antiques,* VI (De-

cember, 1924), 310–311; *Three Centuries of Connecticut Furniture,* No. 92.

38 *The Cabinet-Maker and Upholsterer's Guide* of 1788; Hepplewhite's statement occurs on the second page of his description of the plates.

39 The set of six similar chairs from Massachusetts were offered for sale by John S. Walton, of New York City, in 1963.

40 The pair of similar chairs, found in New England, were offered for sale by David Stockwell, Inc., of Wilmington, Delaware, in 1964.

41 Albert Sack, *Fine Points of Furniture* (New York: Crown Publishers, Inc., 1950), pp. 54–55.

42 Hipkiss, op. cit., Supplement 102.

43 Lemuel Adams' original bill in the Connecticut Historical Society is not dated, but was sworn to and presented for payment in June of 1796.

44 *The London Chair-Makers' and Carvers' Book of Prices for Workmanship* (1802), p. 51, Pl. 7, Fig. 4.

# New York Chairs 1790–1805

*Side Chairs, Armchairs, and Chair-back Settees*

The earliest known illustration of an American chair in the new style of the Federal period is in an advertisement in the *New York Daily Advertiser,* March 15, 1790. George Shipley, cabinetmaker and house carpenter from London, included in his notice a vase-back chair with bell-shaped seat, turned legs, and three feathers in the banister. In the same year, George Washington purchased two chairs from Thomas Burling, similar to No. 57. New Yorkers seem to have favored in the 1790's and early 1800's three types of shield-back chairs: those with banisters divided into three splats, centering a fan (Nos. 55, 56) or Prince-of-Wales feathers with drapery (No. 50), and those with four ribs, usually carved as in No. 57. Equally popular but perhaps a few years later in inception were the square backs with center banister of angular urn, feathers, and drapery set between vertical colonnettes (No. 58); those with three urn splats (No. 65); and those with four turned colonnettes fanned out at the top to form "Gothic arches" (No. 61).

About 1805, scroll-back chairs with either turned or outflaring saber legs were introduced. Sometimes the legs were carved with pointed leaves and ended in carved paw feet. These beautiful and fragile-looking chairs often had a minimum of bracing and required the finest, close-grained mahogany to be serviceable. Unquestionably Duncan Phyfe made large numbers of them (No. 66). The usual back featured a cross, a trellis, or a horizontal rounded splat, often "with double Prince of Wales feathers" at the ends. Less common but surviving in some numbers are eagle, harp, and lyre backs. On the chairs made after about 1815, the backs often have only plain, horizontal bars of figured woods.

For the documentation of the most popular types of chairs and the dates when they were commonly manufactured, the successive editions of the cabinet- and chair-makers' books of prices published in New York in 1796, 1802, 1810, 1817, and 1834 offer information nowhere else available. Each edition describes and gives the wages to be paid cabinet- or chairmakers for making several kinds of chairs. It may be assumed that those listed were the most popular and the staple chair forms in daily production, but that other forms were being made is indicated by a sentence at the end of the chair section in the 1802 edition: "Any different pattern chairs or sofas to be paid for in proportion to the above."

To make the information in the price books readily available to the reader, the chair descriptions have been excerpted and listed below. The "extras" under some entries clearly indicate not only that additional ornament was readily available, but that the most commonly used ornament and refinements included bordering; veneering; inlays and stringing; turning; carving; reeding; fluting; sweeping (curving) of legs, seat frame, or back; and therming of legs. Not included in these entries but

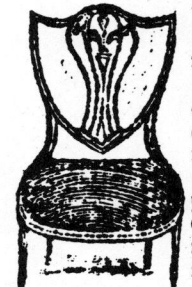
shown elsewhere in the price books are tables giving the price to be paid by the inch or by the foot for banding, string inlays, cock beading, and moldings. Veneering, for instance, four inches wide or under, cost two pence for a strip up to six inches long, three pence from six inches to a foot in length, etc., but, "on round work," to be an extra two-thirds, and double "on hollow or elliptic." The increase in wages for the latter makes perfectly good sense when one considers the extra time consumed on the more complicated contours.

Comparison of the New York chairs here illustrated with those of other regions shows that carving is more prevalent on New York examples, that paterae and other inlays occasionally were used, but that stringing is uncommon. Reeding on legs, backs, banisters, or seat frames was more frequently employed by New York chairmakers than by those of other centers, although this ornamental device was also used in Philadelphia and sometimes in Massachusetts, particularly on square-back chairs. Because an additional charge was made for all such ornament, it would seem that the customer determined the kind and amount of it. However, the maker determined structural features. According to the 1796 New York price book (p. 77), either "block'd or braced" seat frames were standard practice in that city, though "each nail'd block" cost two pence more than "common blocks." These specific references to blocks or braces, apparently for all four corners, indicate a different American norm from that expressed in the 1802 edition of *The London Chair-Makers' and Carvers' Book of Prices,* where the standard was "two open braces" per chair, and blocks or more braces were not offered as extras.

In the New York 1802 price book, it is noted (p. 56) that all "chairs and sofas [are] to start with sweep braces and blocks in the corners." "Sweep braces" (curved medial braces running from front to back of the seat frame) are more frequently found in

New York chairs than in those made elsewhere. In fact, their presence is strong evidence of New York workmanship. "Mortising the back feet through each chair" (open tenons) is listed as an extra at six pence in the New York price book just as it was in Philadelphia, but it is an option that seems not to have been so often exercised in New York as in the Quaker City.

Slip seats are seldom found on New York chairs of the early Federal period. All chairs in the price books prior to 1817 are listed as "made for stuffing over the rail," and every New York chair identified as such in the book has this feature except those of Klysmos, Grecian, or French design.

## New York Price Book 1796

### Chairs.

A plain bannister chair cover'd over the rail either block'd or braced, no holes in the bannisters, strait seat, no low rails,     £.0 11 9

### Extras.

| | | | |
|---|---|---|---|
| Each hole in the bannister, | 0 | 0 | 2½ |
| Each ditto in the top rail, | 0 | 0 | 4 |
| Each hole in upright or cross splatts, | 0 | 0 | 2½ |
| Each scroll in the bannister, | 0 | 0 | 1 |
| Each scroll in upright or cross splatts, | 0 | 0 | 1 |
| Each scroll in top rail or back foot, | 0 | 0 | 2½ |
| Each square in bannister, or splatts forming a break, | 0 | 0 | 1 |
| Each ditto in the top rail or hollow to form a break, | 0 | 0 | 2 |
| Each nail'd block in corner of chair seats, extra from common blocks, | 0 | 0 | 2 |
| A serpentine or circular front, | 0 | 0 | 9 |
| If made with hollow seat, each rail, | 0 | 0 | 2½ |
| Sweep side rails, | 0 | 1 | 0 |
| A loose seat, strait, | 0 | 3 | 0 |
| If made with hollow seat, | 0 | 2 | 0 |
| Ditto with circular front, | 0 | 4 | 0 |
| Ditto with serpentine, | 0 | 5 | 0 |
| If with sweep side rails, extra, | 0 | 1 | 3 |
| Low rails to ditto, | 0 | 3 | 9 |
| If no low back rail, deduct, | 0 | 0 | 9 |
| Veneering the top edge of each, | 0 | 0 | 2½ |
| Each slip between the back feet, with a bead on each side, | 0 | 0 | 2½ |
| Ditto a toad back moulding, | 0 | 0 | 3½ |
| Tonguing each stay rail together in chairs, | 0 | 0 | 4 |
| If dove-tailed, | 0 | 1 | 0 |
| For tapering, plinthing, therming, moulding, or pannelling the feet, see tables of ditto. | | | |
| Veneering each back rail, | 0 | 0 | 2 |
| Mortising the back feet through each chair, | 0 | 0 | 6 |

### A Splatt back Chair with three cross Splatts,

Made for stuffing over the rail, strait seat, no low rails,     £.0 13 0
Other extras not inserted here, see plain bannister chair.

### A Splatt back Chair,

Honey suckle pattern, made for stuffing over the rail, strait seat, no low rails,     £.0 15 6

### A Heart Back Stay Rail Chair,

With a bannister and two upright splatts, strait seat made for stuffing over the rail, no low rails,     £.0 16 6

### A Stay Rail Chair,

With serpentine top rail five upright splatts, strait seat, made for stuffing over the rail, no low rails,     £.0 16 0
Other extras, see plain bannister chair.

### An Urn Back Stay Rail Chair,

With three upright splatts, strait seat, made for stuffing over the rail, no low rails,     £.0 17 6
Other extras, see plain bannister chair.

### A Vase Back Stay Rail Chair,

With serpentine top and three upright splatts or bannister in ditto, strait seat, made for stuffing over the rails,     £.0 16 6

### A Square Back Chair,

| | | | |
|---|---|---|---|
| With strait top and stay rail, three upright splatts, strait seat, made for stuffing over the rails, no low rails, | £.0 | 14 | 6 |
| If the top and stay rail are sweeped in the front, extra, | 0 | 0 | 6 |
| If the above is made with a long vase splatt in the middle, and an arch in the top rail, to be extended between the two outside splatts, extra | 0 | 0 | 9 |
| Diminishing each back foot with a hollow front, the seat rail up, extra from plain taper, | 0 | 0 | 3 |

### Elbows for Chairs.

| | | | |
|---|---|---|---|
| The old scroll'd elbow, | 0 | 10 | 6 |
| Plain twisted ditto, | 0 | 11 | 10 |
| Plain elbows | 0 | 9 | 6 |
| French elbows for strait side rail, the elbows mortis'd on the stump of front foot, | 0 | 13 | 6 |

## 1802     [56]

### A Square Back Chair, No. I.   £. s. d.

| | | | |
|---|---|---|---|
| With straight top and stay rail; four upright splatts; straight seat, made for stuffing over the rail; plain taper'd legs | 0 | 12 | 0 |

### A Square Back Chair, No. II.

| | | | |
|---|---|---|---|
| With three urn splatts, sweep stay and top rail, with a brake in ditto; the splatts pierc'd; sweep seat rails, and plain taper'd legs, for stuffing over the rail | 0 | 17 | 0 |
| *[For Extras, see No. I.]* | | | |

### A Square Back Chair, No. III.

| | | | |
|---|---|---|---|
| With gothic arches, and four turned columns, sweep stay, and top rail, with a brake in ditto; plain taper'd legs | 0 | 18 | 6 |
| If made with a sweep top rail, extra | 0 | 2 | 0 |
| *[For other Extras, see No. I.]* | | | |

### A Square Back Chair, No. IV.

| | | | |
|---|---|---|---|
| A drapery bannister, with feather top; a splatt on each side, to form an arch with the top rail; bannister and splatts pierc'd; sweep stay and top rail, with a brake in ditto; sweep seat rails, for stuffing over ditto; plain taper'd legs | 0 | 19 | 6 |

All chairs and sofas to start with sweep braces, and blocks in the corners. Any

different pattern chairs or sofas, to be paid
for in proportion to the above.

### Elbows for Chairs.

| | | | |
|---|---|---|---|
| A pair of plain elbows | 0 | 8 | 6 |
| A pair of plain twisted ditto | 0 | 10 | 0 |
| French elbows for straight side rail, the elbows morticed on the stump of front feet | 0 | 12 | 0 |

| | | | |
|---|---|---|---|
| Each upright splat, as marked A in plate | 0 | 1 | 0 |
| A plain cross bannister lapped together | 0 | 2 | 3 |
| A rose in the centre of the cross | 0 | 0 | 9 |
| Ogee bannisters, lapped, marked B in plate | 0 | 5 | 3 |
| Ditto      ditto,   marked C in plate | 0 | 6 | 9 |
| A harp bannister, with turned column, as marked F in plate | 0 | 7 | 8 |
| Stringing lyre or harp with brass, each string | 0 | 0 | 3 |

## 1810

### A Scroll Back Chair.

| | | | |
|---|---|---|---|
| With straight rails for stuffing over, one cross bannister in the back, | £.1 | 2 | 8 |
| Common sweep rails, extra | 0 | 1 | 6 |
| Bell seat, extra from sweep rails | 0 | 4 | 3 |
| Each extra cross bannister, | 0 | 2 | 0 |
| Each rose in the centre of the cross, | 0 | 0 | 9 |
| Scroll sweep elbows, | 0 | 11 | 0 |
| An ogee splat instead of a straight one, | 0 | 2 | 9 |
| Springing the front legs one way, each leg | 0 | 0 | 6 |
| Preparing the front legs for lion's paws, each | 0 | 1 | 0 |

## 1817

### A Square Back Chair,

| | | | |
|---|---|---|---|
| With straight top and stay rails in front, one inch deep or under, back legs as in plate No. 6, figure 1; straight mahogany seat rails, plain tapered front legs, without braces | 0 | 17 | 0 |
| Working a scroll on front legs, marked 1 or 2, extra | 0 | 0 | 6 |
| Preparing ditto for lion's paws, each leg | 0 | 1 | 0 |
| Shaping the stay rails with double Prince of Wales feathers, tied with a gothic moulding, (as D in plate,) three inches wide or under, straight in front, extra from start | 0 | 4 | 3 |
| A scroll top rail, two inches and three quarters deep or under, for a straight back, extra from start | 0 | 1 | 9 |
| Bell seat ash rails, extra from start | 0 | 6 | 0 |
| Mahogany rails, extra | 0 | 0 | 10 |
| Lyre bannister, with a turned stretcher, sweep piece at bottom, with a quarter round on front, and returned at the ends, as in plate, letter E. | 0 | 7 | 8 |
| Sweeped stretcher at top, with an astragal in front, extra | 0 | 0 | 7 |

**PLATE N⁰ 6.**

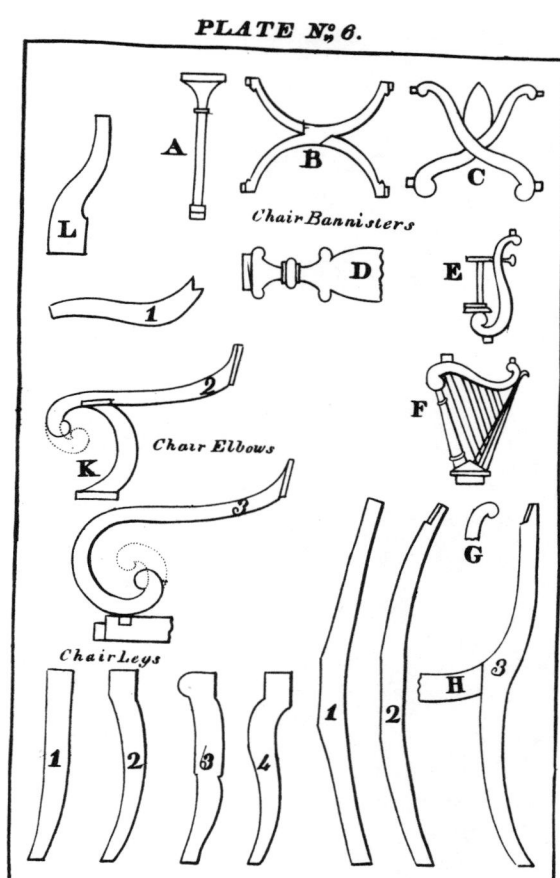

X

# Corner of the Montmorenci Stair Hall

*Against an off-white background of painted and paneled dado from Montmorenci are a stylish New York sofa (No. 265) and side chair (No. 71), upholstered in black antique haircloth, and one of the daintiest American gilded looking glasses (No. 231). At the right is the Conservatory filled with flowering plants and shrubs.*

**50 ARMCHAIR** with vase back or shield back
(one of a pair)
*1795–1800  New York*

A sofa (No. 265), a side chair, and this armchair
are part of a large set—six side chairs, a pair of
armchairs, and a pair of sofas once owned by the
Montgomery family of Dutchess County, New
York, and all now at Winterthur. The design of the
vase back is one long associated with the name of
Duncan Phyfe because of the character of the finely
carved ruffled leaf from which the drapery depends.
However, clear proof of his authorship is yet to be
set forth. Few chairs show the high quality of
workmanship seen here. All front surfaces are
molded, beaded, carved, or inlaid. Both the hollowed arms (elbows) and the supports (ogee stumps
screwed to the frame) are serpentine—the kind
most frequently seen on New York armchairs.

Dimensions: height 38⅜; width 21¾; depth 18.
Materials: front and side rails, ash; rear rail and two
   medial braces, cherry; corner blocks, (type IV) tulip;
   upholstery, black haircloth, English, about 1800.
Provenance: Eglinton Montgomery.
Accession: 57.673

**51 SIDE CHAIR** with vase back or shield back
*1795–1800  New York*

This beautiful chair is closely related to the preceding one but stretchers are added and reeding is
substituted for string inlay on the front legs. Close
comparison of details of the back design will reveal
less successful handling here of the upper part of
the splat (or banister, as this part of the back was
known to cabinetmakers if made of one piece of
wood). The upper leaf, or feather, does not extend

over the top of the shield back and, like the dominant central oval, seems a little crowded and confined.

Dimensions: height 39½; width 21⅛; depth 16.
Materials: mahogany; open braces (type I) red gum and small blocks (type II) white pine, all four corners; rails, ash; upholstery, black haircloth, English, about 1800.
Accession: 57.936

## 52 ARMCHAIR with vase back
*About 1800   New York*

The parts and ornamentation of this armchair conform with one exception to those usually found on chairs made in New York. The spade feet, reeded legs, concaved, outflaring arm supports screwed to the bowed seat frame and ending in carved rosettes at their junctions with the serpen-

tine and hollowed arms, and the carved fan at the base of the banister are all in the New York idiom. However, the shaping of the top of the vase back is more complex than the normal American serpentine crest. It is described as "a back, with a circular joint and two squares in the top" (p. 51) and illustrated as Fig. 3, Plate 7 in *The London Chair-Makers' and Carvers' Book of Prices* (1802). Neither the carving nor the quality of the mahogany are up to the usual New York standard. This and the delicacy of the banister may account for several breaks which have been repaired. The side rails are tenoned through the rear legs.

Dimensions: height 36⅞; width 21½; depth 17¾.
Materials: mahogany; front seat rail, American ash; rear seat rail, tulip; front corner blocks (type IV), white pine; rear corner blocks (2-part type IV), tulip and white pine; upholstery, brown silk and cotton, woven

in floral and leaf pattern resembling haircloth, about 1800.
Accession: 53.9

**53** ARMCHAIR with vase back or shield back (one of a pair)
*1790–1800   New York*

On the label of Elbert Anderson,[1] a side chair with this type of vase back is illustrated; and, for many years, such chairs have been attributed to his hand. However, since this pattern was a popular one in Manhattan, with several variant examples known,[2] there is little certainty that this or any other chair without his label or stamp was made in his shop. The inlaid light wood patera under the serpentine cresting rail; the whorls inlaid on the fronts of the arms; the beading which outlines each member of

the back; the stylish arms and the arm supports; and the outsweeping front legs mark this as a chair of quality. Carved, pointed leaves ornament the upper face of the arms where they meet the back. Except on New York chairs, such flaring front legs are seldom seen in American furniture.[3]

Dimensions: height 37¾; width 21; depth 17¼.
Materials: mahogany with satinwood inlays; rails and seat frame, ash; medial braces, red gum; original corner blocks missing; upholstery, black haircloth, English, about 1800.
Accession: 57.672.1, 2

**54** SIDE CHAIR with vase back or shield back
*1790–1800   New York*

Until recently, all American vase-back chairs, whether with serpentine or truncated tops, if inlaid with festoons, were supposed of New York origin. In January of 1964, Eleanore Bradford Monahon put forward a strong case for reattributing one kind with flat-top shields to Providence.[4] However, on those chairs, the inlaid festoons are not made of bellflowers as are those seen here but of abstract elements (from dart and other bandings) arranged in petaled forms. Several floral elements in this inlay and that on No. 55 seem identical, and the backs of the shield are worked in much the same way. The same shop, perhaps the same man, may have made both chairs.

Dimensions: height 38; width 21½; depth 17¾.

Materials: mahogany with light wood inlays; seat rails, front and side, ash; seat rail, rear, mahogany; front, open braces (type I), curly soft maple; rear, large nailed open braces, white pine; upholstery, black haircloth, English, about 1800.

Accession: 57.937

## 55 SIDE CHAIR with vase back, truncated top
*1790–1800   New York*

Perhaps derived in form from a stuffed-back chair with straight top shown in Plate 11 of *The Cabinet-Maker and Upholsterer's Guide* by Hepplewhite, this striking interpretation of the more usual arched top, shield- or vase-back chair is one of four variants known. All of them have the same intricately inlaid festoons of husks, each of which is "engraved" with fine black lines. Three have fans inlaid at the base of the back. A matching pair of chairs in the Charles K. Davis collection was originally owned by Elizabeth (Schuyler) and Alexander Hamilton and used at *The Grange* in New York. The details of the inlay, with the exception of that on the front legs, more nearly approximate those of New York than inlays found on furniture made elsewhere.[5]

Dimensions: height 36¼; width 20¾; depth 17¼.

Materials: mahogany with light wood inlays; front seat rail, beech; side rails, hard maple; rear rail, mahogany; upholstery, green silk, about 1800.

Accession: 52.131

## 56 SIDE CHAIR with vase back or shield back (one of a pair)
*1790–1800   New York*

Other New York chairs with similar vase backs are known,[6] but this pair presents an unusual combination of elements. Inlays and carving are not often found together, especially with such dominant

accents; double-serpentine back supports occur on a few chairs with New York or Albany histories, but are rare; and this type of back with three upright splats—the center one pierced and fan-shaped at the top—is more often seen on Baltimore (No. 101) and Philadelphia chairs.

Although no other inlaid American chair backs can match the finesse of these restless, leafy, inlaid vines, the undulations of the back supports and the rather florid carving of the clustered leaves on the splats (cut in concave and convex ribs in the New York manner) give these chairs an exuberance that this observer finds fortunately not typical of early Federal furniture.

Dimensions: height 39½; width 21½; depth 17½.

Materials: mahogany, light wood inlay; seat rails, ash;

four original open braces missing; upholstery, pale-blue silk with white satin stripes and floral sprigs brocaded in colored and silver threads, French, late eighteenth century.
Accession: 51.34, 35

**57** ARMCHAIR with vase back or shield back
*1790–1800   New York City*

The reeding of the front legs, arm supports, and splats gives unity and distinction to this fine armchair, a variant of the design shown in Plate 2 of Hepplewhite's *Guide*. Ten side chairs and two armchairs identical in every detail, including the highly unusual beading and the carved scalelike ornament on the splats, have been until recently in the Glen Sanders House in Scotia, New York. An original

bill, recently found in the attic of that house, from "Robt Carter," a New York cabinetmaker, to "Mr. Elmendorf," is believed to be for those chairs.[7] Dated "New York 28 Aug 1793," it reads in part:

| 10 Mahogany Chairs at 66/. | - - - - | 33. 0 0 |
| 2 D° with Arms at      82/. | - - - - | 8. 4 0 |

Such chairs may have been made by several New York cabinetmakers inasmuch as another pair, at Mount Vernon, are believed to have been made by Thomas Burling of New York.[8]

Dimensions: height 38⅝; width 22¼; depth 18½.
Materials: mahogany; front and side rails, ash; rear rail, maple; a fragment of one of the four missing corner braces is cherry; upholstery, green silk, about 1800.
Provenance: Museum Purchase, 1953.
Accession: 53.170

**57**

**58**

**58** ARMCHAIR with square back (matches side chair No. 60)[9]
*About 1800   New York*

Variants of the square-back design from the 1794 edition of Sheraton's *Drawing Book* (Plate 36, No. 1) were highly popular in New York. The price paid journeymen cabinetmakers for making the simplest version of this type of chair, a "Square Back Chair No. IV," (*The New York Book of Prices for Cabinet and Chair Work,* 1802), was nineteen shillings and six pence. Beading the outlines of the back, arms, and front legs; carving the fans, the drapery banister with feather top, and the pointed leaves which ornament the upper surface of the arms where they meet the back (see also No. 53); and shaping the spade feet would have been extras. A pair of "plain twisted elbows [arms]" cost ten shillings for workmanship. Chairs with this kind of back more often have reeded than paneled legs, although paneled ones are seen here. Other examples with molded and inlaid legs are known. The latter may have been made in Philadelphia.

Dimensions: height 35½; width 23; depth 18.
Materials: mahogany; front and side rails, ash; rear rail and medial seat brace, birch; four open braces (type I), cherry; small blocks (type IV) front and (type II) rear, white pine; upholstery, brown satin with floral sprigs embroidered in colored silks, French, late eighteenth century.
Accession: 57.631

**59** ARMCHAIR with square back (one of a pair)[10]
*1790–1800   New York or Albany*

These sophisticated chairs, of the same design as the preceding one, differ in several respects beyond the obvious use of stringing and "engraved" inlays instead of carving for ornament. The backs are curved or hollowed, the rear legs flare out at a sharp angle, and the arm supports are fastened to an extension of the front legs instead of being screwed to the seat frame as in the usual New York City practice. Despite these exceptions, these fine chairs were probably made in New York City, or possibly Albany.

Dimensions: height 35⅞; width 23¼; depth 18⅞.
Materials: mahogany with light wood inlays; seat rails, ash; in front are open braces (type I), beech; upholstery, dark-blue satin with floral trails, stripes, and lace in colors, English or French, late eighteenth century.
Provenance: Museum Purchase, 1953; Lammot du Pont Copeland Fund.
Accession: G 53.153.3, 4          see Inlay Fig. 112

**60** SIDE CHAIR with square back (one of three)
*About 1800   New York*

This is one of the finest interpretations of the commonest surviving New York chair form. All front surfaces of the back and front legs are outlined with a bead; and the carving of the Prince-of-Wales feathers, the fans, and the swags of drapery festooning the pierced urn is skillfully handled. Of these three chairs, so nearly identical as to be indistinguishable, two are carved by the same hand, one by another. One has a medial brace, the others none.

Dimensions: height 35¾; width 21; depth 17½.
Materials: mahogany; seat rails, ash; four original open braces (type I) and medial brace, cherry; front corner blocks (type II), white pine; small rear corner blocks

59

(type IV), white pine; upholstery, dark-blue satin with floral trails, stripes, and lace in colors and white, English or French, late eighteenth century.
Accession: 57.632.1–3

**61** SIDE CHAIR with square back (one of a pair)
*1800–1810　New York　Possibly made by Abraham Slover and (?) Taylor (working 1802 to 1805)*

With the exception of minor variations in the turnings of the "columns" and the addition here of carved rosettes at the lower corners of the back, this chair seems identical to a chair with the partial label of "S over and Taylor" first published in *Antiques*, November, 1923. The first named partner, then assumed to be Stover, has since been properly identified as Slover.[11]

Many variants of this kind of chair with New York histories of ownership are known (No. 62).[12] They were probably made in most chairmaking shops since the back is unmistakably described in *The New-York Book of Prices for Cabinet and Chair Work* for 1802 as a "Square Back Chair, No. III With four gothic arches, and four turned columns, sweep stay, and top rail, with a brake in ditto; sweep seat rails, for stuffing over ditto; plain taper'd legs." There are many extras on this fine example: the carving of the sunburst, the tops of the columns, and the rosettes at the four corners of the back; the reeding of the columns; the beading around the back; the reeding of the legs; and the spade, or thermed, feet.

Dimensions: height 36⅝; width 21½; depth 18.
Materials: mahogany; all rails, ash; medial brace, cherry; corner blocks (type VI), white pine; upholstery, yellow

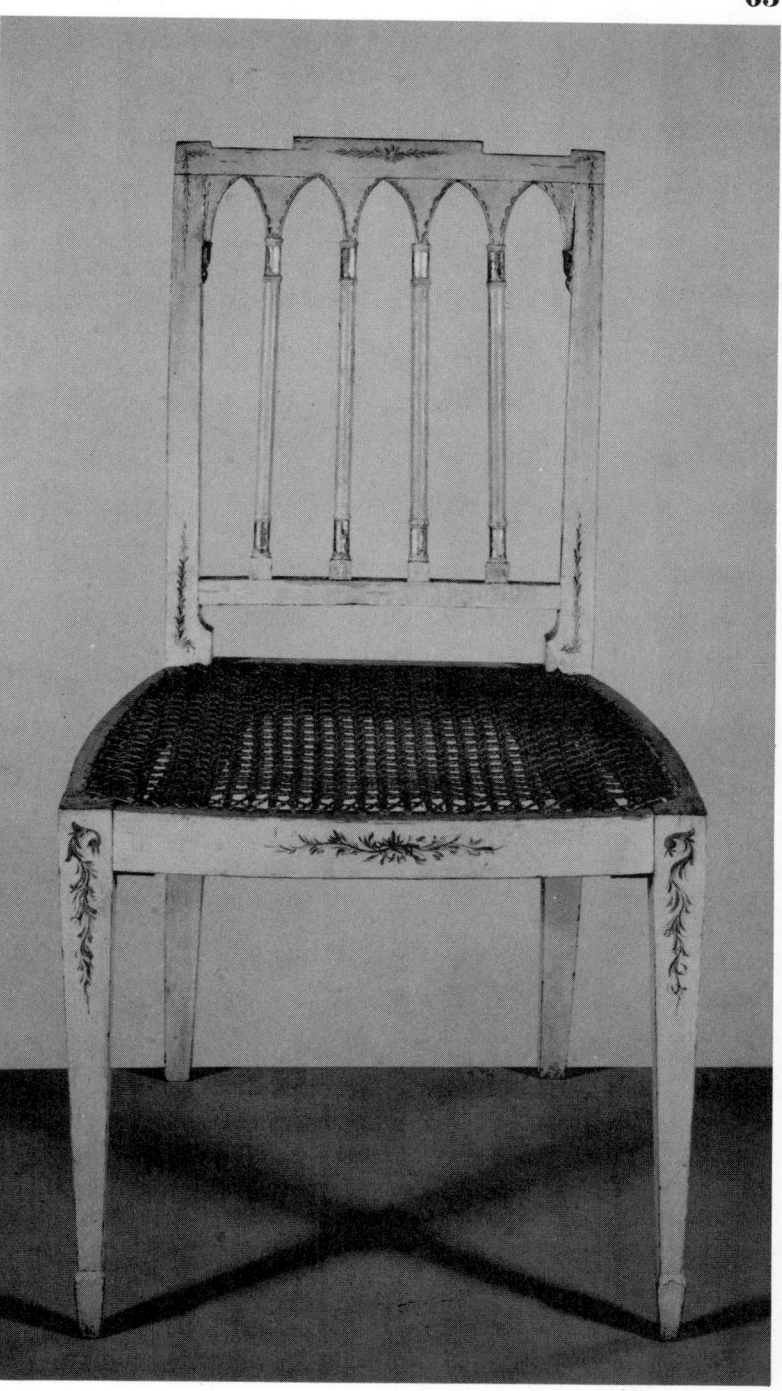

during the following three-year period included charges for satinwood and black holly veneers, cherry plank, a portable desk, and eleven "Side Board Tops."[14] This is but another instance of the close working relationships between cabinetmakers. The fact that Lyell made chair frames for Slover and Taylor and a variety of furniture for other well-known cabinetmakers emphasizes the weakness of attributions based on stylistic grounds.

Dimensions: height 36½; depth 16½; width 20¾.

silk taffeta with polychrome sprigged stripes, floral trails and garden hats, English or French, late eighteenth century.

Provenance: Gift of Mr. Charles K. Davis, 1954.

Accession: G 54.74.8, 9

**62** ARMCHAIR with square back

*1800–1810   New York*

This variant of No. 61 differs mainly in the substitution of carved drapery for the sunburst in the upper rail.[13] On March 25, 1805, Fenwick Lyell, New York cabinet and chairmaker charged "Slover and Taylor" twenty-seven pounds, twelve shillings, for twelve mahogany chair frames. His charges to this partnership began on October 16, 1802, with a debit, "35 feet St. Domingo, Table Wood," and

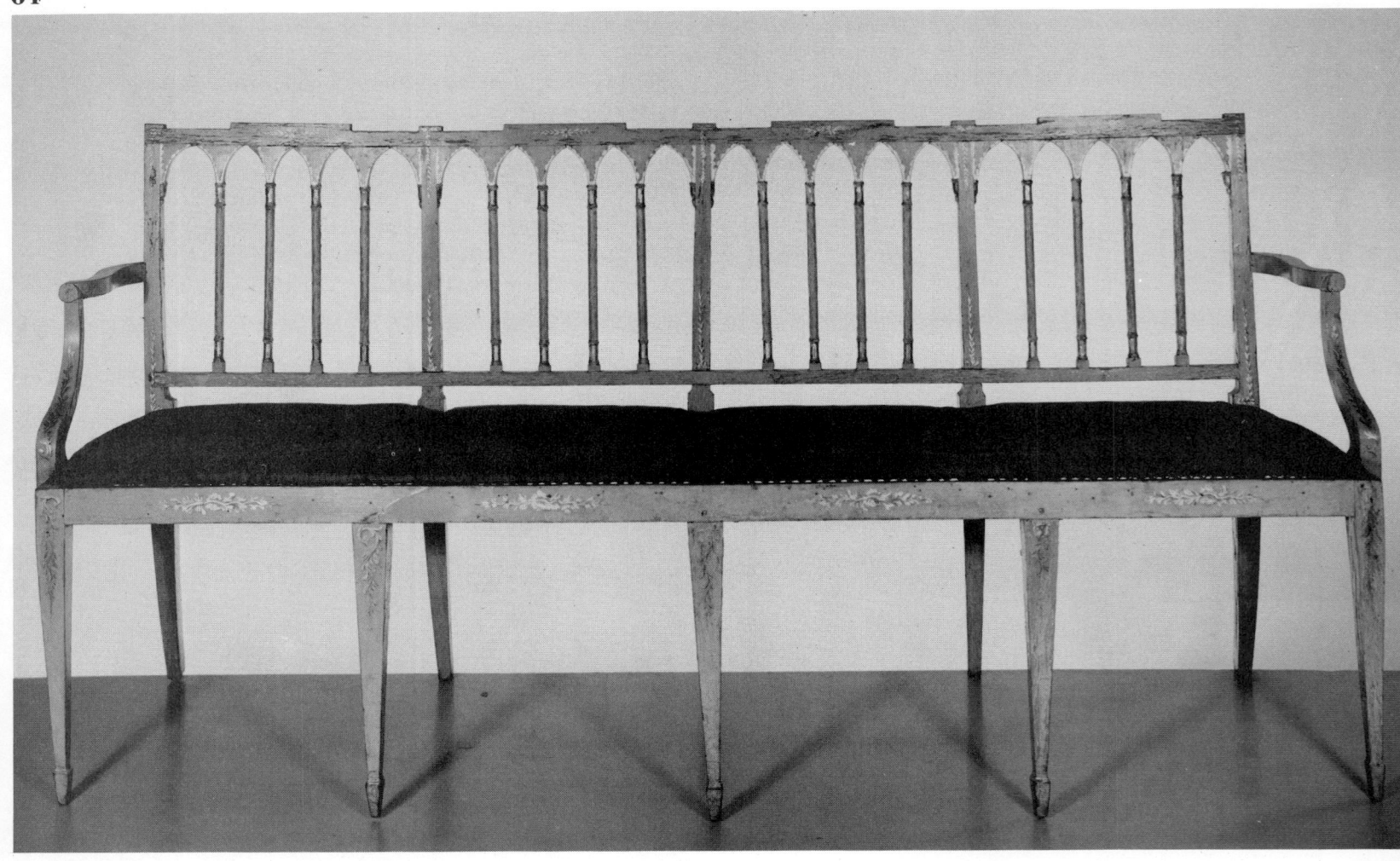

# 64

Materials: mahogany; all rails, ash; right front corner block (type VI), white pine; medial seat brace, cherry; upholstery, green silk called *droguet*, woven in stylized leaf-and-fruit pattern, French, second half of eighteenth century.
Accession: 57.949

### 63 PAINTED SIDE CHAIR with square back
*1800–1810   New York City or Albany*

These side chairs with caned seats and five "Gothic arches" are sophisticated variants of a popular New York chair style discussed under No. 61. They were a part of a large set (see also No. 64) which was painted white and decorated with garlands and streamers in red and gold.[15] With the same history of ownership, by Governor and Mrs. Yates of Albany, as the painted bed (No. 4), they may possibly have been made in Albany; but New York City seems the more likely place of origin.

Dimensions: height 35⅛; width 18¾; depth 14¼.
Materials: seat rails, birch; legs and splats, cherry.

Provenance: Gov. and Mrs. Joseph C. Yates; Jane Josepha DeLancey Neill; Edward Montandevert Neill; Anna DeLancey Neill Grinnell (Mrs. Edward).
Accession: 57.962.1

### 64 PAINTED SETTEE
*1800–1810   New York City or Albany*

This handsome chair-back settee with caned seat and its mate (see footnote No. 15) are believed to be unique in American furniture. However, the 1802 and later editions of *The London Chair-Makers' and Carvers' Book of Prices*, which were followed closely by New York chairmakers, gives specific directions and charges (pp. 95–97) for framing square- and vase-back settees following the patterns of sofas but with "banisters or splats in the backs, to be charg'd one third more than for ditto square-back [or vase-back] chairs." The paint and decoration matches the side chair No. 63 of the same set.

Dimensions: height 36; width 75; depth 19.

Materials: seat rails, birch; legs and splats, cherry; cushion, green silk, French, late eighteenth century.
Provenance: The same as for No. 63.
Accession: 57.957

**65** ARMCHAIR with square back, one of a set of two armchairs and ten matching side chairs
*About 1800   New York City*

This large set of chairs and a sofa (No. 275), originally owned by Victor Marie du Pont, were possibly acquired by him when associated with the French Ministry to the United States in 1787 and from 1791 to 1793. More likely, they were bought after his return to New York in 1800 when he established a commission house; and possibly part or all of them are those entered in his "Book of personal Family expenses" (p. 3), "October [1802] chairs for dining room $36.00" (see Plate XXII). The sofa and perhaps additional chairs may have been included in the same book (p. 6) in the entry "April, 1803... Dove's bill for dining table and other article 166.00."[16] (William Dove, cabinetmaker and upholsterer, at No. 161 William Street, New York City, advertised "a general assortment of Cabinet Furniture made to the most fashionable manner on moderate terms" in 1801.[17])

This type of chair was a popular one in New York (there are twelve other variant examples in the Winterthur collections) and is well described in *The New-York Book of Prices for Cabinet and Chair Work* for 1802 where on page 56 is listed "a square back chair, no. II With three urn splatts, sweep [curved] stay and top rail, with a brake in ditto; the splatts pierc'd; sweep seat rails, and plain taper'd legs, for stuffing over the rails. 17 shillings." An additional charge was made for the carving in the "brake" in the top rail and at the top of the urn splats, as well as the sweeping of the front legs. Such outcurving legs showing French influence are rare and unusual on American chairs. A pair of plain, twisted elbows (arms) cost ten shillings. The sweeped or hollowed back (as on these chairs) is another refinement not found on many American chairs.

Dimensions: height 35; width 21½; depth 18½.
Materials: mahogany; rails, white oak; blocks, not original; medial brace, soft maple; upholstery, silk satin, cream ground with yellow, green, salmon, and black stripes, French, late eighteenth century.
Provenance: Victor Marie du Pont; Sophie Madeleine Dalmas du Pont; Henry Algernon du Pont; Henry Francis du Pont.
Accession: 57.835.1, 2

FOOTNOTES

1 The trade card, or furniture label, of Elbert Anderson was engraved by Cornelius Tiebout. Photographs of two examples of this label are in the Decorative Arts Photographic Collection.
2 See page 50, *New York Furniture Before 1840* (Albany Institute of History and Art, 1962), for an armchair with almost identical back, but with different types of legs and arm supports.
3 In "Providence Cabinetmakers," *Rhode Island History*, XXIII (January, 1964) 12, Eleanore Bradford Monahon illustrates a flat-top, vase-back side chair with inlaid festoons and *outflaring* legs. She makes a strong case for the theory that this chair was made in Providence, Rhode Island, by Thomas Howard, Jr.
4 *Ibid.*, pp. 1–22.
5 According to Joseph Downs, a set of six lattice-back chairs with the same detail of inlay, formerly in the John

**65**

F. Bernard Collections (see *John F. Bernard Collection Sale Catalogue*; Albany, New York: September 14–15, 1938), Nos. 62–67, was stamped Anderson on the inside ash seat rail between the cherry medial braces of each chair. It is uncertain whether that name is Elbert Anderson's, whose ambitious trade card on a Hepplewhite sideboard gives him importance, or that of Alexander, Andrew, or Samuel Anderson, his competitors, all of whom had their own shops in Lower Manhattan in the 1790's and are listed in the New York directories together. Of the group, Elbert Anderson & Son seems to have had the longest period of activity, beginning in 1786 at 5 Maiden Lane and ending in 1821 at 28 Provost Street.

6 The label of Andrew Anderson, cabinet and chairmaker, 50 Beekman Street, New York City, illustrates a side chair with closely related back (Decorative Arts Photographic Collections, Winterthur); No. 130, *New York State Furniture* (Metropolitan Museum of Art, 1934), is a similar chair (with carved back, no inlay), at that time in the famous Glen Sanders House in Scotia, New York; and No. 697 in the Catalogue of the *Girl Scouts Loan Exhibition* (New York, 1929) is almost identical in form, but has carved ornament instead of inlays. The latter is said to have been originally in New York City in the Morris House, now known as the Jumel Mansion.

7 Colonial Williamsburg now owns "Mr. Elmendorf's chairs." Their maker's prominence is indicated by his position in the New York Federal Procession of 1788 celebrating the ratification of the United States Constitution: "...The Cabinetmakers [were] headed by Messrs. Carmer, Rucker, and Anderson. Robert Carter bearing the arms of the procession..." (from The Impartial Gazeteer, August 9, 1788, Gottesman, 1777–1799, No. 335).

8 Two armchairs once owned by George Washington at Mount Vernon are thought to be the "2 armed Ch$^{rs}$" for which he paid Thomas Burling, New York City cabinetmaker, 7 pounds in 1790. Although the carving on the sectors at the base of the splats and the arms of that pair differ, the carving of the back splats seems identical to that on this chair. These are now in the Lewis Collection, United States National Museum, Smithsonian Institution.

For an illustration of one of the chairs in the Smithsonian, see Helen Comstock's article, "Mount Vernon Centennial," *Antiques*, LXIV (July, 1953), 36.

9 An armchair of the same design, but with reeded front legs and less luxuriant carving is illustrated as No. 107 in Hipkiss, op. cit.

10 A closely related side chair, also with stringing and inlays on the back and legs but without spade feet, is illustrated as No. 108 in Hipkiss, op. cit.

11 Phelps Warren, "Setting the Record Straight: Slover and Taylor, New York Cabinetmakers," *Antiques*, LXXX (October, 1961), 350–351.

12 Of this style of chair, Joseph Downs noted in the *Bulletin of the Metropolitan Museum of Art* (April, 1938), p. 108n: "In the latter part of the nineteenth century Sypher and Company, established on Broadway in 1867, had many chairs and double-chair settees made after this pattern. The reproductions are easy to identify, however, as close scrutiny soon reveals that the carving is thin and mechanical, the finish too red and overpolished, and the seat construction different from the old models."

13 What appears to be an identical chair with carved drapery on the rail is credited by Thomas Ormsbee in *Early American Furniture Makers* (New York: Tudor Publishing Company, 1930), Plate XXXI, as being Duncan "Phyfe's own furniture."

14 Manuscript account book of Fenwick Lyell, Monmouth County Historical Society, Freehold, New Jersey.

15 In 1958, Israel Sack and Sons of New York offered for sale chairs and a settee which matched these and No. 64 except for the feet which may have been cut.

16 Other entries in the same book record payments to "Turcot the upholsterer." Peter D. Turcot was in business as upholsterer and paper hanger at 108 Water Street in 1800 and at 21 Maiden Lane in 1804. Winterthur Manuscripts, Group 3, Box 29. The gift of Henry Francis du Pont to the Eleutherian Mills Historical Library, Greenville, Delaware.

17 Rita Susswein Gottesman, *The Arts and Crafts in New York, 1800–1804* (New York: The New-York Historical Society, 1965), No. 341.

# New York Chairs 1805–1825

*Side Chairs, Armchairs, and Chair-back Settees*

A new style in seating furniture, embodying Grecian influences, was introduced in New York soon after 1800. A forerunner of what is usually called Empire furniture today, its makers nevertheless did not so designate it, nor did they often acknowledge French attributes in most names for it. One of the earliest documented groups of furniture in this mode is included in a bill dated November 21, 1807, from Duncan Phyfe to William Bayard for Bayard's New York house at No. 6 State Street. Ten pieces most assuredly from this group—ten side chairs (No. 66), and two armchairs (No. 67), and probably a cane-seated sofa (No. 278), and a window stool (No. 69)— are now at Winterthur in the Phyfe Room.

Although the history of the introduction in New York of the new styles based on Greek and Roman furniture is yet to be worked out, the writer believes that Duncan Phyfe played an active part in the popularization of the new forms with Grecian front and back legs and that the immediate source for all of these is *The London Chair-Makers' and Carvers' Book of Prices for Workmanship*, first published in 1802 with an important supplement added in 1808. Virtually every feature of the scroll-back chairs and sofas such as those seen in Plate XI and the following illustrations can be traced directly to this London book. The writer is convinced that Phyfe's importance rests on his influence as an introducer of a new style rather than as an inventor or innovator as heretofore thought. The delicate and fragile scroll-back chairs and sofas required expert cabinetwork and strong, fine-grained mahoganies. With a large shop in which many men were employed and a following of eminent New Yorkers who relied upon him for their furniture, Phyfe was in an excellent position to assume leadership in the introduction of the style. He probably also had much influence in the rapid dissemination of new forms, ornament, and idioms. As has already been shown, journeymen cabinetmakers were an itinerant lot, and there is no reason to think that the men who worked in Phyfe's shop stayed there for long periods. Some unquestionably moved on to work for others or to set up shops for themselves. With such moving about of the workmen who actually made furniture, it becomes virtually impossible in most cases to determine whether a piece was made in Phyfe's shop or by men who had been exposed to his interpretations of the London book of prices. In that book, the square-back chair, hollowed and scrolled in outline, is described; and there are illustrations of many details. Many of these attributes are incorporated in *The New-York Book of Prices for Manufacturing Cabinet and Chair Work* published in 1817.

The cross, or lattice, back, the ogee scroll back, and the lyre and the harp, combined with Grecian front and rear legs, became the standard for New York chair designs. The most costly examples of scroll-back chairs have carved front legs that end in paw feet. In none of the price books is there reference to French features or the

Empire style. And although there are references to broad slat backs (as seen in No. 389) which, when combined with Grecian front and rear legs, would have produced the Klysmos-type chairs, of which some examples were produced in Philadelphia, these apparently were not favored in New York.

Catalogue entries, Nos. 67, 68, and possibly 69, deal with chairs owned by William Bayard and mentioned in Phyfe's bill which follows. It illustrates the kind of information provided by original manuscripts and the problems connected with their study.

| 1807 | | | MR WILLIAM BAYARD | | |
| | | | TO D. PHYFE D[R] | | |
| Nov. 21 | To 28 | Mahogany Chairs | $12 \frac{50}{100}$ | 350 | – 00 |
| | 14 | D° D° | 15 | 210 | – 00 |
| | 3 | Sofas | 65 | 195 | – 00 |
| | | Sideboard | | 125 | – 00 |
| | | Set Dining tables | | 160 | – 00 |
| | | Dressing table | | 65 | – 00 |
| | | Ward Robe | | 100 | – 00 |
| | | Pair Card tables | | 75 | – 00 |
| | | Pair D° D° | | 80 | – 00 |
| | | Tea table | | 30 | – 00 |
| | | one D° | | 35 | – 00 |
| | | Bason Stand | | 9 | – – |
| | | | | $1434 | – – |

To know the prices Phyfe actually charged is interesting although there is some question about the nature of the chairs included in the bill. Twenty-eight mahogany chairs are charged at $12.50 each. Fourteen are charged at $15.00. Were some of them side chairs? Were some armchairs? Were all of the same design? At the time of the death of Bayard's granddaughter, Miss Marie Louise Campbell, in 1912, she possessed a substantial amount of furniture which she had inherited from her mother and which, according to family tradition, had been made by Phyfe for Bayard. The veracity of this tradition was strengthened by Phyfe's bill. The furniture in Miss Campbell's estate was sold at private sale to her relatives in April of 1912. Ten side chairs (No. 66), two armchairs (No. 67), and the above bill were acquired by Horace Townsend, nephew of Miss Campbell. In 1931, he sold these to Henry Francis du Pont.

Also included in Miss Campbell's estate were other side chairs with scroll backs (a single cross instead of a double cross) and with the same carving of reeds and ribbon as on Nos. 66 and 67. These also were believed to have been made for William Bayard by Phyfe. No. 68 is like these chairs and may be one of them. Of the same design as the chairs is the sofa (No. 277). It, too, may have been purchased from Phyfe by Bayard (see Hornor, *The Antiquarian*, XIV [March, 1930], 38).

Not enough information is at present available to the writer to interpret properly the above bill. Most sets of six or more chairs included armchairs; and there were armchairs in the set owned by Bayard. Armchairs were normally charged at about fifty percent more than side chairs. Phyfe makes no reference in his bill to armchairs, nor is there an extra charge for them. In his 1816 bill to Charles N. Bancker, twelve mahogany chairs are also charged with no reference to armchairs. Perhaps it was Phyfe's practice to include the necessary armchairs along with side chairs at one unit price for the whole lot. If such was his custom, this bill accounts for two types of chairs which were passed on from one generation to another of Bayard's descendants.

# XI

## Phyfe Room

*At least ten pieces of furniture in this drawing room are well documented as having been made by Duncan Phyfe (1807) for William Bayard who lived at No. 6 State Street in New York City, next door to the house of Moses Rogers from which the architectural elements of this room (1806) were taken. All of the furniture is in the mode associated with and represented by the Phyfe style in the United States. The pair of glass chandeliers and wall sconces of about 1815–1825 are English or American; the Aubusson-type carpet of tapestry weave is French and about the period of the architecture.*

### 66   SCROLL-BACK SIDE CHAIR
(one of ten)[1]
*1807   New York City   Made in the shop of Duncan Phyfe*

These ten side chairs and the following pair of armchairs (No. 67) are believed to be part of one of the lots of chairs and other furniture charged by Duncan Phyfe to William Bayard, a wealthy New Yorker, in 1807 (see page 118). Because the writer thinks chairs with these outflaring feet and an extra cross in the back were more expensive to make than such chairs as No. 68, he believes these to be twelve of the fourteen charged at $15 each. They stood originally in Bayard's house at 6 State Street, New York City, next door to the house of Moses Rogers. Today they stand in a room from Rogers' house installed in Winterthur and known as the Phyfe Room.[2]

The following description for a "Scroll Back Chair" in the 1810 New York book of prices obviously applies to this set of chairs:[3]

> With straight rails for stuffing over, one cross bannister in the back,...
>
> Bell seat, extra from sweep rails...
>
> Each extra cross bannister,...
>
> Each rose in the centre of the cross,...
>
> Springing the front legs one way,...

Although there is no mention of "Grecian" in connection with this chair in the New York book, a "Grecian" sofa is listed on the following page; and it has elements then called "Grecian," as is evident from the more detailed descriptions in the 1802 edition of *The London Chair-Makers' and Carvers' Book of Prices for Workmanship*. There, options for a "Scroll Back Chair" included the following features found in this chair: the "Bell-shaped seat," "the sweep'd Grecian back legs ... with square and hollow at the bottom above the seat." The "Grecian front legs" and cross banisters are all illustrated and prices are given for the manufacture of each. The London rate for each reed on "sweep'd front legs" was one and a half pence; for reeding "back legs upper ends" (Plate 2, Fig. N) with five reeds as in "17" and "18" Plate 1 (as on this chair) the cost was five pence per leg.

The design of this chair was a popular one in New York. As noted above, its elements were clearly set forth in the New York book of prices used by most, if not all, New York cabinetmakers. Unquestionably such chairs were made by many New York cabinetmakers. Until a detailed study is made of many documented pieces of New York cabinetwork by others than Phyfe, no one can say that his competitors equaled his standards of workmanship to which these superbly made chairs testify.

Dimensions: height 33; width 19; depth 16½.
Materials: mahogany; back, front, and side seat rails, ash; medial seat brace, red gum; upholstery, light-blue satin with stylized floral-and-leaf medallion in white and yellow, French, Empire style, early nineteenth century.
Provenance: Originally owned by William Bayard; Mrs. Duncan Pearsall Campbell; Miss Marie Louise Campbell; Horace Townsend.
Accession: 57.719.1–10

## 67 SCROLL-BACK ARMCHAIR
(one of a pair) [4]
*1807   New York City   Made in the shop of Duncan Phyfe*

Few American armchairs can match the grace and over-all composition of these chairs. Each member is delicate and refined. The hollowed top rail looks comfortable; the scrolled arms are inviting. Outflaring reeded legs give a sense of stability. Five reeds with a ribbon tied in a bowknot are crisply carved on the beaded sunken panel of the hollowed upper rail of each of fourteen pieces at Winterthur—the pair of chairs shown here, ten matching side chairs (No. 66), a sofa (No. 277), and window stool (No. 69). The fine carving is typical of that found on many chairs either documented as Phyfe's work or attributed to him.

The anatomy of the elbows shown here is presented in the 1802 *London Chair-Makers' and Carvers' Book of Prices* as "framing with turned stumps ... screwed to the outside or mortised into the upper

edge of the side rail ... and scroll elbows sweeped toward the tops of the back legs."

An arm with serpentine flare like these is shown as Figure 3, Plate 6, in the same book; and the shaping is described on page 47 as "sweeping the elbows ... by a mould." "Scroll sweep elbows" cost eleven shillings (about $1.38) for labor in the New York price book of 1810 (p. 56). The turnings on the stumps (arm supports) are the same as on the sofa (No. 277).

Dimensions: height 33; width 21¼; depth 21.
Materials: mahogany; front and side seat rails, ash; medial seat braces, cherry; upholstery, light-blue satin with stylized floral-and-leaf medallion in white and yellow, French, Empire style, early nineteenth century.
Provenance: William Bayard; Mrs. Duncan Pearsall Campbell; Miss Marie Louise Campbell; Horace Townsend.
Accession: 57.720.1–2

**68**

# 69

**68**  SCROLL-BACK SIDE CHAIR
*1807  New York City  Strong evidence for attribution to the workshop of Duncan Phyfe*

To all appearances, this chair is identical to chairs which descended from William Bayard to Miss Marie Louise Campbell and which were bought by various members of her family at the private sale of her effects[5] (see page 118). Like the other set of scroll-back chairs (Nos. 66, 67) billed by Phyfe to Bayard in 1807, this one has carved reeds and ribbon on the upper rail and a cross banister (though only one cross instead of two as on the other set) with carved rose and a bell-shaped seat. In contrast, the back legs of this one are turned above the seat, the front legs are turned and reeded, and the seat is caned. All of these are variations

that might be expected among chairs made in New York at that time. The chairs in the set which this one matches are believed to have cost $12.50 each (see No. 66). The cost of labor in 1810 for "Liping or rabbiting for cane" was nine pence and "Boreing the seat for cane" one shilling, six pence.

Dimensions: height 33; width 18½; depth 16½.
Materials: mahogany; medial seat braces, red gum; caned seat.
Accession: 57.1046

**69**  WINDOW STOOL with scroll ends[6]
*1805–1815  New York City*

The entry following "Scroll Back Chair" in the 1810 book of prices for New York is for a "Window

Stool—Each end to start as a chair; deducting [one shilling] for each front foot." Many similarities exist between the preceding chairs, Nos. 66, 67, and 68, and this window stool, or window seat, as the form is called today.

This stool is a good example of the way various standard elements listed in the price books could be combined in different forms and for different effects and the whole unified by a common motif. Turned legs, a back with turnings above the seat (see No. 68), a splat "with an extra cross banister," and a hollow rail carved with reeds and ribbons (Nos. 66 and 67) are unified by reeding.

Dimensions: height 30; width 41¼; depth 16¼.

Materials: mahogany; medial seat braces, cherry; upholstery, caned seat with cushion covered in gold silk damask with basket of flowers, English or French, early nineteenth century.

Provenance: Louis Guerineau Myers.

Accession: 57.735

### 70 SCROLL-BACK ARMCHAIR
*1805–1815 New York City*

Many subtle variations and relationships are to be found in New York scroll-back chairs, as in the inverted urn turnings repeated on the arm supports and back legs above the seat and in the reeding on flat, curved, and turned members of this interesting armchair.[7] The turned and reeded legs and turned feet are standard for New York cabinetwork, but the reeded panels on the hollow yoke, or curved top rail, are unusual, as are the rather stiff "common elbows sweep'd towards the tops of the back legs."[8]

The height, abrupt terminals, and squarishness of the arms (despite their upward curve), and the bowed lines of the seat frame give the chair a foursquare quality lacking the grace of No. 67.

Dimensions: height 33; width 19; depth 16¾.

Materials: mahogany; seat rails, ash; medial braces, cherry; corner blocks (type II), white pine; upholstery, pink-and-black-figured silk.

Accession: 57.1043

### 71 SCROLL-BACK SIDE CHAIR
*1810–1815 New York City*

Although this chair could have been made in Duncan Phyfe's workshop because the back and the bell-shaped seat are so similar to No. 66, which is documented as having been made in the shop of that famous cabinetmaker, it is well to remember that this was a standard form for most New York

cabinetmakers. It follows closely the description for scroll-back chairs given in the 1810 New York price book. Since such chairs were being made in many shops, the one shown here cannot with justification be attributed to Phyfe simply on the basis of No. 66. There are too many variations. Instead of the standard "one cross bannister in the back, with extra cross bannister," it has an "ogee splat instead of a straight,"[9] a different "rose in the centre of the cross," carved drapery with tassel instead of reeds, and turned and reeded front legs instead of Grecian supports.

Dimensions: height 33; width 18½; depth 16⅜.

Materials: mahogany; front and rear seat rails, ash; front corner blocks (type II), ash; rear corner blocks (type II), white pine; medial seat braces, cherry; upholstery, white silk taffeta with pink-satin stripes and sprigs of

**70**

flowers brocaded in colors, English or French, late eighteenth century.

Provenance: Margaret Haskell Waring; Museum Purchase, 1953.

Accession: 53.162.2–3

## 72 SIDE CHAIR, curule form with "Grecian-cross" legs at the sides (one of a pair)
*1810–1815 New York*

Only a few sets of "chairs with Grecian Cross Fronts" are known in American furniture. All bear unmistakable evidence of New York workmanship and all have been attributed to the workshop of Duncan Phyfe. In support of such an attribution is a sketch of such a chair (see page 126) in Phyfe's hand, believed to have accompanied his letter of

**71**

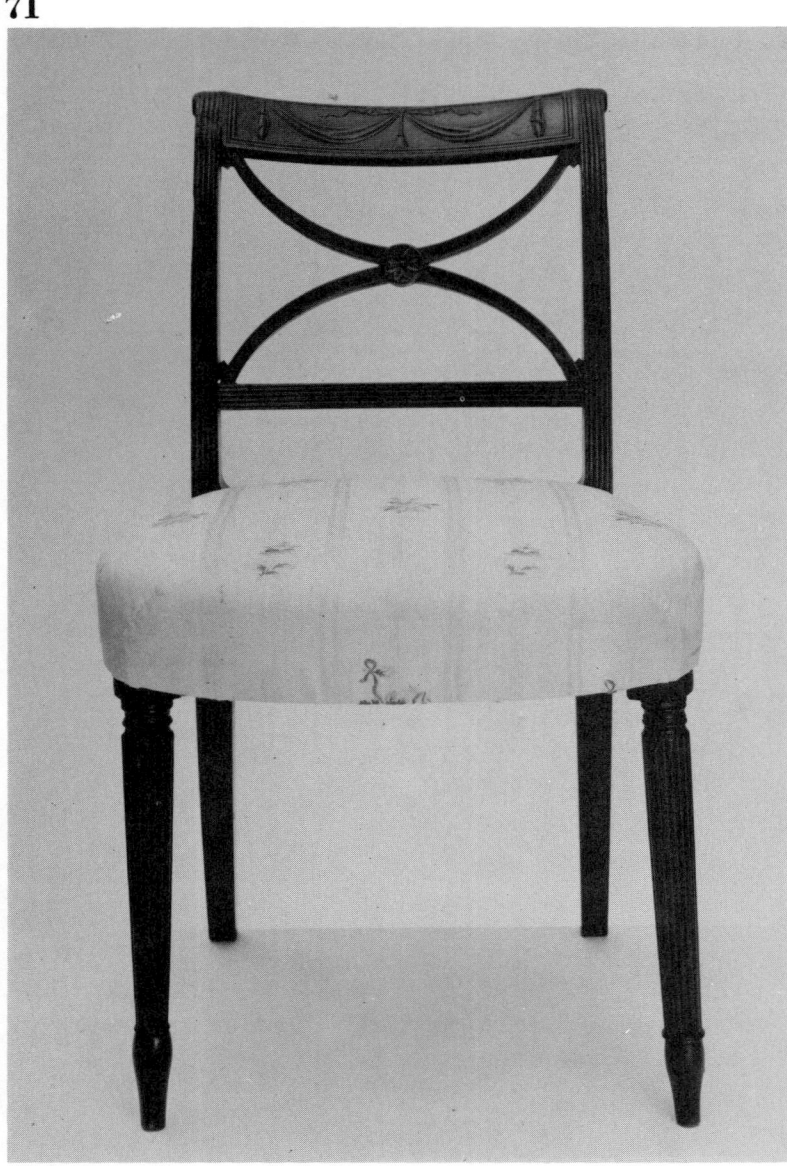

January 4, 1816, to Charles N. Bancker of Philadelphia. That chair has a back like this one with ogee cross splats, but the cross is at the front and the rear legs are the conventional type. Until proof to the contrary is forthcoming, the writer is content to believe Phyfe's shop made this pair of chairs—surely the noblest of early nineteenth-century chairs.

As early as 1800, La Mésangère in *Meubles et Objets de Goût* illustrated (No. 13) a stool based on the Roman curule. In a plate dated 1807, George Smith illustrated three Drawing Room *X* Seats, and two plates of the same year in Thomas Hope's *Designs for Household Furniture* show interiors furnished with stools and chairs of curule design. Like the "Chairs with Grecian Cross Fronts" in the 1808 *Supplement to The London Chair-Makers' and Carvers' Book of Prices for Workmanship*, all of the above chairs have the cross *at the front* with sometimes a cross and sometimes, as in Phyfe's sketch, conventional legs at the back.

The pair of Winterthur chairs is a distinct innovation. The crosses are at the sides instead of the front. The back is spliced not to one pair of legs but to both pairs in differentiation from the explicit directions given in the London book of prices for "splicing a square back" to a pair of legs. These chairs are adaptations of two stools shown in the 1808 supplement mentioned above (Figs. 3 and 6, Pl. 6). The design of the present chairs was arrived at by eliminating one set of scrolled arms of the stool designs and framing the other as a chair back with ogee splats. Of particular interest is the fact that on the same plate, near the foot of the stool, is a separate lion's paw, identical in appearance to those on the Winterthur chairs. And, on page 63, six and one half pence is listed as the workman's wages for "fitting and fixing lion's paw's to receive pins."

A splendid set of furniture consisting of a sofa, two armchairs, and ten side chairs, the latter so like this pair as to be indistinguishable from them except for the carving, were made, according to family tradition, for Thomas Cornell Pearsall of New York[10] in Duncan Phyfe's shop. Chairs of this type are nevertheless quite rare.

Dimensions: height 33; width 17⅞; depth 18.

Materials: mahogany; braces, soft maple; rear seat rail, birch; seat block, white pine; upholstery, green silk twill with applied border in Empire style, French, early nineteenth century.

Provenance: Museum Purchase, 1964, from Charles K. Davis Fund.

Accession: 64.24.2

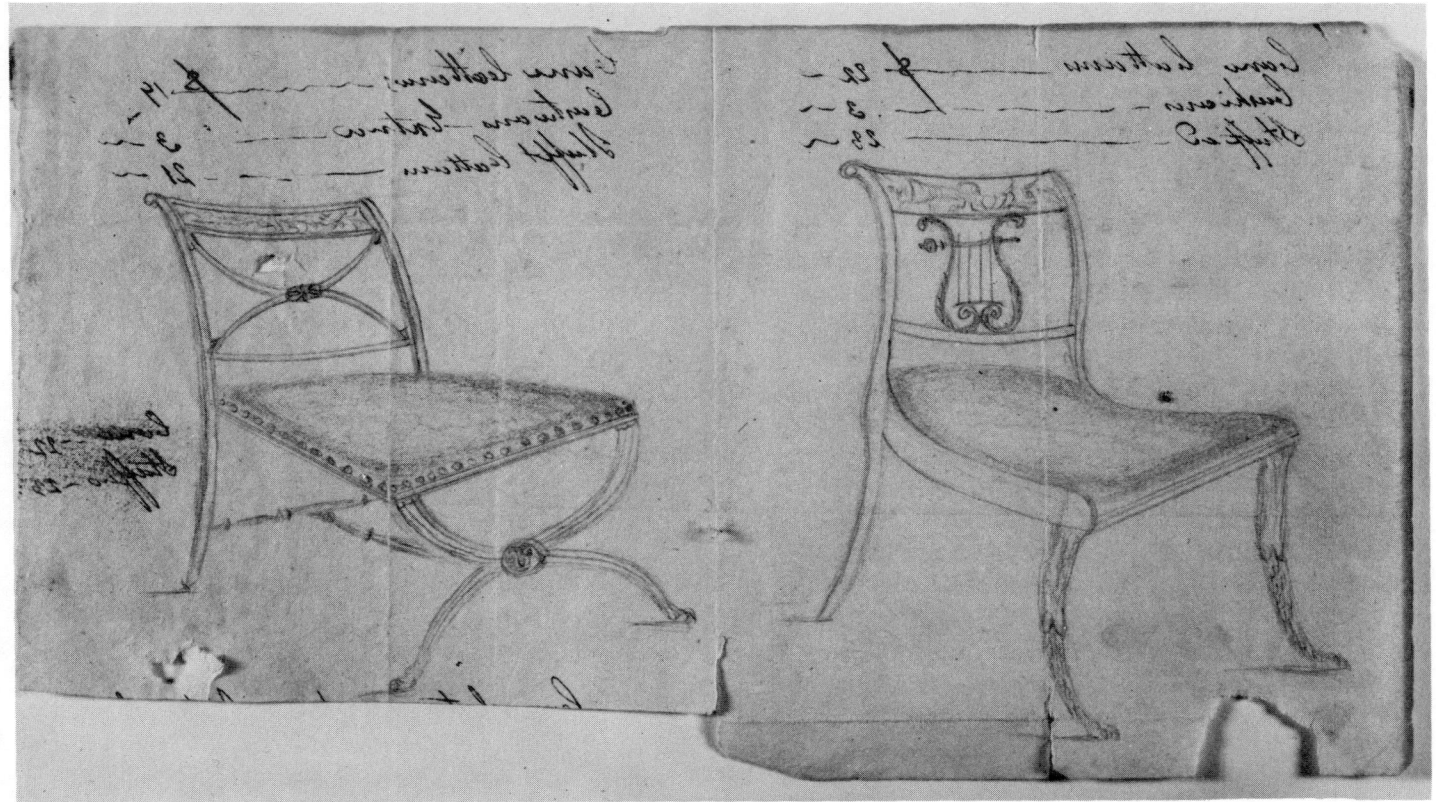

**72a** SKETCHES ATTRIBUTED TO
DUNCAN PHYFE

Sketches of a lyre-back chair and a Grecian cross-front chair with the following price notations.

Above the lyre-back chair:   "Cane bottoms $22
                            Cushions       3
                            Stuffed       23"

Above the Grecian cross-front chair:
                            "Cane bottoms $19
                            Cushions Extra   3
                            Stufft bottoms  21"

Although these sketches have for many years accompanied a bill from Phyfe to Charles N. Bancker of Philadelphia and have been published as being on the reverse side of that bill,[11] this is not true. The sketches and the bill, now in the Joseph Downs Manuscript and Microfilm Collections at Winterthur, are separate and distinct. It is the writer's supposition that the sketches accompanied an earlier letter of Phyfe's to Bancker (1815 or 1816) as an illustration of then fashionable chairs and his prices for them.

**73** SCROLL-BACK SIDE CHAIR with lyre banister

*1810–1820   New York*

Lyre-back chairs were known at an early date in the United States. In 1794, after his visit to the great and fashionable house of William Bingham in Philadelphia, Henry Wansey commented in his journal: "I found a magnificent house and gardens in the best English style, with elegant and even superb furniture: the chairs of the drawing room were from Seddons's in London, of the newest taste; the back in the form of a lyre adorned with festoons of crimson and yellow silk, the curtains of the room a festoon of the same."[12]

Although lyre-back chairs may have been made in this country as early as 1805 or 1810, the earliest offering by an American cabinetmaker of chairs in this style is the sketch with prices shown on the facing page. It is thought to have accompanied a letter from Duncan Phyfe to Charles N. Bancker in 1816 or a little before. As will be noted, that sketch also shows carved legs and lion's-paw feet. To the

**73**

**74**

writer's eyes, this connotation of the *antique*,[13] which was then highly fashionable and increased the cost, detracts from the harmony of the chair by its incongruity. The watercolor of Phyfe's shop owned by the Metropolitan Museum of Art depicts an interesting episode in the doorway: one fashionable lady pulls another away from a chair with an ogee splat to see a lyre back.[14]

A lyre banister, slightly different from this one, is illustrated in *The New-York Book of Prices for Manufacturing Cabinet and Chair Work* for 1817 (E, Plate 6). On page 107, the extra labor charge of seven shillings, eight pence, is quoted for a "Lyre banister, with a turned stretcher, sweep piece at bottom, with a quarter round in front, and returned at the ends, as in plate, E."

Dimensions: height 32½; width 19½; depth 17¼.

Materials: mahogany; front and rear seat rails and seat frame, ash; upholstery, gold-and-white silk damask, Regency style.
Accession: 57.716.1–2

## 74 SCROLL-BACK CHAIR with harp banister
*1810–1820   New York*

The statement is made in the Catalogue of the *Girl Scouts Loan Exhibition* concerning a pair of chairs from the same set as this one: "No one but a Phyfe could have used such an unbalanced form as this one with any degree of success. Doubtless the experiment did not altogether please him, for no other examples are known to collectors." To the present writer there seems little evidence for attributing the chairs to Phyfe. Scroll-back chairs were made by many, perhaps all, New York chairmakers at that time; and front legs with cross-banded edges above poorly carved shanks and feet are out of character with the better quality chair work of the city and below the standard expected of Phyfe.

Although harp-banister chairs remain much rarer today than lyre-back chairs, they were, nevertheless, a standard article in the trade, and an illustration of a well-proportioned harp made to stand symmetrically as a *V* can be seen in F, Plate 6 of the 1817 edition of the New York price book. It is described on page 108 as a "harp bannister, with turned column, as marked 'f' in plate" and cost seven shillings, eight pence. "Stringing lyre or harp with brass" cost three pence for each string, and four pence if with ebony.

Dimensions: height 32¾; width 18½; depth 15¾.
Materials: mahogany; front and rear seat rails, ash; seat framing, cherry; upholstery, gold-and-white silk damask, Regency style.
Provenance: W. G. Higgins Family.
Accession: 57.717.1–2

## 75 SCROLL-BACK SIDE CHAIR with eagle splat
*1810–1820   New York City*

Few chairs of any period excel either this one or No. 76 in beauty. As a solution to the problem of seating, each is the ultimate in simplicity. There are no meaningless parts. Legs, back, and seat are streamlined and reduced to essentials that are not individual parts but parts of a whole. The molded outline of the back, seat, and front legs is one of rhythm in its unbroken downward movement from the scroll at the crest to the tip of the front feet.

Carved eagles may sometimes seem incongruous when they appear on tables and sofas. Here and in No. 76 they are so composed as to give a sense of strength to a fragile form.

Dimensions: height 32; width 18¼; depth 15¼.
Materials: mahogany; front and rear seat rails, ash; upholstery, pillar print, green ground with pink-and-black, roller-printed cotton, English, 1830–1835.
Accession: 57.562.1–2

## 76 SCROLL-BACK SIDE CHAIR with eagle splat (one of five)
*1810–1820   New York City*

What has been said of No. 75 pertains equally to this chair. Here the eagle is bolder, the carving more flamboyant, the statement stronger.

Several sets of eagle-back chairs of mahogany and some of other woods, painted or decorated, are known; they were apparently produced in number. However, the writer has been unable to find any reference to eagle backs in American price books. Eagle supports for tables are listed and illustrated. Lyres and harps are shown for chairs—but no eagles.

Dimensions: height 33½; width 18¼; depth 15.
Materials: mahogany; front and rear seat rails, ash; upholstery, bright-blue satin with white medallion, rosettes, and applied border in Empire style, French, early nineteenth century.
Accession: 57.939.1–5

77

conveyed by the spread eagle over the pair of eagle-headed cornucopia. It is the same message spelled out on the banner under the spread wings of a great eagle over an 1803 view of New Orleans:[15] "Under my wings everything prospers."

Dimensions: height 32⅛; width 18; depth 16.
Materials: maple; front rail, soft maple; painted to imitate rosewood and decorated with gold leaf; cane seat.
Accession: 57.890

**78** SCROLL-BACK SIDE CHAIR
*1815–1825   New York City*

Despite the fact that details differ and carving is seldom found on the scrolls of New York chairs, the over-all character of this chair and No. 77 so closely approximates the idiom of New York scroll-back chairs that there appears little doubt that it was made there.

Gilt ornament was widely used in the United States as a substitute for the more expensive fire gilt or ormolu appliqués generally used on French

# 79

**77** SCROLL-BACK SIDE CHAIR painted
and decorated
*1815–1825   New York City*

Early in the nineteenth century, "fancy chairs" with painted or japanned decoration became very popular and were made widely in both city and country shops. Numerous illustrated advertisements of fancy-chair makers are to be found in newspapers published after 1815 all up and down the Atlantic Coast. The carving on the paw feet of both this chair and No. 78 is of excellent quality, as is the delicate and precise gilt decoration.

Because this chair and No. 78 were made with the same fine high-style carving of mahogany chairs and were painted to imitate rosewood, they are included in this section instead of that on painted furniture.

There can be little doubt of the sentiment to be

furniture and by such French cabinetmakers as Charles-Honoré Lannuier working in this country.

At this time, not enough information about regional practices of American cabinetmakers working after 1815 is known to permit generalization; but the quality of gilt design on New York work seen by the writer surpasses that done elsewhere.

Dimensions: height 32; width 17¾; depth 16⅝.

Materials: soft maple; front and rear seat rails, soft maple; seat frame, hard maple; upholstery, medallion in gold woven on dark-green satin or cotton and silk, Empire style, early nineteenth century.

Accession: 57.742.1–2

## 79 ARMCHAIR with scroll back
*1815–1825   New York or Philadelphia*

The American maker of this large, gilt-ornamented armchair utilized but exaggerated the prevailing forms of his time (1815–1825) to achieve a unique expression of tension and movement. Taut, carved animal legs in back as well as in front and enormous voluted arms combined with superbly executed gilt ornament create an effect that is rich, grotesque, and powerful. The chair seems never at rest. Carved animal legs and foliated gilding of this type are commonly found on New York chairs, but the carving approximates Philadelphia work.

Dimensions: height 38; width 26½; depth 22¾.

Materials: maple, painted and gilded; rails and front legs, maple; slip-seat frame, walnut; medial brace, hickory; upholstery, green satin woven with a raised pattern of Empire motifs, French, early nineteenth century.

Accession: 57.739

## 80 SIDE CHAIR (one of a pair)
*1815–1825   Probably New York*

The names used in the early nineteenth century for various types of chairs are almost as diverse as the names used for automobile models today. This chair with its overhanging splat (scrolled in contour and then referred to as a "tablet top") more closely approximates the Greek klysmos chair than do others in the Winterthur collections, but the name klysmos seems not to have been generally used, if it was used at all. In all editions, *The London Chair-Makers' and Carvers' Book of Prices* illustrates and refers to front and rear legs such as found here as Grecian. The name used in the book for this general kind of chair is Trafalgar. Drawings in the "General Sketch Book" of the Gillow Company show several chairs with topical names—a "Wellington Chair" with ball-turned legs of diminishing sizes to represent cannon balls, a "Trafalgar Chair" similar to this one but with slip seat (then called a French seat) and no splat in the back, and a "Bouneparte Chair." The latter approximates this one in that it has a tablet top with scrolled decoration, cross splat of fancy outline, and a front seat so upholstered as to reveal no front rail.

Ash and cherry secondary woods, fine quality gilt decoration, and the high level of workmanship suggest New York chairmaking practice; and the gadrooning across the seat rail recalls similar treatment of New York Chippendale chairs.

Dimensions: height 35; width 19; depth 16.

Materials: mahogany; side seat rails, mahogany; front and back seat rails, ash; lower lamination of front seat rail, cherry; upholstery, bluish-green silk with an applied border of green and white.

Accession: 57.741.1–2

## FOOTNOTES

1 Illustrated in Nancy McClelland, *Duncan Phyfe and the English Regency, 1795–1830* (New York: W. P. Scott, Inc., 1939), Pl. 244, p. 258.

2 Oddly enough, Moses Rogers' son, Benjamin, married the girl next door, Susan, the daughter of William Bayard.

3 Henry Francis du Pont acquired Duncan Phyfe's own copy of *The New-York Revised Prices for Manufacturing Cabinet and Chair Work*, June, 1810. Phyfe's signature appears on its flyleaf.

4 McClelland, op. cit., Pl. 245, p. 259.

5 W. M. Hornor, Jr., "A New Estimation of Duncan Phyfe," *The Antiquarian*, XIV (March, 1930), 38.

6 Catalogue of the *Girl Scouts Loan Exhibition* (New York, 1929), No. 791.

7 A matching side chair, formerly in the collection of Allan B. A. Bradley of New York, is illustrated in Plate 158 of Nancy McClelland's *Duncan Phyfe and the English Regency, 1795–1830*.

8 *The London Chair-Makers' and Carvers' Book of Prices for Workmanship*, 1807, p. 45.

9 The splat in No. 71, termed an ogee splat in the New York book of prices for 1810, is illustrated and called a "Grecian cross lapped in the middle" in *The London Chair-Makers' and Carvers' Book of Prices for Workmanship*, p. 7.

10 McClelland, op. cit., pp. 289–290 and Plate 276.

11 *Ibid*, pp. 255–256.

12 Henry Wansey, *An Excursion to the United States of North America in the Summer of 1794* (Salisbury, England, 1798), p. 123.

13 On page 9 of his *Cabinet Dictionary*, Sheraton points out, "Antique is generally applied to such painting and sculpture, or architecture, as were executed at the period, when these arts arrived to their utmost perfection amongst the Greeks and Romans." "Antiques [are] an irregular composition of men, beasts, birds, fishes, flowers, and such like, merely fanciful, as on the walls of the Vatican at Rome, painted by Raphael—These kind of ornaments had their origin amongst the Grecians, who adorned the friezes of their temples with such kinds of figures as best suited and represented the idols that were worshipped in them."

14 Hornor, op. cit., p. 36.

15 An aquatint with the inscription *A View of New Orleans taken from the plantation of Marigny. Boqueta De Woiseri fecit in New Orleans in Nov. 1803*. The print is illustrated in Marshall B. Davidson's *Life in America* (New York: Houghton Mifflin Company, 1951), II, 117, although called a watercolor there.

# Philadelphia and Southern Chairs

Despite restraining Quaker influences, several factors made Philadelphia the American style and cultural center in the years immediately following the Revolution. The largest city and most important port in the new nation, the seat of government, and for many months of each year the home of the leaders from every state in the new union, it was a crossroads where new ideas were brought by travelers and emissaries from abroad and from which these ideas were disseminated.

It is no accident that the earliest piece of American silver in the Adamesque style was made in Philadelphia in 1774 by Richard Humphreys to be given by the "Cont.[inental] Congress to Cha⁵ Thomson Secrʸ: in Testimony of their Esteem and Approbation..." and that the first intimation of the new furniture styles appears in a small desk made in Philadelphia in 1776 by Benjamin Randolph for Thomas Jefferson. Although this writing box (now in the Smithsonian Institution) upon which Jefferson wrote the Declaration of Independence has only an inset keyhole escutcheon and cock bead around the drawer of light wood, it anticipates the use of inlays as a major decorative element. The next earliest known piece of furniture in the new style that can be dated was also made in Philadelphia—a handsomely and elaborately inlaid case for a piano made by Charles Albrecht and dated 1789.[1]

In the 1780–1800 period, the most popular type of chair was what we know today as the ladder-back but then called "Splatt-back" or "Slatt-back" chairs. A "Splatt back Chair, Honey suckle pattern, made for stuffing over the rail" and a "Splatt back Chair with three cross Splatts" were each given a separate listing in the 1795 Philadelphia price book. Examples reproduced are Nos. 81, 82, 83, and 84. The first public record of vase- or shield-back chairs is John Aitken's advertisement in the *Federal Gazette* (Philadelphia) of June 9, 1790. It illustrates a chair similar to No. 101, which the writer believes may have been made in Philadelphia, rather than in Baltimore.

The description of a "square-back Chair" listed in the Philadelphia price book for 1795 "with straight top and stay rail, three upright splatts, straight seat, made for stuffing over the rails" seems to fit the most widely recognized type of Philadelphia chair (see No. 91) with turned legs and bulb or round spade feet. Though often attributed to Henry Connelly or Ephraim Haines, these were probably made by many Philadelphia chairmakers as were variants with four turned bars in the back.

Other square-back chairs in the 1795 price book included ones with "a hollow corner'd top rail and straight seat rail," "three upright splatts or bannister in ditto" (No. 105), and "straight top rail and ... three upright splats" with a long vase splat in the middle and an arch in the top rail between two outside splats (No. 98). Another square-back type of chair with vase is well illustrated by Nos. 96 and 97. Both of these with carved drapery and S-scrolls flanking the urn are similar to a number of chairs now at Mount Vernon and the Smithsonian Institution, which are a part of the two dozen for which Washington paid John Aitken on February 21, 1797.[2]

Among the most sophisticated surviving Philadelphia chairs of the Federal period are painted chairs made for Elias Hasket Derby and John Derby (Nos. 17 and 18) and two cabriole armchairs (Nos. 92 and 93) with upholstered backs and excellent well-carved turnings. These four chairs are among the finest surviving Federal examples. The armchair (No. 92), painted white and highlighted in gilt, is of particular importance because it illustrates a type of chair almost unknown today, but once the height of fashion. Because of their fragile ornament, few such chairs have survived.

As one moves from chairs and other furniture made in Philadelphia to that believed to have been made in Baltimore and southward, our information is less exact. With close commercial ties between Philadelphia and Baltimore, Charleston, and other southern cities, with many recorded instances of Philadelphia cabinetmakers migrating to those cities, with a key instance of one of Philadelphia's most gifted cabinetmakers, Joseph Barry, maintaining a branch shop in Baltimore for a few years (see No. 354), and with innumerable references in the Baltimore newspapers to the sale at auction and otherwise of furniture imported from Boston, New York, and Philadelphia, it is obvious that long Baltimore ownership is insufficient to establish Baltimore manufacture.

In 1814, *Niles Weekly Register* published statistics on American manufactures for the year 1810. For Pennsylvania, the number of cabinetmakers at work is listed as 482, and the total value of their production as $657,870. Maryland is credited with having only fifty cabinetmakers who produced furniture worth $237,043. (Unfortunately, neither of these states reported the number of chairs produced, as did Massachusetts, credited with 699 dozen valued at $96,060. Quite surprisingly, 507 dozen chairs are listed as made in Virginia worth only $9,125.) From directory listings, it appears that the differential between the number of cabinetmakers in Baltimore and Philadelphia was even greater in the year 1800. In the light of these facts, it appears that a thorough review is in order of all furniture now attributed to Baltimore. Much of it may have been made in Philadelphia or elsewhere.

Of signal importance is the side chair (No. 100) bearing the label of John Shaw of Annapolis, one of the few Maryland cabinetmakers by whom labeled furniture has been found. Although Shaw's chairs are usually upholstered over the seat frame, Baltimore chairmakers seem often to have left about half the seat rail exposed and to have finished the lower part with veneer, normally edged with patterned stringing or banding. Front legs on surviving Maryland chairs are often inlaid, though they are sometimes carved, as on the set believed to have been made for Charles Carroll (No. 99).

Perhaps other chairs in the Winterthur collection may eventually be recognized as having been made in the South. At present, No. 106 appears to be the only possibility.

---

1 Jefferson's desk is illustrated in Marie Kimball, "The Furnishing of Monticello," *Antiques*, XII (November, 1927), 380. Thomson's urn is illustrated in *Philadelphia Silver 1682–1800* (The Philadelphia Museum of Art, 1956), p. 5. Albrecht's piano, now owned by the Historical Society of Pennsylvania, is illustrated in N. E. Michel, *Historical Pianos, Harpsicords, and Clavichords* (Pico Rivera, California, 1963), p. 81.
2 Comstock, "Mount Vernon Centennial," *Antiques*, LXIV (July, 1953), 30–37.

XII

# South Alcove of the Billiard Room

*In the south alcove of the Billiard Room before a majestic scene painted on canvas stands a mahogany chair with many Philadelphia features: vase-shaped back, slip seat, serpentine front, and molded legs with stretchers. The romantic view is one panel from a set of wall hangings painted about 1800 by Michel Felice Corné for a room in New England. Fine inlays and veneers distinguish the Baltimore side table which stands beneath a delicate gilt oval looking glass.*

**81** SIDE CHAIR with slat or splat back
*1785–1800   Philadelphia*

The pronounced ears and sturdy outflaring molded stiles remind one immediately of many Philadelphia Chippendale chairs, but the slightly tapered and molded front legs with two beads and a hollow suggest a late eighteenth-century date for this handsome forthright chair of a type often called pretzelback today. In many ways it conforms to the brief description given in the 1795 and 1796 editions of the Philadelphia price book with its three "scroll'd splatts," "stuffing over the rail" upholstery, and "commode" or serpentine front. Such chairs probably continued to be made through the first years of the nineteenth century.

The name "Peter Kline" branded twice on the inside of the back seat rail may be that of the original owner. A bricklayer of this name is listed from 1797 to 1822 in the Philadelphia directories—first on Third Street between Green and Coates's Street and in 1801 on Third Street above Vine, two houses away from John Lentz, listed in the directories as a "cabinetmaker."

At Mount Vernon, five chairs with what appear to be identical backs but with plain marlboro legs are believed to be a part of a set of "two doz. strong neat and plain but fashionable Table Chairs" purchased by Martha Washington on her way through Philadelphia in 1783[1] and about which the General had correspondence with Bushrod Washington in the same year.[2] Another chair, so like the Mount Vernon chairs that it may be from the same set, is labeled by Jonathan Gostelowe.[3]

The side rails are tenoned through the rear legs.

Dimensions: height 37¼; width 21; depth 19.
Materials: mahogany; left front seat block (type IV), white pine; left rear seat block (type II), tulip; front rail, a white oak; rear rail, hickory; side rails, walnut; upholstery, dark-red silk damask, Italian, early eighteenth century.
Accession: 59.1487

**82** SIDE CHAIR with slat or splat back
*1785–1800   Philadelphia   Attributed to Daniel Trotter
(working 1769 to 1800)*

The one chair design that has retained its popularity in America from the seventeenth century to the present is the slat back. During the eighteenth and much of the nineteenth century, most slat-back chairs had turned legs and stretchers and were made of native woods such as hickory, ash, and maple and were often stained or painted. However, during a brief period from about 1780 to 1800, as the Chippendale style waned in popularity, an adaptation of the slat-back form was made of mahogany. In this interesting new style, called ladder-back today, horizontal members, or slats, took the place of the vertical, pierced splats common to the earlier Chippendale chairs. Although English examples exist, the writer has not seen designs for such chairs in the English furniture-design books. The type illustrated here, with pierced slats to resemble drapery swags and featuring a carved, central flower with rosettes at the top of the stiles has long been associated with the name of Daniel Trotter. Usually combined with this type of back are fluted front legs—stop-fluted at the tops—terminating in spade feet. However, examples with plain or molded legs are known.[4]

# 82

So far as can be ascertained, this particular interpretation with draped and openwork slats was made only in Philadelphia, although other variants of the basic idea seem to have been produced in most American cabinetmaking centers. The side rails are tenoned through the back legs.

Dimensions: height 38; width 24¼; depth 18¼.

Materials: mahogany; slip-seat frame, hard pine; corner blocks (type II), mahogany; upholstery, dark-red silk damask, Italian, early eighteenth century.

Accession: 57.871.2

**83** SIDE CHAIR with slat or splat back (one of a pair)

*1790–1800 Philadelphia*

Two types of handsome and sophisticated slat-back chairs seem to have been made exclusively in the Philadelphia area. One type is illustrated by No. 82 and the other, with round shoulders, by this example. William Macpherson Hornor, Jr., states that Thomas Tufft made a set of twelve of this kind for Deborah Norris Logan of Stenton in 1783 and that six others were fashioned by Jacob Wayne for Captain Thomas Mason in 1790. An example of each set is illustrated in *The Blue Book of Philadelphia Furniture*, Plates 289 and 101, respectively. Both chairs are virtually identical to the one shown here. All three have stretchers, molded tapered legs, slip seats, and serpentine front rails. Two other side chairs in the Winterthur collection, almost identical to this pair except for having straight seat fronts, have the side rails tenoned through the back legs in the normal manner of Philadelphia chairmaking. These are not tenoned through the rear legs.

Dimensions: height 37; width 21; depth 17.

Materials: mahogany; slip-seat frame, hard pine; corner blocks, replacements; upholstery, slate-blue moreen (wool), English, probably early nineteenth century.
Accession: 58.2769

**84  ARMCHAIR** with slat or splat back (one of a pair)
*1790–1800   Philadelphia*

As indicated in *The Philadelphia Cabinet and Chair-Makers' Book of Prices* for 1796 (p. 21), armchairs cost fifty per cent more for labor than side chairs, and the purchaser had the option of "the old scroll'd elbow" (arm), "plain twisted ditto," or "plain elbows." These may well represent the latter since they obviously are not the first two—

**84**

**85**

and they are indeed plain. The standard model of nine versions of Philadelphia chairs listed in 1795 was "made for stuffing over the rails [and with a] straight seat." With the exception of a "Vase back stay rail Chair" and one type of "Square Back Chair," all are cited with "no low rails," that is, without stretchers. Low rails added three shillings, nine pence, to the cost of labor and "mortising the back feet through each chair" cost six pence extra. That additional charge was made for stretchers and such mortising seems amazing since the back legs of most chairs made in Philadelphia are mortised through as these are, and more than half of the chairs believed to have been made in that city around 1800 have stretchers.

Dimensions: height 37; width 22½; depth 17½.

# 86

Materials: mahogany; front and side rails, ash; rear rail, mahogany; front corner blocks (type II), tilia; rear corner blocks (type II), mahogany; upholstery, slate-blue moreen (wool), English, probably early nineteenth century.
Accession: 58.2767–.2768

## 85 SIDE CHAIR with vase back
*1790–1800 Philadelphia*

The graceful back of this chair is a free interpretation of Plate 7 of Hepplewhite's *Guide*. The elements of the banister spring from a neatly carved pedestal, broaden naturally and flow into leafy scrolls at the top—establishing a nice rhythm within the bead-outlined, shield-shaped back. Features seen on

many Philadelphia-made chairs are the rather deep, serpentine front; side rails mortised through the back legs; and front legs molded with two beads and two hollows. A pair of chairs with similar backs, seen recently by the writer,[5] has another and even more conclusive Philadelphia feature—front legs stop-fluted at the top with short spade feet—the leg type found on No. 82. So far as the writer knows, such stop-fluted legs are found only on Philadelphia chairs. The chair is numbered "IV."

Dimensions: height 38¾; width 21¾; depth 18¾.
Materials: mahogany; seat rails, mahogany; slip-seat frame, hard pine; front corner blocks (type IV), hard pine and mahogany; rear corner blocks (type II), tulip; upholstery, red-and-white resist-dyed cotton, French, late eighteenth century.
Accession: 57.991

## 86 SIDE CHAIR, vase back (one of a pair)
*1790–1800 Philadelphia or the South*

The design for this chair derived from Plate 4 of Hepplewhite's *Guide* is uncommon, though not rare. Like that of the preceding chair, the shield-shaped back is broad and very rounded at the bottom with a large amount of open space on either side of the banister. Although the molding on the legs and the beading on the back and supports are competent, the edges of the banister have been left plain, and the carved leaves and husks at the center have not the quality seen on the best work of this period. The stretchers are also somewhat heavier than most chairmakers thought necessary. Although the side rails are not tenoned through the back legs, the corner blocks of hard pine suggest a Philadelphia or southern origin. The chairs are numbered "III" and "XIII."

Dimensions: height 38¾; width 21½; depth 18.
Materials: mahogany; corner blocks (type IV), hard pine; upholstery, red-and-white resist-dyed cotton, French, late eighteenth century.
Accession: 57.993.1, 2

## 87 SIDE CHAIR with vase back[6]
*1790–1800 Philadelphia*

This chair is a combination of two types of backs listed in *The Journeymen Cabinet and Chair-Makers Philadelphia Book of Prices* for 1795: "A Stay rail chair with serpentine top rail and five upright splats, straight seat made for stuffing over the rail" and "An Urn back." The term shield back seems not to have been used by the makers. "Vase back" was a back of this type with a pointed or rounded bottom. Many refinements are found here: the stay rail, in this case the arc at the bottom of the back, and the splats are carved; the front of the seat has been shaped into serpentine form; the side rails are "sweeped" and the front feet tapered and molded with two beads and two hollows. Molded, tapered front legs are more commonly found on Philadelphia and New England chairs than on those of New York and Baltimore. On this chair, the side rails are not mortised through the rear legs.

Dimensions: height 39¼; width 20⅞; depth 18.

Materials: mahogany; front rail, red oak; side and rear rails, white oak; front corner blocks, replacements; rear corner blocks (type II), white cedar; upholstery, blue-green silk with stripes and sprigs, late eighteenth century.

Accession: 57.992

**87**

**88**

**88** SIDE CHAIR with vase back
*1790–1800   Philadelphia*

With the exception of a slip seat instead of a stuffed seat and carved leaves at the base of the five splats instead of flutes, this chair varies little from No. 87. The side rails are not mortised through.

Dimensions: height 39¼; width 21; depth 18.

Materials: mahogany; blocks missing; slip-seat frame replaced; upholstery, red-and-white resist-dyed cotton, French, late eighteenth century.

Accession: 57.1008

**89** SIDE CHAIR with vase back
*1790–1800   Philadelphia or the South*

The back of this well-made and nicely finished chair of excellent mahogany is an unusual one; a

chair from the same set, possibly this one, was formerly owned by Mr. Howard Reifsnyder.[7] Although the back is broader and more rounded than those seen on most Philadelphia urn-back chairs, the carving of the rosettes on the banister, the front legs molded with two beads and two hollows, and the serpentine front with molded upper edge are common to other chairs from that area. The side rails are not mortised through the back legs; and, unfortunately, hard pine does not give a specific clue as to the origin and the original blocks are missing. The chair is marked "IIII" inside the seat frame.

Dimensions: height 37; width 21½; depth 18.
Materials: mahogany; corner blocks missing; slip-seat frame, hard pine; upholstery, red-and-white resist-dyed cotton, French, late eighteenth century.
Accession: 57.994

## 90 ARMCHAIR with oval back
*1785–1795 Philadelphia or Maryland*

Oval-back chairs are more frequently found in England than in America. Robert Adam designed and used the form more often than Hepplewhite and Sheraton and its greatest vogue was probably in the 1770's and 1780's, a period when the Chippendale style was still at its height in this country. However, a few notable American examples survive such as those numbered 16, 17, and 18 in this catalogue. The latter two are believed to have been made in Philadelphia, the city to which this fine but unusual chair can be linked.

Typical of Philadelphia chairmaking practice of the 1780's and early 1790's are: the carved paterae on the splats; the sturdy grooved tapered front legs with short spade feet; the serpentine front rail and especially the character of the serpentine arms (though here hollowed more deeply than usual) terminating in a knuckle where they meet the ogee arm supports screwed to the frame. An oval-back armchair with curving wheel-like splats originally owned by Major General Isaac Trimble of "Ravenshurst," Maryland, parallels this chair in some ways, but the features described above suggest a Philadelphia rather than Baltimore or Annapolis provenance.

Dimensions: height 39¾; width 23½; depth 20½.

Materials: mahogany; slip-seat frame, hard pine; original seat blocks missing; upholstery, pale-blue silk with white satin stripes and floral sprigs brocaded in colored and silver threads, French, late eighteenth century.

Accession: 52.235

**91**

## 91 ARMCHAIR with square back
*About 1805–1815   Philadelphia*

This fine chair is similar in design to the armchairs from the famous set of ebony seating furniture made by Ephraim Haines in 1807 for Stephen Girard of Philadelphia (now owned by Girard College); attribution to the same maker might thus seem reasonable. The rectangular back with its carved and reeded spindles, the turned and reeded arm supports, and the profile and details of the front legs are all closely related to features on the Girard set. But one important detail is an exception: a crisp turned spade foot here takes the place of the concaved and tapered foot with bulb of the documented set made by Haines for Girard. Similar turned spade feet are used on a sideboard labeled by Henry Connelly. Writers in the past have called one (bulb) the Haines foot, the other (round spade) the Connelly foot. This writer feels that both of these men and many others probably used both kinds of feet at one time or another, since they probably patronized the same independent turners.

The following entry (p. 81) in the Philadelphia book of prices for 1795 suggests the Philadelphia name for the arms on this chair: "French elbows, ... the elbows mortis'd on the stump of front foot 13-6." When made for "sweep side rails" as here, they cost three shillings extra. This labor charge of sixteen shillings, six pence, for such arms in comparison with the charge of fourteen shillings for making a complete square-back side chair indicates the craft problems connected with making satisfactory arms. And today most connoisseurs gauge the quality of an armchair by the quality of its arms. Chairs of this type (usually with less carving than this one) seem to have been made only in Philadelphia. Here the rear legs are turned in a simplified version of the front legs, an unusual deviation from the squared rear legs of other Philadelphia chairs (No. 95).

Dimensions: height 33¾; width 19⅞; depth 17¾.

Materials: mahogany; no secondary woods; upholstery, green silk, about 1800.

Provenance: Museum Purchase; Lammot du Pont Copeland Fund.

Accession: G 53.58

## 92 CABRIOLE ARMCHAIR, painted white and gold
*About 1800   Philadelphia*

This sumptuous painted armchair with upholstered back, carving, and applied composition orna-

ment highlighted with burnished gold was one of the most fashionable chairs when made, and stands today as a monument of early American chairmaking. Hepplewhite called chairs with upholstered backs cabriole chairs, and this term seems to have been generally used. However, Sheraton used the name "Drawing-Room Chairs" for these chairs; and that name was retained by the Philadelphia cabinetmakers, Joseph B. Barry & Son, when they had two of Sheraton's armchairs reengraved on their trade card.[8] Of two related chairs, Plates 32 and 34 in his *Drawing Book*, Sheraton remarked: "These chairs are finished in white and gold, or the ornaments may be japanned; but the French finish them in mahogany, with gilt mouldings.... Chairs of this kind have an effect which far exceeds any conception we can have of them from an uncoloured engraving, or even of a coloured one."[9]

Mahogany furniture is commonly regarded today as being in the highest style, but it was not always so. In Jefferson's inventory of the White House furnishings taken when he left the Presidency in 1809, twelve lots of chairs variously described as "crimson and Gold," "blue and Gold," "Gold and green," and "black and Gold" are called fashionable; but not a single listing of mahogany chairs, even those with "crimson damask bottoms," merit that accolade from the leader who, perhaps more than any other of his time, merits the term a man of taste. The vogue for painted and gilt furniture was probably heightened by the popularity of French furniture among United States leaders. From 1790 onward, Jefferson, Monroe, John Adams, and others acquired it while in France. Washington bought it at the dispersal of the effects of Count de Moustiers, the first French Minister to the United States. Much of it was finished in gold leaf or painted white or gray or sometimes enlivened with gilt.

As early as 1787, William Long, "Cabinetmaker and Carver, Late of London," informed Philadelphians that he made "French Sophas in the modern taste, on as reasonable terms as them of the oldest fashion; one he has finished within these few days has been approved of by competent judges; Cabriole and French Chairs on reasonable terms..."[10] Among Long's stock advertised after his death in 1794 were "a few sets of fashionable elbow painted chairs" and "a set of Mahogany cabriole chairs."[11] Several factors point to Philadelphia as the place where this superb chair was made. The general outline and the stepped down arms, although here fitted with pads, are compa-

rable to those on other fine armchairs made in that city (No.93). Philadelphia chairs are frequently found with straight tapered and reeded legs with a drum at the top and a turned spade foot, and many are made partially of ash.

Dimensions: height 36½; width 20¼; depth 18¼.
Materials: ash; no secondary woods; upholstery, green taboret, silk with moiréd and satin stripes, about 1800.
Provenance: Museum Purchase, 1960.
Accession: 60.331

**93** CABRIOLE ARMCHAIR with square back and elliptic top (one of a pair)
*About 1810   Philadelphia*

These handsome, richly carved chairs must be numbered among the richest expressions of the American cabinet- and chairmaker of the Federal period. They were probably made for a drawing room and were part of a large set since they are numbered "VI" and "VII."[12]

Hepplewhite commented that "chairs with stuffed backs are called cabriole chairs."[13] Sheraton illustrates and calls similar stuffed-back chairs "drawing room chairs." In his *Dictionary*, he remarks that "drawing room chairs should always be the produce of studied elegance, though it is extremely difficult to attain to anything really novel."[14] He obviously had strong feelings about the drawing room for elsewhere he ordained that it "concentrate the elegance of the whole house, and is the highest display of richness of furniture.... The grandeur then introduced into the drawing-room is not to be considered, as the ostentatious parade of its proprietor, but the respect he pays to the rank of his visitants."[15]

The knuckled arms, each with a double curve, are adapted from designs for two "Drawing-Room Chairs" in the *Appendix* to Sheraton's *Drawing Book* of 1802 (Pl.6). They may seem quite high at the present time, but when they were made they must have been extremely fashionable for Hepplewhite noted in the 1793 edition of his *Guide:* "The arms... though much higher than usual, have been executed with good effect for His Royal Highness, the Prince of Wales."

Dimensions: height 36; depth 21; width 19⅛.
Materials: mahogany; seat rails, black ash; upholstered backing in splat, white pine; all corner blocks replaced; upholstery, dark-blue-and-white-striped imberline (part silk), French, late eighteenth century.
Provenance: Warren E. Doran; Josephine L. Doran; Museum Purchase, 1963.
Accession: 63.31.1, 2

**94** SIDE CHAIR with square back and bell-shaped seat
*1805–1815  Philadelphia*

"Bell Shaped Seat" is the name given for this shape of stuffed seat in *The London Chair-Makers' and Carvers' Book of Prices for Workmanship* in the 1802 and later editions. Bell-shaped seats and square backs with reeded banisters set on pedestals found more favor in New York and Philadelphia than elsewhere in the United States. Reeded front legs—more often with bulbs at the top than the straight ring-turned drum found here—and bulb-shaped terminals at the bottom of the legs have often been attributed to the hand of Ephraim Haines in the past upon the basis of the ebony furniture he made

for Stephen Girard in 1807. But, as already noted, many Philadelphia chairmakers probably used similar designs. Although the carving at the top of the banisters is unusual, the bead outlining the back is found on many Philadelphia chairs.

A drawing in the Gillow Records[16] of a square-back chair with three colonnettes suggests that the old name for this kind of chair is "Spanish back." Spanish chairs are listed in the 1828 Philadelphia book of prices but cannot be identified on the basis of the description given.

Dimensions: height 33⅝; width 19½; depth 17.
Materials: mahogany; rails, ash; rear corner blocks (type V), cherry; upholstery, pale-blue silk with white satin stripes and floral sprigs brocaded in colored and silver threads, French, late eighteenth century.
Accession: 51.44

**95** SIDE CHAIR with square back and bell-shaped seat (one of a pair)
*1805–1815  Philadelphia*

Basically this is the same type of square-back chair as No. 94 with the substitution of a banister featuring an urn with interlaced scrolls and drapery. To correct the error of an earlier writer that the beautiful back of this chair is the *Honeysuckle pattern* it should be pointed out that this name was reserved in both the 1795 and 1796 Philadelphia price books for a "slatt back" or "splatt back with three [or more] Cross Splatts," a chair which is called a ladder-back chair today—presumably one with an anthemion carved on the slat as Nos. 11 and 13.[17]

Chairs with turned spade feet have long been attributed to Henry Connelly on the slimmest of evidence—one sideboard with this kind of feet and bearing his label![18] Some may have been made in his shop, but assuredly, many other Philadelphia cabinetmakers made them also. Excellent chairs from at least four and probably many more sets with this type square back and variant legs are known. Two other examples illustrated in Hornor's *Blue Book of Philadelphia Furniture* (Pls. 419 and 422) have similar concaved drums at the tops of the legs, but neither of those drums are carved as is the case on these chairs.

Dimensions: height 33⅞; width 18⅞; depth 17⅛.
Materials: mahogany; front and rear seat rails, an ash (American); right rear corner brace, a hard pine; upholstery, blue silk damask with pattern of basket of flowers, drapery, and tassels, English or French, early nineteenth century.
Accession: 51.2.1, 2

**96** SIDE CHAIR with square back (one of a pair)

*About 1800    Philadelphia or New York City*

Chairs with this type of back, related to several illustrations in Sheraton's *Drawing Book* (Pls. 25, 33, and 36), were apparently made in both New York City and Philadelphia. George Washington paid John Aitken for two dozen such chairs on February 21, 1797.[19] Surviving examples of that set have front legs with "stringing" seemingly identical to No. 97, and the backs have the same "elliptic cornered tops" as the chair shown here, but use a different design at the bottom of the vase instead of inverted carved leaves in the oval. Many American variants of this chair have been frequently illustrated,[20] some with histories associated with Philadelphia and some associated with New York; but none have backs so delicate and lively as this one. Inasmuch as molded front legs are seldom found on New York chairs, one is tempted to attribute this pair to Philadelphia; but red gum is found in New York chairs and seldom if ever in Philadelphia chairs. Hence an attribution to either city is tentative.

Dimensions: height 36½; width 30⅛; depth 17⁹/₁₆.

Materials: mahogany; side rails, soft maple; rear rail, red gum; right front corner block (type IV), arbor vitae; rear corner block (type II), tulip; upholstery, cream-colored silk with polychrome stripes, floral trails and sprigs, French, Louis XVI style, late eighteenth century.

Provenance: Museum Purchase, 1962.

Accession: 62.105.1, 2

**95**

**96**

**97** SIDE CHAIR with square back (one of a pair)

*About 1800   Philadelphia*

In this somewhat simplified version of No. 96 are a number of characteristics of workmanship that are more frequently found in Philadelphia than in New York: line inlaid tapered legs without spade feet, carving with less modeling of leaves and drapery, and corner blocks instead of open braces inside the seat frame. And indeed several similar chairs have been found in Philadelphia.

Dimensions: height 35¾; width 21⅝; depth 17⅝.
Materials: front and side rails, black ash; rear rail, mahogany; front corner blocks (type IV), tulip; upholstery, brown-and-white dotted-and-striped silk with floral sprigs embroidered in silk and metal threads, French or English, late eighteenth century.
Accession: 57.1029.1, 2

**98** SQUARE-BACK CHAIR with a vase splat
*About 1800   Philadelphia*

A number of chairs of this type have survived in the Philadelphia area and they were made there frequently enough to have a special listing in the cabinetmakers' price book of that city in 1795. It reads:

> A Square Back Chair,
> With straight top and stay rail three upright splatts, straight seat, made for stuffing over the rails.                    0 14 0
> If the above is made with a long vase splatt in the middle and an arch in the top rail to be extended between the two outside splatts extra,                    0 9 0

Other structural extras included "sweep" side rails and front seat rail at one shilling, three pence, each for labor. The unusual double bead around each

Maryland)[21] is the finest. Beautifully conceived, superbly carved, and of excellent craftsmanship, they are constructed of close-grained mahogany. As with many Maryland chairs, they are upholstered over only the upper part of each seat rail. The lower and exposed part is richly veneered, finished at the bottom with a band of satinwood and at the top with a bead. All prominent surfaces of the front legs and back are carved with an ornamental bead to enrich the over-all outline and frame the exquisite carved husks, flowers, leafage, Prince-of-Wales feathers, and drapery. One might suppose the design source, if found, would be Hepplewhite, and indeed the source for the husk carving on the legs is illustrated on Plate II of his *Cabinet-Maker and Upholsterer's Guide;* but contrary to expectation the design for the back is taken from Plate 36, No. 5 (p. 388) of Thomas Sheraton's *Drawing Book* of 1793.

From the cabinetmaker's drawing, the carved ornament on a mahogany side table made by Gillow and Company of Lancaster, England, appears to be identical.[22] In August of 1792, they paid for the following:

|  |  |
|---|---|
| making by Peter Briscoe complete | 1-10 |
| carving the husks by Mr. Gibson | 8-2 |
| carving 4 pateras by  „      „ | 10 3-4 |

Dimensions: height 36½; width 20¾; depth 19.
Materials: mahogany with satinwood banding; side and front rails, walnut, with upper lamination of cherry, and lower lamination of tulip; rear rail, mahogany; open braces in front (type I) missing in rear; upholstery, striped blue silk, late eighteenth century.
Provenance: Charles Carroll of Carrollton.
Accession: 57.770.1, 2

member of the back, and the vase and fleurs-de-lis are delicate and sophisticated in conception but rather coarse in execution. The carving was probably done on a time or piecework basis.

Dimensions: height 35½; width 20; depth 17⅜.
Materials: mahogany; corner blocks (type III), tulip; right seat rail, white oak; front and rear seat rails, ash; upholstery, brown silk woven in floral and leaf pattern resembling haircloth, about 1800.
Provenance: Gift of Charles K. Davis, 1952.
Accession: G 52.298

## 99 SIDE CHAIR with vase back (one of a pair)
*About 1800   Baltimore or Annapolis*

Of all known Maryland chairs, this pair (and other matching chairs in the original set believed to have been owned by Charles Carroll of Carrollton,

## 100 SIDE CHAIR with vase back and eagle banister [23]
*1790–about 1797   Annapolis   Label of John Shaw (working before 1773 to about 1800)*

Of three American designs for chair backs utilizing the American eagle, the most ambitious is this one with the label of John Shaw pasted inside the rear seat rail.[24] Presumably this chair and eleven others, all collected by the late Mrs. Breckinridge Long, were designed by Shaw himself. They are believed to have been originally owned by Robert Bowie who was elected Governor of Maryland in 1803.[25]

There seems little doubt of the nationalistic significance of this highly effective banister which features within the shield back a symmetrical composition of two eagles' heads, and a carved glory, or sunburst. A line-inlaid panel accentuates the

sharp taper of the front legs, a feature found on several other pieces labeled by Shaw.

Dimensions: height 37⅝; width 20; depth 19.

Materials: mahogany; rear corner blocks (type V) and seat rails, tulip; front open braces (type I), white oak; upholstery, polychrome striped-and-sprigged silk, English or French, late eighteenth century.

Provenance: Mrs. Breckinridge Long; Museum Purchase, 1958.

Accession: 58.96

**101** SIDE CHAIR with heart back (one of a pair)

*1790–1800   Philadelphia or Baltimore*

"A Heart back stay rail Chair, with a bannister and two upright splatts, straight seat made for stuffing over the rail [and] no low rails" is listed in

the 1795 Philadelphia book of prices and the following year in the price book for New York. Such chairs were apparently made in Salem as well for there are charges for three sets of "Ht back" chairs on a single bill of Daniel Clark to the Sandersons in 1794.[26] Heart-back chairs with eagles inlaid in the center of the banister have long been attributed to Baltimore,[27] but the writer believes this chair was made in Philadelphia. Molded legs are common to many Philadelphia chairs but seldom found on Baltimore work. The carving at the top of the splats is like more Philadelphia work than Baltimore (compare Nos. 88, 98, and 99). Some may object that the inlaid eagle is a Baltimore eagle and so it is like many eagles on furniture attributed to Baltimore. But its mate is also to be found on a fine tall clock case with "works" by Solomon Parks of Germantown, a suburb of Philadelphia.[28] It

**102**

the crest of each splat, and a string of plump, three-part husks hung from a loop, add color and intricacy to the composition. The seat, bowed at the sides, is serpentine in front. The plain legs are chamfered on the inner corners. Related chairs with Maryland histories of ownership suggest an attribution of Baltimore workmanship—an attribution supported by the structural features.

Dimensions: height 39; width 21; depth 18.
Materials: mahogany with satinwood inlays; front and side seat rails, tulip; rear rail, mahogany; four open braces (type I), mahogany; upholstery, yellow-and-beige-striped silk satin, early nineteenth century.
Provenance: Museum Purchase, 1963.
Accession: 63.40.1, 2

**103**

must not be forgotten that one of Philadelphia's outstanding cabinetmakers of the early 1800's, Joseph B. Barry, maintained a branch in Baltimore for at least two years; and there were undoubtedly many other close trade relationships between the two cities.

Dimensions: height 38¾; width 20¼; depth 17½.
Materials: mahogany; front and side seat rails, maple; rear rail, mahogany; corner braces (type I), tulip.
Accession: 57.771.1, 2 see Inlay Fig. 119

**102** SIDE CHAIR with heart back (one of a pair)
*1790–1800 Baltimore*

Satinwood inlays give distinction to the heart back of this chair. A fan at the base, flamelike leaves at

**103** SIDE CHAIR with vase back (one of four)
*About 1800   Baltimore or Annapolis   Possibly by War-
wick Price, "foot of high street, old Town Baltimore"
(working about 1790–1810)*

In many ways, these chairs are a comparatively
simple statement of normal Maryland chairmaking
practice, but a single decorative device raises a
competent expression to one of brilliance. Inlaid,
shaded satinwood leaves at the top of each scratch-
beaded banister create the effect of three torches
and illuminate the over-all appearance. According
to family tradition, these chairs, (never out of the
family until purchased by Mr. Joe Kindig, III),
were made by Warwick Price, great granduncle of
Mr. Tolley A. Biays from whom they were acquired.

Dimensions: height 37¾; width 20¼; depth 17½.

Materials: mahogany and light and dark wood stringing;

seat rails, tulip; corner blocks are replacements; upholstery, green-and-yellow-printed moquette (wool
velvet), late eighteenth century.

Provenance: Tolley A. Biays.

Accession: 57.696.1–4

**104** SIDE CHAIR (one of three)
*About 1800   Annapolis or Baltimore*

Several variants of this unusual, modified shield-
back chair are known, and most if not all have
Maryland histories of ownership or are at present
in Maryland collections.[29] This does not necessarily
prove them to be of Maryland workmanship, but
certainly implies a common source or preference.
Found on other chairs in that area are: similar
leaf carving in low relief at the top of the outer

**104**

**105**

splats; carrot-shaped cutouts in all three splats; and chamfered inner corners of the plain, unornamented, stretcher-braced legs.

Dimensions: height 38¼; width 20¾; depth 18.

Materials: mahogany with satinwood inlays; front and side seat rails, white oak; rear rail, tulip; four open braces (type I), hard pine; upholstery, striped silk, about 1800.

Provenance: Charles Carroll (barrister);[30] R. T. Haines Halsey; Francis P. Garvan; Mabel Brady Garvan Collection, Yale University Art Gallery; Museum Purchase, 1963.

Accession: 63.29.1–3

## 105 SIDE CHAIR, square back (one of three)
*About 1800    Baltimore or Annapolis*

Plate 28 (lower left) of Sheraton's *Drawing Book* provides the source for the design of this back with hollow corners and a banister with racquet-shaped central motif between two colonnettes. Variants of this back are found on Philadelphia and New York chairs. This handsome Maryland interpretation includes several ornamental features seldom found on furniture made elsewhere: a splayed back; an elliptic seat stuffed over half the rail, the other half veneered; a bead at the upholstery line; and a band of inlay on the lower edge. Such bands of triple stringing interrupted at about half-inch or inch intervals by squares or sometimes circles are a Maryland hallmark. Another feature often found on Maryland furniture is the dependent teardrop, or carrot-shaped panel, framed in broken line inlay seen on each front leg. The satinwood cuffs were probably originally only about half as wide.

Dimensions: height 36½; width 21; depth 17.

Materials: mahogany; seat rails, mahogany; original open braces (type I) missing and present blocks are replacements; upholstery, green-and-beige-striped silk with floral trails, French, late eighteenth century.

Accession: 57.772.1, 2

## 106 SIDE CHAIR with square back
*About 1800    South Carolina (?)*

This chair contains secondary woods normally used south of Philadelphia, but where it was made is impossible for the writer to say. For, although the carved husks and flowers are related to those on the side chair (No. 99) attributed to Baltimore, the carving on both chairs follows English precedent; and it should be noted that the hollow seats and molded tapered legs of this chair are not normally found on Baltimore chairs. However, a

clue to its origin is offered by ten side chairs which from the catalogue illustration appear to be identical to this one (although possibly without serpentine front seat rail) and which were sold in the Roland V. Vaughn sale in 1931.[31] That set was documented as having originally belonged to Capt. John Singleton of Sumter County, South Carolina. This chair may have been made in that locale.

The opulence of the rather broad carving of the drapery and ribbons with their irregularity of outline detracts from an otherwise handsome and strictly rectangular composition.

Dimensions: height 36½; width 20; depth 18½.

Materials: mahogany; front and side seat rails, tulip; rear rails, oak; corner braces (type I), hard pine; upholstery, black haircloth, English, about 1800.

Accession: 57.773

## FOOTNOTES

1 Information from correspondence with Charles C. Wall, Resident Director of Mount Vernon (April 13, 1964).

2 Illustrated in Helen Comstock's article "Mount Vernon Centennial," *Antiques*, LXIV (July, 1953), 30.

3 Illustrated Pl. 5 in "Jonathan Gostelowe, Philadelphia Cabinetmaker" by Raymond B. Clark, Jr.

4 Milo M. Naeve, "Daniel Trotter and his Ladder-Back Chairs," *Antiques*, LXXVI (November, 1959), 442–444.

5 In the shop of Harry Arons, Ansonia, Connecticut, February, 1964.

6 Another chair which appears to be from the same set was illustrated as Pl. 397 in W. M. Hornor, Jr., *Blue Book of Philadelphia Furniture*. At that time, it was owned by Mr. and Mrs. Lambert Cadwalader.

7 Illustrated No. 2340 in Wallace Nutting, *Furniture Treasury* (New York: The Macmillan Co., 1928).

8 Hornor, *Blue Book of Philadelphia Furniture*, Pl. 432.

9 Sheraton, *The Cabinet-Maker and Upholsterer's Drawing Book* (London, 1802), p. 387.

10 *Pennsylvania Packet* (Philadelphia), April 30, 1787. Prime, II, 188.

11 *Pennsylvania Packet* (Philadelphia), February 15, 1794. Prime, II, 189.

12 One of Winterthur's pair is illustrated in Hornor's *Blue Book of Philadelphia Furniture* (Plate 417), and a similar chair was sold (Lot 180) in Part V of the Americana Collection of the Late Mrs. J. Amory Haskell, December 6, 7, 8, 1944, at the Parke Bernet Galleries, Inc., New York.

13 Hepplewhite, *The Cabinet-Maker and Upholsterer's Guide* (1788) in the introductory essay.

14 Sheraton, *The Cabinet Dictionary* (1803), p. 201.

15 *Ibid.*, p. 218.

16 Gillow Records, ES, A 68–812, No. 555, dated 23 December 1789.

17 See caption for Plate 421 in Hornor's *Blue Book of Philadelphia Furniture*.

18 W. M. Hornor, Jr., in an article, "Henry Connelly Cabinet and Chairmaker," *International Studio*, XCIII (May, 1929), 43, illustrates several chairs and a sofa with the intimation that they were made by Connelly.

19 A chair from the Washington set, now in the Lewis Collection of the National Museum, Smithsonian Institution, is illustrated in *Antiques*, LXIV (July, 1953), 36.

20 No. 190 in *The Hudson-Fulton Celebration Catalogue of an Exhibition held in the Metropolitan Museum of Art* (New York, September to November, 1909) has similar but heavier back legs with plain instead of molded front legs.

21 *Baltimore Furniture 1760–1810*, p. 95.

22 Gillow Records, ES, 813–1140, No. 895.

23 *Baltimore Furniture 1760–1810*, p. 94.

24 Others are the type with inlaid eagle (No. 101) and a set of chairs of the Federal period in the New London (Connecticut) Historical Society. In those, eagles with outspread wings are shown in silhouette.

25 In support of this tradition, it may be worth mentioning that a large set of French china elaborately decorated with American symbols (owned until a few years ago by Mrs. Miles White of Baltimore) also has a history of ownership by Governor Bowie. Both the set of chairs and the china indicate patriotic enthusiasm.

26 Many years ago, Mabel M. Swan, in *Samuel McIntire, Carver and The Sandersons, Early Salem Cabinet Makers*, p. 14, suggested the "Ht" stands for Hepplewhite but "Hepplewhite back" makes rather less sense than "heart back." This writer has not seen a single instance of the use of Hepplewhite's name in early American cabinetmaking records. Heart back occurs repeatedly.

27 *Baltimore Furniture 1760–1810*, p. 98, where a similar though not identical chair is illustrated and discussed.

28 Photograph courtesy of David Stockwell in D. A. P. C.

29 Edgar C. Miller, Jr., *American Antique Furniture, A Book for Amateurs*, I (New York: M. Barrows & Company, Inc.), Nos. 192, 193, 217, 218, 219.

30 Original ownership of a chair which seems to be from the same set to Charles Carroll, barrister, was ascribed by Dr. Henry J. Berkley in his article "Early Maryland Furniture," *Antiques*, XVIII (September, 1930), 208, Fig. 4.

31 Sale Catalogue of the *Roland V. Vaughn Private Collection*, November 14 (New York: American Art Association Anderson Galleries, Inc., 1931), Lot No. 122, p. 68.

# Martha Washington or "Lolling" Chairs

A type of chair that seems to be the most distinctively American of the furniture forms used in the Federal period is the "Martha Washington" chair. Exactly when and by whom this name was given to such high-back, open-arm chairs is unknown today, but certainly this was a popular form with early American householders and was produced in considerable numbers in this country. One author noted that Joseph Short, Newburyport cabinetmaker, included the phrase "he also makes Martha Washington chairs" on one of his labels.[1] The writer has been unable to locate such a label and wonders if that usually meticulous author actually saw such a label or was possibly misled by "hearsay."

In recent years, collectors and scholars have repeatedly asked, "What is a lolling chair?" "2 Mahog$^y$ Loll$^g$ Chairs w$^{th}$ Copper plate covers" and window curtains to match were priced at $12 and found in the parlor when the inventory of the estate of Elizabeth Senter, widow of Dr. Horace Senter, was taken on December 10, 1802, in Newport, Rhode Island.[2] Four lolling chairs were shipped to Havana in 1799 by David Clarke; and he was only one of several Salem, Massachusetts, cabinetmakers who made what seems to have been a popular form in New England.[3] At first, the writer decided that chairs with reclining back and footrest such as No.119, answered the definition of "loll" given in *The Oxford English Dictionary* as: "to lean idly; to recline or rest in a relaxed attitude." But with so many early references to "lolling chairs," one would expect more to have survived than just this unique example. Slowly the writer came to the conclusion that all "Martha Washington" chairs were known as lolling chairs. Happily, just before this book was to go to press, Mr. Dean A. Fales, Jr., Director of the Essex Institute, confirmed the idea. He says that the term lolling chair is still recognized by older New Englanders as the name for open-arm upholstered high-back chairs and that about 1900 when Mr. George Rea Curwin bequeathed a fine group of furniture to the Essex Institute, one armchair similar to No.108 was specifically referred to as a "lolling chair" in the bequest.

High-back, open-arm chairs with upholstered backs and seats were made in England and France from the seventeenth century through about the third quarter of the eighteenth century. Although by the 1750's and 1760's their vogue in France was past, numerous variant designs for these comfortable chairs were illustrated in Chippendale's *Directory* [1754 and later editions], Ince and Mayhew's *Universal System of Household Furniture* [1762], and *Household Furniture by a Society of Upholsterers, Cabinetmakers*, etc. [1760]. Commonly designated in these books as French chairs or "French Elbow Chairs," most are shown with upholstered arms, although plain wooden arms are also included with either cabriole or variants of marlboro legs with bases. In America, as in England, armchairs were made in accord with these designs, but those made in colonial cabinetmaking centers usually had higher backs. Depending upon the style of leg, we refer to these earlier chairs as being in the Queen Anne or Chippendale style. Some had cabriole supports with pad, trifid, or claw-and-ball feet; others had either plain or molded straight legs.

Armchairs, smaller in scale and with oval backs in the Louis XVI style, are illustrated in the published designs of Robert Adam. Strange as it may seem, designs for the high-back form are not shown by either Adam or his followers—Hepplewhite, Sheraton, and Shearer; nor is the form usually found in antique English furniture of these styles. Apparently, by about 1775, this type of tall armchair had lost its appeal to Englishmen. The "Martha Washington" armchair is a modification and continuation of the earlier form and seems to be an American development—one of the few American innovations of the Federal period. Like the Chippendale-style highboy in America, it is a continuation of a form once popular in England but continued and reinterpreted in the hands of the American cabinetmaker after having become passé in the mother country.

The ultimate in comfort in a "Martha Washington" chair is exemplified by two chairs believed to be unique: No. 119 with adjustable, reclining back and leg rests, and No. 120 which in its free form anticipates the modern contour chair. Both chairs seem to fit perfectly the idea of lolling and taking one's ease.

The term "Martha Washington" chair will probably continue to be used for a long time, but the writer is confident that the old name was indeed lolling chair. The usual form seems to have been more widely made in Massachusetts than elsewhere; and at the present writing, no documented example made outside New England is known to the writer except for No. 120 which is really a different kind of chair though used for the same purpose.

1 Swan, "Newburyport Furnituremakers," *Antiques*, XLVII (April, 1945), 222–225.
2 Wills and Inventories Newport City Hall, Newport, Rhode Island, December 6, 1779, to March 7, 1803. Microfilm Copy M83 in DMMC.
3 Swan, *Samuel McIntire, Carver, and The Sandersons*, p. 17. The number of lolling chairs in contemporary records, recorded by Mrs. Swan, indicates their great vogue.

# XIII

# Dining Room Cross Hall

*Characteristic of the early Federal style are the refined lines found in this crisply carved sofa from Salem, Massachusetts (No. 262), a pair of barrel-back armchairs from the Boston area (No. 115), and a mahogany work table from Rhode Island or Connecticut (No. 398).*

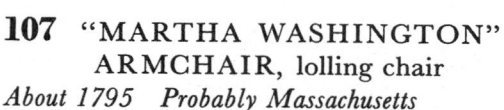

**107** "MARTHA WASHINGTON"
ARMCHAIR, lolling chair
*About 1795   Probably Massachusetts*

The generous width of seat, slightly lower than usual back, deep seat frame, and upholstered arms with supports set back from the front legs suggest the Chippendale prototype from which this form developed. Later features in accord with the neoclassical style are the boldly serpentine crest and tapered front legs molded to conform with the arm supports.

Birch rails and nailed white-pine triangular corner blocks point to Massachusetts as the place of origin of this chair.

Dimensions: height 43½; width 28¾; depth 22¾.
Materials: mahogany; seat rails, birch; corner blocks, front and rear (type III), white pine; upholstery, Winterthur leather bound with brass round-headed nails.
Accession: 57.1039

**108** "MARTHA WASHINGTON"
ARMCHAIR, lolling chair
*About 1795   Massachusetts or possibly New Hampshire*

The rounded crest, with slight serpentine, and the flat, outflaring arms with supports set well back from the front legs are early features which link this chair stylistically to its antecedents of the Chippendale era.

The use of birch, a secondary wood much favored by Salem and Boston cabinetmakers, suggests a Massachusetts origin, as does the S-shaped outline of the arms so carefully rounded on the underside and skillfully hollowed on the upper surface.

Dimensions: height 43½; width 24; depth 20.
Materials: mahogany; seat rails, birch; original open braces at front, missing; upholstery, green silk called *droguet*, woven in stylized leaf-and-fruit pattern, French, second half of the eighteenth century.
Accession: 57.950

### 109 "MARTHA WASHINGTON" ARMCHAIR, lolling chair

*About 1795   Massachusetts*

The crisp serpentine of the crest, sharply receding concaved arm supports, prominent outline of the string inlay, and fine dark mahogany give this chair its special quality. Such concave arm supports were known as "hoop stumps mortic'd on the top of the front legs."[1] The sharp, quick taper of the front legs below the inlaid cuffs suggests a Massachusetts origin. American beech was sometimes used there as a secondary wood.

Dimensions: height 43; width 26½; depth 23.
Materials: mahogany; light and dark wood stringing; seat rails, American beech; no front or rear corner blocks or indication of any; upholstery, green silk with floral and lace pattern, style of mid-eighteenth century.
Accession: 57.798

### 110 "MARTHA WASHINGTON" ARMCHAIR, lolling chair

*About 1795   Dorchester, Massachusetts   Stamp of Stephen Badlam (working 1790 to 1815)*[2]

This chair and the following are two of three "Martha Washington" chairs of which the maker is known. This one bears the stamp of Stephen Badlam, as do a variety of other pieces including at least two card tables, a dining table, and several side chairs (see No. 30). All are embellished with close variants of the carved ornament seen here, and all bear Badlam's stamp. On each are features favored by Hepplewhite—the side chairs have shield backs, the legs are tapered, the ornament is carved.

For fine workmanship, Badlam will always be remembered for the double chest he billed to Elias Hasket Derby in 1791—one of the finest examples

**109**

**110**

### 111 "MARTHA WASHINGTON" ARMCHAIR, lolling chair

*About 1800   Massachusetts*

Unity is gained in this successful chair by continuing the molded contours of the tapered front legs upward through the arm supports and shading them into the slightly scooped arms. The arms with supports screwed to the sides of the seat rails are typical of those found on many Massachusetts chairs of this kind—often, as here, with seat rails made of birch. Usually such chairs are made of mahogany, but cherry and maple examples are occasionally found. In the Lebanon Bedroom at Winterthur, there is another of the same design made completely of birch.

Dimensions: height 44½; width 26½; depth 22½.
Materials: mahogany; seat rails, birch; no rear blocks, front not original; upholstery, pink-and-white-striped lampas with polychrome floral sprigs and bowknots,

### 112

of American neoclassical furniture, now in the Mabel Brady Garvan Collection, Yale University. For the carving of that chest, Badlam employed John and Simeon Skillin, reputed to have been the best carvers in Boston; and perhaps on other occasions[3] he employed their services for the excellent carving which appears on much of his work. The *S.F* stamped inside a seat rail may be the initials of an early owner or possibly those of a journeyman who made the chair for Badlam (see Nos. 30 and 35).

Dimensions: height 41; width 25½; depth 21.
Materials: mahogany; seat rails, hard maple; at front open braces (type I), birch with additional triangular corner blocks (type III) of white pine; no rear blocks; upholstery, cream-colored silk, with stripes and floral sprigs in dark-blue and white, English or French, late eighteenth century.
Provenance: M. E. L. Lynch.[4]
Accession: 57.653

French, Louis XVI style, third quarter of the eighteenth century.
Accession: 57.929

## 112 "MARTHA WASHINGTON"
ARMCHAIR, lolling chair
*About 1800   Northeastern Massachusetts or Portsmouth, New Hampshire*

The inlaid flower motif and light wood stringing give individual character to this handsome chair. Such bellflowers made of one piece of wood, sometimes accompanied by white or black dots, were often used by Massachusetts cabinetmakers, who also frequently chamfered the front edges (below the stretchers) of the back legs of chairs, as here. Therefore, a Massachusetts attribution is suggested for this chair despite the presence of hard pine as a secondary wood, a wood frequently employed for this purpose in New Jersey, Maryland, and

**113**

farther south—but not one normally found in Massachusetts furniture of this era, except on sofas such as No. 271.

Dimensions: height 43⅞; width 26; depth 19¾.
Materials: mahogany; light wood inlays; seat rails, hard pine; corner blocks front and rear (type II), white pine; upholstery, silk satin with polychrome stripes and floral sprigs, French, third quarter of the eighteenth century.
Accession: 57.989

## 113 "MARTHA WASHINGTON"
ARMCHAIR, lolling chair
*1800–1810   Massachusetts or Rhode Island*

The origin of this highly unusual chair with boldly serpentined back and seat front has been a puzzle for a long time. The inlays are not unlike those found on several chairs and tables made by Jacob Forster of Charlestown, Massachusetts, though they are also related to sprigged inlays with ebony center line seen on Portsmouth and Providence furniture. Birch, soft maple, and white pine were used as secondary woods in both Boston and Providence, as was similar black-and-white segmental stringing which is used here to form the cuffs.[5]

Dimensions: height 44; width 26; depth 22.
Materials: mahogany; light wood and ebony inlays; side seat rails, birch; front and rear seat rails, soft maple; corner blocks, both front and rear (type III), white pine; upholstery, striped satin in light blue, yellow, and brown, French or Spanish, late eighteenth century.
Accession: 57.652

## 114 "MARTHA WASHINGTON"
ARMCHAIR, lolling chair
*About 1800   Massachusetts*

The absence of stretchers, the flowing S-curve of the arm supports repeated in the shape of the arms and the crest of the back, and the line inlay hollowed at the bottom to repeat the molding of the leg and rounded at the top to accord with the finish of the arm terminals, mark this as one of the most sophisticated chairs of its kind. Maple and birch were commonly used by Massachusetts cabinetmakers as secondary woods.

Dimensions: height 44¾; width 25¾; depth 22.
Materials: mahogany; light wood inlays; seat rails—rear, soft maple, front, birch; corner blocks, front and rear (type III), basswood; upholstery, light-blue taffeta, with lace and floral trails brocaded in polychrome, French, Louis XV style, mid-eighteenth century.
Accession: 57.990

**115** "MARTHA WASHINGTON"
ARMCHAIR, lolling chair (one of a pair)
*1800–1810   Boston or North Shore Massachusetts*

The flaring backs and the severe vertical and recti-linear quality of the pair of chairs, illustrated in Plate XIII, give them a flamboyance seldom seen in furniture of the Federal period. Although the large satinwood panels on the front legs are unusual and possibly unique, the rich contrasting effect of satin-wood, or figured birch, and mahogany was well known to Boston and North Shore cabinetmakers; also, the sharp, tapered foot is a characteristic so frequently found in their furniture as to be regarded as a hallmark. However, it must be noted that some pieces of Maine furniture are indistinguishable from pieces made in northeastern Massachusetts.

Dimensions: height 44¾; width 24¾; depth 20.
Materials: mahogany and light wood; seat rails, soft maple; corner blocks, front and rear (type III), white pine, rear ones, curved to conform to seat rail; up-holstery, striped and sprigged satin in shades of rose, green, and yellow, possibly French, third quarter of the eighteenth century.
Provenance: William C. Whitney of Portland, Maine, orig-inal owner. From Mr. Whitney (married in 1799), land agent for Andrew Craigie of Brattle Street, Cambridge, Massachusetts, the chairs descended to Mrs. Ralph W. Booker.
Accession: 60.327.1, 2                    see Inlay Fig. 51

**116** "MARTHA WASHINGTON"
ARMCHAIR, lolling chair
*About 1805   Boston   Label of Lemuel Churchill (work-ing 1805 to about 1828)*

Lemuel Churchill, cabinetmaker, was listed in the Boston directory of 1805 at 26 Orange Street, where he worked, and at 114 Orange Street, where he lived. His printed label (see p. 475) announces that he "makes and sells" cabinet furniture and chairs and offers "the newest fashions and best of work." This chair is his only known documented piece.

The flared lines of the concaved back and rear legs, the refined shaping of the arms, and the subtle carved outline of the front legs and arm supports mark Lemuel Churchill as a master of proportion.

Dimensions: height 44¼; width 24½; depth 20⅞.

Materials: mahogany; front seat rail, birch; side and rear rails, soft maple; original corner blocks missing; upholstery, polychrome lampas with stripes and floral sprigs in pink, blue, and light green, French, Louis XVI

style, third quarter of the eighteenth century.
Accession: 57.769

### 117 "MARTHA WASHINGTON" ARMCHAIR, lolling chair
*About 1805    Massachusetts*

"Hollow back" upholstered armchairs usually have backs of keystone shape, wider at the top than at the bottom, as seen here. This fine example, though lacking the flamboyance and pronounced flare of the back of No. 115 and the subtlety of arm and support of No. 116, ranks as one of the best expressions of the "Martha Washington" armchair.

Dimensions: height 45; width 24¾; depth 21¼.

Materials: mahogany; frame and top rail, birch; side

**116**

**117**

rails, maple; original front corner blocks missing; rear seat rail now reinforced with flat rectangular iron bar; upholstery, polychrome lampas with stripes and floral sprigs in blue, white, salmon, light green, and purple, French, Louis XVI style, third quarter of the eighteenth century.

Provenance: Museum Purchase, 1956.

Accession: 56.83

## 118 "MARTHA WASHINGTON"
ARMCHAIR, lolling chair (one of a pair)
*About 1805   Salem*

These handsome armchairs may have been made *en suite* with a sofa in the Karolik Collection.[6] That sofa, as does No. 270, follows the basic design of Plate 35 in all the editions of Sheraton's *Drawing Book*. The likeness is striking, inasmuch as the center panel of crossed arrows on a plain ground is far less usual than the variety of baskets carved on Salem sofa crests. The style of arm and crest seen here also relates closely to Sheraton's design. The exact counterpart of these arms, called "common cabriole elbows," as well as their supports, called "turned stumps," are illustrated on Plate 6, No. 3 of the 1802 edition of the *London Chair-Makers' and Carvers' Book of Prices*. Each pair cost two shillings, seven pence, without carving, and is described as follows: "Framing ditto [and fitting a pair of common cabriole elbows] with turn'd stumps and front legs in one piece, the elbows sweep'd towards the top of the back legs, as No. 3. Plate 6..."

A similar chair is in the Pingree House in Salem, but apparently the type was not a popular one in spite of its highly successful interpretation.

Dimensions: height 43; width 22½; depth 21.

Materials: mahogany; seat rails, birch; corner blocks, front and rear, triangular (type III), white pine; upholstery, yellow satin with fleurs-de-lis woven in mauve and white, French, Empire style, early nineteenth century.

Accession: 57.882.1, 2

## 119 LOLLING CHAIR (?)[7]
*1790–1810   New England*

The term lolling chair seems indeed appropriate for this chair with reclining back and adjustable footrests. Reminiscent of an earlier period are the heavy, old-fashioned arm supports and flat arm rests. But the reeded rails of the leg rests and the light, tapered front legs are in the new vogue. Ratchets under the seat and between the seat rail

and arm rests allowed the back and the leg rests to be adjusted and locked in any of several positions. The upholstery is not original but is perhaps suggestive of an original covering of leather.

Dimensions: height 51; width 24½; depth 35¼.

Materials: mahogany; footrest frame and rear rails, maple; medial seat brace and lower back rail, birch; upholstery, artificial leather.

Accession: 51.27

## 120 LOLLING CHAIR (?)
*1810–1820   New York City*

Since this unusual, outstanding, and perhaps unique open armchair may have been known as a lolling chair when made, it is included in this section even though it is not a "Martha Washington" chair in today's ordinary sense of the term. Closely related in its curvilinear shape to the "campeachy chairs" of New Orleans so highly prized by Thomas Jefferson,[8] it anticipates the contour chairs of the last century and this. As a piece of design, it is a fascinating study in harmony in its interplay of curve and countercurve. Based on the curule form, it is an ingenious modification of a "Grecian stool," with one set of the scrolled upper ends of the "Grecian cross" supports greatly

**119**

**120**

extended to form the frame of the back. The fine reeding outlining the seat, scrolled back, padded arms, and scrolled arm supports as well as the shape of each of these elements are so suggestive of the best early nineteenth-century New York chairmaking that it appears this chair was made in that city.

Dimensions: height 40½; width 21⅝; depth 29½.
Materials: mahogany; front seat rail, tulip; bottom

stretcher, hard pine; upholstery, blue silk twill, early nineteenth century.
Provenance: Museum Purchase, 1964.
Accession: 64.143

### FOOTNOTES

1 *The London Chair-Makers' and Carvers' Book of Prices for Workmanship* (1802), p. 57 and illustrated Plate 6, No. 5.
2 Mabel M. Swan, "A Revised Estimate of McIntire," *Antiques,* XX (December, 1931), 338–343.
3 The best article on Badlam and one in which this chair is illustrated is "General Stephen Badlam—Cabinet and Looking Glass Maker," by Mabel M. Swan, *Antiques,* LXV (May, 1954), 380–383.
4 Mrs. Lynch of Halifax, Canada, wrote the Winterthur Museum on April 1, 1956, that this chair "came from my late husband's family ... we know that it also came from Salem but whether from the Pickmans or not I am not sure. It has always been my impression that it did come to us from them. It was spoken of in our family as the La Fayette chair as he once sat in it when visiting in Massachusetts."
5 Eleanore Bradford Monahon, "Providence Cabinetmakers," *Rhode Island History,* XXIII (January, 1964), 1–22. Inlays used by Thomas Howard, Jr., and illustrated in this article are related to those seen in No. 124.
6 No. 122 in Edwin J. Hipkiss, *Eighteenth-Century American Arts. The M. and M. Karolik Collection* (Boston: Harvard University Press, 1941).
7 This chair was illustrated in "The Editor's Attic," *Antiques,* LXII (May, 1950), 385, when owned by Robert G. Hall, Dover, Foxcroft, Maine.
8 Marie G. Kimball, *Furnishings of Monticello* (Charlottesville, Virginia: Thomas Jefferson Memorial Foundation, 1954), p. 11.

# Easy Chairs

The easy chair was a popular form in England and America throughout the eighteenth century. Its shape changed less during that time than any other chair form. True, the legs were modified to accord with prevailing styles, but the upholstered part remained much the same from about 1725 to 1810. Later developments included the thinning of the lines of the arms and wings and the introduction, some time in the last half of the eighteenth century, probably after the Revolution, of the tub, or rounded, back as in Nos. 128 and 129. In a sense, the elimination of the back corners in the tub and circular back forms corresponds to the elimination near the end of the century of the corners in the backs of more sophisticated sofas. But, as with other furniture, old forms lingered on and continued to be made concurrently with newer models. In the pamphlet of prices agreed upon by the cabinetmakers of Hartford in 1792, easy chairs with plain or fluted legs and also with claw feet are listed. These features, associated with the Chippendale style, then out of date, mark the chairs as old-fashioned. We have no way of knowing how much longer they continued to be made in this manner.

In a plate dated 1787, Hepplewhite shows an easy chair with stretchers, spade feet, horizontal rolled arms, and serpentine crest and wings, which he describes as "a design for a Saddle Check or easy chair: the construction and use of which is very apparent: they may be covered with leather, horse-hair; or have a linen case to fit over the canvas stuffing as is most usual and convenient." The writer is convinced that "Saddle Check" is a misprint for "Saddle Cheek," the serpentine wings being shaped somewhat like the cheeks of a saddle. This conviction is supported by the 1802 *London Chair-Makers' and Carvers' Book of Prices* where (pp. 65–66) the standard model for "Square Easy Chairs" and "Tub Easy Chairs" is one with "straight cheeks," and "Saddle-tree cheeks" are offered as an option. Curiously, the printer's error in Hepplewhite has resulted in a misnomer in the English language. "Saddle-check chair" is defined in Webster's *New International Dictionary* as "A wing chair;—an eighteenth-century name."!

It seems fairly certain that what the English cabinetmaker referred to as a "tub back easy chair" was known to the American cabinetmaker as a "circular easy chair" such as Nos. 129 and 130. Now they are often called "barrel-back chairs" to differentiate them from those with straight backs, then called "square easy chairs."

The majority of American easy chairs of the early Federal period have horizontal rolled arms, with wings either straight or serpentine in silhouette as viewed from the front. However, chairs were made in New York with both vertical and horizontal rolls of the type found on American easy chairs in the William and Mary and the Queen Anne styles; but the vertical rolls of the later examples are usually very small as in Nos. 123 and 124. A few chairs have dominant vertical rolled arm supports with no wing at all, as in No. 122, or wings of reduced size as in No. 121.

All the earlier versions of American books of prices list easy chairs, but the descriptions are succinct until the 1817 edition of the New York book, which in its detailed listings offers excellent proof of the forms in vogue at that late date. The first entry (p. 109) for an "Easy Chair" seems clearly for a "square easy chair" as opposed to the "circular" one (barrel back) which follows it (p. 110). Both offer so many details of construction that the descriptions (without extras) for the basic forms are quoted.

### AN EASY CHAIR,

Two feet four inches long in front, two feet at the back, one foot ten inches from front to back, two plain legs in front, two sweeped ditto at the back, hard wood seat rails, pine back and cheeks, scrolls on the cheeks and top end of front legs, pine pieces glued on the cheeks over the joints                                            1 3 0

### A CIRCULAR BACK EASY CHAIR,

Two feet two inches in front, two feet from front to back, straight front rail, two plain legs in front, two sweeped ditto, at the back; hard wood seat rails lapped together or framed in the back legs, hard wood cheeks, shaped as in common easy chair, pine top rail glued up in thicknesses, three pieces to support ditto, or one piece and the back legs, to continue up, plain arms shaped to the side rails, tenoned on the front leg, and screwed fast to the cheek, for stuffing, over                          2 5 0

Both English and American price books include as an option "a close stool... slider clamp'd." This may be the board with a hole cut out in the center sometimes found under the seat to accommodate a china or pewter pot. Apparently a good many easy chairs were fitted for this accommodation.

Variant kinds of easy chairs are the bergère and fauteuil. A fauteuil to the French meant an armchair, usually an open-arm chair; and this connotation appears to have carried over to English interpretations. Both are listed in the 1802 and later editions of *The London Chair-Makers' and Carvers' Book of Prices,* and there are illustrations or references to both in the books of Sheraton and Hepplewhite. A basic different between the bergère, the fauteuil, and the normal easy chair seems to be one of height. Easy chairs are approximately four feet high and the usual bergère and fauteuil about three feet. Rarely, as in No. 132, are bergères taller. Despite Sheraton's illustration of one square-back example (*Cabinet Dictionary,* Pl. 8, No. 2), the bergère usually had a round or barrel-shaped back with a sharply arched top which dips downward and forward to meet the front legs as in Nos. 131 and 133. In England bergère and "cabriole bergère" seem to have been interchangeable terms, and the form is listed under the latter heading on page 57 in the 1802 London chairmakers' book of prices.

A fauteuil easy chair as interpreted by English cabinetmakers had a comparatively low and broad upholstered square back slightly hollowed, with turned or square stumps supporting the ends of the arms. One is described on page 62 and illustrated in Plate 8 (No. 2) of *The London Chair-Makers' and Carvers' Book of Prices* for 1802. The chair in that illustration is similar to No. 135 but without the rolled cresting rail. In summary, although the difference between a fauteuil and a bergère is slight and not always clear, the English and probably American cabinetmakers who made them seemed to think of a fauteuil as an upholstered chair, square in plan and silhouette, and the bergère as one approximating a half circle in plan with a rounded top. On occasion, but infrequently, both bergères and fauteuils were made by American cabinetmakers, but square and circular easy chairs were the normal forms produced.

# xiv Music Room

*In a room which takes its name from the presence of a high-style New York barrel organ (No. 470), a New York tilt-top table is laid out for tea with an English basalt ware tea set. The easy chair (No. 125) is from Philadelphia, as are the sewing table (No. 426) and oil painting, Election Scene, State House, Philadelphia, painted in 1815 by the earliest genre painter in the United States, John Lewis Krimmel. Of interest is the Sheffield-plate Argand lamp, which is like others now at Mount Vernon originally owned by George Washington; the history of this one is unknown. The cotton curtains, roller-printed in pink, portray the first seven presidents of the United States. On the floor is an Aubusson-type tapestry-weave French carpet of the late eighteenth century.*

### 121 EASY CHAIR
*1790–1810   New England, possibly Connecticut*

If one disregards the slip seat and exposed seat frame as innovations seldom seen on American easy chairs of any period, the only features which relate this chair to the styles of the Federal period are the marlboro legs which have been sharply tapered on the inside legs. The thickness of the arms, the slightly bowed crest, and the heavy vertical rolls are all in accord with those found on many New England easy chairs of the Queen Anne style.[1] This chair could have been made anywhere in New England, but the use of cherry as the primary wood gives the edge to Connecticut as the possible place of origin.

Dimensions: height 44½; width 27¾; depth 20¾.

Materials: cherry legs; seat rails, cherry; front corner blocks (no rear blocks used), white pine (type IV); upholstery, cotton, about 1785, printed by copperplate in red after the design "L'Hommage de l'Amérique à la France," by Jean-Baptiste Huet, Jouy, France.

Accession: 57.602

maple was also used in each of these areas, but is more commonly found in furniture of New England origin.

Dimensions: height 45½; width 28½; depth 16½.

Materials: mahogany legs; seat rails, beech; corner braces (type I), soft maple; upholstery, cream-colored striped silk with flowers brocaded in colors, French, Louis XVI style.

Accession: 57.1059

### 122 EASY CHAIR
*1790–1810   Probably Massachusetts*

By eliminating the wings and sweeping the arms into a curvilinear form of inviting shape, the maker of this easy chair produced not only an unusual, but perhaps a unique American easy chair. Although beech is infrequently found in American furniture, a few instances of its use are known in Massachusetts, New York, and Pennsylvania. Soft

### 123 SQUARE EASY CHAIR
with straight wings
*1800–1810   New York*

This easy chair is an outgrowth of an older common form. New-style turned legs have been substituted in front for the earlier turned, cabriole, or heavy marlboro supports, and the lines of the upholstered frame made lighter and thinner. The inverted cones above the front legs are slimmer, the rolls of

the arms smaller in diameter, and the C-scroll connecting the two are longer and more vertical than on earlier chairs. On later chairs, the line of the crest is often serpentine, as here.

Dimensions: height 47; width 30; depth 22¼.

Materials: mahogany; seat rails, soft maple; upholstery, pale-blue silk satin, *camaieu* type with amorini, bowknots, ribbons, and flowers, patterned after material brought from France in 1800 by Eleuthère Irénée du Pont.

Accession: 57.1045

## 124 SQUARE EASY CHAIR
with straight wings
*About 1800–1810   New York*

In this chair, the same form as No. 123, an elliptic top takes the place of the serpentine crest and reeding adds refinement to the front legs. Their outline (see also Nos. 123 and 135) admirably illus-

trates a type of turned leg and foot that seems to be found only on furniture made in New York City or by men trained there. Such legs or feet occur on furniture labeled by Michael Allison (No. 198), George Woodruff (No. 330), John Dolan,[2] and others, as well as on chairs attributed to the workshop of Duncan Phyfe. Standard elements of these turned legs are a distinctive foot of ogee outline (often tipped with brass ball feet or casters), separated by a turned ring from an inversely tapered shaft (reeded, as here, or plain as in No. 123), surmounted by a double hollow, and square at the top of the leg.

Dimensions: height 44½; width 30; depth 22.

Materials: mahogany; seat rails, soft maple; small inner rails, tulip; corner blocks (triangular type III), white pine; upholstery, gold-colored silk damask with pattern of urns of flowers, drapery, and tassels, English or French, early nineteenth century.

Accession: 57.1102

**125** EASY CHAIR

*1800–1810 Philadelphia*

The wings of this square easy chair with serpentine crest and elliptic seat are fastened to the outside of the horizontal rolls which form the arms. This structure is found on many easy chairs of the late eighteenth and early nineteenth centuries but is not common on earlier chairs. Here the dominant inner lines of the rolls continue unbroken all the way to the back of the chair, whereas in earlier examples the lines of the arms fade subtly into the lines of the wings. Such bulb-turned feet and reeded legs are found on much Philadelphia furniture.

Dimensions: height 46; width 34; depth 34.

Materials: mahogany; front seat rail, cherry; right seat rail, red oak; rear seat rail, soft maple; upholstery, silk with polychrome sprays of flowers brocaded on white ground, English or French, third quarter of the eighteenth century.

Provenance: T. B. O'Toole.

Accession: 56.18.1

**126** EASY CHAIR

*1810–1820 Northeastern Massachusetts*

During the second decade of the nineteenth century, earlier furniture forms lingered on while "Grecian" furniture styles came into prominence and popularity. In many cases the earlier forms remained almost unchanged; but often, as in this chair of ample dimensions and curvaceous outline, the contours of the turned front legs became heavier. Except for the front legs, this design with horizontal rolled arms, serpentine crest, and half-serpentine wings is a close parallel to that shown in Plate 15, dated 1787, of Hepplewhite's *Guide*. His chair is equipped with tapered legs and spade feet. Sharply tapered rear legs and the presence of birch in the seat rails suggest Boston, Salem, or some other city of northeastern Massachusetts as the place of origin. The use of the eagle motif in the English roller-printed cotton upholstery is interesting as an appeal to the American market in an era when American cotton manufacturers were beginning to offer serious competition to overseas producers.

white corded silk with flowers brocaded in colors, English or French, mid-eighteenth century.
Accession: 57.1273

## 128 CIRCULAR EASY CHAIR
*1805–1815   Probably Philadelphia*

The reeded front legs of this chair with their bulb-turned feet and carving at the top are similar to those on the famous set of ebony furniture made by Ephraim Haines for Stephen Girard in 1807.[4] These features and the turned rear legs matching the contour of those in front have long been accepted as hallmarks of Philadelphia workmanship; there can be little doubt that this comfortable-looking easy chair was made in that city, where circular easy chairs were listed in the price books issued there in both 1811 and 1827.

Dimensions: height 46; width 33½; depth 24½.
Materials: mahogany; front seat rail, cherry; left and rear
    seat rails, American ash; lower lamination rear seat

Dimensions: height 44½; width 30; depth 24½.
Materials: mahogany legs; seat rails, birch; triangular
    corner blocks (type III), white pine; upholstery, roller-
    printed cotton with American eagle surrounded by
    floral wreath in red and black on tan blotch ground,
    English, about 1835.
Accession: 57.1095

## 127 EASY CHAIR
*1790–1800   Baltimore*

Several easy chairs which have Baltimore histories and have been attributed to the cabinetmakers of that city have outflaring and downward raked arms such as those found on this chair.[3] This appears to be a Baltimore characteristic—one that the writer has not seen used by chairmakers elsewhere in the United States.

Dimensions: height 49¼; width 29; depth 25¼.
Materials: mahogany; wing, arm, back stile, and crest
    rail, tulip; seat rails, tulip and hard pine; upholstery,

rail, white pine; upholstery, pale-blue-and-white-striped silk with polychrome floral trails and sprigs, English or French, late eighteenth century.
Accession: 60.574

## 129 CIRCULAR EASY CHAIR
*1805–1815 Philadelphia*

On the basis of the front legs, this easy chair and two other ones in the Winterthur collections (Nos. 125 and 128) can with assurance be ascribed to Philadelphia workmanship. On these chairs, the legs are turned, reeded, and in one case carved in familiar Philadelphia fashion. All three have elliptic front seat rails which bow out rather sharply at the ends and are made of cherry. The two with circular backs have outflaring rear legs. The writer believes these characteristics to have been in common practice among Philadelphia easy-chair

makers and they may be found on many of their products.

Dimensions: height 47½; width 28; depth 23.

Materials: mahogany; front seat rail, cherry; sides and back, 2-inch ash glued upon one inch of cherry; upholstery, American eagle surrounded by floral wreath, cotton, roller-printed in red and black on tan blotch ground, English, about 1830.

Accession: 57.1094

## 130 CIRCULAR EASY CHAIR
*About 1795–1815 Philadelphia*

The flowing lines of this chair make it one of the most successful of American easy chairs of this period. Each independent curving member is in harmony with the others, producing a remarkable over-all fluid effect. The ample size of the front legs and the outward sweep of the rear legs give stabil-

**128**

**129**

ity; but, as the legs move downward or outward, they are diminished slightly to free them of heaviness. Like others in the group discussed under No. 125, its elliptic front seat rail is of cherry.

Another large circular easy chair in the Winterthur collections (Acc. 57.638), almost a mate to this one, also has an elliptic front seat rail of cherry; the writer believes that it, like this one, fits into the group of Philadelphia chairs discussed under No. 125.

Dimensions: height 48¼; width 26; depth 20¾.
Materials: mahogany; front seat rail, cherry; rear and side rails, mahogany; front corner blocks (type IV), tulip; upholstery, dark-blue-and-white-striped *imberline* (part silk), French, late eighteenth century.
Provenance: Ashbridge Family (Chester County, Pennsylvania).
Accession: 57.988

**130**

## 131 EASY CHAIR, bergère type
### *1805–1815 Philadelphia*

Philadelphia may claim this restrained and sophisticated chair because of the character of the turned legs. Those at the rear are particularly significant because rear turned legs are so seldom seen on mahogany American chairs except in Philadelphia. Those on No. 91, also made in Philadelphia, have similar round spade feet. Although restricted here to the bottoms of the arm supports, leaf carving appears frequently on the arm supports of Philadelphia sofas of this period and occasionally on easy chairs (No. 132); but it was seldom used in this way elsewhere in the United States.

Dimensions: height 33½; width 23⅛; depth 18¾.
Materials: mahogany; left seat rail, ash; original front corner braces (type I), missing; left corner block, tulip; upholstery, pale-blue-and-beige velvet, French, early nineteenth century.
Accession: 57.1044

pattern, French, first half of the eighteenth century.
Accession: 57.517

### 133 EASY CHAIR, bergère type
*1790–1800   Probably Massachusetts*

The so-called bergère, a low-backed upholstered armchair, was less common in the United States than in France and England. Here the arched back, the serpentine line of the armrests, and the curve of the seat front give grace to a utilitarian form. "Various easy Chairs with their sizes in Inches" shown on Plate 8 of Sheraton's *Cabinet Dictionary* (p. 19) include an example (No. 1), similar in outline to this chair. He calls it "a cabriole arm-chair stuffed all over." Though this is a unique example, it is tentatively attributed to Massachusetts on the basis of the maple seat frame and

**133**

### 132 EASY CHAIR, bergère type
*1805–1815   Philadelphia*

This practical form of easy chair is unusual in having a high, curved barrel back without wings. The bowed front gives additional depth to the narrow seat. Although this chair may have been made for a lady, as is suggested by its narrow proportions, a high-back chair of similar proportions and style was used by Thomas Jefferson when he was Vice-President. It is at Monticello today.

Panels of foliated carving with stiff leaves rising from them and the reeded bulbous supports parallel those on a Philadelphia card table (No. 316) and a number of Philadelphia sofas.[5] On the latter, mahogany scrolled arms carved in similar fashion and backs and seat rails with molded veneered edges are often found.

Dimensions: height 44; width 23¼; depth 21½.
Materials: mahogany; seat rails, oak; interior framing, tulip; traces of original corner blocks, mahogany; upholstery, dark-green silk damask, large floral-and-leaf

triangular corner blocks of white pine.

Dimensions: height 38; width 25; depth 22.

Materials: mahogany legs; seat rails, American soft maple; corner blocks (type III), white pine; upholstery, green silk twill, edged with red-and-green silk fringe, about 1800.

Accession: 57.516

## 134 EASY CHAIR, bergère type

*1797 Boston Attributed to George Bright (working from about 1750 to 1805)*

Since 1948 it has been known that George Bright, a Boston cabinetmaker, billed the State of Massachusetts in December of 1797 for thirty mahogany chairs at $8 each, for the new State House.[6] When first published, this information was mistakenly linked to a later style chair. But as early as 1930,

**134**

Henry Francis du Pont bought at the Philip Flayderman Auction Sale at the Anderson Galleries an armchair like this one with a history of having been handed down in the Cushing family from Judge John Cushing of Boston and as being a "part of the original furnishings of the old Boston State House."[7]

Not until 1964 was the eminent position of George Bright as a Boston cabinetmaker recognized or the quality of his craftsmanship assessed. In a masterful article in the *Art Quarterly*,[8] Richard H. Randall, Jr., showed that in 1787 George Bright was "reckoned a very honest Man and an extraordinary good Workman" and was "esteemed the neatest workman in town." Although as yet this chair cannot be conclusively proved to have been made by George Bright, there appears little doubt to this writer that it is one of the thirty chairs he made for the Boston State House; and it is certain that it is one of the neatest surviving chairs of its type. The hollowed back of this dignified bergère form, originally derived from the French by the English, is outlined in wood and continues forward almost to the turned stumps above the front legs in the manner of many American sofas (see Nos. 271, 272, 276, 277).

Dimensions: height 34; width 22; depth 24.
Materials: mahogany; no secondary. woods; original brass, iron, and wood casters; upholstery, black leather, modern.
Provenance: Gift of Mr. and Mrs. David Stockwell, 1964.
Accession: G 64.147

## 135 EASY CHAIR, fauteuil type
*1805–1815 New York City*

A chair of similar design with variant details is illustrated under the heading: "Various easy Chairs" in Sheraton's *Cabinet Dictionary* (Pl. 8, No. 2). He states: "Arm-Chair, No. 2, is a fauteuil, having a molded top rail and arm, and turned stumps...."

The carved back, serpentine-scrolled arms with turned supports, reeded frame, and turned and reeded legs of this fine armchair are elements found on upholstered New York sofas (No. 277), long attributed to Duncan Phyfe's workshop.[9] This chair approximates a shortened version. On first sight it matches the sofas, but in several details the difference is quite marked: the turning and the long pointed leaves on the arm supports are unlike those on the sofas, no "buttons" appear on the back and arm ends; and the relief of the carving on the top panel is softer and different in character than that on most sofas. It is well known that George Woodruff and Charles-Honoré Lannuier labeled work matching that formerly assumed to

have been made by Phyfe, and undoubtedly furniture in this idiom was made by many other New York cabinetmakers.

Dimensions: height 37½; width 30½; depth 32.
Materials: mahogany; seat blocks and left seat rail, American ash; front seat rail, American black ash; upholstery, light-blue satin with stylized floral-and-leaf medallion in white and yellow, French, Empire style, early nineteenth century.
Provenance: Museum Purchase, 1952.
Accession: 52.93

## FOOTNOTES

1 For New England Queen Anne chairs with similar arms and back, see Joseph Downs' *American Furniture, Queen Anne and Chippendale Periods* (New York: The Macmillan Company, 1952), Nos. 74, 79, 80, 81, 82.
2 A table formerly in the collection of Israel Sack, Inc. Photograph in Decorative Arts Photographic Collection, Winterthur Museum.
3 See *Baltimore Furniture, 1760–1810* (Baltimore, Maryland: The Baltimore Museum of Art, 1947), Nos. 66 and 67, pp. 103 and 104.
4 Hornor, *Blue Book*, pp. 243–244, 250. See also Marian Carson, "Sheraton's Influence in Philadelphia," *Antiques*, LXIII (April, 1953), 342–345.
5 Hornor, op. cit., Plates 415 and 429.
6 Swan, "Boston's Carvers and Joiners," *Antiques*, LIII (April, 1948), 281–285.
7 Sale Catalogue of the *Collection of the Late Philip Flayderman* (New York: American Art Association Anderson Galleries, Inc., January 2, 3, 4, 1930), No. 460.
8 "George Bright, Cabinetmaker," *Art Quarterly*, XXVII (No. 2, 1964), 135–149.
9 A similar and perhaps identical example, possibly this very chair, is illustrated as 2367 in Nutting's *Furniture Treasury*, II.

# Chests of Drawers

At least as early as 1792, the term "bureau" was used in the United States to describe a four-drawer chest of drawers. In contrast, the English appear to have reserved the name "bureau" for a slant-top desk and to have used the name "dressing chest" for the four-drawer chest of drawers.

The following excerpts from cabinetmakers' price books help clarify the difference between American and English nomenclature. The piecework prices noted at the right represent the amount to be paid the journeyman for making each form in its simplest state with little or no ornament. As noted before, the daily wage for journeymen was approximately a dollar a day, hence the number of dollars quoted approximate the number of days required to make that particular item.

Hartford, 1792

| | £ s d | Approx. $ |
|---|---|---|
| A plain Bureau, plain feet, 3 feet long | 2-18-0 | 7.73 |
| ditto with swelled feet [ogee bracket], 3 feet four inches long | 3- 6-0 | 8.80 |
| ditto with swelled front | 5- 0-0 | 13.33 |
| ditto with claw [claw and ball] feet | 5-10-0 | 14.67 |
| ditto with columns, claw feet and carved mouldings | 6- 0-0 | 16.00 |

Hatfield (Massachusetts), 1796

| | Approx. $ |
|---|---|
| Plain Bureau, 3 feet long | 8.33 |
| ditto with swelled feet and columns | 10.00 |

Chests with more than four drawers were listed as a high or low case of drawers; viz:

| | Approx. $ |
|---|---|
| a *High Case with 8 drawers*, Square head | 20.00 |
| Scroll head | 25.00 |
| a *Low Case, 5 drawers* | 9.17 |

The above descriptions suggest chests of drawers in the Chippendale style. Those that follow for New York are in the new style.

New York, 1796

| | £ s d | Approx. $ |
|---|---|---|
| A Dressing Chest, or Beaureau [straight front] | 2-11-0 | 6.37 |
| A Round Front Dressing Chest, or Beaureau | 3-16-0 | 9.50 |
| A Serpentine Dressing Chest, or Beaureau | 5-12-0 | 13.75 |

All of these are described as being three feet six inches long, as having four drawers, cock-beaded, an ogee and square on the edge of the top, or the edge veneered, a string in the upper corner, square corners. For the straight-, round-, or serpentine-front bureaus, the feet are described, respectively, as "straight brackets, all solid, French Feet, or common brackets, all solid; French feet, or common brackets, front veneered."

The listings in the 1793 and 1797 London books of prices are essentially the same as the entries cited above for New York except that the alternative name "bureau" is omitted. Under the separate heading for a Bureau in the London books, such details as six small drawers and six letter holes inside lead one to believe that a slant-top desk is meant.

|  | £ sterling | Approx. $ |
|---|---|---|
| A Dressing Chest | 0-18-0 | 4.00 |
| A Round-Front Dressing Chest | 1- 6-0 | 5.77 |
| A Serpentine Dressing Chest | 1-17-0 | 8.32 |

All to be "Three feet long, four drawers in ditto, cock beaded, astragal or stone molding on the edge of the top, or the edge veneer'd and a string in the upper corner, French feet or common brackets," except for a plain Dressing Chest which specifies "a fast plinth, on common brackets" [feet]. It will be noted that the standard size for London was six inches narrower than that for New York.

In comparing the prices paid journeymen, it may be well to keep in mind that not only were London wages lower, but the English pound sterling was worth about $4.44 compared to $2.50 for the New York and $2.66⅔,[1] for the Philadelphia pound. Stated in another way, twenty-one shillings sterling were equivalent to thirty-seven shillings of New York money and thirty-five of Pennsylvania currency.

Regional preferences for chests of drawers is indicated to some extent in the captions which follow, but a special word is in order on those made in Connecticut. The ingenuity of Connecticut cabinetmakers is incredible. More variety can be found in case forms made there than in the output of any other locale. Prior to 1800, Lemuel Adams, Benjamin Burnham, Aaron and Eliphalet Chapin, Silas Cheney, and a host of others produced, one or another until about 1800, almost every façade imaginable on case pieces—the straight front, the block front, the round or bowed front, the serpentine, and the reverse serpentine. Only the bombé (puffed, round, or bulged front) favored by Massachusetts cabinetmakers in the Chippendale period, but apparently not made elsewhere in the United States, had been overlooked. However, in the Federal era one or more Connecticut cabinetmakers may have compensated for this oversight. At least five chests of drawers of partial bombé form, bulged or bellied on the front but with straight ends are known.[2] Although highly unusual they have many features found in Connecticut cabinetwork and have often been attributed to that state. However, very recently an infra-red photograph revealed the complete inscription on the chest of this type in the Winterthur collection (No. 147) to show that it was "made by G. Stedman Norwich Vermont" instead of Norwich, Connecticut as had been supposed. Since there is no record of Stedman in Vermont, he may have been an itinerant cabinetmaker who traveled northward from Connecticut along the river valley.

---

1 The DMMC, 59 × 9.177. List of currency values, undated but believed to be in the 1790's.
2 One of these is in the Henry Ford Museum, two more are in private collections, another was owned by John S. Walton in the late 1950's, and still another by Israel Sack and Sons in 1964.

## xv Corner of the Blue Room

*American bureaus with the upper drawer fitted with a looking glass and many small compartments for toilet articles are extremely rare. One of the finest of its kind, this bureau (No. 142), believed to have been made in Rhode Island, was given to the Museum by Commander and Mrs. Duncan I. Selfridge. Also outstanding is the gilt looking glass (No. 227), a close interpretation of a Hepplewhite design; it was probably made in England since its secondary woods include oak, cottonwood, and hop hornbeam. The cheval glass or "screen dressing glass" (No. 247), as it is termed in The Cabinet-Makers' London Book of Prices of 1788, may have been made in Philadelphia. As early as 1808, George Smith in Collection of Designs for Household Furniture and Interior Decoration referred to such glasses as "cheval glasses," the term we still use today. They were often termed "swingers" by the men who made them.*

### 136 CHEST OF DRAWERS
#### or serpentine bureau
*About 1800   Massachusetts*

Serpentine-front chests of drawers of any wood are uncommon, but this one of unusually bold contours and made of brilliantly figured "tiger striped" maple is extraordinarily rare, perhaps unique. The serpentine form offered opportunity for highly in-

dividualistic expression on the part of the cabinet-maker, as is shown by examples labeled by William King of Salem and Jonathan Gostelowe of Philadelphia, but none is more flamboyant than this one of the highly prized striped maple.[1]

A serpentine bureau cost fifty per cent more to make than a round front and twice as much as the straight front. To "cant" the front corners, base, and bracket feet cost an additional twenty shillings[2] (approximately twenty per cent more). Thin chamfered and fluted front corners with conforming bracket feet are occasionally seen on chests made in Massachusetts where white pine is the normal secondary wood for case pieces.

Dimensions: height 36¼; width 44¼; depth 21⅛.
Materials: Curly maple top and façade; maple ends; secondary woods, white pine.
Accession: 56.532

### 137 CHEST OF DRAWERS
#### or round-front bureau
*1795–1810   Rhode Island or Southeastern Massachusetts*

The original purchaser of this piece of furniture was willing to spend more than was required for a common "dressing chest or beaureau." It is, however, an expression of the standard "round-front bureau" with no extras for veneering its top, front, or bracket feet. One concession to luxury was the choice of mahogany over the less costly

**136**

**137**

and more frequently encountered maple and birch. A rounded bead frames the drawers, a departure from the cock-beading on the edges of drawers listed in cabinetmakers' price books. The use of chestnut for the dividers between the drawers suggests that this chest was probably made in Rhode Island or a contiguous area. All four drawers are lined with pages of the *Columbian Centinel* (Boston newspaper) dating from July to September, 1795. The sailing ship on the backplates of the drawer pulls which are framed by rope-twisted handles may possibly have been a conscious choice to reflect the maritime activity of the owner.

Dimensions: height 33; width 41; depth 22½.
Materials: mahogany; framing and dust boards, chestnut; back panel and drawer sides and bottoms, white pine.
Accession: 57.520

## 138 CHEST OF DRAWERS
or round-front bureau
*1790–1810     Northeastern Massachusetts or New Hampshire*

In contrast to the original owner of No. 137, the first purchaser of this chest of drawers paid extra to have the front, the drawers, and the "French feet" veneered. Oval and rectangular panels of

figured birch set in mitered frames of mahogany veneer give a handsome effect that is characteristic, both in contrast and arrangement, of the best cabinetwork produced between Salem and Portsmouth about 1800. In that locale, a center "drop-panel," or tablet, on the skirt was also occasionally used on bureaus and much patterned stringing employed on all case pieces. The bowed drawer fronts are contrived with laminated strips of white pine, as a base for the veneers. Cock-beading was the normal practice for finishing and protecting the edges of the drawers. The brasses are old but not original.

Dimensions: height 37¾; width 41; depth 22.
Materials: mahogany; figured birch and mahogany veneers; secondary woods, white pine; patterned stringing of light and dark woods, probably of natural and stained holly.
Provenance: Wingate Family, Hampton, New Hampshire.
Accession: 57.564          see Inlay Figs. 26, 50

## 139 CHEST OF DRAWERS
or elliptic-front bureau
*1810–1820     Northeastern Massachusetts or New Hampshire*

Many of the features of this slightly later type of round-front chest of drawers, or bureau, would have been listed as extras in the price books for workmanship in New York in 1810. Framing the case to provide for "stump feet" was included in the price for the standard form, but "three quarter-round corners in front legs, and half-round on back, the top shaped to ditto, and edge banded" added twelve shillings, and the "elliptic sweep, extra from round front," five shillings. Veneered drawer fronts and reeded legs were also options and further increased the cost.

The principal parts of this chest are made of birch, a wood often stained to simulate mahogany in northern New England. Also common to that area on cabinetwork of the 1810 to 1830 period are bowed drawer fronts with engaged reeded colonnettes at the corners. The disposition and placement of the flamelike figured-birch veneers is a brilliant achievement, overshadowing the uninspired treatment of the lower section of the reeded colonnettes, which are weak in contrast to those seen on a similar form (No. 144). Ivory escutcheons and broad cross-bandings of rosewood dramatize the over-all effect.

Dimensions: height 39; width 42⅝; depth 19⅞.
Materials: birch legs and ends; front, mahogany and figured-birch veneers with rosewood bandings on birch; other secondary woods, white pine.
Accession: 57.907

## 140 CHEST OF DRAWERS
### or elliptic-front bureau
*1810–1820   New York*

Although this chest of drawers has been published as a serving table and attributed to Duncan Phyfe,[3] it is more likely a "Round front bureau with elliptic sweep" listed in the 1810 *New York Book of Prices*. In the 1817 edition of the same book, the following options are illuminating: "Half or feint rounding front legs, the top shaped to ditto" and "Preparing and fixing paws, see table No. 30."

The contour of the lower turning on the legs is so frequently seen on New York furniture that it has come to be regarded as a hallmark. Paw feet (here of wood, but often of brass), reeding, and lion's-head brasses were also commonly favored by that city's cabinetmakers.

Dimensions: height 38; width 36; depth 21.
Materials: mahogany; bottom board, drawer linings, tulip; lower side rails and sides of frame, white pine.
Provenance: Freylinghuysen Family, Hillside, New Jersey.
Accession: 57.1047

## 141 CHEST OF DRAWERS or bureau[4]
*1795–1810   Baltimore*

In terms of surviving examples, the straight-front bureau must have been the standard for chests of

**140**

**141**

drawers in the United States because there seem to be at least ten times more extant today than all other types combined. Most examples are of solid wood—mahogany, maple, birch, cherry, or walnut. Finer examples such as this one have matched veneers over other woods, in this case over mahogany. In New England, the basic wood used for veneered drawer fronts was usually white pine. But in New York and southward, mahogany veneers are often laid on tulip as in this case.

Features seen on other Baltimore furniture and repeated here are the serpentine skirt inlaid in the center with a large floral-and-leaf motif in a half oval and the large inlaid eagle in oval at the center of the top. The stringing on the skirt comprised of light-colored squares separated by three light lines seems to be a type not found on any furniture except that of the Baltimore area. Cross-banded mahogany veneers are used on the fronts of the rails between the drawers, the faces of the ends, and the edges of the top. There are dust boards between the drawers, and the brasses are old but not original to this bureau.

Dimensions: height 37¼; width 38; depth 21½.
Materials: mahogany front, ends, and top; bottom board and blocks, hard pine; dust boards and other secondary woods, tulip.
Accession: 55.560     see Inlay Figs. 78, 124, 125

**142** CHEST OF DRAWERS or a serpentine bureau with dressing drawer
*1780–1795   Probably Rhode Island*

Beautifully finished in every detail with figured drawer fronts of matching mahogany veneers, edged with cross-banding, and enlivened with fans and figured stringing, this serpentine bureau is further distinguished by the presence of a "dressing drawer" of great beauty. In the *Cabinetmaker and Upholsterer's Guide*, Hepplewhite illustrates a chest of drawers and a detail of the top drawer. He refers to this in the text under the heading "Dressing Drawers" with the following remark: "Plate 74 shows a design for this article; the top drawer in which contains the necessary dressing equipage." The compartments shown, like those of his Ladies Dressing Tables, Plate 73, have "partitions or apartments in which are adapted for combs, powders, essences, pin cushions...the glasses rise on hinges in the front, and are supported by a foot affixed in the back." Plate 8 in most editions of the London books of prices illustrates designs for two similar drawers. But such a drawer is rarely found

in an American bureau, and no other with an interior so prettily ornamented with colored bandings (white, green, and mahogany) is known to the writer. To prevent the dressing drawer from sagging, its sides are fitted with slides.

Largely on the basis of early ownership, this chest is attributed to Rhode Island since red cedar was occasionally used for drawer linings in most East Coast cabinetmaking centers. The handles are original.

Dimensions: height 36⅜; width 40¾; depth 22¾.
Materials: mahogany; upper drawer sides and partitions, mahogany; other drawer sides and backs, red cedar; other secondary woods, white pine.
Provenance: Commodore Duncan N. Ingraham, Newport, Rhode Island; Gift of Commander and Mrs. Duncan I. Selfridge, 1957.
Accession: G 57.32.2     see Inlay Figs. 8, 44

**143** CHEST OF DRAWERS or bureau with serpentine front and ovolo corners
*1795–1810   Philadelphia or Baltimore*

The contours of the façade and drawer fronts of this bureau are more highly developed than those of any other American example of the Federal period known to the writer. The whole is comparable in complexity to the serpentine chests of drawers with half-serpentine or ogee ends frequently illustrated in English price and design books of about 1800. Of these, no American examples are known to exist. Although no printed

prototype for this one has come to light, the individual elements of the façade are not uncommon. The center section of the drawers (and conforming frame) is the normal serpentine, with large ovolos at either end to form the front corners. The rounded ends of the undulating skirt have been carried down to meet the heel of the outflaring French feet. Seldom have matched crotch mahogany veneers been used to such good advantage as on the curved surfaces of the front.

The stamped brasses, which are original, are distinguished by a temple motif in a central me-

dallion. The inlaid escutcheons are of ivory. Tulip, white pine, and hard pine were used in Pennsylvania, Maryland, and other southern cabinet-making areas. However, reliance on matched veneers and stringing rather than on ornamental inlays suggests a Philadelphia origin.

Dimensions: height 38⅜; width 38¾; depth 23¼.
Materials: mahogany top and ends; matched mahogany veneers over tulip drawer fronts; light-colored stringing; back board, white pine; right side and bottom of frame, hard pine; other secondary woods, tulip.
Accession: 57.600

**144** CHEST OF DRAWERS or elliptic-front bureau and dressing glass[5]

*1813–1816   Boston   With label of Levi Ruggles, working 1813–1855*

Dressing glasses (usually small ones, sometimes with and sometimes without drawers) were made and used during much of the eighteenth century. It is believed they normally stood on tables or chests of drawers. During the Federal period, it became the practice in Massachusetts to fasten a large dressing glass with drawers to the top of a long-legged bureau; and a new and useful form of bedroom furniture evolved. Several pieces of this kind have been attributed to Nathaniel Appleton, of Salem, and to John Seymour and Son, in Boston; but this labeled example shows clearly the shop where it was made. Levi Ruggles worked at No. 2 Winter Street, Boston, from 1813 to 1816.

Little is known of Ruggles other than that he made panels for Gilbert Stuart in Boston in 1810,[6] and from the details he employed on this bureau, it seems likely that he learned the practice of furniture-making in that city. Similar triple bands of reeding on engaged columns are to be seen on the semi-elliptical commode that Thomas Seymour made for Mrs. Elizabeth Derby in 1809.[7] Fluted drums and scrolled brackets like those found here also appear on sideboards and chests that have been attributed to the Seymours. However, the rounded drawer front with "elliptical sweep" veneered with figured birch is a shape unknown on any of the Seymours' case pieces. The quality of these proves that Ruggles' standards were above the average. The scrolled brackets flanking the looking glass are outlined in gilt. The dovetails of all the drawers are overlaid by mahogany strips which carry the beading on the drawer edges. The ceramic knobs on the small drawers are replacements, and the old pulls of Sheffield plate, on the long drawers, may not be original to the piece.

Dimensions: height 74½; width 38½; depth 23¼.

Materials: mahogany; mahogany and figured birch veneers; secondary woods, white pine.

Accession: 57.567

**145** CHEST OF DRAWERS or bureau and dressing glass

*1810–1820   Boston*

This handsome chest of drawers does not bear the label of Levi Ruggles, despite the fact that it has been so published at least twice.[8] With a straight front and with veneers of bird's-eye and flaming

maple instead of the bowed contours and figured birch of No. 144, this example has, nevertheless, similar brackets, fluted drums, and turnings of ogee outline on the legs just below the lower drawer. It may have been fashioned in Ruggles's shop, but details of the richly figured half-rounded veneers which frame the glass and edge the top, and the shape of the looking glass cresting and the turnings and reedings of the legs appear to be almost identical to features found on furniture attributed to the Seymours.[9] But, alas, those attributions have been loosely made, and undoubtedly

144

the same turner or turners did work for several Boston cabinetmakers, and the same veneers were available to all from the shop of John Dewhurst[10] and others. The use of mahogany for the sides and backs of the small drawers and ivory for the keyhole escutcheons is, however, a practice found on documented Seymour work (see No. 184). When more is known of Boston cabinetmaking, the maker of this superbly made piece may be discovered. For the present, he must remain anonymous.

Dimensions: height 71; width 38; depth 21¼.

Materials: mahogany; mahogany and maple veneers; small drawer back and sides, mahogany; other secondary woods, white pine.

Accession: 57.883

## 146  CHILD'S CHEST OF DRAWERS
### or reverse serpentine-front bureau
*1800–1810   Probably Massachusetts*

The reverse serpentine front, often called ox-bow today after the shape of the ox-yoke, is not an uncommon form for New England bureaus, high chests of drawers, or desks of the last half of the eighteenth century. But no other child's bureau of this form is known to the writer. It has all the finesse and fine workmanship of a full-scale piece: the shaped front is veneered with matched branch mahogany, the drawers are edged with a cock

bead, and the top and base finished with an ogee molding. Only the bracket feet are simplified to follow the curve of the base.

Dimensions: height 25⅝; width 25½; depth 16½.

Materials: mahogany; drawer fronts, mahogany veneer over white pine; secondary woods, white pine.

Accession: 57.1100

## 147  CHEST OF DRAWERS or bureau
*1800–1820   Norwich, Vermont   Inscribed in pencil "Made by G. Stedman Norwich Vermont"*

The "Norwich" in the inscription on a drawer of this chest can be clearly read, but infrared photographs show it is Norwich, *Vermont,* not Connecticut, which might be inferred because the chest is of cherry and the design a novel one as is often the case with Connecticut furniture. Four other cherry chests, one in the Henry Ford Museum and three privately owned, are of the same unique bombé design, though differing in inlaid details. They also may have been made by Stedman, about whom nothing is known.[11]

On the top and drawer fronts are fan inlays with wavy segments. They further intensify what must be regarded as a bizarre conception. Also unusual on a piece of cherry furniture are the cross-bandings of mahogany (outlined with light stringing) on the edge of the top, drawer fronts, and upper line of the skirt. The handsome stamped eagle brasses, original to this piece, are marked "H.J." on the bails. As yet their maker is unidentified, but it appears to have been an English firm with a large export trade since this mark appears frequently on mounts original to American as well as English furniture.

Dimensions: height 34⅞; width 41¾; depth 20⅛.

Materials: cherry with cross-bandings of mahogany; light wood stringing and inlays; cherry veneer on skirt; blocks, drawer sides and bottoms, white pine.

Accession: 51.25

## FOOTNOTES

1 "The Editor's Attic: Finding Feet for Serpentines...," *Antiques*, XII (September, 1927), 201–203; and Clarence Wilson Brazer, "Jonathan Gostelowe: Philadelphia Cabinet and Chair Makers," *Antiques*, IX (June, 1926), 385 to 392.

2 *New York Book of Prices*, 1796.

3 Nancy V. McClelland, *Duncan Phyfe and the English Regency, 1795–1830* (New York: W. R. Scott, Inc., 1939), Pl. 89, p. 103.

4 Illustrated in *Baltimore Furniture, 1760–1810*, Pl. 83, p. 133.

5 Illustrated in Richard H. Randall, Jr., "Works of Boston Cabinetmakers, 1795–1825," *Antiques*, LXXXI (February, 1962), Fig. 2, 187, giving Ruggles' working dates and dating the piece on the basis of the location at "No. 2 Winter Street"; also illustrated in Wallace Nutting's *Furniture Treasury*, I, No. 289; and in the Catalogue of the *Girl Scouts Loan Exhibition*, No. 713.

6 Swan, "Boston's Carver and Joiners," *Antiques*, LIII (April, 1948), 285.

7 Now in the Museum of Fine Arts, Boston. See Edwin J. Hipkiss, "A Seymour Bill Discovered," *Antiques*, LI (April, 1947), 244–245.

8 Illustrated and erroneously ascribed to Levi Ruggles by Paul H. Burroughs, "Two Centuries of Massachusetts Furniture," *American Collector*, VI (September, 1937), 5; and by Randall, op. cit., 187; also in Nutting's *Furniture Treasury*, I, No. 288.

9 Vernon C. Stoneman, *John and Thomas Seymour, Cabinetmakers in Boston, 1794–1816* (Boston: Special Publications, 1959), Plates 173 and 176.

10 Randall, "Works of Boston Cabinetmakers, 1795–1825," *Antiques*, LXXXI (April, 1962), 412.

11 For kind assistance the writer is indebted to Mr. Houghton Bulkley of Hartford who with the assistance of Mrs. Albert H. Chase, of Norwich, made the most meticulous and careful search of Connecticut records in an effort to find a Stedman clearly identified as a cabinetmaker in Norwich at this time.

# Clocks

Clocks have always been highly prized. This may account for the number surviving, despite the fact that their early ownership seems to have been very limited. In 1786 William Bentley, Salem's famous diarist, noted, "At one, Public notice is given through the town of the hour & as there are few clocks & watches in the Town in families, there can be no other certain time of collecting."[1] Ten inventories of prosperous New York households from 1800 and 1820, containing 482 chairs, list but one clock. Although the first three decades of the nineteenth century showed vastly increased clock production (Eli Terry's factory alone produced four thousand wooden movements from 1807 to 1810[2]), thirty inventories taken in Boston, Newport, and New York City between 1800 and 1830 show a total ownership of thirteen clocks and five watches. The largest of these—in Newport with assets of $70,000—included a single clock. Only one estate of the thirty contained as many as three timepieces, but two of these were watches.

From cost alone one may conclude that any clock of the pre-Federal or Federal period constituted a highly desirable and expensive object. However, certain factors made some clocks more desirable than others. Long-running movements (eight-day as against thirty-hour) were preferred as, of course, were movements of greater accuracy. Fancy movements—those with second hands or with alarms, that struck the hour and even played tunes or chimes, that showed the dates of the month and the phases of the moon—were more coveted than their plainer counterparts. Lastly, the production of the small but costly bracket clock shows that compactness and portability were sometimes factors influencing desirability.

Tall-case clock designs did not change rapidly in the Federal period. Descriptions of such cases vary little in New York cabinetmaking price books between 1796 and 1834. "Arch'd head and scroll pediment," which was an option in 1796, had become the standard by 1802 and remained so until at least 1824. "Column corners in body and head" and "French feet" were offered for periods of thirty-eight and thirty-two years respectively.

Willard "patent timepieces" from their inception in 1802, as well as the later girandole variation introduced by Lemuel Curtis, relied for their ornamental effect on gilding, painting, and sometimes carving. However, being "in the latest mode" may have played a strong part in enhancing their vogue. With the advent of the Massachusetts wall clock, introduced by Simon Willard, it became apparent that there was a large and enthusiastic public for a comparatively inexpensive clock.

Clockmakers learned their craft through apprenticeship either before coming to America or from established craftsmen here. English types of movements prevailed until the late eighteenth- and early nineteenth-century innovations of the Willards and

Eli Terry. A number of English horological design books seem to have been used in this country, including Alexander Cumming's *The Elements of Clock and Watch Work Adapted to Practice* (London, 1766) and Charles Leadbetter's *Mechanick Dialling* (London, 1773). Apparently most, if not all, plates and gears were cast and worked locally, sometimes by the clockmaker himself. One brass worker, William C. Hunneman (1769–1856), after serving his apprenticeship with Paul Revere, made brass andirons, kettles, warming pans, candlesticks, and copper teakettles for general sale and castings for the Willards.[3] Some tools were made locally, but most seem to have been imported from England (particularly fusee engines and gear cutters) as were many painted sheet iron dials from the large Birmingham manufacturies.

Tall and bracket clockcases conformed in large part to English design although American tall clocks were generally less ponderous and had smaller dials. Design books, or infrequently imported cases, may have provided models for tall and bracket clocks. Massachusetts shelf and wall clocks, the Willard "patent timepiece" or banjo clock with its many variations, and later the "pillar and scroll timepiece" of Eli Terry were all American innovations.

### TALL CLOCKS

First produced in Europe about 1660 and probably introduced into America not long afterward, the tall-case clock was then, and has remained to this day, the Cadillac of clocks. The form developed organically in order to protect the movement from dust and damage as well as to protect the weights and the pendulum (which after 1671 was usually 39.19 inches long to give a one-second sweep).

Handmade movements of the Federal period did not differ substantially from their predecessors and ranged in complexity from thirty-hour to one-year types. Regional variations in movement are hard to ascertain; but some groups of clockmakers show definite attributes—for example, the Dominy family used cast skeletonized plates, and the "school" composed of Griffith Owen, the Hoffs, and Jacob Hostetter in Lancaster, Pennsylvania, used "lantern" instead of cut pinions.

In clockcases, definite regional characteristics do, however, exist. The "Roxbury" type case, used throughout New England between 1780 and 1820, is distinguished by open fretwork over a rounded hood with three cup or urn finials of brass. Inland Pennsylvania cases are characterized by heavy bases and tops separated by a slender waist, and hoods protruding in pouting fashion at the front.[4] Although New York and northern New Jersey cases are not represented in the Winterthur collection, No. 154 is a close parallel to a type distinctive of that area, characterized by high swan-neck pediments and many inlaid ellipses and circles. In Philadelphia particularly, inlaid geometric panels are often heavily outlined by cross-banding or patterned stringing. High scrolled pediments ornamented with pierced fretwork and naturalistic vine, leaf, and flower inlay are often found on Baltimore cases. Despite these fairly strong regional variations, price books for New York and Philadelphia gave similar specifications for a clockcase and offered virtually the same extras to convert a simple form into an elegant case design.

### DWARF TALL CLOCKS

Dwarf tall clocks, usually from three to five feet tall and incorporating a smaller version of the standard eight-day tall clock with striking movement, originated in

England. They had a limited popularity in this country, possibly because a tall clock gave a much grander effect at little advance in cost. Reuben Tower and his brother-in-law, Joshua Wilder, both working in Hingham, Massachusetts, between 1810 and 1830, made a specialty of these small clocks, which are eagerly sought by collectors today.

## BRACKET CLOCKS

Bracket or "spring" clocks are a comparatively rare American form and survive in about the same number as dwarf tall clocks. Many American bracket clockcases hold English movements, a fact readily accounted for by the difficulty in turning (by means of a special engine) the complex conical fusees which equalize the rate at which the spring unwinds. These movements were the only non weight-powered clocks produced in America until the 1840's. They were usually fitted with a crown wheel and short bob escapement to prevent damage when being carried from place to place. Their handsome cases with handles at the tops, which are very close to English prototypes, suggest their presence in the parlor (a fact confirmed in inventories); and the frequent incorporation of alarm devices seems to point to their use, by night, in bedrooms.

## MASSACHUSETTS WALL CLOCKS

Made by hand in small numbers between 1775 and 1795, the Massachusetts wall clock was an attempt to provide a cheaper timepiece. Their light thirty-hour movements of few parts employed a dead-beat escapement with short pendulum connected directly to the verge shaft. Although definitely of American origin, some question remains as to whether the type was first designed by the Willards or the Mullikins of Massachusetts. By 1800 this form was superceded by the "patented timepiece" of Simon Willard as well as by Massachusetts shelf clocks.

## MASSACHUSETTS SHELF CLOCKS

Without counterpart in the Middle-Atlantic or Southern regions, Massachusetts shelf clocks—usually with eight-day movements similar to those used in "banjo" timepieces—were being made by most of the important New England clockmakers by 1800. Designed for a less affluent market than the purchasers of tall clocks, the shelf clocks required but one third the quantity of brass needed for tall clocks; and, although some cases, notably those for David Wood and Willard movements, were elegant indeed, many were but simple pine boxes. Their popularity waned by 1830 when the market was filled by inexpensive machine-made shelf clocks.

## WALL CLOCKS

Wall clocks of the "patent timepiece" (banjo) type, an innovation developed by Simon Willard about 1795, incorporated movements similar to those of Massachusetts shelf clocks in novel cases designed by Willard and fabricated, painted, and gilded for him by a number of craftsmen in the Roxbury-Boston area. Willard (who is reported by his biographer, John Ware Willard, to have made four thousand movements himself) permitted a number of his favorite former apprentices to use his patented design and to make and sell clocks bearing the phrase "Willard's Patent." One of these apprentices, Lemuel Curtis, developed the so-called girandole variation which, like the "banjo" timepiece, sold at about two thirds of the price of an average tall clock.

## OTHER TYPES

Several clocks in the Winterthur collection are novelties which do not conform to any popular or widely made type. Among these is the well-known Eddystone lighthouse alarm timepiece patented by Simon Willard in 1822, when he was sixty-seven years old. This form, with beautifully grained base surmounted in glass bell, is apparently original to Willard. Another New England clock, "The Bunker Hill Clock," is, in design of case and of movement, an innovation of Benjamin Clark Gilman and made only by (or for) him.

The above clocks were all made individually and by hand. For this reason, they were expensive, and only a fraction of the population could afford them. In 1806 or 1807, Eli Terry set up a factory with water-powered machinery in Connecticut to make clocks by mass production. At first he produced wooden thirty-hour movements with printed paper dials for tall clocks to be sold without cases. Between 1807 and 1810, Terry's factory completed four thousand of these movements, which were often hung on a wall bracket until the owner could afford a case.

By 1814, Terry had devised and introduced a wooden-movement shelf clock, complete with case, which sold for fifteen dollars.[5] During the next several decades, clocks of this type were made by many New England (particularly Connecticut) factories in vast quantity. In rural Pennsylvania, brass movements continued to be produced by hand until 1850, but elsewhere the era of the handmade clock had passed by 1830.

1 William Bentley, *The Diary of William Bentley* (Salem, Massachusetts: The Essex Institute, 1905), I, 32, entry for March 19, 1786.
2 Brooks Palmer, *The Book of American Clocks* (New York: The Macmillan Co., 1950), p.290.
3 Swan, "The Man Who Made Brass Works for Willard Clocks," *Antiques*, XVII (June, 1930), 524–526.
4 For this and other information in this section and especially in the catalogue which follows, I am deeply indebted to Edward F. LaFond, Jr. His study "The Henry Francis du Pont Winterthur Museum Collection of American Clocks: A Catalogue of the Collections and an Interpretation of How It Illustrates Clockmaking in America from 1640 to 1840," was submitted as a thesis in 1964 to the Faculty of the University of Delaware as one of the requirements for his master's degree in the Winterthur Program of Early American Culture. This thesis and Mr. LaFond personally have guided me in the preparation of this section.
5 Carl W. Dreppard, *American Clocks and Clock Makers* (Boston: C.T. Branford Co., 1958), p.79.

# xvi Library Cross Hall

*New England sailing ships brought back luxuries from all over the world for the homes of Salem, Boston, and the surrounding countryside. From France came the wallpaper, The Monuments of Paris; from the Middle East, the Joshaghan carpet on the floor; from the West Indies, the mahogany for the furniture along the wall. Chairs from the Boston shops of Stephen Badlam (No. 30), and Stone and Alexander (No. 31) are upholstered in silk from Europe. Also from Boston is the lady's desk (No. 193). Simon Willard made the outstanding tall clock (No. 148).*

**148** TALL CLOCK
*1790–1810 Roxbury, Massachusetts "Simon Willard" (working 1766–1839) painted on dial and his printed label pasted inside door*

Typical of the tall clock case form known as the "Roxbury" type, this example, with eight light wood fans on the door and base, has more inlaid ornament than is usual. The inlaid fans, like those found on other Boston furniture but not unique to cabinetmaking of that locale, have scalloped outer edges inset with ebony. Standard elements of such cases are: ogee bracket feet, fluted quarter columns on the waist and colonnettes on the hood, both with brass bases and capitols and stop-fluted reeds of brass; an arched head ornamented with scroll work; and three cup-shaped brass finials set on line-inlaid plinths.

Like so many other clockmakers working about 1800, Simon Willard imported many of the painted iron dials he used. The decoration on this one is typical of that found on English enamelled iron dials used in America after 1785 and into the first years of the nineteenth century. A maiden with a bird and birdcage is painted in an oval on the lunette, and a spray of flowers ornaments each corner. A sub-dial (below the "XII") marks the passage of seconds, and an opening in the lower half of the dial and above "Simon Willard" tells the day of the month.

Skillfully fashioned from locally prepared brass castings, the fine quality of the eight-day movement, the rack-and-snail strike, and the anchor-recoil escapement are typical of the work of the Willard shop in Roxbury, a suburb of Boston. The workmanship reflects the standards set by Simon Willard for his many journeymen and apprentices. The case may have been made in the shop of William Fisk, John Doggett, or any of the several other nearby cabinetmaking shops, but the use of

chestnut and hard pine are not typical secondary woods in Boston furniture. The label, printed by Isaiah Thomas, Jr., of Worcester, Massachusetts, advertises the various types of clocks made by Simon Willard at his "Clock Manufactury" and gives "directions to set clocks in motion."

Dimensions: height 88; width 19⅛; depth 9¾.
Materials: mahogany; light wood and ebony inlays; door and front of case, mahogany veneer on chestnut; inner bottom, a hard pine; backboard, white pine.

Provenance: Gift of Charles K. Davis.
Accession: G 53.155.64

## 149 DWARF TALL CLOCK
*1815–1825 Hingham, Massachusetts "Jo. [ Joshua] Wilder, Hingham" (working 1810–1830) painted on dial*

Highly figured dark crotch mahogany veneers are used effectively in this smaller version of the New

**151**

England tall clock case. The brass movement, also smaller in scale than those used in the normal tall clock, is of the standard eight-day weight-driven variety with rack and snail striking system and anchor-recoil escapement. However, the pendulum is shorter (eighteen inches) and beats in roughly two thirds of a second instead of the precise second of the 39.14 inch pendulum.

The red, white, and blue shields which ornament the corners of the painted iron dial are a motif (see also No. 150) often found on the clocks of both Wilder and Tower. Their dials were probably painted by a local craftsman instead of being imported from Wilson, Osborn, Owen, or another of the many English dial-making specialists in the Birmingham area who furnished faces for the clocks of many American makers. Paint loss as found on this dial is not uncommon on American-made examples, perhaps because American craftsmen had less experience and skill than their English competitors in making and applying a durable enamel.

Dimensions: height 50½; width 11; depth 5½.
Materials: mahogany; door and base panel, mahogany veneer on white pine; backboard, white pine.
Accession: 59.769

**150** DWARF TALL CLOCK
*1815–1825  Hingham, Massachusetts*
*"Reuben Tower" (working 1808–1845) painted on dial*

With the exception of such minor details as variant brass finials and the addition of brass bases and capitols to the inset quarter columns on the waist, the handsome case of this small tall clock is essentially a replica of No. 149 and was probably made by the same cabinetmaker. A clock with dial decorated in similar fashion but with a case which may be slightly earlier than this one is inscribed "This clock was made by Ruben Tower of Hingham for Isaac Wilder in 1816."[1] That gives a clue to the date of this and the preceding clock.

The movement is almost identical to No. 149, though of slightly inferior workmanship; and the dials of the two clocks, though differing in ornament, appear to have been painted by the same hand. Both movements are made of cast brass parts and are beautifully finished, approaching in quality those found in fine French clocks.

Dimensions: height 50; width 11½; depth 5¾.
Materials: mahogany; door and base panel, mahogany veneer on white pine; backboard, white pine.
Accession: 55.622

### 151 TALL CLOCK

*1799   East Hampton, Long Island   New York*
*"N. Dominy [Nathaniel IV]  E. Hampton 1799,"*
*(working 1769–1812) engraved on notched brass*
*alarm disc[2]*

Replicas of the clockmaking and woodworking shops with the original tools used by three generations of Dominy craftsmen of East Hampton, Long Island, are now on display at Winterthur. This clock made in 1799 for David Gardiner of Flushing, Long Island, stands in the tiny shop surrounded by the tools with which its movement was made. Nearby is located the duplicate of the woodworking shop in which the case was fashioned by Nathaniel Dominy V (1770–1852), an ingenious and skillful member of this remarkable family and son of Nathaniel Dominy IV, maker of the movement. Few nonurban American-made clocks are so complex as this eight-day movement equipped with an alarm system which can be set to ring at an appointed time. The dial is fitted with two subdials, one (below the "XII") with second hand, and the other (above the "VI") to show the date of the month. Like most rack-and-snail striking systems, this one is fitted with a "night string" which when pulled caused the clock to strike the nearest hour—a convenience often incorporated in clocks before the invention of the sulphur match. The Dominys called this type of clock a "Horologiographical, Repeating, Alarm, Monition-Clock."[3]

The movement is extremely beautiful, a beauty created in large part by the fact that the plates are skeletonized in pleasing abstract patterns. The voids were achieved through use of more intricate mold patterns by the Dominys for their castings than those normally used by American clockmakers. The straightforward lines and dynamic curves give the mahogany case dignity and distinction.

Dimensions: height 92; width 17; depth 9.
Materials: mahogany; seat board for movement, cherry; backboard, white pine.
Provenance: Museum Purchase, 1957.
Accession: 57.34.1

### 152 TALL CLOCK

*1800–1810   Pennsylvania, probably Lancaster   Probably made by John or George Hoff, Jr. (John, working 1800–1819; George, Jr., working 1790–1816)*

This eight-day, quarter-hour chiming, hour-striking movement with musical attachement is one of the most intricate and beautifully made American clock mechanisms of its era. By means of eleven bells and twenty-two hammers, the clock plays seven tunes. A knowledgeable clock collector[4] has told the writer that the only American clocks he has seen with "lantern pinions" such as found in this clock were made by Griffith Owen, the Hoffs of Lancaster, and Jacob Hostetter. All of these men were trained in the German tradition of clock-making in which the lantern pinion was commonly used as opposed to the English and French custom of using cut pinions. The movement is attributed to one of the Hoffs on the basis of the unusual method of tripping the moon disk by a cam and counterbalanced weighted ratchet, and a unique method of supporting the pendulum from a turned post screwed to the backplate of the movement.[5]

Although the line-inlaid colonnettes and chamfered corners, the crosshatched stringing above the door, the handsome eagle inlay on the door, and the large patera on the base are related to Baltimore cabinetwork, frontally protruding hoods are most often found on inland Pennsylvania-made cases.

Dimensions: height 106½; width 22; depth 15½.
Materials: mahogany and mahogany veneers on hard pine with inlays of zebra wood and satinwood; backboard, white pine; blocks, hard pine.
Accession: 57.1026                    see Inlay Figs. 77, 81

## 153 TALL CLOCK
*1810–1820   Manheim, Pennsylvania   "Jacob Eby" (working dates, unknown) and "Manheim" painted on dial*

The design and workmanship of this large and handsome case and carefully made movement bear testimony to the taste and skill of two inland Pennsylvania craftsmen. Although the maker of the case is unknown, that he was an able cabinetmaker is certain. Not only is the bowed façade extremely ambitious, it is successful. The curved front is carried upward from the base through the long door and waist to the satinwood cross-banded shelf for the hood. The latter extends far forward in the Pennsylvania manner. Three ovals of ropelike stringing emphasize the patterns of carefully chosen mahogany veneers. A fourth oval frames a great inlaid spread eagle which, like the fine shell on the skirt and swastikas on the volutes, may have been purchased ready-made from a Philadelphia or Baltimore specialist in inlays.

A Jacob Eby is listed in various clock books as son of Christian, a brother of George Eby, and as

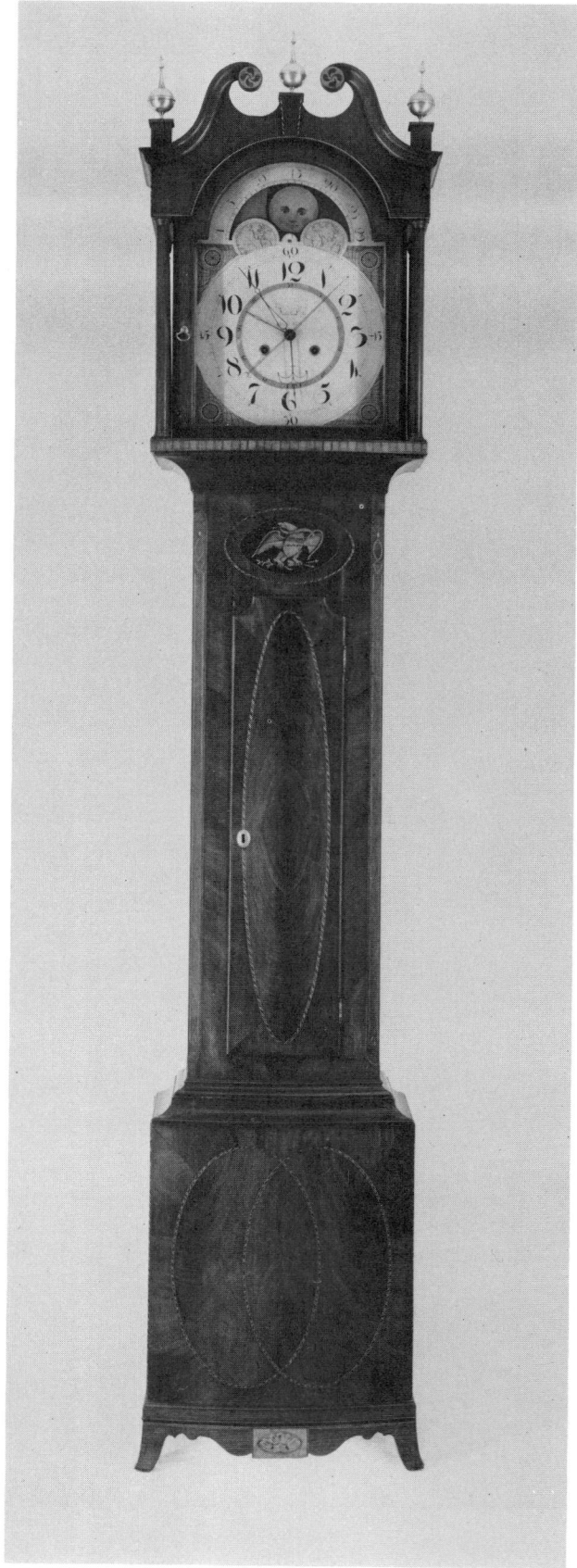

working from 1830 to 1860 in Manheim,[6] but the maker of this clock must have been of an earlier generation. The case has every appearance of being original to the movement and appears earlier than 1830. But better supporting evidence for an earlier date is offered by the iron false plate which is stamped "Patton and Jones, Philadelphia." This partnership was in business in that city only between 1804 and 1814. Less conclusive is the name "New Holland" on one of the hemispheres at the base of the lunette. Although it was renamed Australia in 1814, the dial painter might have used an old atlas as his source.

The eight-day movement has a dead-beat escapement, rack-and-snail striking system, and the standard 39.14 inch pendulum. The lacy hands are most unusual as is the mounting of the sweep second and date-of-month hands at the center of the dial along with those which indicate the minutes and hours. The phases of the moon are shown in the lunette.

Dimensions: height 105; width (bottom of hood) 20; depth 10¼.

Materials: mahogany; light and dark wood inlays; backboard, tulip; other interior woods, white and hard pine.

Accession: 57.627

## 154 TALL CLOCK
*1810–1820 Wilmington, Delaware "George Jones, Wilmington, Del." (working 1803–1850) painted on dial*

The case of this tall clock is one of the most handsomely inlaid and ornamented American examples. As on some other fine furniture with Wilmington associations or histories of ownership, the ornament bears close relationship to that used in both Baltimore and Philadelphia.[7] Inlaid astragal-ended satinwood rectangles with dark elliptical centers are more often found on the finest Philadelphia and New York furniture. Geometrically shaped panels bordered by patterned stringing of such prominent outline are seldom found except on Philadelphia furniture.[8] The shape of the case with its high pitched and narrow swan-neck pediment and French feet is more like cases made in New York and northern New Jersey and Philadelphia than those known for Baltimore. There is an excellent chance that the case was made by a Philadelphia-trained cabinetmaker working in Wilmington.

The dial is richly ornamented with the figure of a girl representing the seasons in each corner and two hemispheres painted at the base of the lunette.

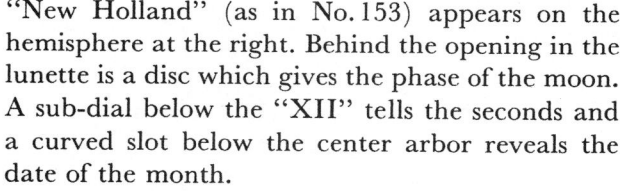

"New Holland" (as in No. 153) appears on the hemisphere at the right. Behind the opening in the lunette is a disc which gives the phase of the moon. A sub-dial below the "XII" tells the seconds and a curved slot below the center arbor reveals the date of the month.

The twenty inlaid stars in the pediment and the two under the volutes may be purely decorative or they may have historical significance. If each star represents a state (there were twenty states in the Union between December 10, 1817, and December 3, 1818), the clock must be rather later than its cabinetwork would indicate. The style of the hands which appears to be of about 1820 supports this view. The eight-day brass movement with rack-and-snail striking system, anchor-recoil escapement, and 39.14 inch pendulum are something of a disappointment since the level of workmanship is below that of the brilliant case.

Dimensions: height 97; width 20½; depth 9¾.

Materials: mahogany and mahogany veneers on cherry; satinwood inlays; backboard, tulip.

Accession: 57.1013

## 155 MASSACHUSETTS WALL CLOCK

*1775–1780　Grafton, Massachusetts　"A. [Aaron] Willard Grafton" (working about 1770–1823) engraved on dial*

Although these ingenious wall clocks were made during the latter part of the Chippendale era, they mark the beginning by the Willards of the trend toward smaller wall clock movements; this ultimately led to the successful development of the relatively inexpensive "patent timepiece" by Simon Willard, elder brother of the maker of this clock.

Perhaps the acute shortage and high price of brass during the American Revolution motivated clockmakers to seek designs for simpler movements requiring a minimum number of parts and the smallest quantity of metal. The movement used in this example has fewer than thirty parts, including screws. This saving of materials and probably of labor was accomplished by sacrificing running time (only thirty hours) and by eliminating the second hand and day-of-the-month indicator. This clock strikes but once an hour.

The version of dead-beat escapement (found on this clock), with pendulum hung directly from the verge shaft, seems to be an innovation of the Willards and is unique to American clocks of this type.

Dimensions: height 28; width 8¾; depth 3½.
Materials: mahogany; no secondary woods.
Provenance: Mrs. Miles White.
Accession: 57.908

## 156  MASSACHUSETTS WALL CLOCK

*About 1780  Roxbury, Massachusetts  "Simon Willard" (working 1766–1839) engraved on brass dial*

The cases of Willard Massachusetts wall clocks of this type give the appearance of being bracket clocks with scroll feet resting on a wall bracket. Bracket clocks were, because of their mechanism, complex and therefore costly; perhaps they served to indicate the elevated status of their possessors. Apparently, the Willards and/or their customers felt that owning something that looked like a bracket clock (even if the simulacrum lacked the bracket clock's mechanical advantages) was almost as good as owning a real bracket clock. This same kind of thinking caused false winding staffs to be painted on the dials of thirty-hour tall clocks (worked by a chain within the case) so that they would appear to be eight-day clocks. Although incorporating a movement with escapement and striking mechanism similar to No. 155, this example is rather more complex since it has a seconds dial (below the "XII") and a date-of-the-month indicator (above the "VI").

Dimensions: height 24; width 8⅞; depth 3¾.
Materials: mahogany; no secondary woods.
Provenance: Frothingham Family (Boston).
Accession: 57.1080

## 157  SHELF CLOCK

*About 1820  Concord, New Hampshire  "T.[Timothy] Chandler (working 1800–1829) Concord" painted on dial*

By the 1820's when this clock was made, Connecticut clocks, mass produced by water power, were already strong competition for movements largely produced by hand. Clockmakers such as Major Timothy Chandler, the maker of this clock, resorted to a number of time- and money-saving short cuts in an effort to survive this competition. Instead of the sawed wooden pierced fretwork familiar in the Roxbury type cases, cast pewter frets

are used here on either side of the simple plinth supporting a cast pewter eagle. Wrought iron plates, with brass inserts at the pivot holes, are used instead of all brass plates for the simple thirty-hour movement, with anchor-recoil escapement which, unlike that of the Massachusetts shelf clocks, has the pendulum hung from the front plate. Apparently to save labor, the brass gears are not spoked, but solid. The sprays of roses which appear to be painted on the boldly numbered dial are actually painted on the glass of the door. Perhaps this was another labor-saving technique. The painting on the dial has been retouched.

Dimensions: height 43½; width 10¼; depth 4¾.
Materials: basswood.
Accession: 57.574

## 158  EXPERIMENTAL CLOCK

*About 1790–1800  Roxbury, Massachusetts  "Simon Willard, Roxbury Street" (working 1766–1839) engraved on plate below dial*

As an example of American interest in the natural sciences and as an earnest of the attempts of Simon

**157**

**158**

Willard to produce instruments that did more than keep time, this clock is important.[9] The evolution of the case from the preceding wall clocks (Nos. 155 and 156) to this extraordinary shelf clock is evident. The shape and treatment of the glazed opening remain the same; but pilasters and feet have been added to the base, the hinged front of which opens to reveal an engraved dial and equation tables for relating mean and solar time. Directions are given to find the day of the month for any day of the week from 1780 to 1860. A pointer and part of the original mechanism, which may have been driven by the clock movement, are missing. The clock, which runs for two days on a winding, has a dead-beat escapement; connected to the verge shaft, a two-piece pendulum rod swings behind the hollowed lead weight which is suspended on a compounded weight cord. The plates anticipate those of Simon Willard's patent timepiece, now known as the "banjo clock."

Dimensions: height 28¾; width 11½; depth 4.
Materials: mahogany; white pine.
Accession: 65.2275

**159** WALL CLOCK or "Patent Timepiece"
*1802–1810   Roxbury, Massachusetts   "S. Willards Patent" painted on door*

Although he permitted others to sign their clocks "S.Willards Patent," several features of the movement of this fine "presentation" clock (called a "patent timepiece" by Simon Willard, and patented in 1802) suggest that it was actually made in his "Clock Manufactory." The thin spearlike hands, the "T"-bridge method of hanging the pendulum, the slight rounding of the tops of the brass plates of the larger-than-usual movement, the curved teeth of the escape wheel, and the well-finished lead weight are all in accord with practices followed in Simon Willard's shop. The escapement on this clock is the normal anchor-recoil type. (He did not always use the dead-beat escapement.)

Presentation clocks, believed to have been made for weddings or other special occasions, were sometimes ornamented chiefly in white and gold. On this one, the sides of the case, the dial, and the background of the glass tablets are all painted white. The well-carved eagle, original bracket, facings, and ornament are in gold leaf. The face of the "man in the moon" and silhouetted eagle on the upper and lower tablets are special touches. Both tablets are signed on the reverse in red paint "Willard & Nolen, Boston." Aaron Willard, Jr., and his brother-in-law Spencer Nolen were ornamental painters in partnership in Boston from about 1805 to 1809.

Dimensions: height 42; width 10¼; depth 4.
Materials: mahogany painted white; eagle, "twist," and corner blocks, white pine ornamented with gold leaf.
Provenance: Mrs. William Page Andrews; Karl E. Weston.
Accession: 57.952

**160** WALL CLOCK
*About 1813–1815   Boston, Massachusetts   "Willard's Patent" painted on glass mid-section*

The dial of this clock, ornamented only by very stylish arabic numerals and thin spearlike hands, provides a foil for the center glass which is stencilled and painted with multicolored flowers, leaves, and stringing. At the bottom of this glass is written "Willard's Patent" indicating that the clock may well have been made by a former apprentice of Willard's since Simon Willard himself adhered to far plainer and more geometric designs for the glass tablets in the waist and bottom door.

A naval battle between two ships (identified

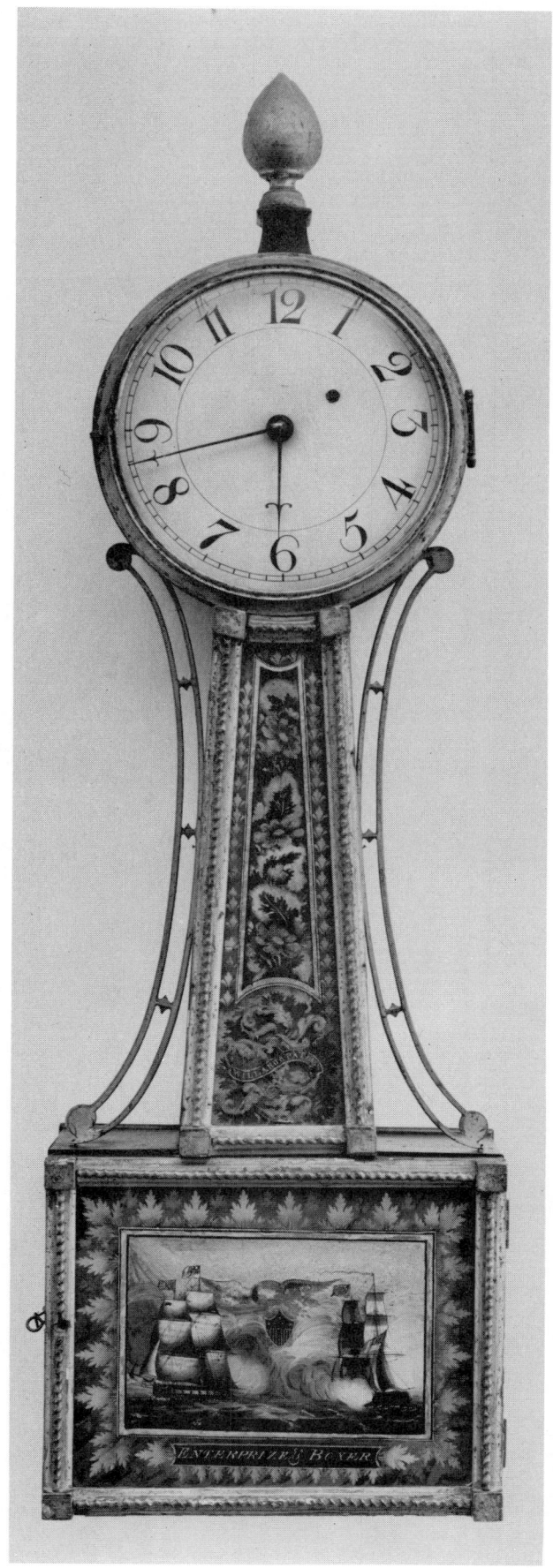

**161**

beneath the scene as the *Enterprise* and the *Boxer*), which are separated by a stylized eagle and shield, is painted in a rectangle centered in the lower glass and framed by a stencilled border of leaves. The clock probably dates within a few years of the naval battle. The eight-day movement with anchor-recoil escapement is similar to the movements of Simon Willard although it lacks the usual T-bridge suspension as well as plates with curved tops characteristically used by him.

Dimensions: height 33; width 10; depth 4.
Materials: mahogany; door, white pine; corner blocks, mahogany.
Accession: 57.1062

## 161 WALL CLOCK
*1810–1820    Salem or Boston    "Jabez Baldwin" (working 1800–1829) painted on lower glass*

Dark mahogany has been used for the case of this "diamond head banjo clock," a rare variant of a form usually finished in gold leaf. The effect is rich and imposing and one of contrast between the figured mahogany and the gracefully ornamented painted dial and tablet in the lower door. The severity of the flat surfaces is relieved by reeding on the upper part of the waist panel and on the plinth for the original turned gilt finial.

Whereas the improved timepiece patented by Simon Willard in 1802 had the escape wheel and verge located near the top of the movement, in this eight-day movement with anchor-recoil escapement they are positioned near the bottom of the front plate. Jabez Baldwin, who was apprenticed to Thomas Harland in Norwich, Connecticut, settled in Salem, Massachusetts, about 1800. He moved to Boston around 1815.[10]

Dimensions: height 39; width 11½; depth 4.
Materials: mahogany; mahogany veneers over white pine; back, white pine.
Accession: 57.645

## 162 WALL CLOCK
*1825–1840    Boston, Massachusetts*

Lushly carved side brackets with rich, bronze powder stencilling give this timepiece something of the appearance of the lyre clocks which were popular after about 1820 and relate the case to the stencilled furniture being produced in quantity from the 1820's through the 1840's. Scratched on the front plate is the following: "Cleaned by E. Taber March 16, 1847" and "Tho⁵ Taber Aug

**164**

**WALL CLOCK**, Girandole Case
*1820–1825   Northern New England*

This may be a unique girandole clock. The most ornate and elaborate of American wall clocks, the girandole is essentially a banjo clock with a round convex glass at the bottom and with scrolled side brackets and support. It takes its name from the circular mirrors with convex glasses popular at the time of its manufacture. Designed and patented by Lemuel Curtis in 1816 while he was still in Concord, Massachusetts, and before he moved to Burlington, Vermont (in 1821), the girandole type is rare today and much admired by collectors. This clock by an unidentified maker lacks the finesse of painting, carving, and details of construction of movement—especially the beautifully machined gears and plates, intricate hands, and small neat figures on the painted dials—found in documented Curtis examples.

Vestiges of a nicely painted scene depicting three girls in neoclassical costume playing "blindman's buff" are found on the convex bottom glass ringed by a glory of gilt composition balls. Above this, the glass waist panel, ornamented with grape leaves and tendrils stencilled in gold leaf and colors, is delicate in comparison to the flamboyant carved and gilt wood scrolls which frame all but the dial of the clock. The eight-day movement, similar to that of a banjo clock, has an anchor-recoil escapement, and the pendulum is hung from the front plate.

Dimensions: height 44; width 15.
Materials: mahogany; eagle, side brackets, frames at lower door, and waist panel, white pine.
Accession: 57.713

**164** **WALL CLOCK**
*1800–1830   Exeter, New Hampshire (?)   Attributed to Benjamin Clark Gilman, Exeter, New Hampshire (working about 1785–1835)*

This rare and interesting clockcase matches one owned, as of 1943, by a descendant of Benjamin Clark Gilman, a versatile engineer, silversmith, and clockmaker of Exeter, New Hampshire.[11] It was known in the family as the "Bunker Hill Clock," and said originally to have "possessed a brass face with the maker's usual legend 'B. C. Gilman/ Exeter.'"[12] Neither case bears more than a tenuous resemblance to the Bunker Hill monument which was constructed in the years following 1825; but, if Gilman designed the clock after the monument, he must have done so in the last ten years of his

1858." Elnathan Taber (1768–1854) and Thomas Taber, his son, were both Roxbury clockmakers. Elnathan served his apprenticeship under Simon Willard and, although he had his own shop, made many clocks for both Simon and Aaron Willard. Possibly he made this clock, but there is no evidence to that effect.

The bottom glass, with pendulum peephole, is decorated with a lively scene of either Aurora or Colombia drawn by two horselike beasts. The eight-day movement has the standard anchor-recoil escapement.

Dimensions: height 40; width 11; depth 4.
Materials: case, mahogany; back and frames of center panel and lower door, cherry; corner blocks, white pine.
Accession: 57.978

life. It is not definitely known whether Gilman himself made either of the cases although they appear to be the product of the same hand. The gears and teeth in the matching Gilman family clock and in others bearing his name are described as being smaller and finer than is usual in wall-clock movements. Such is the case with those in this small eight-day movement related to those found in "banjo" clocks. It has an anchor-recoil escapement with the pendulum supported behind the pierced backplate on a metal strap, with a nut on the top of the case for adjustment. The dial of the clock shown here (lacking hands) is protected by the glass and rim of a pocket watch hung from a brass pin, therefore giving the impression of a watch hung from an oversized watchbox. A keen sense of humor is evident in Gilman's correspondence; a sense of humor to which the idea of an eight-day "watch" might have appealed.

The Greek-key border inlaid on the upper molding is similar to inlays found on several pieces of furniture of northeastern Massachusetts and New Hampshire provenance.

Dimensions: height 30½; width 9; depth 4½.
Materials: mahogany veneers on tilia (basswood) with cross bandings of rosewood; light and dark wood stringing; seat board for movement, cherry; baseboard, white pine.
Provenance: Miss Mary Hatch, granddaughter of Thomas Hatch of Exeter, New Hampshire.
Accession: 57.605

### 165  BRACKET CLOCK
*1800    Roxbury, Massachusetts    "Aaron Willard" (working 1780–1823) painted on dial*

Probably only a few movements for bracket clocks were made in the United States during the Federal period, and not many with the name of an American clockmaker on their dials exist today. But of those known, perhaps as few as one in five were made in this country, the rest having been imported and the name added here by the seller. Therefore, this clock and the two following (Nos. 166 and 167), whose identification is less secure but which are believed to have been American made, are exceptionally rare. Their infrequent manufacture here is probably due to the difficulty of tempering the steel spring and of making the brass fusee and spring barrel. This eight-day movement is an innovation. It employs the usual anchor-recoil type escapement, common to eighteenth-century and later tall clocks, instead of the crown wheel and verge with short bob pendulum nor-

mally used by English clockmakers on this kind of clock.

As in a tall clock, the pendulum is lens shaped and suspended from a balance cock on a flattened spring. The iron dial, painted with an urn of flowers in the lunette and complementary sprays in the spandrels, is pierced above the "VI" with a slot to reveal the date of the month. The mahogany case is similar to many English bracket clockcases except for the rather large wooden ogee bracket feet and the brass inlaid quarter columns which are similar to those used on Roxbury tall clocks.

Dimensions: height 22; width 13½; depth 7⅝.
Materials: mahogany and mahogany veneer over white pine.
Accession: 57.1081

### 166  BRACKET CLOCK
*1797–1799    New York City    "Stephen Van Wyck New York" (working 1797–1824) engraved on dial*

Such handsome brass dials as that on this clock were rarely made as late as this one seems to have

**165**

**166**

**167**

been. The name of Stephen Van Wyck, its maker, is listed in the New York City directories from 1797 to 1799 as both a clock- and watchmaker; after that time until 1824, as a watchmaker only.

The well-made eight-day, spring-powered movement has a crown wheel and verge escapement and short bob pendulum. As is normal in bracket clocks, the power of the springs is equalized by the use of fusees connected to the great wheel. A switch in the lunette permits the striking mechanism to be turned off at night; the date of the month is shown on a small dial above the "VI." The backplate as well as the dial is engraved, the latter with rosettes and a garland, the former with floral bands and a lozenge. The mahogany case with brass bracket feet and cast-brass grills in the sidelights is similar to English examples of the last quarter of the eighteenth century and may have been refitted with an American movement.

Dimensions: height 19; width 12; depth 8.

Materials: mahogany veneer on white oak; inner shelf, mahogany supported on spruce blocks.

Accession: 57.1091

**167** BRACKET CLOCK

*1795–1810   Philadelphia (?)   "Tho: Parker Philadelphia" (working 1783–1835) engraved on backplate*

The unornamented painted iron dial on this clock has a switch in the lunette with two positions, "Strike" and "Peace," for activating or silencing the striking mechanism. That "Peace" is used instead of "Silent" suggests Quakerly overtones for this Philadelphia clock. Both the plain dial which has been overpainted and the highly engraved backplate are in accord with English usage. On the latter, amidst lavish rococo ornament, "Tho: Parker Philadelphia" is engraved in flourishing script. Thomas Parker, born in 1761, started his own shop in 1783 after serving his apprenticeship under the great Philadelphia clockmaker, David Rittenhouse.

The fine eight-day movement retains its original crown wheel with horizontal verge escapement, but the pendulum bob is missing, as is the date-of-the-month hand. The case is typical of English examples.

Dimensions: height 19; width 9½; depth 6½.
Materials: mahogany veneers on a hard maple of an as
   yet unidentified species.
Accession: 59.641

### 168 MASSACHUSETTS SHELF CLOCK
*1790–1795    Newburyport, Massachusetts    "Dan!
Balch Jn! Newbury Port" (working 1790–1835) engraved on the dial*

The case of this shelf clock must be ranked as one
of the most original and unusual of all American
clockcases. Its maker and presumably its originator
also probably furnished the cases of similar design
found containing movements made by David Wood
of Newburyport[13] and William Fitz of Portsmouth,
New Hampshire.[14]

Architectonic in quality, the case with scrolled
pediment, engaged and reeded pilasters, arches
and base moldings reminiscent of steps, resembles
a miniature clock tower. Architectural treatment
of clockcases seems only logical since a high proportion of the first mechanical clocks were made
for towers. Although the style of this clockcase
(except for the banding and fans) is suggestive of
an earlier date, it was actually made after 1790
since Daniel Balch, Jr., succeeded his father in
business in that year.

The movement is essentially a small-scale version
of a standard tall-clock movement with rack and
snail striking system, anchor-recoil escapement and
pendulum hung in tall clock fashion from the
balance cock on the backplate. The trains for the
weight-driven, full-striking movement which runs
only two days are both wound through staffs in the
silvered brass dial.

Dimensions: height 29; width 16; depth 6½.
Materials: mahogany inlaid with lighter woods; curved
   hood and backboard, white pine.
Accession: 57.628

### 169 MASSACHUSETTS SHELF CLOCK
*About 1800    Newburyport, Massachusetts    "D.[David]
Wood" (working 1792 until after 1824) painted on
dial*

The articulated quality of the deep cove above the
door, the lively tracery of the cresting, the cast
brass eagle, the select mahogany used in the lower
door, the chaste stringing, and the shield-shaped
inlays give special character to this fine clock with
a movement by the versatile and prolific Newburyport clockmaker David Wood. The finely painted

dial, the rococo hands, and the brass handles at the sides—usually found only on large case furniture—further the impression of richness.

The two-day movement with the usual anchor-recoil escapement has a pendulum which hangs from the balance cock mounted on the back side of the rear plate. The bell, affixed to the left of the movement, is struck once on the hour. The great wheel is mounted at the 8:45 o'clock position instead of the 3:15 o'clock position as is standard in David Wood movements. On the backboard is pasted a label reading, "Daniel T. Smith, formerly Jesse Smith, watches, clocks, spectacles, eye glasses etc. 241 Essex St. Salem, Mass." Since Daniel Treadway Smith was born in 1824 and is not recorded as being in business before 1846,[15] this label must have been added at a time of a repair or a cleaning.

Dimensions: height 35; width 13; depth 6½.
Materials: mahogany veneer over white pine, inlaid with light and dark woods.
Accession: 57.1092

**170** MASSACHUSETTS SHELF CLOCK

*1810–1820 Newburyport, Massachusetts "Newburyport" painted on dial Attributed to David Wood, Newburyport (working 1792 until after 1824)*

Despite the rather naive quality of the inlaid drapery and bumpy outline of the crest, the maker of this clock was well aware of the fashionable attributes of early nineteenth-century furniture. Patterned stringing and dentiled inlays have been used to good effect as a frame for the handsome dial with illusionistic fan decoration in the spandrels and a dramatic marine view in the lunette. A broad panel of figured maple in the lower door, French splayed feet, cast-brass lionhead side handles, and quarter columns with bases and capitols of brass are all indicative of the pains taken to make this a stylish clock.

Signs of the Zodiac are revealed one at a time as they revolve briskly on a disk behind a slot under the "XII." This unusual device seems only to indicate that the clock is running. The two-day movement has an anchor-recoil escapement, and its pendulum is located behind the weight directly in front of the backboard. Although the dial of this clock is marked only "Newburyport," the similarities between it and signed David Wood clocks (see No. 171) are so close that the attribution seems a firm one.

Dimensions: height 36; width 12; depth 6.
Materials: mahogany; white pine veneered with mahogany inlaid with figured maple and other woods.
Accession: 57.801                    see Inlay Fig. 12

**171** MASSACHUSETTS SHELF CLOCK

*About 1815 Newburyport, Massachusetts "D. [David] Wood" (working 1792 until after 1824) painted on dial and engraved label of David Wood is pasted inside the door*

This David Wood clock, although less richly ornamented than the two preceding examples, is of special significance because of its original bracket whose inlays match those on the clockcase. The upper section seems plain in comparison with the base, but the over-all character of this case is similar to that of No. 170. The dial bears only traces of the maker's name. However, a watch paper with his name and directions for regulating the clock is pasted inside the lower door. The two-day movement with an anchor-recoil escapement is almost identical to the movement of No. 170. An interesting touch is the inclusion of a naval engagement painted in the arch above the dial. Unfortu-

nately, its condition, like that of the dial, is somewhat faded.

Dimensions: height 32½; width 11⅝; depth 5¾.
Materials: mahogany and mahogany veneers on white pine with satinwood and dark wood inlays; corner blocks, seat board, and back, white pine.
Accession: 57.995

**172** MASSACHUSETTS SHELF CLOCK

*1800–1810 Boston, Massachusetts "Aaron Willard" (working 1780–1823) and "Boston" painted on face*

The circle of the restrained dial of this clock is echoed by the roundel of fine mahogany veneer in the base; complex two-dimensional curves in the cresting are answered by the three-dimensional curves of the French bracket feet. The convex moldings at the top and base find correspondence in the concave molding at the waist. Sparing but refined inlay further enhances and repeats larger and more obvious shapes, and a gilt cartouche below the dial relieves the mass of rich mahogany. The eight-day movement with anchor-recoil escapement and half-second pendulum in this clock

**171**

**172**

**173**

is essentially the same as those used in the Willard "Patent Timepieces" ("banjo clocks") with the differences that here the weight falls in front of the pendulum (unlike the banjo clock whose pendulum swings in front of the weight which runs in a channel flat against the backboard) and the pendulum is hung from a balance cock which, as in the case of tall clocks, is mounted on the back side of the backplate.

Dimensions: height 36; width 14½; depth 6½.

Materials: mahogany inlaid with light and dark woods; back panel and bottom, white pine; base framing, a spruce.

Accession: 57.920          see Inlay Figs. 17, 55

### 173  MASSACHUSETTS SHELF CLOCK
*1810–1820  Boston, Massachusetts  "Aaron Willard" (working 1780–1823) and "Boston" painted on face*

The case of this clock is a later and far less brilliantly conceived version of No. 172. The movement is nearly identical to that one and other Aaron Willard shelf clocks. Both have anchor-

recoil escapements and half-second pendulums which swing behind the weight. On this movement are scratched two inscriptions, "E. G. Brewster 1820" and "... M. Shearman March 27, 1829," which are presumably the marks of clock cleaners. The hour hand is a replacement.

Dimensions: height 33; width 13¼; depth 6.

Materials: mahogany; mahogany veneer and light wood inlays; secondary wood, white pine.

Accession: 61.1732

### 174  PARLOR TABLE CLOCK
*About 1800  English (?)*

Stop-fluted columns, sophisticated brass swags, a cast-brass eagle, and a mirror behind the pendulum give this table clock of mahogany with light wood inlays a handsome effect. If the case is American, it must be classified as unique. The partially repainted mahogany dial is screwed to an iron false plate. The eight-day movement is very much like those used in bracket clocks but lacks a striking mechanism. Although the move-

ment is by and large well finished, the presence of several casting flaws may point to an American origin though the use of spruce as a secondary wood suggests an English origin.

Dimensions: height 33; width 14; depth 7¼.
Materials: mahogany; back panel for mirror, spruce.
Accession: 59.578

## 175 EDDYSTONE LIGHTHOUSE ALARM TIMEPIECE

*1819–1830   Roxbury, Massachusetts   "Simon Willard" (working 1766–1839) painted on dial*

The dial of this clock, mounted in a glass dome (replaced), is capped by a silvered bell with matching knob. The dial itself, banded by a cast-brass rim, has at its center an "alarm set" dial. The movement, with a dead-beat escapement and half-second pendulum, does not strike the hour, serving only for the alarm which sounds but briefly. The glass dome need be removed only for the weekly winding as the alarm can be wound by pulling a string which runs under the dome.

Patented by Simon Willard in 1819 (according to his biographer John Ware Willard), the idea of the "Eddystone Lighthouse Alarm Timepiece" is believed to be, in both movement and case, original to Willard. Apparently less popular when introduced than was his other patented timepiece—the banjo clock—only a few original examples are known, probably less than thirty. But these clocks, with their lustrous grained mahogany and cast-brass mounts, as finely finished as on French clocks, are so desirable today that even replicas are highly coveted.

Dimensions: height 30; width 9½; depth 9½.

Materials: mahogany and mahogany veneer on white pine; bottom, white pine.

Accession: 57.1011

## FOOTNOTES

1 Sale Catalogue of the *Property of Mr. and Mrs. Norvin H. Green* (New York: Parke-Bernet Galleries, November 29 and 30, December 1 and 2, 1950), p. 108, No. 487.

2 Identification of the makers of the movement and case as the work of father and son is possible through an outstanding study by Charles F. Hummel of this family of craftsmen, their records, tools, cabinetwares, and clocks. It will be published in the near future and will provide much new information on the work and methods of non-urban craftsmen in the United States.

3 So called on original bill. DMMC. M-310, microfilm copy of the original in the East Hampton (New York) Free Library. It reads:

David Gardiner to Nath.! Dominy

To an Horologiographical, Repeating, Alarm, Monition-Clock

| | | |
|---|---|---|
| at 90 Dollars – – – – – – – – – – – – – – – | £36-0-0 |
| Per Contra | – – – – |

By the Face which is on the above s<sup>d</sup>

| | |
|---|---|
| Clock – – – – – – – – – – – – – – – – – – – | 1:16:0 |
| By Weights that I expect him to procure | 0:8:0 |

By Cash which I Rec<sup>d</sup> of Josiah Hedges Viz

| | |
|---|---|
| 60 Doll<sup>s</sup>, | 24:0:0 |

Easthampton        Nathaniel Dominy
Nov. 6th 1799

At the bottom of the bill is a letter of instructions:

Sir I send the Clock by Capt. Moses Clark with the following (but perhaps needless) instructions for seting it up—Viz 1st Take out those things which are deposited in the bottom of the Case—then take it out of the Box and rear it where you intend it shall stand—next relieve the Pendulum Rod & hang the Bob thereon—erect the Case by the lower end of the Bob spear & the black perpendicular line on the middle of the Back, leaning it a little back, that the Alarm Weight may bare lightly against the back & also that the large Weights may the better clear the top of the Pedestal. Thus fix<sup>d</sup>, secure it to the Wall thr'o the back near the top of the lower Door, & at bottom steddy it by Cleats on the Room floor. Now relieve the Cords, let the staples over the Alarm-cords remain, hang the Weights on & put her in motion – – – –

Easthampton        From your Friend Nath.! Dominy
6 Nov. 1799

N.B. You must draw the Nails from the top of the Head & the Key at the bottom within the front of D° before the S<sup>d</sup> head can be taken of—also the Bolt which peeps thr'o the Face must be drawn downward before she'll Strike

4 Edward La Fond, Jr., Curator of the Chester County Historical Society.

5 The only other clock known to Mr. La Fond with these unusual characteristics is one signed by "George Hoff Lancaster" on its brass dial, owned by Stanley Todd of Churchtown, Pennsylvania.

6 Brooks Palmer, *The Book of American Clocks* (New York: The Macmillan Co., 1950), p. 186.

7 Three secretaries with bookcases owned in Wilmington and with Wilmington histories have pierced fretwork, scrolled pediments, and inlaid fret designs on the friezes. The latter are much like work attributed to Baltimore, but they seem more likely to have been made in Wilmington or possibly Philadelphia.

8 A tall clock made in Germantown, Pennsylvania, now in the collection of Mrs. Duncan I. Selfridge, is similar to this one in general form and type of ornament.

9 A similar example (complete with astronomical disk) owned by the Historical Society of Dedham, Massachusetts, is illustrated and discussed by Lockwood Barr in "An 'Unique' Willard Timepiece," *Bulletin of the National Association of Clock Collectors, Inc.,* IX (December, 1959), 16.

10 Brooks Palmer, op. cit., p. 143.

11 Frank O. Spinney, "An Ingenious Yankee Craftsman," *Antiques,* XLIV (September, 1943), 116–119.

12 *Ibid.* See also an article on this clock by Hugh Grant Rowell in *American Collector,* August, 1943.

13 Albert Sack, *Fine Points of Furniture: Early American* (New York: Crown Publishers, 1950), p. 131.

14 Carl W. Dreppard, *American Clocks and Clockmakers* (Boston: C. T. Branford Co., 1958), p. 184.

15 Information furnished by Dean A. Fales, Jr., Director of the Essex Institute, and from Brooks Palmer, op. cit., p. 228.

# Desks and Bookcases

*Including Secretaries and Writing Tables*

In 1788, Hepplewhite illustrated several slant-top "desks and bookcases" and remarked, "The dimensions of this article, will in general, be regulated by the height of the room, the place where it must stand, or the particular use to which it is destined." But by about 1800 the slant-top desk had become old-fashioned and was infrequently made except in rural areas. Under the heading, "Bureau," the name generally used by the English to denote a slant-top desk, Sheraton noted in his *Cabinet Dictionary*, "These pieces of furniture are nearly obsolete in London; at least they are so amongst fashionable people. I have, however, endeavoured to retrieve their obscurity, by adding to them an open book case, and modernizing the lower part, as in plate 23, where they are called Bureau Bookcases."[1]

The many new forms devised to provide facilities for writing seem to parallel the new emphasis on education and, particularly, the rise in the number of girls' schools. Sheraton illustrates several designs that are feminine in appearance and small in scale, such as a "Ladies Drawing and Writing Table," a "Ladies Cabinet and Writing Table," a "Ladies Writing Table," and a "Ladies Cylinder Writing Table." He devotes six pages in the *Cabinet Dictionary* to a "narrative of the origin of books" and paper, and notes "the multiplied demands that have been [made] for bookcases of late years, which in some manufactories have been the leading articles of employ."[2] One goal of the writer has been to determine, where possible, the old names current when the pieces were made. Those listed and described below seem to be the formal and better-known ones. The term "writing table" seems to have been reserved for those pieces with not more than one long drawer in the lower section and long legs. The price books made a clear differentiation between a "tambour" writing table with one long drawer (which might be divided into shorter ones) in front and plain taper legs and a tambour desk with three drawers in front and common bracket feet. Exactly the same differentiation in specifications is made for a "cylinder fall writing table" and a "cylinder fall desk," a new English form which never became widely popular in the United States, illustrated here by Nos. 194 and 195.

The chief innovation introduced in the last quarter of the eighteenth century is the "secretary drawer" for writing. This type of drawer was often incorporated in a bookcase (No. 178) or as the upper drawer in a chest of drawers. In contrast to the then outmoded slant-top desk, this drawer is not sloped in front and in Hepplewhite's words provided accommodations for writing "by the face of the upper drawer falling down by means of a spring and quadrant, which produces the same usefulness as the flap to a desk."[3]

*Gentlemen's Secretary.* For this, there is not a good modern name, though a common American version is usually known as a Salem secretary after its place of origin.

Similar forms (No. 182) which also may be of Salem or possibly Boston workmanship have turned legs of about the same length.

*Secretary, Escritoir* (also known as *Scrutoir*). A chest of drawers with a secretary drawer at the top and known today as a "butler's desk."

*A Lady's Cabinet and Writing Table*. A design for this very feminine furniture form, derived from the French *Bonheur de Jour,* is illustrated as Plate 50 in Sheraton's *Drawing Book,* 1794, and almost exactly repeated in this collection by No. 188.

Another type of writing drawer is frequently found in sewing tables and small multiple-purpose tables called writing tables. This writing drawer is fitted with compartments for pens, ink, and other writing equipment (No. 198) and an adjustable writing surface, finished with baize or leather, that may be raised or lowered.

Tambour Desk is the modern term for a popular form frequently made in New England. Apparently without exact English antecedents, it is more closely related to the above Lady's Cabinet and Writing Table than the English Tambour Writing Tables illustrated in Hepplewhite's *Guide* and most English editions of the cabinet-makers' price books. The American tambour desk has upright reeded or slatted shutters that cover up the "nest of drawers" and pigeonholes. These shutters slide from the center outward in a vertical plan in contrast to those of the English tambour writing table. The latter usually is a modification of the cylinder desk with tambour shutters instead of a curved solid cylinder. Two labeled examples, No. 184 in the Winterthur collection and the well-known satinwood *tour-de-force* in the George Cluett estate,[4] provide clues for the identification of many desks of this type as the work of John Seymour and his son, Thomas, cabinetmakers first in Portland, Maine, and later in Boston. However, labeled examples of ladies' desks and ladies' desks and bookcases by other cabinetmakers working in the Boston and Salem areas are known.

The cost of desks ranged from twenty to one hundred dollars. Considering their cost, it is surprising how many were made and how many have survived today.

1 Sheraton, *The Cabinet Dictionary* (London, 1803), p. 111.
2 *Ibid.,* pp. 70–71.
3 *The Cabinet-Maker and Upholsterer's Guide,* 1788.
4 Stoneman, op. cit., pp. 48–51.

## XVII Federal Parlor

*In 1788 Oliver Phelps purchased the Burbank House (now known as the Phelps-Hatheway House) in Suffield, Massachusetts. In the 1790's having become rich as a speculator in western land, he remodeled the existing structure and added a wing containing, on the ground floor, a hall and two parlors. This neoclassical woodwork with composition ornament and the French wallpaper in the "Etruscan style" came from one of the parlors. Phelps patronized local craftsmen and bought furnishings in New York and Boston as well. The furniture illustrated, although not original to the room, was probably made nearby. Both the desk and bookcase (No. 177) and the shield-back chairs (Nos. 46 and 48) reflect the highest style of southern New England design and craftsmanship.*

**176**

## 176 DESK AND BOOKCASE
*1785–1795 Massachusetts, Boston Area*

Joseph Barrell, a wealthy Boston merchant, completed in 1793 a country seat known as Pleasant Hill. Located between Boston and Charlestown and built after plans prepared by Charles Bullfinch, it was described by a traveler while it was under construction. "It will be the largest, ... [and] I think it will be infinitely the most elegant dwelling house ever yet built in New England. It commands the most beautiful views imaginable."[1] Barrell's fabulous gardens were tended by gardeners brought from Holland, and his greenhouse is reputed to have been two hundred feet long.

This desk and bookcase, originally owned by Barrell, may have been made for his new house, or slightly earlier for his fine house "elegant in all its furniture"[2] on Summer Street, at that time the most beautiful street in Boston. In terms of craftsmanship and flamboyance, this piece of furniture matches the legendary exploits of a man with the means and the will to command the best—a man who repeatedly in orders for furnishings used such phrases as "be sure the mirrors [from France] are without any flaw or defect of any kind"; "I want an elegant Lustre for my oval room ... that is light airy and elegant"; "If you meet with a handsome cover for a [dining] table of looking glass, and a pyramid of handsome cut glass for the middle of the table ... I wish you would buy them."[3]

There is little doubt that this desk and bookcase and that illustrated in Downs, No. 227, are from the same shop. The design and construction of the bases are identical in almost every detail except for the brasses. Also, the unusual design and the conception of the bookcases are similar—in each a broad mirrored door conceals bookshelves, and on either side behind hinged pilasters are narrow compartments with shelves. But whereas the bookcase of Downs is highly rococo and in accord with the base, the cabinetmaker saw fit to bring the bookcase of this later example up to date, utilizing a higher pitched arch and a wealth of superbly carved neoclassical ornament, including round and oval paterae, wreaths, ribbons, festoons of beading and husks, a ram's head, and ox skulls. For the pilasters, instead of the composite, he used the Corinthian order. The figures, perhaps Commerce flanked by Justice and Agriculture, are among the finest American examples of the carver's art. Although they cannot be attributed to a specific hand, there were in Boston at this time several highly skilled carvers, including John and Simeon

Skillin.[4] The silvered glass is old but a replacement. The ends of the long drawers conform in shape to the curve of the carcass, and there are "dust boards," or full dividers, between each drawer, the upper two of which originally were divided into several sections.

Dimensions: height 95; width (desk) 34, (bombé) 37, (bookcase) 31½; depth 19½.

Materials: mahogany, including interior shelves, back panels, and sides of small drawer in upper section.[5] The bottoms of these drawers are of white pine, as is all other secondary wood.

Provenance: Originally owned by Joseph Barrell; later owned by Hannah Barrell Joy, John B. Joy, Charles H. Joy, Benjamin Joy.

Accession: 56.23

## 177 DESK AND BOOKCASE
### *1790–1810    Connecticut or Rhode Island*

Among the first rank of furniture in the Federal period stands this desk and bookcase. Of moderate size, it is shaped with an exacting nicety, and each element is given emphasis by an appropriate amount of ornament calculated to suit its position. The ropelike stringing outlining the bracket feet, the airy vines accenting the drawer escutcheons, the flowering sprays in contrasting colors on the old-fashioned sloping desk lid, and the pendants of the chamfered corners deftly balance the more spectacular doors of the bookcase and the fantastically intricate tracery of the pediment. The whole work is a *tour-de-force*, closely related to a desk and bookcase, with flat top and undoubtedly by the same hand, in the Barbour Collection of the Connecticut Historical Society.[6] Two details, the carved urn at the top and the inverted "icicle" inlaid on the corners, are reminders of the Hepplewhite chairs made for the Hartford State House in 1796 by Kneeland and Adams. This at least suggests a regional affinity, but the over-all treatment of inlay is so similar to that of a desk and bookcase labeled by Webb and Scott of Providence, Rhode Island,[7] as to suggest that locale as its place of origin.

The interior of the bookcase is divided into six compartments to hold ledgers, and the interior of the desk has eight scallop-topped pigeonholes, centered on a cupboard door inlaid with a wavy patera in a diamond-shaped form. For added strength, the pierced scrolls of the pediment are laminated in two layers. No locks were applied to two of the lower drawers; the false keyhole escutcheons played their part as ornament.

Dimensions: height 92½; width 41¼; depth 20½.

Materials: cherry inlaid with mahogany and light and dark woods; all secondary wood, white pine.

Provenance: Wheelwright Family of Boston.

Accession: 57.885        see Inlay Figs. 64, 65, 103, 108

## 178 SECRETARY AND BOOKCASE
### *1795–1804   Salem, Massachusetts   Label of William Appleton (working about 1794–1822)*

Inasmuch as William Appleton was located at the corner of Charter and Liberty Streets in Salem (the address on the label) only from 1795 to 1804, this desk may be one of the earliest American examples with the then-new secretary drawer. The first illustration of such a "secretary and bookcase" appears in Hepplewhite's *Guide* (Pl. 44, dated 1787). It is of the same general design as this one, but with different doors (see No. 181) and without the swan-neck pediment.

Two other secretary and bookcases can be attributed to Appleton's shop by comparison with this one.[8] Not only do they have the same form, but ornamental stringing is employed in the same way

**178**

**179**

to emphasize the outlines of the bracket feet, drawers, doors, and tympanum. All three include the interlacing and diamond motif on the frieze. The cornice is detachable.

In 1803, William Appleton was one of the ten Salem cabinetmakers who shipped furniture to the coast of Brazil "in trust," aboard the brig *Welcome* in charge of Jeremiah Briggs, master. Among the fifty cases of mahogany furniture, the largest consignments, from Elijah and Jacob Sanderson and Nehemiah Adams, were valued at $1337, $975, and $1187 respectively, and that of Appleton at $450.50.[9] In another shipment sent out by Appleton with the Sandersons in 1805, the most expensive item is "one secretary bookcase—$60."

An inscription on the bottom of a small drawer reads:

Lewis B. Ziegler
Woodland Heights
February 22, 1800

The identity of Ziegler and the exact location of

that follow have been called Salem desks or Salem secretaries.[10] A dozen or more examples are known. Three, including this secretary, all with the label of Edmund Johnson, display the same form and concept of ornament. One of these, owned by Mrs. Walter Wright in 1926,[11] appears identical to this one except for variations in the stringing. The other secretary, in the Henry Ford Museum,[12] substitutes heavier ebony line stringing on the pilasters for the light fulsome bellflowers and intervening ebony dots and pointed ovals seen on this example.

The use of single-line stringing, often of light wood but sometimes of triple stringing (ebony or stained holly between two white lines), to form panels is a feature frequently found on Salem and North Shore cabinetwork. Occasionally, on furniture feet of that area, as on the piece shown here, the stringing lines run into the floor. The eagle finial, which is like that on the Wright secretary, and the brasses appear to be original. The brass, spired, ball-shaped finials are probably replacements, as are the old drawer pulls stamped with a classical figure with a ship in the background.

Dimensions: height 94; width 66¼; depth 18½.

Materials: mahogany and mahogany veneer inlaid with light and dark woods over white pine; secondary woods, white pine.

Accession: 57.844                    see Inlay Fig. 93

## 180  GENTLEMAN'S SECRETARY
### Secretary and Bookcase
*About 1800   Salem or, possibly, Newburyport, Massachusetts*

Such secretary and bookcases as this one and Nos. 179, 181 and 182 are probably among the most important forms made by Salem and nearby cabinetmakers.[13] There is comparatively little variation in the over-all form of such pieces; but, as may be observed in these four and in others in public and private collections, they consist of two or sometimes three principal parts: an upper section, which may be one or two parts depending on whether the cornice of undulating outline is fixed or removable, and a lower section with drawer and cabinet at either end, which is fitted with a long "secretary" drawer in the middle. The disposition of the space below the writing drawer accounts for the chief variation of form. In some the space is left open (No. 181), in some it is fitted with one or two more long drawers (Nos. 179, 182). In others, the bottom is closed in with cupboard doors, as it is here, or with tambour shutters. Usually the

Woodland Heights are at present unknown.

Dimensions: height 99½; width 42; depth 24½.

Materials: mahogany inlaid with holly and ebony; drawer bottom and sides, backboards, white pine.

Provenance: J. Hall Davis; Museum Purchase, 1953, Lammot du Pont Copeland Fund.

Accession: 53.57                    see Inlay Figs. 1, 89

## 179  GENTLEMAN'S SECRETARY
*1793–1805   Salem, Massachusetts   Label of Edmund Johnson (working about 1793–1811)*

"This piece is intended for a gentleman to write at, to keep his own accounts, and serves as a library. The style of finishing is neat, and sometimes approaching to elegance, being at times made of satinwood, with japanned ornaments." So wrote Sheraton of a form similar to this one, but with variant details, entitled "Gentleman's Secretary," illustrated as Plate 52 in his *Drawing Book*. For a long time such pieces of furniture as this and those

upper section has four glazed doors to enclose the bookshelves, with the center set of shelves slightly deeper than those on the side. As a result, the appearance is that of a small break-front bookcase.

On most of these "Salem secretaries," ornamental effect is achieved through the contrast of dominant geometrical figures of light-colored banding or stringing against dark and richly figured conforming veneered backgrounds. The pilasters above the front feet are usually emphasized with inlaid one-piece husks and stringing; though sometimes, as in No. 182, light-colored panels are inlaid in the pilasters to achieve the same effect of verticality. A horizontal motif of intertwining panels of stringing usually dominates the frieze of the upper section, and a dentilled cornice as used on this example is rare.

The brasses stamped with a lion motif are old but not original. The turned wooden urns and carved-and-gilded eagle are replacements. It is of special interest that the eagle with downspread wings, which is an old one, is in the style long associated with Samuel McIntire. An eagle of similar design was carved by McIntire for the cupola of Lynn Academy. The original bill, in McIntire's hand, is preserved at the Lynn Historical Society.[14] Some of the interior linings of white pine of this piece and No. 181 and several other pieces of New England origin in the collection appear to have been stained red or pink when made. An old inscription on the back of the secretary drawer reads "Secretary Back."

Dimensions: height 94⅜; width 67; depth 21.

Materials: mahogany inlaid with light and dark woods; shelves and lower unit backboard, white pine; upper unit backboard, Scots or red pine; lower unit doors, birch with mahogany veneers; backboards fastened with hand-wrought nails.

Accession: 57.630      see Inlay Fig. 11

## 181   GENTLEMAN'S SECRETARY
### Secretary and Bookcase

*1795-1798   Salem, Massachusetts   With two labels of Nehemiah Adams pasted on back, one on upper and one on lower section*

This remarkable secretary and bookcase has a most interesting history of ownership that offers fascinating opportunities for conjecture concerning the exportation of furniture as venture cargo by Salem cabinetmakers. It was found and purchased for Henry Francis du Pont in Capetown, South Africa, more than twenty-five years ago. There is pasted on the inside of the back what appears to be a

printed page from a sales catalogue. Headed "An Interesting Piece of Furniture," the description concludes with the statement, "This unique and charming piece of furniture was made in the United States, as gathered from the labels on the back, and was bought by Mr. Keene in the Colony where it must have been for a 100 years." In script are two penned notations, "Sold at Kaleb Keane's Sale Aug. 9, 1912" and "£36 Parliament St. Capeton, bought at auction there by Scarborough."

Nehemiah Adams, a member of a cooperative furniture enterprise with Jacob and Elijah Sanderson, William Appleton, and others, regularly made furniture for export. That he was deeply involved in trade and shipping is indicated by his part ownership of a brig, a brigantine, and a schooner between 1800 and 1804 and by a number of records of shipments[15] he made. One shipment made in 1804, some six years after his shop on Newbury-street was burned (the address on this label), included twenty-one pieces of furniture invoiced at $1036 to Captain James Devereux of the ship *Franklin*.[16] Each of nine pieces was listed as a "Ladyes sectary and bookcase" (eight at $50, one at $20). Of the other three listed as "Sectary and Bookcase," two were listed at $50 each—the other at $100 was the most expensive piece in the shipment. Perhaps that was a secretary such as this one? The agreement between Adams and Captain Devereux is interesting. "The above goods are to be sold for the most they will bring at the Isle of France [Mauritius] or elsewhere and the neat proceeds to be placed to the owners of & they to have the euse of any money soomes [sums?] for the freight out & the shipper to risk them out & home. Salem May 9th 1804. Neha Adams." Devereux's sales for Adams amounted to $842. Commissions and expenses reduced this to a net of $740.11. There seems every likelihood that this was but one of many voyages to Mauritius, and it is easy to speculate that on an earlier venture this secretary and bookcase was sold enroute to or on return from Capetown.

Not often seen on American furniture is the pattern of the pointed-oval mullions.[17] Here the cross-banded divisions are boldly edged with satinwood to accent the interplay of curvilinear and rectilinear elements and to emphasize the feeling of surface movement. Each lower cupboard contains a bookshelf; beneath that on the left are vertical dividers to provide spaces for ledgers. The brasses and finials are replacements, and the back was originally stained red. What appears to be the original green baize covers the writing surface of the secretary drawer.

Dimensions: height 90; width 67¾; depth 18 in the middle and 16¼ at the ends.
Materials: mahogany veneer on white pine, inlaid with light wood stringing; backboards and top of lower unit, white pine.
Accession: 57.796          see Inlay Figs. 3–6, 91

## 182 GENTLEMAN'S SECRETARY
Secretary and Bookcase
*About 1800  Northeastern Massachusetts*

Honey-colored mahogany, satinwood pilasters, trellis-like mullions, and painted, gilded, and silvered glass panels give this secretary a very different aspect than that of the preceding ones.[18] The composition seems lighter and looser. The lift of the turned legs, the arc of the skirt, and upward thrust of the figured veneers on doors and drawers carry the eye to the centers of interest—oval mirrors, and eglomisé vases, bouquets, and scenes of ladies picking and arranging flowers.[19] The broad

and distinctive dark cross-banding around the doors and drawers and the fret, or dentil-like bandings, on the mullion and frieze are distinctive and unusual; but the patterned stringing on skirt and shelf is typical of those found on many pieces of furniture made in Boston and on the North Shore of Massachusetts. The upper middle drawer is fitted as a secretary drawer for writing, and a mahogany bookshelf divides the compartment behind each cupboard door. The meaning of the inscription in a small interior drawer is uncertain. It reads: "$79 Nov 1 1819 August."

Dimensions: height 92½; width 75¼; depth 22½.
Materials: mahogany; mahogany and satinwood veneers on white pine; light and dark wood stringing; secondary wood, white pine; eagle-stamped brass knobs on large drawers appear to be replacements.
Provenance: R. H. Maynard; Helen T. Cooke.
Accession: 57.845          see Inlay Figs. 9, 29, 57

## 183 LIBRARY BOOKCASE with wings and
secretary drawer
*1796  New York City*

In *The Journeymen Cabinet and Chair Makers' New-York Book of Prices* for 1796, the wages for making a "Library Book-case with wings" is listed as £16.10.9 ($41.34). That one is described as:

Six feet long, 7 feet 4 inches high between the plinth and cornice, the middle ends of the lower part one foot seven inches wide, the middle ends of the upper part one foot two inches wide, flat pannel'd doors to the upper and lower part, the pannels plow'd in, the lower part made in one carcase, three clothes press shelves in the center, and one book-shelf in each wing; the upper part made in three carcases, with 9 book-shelves in ditto, framed backs, loose cornice and fast plinth, all solid (for cornice see plate).

Except for a "Wing'd Wardrobe" at £17.5.11, this is the highest "start price" in the entire book. But the making of such fancy glazed doors as seen here (the design is illustrated in Plate VI, No. 21, of the same publication), instead of the "flat pannel'd doors to the upper part," would have added at least £10, and the secretary drawer another £5 to the journeyman's wages.[20]

In 1931, this bookcase, owned just prior to that time by H. G. Hunter of Doswell, Virginia, was published as a Virginia-made piece of furniture of about 1790.[21] Considering its sophistication and outstanding workmanship, this writer doubted that it could have been produced in that area at

that time. It has the look of an urban product. But where was it made? New York or Philadelphia? Such cross-banding and light-wood crestings to letter holes is found in the finest furniture of both cities. The use of tulip as a secondary wood is also common to both, as is white pine, though the latter is less frequently found in Philadelphia furniture.

At the time of its purchase in 1930, Mr. Hunter advised that this piece was made for his forebears, who owned Hunters Island near New York. Happily, the writer discovered recently a contemporary penciled inscription on the bottom of the lower drawer behind the left door. It reads:

> For Mr. Robert Hunter
> No. 5 State Street
> N.Y.
> July 1, 1796

When closed, the front of the secretary presents the appearance of two smaller drawers, simulating companion end drawers. The oval handles appear to be original. The brass finials may be replacements.

Dimensions: height 110⅝; width 98½; depth 22¼.

Materials: mahogany inlaid and veneered with light woods; large drawer lower, door fronts, mahogany veneered on white pine; drawer linings and back of lower unit, tulip.

Provenance: Robert Hunter; H. G. Hunter.

Accession: 57.1024          see Inlay Fig. 66

### 184 TAMBOUR DESK, Lady's Writing Table
with tambour shutters
*1794–1804   Boston   Label of John Seymour and Son (working 1794–1804 in Creek Square)*

This superb desk epitomizes the refinement, skill, and quality of workmanship of New England cabinetmakers in the Federal period.[22] The easy grace of the festooned husks inlaid on the tiny ribs of the tambour sliding doors sets the tone of the entire piece, in keeping with the varied inlays, meticulous joinery, colorful enamel pulls of the four seasons, letter boxes painted a robin's-egg-blue, and the choice of grain of the wood. Numerous details of fine cabinetmaking, for which John and Thomas Seymour have long been celebrated, are not visible in the accompanying photograph. Drawer bottoms and sides of the upper section are thin and light. Delicate but precise dovetails join the pieces together. In contrast, the drawer members of the lower section are quite thick, but their construction is fine. Chisel marks were used to number the vertical dividers of the letter boxes with corresponding marks chiseled or penciled on

the bottom boards of this section. This small masterpiece stands supreme to perpetuate the Seymour name. Under the bottom drawer a printed label reads:

> JOHN SEYMOUR & SON,
> CABINET MAKERS,
> CREEK SQUARE

A chalk initial or initials written with great flourish appears on the back of the upper section. The letter or letters could be "CS" or "JS."

Dimensions: height 41⅝; width 37¾; depth 18½.

Materials: mahogany inlaid with light wood; secondary woods, white pine; small drawer sides of mahogany; large drawer fronts of white elm with mahogany veneer.

Provenance: Col. Thomas Foxhall Cutts; Judge George Addison Emery; Philip Flayderman.

Accession: 57.802          see Inlay Figs. 23, 42, 43

### 185 TAMBOUR DESK, Lady's Writing Table
with tambour shutters
*About 1800   Boston   Attributed to John Seymour and Son*

In outline and form this desk and the preceding one are among the most delicate and graceful of all American furniture. Attributed to the hand of John Seymour and Son, this small desk bears close

similarity in form, workmanship, and decoration to the labeled example, No. 184. The same technique of using a chisel to number the dividers of the letter boxes was employed; dovetails used in the drawer construction are small and delicate; and several parts of this desk bear a penciled inscription "nᵒ 1," "nᵒ 2," and so forth. The letter N found in both desks is "in the hand" of the same person. The dependent husks on the legs (composed of three overlapping ovals), separated by inlaid discs and framed by string-inlaid panels with rounded top, the use of ivory escutcheons, and the robin's-egg-blue interior are all repeated here. The lunette inlay on the top and on the front of the folding writing lid, the pilasters of satinwood, and the tambour strips instead of reeds relate more closely to the labeled desk in the George Cluett estate.[23] An example of the maker's attention to decorative detail is the repetition of the same wood sequence on the pilasters and tambour strips. However, it should be noted that whereas the strips in the Cluett desk are all satinwood, those seen here are alternately satinwood and mahogany, providing an exciting contrast of color. The ornamental ivory ovals for penciled labels are similar to those inlaid above the letter holes in No. 186.

Dimensions: height 44¼; width 36⅛; depth 19.

Materials: mahogany inlaid with satinwood, ebony, and ivory; secondary woods, white pine; large drawer fronts, walnut with mahogany veneer.

Provenance: Helen T. Cooke.

Accession: 57.909

## 186 LADY'S SECRETARY AND BOOK-CASE, Lady's Desk and Bookcase[24]

*About 1800   Boston   Probably made by John Seymour or Thomas Seymour*

Although as yet it is impossible to distinguish between the individual work of father (John Seymour), son (Thomas Seymour), or their partnership, those pieces which can with certainty be documented as theirs[25] are distinguished by the brilliant organization and arrangement of veneered and inlaid motifs, unrivaled by any known work of their many gifted Boston and Salem contemporaries. Each part is dramatic. Contrasting woods, carving, and inlays provide an allover effect of richness and sparkling detail, knit together through the arrangement of intricate borders and the pattern of figured veneers.

Certain features both external and internal occur again and again in furniture attributed to these two masters. For example, many details of this

three-section desk and bookcase with tambour shutters, an extraordinary piece of fine cabinetwork, are duplicated in No. 185, which it closely resembles. The tambour sliding doors are constructed of flat strips (instead of reeding) of mahogany and satinwood, accented by flat lines of ebony. Seen on the small drawers behind the tambour doors of both desks is the same highly individual quirk in the shaping of the fine dovetails. On both, the interiors of the pigeonholes are painted the familiar robin's-egg-blue color, and the lettering scratched on the bottoms of the drawers appears to be by the "same hand." Ivory urn-shaped escutcheons of classic refinement are used on several desks attributed to the Seymours. As on this piece, the escutcheon for the doors is frequently located in the pediment block. On furniture with these attributes (presumably made in the Seymours' shop or shops), one occasionally finds corner brackets used to break the sharp angle at the juncture of leg and skirt (see No. 344). In this case the brackets are carved with heads of wheat and inset with shaped veneers of satinwood. The finials and oval brasses are replacements.

Dimensions: height 76; width 37½; depth 19½.

Materials: mahogany inlaid with satinwood and ivory; large drawer front, walnut; drawer linings and backboards, white pine.

Provenance: Originally owned by Eben or Gorham Parsons of Boston and Byfield, Massachusetts; Gorham Parsons Sargent; Mary W. Sargent Hoffman; Schuyler Hoffman, Jr.

Accession: 57.570        see Inlay Figs. 15, 35, 36, 58, 94, 97

## 187 TAMBOUR DESK with perspective glass

*1793–1811    Salem, Massachusetts    Attributed to Edmund Johnson (working 1793–1811)*

Except for minor details, this desk appears to be identical to one labeled by Edmund Johnson of Salem, Massachusetts, illustrated in "The Perspective Glass" by Joe Kindig, III.[26] As pointed out by Mr. Kindig, perspective glasses were devices that "served the same purpose of visual entertainment as the nineteenth century's stereopticon and the twentieth's television set." Large prints laid on the shelf behind the lower tambour doors and illuminated with a candle could be viewed in the large glass lens revealed by opening the upper door. According to family history, this desk was taken by Francis W. Pickman from Salem to Nova Scotia in the early nineteenth century.[27] When it was found there in 1955, there were thirty-four mounted prints of European scenes in the long drawers.

Dimensions: height 52; width 38¾; depth 20.

Materials: mahogany; secondary wood, white pine.

Provenance: Benjamin Pickman, Francis W. Pickman, through descendants to M. E. L. Lynch; Museum Purchase, 1955.

Accession: 55.96.4

## 188 LADY'S CABINET AND WRITING TABLE

*1795–1810    Baltimore*

A "Lady's Cabinet and Writing Table," Sheraton's designation for a design shown in Plate 50 of his *Drawing Book* is closely related to this piece, one of the most sophisticated examples of American cabinetmaking of the Federal period. Modifications on this cabinet are the addition of the oval mirror in a broad satinwood frame,[28] veneered satinwood door fronts mitered at the corners and inset with painted and gold-leafed glass ovals of biblical and mythological figures done in the Baltimore manner, and the satinwood outlines of drawers and skirt. These combine to make this colorful in contrast and one of the most extraordinary of a small group of rare Baltimore desks.[29] The source for these figures, as yet undiscovered,

would be of great interest since the figure in the lower center oval is seated on a klysmos-type Grecian chair and there is the possibility that this is the earliest illustration of this type chair in the United States. The design by Henry Latrobe for Grecian chairs for the President's house was not executed until 1809 and has been shown by Robert Raley to have been derived in all probability from *Household Taste* by Thomas Hope, published in London, in 1807.[30]

As yet the identity of S. E. WAITE 1812 (hand lettered in ink at the rear of the top drawer in the lower section) is unknown.

Dimensions: height 62⅛; width 30⅞; depth 22¼.

Materials: mahogany inlaid with satinwood; drawer backs and bottoms, red cedar; drawer sides, mahogany.

Provenance: Coralie E. Phipps (whose mother purchased it near Baltimore about 1915); Museum Purchase, 1957.

Accession: 57.68

## 189 LADY'S SECRETARY AND BOOKCASE, Lady's Desk and Bookcase

*1800–1810    Massachusetts*

Though of small size and good proportions, what would otherwise be a rather modest secretary and bookcase is given distinction through the inspired use of ornamental edging. Light wood and variegated cross-banding frame three real and two sham drawer fronts, and light wood edging gives drama to innumerable geometrical shapes in the door divisions. The brass knobs stamped with a portrait of Washington appear to be original, and the finials replacements.

Dimensions: height 78½; width 39; depth (desk) 20½; depth (bookcase) 11.

Materials: mahogany; drawer fronts, mahogany veneers over white pine; bandings of walnut; light and dark wood patterned stringing.

Accession: 57.521        see Inlay Fig. 2

## 190 LADY'S SECRETARY AND BOOKCASE, Lady's Desk and Bookcase

*1800–1810    Northeastern Massachusetts*

Curly-maple veneers, variegated bandings, and dash, dot, dot, dot, dash patterned stringing is found on much Boston and north-of-Boston furniture. Although enlivened with such ornament, this excellent small desk and bookcase nevertheless lacks the flair of the preceding examples. Legs sharply tapered below the cuff are common to much northern New England furniture.

Dimensions: height 65; width 37⅞; depth 18⅞.

Materials: mahogany; bird's-eye-maple veneers and variegated American-walnut bandings on white pine; secondary woods, white pine except for lower front rail of red oak.

Accession: 57.953　　　　　　see Inlay Figs. 16, 27, 34

### 191 LADY'S WRITING TABLE AND BOOKCASE[31]

*About 1810–1820　Providence, Rhode Island　Label of Joseph Rawson and Son*

This form was contrived from one first illustrated by Sheraton, who shows several variations, dated 1792, in his *Drawing Book*. At the turn of the century, writing tables were widely made by Federal

cabinetmakers, not only in New England, but in New York, Philadelphia, and Baltimore, sometimes with a cylinder-front desk, but more often with this type of folding baize-lined flap. Niceties of Rawson's work are the half-round molded bead mullions of the glazed doors and a variety of sophisticated patterned stringing to provide horizontal accents. At the top of the bookcase are eight letter slots above two tiers of short drawers. Finials, escutcheons, and drawer pulls are replacements.

Dimensions: height 73; width 34; depth 20.
Materials: mahogany inlaid with light wood; doors, cherry; backboards and top of lower unit, white pine; drawer linings, chestnut.
Accession: 57.601　　　　see Inlay Figs. 20, 28, 37, 53

bearing the label of Webb and Scott, cabinet- and chairmakers in Benefit Street in Providence.[33] The right small drawer has mahogany sides and is fitted for writing, with spaces for inkpot and sand shaker. Old red stain remains on several surfaces.

Dimensions: height 55½; width 27; depth 20½.

Materials: mahogany; long drawer fronts, mahogany veneer on white pine; backboard lower unit, walnut; other secondary wood, white pine; the wooden knobs are replacements.

Accession: 57.968

### 193 LADY'S DESK
*About 1800   Massachusetts*

Ingeniously conceived and handsomely ornamented, this writing table gives the effect of a

### 192 LADY'S DESK AND BOOKCASE
*1810–1820   New England*

Composed of three sections, this small desk and bookcase without a pediment appears to be a simpler version of No. 191, but there are important differences. Instead of a flap, as on that example, a sloping writing surface is achieved in the same way as in a portable desk, half of the lid being hinged to fold forward, exposing a baize-covered writing surface and three small drawers.[32] Bold, light-colored stringing is used to highlight the divisions in the bookcase doors in a manner not commonly used by Providence cabinetmakers, although the "rope-inlaid" border around the long drawer is similar to that on a desk and bookcase

actual execution by the cabinetmaker. He gave more height to the bookcase, introduced a pediment, and added rich veneers and inlays of satinwood, zebrawood, and ebony on a mahogany ground. Hard pine and oak as secondary woods are found in pieces of furniture with Maryland histories as are teardrop-shaped satinwood inlays seen on the legs of this desk. It may have been made in that locale.

A large inlaid eagle, unmistakably the national symbol, is prominently centered on the cylinder desk front, and again the Seal of the United States is echoed in the spirited carved eagle finial. When the cylinder desk front is rolled back, the writing board, or slide, may be pulled forward, but it is not coordinated with the cylinder fall as in some desks. Satinwood is used to outline the interior drawers and pigeonholes, and the center door, the latter inlaid with an oval frame and the initials S.B.

Dimensions: height 102; width 42½; depth 23.

Materials: mahogany inlaid with ebony, satinwood, and zebrawood; backboards, tulip; lower back rail, hard pine; large drawer linings, oak; small drawer linings, mahogany; paneled backboards are fastened with hand-wrought nails; the brasses are replacements.

Provenance: Descended in Faulkner Family of Albemarle County, Virginia, to Mrs. George (née Faulkner) Ferguson.

Accession: 57.775          see Inlay Figs. 75, 126

small chest on long legs when the hinged top is closed.[34] Variegated cross-banding—in this case of rosewood—is occasionally seen on Boston furniture, where it is used as edging or to outline drawer fronts. Far more frequently used there, however, is this type of reeded leg with tapered profile, ring turnings, and rather long straight foot. Perhaps an inch has been lost from the tip of each foot.

Dimensions: height 34½; width 30; depth 19⅛.

Materials: mahogany banded with rosewood veneer; secondary wood, white pine.

Accession: 57.865          see Inlay Figs. 18, 22

## 194  CYLINDER-FALL DESK AND BOOK-CASE

*1790–1800   Maryland (?)*

Of all American desks and bookcases, this is to the eyes of the writer the most beautiful and successful. Based upon illustrations in both Hepplewhite's and Sheraton's books, with plates dated between 1787 and 1793, and the 1788 edition of *The Cabinet-Makers' London Book of Prices, and Designs of Cabinet Work,* the design has been greatly improved in the

## 195  CYLINDER-FALL DESK

*1800–1810   Massachusetts, Probably Salem*

Despite the fact that the roll-top desk of oak was very popular with American businessmen in the early twentieth century, its antecedent—the cylinder desk—seems to have been made infrequently in this country. This rare and small example is linked to other cabinetwork of Salem, Massachusetts, by the style of the carving at the top of the long legs and the knurled ornament around the base and opening for the lid. Related leaf carving and what appears to be identical knurling occur on a sideboard believed to have been made by William Hook in 1809 as a wedding present to his sister.[35] But much closer in character is the carving found on the pair of side tables (No. 343) bearing the label of William Haskell. On those tables and this desk, similar feathery leaves with pronounced spines and wavy edges are separated by star-punched fillings. The drawer pulls are of the period of the desk but are replacements.

Dimensions: height 42½; width 28¾; depth 22½.
Materials: mahogany; secondary wood, white pine.
Provenance: J. Kenneth Danby.
Accession: 56.38.140

**196** CYLINDER-FALL DESK
*1810–1830  Pennsylvania*

The nicety of workmanship apparent in the curved
lid of this cylinder desk (so coupled with the writing slider that when the lid is opened the latter is
pushed forward) and the skillful handling of richly
figured mahogany veneers on the drawers, lid, and
frame indicate that it was made by an extremely
able craftsman with access to fine woods. Imagination is also shown in the treatment of the stump
supports inspired by the Roman foot that became
stylish about 1810. The interior may be unique in
both ornament and arrangement: instead of one
"prospect door," there are two, one at either end;
the center space is an open recess with ionic colonnettes at the corners and a mirror at the back to
reflect an intricate floor inlaid with a large tattered-

shell patera; both the doors and six small drawers
are framed within an elaborate inlaid "cabling of
ribbons."

Despite the profusion and ambitious quality of
the inlays, they lack the sophistication of English-
inspired work. The pots of flowers are so strongly
reminiscent of the pen-and-wash drawings called
"Frakturs" as to suggest that this is the work of a
gifted Pennsylvania German.

Dimensions: height 49¼; width 48¼; depth 24¼.
Materials: white and hard pine with mahogany veneer;
    drawer bottoms, backs, and bottom panel, tulip;
    drawer fronts, frame, and stiles, white and hard pine.
Provenance: Museum Purchase, 1958.
Accession: 58.136

**197** MINIATURE, OR CHILD'S,
CYLINDER-FALL DESK
*1800–1810  Maryland or Pennsylvania*

Children's furniture of any sort has great appeal
to the collector and is not common. Far rarer,
however, are miniature examples of high-style
forms. Not only is the scalloping of the skirt of this
small desk (with dominant inlaid motif in the
center) in accord with the lines on many Baltimore
(see No. 141) and some Philadelphia chests of
drawers and desks, but teardrop inlays and the

patterns of the stringing are also seen on much Baltimore furniture.

Dimensions: height 16½; width 15; depth 8.

Materials: walnut with light and dark wood inlays; drawer linings and backboard, hard pine.

Accession: 58.2057

## 198 TABLE DESK

*About 1823   New York   Label of Michael Allison (working 1800–1847)*

Michael Allison was one of the most prolific and long-lived cabinetmakers of the Federal period. His name appeared in the New York directories from 1800 to 1847. Among a number of extant case pieces bearing his labels, the earliest in style is a shapely Hepplewhite chest of drawers (Metropolitan Museum of Art) made of light, figured mahogany and inlaid with an American eagle, nimbus, and stars.

Allison's printed label, dated 1823, examples of which he may have used for several years, is pasted in the lower drawer. The side drawer offers a baize-covered reading-and-writing board supported by ratchets. This table, made several years later than No. 306 by Lannuier and No. 331 by Woodruff, continues certain features that characterize the New York Sheraton school of work, namely, the shape of the foot and cut reeding of

the upper legs. Late Sheraton features are the enlarged corner posts with repetitive ring turnings; coarse acanthus-leaf carved bases; and a fattened version of the familiar New York turned foot.

Dimensions: height 29¾; width 25; depth 17.

Materials: mahogany; framing and drawer fronts, white pine; drawer bottoms, tulip.

Accession: 57.1057

## 199 DRAWING TABLE

*About 1800   Salem, Massachusetts   Label of Thomas Needham (working 1775 to after 1827)*

"This table will be found highly useful to such as draw, it being designed from my own experience of what is necessary for those who practice this art. The top of this table is made to rise by a double horse, that the designer may stand if he please, or he may sit, and have the top raised to any direction....The long drawer holds paper, square and board, and those drawers which form the kneehole are fitted up for colours." So wrote Thomas Sheraton of a "Drawing Table" (pages 49 and 50 and Plate 30, dated 1793) in the appendix of the 1802 edition of his *Drawing Book*, which served as a general source for this design. Under the top of the table is the printed label of Thomas Needham. On this example, the small compartments under the top may have been used for "colours." Added

storage space for "paper, square and board" is available in drawers on either end as well as the one in front. For balance of composition, sham drawers are added above the real drawers at the ends and beneath the one on the front.

This rare drawing table may be unique, but several of its features are to be seen on much other Salem furniture: long, slightly bulging, tapered legs (here without reeding) with elongated swelled feet; knurled edging on the top; each leg so engaged at the corner as to stand partially free of the case and the top shaped outward in a partial circle to cover it. The interior and small drawers are stained pink, and the brasses and castors are the original ones.

Dimensions: height 31; width 34¾; depth 22⅞.
Materials: mahogany; white pine; original baize covering on the top.
Accession: 57.635

## 200 COUNTING DESK
*1790–1800   Hartford, Connecticut*

This desk on a frame follows the contour of merchants' desks of the eighteenth century. It is made

in two sections; the writing lid gives access to the interior, which is furnished with six small drawers above eight pigeonholes trimmed with double cyma curves. Although the desk was found in a sea captain's house in Marblehead, Massachusetts, the sand-shaded light wood paterae inlaid on mahogany, the bellflower pendants flanking the drawers, and the use of cherry as a primary wood are attributes often found on Hartford cabinet-making (see No. 323). The semi-elliptical brasses are unusual in shape; the bails are knurled to match the borders of their back plates.

Dimensions: height 51¾; width 37½; depth 26.
Materials: cherry inlaid with light wood and mahogany; small drawer bottoms and sides, tulip; large drawer bottom and back, white pine.
Accession: 57.875          see Inlay Figs. 102, 104

## 201 WRITING TABLE OR DESK
*1818–1819   Probably Boston*

According to tradition, this desk was part of the furnishings of the New Hampshire State House, completed in 1819, for which furniture costing $875 was bought in the preceding months. For this information, the writer is indebted to Mr. Philip Guyol, former director of the New Hampshire Historical Society. In his letter, Mr. Guyol noted the similarity of this desk to three pieces of furniture in the Historical Society's collections—all of bird's-eye-maple—two curved writing tables to seat six persons each and a slant-top desk. These also are believed to have been State House furnishings. Mr. Guyol suggests, "your desk matches the tables so closely and is so much more elaborate than ours that I would guess it might have been used by the President of the Senate...."[36]

One day the original purchase records may be located to provide proof of its maker. However, the contour of the legs and the intercepted reeding on them suggests Boston or Salem workmanship. In 1866, the new furniture for the State House was purchased from J. L. Ross of Boston.[37] The old furniture may have come from the same city.

Dimensions: height 40½; width 46; depth 25¾.
Materials: mahogany with bird's-eye-maple veneer; rails, drawer sides and bottoms, white pine; cross members, maple; moldings under rear rail, cherry.
Accession: 57.940

## FOOTNOTES

1 "Extracts of a Gentleman Visiting Boston [September 19, 1792]," *Massachusetts Historical Society Proceedings*, XII, 12.

2 *The Diary of William Bentley* (Salem, Mass.: The Essex Institute, 1905), I, 264.

3 From the *Letter Book of Joseph Barrell* in the Massachusetts Historical Society, Boston, Mass.

4 Swan, "A Revised Estimate of McIntire," *Antiques*, XX (December, 1931), 338–343.

5 On the bottom of this small drawer is scratched "Bearing Broth."

6 The Connecticut Historical Society, *Frederick K. and Margaret R. Barbour's Furniture Collection* (Hartford, Conn., 1963), pp. 68–69.

7 Sale Catalogue of the *Collection of the Late Philip Flayderman*, No. 431, pp. 164–165.

8 Collections of the Essex Institute and Mr. and Mrs. Henry T. Bush, Jr.

9 Swan, *Samuel McIntire and the Sandersons ...*, p. 10.

10 Fiske Kimball, "Salem Secretaries and Their Makers," *Antiques*, XXIII (May, 1933), 168–170.

11 Illustrated in *Antiques*, Special Issue: *Antiques at the Henry Ford Museum* (New York, 1958).

12 Illustrated in Luke Vincent Lockwood, *Colonial Furniture in America* (3rd ed.; New York: Charles Scribner's Sons, 1926), I, Fig. XLVI, 376.

13 It is reported that two or three secretaries with inlays similar to these are or were once owned in Newburyport.

14 Nina Fletcher Little, "Carved Figures by Samuel McIntire and his Contemporaries," *Samuel McIntire, A Bicentennial Symposium* (Salem, Mass.: The Essex Institute, 1957), Figs. 44, 45, p. 78.

15 Frank Hitchings and Stephen Willard Phillips, "Ship Registers of the District of Salem and Beverly, 1789 to 1900," *Essex Institute Historical Collections*, XL (April, 1904), 177–200; XL (July, 1904), 217–240; XLII (January, 1906), 89–107.

16 "Furniture exported by cabinetmakers of Salem," from notes left by Henry Wyckoff Belknap, *Essex Institute Historical Collections*, LXXXV (1949), 335–359.

17 Derived from Plate 27, No. 3, of the second edition of *The London Cabinet-Makers' Book of Prices* for 1793.

18 Though this is an unusual interpretation of this form, a closely related example may be seen in an advertisement of Ferdinand Keller of Philadelphia, *Antiquarian*, XVI (March, 1931), 75.

19 The character and treatment of the glass panels and crossed mullions of the center doors are very similar to those on a small cylinder bookcase in the Karolik Collection of the Boston Museum of Fine Arts. (Hipkiss, page 36, No. 22.)

20 The over-all design for No. 183 is an adaptation from illustrations entitled "Library Book-case" (Plates 1 and 3) in the 1788 and subsequent editions of *The Cabinet-Makers' London Book of Prices*, ...

21 Paul H. Burroughs, *Southern Antiques* (Richmond, Va.: Garrett & Massie, Incorporated, 1931), Pl. VIII, p. 108.

22 Illustrated as No. 451 in the Sale Catalogue of the *Collection of the Late Philip Flayderman* therein described as

**201**

from the collection of Judge George E. [*sic*] Emery of Saco, Maine. Proof of Saco association is offered by a penciled notation on the lower drawer of the desk, "Repaired & Shalacked by Chas. W. Holmes, Oct. 1903 No. 47 Pleasant St. Saco." Ownership by Judge George Addison Emery is confirmed by Mrs. H. F. Hamilton, who wrote of this tambour desk on January 30, 1966, to John Sweeney, Curator of the Winterthur Museum: "I always remember the desk as being in the parlor of Cousin Addison Emery, in Saco." Earlier, August 11, 1965, Mrs. Hamilton had written that "Col. Thomas Foxhall Cutts, [was] the original owner of the tambour front desk with the Four Seasons (Battersea Enamel) in the handles that Mr. Du Pont purchased in the Flayderman ... sale some years ago." She stated that Col. Cutts, a "well-to-do gentleman," [who lived] in the "Cutts Mansion" in Biddeford, Maine, was her ancestor.

Illustrated in Stoneman, *John and Thomas Seymour, ...* Pl. 10, pp. 54–55; Swan, "John Seymour and Son, Cabinetmakers," *Antiques*, XXXIII (October, 1937), Fig. 2, 176–179; and McClelland, *Duncan Phyfe and the English Regency*, Pl. 195, pp. 209–226.

23 Illustrated in Stoneman, op. cit., p. 48; Nutting, *Furniture Treasury*, I, Fig. 669; Catalogue of the *Girl Scouts Loan Exhibition*, No. 710.

24 Illustrated in Stoneman, op. cit., Pl. 49, pp. 106–107.

25 Only two pieces bearing the label of John Seymour and son are known; both are outstanding tambour desks (No. 184 in this book and Pl. 4, pp. 48–49 in Stoneman). Four pieces can definitely be assigned to Thomas. Two are the superb commode and "one elegant dressing table" made for Mrs. Elizabeth Derby in 1809. The former is now in the Boston Museum of Fine Arts and the latter in the Pingree House of the Essex Institute. Thomas Seymour's original receipted bill for these two pieces exists and is illustrated (Stoneman, Pl. 157, pp. 246–249). The other two pieces are a lady's work table with the original bill from the Boston Cabinet Manufactury (opened by Thomas in 1812) pasted on the bottom of the first drawer (Stoneman, Pl. 151, pp. 238–239) and a card table with

original bill to Henry Osborn from the Boston Cabinet Manufactury pasted to the underside, now owned by Earl Osborn, Easthampton, Massachusetts.

26 Joe Kindig, III, "Perspective Glass," *Antiques*, LXV (June, 1954), 466–468.

27 Family genealogy compiled from George Francis Dow, *Diary and Letters of Benjamin W. Pickman* (Newport, R. I., 1928).

28 Related in silhouette to the lady's dressing table owned by the Maryland Historical Society, No. 80 in *Baltimore Furniture*.

29 Almost identical in treatment to a small desk illustrated as No. 78 in *Baltimore Furniture*, then owned by Miss Ethel Knight. See also Nos. 77 and 78, *Baltimore Furniture*, 1760–1810.

30 R. L. Raley, "Interior Designs by Benjamin Henry Latrobe for the President's House," *Antiques*, LXXV (June, 1959), 568–571.

31 Illustrated as No. 371 (pp. 130–131), Sale Catalogue of the *Collection of Israel Sack* (American Art Association Anderson Galleries, Inc., 1929), Sale No. 3787, November 7–9, 1929.

32 A number of penned notations on the bottom of the flap offer clues to earlier ownership. They include: "CPH" several times and the date "July 28th, 1852"; "Hill and Pearce"; "Conduit St. Bond St."; "Craddocks Deeds Book N Vol 2, page 517, 18 Common Records."

33 Sale Catalogue of the *Collection of the Late Philip Flayderman*, No. 431, pp. 164–165.

34 A desk of the same unusual form and with rich veneers is illustrated in *Eighteenth-Century American Arts, ...* No. 31. It is also attributed to Massachusetts.

35 Fiske Kimball, "Salem Furniture Makers: III, William Hook," *Antiques*, XXV (April, 1934), 144–146.

36 Letter from Philip Guyol, New Hampshire Historical Society, to Milo M. Naeve, Winterthur Museum, February 20, 1958.

37 Letter from Mrs. David L. Stark, New Hampshire Historical Society, to Milo M. Naeve, Winterthur Museum, July 12, 1963.

# Fire Screens

SCREEN: A piece of furniture used to shelter the face or legs from the fire. Hence the more common name is fire-screen, of which there are a great variety, as tripod fire-screens, horse or safe fire-screens, folding and sliding fire-screens, and table fire screens.
Thomas Sheraton, *The Cabinet Dictionary*, p. 302.

Today it is difficult for the modern American, accustomed to central heating, electric lights, and a night-time level of illumination equivalent to that of daylight, to understand and appreciate earlier attitudes toward heat and light and the necessity felt by our forebears to screen their faces and eyes from them—whether from the fireplace or from artificial illumination. Some may think a young man who could write so feelingly of the problem in an American magazine in the early 1800's was indeed a delicate fellow, but his words are indicative of the sentiments of many if one is to judge by the considerable numbers of surviving fire screens. He wrote: "The glare of candle light so often is very painful to my eyes, and I have made attempts to soften and improve it by a shade so as to bring it nearer to the natural light of day."

Sheraton, more mindful of the complexion than the eyes, observed of a writing table with an adjustable screen: "The convenience of this table is, that a lady, when writing at it, may both receive the benefit of the fire, and have her face screened from its scorching heat."[1]

In addition to softening the glare of light and screening the face from the heat of the fireplace, fire screens also provided a prominent place for the display of needlework and ornamental painting (Nos. 202, 203, 204, 205). Both were popular subjects of instruction in young ladies' schools and seminaries in the 1790's and early 1800's.

On the decoration of screens, Hepplewhite wrote in 1788, "The screens may be ornamented variously, with maps, Chinese figures, needle-work, etc."[2] In Plates 108 and 109 in *Designs for Household Furniture*, George Smith illustrated Greek and Roman interpretations. Happily, perhaps, parallels are not known in American examples, but his remarks (pp. 19–20) are worth noting:

> These articles of general use admit of every species of decoration, viz. of entire gold, bronze and gold, or japanned; of mahogany, rose, or satinwood; as the apartment they may be destined for shall require. The mounts, if expense be not regarded, may be carved solid in wood, and embellished with painted decorations; or painted on silk or velvet. Where the stands are wholly mahogany, the mounts may be covered with lustring in flutes, with tassels to suit.

Professional and ornamental painters in the United States were prepared to furnish a variety of subjects for fire screens. In 1805 John and Hugh Finlay of Baltimore advertised: "Elegant, Fancy, Japanned Furniture...with real Views, Fancy Landscapes, Flowers.... Horse, Pole, Candle and Fire Screens...with Gold and Painted Fruit, Scroll, and Flower Borders of entirely new patterns."

In the 1788 edition of *The Cabinet-Makers' London Book of Prices, and Designs of Cabinet Work,* the title (p. 102) "Pole and Stand for Face Screen" is illuminating. In the 1793 edition and those thereafter, the listing is simplified to a "Pole and Stand."

In the second edition, a new listing appears: "A pole screen to stand on three claws, the claw as No. 1 [a plain arched leg] Table of ditto, the pillar and pole turn'd." However, many other claws were available and included therm'd (or spade) and snake feet. Also illustrated is a "Plain horse fire screen, with plain rails, common claws, cover'd with shalloon, the tacks cover'd with braid." The design of this is similar to that of the horse, or cheval, dressing glasses such as Nos. 247 and 248.

The 1796 New York price book entries include a "Horse Fire Screen," a "Tripod Bottom for a Face Screen," and a "Pole Screen." All are similar to the London listings with the exception of the latter, which is limited to one type "to stand on three claws ... as in No. 2, in plate of ditto [snake feet]." The mounts parallel those in the London book. In 1810, saber-like claws, such as on candlestand No. 386, are specified as standard; and hexagonal and octagonal screens are added as options. In the 1817 and 1834 editions, the designs remain unchanged.

The entry in the 1795 Philadelphia price book (for labor) is exactly the same as that for New York in 1796 except that the basic price is only eight shillings instead of ten shillings, four pence, but that in *The Philadelphia Cabinet and Chair-Makers' Book of Prices* for 1796 (retail prices) is different and revealing and is therefore quoted extensively.

FIRE SCREENS.

| | Mahogany £. S. D. | Walnut £. S. D. |
|---|---|---|
| A pole fire screen, with a plain pillar and feet, a square frame, with a bead mitred round, (exclusive of silk) | 2 10 0 | 2 5 0 |
| —fluting the pillar | 0 7 0 | 0 7 6 |
| —a horse fire screen, about 2 feet 6, by 1 foot 4, to stand upon two double feet, with straight frame, all plain, (exclusive of silk) | 3 0 0 | 2 12 6 |
| —French toe feet, the scrowls relieved | 0 10 0 | 0 9 0 |

From this, it appears that silk was commonly used for screens in Philadelphia. Fluted pillars at this date seem very old fashioned and French toe feet a complete mystery.

Since most pole screens have at most one secondary wood (and usually none), stylistic attributes and family histories are the primary factors taken into consideration in attempting to arrive at the place of origin. In many cases, exact identification is impossible. The group of pole screens at Winterthur is distinguished by their over-all composition, and the harmony of outline of the screen, the turnings of the shaft, and the stance of the legs.

1 Sheraton, *The Cabinet-Maker and Upholsterer's Drawing Book* (1793), p. 388.
2 *The Cabinet-Maker and Upholsterer's Guide.*

# XVIII

# Blue Room Fireplace

*With the easy artlessness of the pottery toys on the mantelpiece, two needlework miniatures are looped in trompe-l'œil from bowknots of ribbon to ornament these silk taffeta fire screens on mahogany stands (No. 206). More formal are the finest of Philadelphia cabriole chairs (No. 93) and the neoclassical composition ornament on the frieze beneath the pale blue mantelshelf. The French Savonnerie carpet may be a century earlier than the brass andirons from Baltimore and Argand lamps from England which were made about 1800.*

**202**

**203** POLE SCREEN with hinged shelf
*1790–1805   Salem, Massachusetts*

Drop-leaf trays appear on but a few American pole screens. This added feature was both useful and ornamental. When dropped down, the half-octagon shape makes an interesting foil to the highly figured wood of the oval screen above. The sharply ridged legs of the stylish tripod are closely related to some found on Salem-made candlestands. A pole screen in the Essex Institute that appears to be a mate to this one has a long Salem history. It has been published as the work of Thomas Hodgkins.[1] Although Dean A. Fales, Jr., Director of the Institute and an expert on Essex County furniture, has written that he cannot verify that attribution,[2] there is a charge under date of December 24, 1802, for $2 to Jacob Sanderson for "one fire Screene with a flap."[3] Three days later, Sanderson charged Captain John Derby $8 for a "Fire Screen with a leaf to sett Candlestick on."[4]

Dimensions: height 57; screen 16 × 12⅞.
Materials: mahogany; no secondary woods.
Provenance: Blin W. Page.
Accession: 57.1031

**204** POLE SCREEN with hinged shelf
*1795–1810   New England*

Like so much of the furniture produced in the 1790's and possibly later, the individual elements of this trim pole screen are later versions of earlier practice. There is no mistaking this stand as a product of the Chippendale era. The delicacy of the legs, the reduced scale of flattened ball turnings, the fragility of the shelf supported by a thin wrought-iron gate, and the small size of the screen with its original painted cloth are refinements consonant with those of the new styles of the late 1800's. The scrolling of the bracket supporting the shelf to repeat the ogee contours of the legs is an interesting touch. The presence of birch as a secondary wood suggests a provenance of Rhode Island or Massachusetts.

Dimensions: height 56½; screen 14 × 11¾.
Materials: cherry and birch.
Provenance: Museum Purchase, 1960.
Accession: 60.176

**205** POLE SCREEN with hinged shelf
*1795–1810   American*

Few American fire screens are more beautifully composed than this example. The eye may focus

**202** POLE SCREEN with shelf
*1790–1805   New England*

The shape of the legs, the bulbous vase turnings, and the vase-shaped screen on this stand all suggest Boston or North Shore cabinetwork. According to its history, the inlaid initials *EP* stand for Elizabeth Peabody of Salem. The attractive line-inlaid screen can readily be adjusted so that the handsome and lively shaded patera will be enhanced by the flame of a candle standing on the shelf.

Dimensions: height 48; screen 13½ × 13⅝.
Materials: mahogany inlaid with maple and holly; no
   secondary woods.
Accession: 57.661                       see Inlay Fig. 85

203

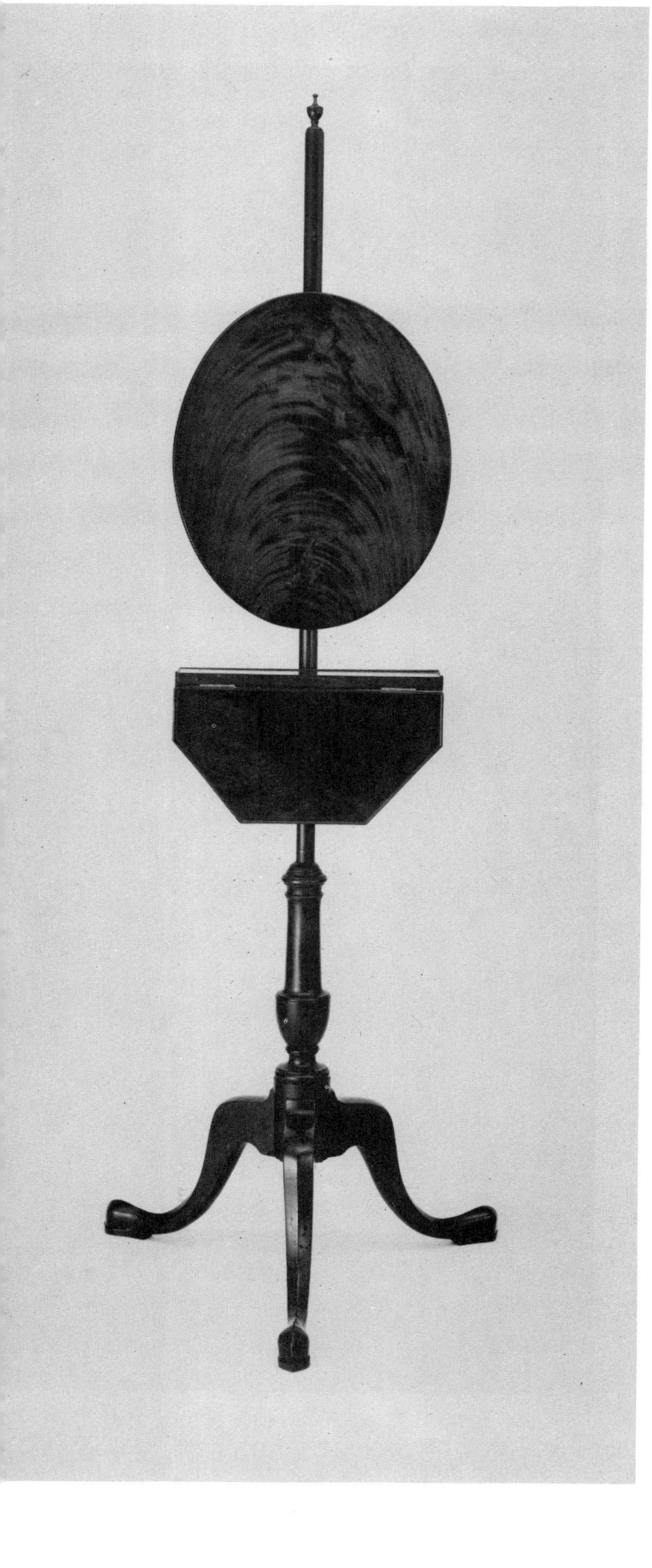

204

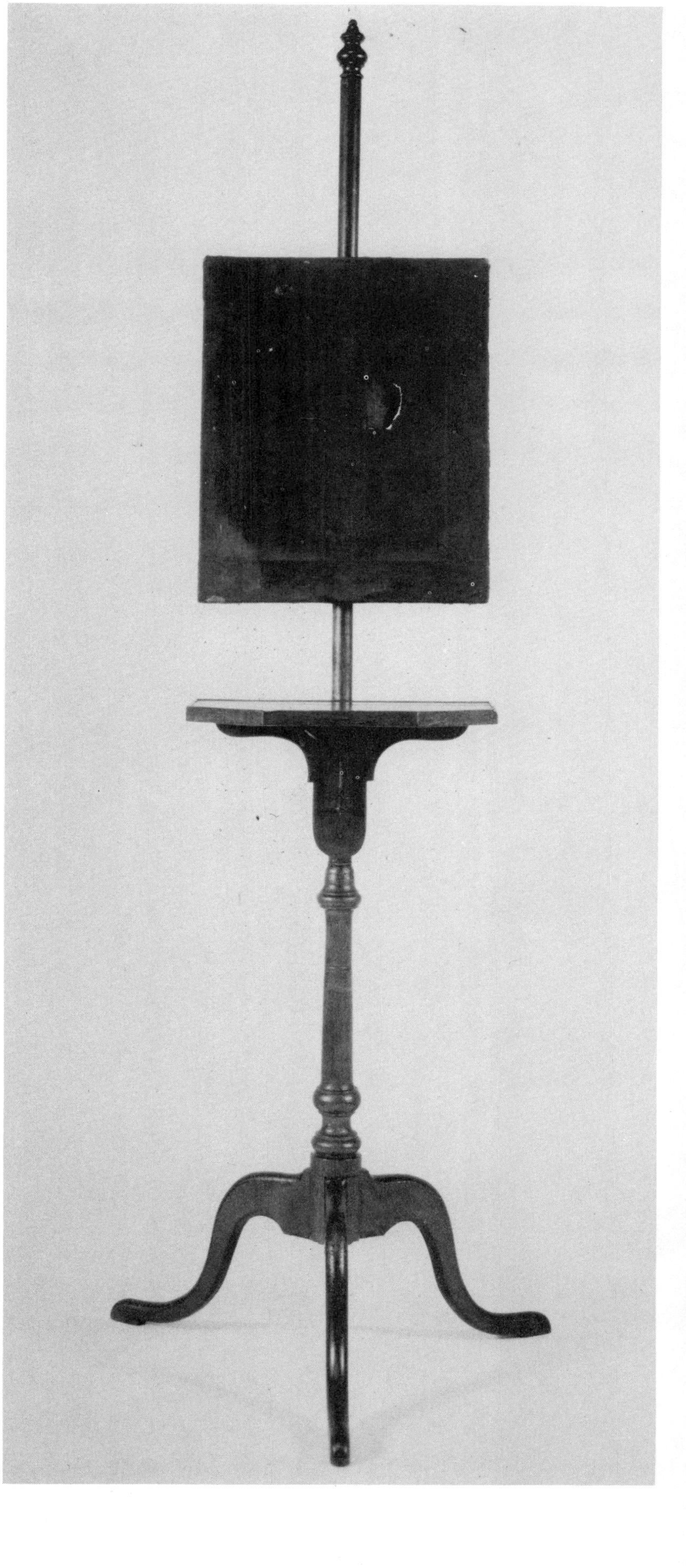

**205**

immediately on the precise eight-sided screen or it may be swept upward through the serpentine line of the claws, there to be captivated for a moment by a turned urn of great beauty and the hinged shelf ready for a candlelight. Each element is a beautiful thing in itself, clearly articulated by ring turnings or other horizontal motifs. A clever over-lapping ring at the top of the legs serves as the base of the urn. The soft curved line of the brackets fading into the shelf anticipates but does not mani-fest the eight-square quality of the octagonal-shaped screen.

Dimensions: height 61; screen $11\frac{1}{8} \times 11\frac{1}{4}$.
Materials: mahogany; no secondary woods.
Accession: 57.979

**206**

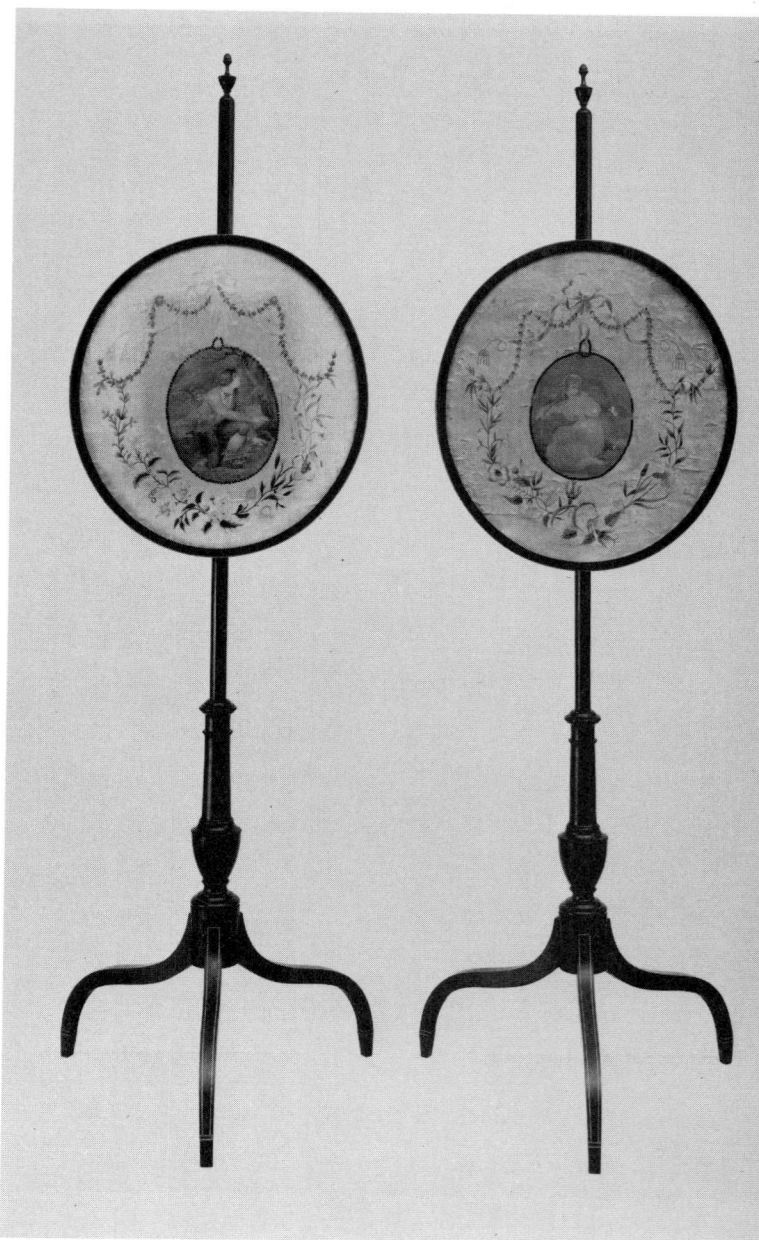

**206** POLE SCREENS (a pair)

*1800–1810   New York or Philadelphia*

Sophisticated, crisp, well-finished details, combined with grace, make this an excellent pair of pole screens and provide admirable supports for two silk needlework pictures probably wrought in a girls' seminary. For their protection, they are covered with glass in accord with the common practice noted by Sheraton: "Such screens as have very fine prints, or worked satin commonly have a glass before them."[5] The presence of tulip in the backing panels, the shape of the urns in the shaft, and the inlaid stringing outlining the cross-banded frames suggest the work of a New York or Philadelphia cabinetmaker.

Dimensions: height 58½; screen 18 × 15¾.

Materials: mahogany with stringing; backing panel, tulip; no other secondary woods.

Accession: 57.997.1, 2

**207** POLE SCREEN

*1800–1810   American*

The design concept of this pole screen is interesting in that it so neatly delineates the role of screen and stand. A dainty vase-shaped screen (of mahogany) painted with a lush basket of fruit, tipped precariously on a yellow background, is casually tied with a ribbon, in *trompe l'œil* fashion, to the pole of the stand. The stand needs to be strong enough for support, delicate enough not to compete. The spade feet, graceful legs, and refined turned shaft fill the need.

Dimensions: height 52¼; screen 16⅛ × 12¼.

Materials: mahogany; no secondary woods.

Accession: 57.558

**208** FIRE SCREEN

*About 1800   Salem*

As a display of the carver's art, cabinetmaking finesse, and for sheer opulence, no other American screen of the early nineteenth century known to the writer can match this one.[6] Derived from a Sheraton design entitled "Horse Fier Screens,"[7] it is carved and fashioned with details similar to those found on Salem furniture. A more brilliant display of carving is seldom found. The leafage rising on each of the tripod legs reminds one of carving seen on sofas attributed to Samuel McIntire; and the vase of leaves with a petalled flower which supports the screen is completely covered with spiny, feathery leaves, strongly reminiscent of those on

the side tables labeled by William Haskell. Sheraton's design includes finials; the fragile ball finials on this example were lost and have been restored to match the ball pendants.

Dimensions: height 46⅜; screen 21⅞×17¾.

Materials: maple and mahogany; stretcher, mahogany; side support and ball finial, a hard maple; upholstery (in screen), pale-blue silk.

Accession: 57.656

### 209 POLE SCREEN (one of a pair)
*1815–1825   New York or Philadelphia*

This pole screen is so different from those of usual design that it presents special problems of dating and provenance. The configuration of the base with its strong emphasis on verticality is not one often seen, but it comes directly from the "Standards for Tripod Face Screens" (No. 9, Pl. 29) illustrated in the 1793 and later editions of the London books of prices. Here carved paw feet are substituted for those shown in the plate, and dominant leaf carving is added on the outer surface of the square legs. The thinness and length of the shaft, the fruit-and-flower finial, and the shaded screen faced with a theorem painting of flowers on velvet suggest a date after 1815.

Carved paw feet are usually associated with New York cabinetmaking work of the early nineteenth century, and these stylish screens may have been made there; but by 1820 paw feet were used in many other places as well. However, the character of the clearly separated carved leaves suggests they may have been done by a Philadelphia artisan.

Dimensions: height 56½; screen 11½×15¼.

Materials: mahogany; no secondary woods.

Accession: 57.747.1, 2

### 210 POLE SCREEN
*1815–1825   Philadelphia (?)*

Curly-maple, scroll-back fancy chairs were made in large numbers in both the United States and England from about 1815 through the 1820's and 1830's. In Baltimore, John Needles made quantities of curly- and bird's-eye-maple furniture—chests of drawers, wash stands, tables, and picture frames. The sturdiness and strength of the base and pillar of this pole screen is more closely allied to Needles' work than to any other work known to the writer. However, the character of the carved leaves on the molded and claw-footed legs approximates that found on much Philadelphia furniture.

Dimensions: height 53½; screen 18½ × 18½.
Materials: curly maple.
Accession: 64.1076

## 211 POLE SCREEN
### *About 1815–1830   New England (?)*

The contrast of elements in terms of size, contour, and shape as seen here in the base of this pole screen with its sharp breaks between arcs, the urn with oversized ball at the lip, and the large screen seems to reflect the eclecticism common to some furniture of the 1820's and 1830's.

Dimensions: height 58¼; screen 13⅞ × 16⅛.
Materials: mahogany; finial, mahogany; screen, spruce (probably); rose, green, and white needlework of wool on wool.
Accession: 57.640

**209**

**210**

FOOTNOTES

1 Thomas H. Ormsbee, "The Sandersons and Salem Furniture," *American Collector*, VIII (August, 1939), 6–7.
2 Letter from Dean A. Fales, Jr., to Charles F. Montgomery, June 5, 1963.
3 Swan, *Samuel McIntire, Carver, and the Sandersons*...p.21.
4 *Ibid.*, p.20.

5 Sheraton, *The Cabinet-Maker and Upholsterer's Drawing Book* (1793), p.391.
6 A superb pole screen believed to have been made for Mrs. Elizabeth Derby West and probably a few years earlier than this one is now in the Boston Museum of Fine Arts.
7 Sheraton, *The Cabinet-Maker and Upholsterer's Drawing Book* (1793), *Appendix*, Plate 13.

**211**

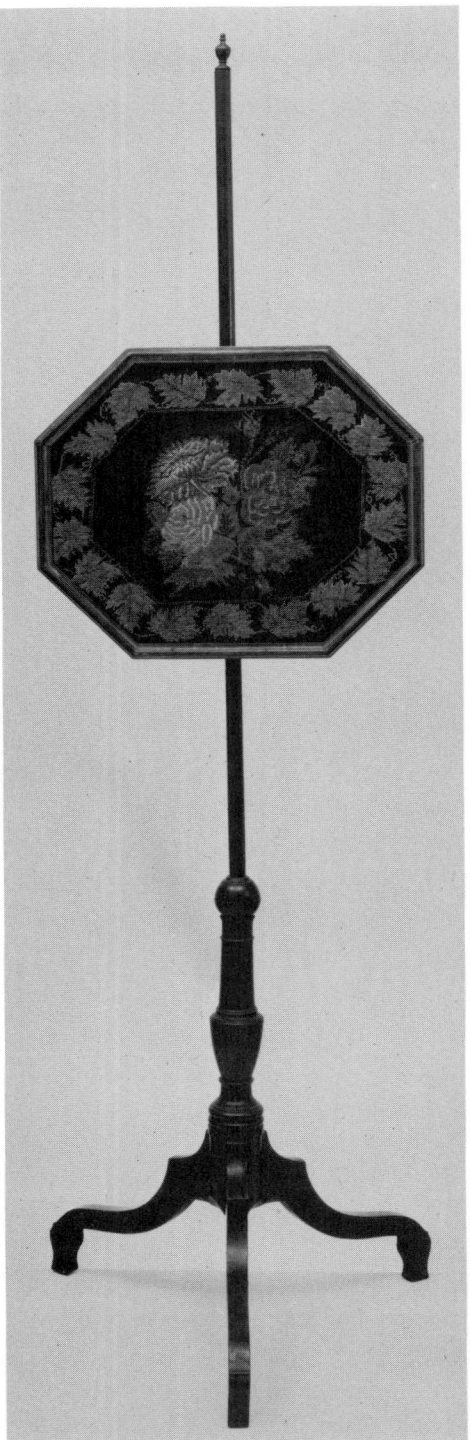

# Looking Glasses

This section includes: (1) looking glasses which, on the basis of stylistic attributes and of micro-analysis of the woods in them, are believed to have been made in America (some of these bear the maker's or seller's label); (2) looking glasses believed to have been made abroad but identified by the seller's label as having been sold in the United States soon after manufacture; (3) a few representative examples of English and European looking glasses imported here in large quantities immediately after manufacture as well as later. In most cases, micro-analysis of the woods in the frames offers evidence for distinguishing foreign examples from the native product.

Because it is well known that large numbers of looking glasses were imported for use in early American homes, such importations and similar examples are, of course, appropriate for use in American period rooms and restorations. The case for the use of such imported frames seems analogous to that for Oriental export porcelain made for the American market, English Delft, Whieldon, salt-glazed and transfer-printed wares, and English chintz and woolens for draperies and upholstery.

Newspaper notices indicate that gilt frames, occasionally oval and presumably in the neoclassical taste, were in use in the United States before the end of the Revolution; and it is the supposition of the author that, because of the large number of imports, looking glasses were au courant with English and European styles. However, the old-fashioned mahogany-and-gilt "Tabernacle" and "architectural frames," but with lighter lines and a streamlined look, continued to be highly popular (No. 213). In fact this type of looking-glass frame with scrolled pediments of the swan-neck variety may well be an American innovation not unlike that of the earlier Chippendale scroll-top highboy which, after the disappearance of the form in England, emerged in America with up-to-date ornament as a new treatment of an old form. In New York, the substitution of composition ornament for all carving except the finial, the addition of inlays and a painted-and-gilded glass panel, coupled with over-all attenuation and lightening of masses, transformed what was essentially an old-fashioned frame (No. 212) into a graceful new idiom (No. 214).

Composition ornament for use on mantels and architectural trim was offered for export by London manufacturers. On occasion the Gillow firm had carved-and-gilded ornaments for their looking-glass frames sent up to Lancaster from London. English furniture brasses were imported in large numbers as mounts for American-made furniture, just as gunlocks were imported for use on American-made rifles. While proof is lacking to support the writer's surmise that there was substantial traffic after 1790 in gilt framing and carved and composition ornaments such as scrolls, urns, leaves, and flowers, it probably is true. If so, it would account for the strange woods that are occasionally found in the ornaments on looking-glass frames that otherwise seem to be of American manufacture.

More looking-glass frames that were made after 1760 and found in America bear labels with the name of the seller and the location of his place of business than any other category of furniture. On some of these labels, such as that of Nathan Ruggles of Hartford (No. 213), the seller specifically calls himself a looking-glass manufacturer. More often, the label merely stipulates, as in the case of Stephen Badlam, Jr., of Boston, that the seller has "a constant supply of Fashionable Looking Glasses, wholesale & retail" (No. 253). Because Badlam was a cabinetmaker, he perhaps made the frames he sold, as his father apparently did before him.[1] On the other hand, when Wayne and Biddle of Philadelphia, who were general merchants, advertised that they "keep constantly for sale, Wholesale and Retail, a general assortment of Looking Glasses, cutlery, etc." (No. 222), one may be sure that someone else made them. Who? As yet this isn't known. But the type of frame and the secondary woods point to an American origin, probably local.

That looking glasses were imported in large numbers during the seventeenth, eighteenth, and early nineteenth centuries can be verified by merchants' and customs' records[2] and supported by advertisements. China and glass merchants and keepers of other kinds of shops frequently offered looking glasses and plate for looking glasses in their newspaper notices. The following are representative advertisements of this kind:

> ...just imported in the Hannah from London... Looking-Glasses... to be sold at Rhinelander's Store, the corner of Burling's Slip. (New York City, 1777)[3]
> Just imported and to be sold by James Reynolds at his Looking-Glass Store, the Golden Boy,...A great variety of English, French, and Dutch Looking-Glasses,...(Philadelphia, 1784)[4]
> J. BILLARD. At the French Store... has just received from France, an Assortment of Looking Glasses in gilt mahogany and walnut frames, with coach and window glass... (Philadelphia, 1784)[5]
> VALCK, ADRIAN. Imported, and for Sale...An Assortment of German Looking-Glasses...(Baltimore, 1789)[6]

Such advertisements, only a few of many, indicate specifically that looking glasses were being imported from England, France, Germany, and Holland. Today not enough information is available about either the styles of the frames or the woods used in them to identify accurately the country of origin of these early imports, or in many cases to differentiate them from the American-made product. Consider, for instance, the difficulty of identifying today the following looking glasses offered in 1802 by William Voight of 92 Maiden Lane, New York, as having just been received "by the latest importations from London and Hamburg, a superb assortment of Looking Glasses, made after the newest London fashion,... Elegant Gilt Frames, with pillars, balls, enamelled frieze and eagle top of all sizes."[7]

An able attempt to differentiate looking-glass frames by country of origin has been made by F. Lewis Hinckley in *A Directory of Antique Furniture*, in which he illustrates numerous looking glasses formerly called American.[8] He suggests that they came from Denmark, Germany, North Germany, Holland, or the British Isles; but, unfortunately, he fails to give enough data to support his attributions.

To assume that looking-glass frames bearing the label of any of the above advertisers were made by the seller or even in America would obviously be unwarranted; the text of advertisements is evidence to the contrary. During the past few years, the secondary woods of many mirrors found in America have been analyzed. The results lead one to the inescapable conclusion that, although a substantial number of looking-glass frames were made in this country after 1790, most of those used here before that time were made abroad. The manufacture of frames in the United States seems to have increased dramatically about 1800, but even then the custom of importing looking glasses was apparently so prevalent that American looking-glass makers normally sold imported examples along with those of their own making. That this was also done in other crafts is well illustrated by orders for English silver in the letter book of the Philadelphia silversmith, Joseph Richardson,[9] and the advertisements of William Poyntell,[10] the prominent wallpaper manufacturer of the same city. Both sold imported articles along with those of their own make.

Why was the trade in imported looking glasses so brisk and that in other foreign-made furniture so slight? A partial answer lies in the nature of the craft and the source of the raw materials. Some cabinetmakers made looking glasses, but most were made by carvers and gilders and, in the Federal period, by frame makers adept in the use of composition ornament and gold leaf.[11] Gilding was a specialized craft, some of whose practitioners were also able to silver and to polish glass. But these were complex and sophisticated operations, and there were comparatively few craftsmen in America who had the necessary skills to perform them and none who could produce glass plates suitable for looking glasses of the first quality. Despite a report in the April 7, 1790, issue of the *Gazette of the United States*[12] about the New Bremen Glass Manufactory of Maryland which noted that "we learn that [glass for] Looking Glasses will be manufactured at these works in the Spring," the following statement in *The Great Industries of the United States*, published in 1872, shows that this optimistic hope was not realized:

> The production of glass and glassware in this country was, by the census of 1860, given as nearly nine millions of dollars, and in 1870, it had reached nearly double this amount, and the business bids fair to increase still further. Though some of the modern processes, as for example, the making of mirrors, are not yet carried on in this country, and we have to depend still upon Europe for the supply of many articles of glassware to meet the demands of artistic cultivation, yet, in time, so surely has American industry become established, there is no doubt that we shall here, as in other departments of industry, attain the ability of supplying the demand. [13]

Even though suitable glass plates could not be made in the United States, large numbers were being imported plain or already silvered and the production of looking-glass frames had increased substantially; but the "most superior" were still "imported from England," as noted by Henry Bradshaw Fearon when he visited New York in 1817:

> Our friend C—— will not be displeased to learn that there are here several large carvers' and gilders' shops. Glass-mirrors and picture-frames are executed with taste and elegance; but still the most superior are imported from England. Carved ornaments are general, though some composition-ornaments are used. Plate-glass is imported from France, Holland, and England, the latter bearing the highest price. Silvering looking-glasses is a separate trade: there is but one silverer in New York, and he is not constantly employed. Carvers and gilders are paid eight-pence three farthings per hour. The sale of prints and pictures is usually combined with this business. There are here two gold-beaters: one of them is a Mr. Jones from London. Leaf-gold is frequently imported; but they consider their own equal to foreign, and it bears the same price, 40 s. 6 d. per packet, containing 20 books. The duty on imported leaf-gold is fifteen per cent. A capital of from 800 £. to 2000 £. would be requisite for a moderately respectable

concern. A journeyman gilder would not succeed; a carver may do so; but neither trades are (to use an Americanism) of the first *grade*.[14]

But, of "carvers and gilders," the compiler of the "trade directory" in Longworth's *New York Almanac* (1805–1806) noted that "work in these branches is performed in this city in a style of elegance which does honor to the taste and ingenuity of the artists."

In New England, the largest looking-glass frame-making enterprise was that of John Doggett in Roxbury, Massachusetts. Situated near the famous clockmaking establishments of Simon and Aaron Willard, his firm produced cases for their tall clocks, and gilt balls, painted-and-gilded glass "tablets," and carved eagles for their new-style banjo clocks. Working for him were the ornamental painters John Penniman, Spencer Nolen, and Aaron Willard, Jr., the carver Thomas Whitman, and numerous cabinetmakers. Some worked for wages and others on a piecework basis.

Although Doggett's records (a daybook for the years 1802–1809 and a letter book for the period 1825–1829[15]) cover but a small part of his activities, they offer many clues to the operation of one large shop. They show that, in addition to his many transactions with the Willards, he supplied glass, gilt balls, gold leaf, and glue and size to frame makers from Portland, Maine to New York City. He sent innumerable looking glasses, usually several pairs at a time, on consignment to merchants in Montreal, Portland, Portsmouth, Hartford, Albany, and New Orleans. He maintained a regular correspondence with glass suppliers abroad. Contrary to Fearon's observation above, in the 1820's Doggett wrote that his best glass (plate) came from the royal Plate Glass Manufactury in Paris, whose director he admonished on one occasion "Have them very well packed with flannel between them." Apparently Doggett determined whether to import his glass already silvered or plain (but polished) on the basis of price differential and import taxes.

Among Doggett's retail customers were those who could afford the best and the finest. For the daughter of Elias Hasket Derby, Mrs. Elizabeth Derby West, he supplied several great looking-glass frames, carved eagles, and a bed cornice with bows, darts, quivers, and arrows, the cornice gilded by William Lemon. At Doggett's service were the most gifted artisans of New England, and it is significant that the main motif engraved on his trade card is a beautiful girandole mirror frame decorated with a flourish of dolphins and surmounted by an eagle with outspread wings. These round or oval frames required greater technical skill than any other looking-glass frames of the Federal period. Probably not half a dozen shops in the whole country could have produced them.

The term "mirror" was uncommon and little used for a normal looking glass. Indeed, the word "mirror" had a special connotation, as indicated by Sheraton's definition in his 1803 *Cabinet Dictionary:* "As an article of furniture, a mirror is a circular convex glass in a gilt frame, silvered on the concave side, by which the reflection of the rays of light are produced, etc."

That this meaning of the term was current in New York is indicated by entries in the inventory and appraisal of the estate of William I. Tillman, New York City looking-glass manufacturer. The word looking glass occurs many times, but the only mention of mirror is in connection with round twelve-inch and fifteen-inch "cornice mirrors" with either "2 lights" or "4 lights" (which would appear to be the mirrors with convex glass that we call girandoles today) and to "1 Broken Convex mirror" valued at eight dollars.[16] Inasmuch as the appraisal of the estate was carried out by Bartholomew

Plain, a New York maker of looking glasses and one familiar with trade names and practice, the following excerpts are especially meaningful.

| Mg [Mahogany] | 24 | 10–8 [10 × 8] | Sconce frames | | [$] 9 75 |
| ,, | 1 | 24–15 | 1  20–12 do | | 1 75 |
| Gilt | 2 | 15 In[ch] | Cornice Mirrors [girandoles] 2 Lights | | 80 00 |
| ,, | 1 | 12 In | do        do | do | 30 00 |
| ,, | 1 | 15 do | do        do | 4 do | 53 00 |
| Mg | 2 | 17–13 | Toilet frames | | 10 00 |
| ,, | 1 | 10–8 | do        without drawers | | 50 |
| Gilt | 7 | 16–10 | Twisted Pillar frame Glass | | 38 29 |
| ,, | | 468 feet | Twist | | 4 68 |
| ,, | 4 | 17–10½ | Single twisted frame glass | | 25 36 |
| ,, | 1 | 34–20 | Twisted chimney frame glass | | 42 35 |
| Mhg | 1 | 18–12 | Piller frame Glass | | 4 16½ |
| Gilt | 1 | 28–16 | Double pillar Double Cornice Glass | | 25 25 |
| Mhg | 5 | 17–12 | Pillester fram[e] Glasses | | 18 30 |
| ,, | 2 | 21–12 | Round Pillar frame do | | 12 64 |
| Gilt | 1 | 32–14 3 In[ch] | Mat· [gold] Hollow frame Glass | | 24 53 |
| Mhg | 1 | 36–20 | Dressing Glass [a cheval glass] | | 39 00 |
| Gilt | 2 | 22–13 | Plum[e] Pillar frames | | 21 54 |
| | 1 | | Broken convex mirror [glass for a girandole] | | 8 00 |

From the above and other inventories and from Doggett's accounts, it appears that the names used by the looking-glass makers themselves were in large part descriptive and based upon one or more of the following elements:
1. Materials: mahogany or gilt.
2. Decorative elements: cornice, double cornice, pilaster, single pillar, double pillar, round pillar, twisted pillar, plume pillar.

Occasionally, references to looking glasses "with balls" can be found in old invoices and accounts. The assumption by several writers that the size of gilt balls used on looking glasses grew gradually larger after 1800 is apparently without foundation. John Doggett stocked four sizes of gilt balls. His daybook shows that his customers, such as Cerminati and Bernarda, purchased different sizes on the same occasion.
3. Function: chimney, dressing, dressing with box or drawer, toilet, swinger, sconce frame glass.

Chimney glass is frequently found as the name of a horizontal glass for an overmantel or chimney piece. In his 1803 *Cabinet Dictionary*, Sheraton states: "This is a piece of household embellishment that has of last years been much in requisition; and certainly they are a pleasing ornament to elegant rooms." Toilet glass, dressing glass, dressing box with glass, swinger—all seem to be synonymous for small adjustable glasses suspended between vertical supports, with or without drawers. The names cheval glass, horse glass, or large swinger were used for dull-length dressing glasses that normally stood on the floor.
4. Size: the size given is usually that of the plate of glass and not of the frame.

These descriptive terms are more useful and accurate than the names "Hepplewhite" and "Sheraton" so often heard today. Carved and gilt frames are frequently and mistakenly called "Hepplewhite" and columnar glasses "Sheraton." Actually, Robert Adam and Joseph Linnell had designed examples, like the so-called "Hepplewhite" frames, almost twenty years before Hepplewhite's *Guide* was published.

Sheraton shows only one looking glass (Pl. 50) in his *Cabinet Dictionary* and it is not in the columnar style. There are no specific designs for looking glasses illustrated in his *Drawing Book*. Although "No. 7, Pl. 4" (Appendix, 1802 edition, plate dated 1794), entitled "A Turkey Sofa," includes a columnar glass with plumed pillars and pictorial tablet, can this single example be sufficient reason to term all columnar glasses "Sheraton"? The common term for any vertical, rectangular, or oval looking glass was "pier glass." Robert Adam used this name for two oval frames and a rectangular one shown in an engraved plate of 1774 of the furniture of Kenwood House. Hepplewhite and Sheraton also used the same term. Specifically, it described a looking glass to hang on the pier, or wall, between two windows; but in practice the name was probably used for any vertical glass of medium to large size; and quite properly all of the larger gilt or mahogany frames with vertical proportions we describe in the catalogue that follows could be called pier glasses. In our descriptions the terms current among the original makers and sellers are generally used.

Hepplewhite's "Plan of a Room, Shewing the proper distribution of the Furniture" (Plates 124 and 125, 1788 edition of his *Guide*) is of general interest for the placement of the furniture, but of special significance in the study of looking glasses since nine are shown in one room—five pier and four oval ones with lights. The latter are termed "girandoles" by him. He suggests that if used for a dining room instead of a drawing room "the glass over the sofa ... might be ommitted"; he continues, "but this is mere opinion, many of the Dining Parlours of our first nobility having full as much glass as is here shown."

1 Stephen Badlam, Sr.'s, inventory (photostatic copy in DMMC) includes more looking glasses than any other item of furniture, and the daybook of John Doggett credited, on November 17, 1804, $38.98 to Stephen Badlam "for Looking Glass frames."

2 R.W. Symonds, "The English Export Trade in Furniture in Colonial America, II," *Antiques*, XXVII (October, 1935), 156–159.

3 *New-York Gazette, and the Weekly Mercury*, July 14, 1777. Gottesman, *1777–1799*, p. 102, No. 312.

4 *Pennsylvania Gazette*, May 12, 1784. Prime, I, 197.

5 *Pennsylvania Packet*, May 22, 1784. Prime, I, 194.

6 *Baltimore Daily Repository*, May 25, 1792. Prime, II, 214.

7 *New-York Evening Post*, November 23, 1803. Gottesman, *1800–1804*, p. 165, No. 414.

8 F. Lewis Hinckley, *A Directory of Antique Furniture* (New York: Crown Publishers, Inc., 1953), pp. 103–105, 116–118, 220, 262–275.

9 Martha Lou Gandy [Fales], "Joseph Richardson, Quaker Silversmith" (unpublished Master's Thesis, Winterthur Program in Early American Culture, University of Delaware, 1954).

10 Prime, II, 282–285.

11 That frame making was a completely separate craft from cabinet- and chairmaking is substantiated by the absence of listings for looking glasses in the cabinet- and chairmakers' and even carvers' books of prices. Only dressing boxes and dressing glasses are listed in such publications.

12 Prime Cards.

13 Horace Greeley, Leon Case, Edward Howland, John B. Gough, et al., *The Great Industries of the United States* (Hartford, Connecticut: J.B. Burr & Hyde, 1872), p. 897.

14 Fearon, op. cit., p. 29.

15 Thanks to the helpfulness of Miss Isabelle French, both of these manuscript books are now in the DMMC at Winterthur, No. 64 × 10 and No. 64 × 11.

16 Inventory of William I. Tillman (taken in New York City, December 13, 1815). DMMC, No. 54.67.206.

# xix Phyfe Room Fireplace

*The handsome and chaste mantelpiece decorated with composition ornament, and the fine detailed cornice, chair rail, and base moldings of the Phyfe Room came from a house in New York City which stood at No. 7 State Street facing Battery Park. This house was remodeled by Moses Rogers in 1806, one year before Duncan Phyfe made a large set of chairs for Roger's next door neighbor, William Bayard (No. 6 State Street). Two of these chairs (No. 66) stand before the marble-faced fireplace.*

*Centered on the mantel shelf is a French ormolu clock given to Pierre Samuel du Pont at the time of his marriage to Anne Alexandrine de Montchanin in 1766. The large gilt and painted chimney glass (No. 235), a unique and beautiful example, was originally owned by Governor Joseph C. Yates and his wife of Albany, New York. It was made there or in New York City. The vases are of oriental export porcelain.*

## 212 LOOKING GLASS (one of a pair) [1]
*About 1795   Probably English   Probably sold in New York by William Wilmerding (who ran a looking-glass store from 1789 to 1815)*

For the past twenty-five years mirrors such as this one, with gilt-scrolled pediment centering a horizontal and beaded oval with flanking leaves of laurel, have been referred to as "made by William Wilmerding" because the original bill of sale for an almost identical looking glass reads: "bot from William Wilmerding in New York, August 15, 1794 for £8:0:0 by Jacob Everson." [2] The limitation of the meaning of the word "bot" has been completely ignored by earlier writers, as has the fact that in Wilmerding's frequent advertisements appear such phrases as *"Has for sale a large and elegant assortment of gilt and wooden framed Looking Glasses and a variety of other articles of the last importation"* (italics the writer's). [3] He was a merchant, he advertised as an importer, and the combination of woods—spruce and Scots pine—is one found in several looking glasses of European origin. These facts leave little doubt that at least some of these mirrors, perhaps all, were imported and sold by Wilmerding rather than made by him. Because several of this design with New York histories are known and are seldom found elsewhere, this design may have been made to special order for William Wilmerding, whose looking-glass store was located at several different New York addresses after 1783.

Dimensions: height 54; width 25¾.

Materials: mahogany and gilt; backing panel, Scots pine; phoenix, spruce.

Provenance: Mrs. Harry Horton Benkard.

Accession: 57.884.1, 2

### 213 LOOKING GLASS, scrolled pediment[4]
*1806–1810   Hartford, Connecticut   Label of Nathan Ruggles (working 1803–1835)*

If the applied pedimental scrolls, superimposed finial, and carved and gilded side ornaments were not included on this looking glass, it would be typical of large numbers produced in this country and abroad from about 1790 to 1820. Although lighter in feeling and construction than the normal Georgian mirror, called "Tabernacle Frames" by Thomas Chippendale and "Architectural Pier Glasses" by Ince and Mayhew, this pedimented type with gilt finial and dependent side garlands is a continuation and direct outgrowth of the common mid-eighteenth-century looking-glass form. Later features are the beaded oval, fret-sawed fancifully cut-out ears, and scrolled bottom. On the backboard is a label which shows a looking glass strikingly similar to this one and that which follows. The label, engraved by Abner Reed, is identical to one also used by Ruggles and Dunbar (1804–1806) except for the name. Probably Nathan Ruggles used this label for only a few years after 1806, the year in which his partnership with Azell Dunbar was dissolved.[5] Since he began using cuts of later-style glasses as early as 1807 in his newspaper advertisements, the long-continued use of this old-fashioned label does not seem plausible.[6]

In 1811, Ruggles advertised that he had just received "at his Looking Glass Factory near the Bridge ... Old Fashioned English Looking-Glass Plates." Plate glass, sometimes beveled, was considered more desirable than the thinner modern glass. On other occasions, he called attention to the receipt of "an importation of Looking Glass Plates and English manufactured Looking Glasses." Obviously Ruggles was both making frames for imported "plates" as well as importing complete glasses.

The presence of white pine as a secondary wood throughout this mirror suggests that this is one of Ruggles' own products.

Dimensions: height 53¼; width 24⅛.

Materials: mahogany; back panel, crest, blocks, frame molding, white pine.

Provenance: Museum Purchase, 1960.

Accession: 60.175

## 214 LOOKING GLASS
*About 1800   Probably New York City, possibly Albany*

This looking glass and that in No. 215 with attenuated swan-neck scrolled pediments are typical of a handsome group of mirrors that frequently have histories of New York or Hudson Valley ownership. Common to this group are the following features: stylized, gilded, composition leaves and flowers strung on a wire down either side; gilt urn finials with gay posies or ears of wheat on wire stems; often an inlaid patera, shell, or eagle under the pediment; and sometimes, as in this and No. 215, a painted-and-gilded glass panel in the upper part of the line-inlaid frame. This type is the most distinguished of all looking glasses made or used in the United States in the Federal period.

Until more documentary evidence, such as looking-glass makers' account books, is available for study, one can but guess that cabinetmakers supplied such frames as this one with inlaid eagle and "stringing" to men like Anthony Renault of New York, who advertised in 1797 that "...He makes all sorts of frames, rich and common, whether for pictures, engravings or looking-glasses. He also gilds, upon glass, and writes inscriptions upon it in such mode or taste as may be pointed out."[7] Renault may, of course, have supplied gilded panels such as this one to other looking-glass makers, as well as using them in his own frames.

The fact that all looking glasses of this type in the Winterthur collection have white pine as the secondary wood suggests an American origin, and the fact that the inlaid eagle on this frame is closely related to eagles found on New York case furniture (see No. 452) supports a New York attribution.

Dimensions: height 72; width 27.
Materials: mahogany; crest, urn, and frame, white pine.
Accession: 57.847          see similar Inlay Fig. 115

## 215 LOOKING GLASS
*About 1800   New York City or Albany*

Varying in detail but similar in concept and execution to No. 214, this looking glass is also believed to have been made in New York or Albany. A very similar example in the collections of Sleepy Hollow Restorations bears a stenciled inscription which reads: "From Del Vecchio Looking Glass & Picture Frame Manufacturers, New York."[8] Several partnerships of various members of this family were in business in New York from about 1800 through 1847. Whether John and Joseph, who also

had a shop in Albany in 1804, specialized in this type of looking glass is not known, but it is a possibility that they were the innovators of this style of looking glass.

Dimensions: height 64½; width 24.

Materials: mahogany; backboard, frame, and crest, white pine.

Accession: 57.846

## 216 LOOKING GLASS

*About 1800    Probably Massachusetts*

Although less elongated and with the ends of the overhanging pediment cut square instead of being scalloped, this frame varies but little from the two preceding ones except in one significant detail— it is inlaid with a large eagle of a type found on several pieces of furniture of Boston or Salem origin. This particular kind of eagle, which has not been seen by the writer on furniture made outside New England, has the following special characteristics: a fierce open beak, a strongly ruffed neck, a body composed of a large shield with ebony scalloped top, a tail shaped like one or more flaring bell-flowers, and a bushy laurel leaf in one claw and a trident-like arrow in the other.

Dimensions: height 59; width 24.

Materials: mahogany; light wood and ebony inlays; crest, urn, and frame are white pine; backboard, spruce.

Accession: 57.522                    see similar Inlay Fig. 96

## 217 LOOKING GLASS

*About 1800    American*

Looking glasses with scrolled outlines at the top and bottom and outflaring ears at the corners, often made of mahogany veneered on a softer wood, have been referred to frequently as Chippendale mirrors. Simplified in concept and execution, they have the restless quality and spirit associated with Thomas Chippendale's designs, but a good many were unquestionably made well into the nineteenth century—many years after his style was outmoded for other pieces of furniture. The intricacy of the fretwork and the reeded surface of flat molding surrounding the glass suggest a date toward the end of the eighteenth century. The secondary wood of tulip attests to its American origin, but the specific locale is unknown.

Dimensions: height 58½; width 27½.

Materials: mahogany and gilt; frame, tulip; pendant, white pine; balls, maple.

Accession: 59.1365

**218** LOOKING GLASS

*1792–1795  Hartford, Connecticut  Label of Kneeland and Adams (working 1792–1795)*

Few pieces of American furniture can be as well documented as this looking glass which is closely related to the preceding example but has a gilt phoenix incorporated in the cresting of the mirror to form an integral part of the crown. On its backboard is pasted the splendid, illustrated label of Samuel Kneeland and Lemuel Adams, cabinet- and chairmakers of Hartford, in partnership from

1792 to 1795.[9] In 1793, they advertised "elegant Looking Glasses from 1 to 30 dollars each"; and, on their label, they call attention to "elegant Looking-Glasses of their own manufacturing." The style of the frame illustrated on the label is quite similar to that of Nathan Ruggles (No. 213).

Dimensions: height 37; width 18½.

Materials: mahogany and gilt; crest and pendant, mahogany veneered on white pine.

Provenance: An inscription on the back of the frame reads "From Thomas Bagg Family West Springfield, Mass."

Accession: 59.794

**219** LOOKING GLASS
*About 1790   English ( ? )*

Although mahogany oval frames for looking glasses are occasionally listed in advertisements in late eighteenth-century American newspapers, only four or five with mahogany frames are known in American collections today. One with scrolled pediment has been attributed to New England,[10] and another very fine example with intricate piercing and elaborately scrolled and gilded pediment is ascribed to New York because of its history of ownership.[11] This attractive example with chevron-like inlay is said to have been found in Baltimore, but the fact that the only secondary wood present

is spruce suggests, but does not prove, Europe as its place of origin. Stylistically it is related to English work.

Dimensions: height 37⅜; width 19.
Materials: mahogany and gilt; satinwood and ebony "stringing"; crest and frame, spruce.
Accession: 59.718

**220** LOOKING GLASS
*About 1800   English or American*

Because this design was commonly used by both American and English frame makers, there seems no way to tell the difference between American and English-made frames of this kind except by determination of the secondary woods. As was noted before, white pine is sometimes found in English furniture made in the last years of the eighteenth century; *but,* when found in English furniture, it is usually accompanied by other secondary woods such as the spruce found here. The flat-surfaced frame (outlined in inlay) is later in type than those of molded contour.

Dimensions: height 37¾; width 20⅜.

Materials: mahogany with light wood inlays; frame, spruce; backboard and brace, white pine.

Accession: 57.967

### 221 LOOKING GLASS

*About 1800   Philadelphia   Label of James Stokes (who ran a looking-glass store 1791 to 1811)*

At first glance, this looking glass and No. 222 look very much alike. Their general outlines are similar, but they differ greatly in their proportions. The head of No. 222 seems large and the ears coarse and lifeless.

For most, if not all, of the time between 1791 and 1811, James Stokes, merchant, ran a store at the corner of Front and Market Streets in Philadelphia, where he had for sale a "General Assortment of Looking Glass, Hardware, Dry Goods & Whole Sale and Retail." [12] In 1811, the business was taken over by Stokes's son-in-law, Charles Biddle, Jr., and his partner, Caleb P. Wayne. Their label appears on No. 222.

White cedar as a secondary wood was much favored by Philadelphia cabinetmakers, and the frame was probably made there for sale by Stokes. The lower ears are restorations.

Dimensions: height 29¾; width 16½.

Materials: mahogany; crest, cleat, and frame, white pine; backboard, white cedar.

Provenance: J. Kenneth Danby.

Accession: 56.38.141

### 222 LOOKING GLASS

*About 1815   Philadelphia   Label of Wayne and Biddle, Philadelphia (who ran a looking-glass store from 1811 to 1822) Successors to James Stokes*

Fretwork frames of this type continued in popularity for a long time and may have been sold throughout the partnership (1811–1822) of the merchants, Caleb P. Wayne and Charles Biddle, Jr., who ran a "Looking Glass and Fancy Store" at the southwest corner of Market and Front Streets in Philadelphia. [13] Who made the frames sold by them is not known, but the presence of white pine as the sole secondary wood (as is the case with No. 245, also bearing their label) points to American workmanship.

Dimensions: height 21; width 12⅝.

Materials: mahogany; underframing and backboard, white pine.

Accession: 57.629

### 223 LOOKING GLASS

*About 1815   Boston   Label of Elisha Tucker (working from about 1809 to 1827)*

Although not many American looking glasses bearing the labels of cabinetmakers are known, this small, pretty frame, without special merit, is probably typical of many produced by cabinetmakers

**222**

in the early nineteenth century. Thin mahogany boards were sawed in scrolled outline and glued to a frame without benefit of the services of gilder or carver. On his label glued to the backboard, Elisha Tucker (see also the handsome card table No. 302) advertises that "Mahogany Looking-Glass Frames of all sizes [are] executed in the neatest manner...," but no larger frames by him are known to the writer.[14]

Dimensions: height 17½; width 11¼.
Materials: mahogany; backing panel and frame, white pine; crest, mahogany.
Accession: 55.92.1

**224** LOOKING GLASS
*About 1807 Boston Label of Cermenati and Bernarda (in partnership 1807, 1808, and possibly later)*

This looking glass is similar to many found in New England—with scrolled outlines, an applied gilded composition ornament on the crest, and distinctive notched inner liner bordering the glass. Several of these small mirrors bear (as does this one) one or another of the Cermenati labels.

As yet, the many partnerships and complex activities of John Bernarda, Paul Cermenati, and G. Monfrino have not been unraveled; however,

**223**

**224**

it is known from the Boston directories and from addresses on their various printed labels that one relative or another of these Italian carvers and gilders had a store in Boston from about 1800 to 1820, as well as occasional branches in Salem, Newburyport, Portsmouth, and London. As indicated on the label pasted to the backboard, theirs was a varied stock, partly imported and partly produced by them in this country. Their looking glasses of this type, cut from thin mahogany boards of $^3/_{16}$- to $^5/_{16}$-inch thickness and braced with white pine, were probably made in this country.

Dimensions: height 25; width 13.
Materials: mahogany; backboard and frame, white pine; pendant, mahogany.
Provenance: Museum Purchase, 1955.
Accession: 55.92.2

## 225 LOOKING GLASS
*Label dated 1826   Utica, New York   Label of Wills M. Gaylord (working 1826 to 1845)*

Picture and looking-glass frames with broad, flat or slightly beveled surfaces, usually veneered in rich mahogany, came into vogue about 1815 and were popular for the next thirty-five or forty years. To find such a frame highlighted with satinwood veneers and embellished with the free-flowing and lively scrolls associated with the Chippendale style, yet bearing the "1826" label of a Utica, New York, looking-glass factory, is a revelation. Whether a folk revival or a new interpretation, it must be regarded as an American creation.

Dimensions: height 36¾; width 22¹/₆.
Materials: mahogany and satinwood; backing panel, tulip; crest, ash.
Provenance: Gift of Mrs. G. Brooks Thayer, 1961.
Accession: G61.410

## 226 LOOKING GLASS
*1790–1800   Probably English*

The "single plume" looking glasses listed in several inventories of looking-glass makers may have been just such creations as this, with a filigree of wire-work ornamented with beads, leaves, flowers, and stalks of wheat rising from what is essentially a gilded frame—like those used for prints and water-colors—with knurled outer edge and beaded liner. Such frames, without crest or drapery, were commonly used for prints and paintings. Except for the presence of what seems to be Scots pine, this

frame might be thought to have been American made.

Dimensions: height 60; width 24.
Materials: gold leaf over gesso, papier-mâché, wire, and wood; frame, Scots or possibly red pine; crest and glued block, white pine.
Accession: 57.681

## 227 LOOKING GLASS, pier glass
*About 1790   English*

Adaptations of basic designs were made so freely during the Federal period that close adherence to

the source of inspiration is not often found. Consequently, this exceptionally fine frame, noteworthy for its formal design and crisp and spirited carving, has the added distinction of closely following Plate 117 in Hepplewhite's *Guide*. The plate, dated 1787, was carried over to the third edition in 1794 from the original publication in 1788.

Dimensions: height 59¾; width 22¾.

Materials: carved wood, gilded; back, spruce; back cleat, oak; pendant, white pine; crest, cottonwood; bottom framing of hop hornbeam.

Provenance: Mrs. J. Amory Haskell; Mrs. Margaret Haskell Waring.

Accession: 57.998

### 227a DESIGN FOR A PIER GLASS

One of three Pier Glasses illustrated in Plate 117 of George Hepplewhite's *The Cabinet-Maker and Upholsterer's Guide,* published in London in 1788, shows the design source for looking glass No. 227. Concerning his pier glass designs, Hepplewhite commented as follows:

> For Glasses, a great variety of patterns may be invented. The frames to Glasses are almost invariably of good carved work, gilt and burnished. Six designs for square glasses are here shown, which is the shape most in fashion at this time; they should be made nearly to fill the pier.

### 228 LOOKING GLASS (one of a pair)
*1790–1800 English*

On Plates 116 and 117 of the 1788 edition of Hepplewhite's *Guide* are six designs for "Pier Glasses." All are similar in concept to this pair—glasses set within comparatively narrow gilt frames, with gilded-wood and composition ornament at top and bottom and sprays of leaves and flowers streaming down wires on either side. This pair, which hung for a long time in the Imlay House in Allentown, New Jersey, may have been purchased in 1794 at the time the house was built. The secondary woods indicate that they were in all likelihood imported, perhaps from England.

Dimensions: height 67½; width 26½.

Materials: gold leaf over gesso, papier-mâché, wire, and wood; crest, alder; back and frame, spruce.

Provenance: John Imlay and descendants.

Accession: 57.776.1, 2

227a

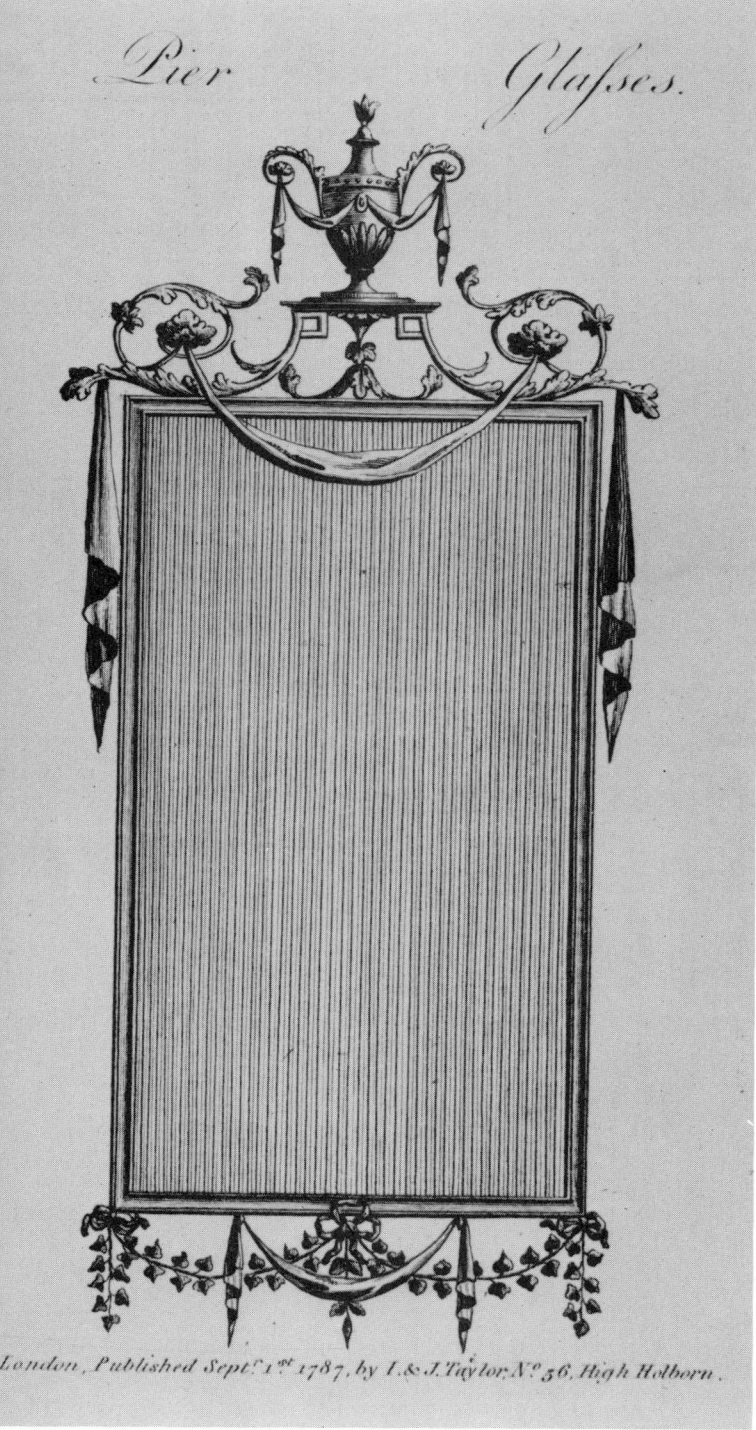

Pier Glasses.
London, Published Sept.r 1.st 1787, by I. & J. Taylor, N.o 56, High Holborn.

227

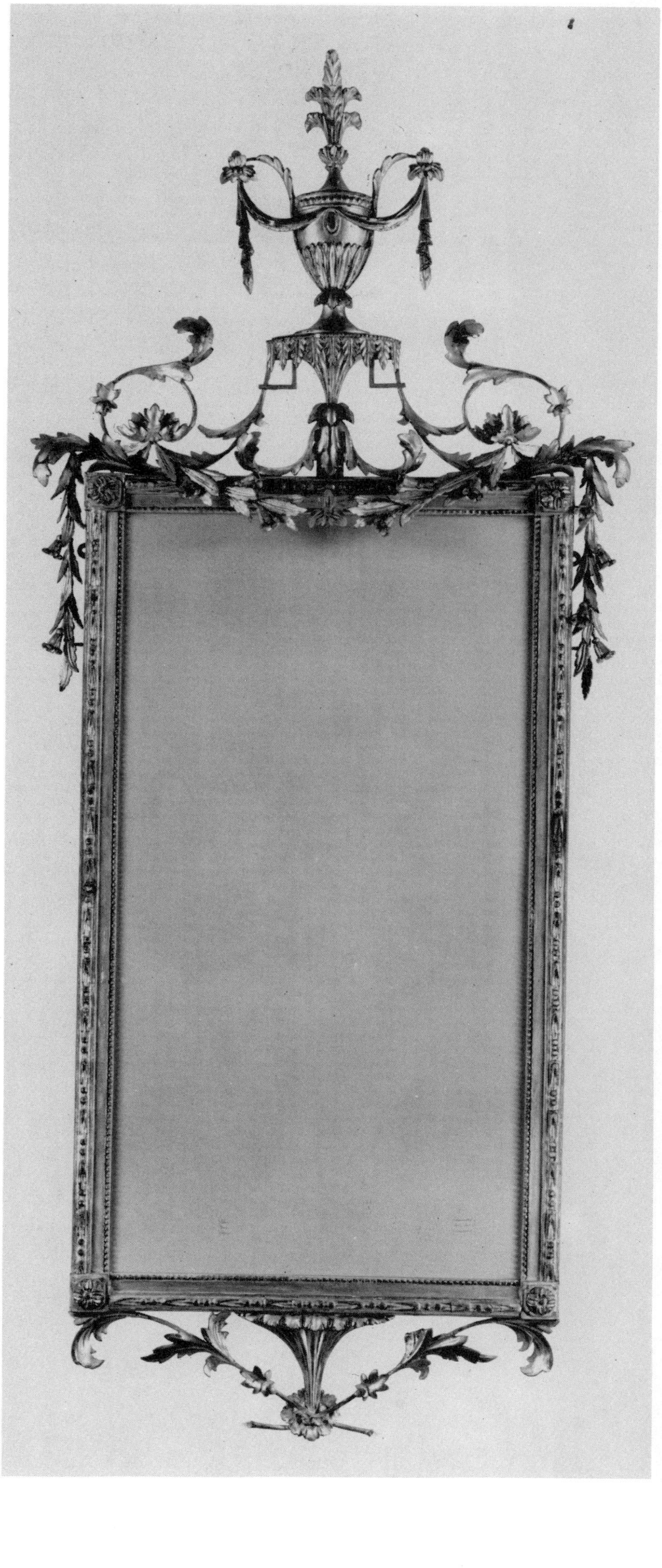

**229** LOOKING GLASS

*About 1800   Probably Continental*

Marble-framed looking glasses of this general description have been called "Bilboa or Bilbao mirrors" for at least fifty years and are thought to have been purchased in Bilbao by sea captains.[15] Some writers have suggested that such looking glasses were made in North Germany and Denmark as well as Portugal, but as yet documentation for their origin is lacking. A painting of a man standing at ease appears within the leaf-carved wreath at the center of the pediment.

Dimensions: height 43; width 20.
Materials: marble; gold leaf over gesso and carved wood;
   back and frame, Scots pine; carved parts, basswood;
   vignette painted in oil on sheet iron.
Accession: 57.911

**230** LOOKING GLASS
*About 1825   Portland, Maine   Label of James Todd*
   *(working 1820–1866)*

That the popularity of neoclassical motifs and
designs lingered for a long time in America is suggested by this gilt looking glass bearing the label of

James Todd's "Portland Looking Glass Manufactory." Seen often in earlier mirrors and repeated here are the urn and gilded festoons ornamented with composition rosettes, ears of wheat, ivy leaves, and daisies. Stylistically this looking glass is earlier than 1820, the date James Todd started working in Portland. Can this be an instance of a "looking glass plate(s) set in [an] old frame(s)" and labeled at that time? Todd advertised this service on his label. The urn seems to be of alder, a tree which grew in America but is not commonly found in American furniture. This ornament may have been imported ready-made for use on an American-made frame.

Dimensions: height 47; width 21.
Materials: gold leaf and gesso over white pine frame; urn, alder; leaf and other ornament is of composition on wire strings.
Provenance: Hyman Kaufmann.
Accession: 57.924

## 231 LOOKING GLASS (one of a pair)
*1790–1800   American*

Comparison of this pair of looking glasses with English ones in the same style reveals no significant differences except that these frames and their delicate carved parts are completely of white pine. The English seem to have favored stronger woods for the latter and to have relied less on composition work especially for leaves and ears of wheat strung on wires for swags and foliated sprays and scrolls.

Under the heading "Girandoles," Hepplewhite notes that this kind of fragile ornament "admits of great variety in pattern and in elegance; they are usually executed of the best carved work—gilt and burnished in parts."

Whether American, as the writer believes, or English, which is a possibility, this pair of glasses with simple frames bordered with beads and tiny leaves and crowned with filigree of gilt composition work are among the most delicate and feminine in the Wintherthur collections.

Dimensions: height 67; width 24.
Materials: frame, pendant, and crest, white pine covered with gesso and gold leaf; leafage is composition work on wires.
Accession: 57.678.1, 2

## 232 LOOKING GLASS
*1800–1810   English, possibly American*

Here, gold leaf and carved leaves and flowers have been used with sensitivity to create not a great glass but a very pretty small one. A nosegay and two trails of leaves and blossoms, tied with a ribbon above a drapery-decked plinth, spill forward and downward over the simple burnished gilt frame. Below, two stems of leaves and buds also held by a ribbon emphasize the horizontal lines of the oval glass. The contours and simplicity of the moldings of the frame remind one of early nineteenth-century picture frames. White pine as the sole wood employed points to an American origin though it does not prove it. There is an outside chance that the frame is American made, but the use of Scots or red pine and the fact that the leaves and flowers are carved (instead of composition) points to England as the place of origin.

Dimensions: height 30; width 26¼.
Materials: Scots or red pine.
Provenance: Museum Purchase from funds given by Charles K. Davis, 1955.
Accession: 55.19.2

## 233 GIRANDOLE MIRROR with convex glass (one of a pair)
*1800   Probably American, possibly English*

Stylized foliage and leaves carved with broad strokes and considerable flair were often used with

**232**

dramatic effect on looking glasses made in England and on the Continent after about 1800. Perhaps because good carving was less readily available to American looking-glass makers in this period, they seem to have relied more on cast composition ornament, which is often less three-dimensional or sculptural than the exquisite carved leaves seen here.

The urn shape of the candle cups and the beading of the frame suggest a slightly earlier date for this mirror than for No. 234. An American attribution is made because of the white pine frame. However, the writer wishes to emphasize that the presence of white pine cannot be regarded as positive proof of American manufacture when found in looking glasses made about 1800 or later.

Dimensions: height 38; width 20.

Materials: gold leaf and gesso over white pine.
Accession: 57.942.1, 2

## 234   GIRANDOLE MIRROR
*1810   American or English*

Round gilt frames with convex glasses are often referred to as girandoles or girandole mirrors. According to Sheraton, a mirror (as an article of furniture) is a "circular convex glass in a gilt frame, silvered on the concave side, by which the reflection of the rays of light are produced. The properties of such mirrors consist in their collecting the reflected rays into a point, by which the perspective of the room in which they are suspended, presents itself on the surface of the mirror, and produces an agreeable effect. On this account, as

well as for the convenience of holding lights, they are now become universally in fashion, and are considered both as a useful and ornamental piece of furniture."[16]

Although these glasses are usually fitted with candle arms, there is an occasional exception that does not have sconces, as is the case with this glass. Because so many girandoles have an eagle as a crest, one might suppose such glasses to be either American made or made specifically for the American market, but that is not always the case. The eagle has been a popular decorative device for centuries. It often appears as a crest on such frames made in England, and may well have been used elsewhere in Europe.

Just where this frame was made is impossible to say. No looking glasses of this type that are documented as made by a particular American maker or in a specific American center have come to the attention of the writer, and regional style characteristics have yet to be worked out. However, the carved eagle is unlike any of known American provenance, and the presence of white pine is inconclusive because some furniture made in England after 1800 has been found with white pine as a secondary wood. The size of balls on looking glasses was thought at one time to offer clues for dating. The accounts of John Doggett show that he was selling them in four sizes throughout the period 1804–1809.

Dimensions: height 43; width 26½.
Materials: gold leaf and gesso over white pine frame and crest; balls, alder.
Accession: 57.750

### 235 OVERMANTEL LOOKING GLASS
chimney glass
*About 1805   New York City or Albany*

This "chimney glass," a delicate confection of pale gilt and tinted glass, flowered latticework, and candy-twist sunbursts, is one of the most beautiful of all American looking glasses.

A dozen or more richly conceived and beautifully executed mirrors embellished with painted and gilded glass panels, often with gilt colonnettes and surmounted with two or more leafy urns (as seen here and in Nos. 236 and 237), have Albany histories and are known in the antiques trade as "Albany Mirrors." Who made them or exactly when they were made is not known, but all that have been examined by the writer are made principally of white pine without the presence of European woods. It seems logical to suppose they are the product of a gifted and as yet anonymous Albany or possibly New York craftsman.

Dimensions: height 55½; width 75½.
Materials: gold leaf over gesso, wood, and wire; all secondary woods are white pine.
Provenance: Gov. and Mrs. Joseph C. Yates; Jane Josepha de Lancey Neill; Edward Montandevert Neill; Anna Delancey Neill Grinnell (Mrs. Edward).
Accession: 57.733

### 236 LOOKING GLASS, double pillar
with twist
*About 1805   Albany or New York City*

Closely related in concept and in detail of ornament and execution to the preceding overmantel mirror, this highly feminine glass is also believed to have been made in Albany or New York. Gilded vases with large ears are seen on virtually all of such frames.

Then, as now, looking glasses were important in a woman's life. Touching indeed are the words of Abigail Adams in a letter written on June 9, 1790, from New York City (then the national capital and her husband, John, the vice-president) to her sister in Braintree, Massachusetts:

> I must request the favour of my good Brother Cranch to get me a case made for my large looking glass, and to be so good as to pack it for me & send it by Barnard...The Glass

I do not know how to do without.... I cannot afford to Buy. Besides I have enough for the Braintree House, & should I purchase here, must sell them again at a loss. This House is much better calculated for the Glasses, having all the Rooms Eleven foot high.[17]

Dimensions: height 62; width 27.
Materials: gold leaf and gesso over white pine frame and urns, composition flowers, leafage, and ears of wheat.
Provenance: The Van Brunt Family, Middletown Township, New Jersey; Mrs. J. Amory Haskell.
Accession: 57.734

**237** LOOKING GLASS, single pillar with beading
*About 1800    Albany or New York City*

Of similar concept, though differing in detail, this glass is a stronger and less delicate expression of the theme so well stated in the two preceding examples and appears to be from the same source. The history of this looking glass is not currently known, but in the caption for it in the catalogue of the *Girl Scouts Loan Exhibition*, No. 739, the remark is made that "this particular one *lived* in Monmouth County, New Jersey, all its life until a few years ago."

painted panel is used above the mirror (as a base for composition ornament standing in relief) instead of a glass ornamented in gilt. Profile busts applied to the architraves above substantial, engaged, reeded and gilt colonnettes are matched in strength by a robust eagle on a hemisphere above a projecting plaque at the top. The effect sought was one of grandeur rather than delicacy. Although this looking glass may have been made in England, it relates to some New England work and seems more likely to have been made there.

Dimensions: height 54; width 27¾.
Materials: white paint or gold leaf and gesso over white pine frame; backboard, fir.
Accession: 57.925

## 239 LOOKING GLASS, single pillar with a single twist
*About 1800   New York City*

At the turn of the century, countless frame and looking-glass makers were busy in well-advertised shops; their work, much of it basically alike, varied mostly in the degree of ornament and the quality of its execution. According to Joseph Downs, Joseph Tallman labeled frames of this pattern, with hollow colonnettes inset with twist, incised festoons, and ball-hung cornice. A Tallman engraved label described by Downs shows a classically robed goddess seated before a pier glass, obviously to call attention to the elegance and high fashion of his frames.[19]

The painted glass panel in brilliant colors shows the first President with the emblems of war against a rolling landscape, and above it all the ubiquitous eagle surveys the scene. The expression of American Independence was a national theme repeated in every medium of the arts, although not always so competently as here.

Dimensions: height 51⅛; width 27½.
Materials: gold leaf on gesso; frame, white pine; backboard, basswood.
Accession: 57.615

Dimensions: height 52; width 26.
Materials: gold leaf and gesso over white pine frame, urns, and eagle and composition flowers and ears of wheat.
Accession: 57.1063

## 238 LOOKING GLASS
*1785–1800   New England (?)*

Essentially of the same form as the preceding looking glasses, this one is, however, more three dimensional, less feminine, and more in the style of Adam than in the mode of Hepplewhite. A white

## 240 LOOKING GLASS, single pillar with a single twist
*About 1810   Possibly New York*

With Mount Vernon in the background and portraits of George and Martha Washington shown on the funerary urn, there can be no doubt that this is a memorial to Washington. Both the oil painting on glass and the looking-glass frame were

**240**

Dimensions: height 38; width 23½.
Materials: gold leaf and gesso over white pine frame and tulip balls; backboard, oak.
Accession: 57.1048

## 241 LOOKING GLASS (one of a pair)
*About 1810   Probably American*

This frame differs from the preceding ones in the use of picture-frame molding for the sides and bottom instead of the more usual pillars, pilasters, or hollowed colonnettes. The pastoral scene in the upper section, painted in oil on a convex oval wooden panel, is set in a gilt sand-surfaced tablet.

Dimensions: height 48¼; width 35; depth 5¾.
Materials: gold leaf over gesso; white pine frame.
Accession: 57.712.1, 2

**241**

probably produced within a few years after his death (December 14, 1799).[20]

Of interest with reference to this frame and related ones are two entries in the 1815 inventory of William I. Tillman, New York looking-glass manufacturer:

| Gilt | 468 feet Twist | [$] 4.68 |
| 5 Patterns [molds for?] balls | | [$] 17.50 |

It seems logical to suppose that these molds were for making balls to be gilded later on. Some found on early nineteenth-century frames are of cast composition (others are of turned wood). As noted before, in the accounts (1804–1809) of John Doggett of Roxbury, Massachusetts, are many charges to other framers for balls in four sizes at 5, 6, 7, and 8 dollars per gross.

**242** LOOKING GLASS (one of a pair)
*1815–1825   New England   Possibly Boston*

The tablets above the glass in each of this all-gilt pair of looking glasses are highly individual and interesting. Two groups of well-modeled figures of cast "composition work" (plaster and glue) are shown in relief. That at the left of a woman in Empire-style dress seated on a klysmos-type chair with a child at her side is entitled "Listen to a Pretty Story." The tableau at the right labeled "Step by Step" shows a kneeling woman in similar low-cut dress beckoning to a toddler.

Soon after 1800 the use of gilt balls in the cornices of gilt looking-glass frames became widespread; and the accounts of John Doggett of Roxbury, Massachusetts, show that he supplied them in large numbers in four sizes to neighboring frame makers as early as 1804. Their use around the sides of covered frames probably parallels the increasing massiveness of frames after about 1810 or 1815. However, one frame maker, Stillman Lothrop, who after working in Doggett's shop went into business for himself, used them on the fronts of the delicate tapered legs of a painted dressing table.[21]

Dimensions: height 49⅜; width 33¾.
Materials: gold leaf and gesso over white pine.
Provenance: Jonathan Hatch Hubbard[22]; Museum Purchase, 1960.
Accession: 60.192.1, 2

**243** LOOKING GLASS, painted pier glass[23]
*1810–1825   England or Europe*

With a long history of ownership in the Rapelye and Totten families of Brooklyn, New York, and with the obvious and explicit connotations of "E Pluribus Unum" on the banderole above the large, carved and painted (brownish-black) eagle— with shield on its breast and arrows and olive branch in its talons—one might assume this splendid and large painted looking-glass frame to have been made in the New York area. There were many looking-glass makers at work there in the early nineteenth century, and there were also family craft ties with one James Rapelye listed in the directories as a cabinetmaker in 1819 and 1820 at 171 Division Street. The frame may have been made in New York, but the use of spruce and Scots pine as the chief structural woods and a wood that defies identification for the carved eagle strongly suggest a European origin.

The well-carved spray of leaves, the baton, the banding on the columns, and the moldings and other details are highlighted with gold leaf. The columns with encircling composition leaves and background surfaces are covered with bronze paint.

Dimensions: height 88¾; width 40½; depth 4¼.
Materials: base of right column, spruce; moldings, Scots or red pine.
Accession: 57.941

**244** LOOKING GLASS, pilaster frame
with cornice
*About 1815   Hartford   Label of Spencer and Gilman (working May, 1808, to at least 1825 as a partnership)*

Almost immediately after Commodore Perry's naval victory on Lake Erie, several prints commemorating the event were produced. Exactly

**242**

which one served as the source for the vignette seen here is not known, but the painter added not only the title, *Engagement on Lake Erie,* but also an American eagle with shield as additional appeal to a victory-hungry people engaged in a controversial war. Just how soon this frame was produced after the engagement, which took place on September 10, 1813, is not known.

Dimensions: height 38; width 18¼.
Materials: mahogany; frame, basswood; backboard, tulip.
Accession: 57.616

**245** LOOKING GLASS, single-pillar frame
with cornice
*About 1815   Philadelphia   Label of Wayne and Biddle
(in partnership from 1811 to 1822)*

The selling of prints seems to have been common practice for looking-glass manufacturers and frame makers as a sideline and stimulus to framing. Among the items listed in the 1815 appraisal of the stock of the looking-glass manufacturer William I. Tillman [24] are large numbers of prints, among

**245**

*About 1815   Philadelphia*

This frame, almost identical in design to No. 245, but with a gilt picture of Mount Vernon instead of Perry's Victory, was probably made in the same shop. Whether it was sold by Wayne and Biddle is uncertain because the design was not made exclusively for them. A similar frame [25] with a different picture but with the same reeded columns, turned bosses, and details of construction bears the label of Earps & Co. of Philadelphia. The Earps were hardware merchants in business from about 1814 to 1825. Their label and Wayne and Biddle's were both printed by P. M. Lafourcade at 273 North Front Street.

**246**

them *Perry's Victory*. One of the prints of this important naval action probably served as a source for the painting on glass seen in the upper section of this frame, which bears the label of the sellers, Wayne [Caleb P.] and Biddle [Charles, Jr.]. As already noted, the looking glasses sold by them were made by others (see Nos. 221 and 222).

Dimensions: height 49; width 25.

Materials: mahogany; back and framing, white pine; moldings, mahogany.

Accession: 57.910

Although frames of this kind date from the middle of the Federal period, the correct architectonic style of engaged columns resting on a plinth and supporting a cornice has the restrained elegance, nice scale, and refinement found on earlier examples.

Inscribed on the backboard in ink is "Mt. Vernon" and a penned label which reads "This glass was my Grandmothers. E.H.I. [his mother] has given it to my son Harry D. Lippincott." Where he lived is not known.

Dimensions: height 40½; width 26.
Materials: mahogany; framing and backboard, white pine.
Accession: 57.963

## 247 CHEVAL GLASS, screen dressing glass
*About 1800    American*

The description "Two Oval Swinging Glasses with Mahogany frames and black and white string edges—one marked on the back 52 s, 6, the other 35 s ... stolen out of one of the stores of the subscribers ... Willing, Morris & Swanwick [on the night of Jan. 26, 1784]"[26] offers a clue to the old name and date of such glasses. "Swingers" is another name occasionally met with in advertisements and inventories. The sophisticated turnings and high quality suggest an urban center as its place of origin. White oak is occasionally found in Philadelphia and Baltimore furniture of this period.

Dimensions: height 58¾; width 38⅛; depth 23⅛.
Materials: mahogany with rosewood inlays; second lamination of molding side and bottom, white oak; splinter from an earlier block, white pine.
Accession: 57.1004

## 248 LOOKING GLASS ON STAND,
   or Cheval Glass
*About 1805    Probably American*

The term "horse," or cheval, glass is explained by Sheraton in his *Cabinet Dictionary* as follows: "a term applied to the feet which supports a rising desk, or which keeps a glass in an inclined position. It is also used to denote a kind of tall dressing-glass suspended by two pillars and claws, and may, when hung by two centre screws, be turned back or forward to suit the person who dresses at them."

The shape of the legs and the applied bosses at their tips suggest a slightly later date than that of No. 247, of which this is a smaller version. Although such frames are more frequently found in New York

than elsewhere, it is at present impossible to relate this one to documented examples.

Dimensions: height 33½; width 16⅝; depth 15.
Materials: mahogany; glass retainer block, white pine.
Provenance: Exhibited in *Accessions 1960*, Henry Francis du Pont Winterthur Museum; No. 15, p. 13, in catalogue of the same title.
Accession: 59.129

## 249 DRESSING GLASS
*1784–1803    Philadelphia or English    Label of John Elliott, Jr. (working from about 1762–1810)*

In looking-glass makers' accounts, one finds such names as a "swinger," "oval dressing glass," or

**247**

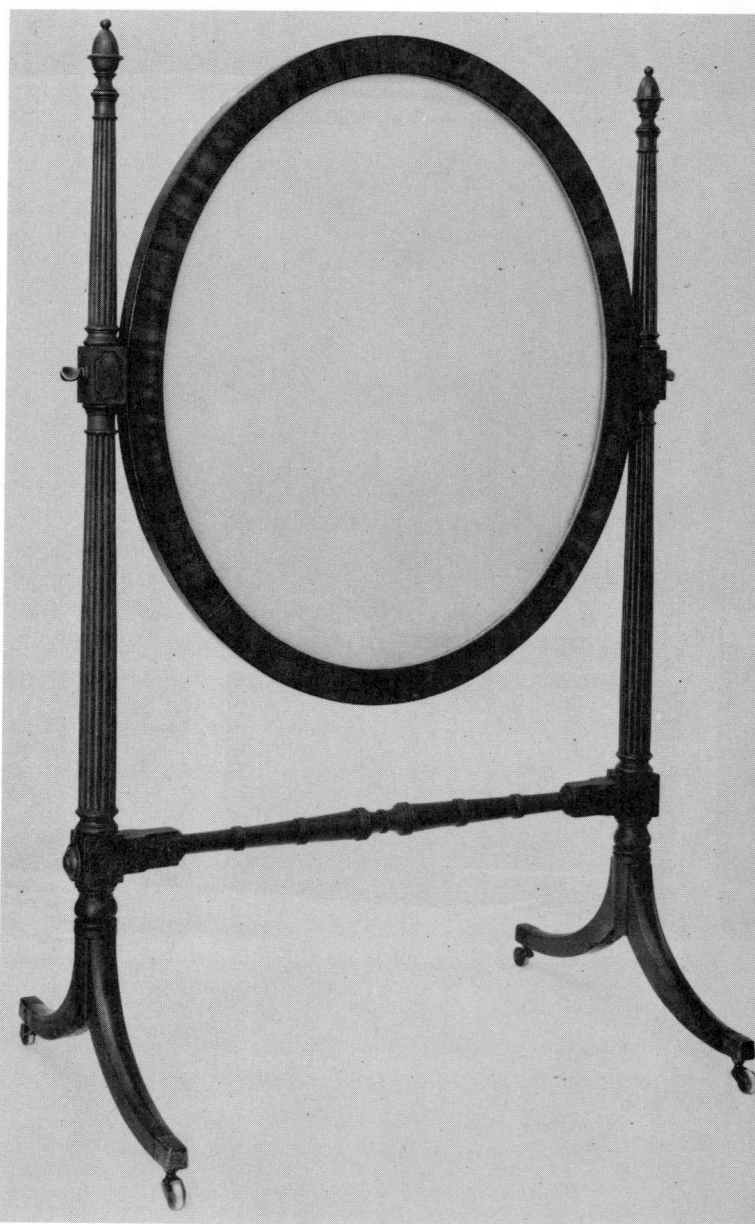

"toilet glass without drawer." Any of these names might properly be applied to this neat oval frame with cross-banded facing edged in satinwood and supported on a curvilinear trestle-based pair of uprights. John Elliott, Jr., whose label it bears, is not known to have made looking glasses himself, although he, like his father, carried on an active business in them. Whereas his father frequently mentions his importing and selling looking glasses, his son—John, Jr.—advertises on his label that he "sells by Wholesale and Retail Looking Glasses in neat Mahogany Frames of American Manufacture." [27] Although he does not state whether he makes these glasses himself or buys them from other Americans, the statement is of special significance because neither the hemlock nor oak used as secondary woods can be positively identified as American or English.

Dimensions: height 13⅝; width 10¼; depth 6⅛.

Materials: mahogany; mirror backing, a hemlock (American or foreign); mirror frame, a white oak.
Provenance: Museum Purchase, 1958.
Accession: 58.85.2

## 250  DRESSING GLASS
*About 1795   American, possibly New York*

Four designs for "dressing glasses" are illustrated in Plates 71 and 72 of *The Cabinet-Maker and Upholsterer's Guide* by Hepplewhite. Of these the author remarks that the ornaments "may be inlaid with various coloured woods, or painted and varnished."

How handsome this dressing glass must have been when new—pristine in white paint set off with gilt. Not only were the box, the standards, and the frame outlined in gold, the old-style claw-and-ball and bracket feet, the scrolls of the pediment, and the new-fashioned composition patera and ornamental rosettes for the pulls were also gilt. Because tulip was not generally used by cabinet-makers in northern New England, this dressing glass probably originated south of Massachusetts. An urban center would account for its sophistication.

Dimensions: height 25; width 15¼; depth 7¼.
Materials: painted wood; brass; drawers, bottom of case, and pediment, tulip; moldings and legs, white pine.
Accession: 57.956

**251** DRESSING GLASS, serpentine front with two drawers
*About 1800    Massachusetts*

Here elements of an old style and a new one are combined to provide a unique new form. The slant top as on a desk, the claw-and-ball foot, and

the serpentine front are features often seen on New England Chippendale furniture. The vase- or shield-shaped frame for looking glasses was first illustrated in Plate 14 of the first edition of *The Cabinet-Makers' London Book of Prices* of 1788.

Dimensions: height 27¼; width 14½; depth 8.
Materials: mahogany and gilt; drawer bottom, back and bottom of case, and mirror-frame molding are white pine; back panel, fir.
Accession: 58.2431

**252** DRESSING GLASS, bow front with two drawers
*About 1810    New Jersey*

The finesse of design and execution of this striking dressing glass with drawers is abundantly evident in the broad outline of satinwood on the edges of

**250**

**251**

the top and drawers; the use of ivory disks to mark the upper terminals of the curvilinear supports; the harmony of outline of supports and oval frame; the rounded veneer used to face the glass; and the spectacular inlaid butterflies silhouetted against ovals of satinwood which are stained green and set in mahogany.

Similar inlaid butterflies in a splendid tall case clock owned by Mrs. Giles Whiting offer a clue to the origin of this piece. The movement of her clock bears the inscription, "Ezra Woodruff, Elizabeth Town [New Jersey]"; and the case bears many of the refinements and features seen in the work of Joachim Hill, Abraham Rosett, and others working in the Elizabeth, New Jersey, area.

Dimensions: height 23⅝; width 17; depth 7½.

Materials: mahogany; satinwood inlays; frame and glass

**252**

backing, hard pine; drawer linings, tulip; cabinet ends, white pine.

Accession: 51.23      see Inlay Fig. 114

**253** DRESSING GLASS,[28] bow front with one drawer

*Early Nineteenth Century   Boston   Label of Stephen Badlam, Jr. (working early nineteenth century)*

Although his label pasted to the board backing the glass does not specify whether he, Stephen Badlam, Jr., actually makes the "constant supply of fashionable looking-glasses [available] wholesale & retail," this dressing glass has all the earmarks of a cabinetmaker's product. The stylish flair of the "french" feet and the serpentine line which sweeps from the feet across the skirt remind one of bow-front bureaus of the period. Features found occasionally on fine American furniture and present on this example are the fan, chevron, and rope inlays, and the cock-beading of drawers.

Little is known of the younger Badlam, but apparently—like his father—he carried on both the cabinetmaking and looking-glass business in the city of Boston.

Dimensions: height 20¼; width 20⅞; depth 9¾.

Materials: mahogany, satinwood and ebony inlays; all secondary woods, white pine.

Provenance: Jerome W. Blum; Museum Purchase, 1958.

Accession: 58.39      see Inlay Fig. 47

**254**

Picture Frame Manufactory," was located at No. 44 Chatham St. New York.[29] Whether or not "fashionable" at that time, it documents the continuance of the straight lines and simplicity of the Hepplewhite style into the third decade of the nineteenth century. The same was occasionally true for other furniture forms.

Dimensions: height 15¾; width 14¼; depth 7.
Materials: mahogany; drawer bottom and front, backing panel, mirror frame (top section), white pine; drawer back and side, tulip.
Accession: 55.553

**256** DRESSING GLASS
*1815–1825   American, possibly Boston*

The reeding and rake of the upright supports, the verve of the scrolled brackets, and the repetition of rounded and spherical motifs give this richly veneered dressing glass great style. The sphere and the circle are repeated again and again in the ball feet, thumbscrews, turned finials, centers of spirals and rosettes, and the strong convex outline of the torus molding framing the glass. Indicative of a date of 1815 or later are the ball-shaped feet,

**254**  DRESSING GLASS, bow front with three drawers
*1800–1815   American   Probably New England*

The veneered ovals centered within mitred borders on the cock-beaded drawer fronts, the ivory escutcheon and pulls, and the bowed façade are in the normal New England idiom for case furniture. Whether affection for the painted and gilt marine scene (probably from a tablet of a gilt looking glass) or ingrained thrift on the part of its owner accounts for the insetting of the irregular shaped fragment of glass on the top of the case, the result is an unusual dressing glass.

Dimensions: height 22½; width 23¾; depth 9.
Materials: mahogany inlaid with glass and ivory; secondary wood, white pine.
Accession: 57.1049

**255**

**255**  DRESSING GLASS
*1830   New York City   Label of Charles Del Vecchio (working 1820 to 1844 and later)*

Charles Del Vecchio advertised on his label "Pier, Chimney, & Dressing Glasses, Framed in the neatest and most fashionable Patterns." This dressing glass may have been termed "neat" from 1830 to 1839 during which time his "Looking Glass and

Similar frames with glasses so cut and silvered as to provide seven or nine individual small circular reflecting surfaces and consequently as many images of the viewer, may be regarded as a kind of "vanity glass." They may have been imported but the woods used in this one suggest an American origin.

Dimensions: height 6¼; length 11; depth ½.
Materials: maple; back, white pine; molding, beech.
Accession: 58.1138

FOOTNOTES

1 Illustrated in the Catalogue of the *Girl Scouts Loan Exhibition*, No. 636.
2 Downs, "Two Looking Glasses," *Antiques*, XLIX (May, 1946), 299. The "Everson" looking glass almost identical to this pair is illustrated in *Albany Furniture by New York Cabinetmakers*, p. 59, No. 71.
3 Gottesman, *The Arts and Crafts of New York, 1777–1799*, p. 142.
4 Exhibited in *Accessions 1960*, No. 16, Fig. 3.
5 See Phyllis Kihn's article "Ruggles and Dunbar, Looking Glass Manufacturers," *Bulletin* of the Connecticut Historical Society, XXV (April, 1960), 56–60.
6 According to the George C. Groce and David H. Wal-

stamped brass pulls and rosettes nailed to the corners of the frame, and the S-shaped brackets. Related brackets are found on Boston-made dressing bureaus.

Dimensions: height 23¼; width 30⅝; depth 7⅞.
Materials: mahogany; all secondary woods, white pine.
Accession: 57.1050

## 257 DRESSING GLASS
*About 1825 American*

Of no great distinction but probably typical of large numbers of such folding dressing boxes made about 1825, this one is unusual in being made of curly maple.

Dimensions: height (raised) 12; height (folded) 4¼; width 12⅛; depth 10⅛.
Materials: curly maple with mahogany feet; bottom and partitions, white pine; top framing, tulip.
Accession: 57.1040

## 258 LOOKING GLASS
*1800–1825 American (?)*

Many painted round frames with turned handles (usually black) survive in the United States today. They must have been used in large numbers.

**258**

lace, *Dictionary of Artists in America* (New Haven: Yale University Press, 1957), p.528, Abner Reed, who engraved the label, left Hartford in 1811 and did not return until 1821.

7 An advertisement from *Argus, Greenleaf New Daily Advertiser*, January 2, 1797, quoted in Gottesman, *The Arts and Crafts in New York, 1777–1799*, No.454, p.141.

8 Photograph of looking glass and inscription in Decorative Arts Photographic Collection, Winterthur Museum. Courtesy of Sleepy Hollow Restorations.

9 "A Kneeland and Adams Mirror" by William Stuart Walcott, Jr., *Antiques*, XIII (January, 1928), 30–32, contains an excellent account of this partnership. Also see

Nos. 173 and 392 in Downs' *American Furniture*, for chest of drawers and label.

10 Sack, *Fine Points of Furniture: Early American*, p.210.

11 Helen Comstock, "The American Looking Glass, Part II," *Antiques*, LXXXV (April, 1964), 438–441.

12 Information from the Philadelphia directories.

13 *Ibid.*

14 For further information on Tucker, see "Works of Boston Cabinetmakers, 1795–1825," by Randall, *Antiques*, LXXXI (April, 1962), 412–415.

15 *The Hudson-Fulton Celebration, Catalogue of an Exhibition Held in the Metropolitan Museum of Art.* No.182, 70.

16 Sheraton, *The Cabinet Dictionary*, p.271.

17 Abigail Adams, *New Letters of Abigail Adams, 1788 to 1801*, ed. Stewart Mitchell (Boston: Houghton Mifflin Company, 1947), p.50.

18 *The Americana Collection of the Late Mrs. J. Amory Haskell*, Part One, April 26, 27, 28, 29, 1944, Parke-Bernet Galleries, Inc., No.719.

19 Somewhere Joseph Downs had seen such a looking glass with a label as described. However, he did not mention in his notes its present whereabouts.

20 That similar scenes were popular for many years after Washington's death is indicated by a needlework memorial in the Winterthur collection (Acc.No.57.784) made by Elizabeth Lane and dated 1817.

21 This table with Stillman Lothrop's label which gives his address as No.29, Court Street [Boston], is in the collection of the writer.

22 Hubbard family history of these looking glasses ascribes original ownership to J.H.Hubbard, born 1768, admitted to the bar in 1790. Congressman, 1809–1811. He lived all his life in Windsor, Vermont.

23 Exhibited in the Brooklyn Museum in 1930 and illustrated in the January issue of *The Antiquarian* of that year.

24 Inventory of William I.Tillman (taken in New York City, December 13, 1815) in the DMMC, MS.54.67.206.

25 In the collection of the writer.

26 This entry from the *Pennsylvania Packet*, January 29, 1784, is listed in Prime, I, 199.

27 Alfred Coxe Prime, "John Elliott," Pennsylvania Museum *Bulletin* (April, 1924), pp.126–140. Cf. especially 134, 137.

28 Illustrated in Swan, "General Stephen Badlam—Cabinet and Looking Glass Maker," *Antiques*, LXV (May, 1954), 383.

29 Sale Catalogue of the *Collection of the Late Benjamin Flayderman*, No.414.

# Sofas and Couches

A cursory examination of estate inventories of the Federal period indicates that sofas, couches, and settees were luxuries. A large number of inventories before 1810 of individuals with small estates contain almost none of these seating forms; in ten "room-by-room" inventories for wealthy Bostonians taken in the year 1800, only two contain these items of furniture. Abigail Howard, the widow of a judge, owned a sofa located in the entry of her house and a black walnut settee with a yellow damask cover in the front chamber. Samuel Bangs, a successful cordwainer, owned a "couch" kept in the front chamber of his home.

The story is much the same for residents of Newport, Rhode Island, where sofas are included in only three out of a sampling of ten inventories (taken between 1800 and 1805) of the estates of relatively wealthy people. A sofa was listed in the parlor of Christopher Champlin, "merchant," William C. Robinson, "merchant," and Mrs. Elizabeth Senter, "widow." Mr. Champlin also owned a couch, located in the upper north entry of his home, and Mr. Robinson had a settee in a second-floor chamber.

In New York City, five out of ten room-by-room inventories of wealthy New Yorkers (1800–1810) included one sofa each. These were all located on the lower floor—in the parlor, back drawing room, or "drawing room." By scanning a considerable number of inventories, the fact comes to light that most sofas were owned by well-to-do individuals. Philip Livingston (1810) died owning a mahogany settee, William Constable (1803), a cane sofa, and George Usher (1810), a settee with a rush bottom.

Mrs. Basil Hall, an Englishwoman who published a book on her travels in the United States, makes clear that by 1828 ownership of sofas was much more widespread. They were to be found even on the frontier. She wrote when in Salem, Illinois (1828):

> One of the things I miss most in this country is a comfortable sofa at the end of a fagging day's work. In the most luxurious houses there is never anything of the kind beyond one of horsehair, not such a one as Mr. Dowgriggin would make, but a miserable, nasty, narrow thing with wood on which to break your elbows at every corner and yet when you go to call upon an American lady she invariably begs you to take a seat on the "sofa" as if there were not more pain than pleasure in such promotion.[1]

As a part of the ethos of house furnishing, Sheraton's remarks on the "anti-room" and the "drawing-room" give us an insight as to why sofas appear most often in the best parlor or drawing room.

> The anti-room, is an introduction to the drawing-room, and partakes of the elegance of the apartment to which it leads, serving as a place of repose before the general intercourse be effected in the whole company. Here may be placed a number of sofas of a second order with a piano-forte or harp, and other matters of amusement till the whole of the company be collected.

The drawing-room is to concentrate the elegance of the whole house, and is the highest display of richness of furniture. It being appropriated to the formal visits of the highest in rank, and nothing of a scientific nature should be introduced to take up the attention of any individual, from the general conversation that takes place on such occasions. Hence, the walls should be free of pictures, the tables not lined with books, nor the angles of the room filled with globes; as the design of such meetings are not that each visitant should turn to his favourite study, but to contribute his part towards the amusement of the whole company. The grandeur then introduced into the drawing-room is not to be considered, as the ostentatious parade of its proprietor, but the respect he pays to the rank of his visitants.[2]

Although sofas are not mentioned in the passage immediately above, they surely are implied; and his plate of a "Plan and Section of a Drawing Room" includes sofas.[3]

In his general remarks under the heading Sofas, Hepplewhite remarked that their "wood-work should be of mahogany or japanned, in accordance to the chairs; the carving also must be of the same. The dimensions of sofas vary according to the size of the room and the pleasure of the purchaser. The following is the proportion in general use: length between 6 and 7 feet, depth about 30 inches, height of the seat frame 14 inches; total height in the back 3 feet 1 inch."

The catalogue of sofas and couches in the Winterthur collection contains most of the types being produced in the United States in the early Federal period. These are arranged more or less according to the dates in which their form was popular. The earliest were those in the Chippendale taste with prominent rolled arms, often with some feature modernized, such as the tapering of the legs (No. 260). From the Chippendale version, more delicate interpretations evolved: some with serpentine backs outlined with wood (No. 264), and some with bowed, or "sweeped," backs such as that illustrated in Plate 22 of Hepplewhite's *Guide*. In the same place and at the same time (1788), Hepplewhite illustrated what the writer considers to be one of the great innovations of the era—four designs for cabriole sofas, curvilinear in both elevation and plan (No. 265). These are obviously copied after Robert Adam's "Design of a confidente for Sir Abraham Hume." The drawing, dated March 1780, still exists.[4] He may have derived the idea from the French.

Three square sofas were illustrated by Hepplewhite, but these do not seem to have become popular in this country, despite the fact that one described as "of the newest fashion" was executed in a highly successful manner by a Massachusetts craftsman (No. 268).

A little later, Sheraton illustrated what was to be the most popular American sofa type—the "square sofa" with free-standing, turned arm supports called "stumps" of one piece with each end leg in front. Stumps were sometimes simply turned and left plain; more often they were reeded or carved, or both.

By far the largest number of American-made sofas of this time have backs outlined with mahogany, often embellished in one way or another. Molding or beading the surface or edges with a plane was common practice, but frequently carving and veneering were used to good effect. Front legs on sofas, like those of chairs, were square, tapered, or turned. Some were carved, others veneered or inlaid. Most, but not all, of the turned legs on fine sofas were reeded. Casters were generally used to give mobility to a heavy and rather large piece of furniture.

"Grecian sofa" is the name for a new design of sofa with scrolled, or outflaring, ends that came into popularity in the first years of the nineteenth century. These sofas are often called "Empire sofas" today, but that name seems to have been unknown then. The earliest published reference found by the author to a Grecian chair was published in *The London Chair-Makers' and Carvers' Book of Prices for Workmanship* for 1802. In 1803 Sheraton attempted to explain the impact of Greek ideas and classical influences on his furniture designs. His three-page essay in his 1803 *Cabinet Dictionary* under "Grecian" may not be crystal clear, but it gives an insight into early nineteenth-century attitudes.

> GRECIAN, properly, is one born in Greece, or that is skilled in the Greek language. I, however, here use it adjectively, to signify any thing executed or shaped in imitation of the taste of the Greeks. Many writers have celebrated the praises of this people, as having left to posterity, models of sculpture and architecture, much superior to any other nation. Particularly the Grecian architecture has always excelled every other attempt; and has been, therefore, the generally allowed example of fine buildings, and the best taste in architecture. In their highest state of improvements, they seem to have regulated most of their conduct by scientific rules, at least the polite part of them aimed at it as much as possible; and hence some of their feasts consisted of guests, to the number of nine, in imitation of their nine graces or muses. It was from this idea that I was led to study the design in plate 47, which I have ventured to call a Grecian dining table, both on account of its figure, and the number it is adapted to accommodate at dinner.... The old Romans sat at meat as we do, till the Grecian luxury and softness had corrupted them; and then they lolled, or reclined at dinner, after the Grecian manner.... The Manner of lying at meat amongst the Romans, Greeks, and more modern Jews, was the same in all respects. The table was placed in the middle, round which stood three beds covered with cloth or tapestry, according to the quality of the master of the house. Upon these the guests lay inclining the superior part of their bodies upon their left arms, the lower part being stretched out at full length, or a little bent.

In Sheraton's Plate 47 (dated 1803) along with the circular "Grecian Dining Table" referred to above, he illustrated three circular Grecian sofas. To date, the writer has no evidence of sofas being used in this country for dining. A little later, George Smith, "upholder extraordinary to his Royal Highness the Prince of Wales," in his preface to *A Collection of Designs for Household Furniture*, 1808, averred, "I flatter myself the work displays a variety of the newest patterns, combined with classic taste, for the plainest and for the most superb articles of modern furniture, studied from the best antique examples of the Egyptian, Greek, and Roman styles; and to augment this variety, some Designs are given after the Gothic or old English fashion, and also according to the costume of China." Plates 5 and 6 of Smith's book, dated 1804, show many articles of furniture in Greek, Roman, and Egyptian taste because, the author says, "as the beauty of the Antique consists in the purity of design, and what was pleasing centuries ago continues to be equally so now; so I do not despair of seeing a style of Furniture produced in this country, which shall be equally agreeable centuries hence."

By 1810, one design for a "Grecian sofa" is listed in a New York book of prices and a year later "a scroll back sofa" appears in the Philadelphia edition of the same book. The design soon became the rage, and by 1815 sofas of this type were being advertised by country as well as city cabinetmakers in the United States. Their popularity continued for nearly fifty years after 1820, the designs growing heavier and more flamboyant, and often incorporating carved eagles as legs or as elements of the back.

With the extensive borrowing of French forms and decoration by English designers in the late eighteenth century, the couch was brought back to popularity. Sheraton in his *Cabinet Dictionary* wrote in 1803, "Couch, from *coucher*, French, to lie down on a place of repose. Hence we have seats that bear this name." George Smith in 1808 illustrated "Four designs for Chaises Longues" noting that they are "an article admissible into almost every room." He commented as follows:

> The present Designs are intended for Drawing Rooms, or Boudoirs, in which case the frames may be of satin-wood, inlaid with other woods, and the ornaments of bronze, as Plates A and B; or in gold, with bronzed ornaments, as Plates 63 and 64. For covering, silks or cloth may be used; and in more moderately furnished apartments calico may suffice, povided the pattern be small and of the chintz kind. The same Designs will answer extremely well for Libraries, Parlors, or Dressing Rooms, executed in mahogany, and divested of the ornaments.

Couches, chaises longues, and day beds were not popular in the United States in the first years of the Federal period, and their use seems never to have been widespread. However, a number of fine examples dating after 1810 are known. This form, both in concept and execution in the early nineteenth century, appears to have been distinguished from a sofa by its lighter lines and the fact that it usually had one high scrolled headrest instead of two. Sometimes there was a low scrolled end at the foot, sometimes none at all. Backs were optional. A couch was primarily an article for reclining rather than sitting. Those included in the catalogue which follows are in the Grecian style with the frame scrolled at both the head and the foot.

1 Mrs. Basil Hall, *Aristocratic Journey*, ed. Una Pope-Hennessy (New York: G. P. Putnam's Son, 1931), p. 282.
2 Sheraton, *The Cabinet Dictionary* (1803), p. 218.
3 Sheraton, *The Cabinet-Maker and Upholsterer's Drawing Book* (1802).
4 Sir John Soane's Museum, London. Illustrated as No. 124, *The Furniture of Robert Adam* by Eileen Harris (London: Alec Tiranti, 1963). According to Mrs. Harris, this type of sofa first appears in Adam's designs about 1773–1774 in his work for the Northumberland House drawing room.

# XX

# Baltimore Drawing Room

*The urbane and sophisticated furniture in this room is of southern origin except for three pieces from New England—the two Martha Washington armchairs (Nos. 116 and 117) and the kettlestand (No. 368) at the end of the sofa (No. 266). Extraordinary examples, perhaps of Baltimore workmanship are the matching (though not a set) marble-top corner tables (No. 350) and side tables (No. 349). Also attributed to Baltimore are the oval table between the armchairs, the great cylinder-fall writing table and bookcase (No. 194), and the chair (No. 105) standing before it. A wide range of classical-derived form and ornament is to be seen in the silver tea and coffee service made by Joseph Richardson, Jr., in Philadelphia, about 1790, and the mantelpiece with composition ornament probably produced by Robert Welford of the same city. The wool velours carpet may have been woven in Utrecht, Holland.*

**259** SOFA

*1795–1805  Probably Massachusetts*

That sofas were still being made in the Chippendale mode in the nineteenth century is well documented by one in the Winterthur collection made by Adam S. Coe in 1812.[1] The Coe example and the excellent small sofa shown here have several features in common. Both have a type of back today called "camel back" because of its serpentine upper line. Both have substantial rolled arms that dip down sharply to the seat, and upholstered ends that seem a little thicker than those of the sofas of the new styles that came into popularity at the end of the eighteenth century. The legs on both sofas are molded, but how different the effect! These are thinner and tapered, and the stretchers have been eliminated. The over-all effect in this case is very much lighter than that of the Coe example, which is earlier in style but later in date.

Dimensions: height 36½; length 37½; depth 21.

Materials: rails, ash; front right seat brace, soft maple; front right seat block, spruce; upholstery, blue-grey silk brocade with pattern of floral trellises in cream and touches of color.

Accession: 59.750

**260**  SOFA

*1790–1800  Probably New England*

Except for the tapered legs, this would be called a Chippendale sofa. The outline, shape, and mass of the seat, back, and arms approximate those of No. 259 and are in the Chippendale style. The half-serpentine upper line of the arms is an unusual subtlety not often found on American sofas. The vigor and size of the rolled arms and the thickness of the nicely finished stretchers relate closely to those found on Philadelphia sofas of the Chippendale era, but birch rails are most often found on Massachusetts seating furniture.

Dimensions: height 36¾; length 65½; depth 26.

Materials: mahogany; seat rails, birch; upholstery, white silk with ribbon stripes and floral trails in polychrome silk and chenille threads, English or French, mid-eighteenth century.

Accession: 57.938

**261**  SOFA

*1790–1795  Probably Philadelphia*

In the over-all evolution of form and supports, this great sofa is one step further from the idiom of the Chippendale era toward that of the Federal period.

Imposing in size, its sweeping lines, especially the peaked serpentine of the back, remind one of the cresting of Martha Washington chairs (Nos. 109, 113) and some easy chairs (No. 125) of the new style. In this connection it is well to remember that for façades and crestings, Hepplewhite and other designers in the late eighteenth century often relied upon a vigorous serpentine line for novelty. Here the arms are thinner than on No. 260 and are in closer harmony with the substantial fluted legs and with the masculine proportions of the spade feet—obviously adequate supports for a sofa of this size and distinction. The rear legs splay backward in a sharply concaved line to give stability and to compensate for the rake of the back.

Because this sofa is in a class by itself and without comparable documented counterparts, the writer has only the secondary woods as a guide for its origin. Soft maple, tulip, and white oak were used in seating furniture from New York southward. The character of the legs and spade feet suggests a strong affinity with the work of Daniel Trotter, Adam Haines, Jonathan Gostelowe, and others in Philadelphia.

Dimensions: height 39½; length 97½; depth over-all 38; depth seat 31.

Materials: mahogany; medial seat brace, soft maple; front seat rail, tulip; rear seat rail, American white oak; upholstery, old leather.

Accession: 57.866

**262**  SOFA

*1795–1800  Salem, Massachusetts   (Carving attributed to Samuel McIntire)*

Robert Adam, at the beginning of the classical revolution in taste, declared himself for "delicacy, gaiety, grace, and beauty" in all that concerned the background and furnishing of rooms. Although his influence in American taste was indirect, it was a force in the early Federal period. The maker of this sofa retained the form common to the Chippendale era. But by straightening the lines a little to make them more gentle, by lightening the thickness of each element, and (in the Hepplewhite manner) by using a facing of mahogany to call attention to the upper line of the back and the front of the arms, he achieved unity as well as the delicacy, grace, and beauty which Adam sought. With crisp, precise motifs—basket of fruit, paterae, floral medallions, acanthus leaves, and streamers of grapes and their leaves—the carver attained surface movement and enlivened the lines of the whole.

259

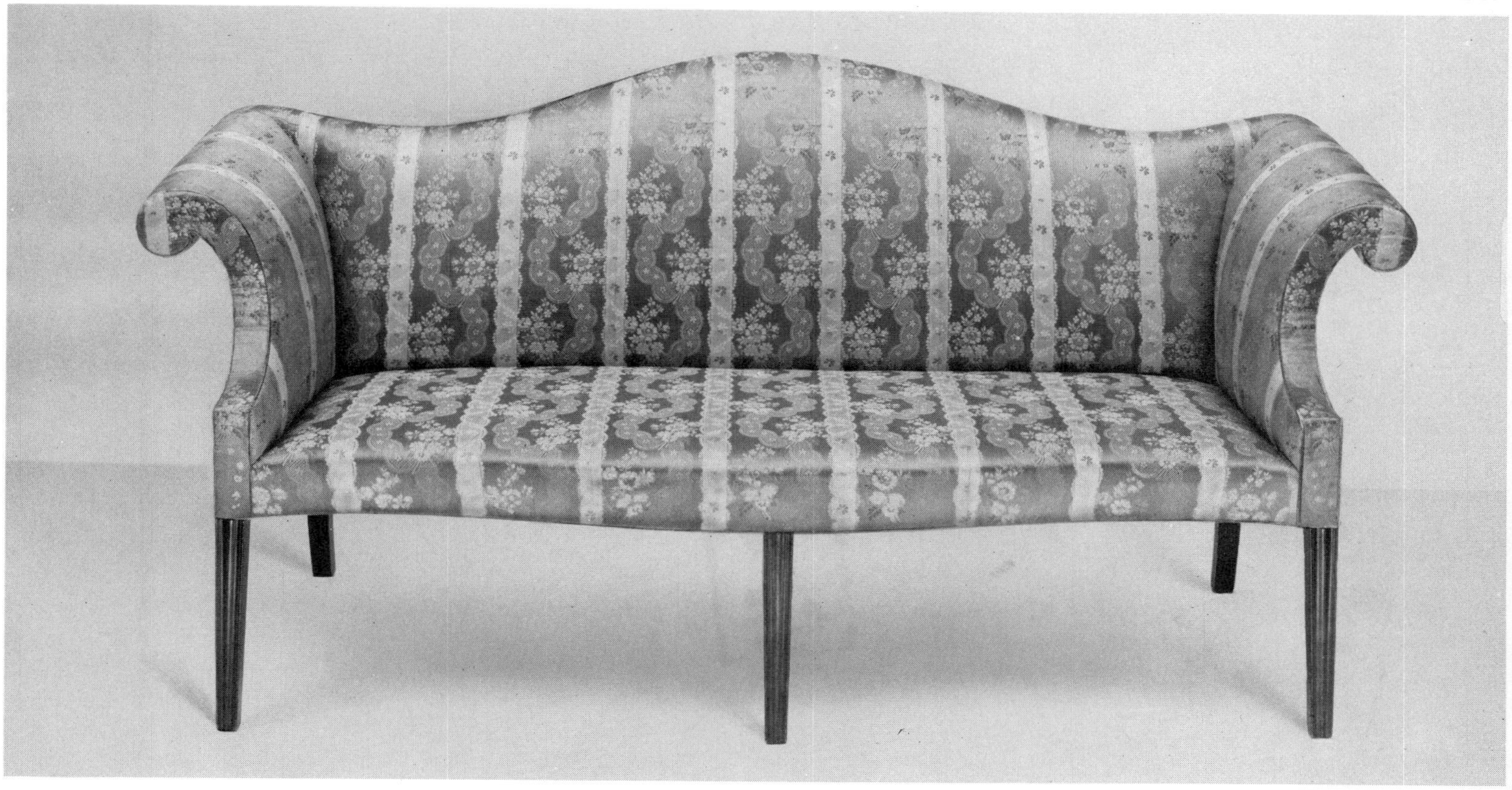

260

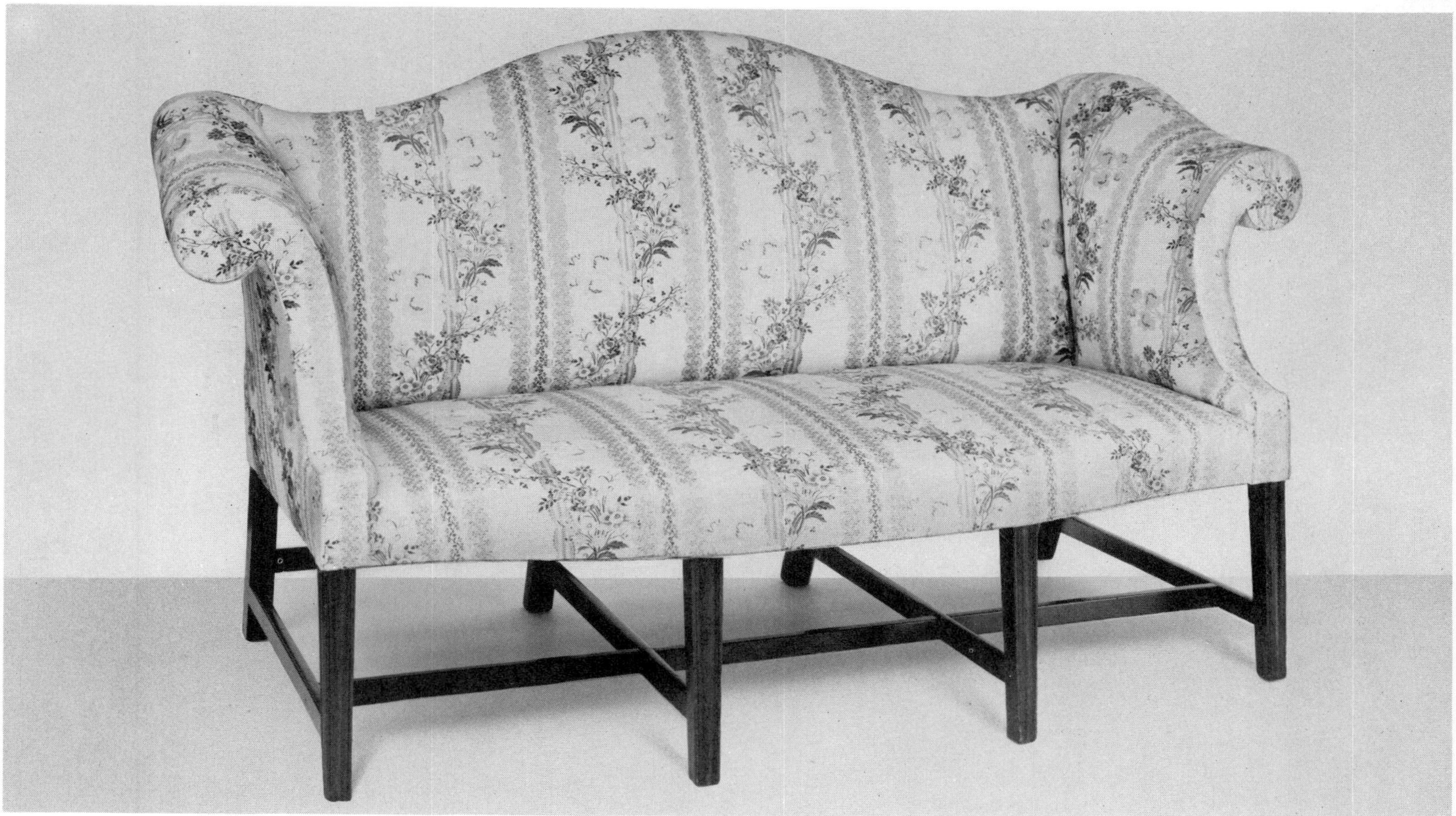

**261**

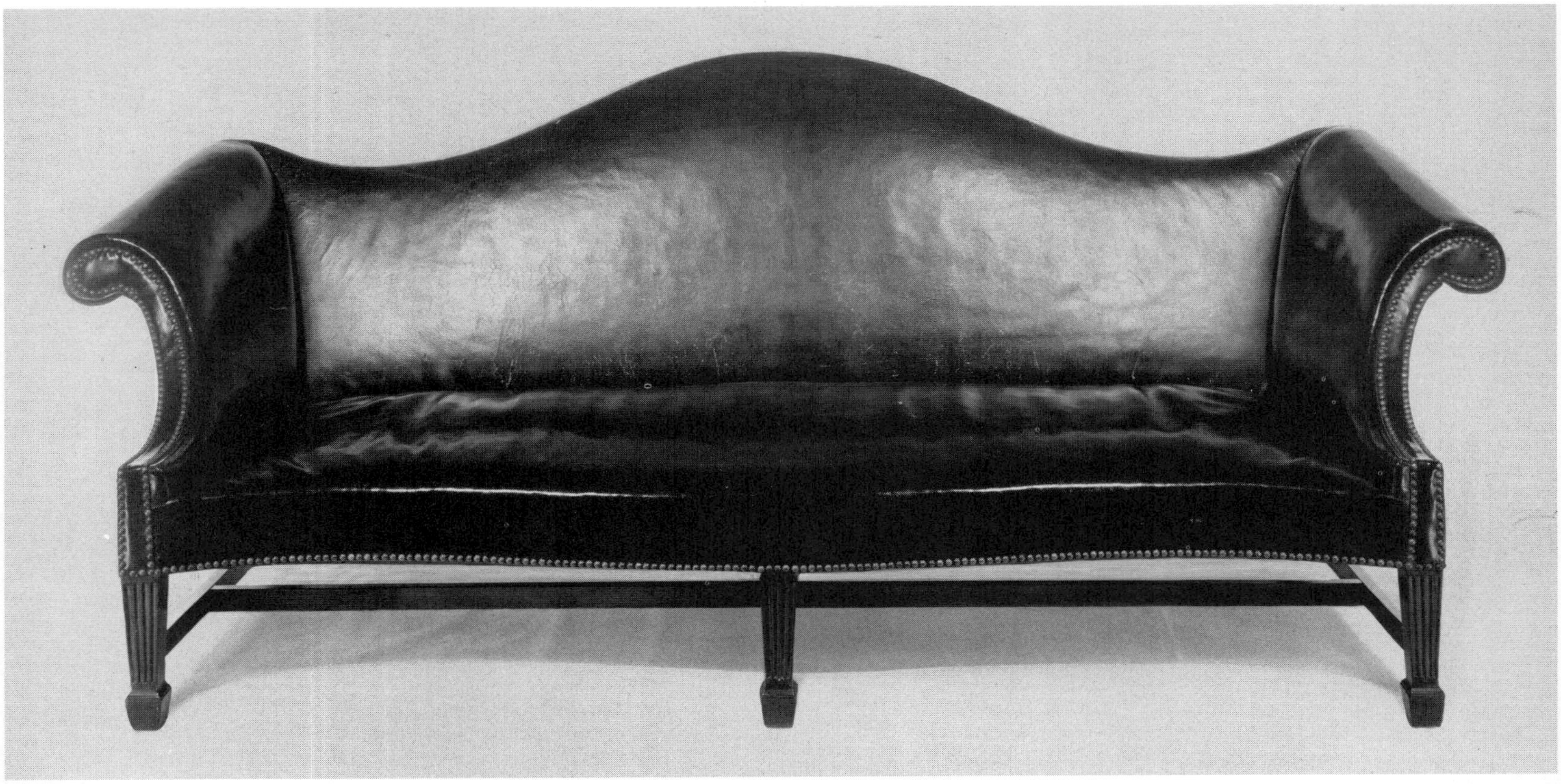

**262**

298

Only one other known sofa of the late eighteenth century is comparable to this one. That one, believed to have been made for Elias Hasket Derby of Salem and now in the Karolik Collection of the Boston Museum of Fine Arts, is also richly carved.[2] On both, the long sweeping line of the back is edged in wood with carved ornament in the center—on the Karolik sofa a pair of cornucopia, on this one a free-standing basket of fruit with flowers spilling along the rail. Such baskets of fruit were not uncommon in eighteenth-century design,[3] but the motif was used more frequently in the Salem area than elsewhere in the United States, and may well have been popularized there by Samuel McIntire.[4] Although lacking the star-punched, or "Salem snowflake," background, the ornament relates closely in kind and execution to that on the great chest-on-chest made by William Lemon and carved by Samuel McIntire for Madame Elizabeth Derby West.[5]

The legs at the front corners are tapered only on their inside edges, and the spade feet are ebony; these are calculated subtleties to indicate strength and stability.

Dimensions: height 39; length 88; depth 29½.

Materials: mahogany; seat rails and four medial braces, birch; corner blocks (type III), white pine; upholstery, pale-blue satin with classical medaillons, pearls, and drapery in white, French, Directoire style, about 1800.
Accession: 57.650

## 263 WINDOW SEAT, window stool
*1795–1800 Salem, Massachusetts (Carving attributed to Samuel McIntire)*

No photograph can do justice to this window seat, the finest example of the form known in American furniture. The appliqués of ebony to shape the spade feet and the carved ornament on the legs and arms are so closely parallel to similar ornament on the sofa No. 262 that the two pieces may have been made ensuite. Of particular note is the diamond shape of the front legs contoured to the serpentine front, a feature often found on the finest serpentine-front sideboards.

According to Hepplewhite, "the size of window stools must be regulated by the size of the place where they are to stand; their heights should not exceed the seats of the chairs."

Four matching window stools of this general

**263**

form, together with two very small matching sofas originally made for the Peirce-Nichols House (Salem, Massachusetts) still stand in its parlor. They may have been made in 1801 when the house was remodeled by Samuel McIntire at the time of the marriage of Jerathmiel Peirce's daughter to George Nichols.

Dimensions: height 28; length 51½; depth 18.

Materials: mahogany and ebony; three medial braces, curved on the upper side, birch; nailed corner blocks (type III), white pine; upholstery, blue silk, late eighteenth century.

Accession: 57.694

## 264 SOFA
*1795–1805 Salem, Massachusetts (Carving attributed to Samuel McIntire)*

Fashioned with the same sweeping and graceful lines of No. 262, this smaller example is less elaborate. It and four similar examples in other collections have tapered legs, carved mahogany frames, and feature a carved basket of fruit and flowers on the top rail.[6] In this case, the background of the meticulously carved basket[7] and the leafy rosettes on the arms is punched with the well-known snowflake design so often seen on the finest Salem work. The face of the arms and legs has been left plain except for carved acanthus leaves which soften the transition from leg to arm.

Dimensions: height 36½; length 72; depth 27½.

Materials: mahogany; seat rails and medial braces, birch; corner blocks (type III), white pine; two rear legs are missing; upholstery, pale-blue satin with classical medallions, pearls and drapery in white (called camaieu), French, Directoire style, about 1800.

Accession: 57.788

## 265 CABRIOLE SOFA (one of a pair)
*1795–1805 New York City*

Six designs for sofas which appear in Hepplewhite's *Guide* of 1788 show great inventiveness. In four of these, the corners where the back meets the

ends have been eliminated so that in both plan and elevation the line is curvilinear. The result is a unified whole, anticipating free-form seating furniture of the twentieth century, many steps removed from the open boxes on legs with which seating furniture began. Such sofas, the writer believes, are the "Cabriole Sofas" referred to in both price and pattern books of the late eighteenth and early nineteenth centuries. In this sophisticated interpretation based on two of Hepplewhite's designs (Plates 22 and 24), the back is higher and the pitch of its slope greater than in either of the plates. The effect is dramatic. Carved rosettes appear on the arms instead of the inlaid whorls seen on armchair No. 50, which is part of a large set used originally with the sofas by the Montgomery family of Dutchess County, New York. Both chairs and sofas may have been made in the same New York cabinetmaking shop, despite the fact that these legs have spade feet and are reeded instead of being line inlaid as are those of the chairs. Both methods of ornamenting legs were common in New York shops.

Dimensions: height 39½; length 72; depth 26.
Materials: mahogany; seat rails, ash; medial seat braces, birch; upholstery, black haircloth, late eighteenth century.
Provenance: Eglinton Montgomery.
Accession: 57.684.1, 2

## 266 CABRIOLE SOFA
*1790–1800   Baltimore*

This sofa is even more closely allied than No. 265 to a design of George Hepplewhite's, Plate 24. The curved lines of its back and serpentine seat give it grace and a fluid quality unrivaled by other sofa forms. A mahogany-outlined back, a half-upholstered, half-veneered seat rail, husk-inlaid front legs, and the same curvilinear form are found on other sofas with Maryland histories. One much like this was formerly at Druid Hill,[8] near Baltimore. The rear legs, here partly restored, are sloped to avoid the exaggerated sweep of outcurving supports at floor level. They are out of the ordinary

**266**

**267**

but are similar in shape to those on another Baltimore sofa from Perry Hall, the country seat of Harry Dorsey Gough.[9]

Dimensions: height 37⅞; length 77; depth 26.

Materials: mahogany; satinwood inlay; seat rails, medial seat braces, and open corner braces (type I), tulip; upholstery, yellow-striped taffeta with floral trails and sprigs in polychrome, French or English, late eighteenth century.

Accession: 53.102

### 267 SQUARE SOFA
*1800–1810   Probably Northern New England*

What appears to be a rural interpretation of city-made sofas is not without certain features that suggest acquaintance with high-style forms. The gentle sweep of the back and the break in the slope of the ends are unexpected subtleties. By staggering the lengthwise stretchers and setting the middle one back a few inches, the maker was able to achieve the necessary mortising with thinner pieces of wood than usual. Curly maple was used by American cabinetmakers through most of the eighteenth and much of the nineteenth century, and occasionally a top-quality piece of furniture was fashioned from this native wood (see No. 136).[10]

Dimensions: height 29¾; length 76; depth 22¾.

Materials: curly maple; seat rails, soft maple; corner

blocks (type III), maple; upholstery, wood-block-printed cotton, roses and jasmine on yellow ground, English, about 1790.

Accession: 57.1085

### 268 SQUARE SOFA
*1795–1805   Probably Massachusetts*

In the first edition of his *Guide*, Hepplewhite remarks of a design with similar free-standing panel back and open arms: "Plate 25 shows a design for a sofa of newest fashion; the frame should be japanned, with green on a white ground, and the edges gilt; the covering of red Morocco leather." As American cabinetmakers so often did, the maker of this sofa took the basic idea and worked it out in his own way. Instead of japanning, he used mahogany. He ornamented the back with a facing of herringbone cross-banding, inset at the top with a central tablet of figured birch. Instead of straight, stiff, sloping arms, he used "crane neck'd elbows [arms]" like those of the finest Martha Washington armchairs, the most distinguished arms to be found on American furniture.[11] Their serpentine shape is outlined by a series of reeds ending in a rosette, and they are fashioned to a finger of polished mahogany where they curve downward to meet the turned and reeded stumps of one piece with the front leg. Martha Washington chairs with such arms have

**268**

long been attributed to the Newburyport-Portsmouth area, but whether they were made there or in Boston or Salem, this writer is unable to say. The source for such arms is illustrated on Plate 6, No. 7, of the 1802 and 1807 editions of *The London Chair-Makers' and Carvers' Book of Prices for Workmanship.* Their construction is described on page 46 of that publication as follows: "Framing with turn'd stumps and front legs in one piece, and crane neck'd elbows sweep'd towards the tops of the back legs."

Dimensions: height 36¼; length 78; depth 20½.

Materials: mahogany; mahogany and figured-birch veneers; seat rails and medial seat brace, birch; corner blocks (type III), white pine; upholstery, green-and-white-striped silk and linen; late eighteenth century.

Provenance: Museum Purchase, 1963.

Accession: 63.25

## 269  SQUARE SOFA

*1800–1810   Salem, Massachusetts   Possibly carved by Samuel McIntire*

Sheraton's *Drawing Book,* published in 1793, documents an important innovation in sofa design, i.e., free-standing arm supports that are a continuation of the front legs. Under the heading "Square Sofas," in the first edition of *The London Chair-Makers' and Carvers' Book of Prices for Workmanship,* 1802 (No. 3, Pl. 11, p. 83), this innovation is described as "Framing with turn'd stumps and front legs in one piece, an upright behind ditto, and elbows sweep'd towards the top." All of the sofas described in the rest of this section incorporate this feature.

The designs of Sheraton and Shearer both contributed to the conception of the example shown here, built in Salem and quite possibly carved by McIntire because the ornament has the particular crispness and spontaneity associated with his hand. The outline of the sofa came from the 1791 edition of Sheraton's *Drawing Book;* the exact shape of this carved basket, seen too on Salem mantelpieces, is illustrated among Shearer's designs on a sideboard, Plate 6 in *The London Cabinet Book of Prices,* published in 1788. The snowflake-punched background sets off the principal carving and appears again on the festooned urns of the arm supports.

Samuel McIntire charged Jacob Sanderson, cabinetmaker, £1.7.0 on July 31, 1802, "to carving Sofa and top rail," and on February 3, 1803, he billed the same client £1.7.0 for "carving Sofa & working top rail."[12]

**269**

Dimensions: height 37; length 75; depth 25³⁄₈.

Materials: mahogany; seat rails, birch; medial seat brace and front corner blocks (type III), white pine; upholstery, silk satin, cream-colored ground with salmon, tan, green, and brown stripes, last quarter of the eighteenth century.

Accession: 57.863

## 270 SQUARE SOFA
*1800–1810   Salem, Massachusetts   Carving attributed to Samuel McIntire*

In describing the design of the sofa shown in Plate 35, Sheraton concluded as follows: "If the top rail be thought to have too much work, it can be finished in a straight rail." As one sees immediately, the top rail of this and other fine Salem-made sofas is more elaborate rather than less, but oddly enough the legs on this type of Salem sofa are often left plain without reeding or other features of embellishment.

On the top rail a carved basket of fruit is often used as ornament (Nos. 262, 264, 269), but here it is replaced by a carved eagle, an expression of patriotic enthusiasm for the new Republic. Although the legs are variants, this sofa and another in the Metropolitan Museum of Art so closely resemble one made in 1810 by Mr. Adams of Salem for Miss Lucy Hill of Billerica, Massachusetts, as to suggest that they were made in the same shop or carved by the same hand.[13] Besides the bill for Miss Hill's sofa, which descended to Mrs. Warren Stearns, a great-grandniece, a letter to the prospective bride from her friend Sally Hemenway also survives. She wrote, "I have purchased a brocade gown for your soffa for thirteen Dollars exactly Such a one as Rebecca Pierce gave fifteen for." This comment documents the use of old dress material for the original covering of a similar sofa.

The carving stands in relief against the snowflake-punched background and includes the festoons of drapery, fruit, and flowers, and paterae and fluting familiar to McIntire's repertoire. The band of flutes and flowers across the top of the back is similar to that on the great chest-on-chest billed by McIntire (1796) to Madam Elizabeth Derby.[14]

Dimensions: height 36¾; length 75½; depth 25.

Materials: mahogany; front and rear rails, birch; upholstery, polychrome striped-and-sprigged silk taffeta, late eighteenth century.

Provenance: Helen Temple Cooke.

Accession: 57.804

**270**

**271** SQUARE SOFA

*1800–1810 Northeastern Massachusetts or Portsmouth, New Hampshire*

In shape and design, this sofa and No. 272 have so many unusual features in common that one might suppose their frames were cut after the same cabinetmaker's patterns.[15] But whether they were made in Portsmouth or Newburyport—as has long been supposed—or Salem or Boston is difficult to determine, and it is impossible to name the maker. However, it is certainly a feminine and sophisticated sofa, reliant upon curves of exquisite proportions. Centered in the broad band of vertical veneers of figured birch across the back is a small ellipse of birch set against a rectangular panel of mitered walnut. So dainty is this panel that it calls attention to the slight sweep of the back capped with a semi-elliptical molding of mahogany, a molding which anticipates the oval contour of the handles, or arms, as they bow forward to meet the reeded and delicate vase supports. These turned supports, a continuation of the end legs, are veneered with a cylinder of birch at the seat line. The shape of the turned-and-reeded legs is comparable to those on the pair of marble-top side tables labeled by William Haskell of Salem (No. 339). The

name, G. C. McClean (the maker or an owner?), is branded on the seat frame of what is said to be an identical or closely similar sofa that is privately owned.[16]

Dimensions: height 36; length 83½; depth 26.

Materials: mahogany veneered with figured birch; rear seat rail, birch, other rails, hard pine; two medial braces, birch; corner blocks (type III), white pine; upholstery, striped satin lampas with floral trails of baskets and bowknots in pink, blue, and gold, French, Louis XVI style, late eighteenth century.

Provenance: Mrs. Freeman Allen; Helen Temple Cooke.

Accession: 57.658

**272** SOFA

*1800–1810 Northeastern Massachusetts or Portsmouth, New Hampshire*

Not often does one see two pieces of furniture so similar in design and form as this sofa and the preceding, No. 271, which present such contrasts of harmony and transitions. Both were made by skilled workmen for buyers willing to pay for the best. Across the top of this sofa is a band of a dark, unidentified, exotic veneer with a pronounced veining of darker hue. But the lateral movement is inter-

rupted in the center by a rectangular island of vertically figured birch. A mantle of scratch-leaf carving instead of reeding highlights the legs, the arm supports, and the elbow of the arms. The flow of line down each leg is nervous and halting, the transition from flattened arm to the too-thin neck of the support hesitant. The maker of this sofa was a talented craftsman. The maker of No. 271 had the eye of the genius.

Dimensions: height 34¾; length 76; depth 24¼.

Materials: mahogany with figured birch and other unidentified veneers; seat rails and three medial braces, birch; corner blocks (type III), white pine; upholstery, white-corded silk with sprigs brocaded in colors, French, late eighteenth century.

Accession: 57.934

**273** SOFA (one of a pair)
*About 1800–1810   Boston, Massachusetts   Possibly made by John and/or Thomas Seymour*

Though this pair of small sofas is similar in form to Nos. 271 and 272, there are several differences in detail that may be significant. The top of the back and ends is upholstered instead of being veneered wood; the back legs break sharply downward an inch or two above the floor; the reeding on the shapely front legs and arm supports is fat, especially at the thickest point; there is no rounding of the handles at the front of the arms; and the light-colored veneered panels behind and below the arm supports (stumps) are bird's-eye maple (the light-wood veneers on the other two sofas are figured birch). All of these may be characteristic of Boston workmanship as opposed to that of a little farther north.

The history of this sofa (that of its mate is not known) is significant. According to an affidavit which accompanied the sofa when it was purchased in 1930 by Henry Francis du Pont,[17] it was originally owned by William Bond, a silversmith and watchmaker, who married Hannah Cranch. They lived in Portland, Maine, but moved to Boston in 1790, four years before the Seymours. Members of the Cranch, Bond, and Seymour families were close friends.[18] A sketch of Portland by John Seymour, Jr., and a desk labeled by John Seymour and Son, formerly owned by Mr. George A. Cluett, descended through these families. The turnings on these legs approximate those on a number of tables attributed to the Seymours' shop.[19] On the basis of circumstantial possibilities, there is reason to believe

that one day proof will be found that this pair of sofas is of their workmanship.

Dimensions: height 35; length 57; depth 23½.

Materials: mahogany inlaid with bird's-eye maple; seat rails and two curved medial braces, birch; original rear corner blocks (type III), white pine; upholstery, pale blue and beige, French, early nineteenth century.

Provenance: Originally made for William Bond, Portland, Maine, and Dorchester, Massachusetts; Hannah Cranch Bond; Dr. William Cranch Bond Fifield; Mary Sanborn Fifield; Philip Flayderman.

Accession: 57.1051

### 274 SMALL SOFA
*About 1800–1810  Rhode Island or Massachusetts*

The turnings and character of the interrupted reeding on the front legs of this rare small sofa are simi-

lar to those found on much Boston and North Shore furniture, as is the use of bird's-eye maple at the top of the front legs on either end. Also found on furniture of that area is light-line, black-dash patterned stringing to surround veneered panels. However, the use of reeding to cap the back and its continuation down the ends and over the handles (common to many New York sofas), the serpentine cresting of the arms instead of the more normal hollow, and the square spade feet are seldom seen in Massachusetts furniture. A Rhode Island card table labeled by Joseph Rawson (No. 296) features an oval veneered panel of figured mahogany surrounded by stringing and inset on a mahogany ground—demonstrating far more subtle design than the normal Massachusetts practice of using light-colored wood for large ovals. A further clue to the origin of this sofa was suggested by the late

Israel Sack, connoisseur par excellence. He thought he had once owned it and that it was made for a "Professor Brown" of Brown University by a famous Providence cabinetmaker whose name he could not recall.

Dimensions: height 37¼; length 64; depth 22.

Materials: mahogany; seat rails, beech; bowed medial braces, birch; no evidence of blocks or braces; upholstery, brown silk with small conventionalized floral figure, about 1800.

Provenance: Benjamin Flayderman.

Accession: 57.872

## 275 SQUARE SOFA
*1800–1810 New York City*

This sofa and a set of twelve urn-back chairs (see No. 65) have been inherited by successive generations of the du Pont family from their original owner, Victor Marie du Pont, who first came to New York City in 1787, a member of the French Legation. He returned to the same post for the period 1791 to 1793, later served as French Consul at Charleston, and emigrated to this country with his father Pierre Samuel du Pont in 1800, when he established a commission house in New York City.

Square reeded legs, square mahogany capping with a bead on the edges, elongated rectangular tablets (fluted here), and sharply dipping concaved ends are characteristics often found on New York sofas of this period. Square sofas are listed in both the 1796 and 1802 New York books of prices. In the 1796 edition, the frame of a "Square Back Mahogany Sofa," five feet long, with six legs (three front and back), a straight seat, and without stretchers cost one pound, ten shillings. Interesting options available included "a sweep front rail with hollow corners," "a hollow corner'd top rail," or "an arch in the top rail to answer the arches in square back chairs." Plain mahogany "elbows" could also be had.

On the back rail of this sofa, the presence of a few rose-headed iron tacks with a shred of old fibers supports the belief that this sofa was made by 1800 or soon thereafter. By 1802 and the publication of the second edition of the price book, a "Plain Square Sofa, No. I" and a "Square Back Sofa, No. II" were popular enough to be listed with many more options. The description of No. II fits the sofa pictured here rather closely: "six feet, six inches long;

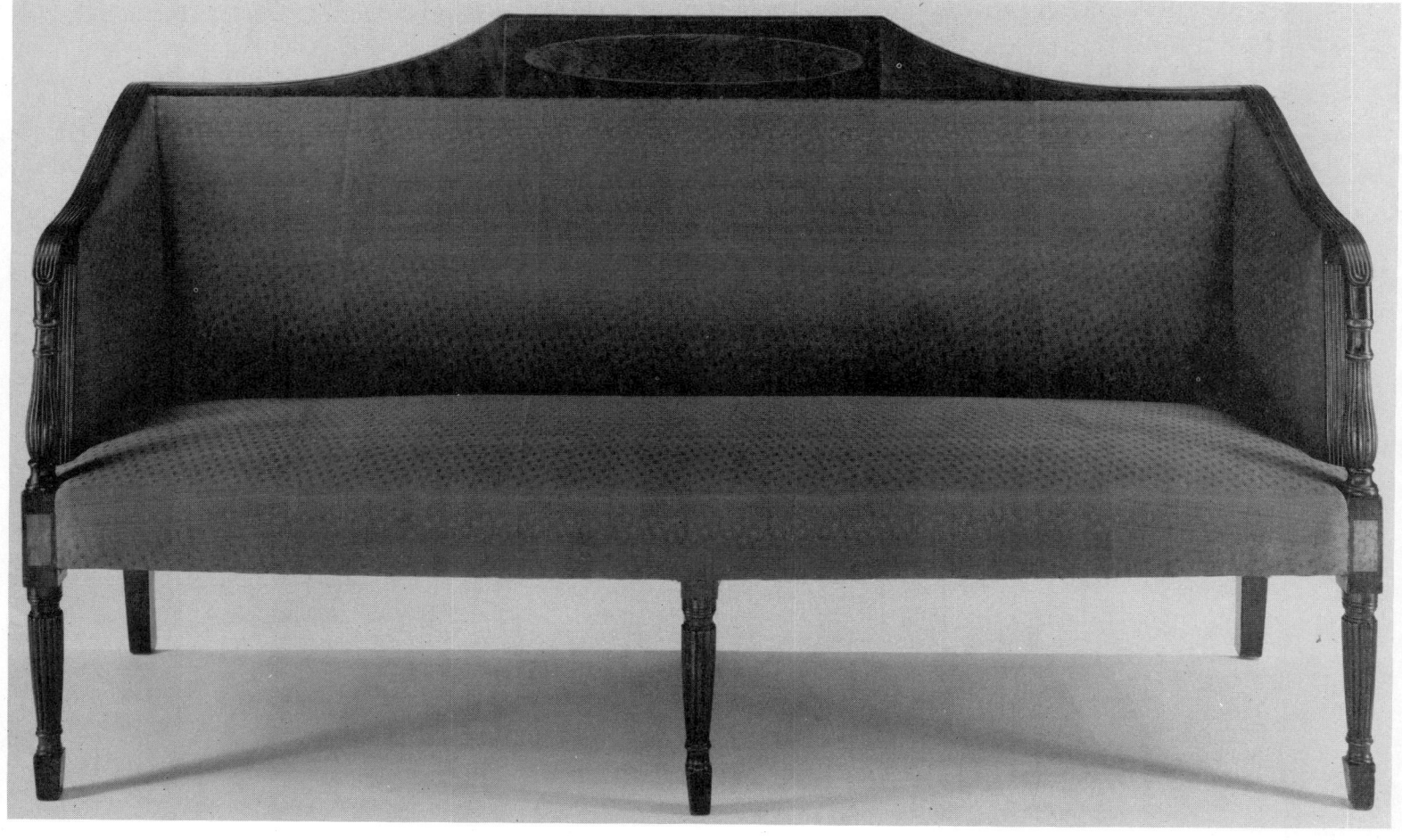

straight front; eight plain legs; two sweeps in the arms; mahogany on the top and down the sweeps." This standard version cost two pounds for the making. Extras on this one included a "brake in the top [a tablet]"... one shilling six pence; "pillars"... four shillings and an unknown amount to be calculated on the basis of the tables in the back of the book for fluting, beading, reeding, tapering, and therming the legs, turning the arm supports, and finishing with oil or wax. The spade feet, the normal terminals on New York sofas and chairs with reeded legs, have been restored.

Dimensions: height 36¾; length 75; depth 26¼.

Materials: mahogany; rails, ash; medial braces and corner braces (type I), cherry; blocks (type VI), white pine; upholstery, red-and-white-striped silk with floral trails, sprigs, and ribbons in polychrome brocade, English or French, late eighteenth century.

Provenance: Victor Marie du Pont; Sophie Madeleine Dalmas du Pont; Henry Algernon du Pont; Henry Francis du Pont.

Accession: 57.864

## 276 SQUARE SOFA with elliptic seat
*1800–1810 New York City*

Of the same form as No. 275 but with important variations, this sofa also was made in New York. The carved daisy, or sunburst, on the tablet in the middle of the back and the carved rosette on the upper "break" and the end of the arm bring to mind at once side chairs labeled by Slover and Taylor of New York.[20] However, no sofas documented as the work of these men have come to light as yet, nor, for that matter, have labeled chairs with turned legs. In all probability, several of the many cabinetmakers and upholsterers working in New York City at this time produced sofas of this type.[21]

Particular niceties on this sofa are the "elliptic front" of the seat and carved leaves on the arm supports.

Dimensions: height 38; length 78; depth 24¾.

Materials: mahogany; seat rails, soft maple; medial braces, cherry; upholstery, striped cotton in red-orange and brown, twentieth century.

Accession: 63.72

## 277 SOFA, with scroll back
*1807–1810 New York Probably made in the shop of Duncan Phyfe*

The epitome of excellence reached by New York cabinetmakers is exemplified in this sofa. To give emphasis to its back-curving upper rail, it is divided into three triple-reeded panels—the end ones highlighted with carved reeds tied with ribbons in bowknots, the center one with stalks of wheat tied in the same way. The curving contours of the reeded arms, arm supports, legs and bowed front emphasize the complexity of the form and also unify the composition. It is indeed a work of art.

In the first edition of *The London Chair-Makers' and Carvers' Book of Prices for Workmanship* (1802), most of the elements combined in this sofa are given and the prices for making them listed. Among these are:

> Framing with turned stumps and front legs in one piece, and scroll elbows sweeped toward the tops of the back legs [p. 46 and illustrated No. 9, Plate 6]
> Sweeping elbows by a mould [making them serpentine in plan, see p. 47 and Fig. 4, Plate 6]
> Scroll back legs [letter b, Fig. 2, Plate 10]
> Forming a "scroll-back sofa" with "a roller along the back for carving."

In the tables of this book, prices are also given for all sorts of reeding in every conceivable place on a piece of furniture. In the New York price book for the same year (1802), scrolls and pillars (stumps, or arm supports) are mentioned in connection with a "Square Back Sofa, No. 2" (p. 55); by the time of the 1810 edition in New York, details of our present sofa are codified for master and journeyman alike. Pertinent details for this sofa (p. 57) are:

Sofas. No. 2.

| | | | |
|---|---|---|---|
| Six feet six inches long, square back, mahogany caping on arms, and on the top rail, | 2 | 6 | 8 |
| [basic price for the making] | | | |
| Pillars | 0 | 4 | 3 |
| Scroll top, and scrolls in front of the arms, | 0 | 10 | 0 |
| Bell seat for stuffing over, | 0 | 16 | 10 |
| Ditto mahogany rails, rabbited for stuffing, extra | 0 | 1 | 7 |
| | [3 | 19 | 4] |

Reeding and carving were paid for on a time basis, but would probably have cost at least two to four pounds more; upholstery was another operation, charged separately.

Dimensions: height 37½; length 81; depth 32.

Materials: mahogany; medial seat brace, rear seat rail, cherry; rear corner blocks, tulip; upholstery, light-blue satin with stylized floral-and-leaf medallion in white and yellow, French, Empire style, early nineteenth century.

Provenance: Louis Guerineau Myers.

Accession: 57.721

275

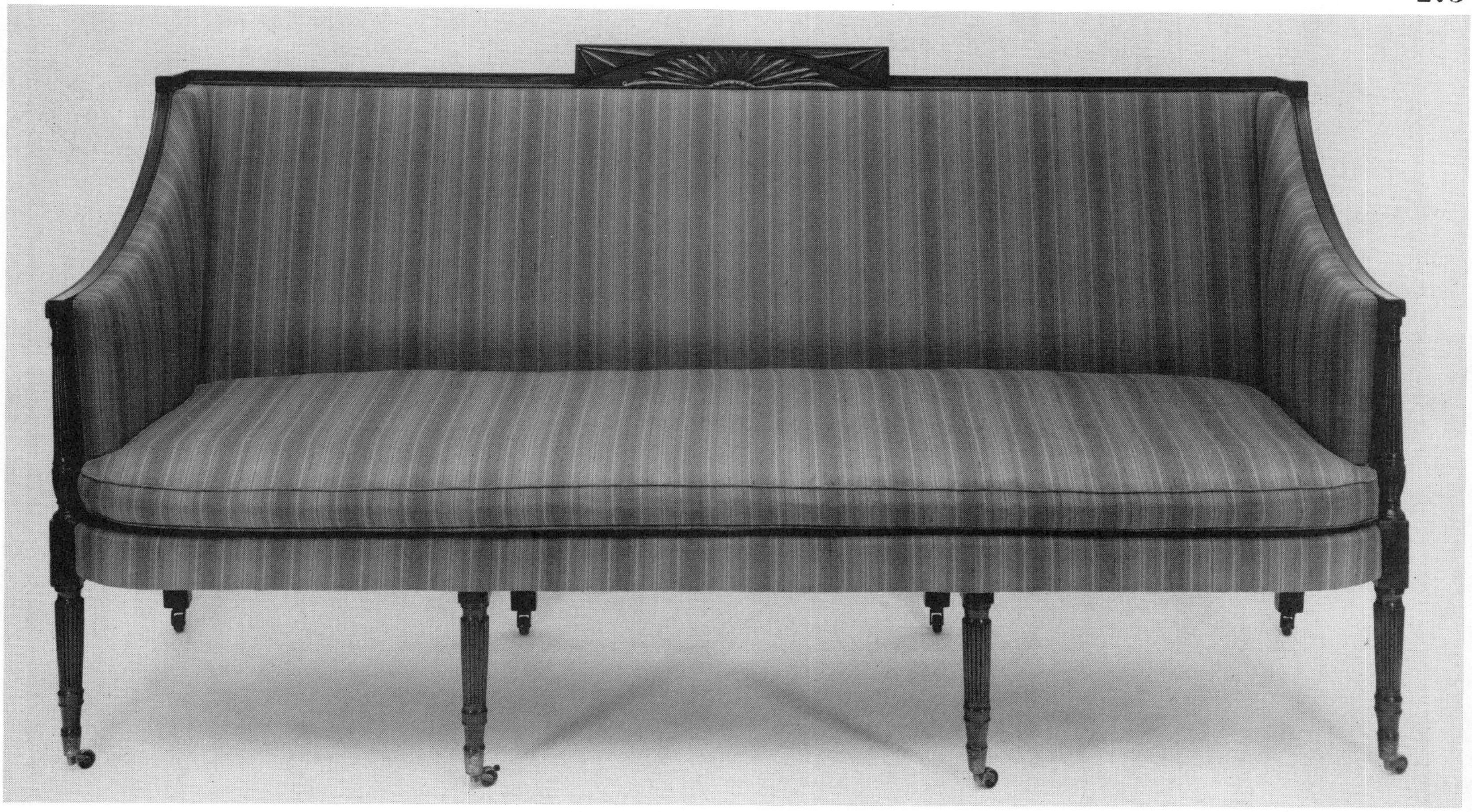

276

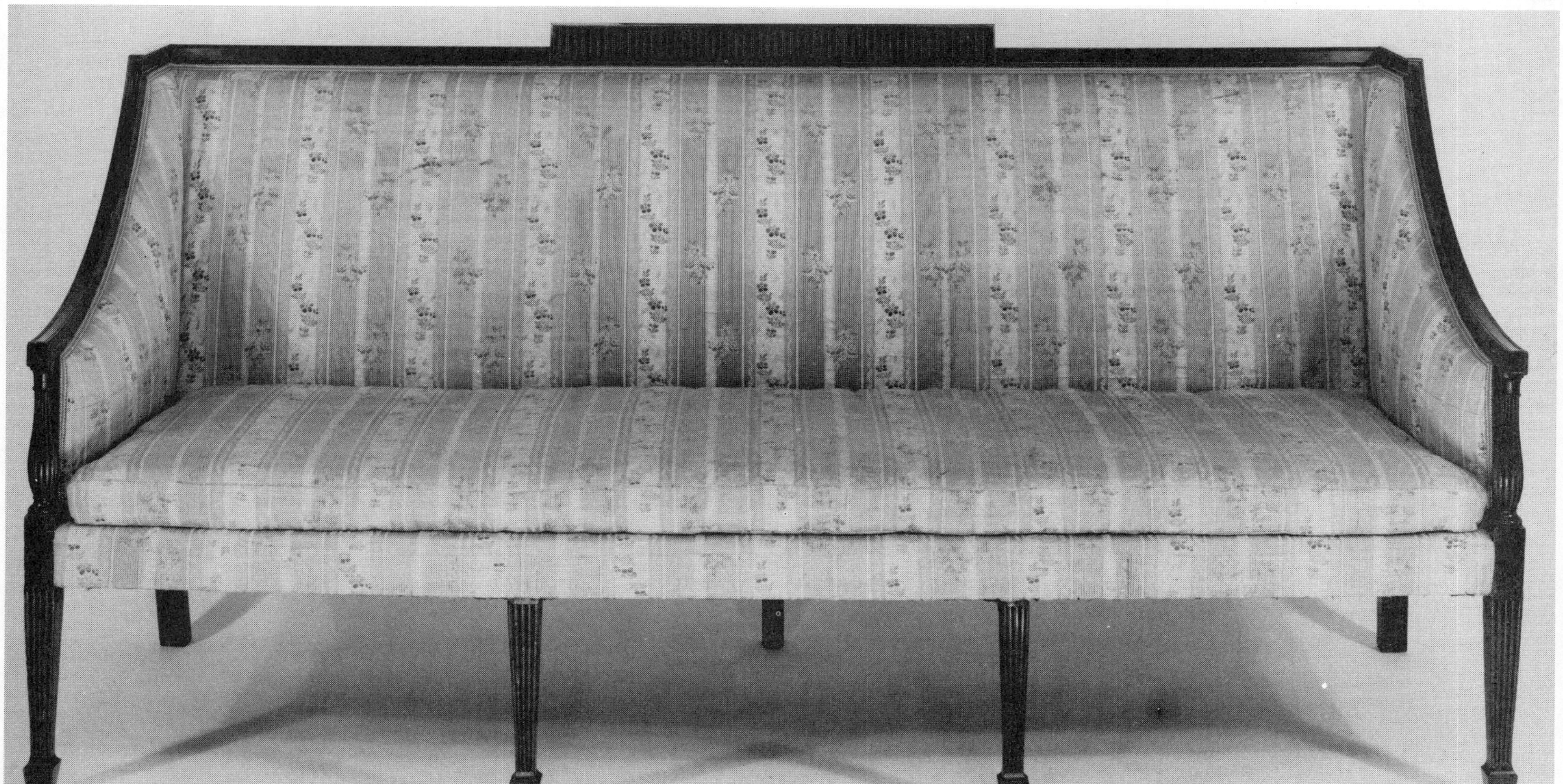

**278** SOFA, a scroll-back cane sofa
*1805–1810   New York City   Probably made in the shop
   of Duncan Phyfe*

In *The New-York Revised Prices for Manufacturing
Cabinet and Chair Work* for 1810 (p. 57), a good de-
scription of this piece is given under the heading,
"A Scroll Back Cane Sofa":

|  |  |  |  |
|---|---|---|---|
| The center legs [back] running up and forming three panels, elliptic front, bored for caning | 6 | 12 | 0 |
| Bell seat [seen here instead of elliptic], extra | 1 | 5 | 0 |
|  | [7 | 17 | 0] |

The carving, caning, reeding, and casters would
also have been extras, hence the cost of its making
may have come to ten or twelve pounds, that is to
say twenty-five or thirty dollars. It would have
taken nearly a month to make, and, on the basis of
known practice, the selling price including materials, overhead, and profit can be estimated at
between three or four times the cost of labor, or
between seventy-five and one hundred and twenty
dollars—seemingly little enough for a great piece
of furniture. However, considering that the selling

price was equivalent to a cabinetmaker's wages for
one hundred days (at the going rate of a dollar per
day), at today's wage rate the cost of making an
identical sofa would be three to four thousand dollars. Probably a more realistic figure of its cost in
terms of today's dollar value would be obtained by
using the conversion factor of ten or twelve (often
used by historians to compensate for the decreased
purchasing power of today's dollar from that of the
early nineteenth-century dollar). At that rate the
current selling price of this sofa would be 750 to
1440 dollars.

Although much rarer than No. 277 because of
the caning, this great sofa follows the lines and
ornament of that one with the notable exceptions
of the substitution of carved drapery and tassels in
the center panel and the tapering, turned arm supports with different carving on their pedestals. This
may have been made in Duncan Phyfe's shop and
possibly was a part of the Bayard set since it
matches so closely Nos. 66 and 67. But there were
many other cabinetmakers capable of turning out
such a piece in the early 1800's, and obviously they
were doing so inasmuch as the wages for making
one are listed in the price book which covered the

work of all men participating in the cabinetmaking business in New York.

Dimensions: height 37; length 76; depth 23¾.

Materials: mahogany and cane; medial brace, maple; upholstery, light-blue satin with stylized floral-and-leaf medallion in white and yellow, French, Empire style, early nineteenth century.

Provenance: Louis Guerineau Myers.

Accession: 57.729

**279** STOOL OR COUCH with scroll ends
*1810–1825   New York City, Philadelphia, or Baltimore*

Stools "with bolster scrolls at each end" are listed after "Grecian Stools" and before "Grecian Couches" in the 1808 edition of *The London Chair-Makers' and Carvers' Book of Prices for Workmanship* (p. 70). Their standard length is given as "from five feet to six feet six inches; width of ditto, two feet." These dimensions could be varied for a slight additional charge.

Few pieces of American furniture are more dashing in appearance than this one. Not only the shape of the frame but its ornament is dramatic. Painted to resemble rosewood, it is decorated in gilt. Be-

ginning with a flourish of brass at the tips of the feet, gilt leaves and honeysuckle ornament outline the curving legs and lead into the animated foliated scrolls and lush rosettes on the frame. The quality of the brass fittings, the gilt ornament, and the spirited outline of the form point to a top flight cabinetmaking shop. The only documented pieces of American furniture with comparable ornament of the same high quality (known to the writer) are a pair of window stools, the gift of Mrs. J. Amory Haskell to the Brooklyn Museum. One is inscribed with the name of Duncan Phyfe, and they appear to be well documented as having been made in his shop in 1823 for Robert Donaldson, then of Fayetteville on the Cape Fear River in North Carolina and later of 15 State Street, New York.[22]

Edgar P. Miller in *American Antique Furniture* illustrates a couch and window seat so much like this one and No. 280 as to leave little doubt they came from the same shop. Although uncertain of their origin, Mr. Miller remarks that such pieces have been inherited in Baltimore families.[23] A pair of superb klysmos-form side chairs with related decoration in the Philadelphia Museum have been attributed to that city.[24]

279

280

314

Although at the present time, the identification of the maker and of the ornamenter of this outstanding group of furniture is impossible. They apparently worked in New York, Philadelphia, or Baltimore. Not normally used as a cabinetmaking wood, the cucumber magnolia grows from Maryland southward.

Dimensions: height 24¾; length 60½; depth 22½.

Materials: base of end supports, front and rear rails, legs, maple; end rails, cucumber magnolia; seat frame, tulip; upholstery, green silk with applied strips woven in Empire design.

Accession: 57.745

### 280 WINDOW STOOL (one of a pair)
*1810–1825 New York City, Philadelphia, or Baltimore*

This pair of window seats of simple construction were designed by a master. With Greek antefixes at the corners (to secure the cushion), high-style gilt ornament on a background painted to simulate rosewood, and elaborate brass mounts for the castors, they were meant to be the equals of the stylish scroll-end couch (No. 279) which they accompany. George Smith's *Collection of Ornamental Designs after the Manner of the Antique* (published in London in

1812) specifically notes on the title page that it is "composed for the use of Architects, Ornamental Painters, Statuaries, Carvers, Casters in Metal, Paper Makers, Carpet, Silk and Printed Calico Manufacturers and every Trade dependant on the Fine Arts." The ornamental painter of this stool and the preceding couch may have used Smith's book as his source for "Grecian foliage and ornament." The designs are similar; but it should be noted they are ones that were in general use after about 1790 in England and France.[25]

Dimensions: height 16½; length 45⅛; depth 14.

Materials: all woods tulip; upholstery, green silk with applied borders woven in Empire design, French or English, early nineteenth century.

Accession: 57.753.1, 2

### 281 GRECIAN COUCH
*1805–1815 Salem, Massachusetts*

The French portrait painted by Jacques-Louis David (1800) of Madame Jeanne Françoise Julie Adélaïde Récamier reclining on a couch shaped like this one is so famous and well known that such couches are often called Récamier sofas today. However, when this form was introduced into

English sofa design about 1800, probably from France, couches and sofas with scrolled ends were called Grecian. Specifications for a variety of interpretations of the form are given in the 1802 and subsequent editions of *The London Chair-Makers' and Carvers' Book of Prices for Workmanship* under the headings Grecian Couches, Grecian Sofas. The lines of the frame of this one are as free flowing as those of the finest American couches.[26] The exposed surfaces are lavishly carved with grapevines, leaves of laurel, stalks of wheat, horns of plenty, fruit, flowers, and ribbons against a punched-snowflake background in what may be Samuel McIntire's last phase before his death in 1811; or the carving may be the work of his son, Samuel Field McIntire. They worked closely together. The younger McIntire (who died in 1819) advertised in the Salem *Gazette* on April 30 and May 3, 1811, as follows: "The subscriber carries on Carving as usual at the Shop of the deceased in Summer Street where he will be glad to receive orders in that line. He returns thanks for past favors."[27]

Here the S-shaped legs are a graceful innovation. In the light of Sheraton's remarks on the Greeks and the Romans and their couches (see page 293), it is interesting that these legs are so placed as to approximate the lower half of the profile of the legs on a Roman curule chair (No. 72) and that the legs on an almost matching couch, formerly in the Cluett collection,[28] are also of Roman form—turned stumps heavily reeded on the upper section.

Dimensions: height 38; length 95; depth 26.
Materials: mahogany; rails, birch; upholstery, yellow satin with fleurs-de-lis in mauve and white, French, Empire style, early nineteenth century.
Accession: 57.912

## 282  GRECIAN COUCH
*About 1820  Salem, Massachusetts  Label of Thomas Needham (working about 1800–1830's or later)*

Although this caned couch is less curvaceous than No. 281 and has less harmonious legs and backboard, the fluid lines of its frame are emphasized with heavy reeding, which neatly diminishes as it flows into the circular scrolls at the head and foot. Comparison of this couch with the labeled drawing table (No. 199) from the same shop reveals the dramatic changes in American furniture design which took place in the first two decades of the nineteenth century. Not only did the individual elements of the new forms become heavier, but the over-all effect became more vigorous and less effete. Since only the front side is finished with reeding, this couch was probably made for a wall rather than to be free-standing. The address given on Needham's label is Charter Street, Salem.

Dimensions: height 31; length 72; depth 25½.
Materials: mahogany and cane; two medial braces, aspen; upholstery, green silk moiré, English or French, late eighteenth century.
Accession: 57.575

## 283  GRECIAN COUCH
*About 1825–1835  New York State (?)*

With all the stately grace of a pleasure barge, this couch, designed in the Grecian manner, represents, in its graceful line and robust carving, the finest quality workmanship of its era. Although the strong diagonal reeding, acanthus leaves, sunflower blossoms, and melons (the latter two crosshatched in the manner of carving found on New York furniture of seventy-five years before) may seem unrefined to modern eyes, the exuberant over-all effect was very much the accepted fashion of the time and is surprisingly close in motif and feeling to the carving found on many Spanish Romanesque capitals.

The clawed feet at first view could be taken for lions' paws, but it is more likely that they are eagles' claws since there are many couches and sofas with similar feet sprouting large eagles' wings which are here replaced by cornucopias. Perhaps the eagles' feet and the cornucopias may have been regarded as only decoration, but it seems likely that for maker and owner there are implications of nationalism and abundance in an era when "peace and plenty" was the common slogan and the Erie Canal had opened the way to the rich resources of the then western farmlands.

The name "Roch" is branded and "R. Rosch CR" scratched on the underside of the seat frame. They may be the name of an as yet unidentified cabinetmaker.

Dimensions: height 27½; length 80; depth 25½.
Materials: mahogany and mahogany veneers; framing, tulip and white pine; upholstery, light-blue lampas with Empire floral and leaf medallions, French, about 1810.
Provenance: Gift of Mrs. John T. Tenneson, 1963.
Accession: G63.94

FOOTNOTES

1 Downs, No. 276.
2 Hipkiss, Fig. 120, p. 182.

282

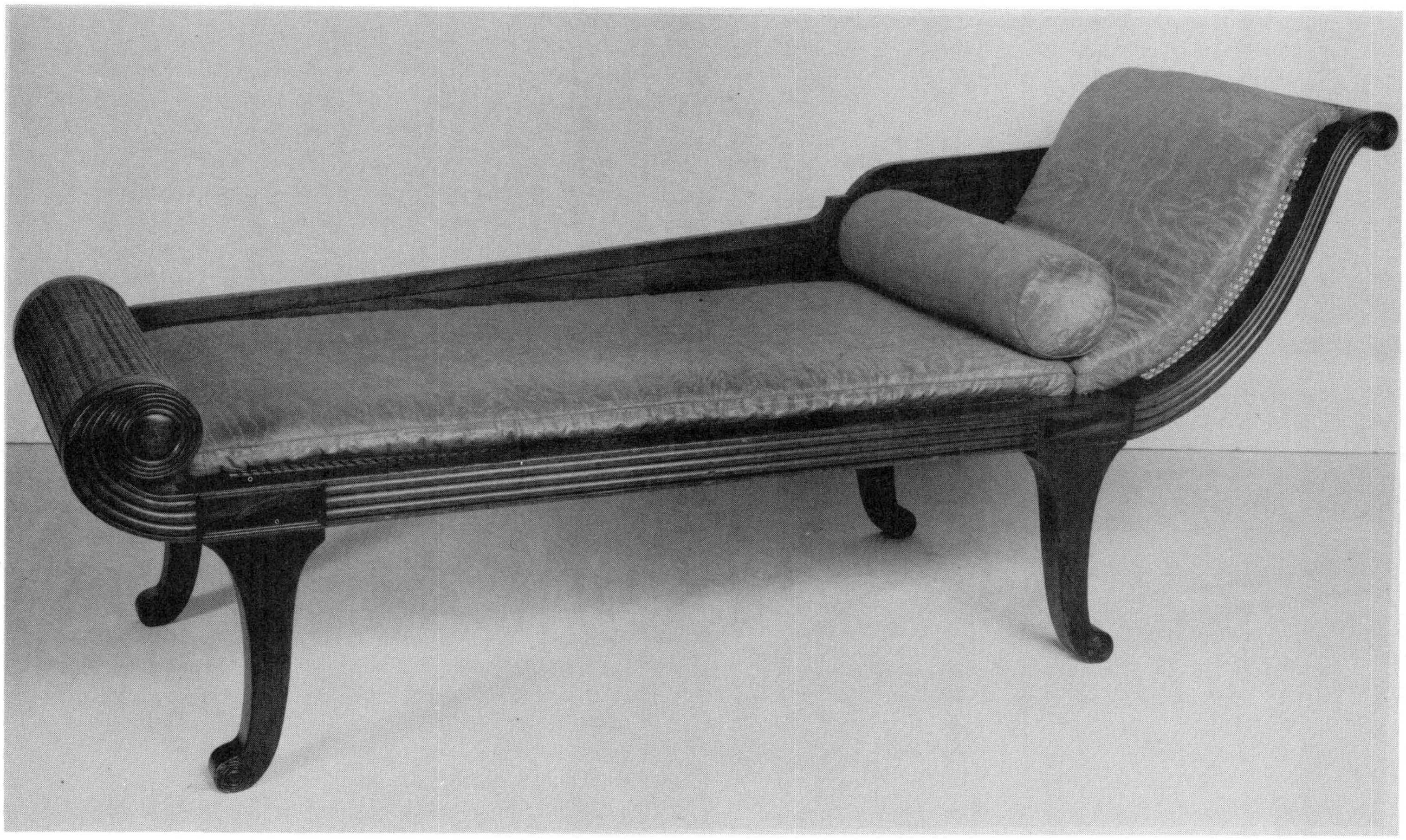

283

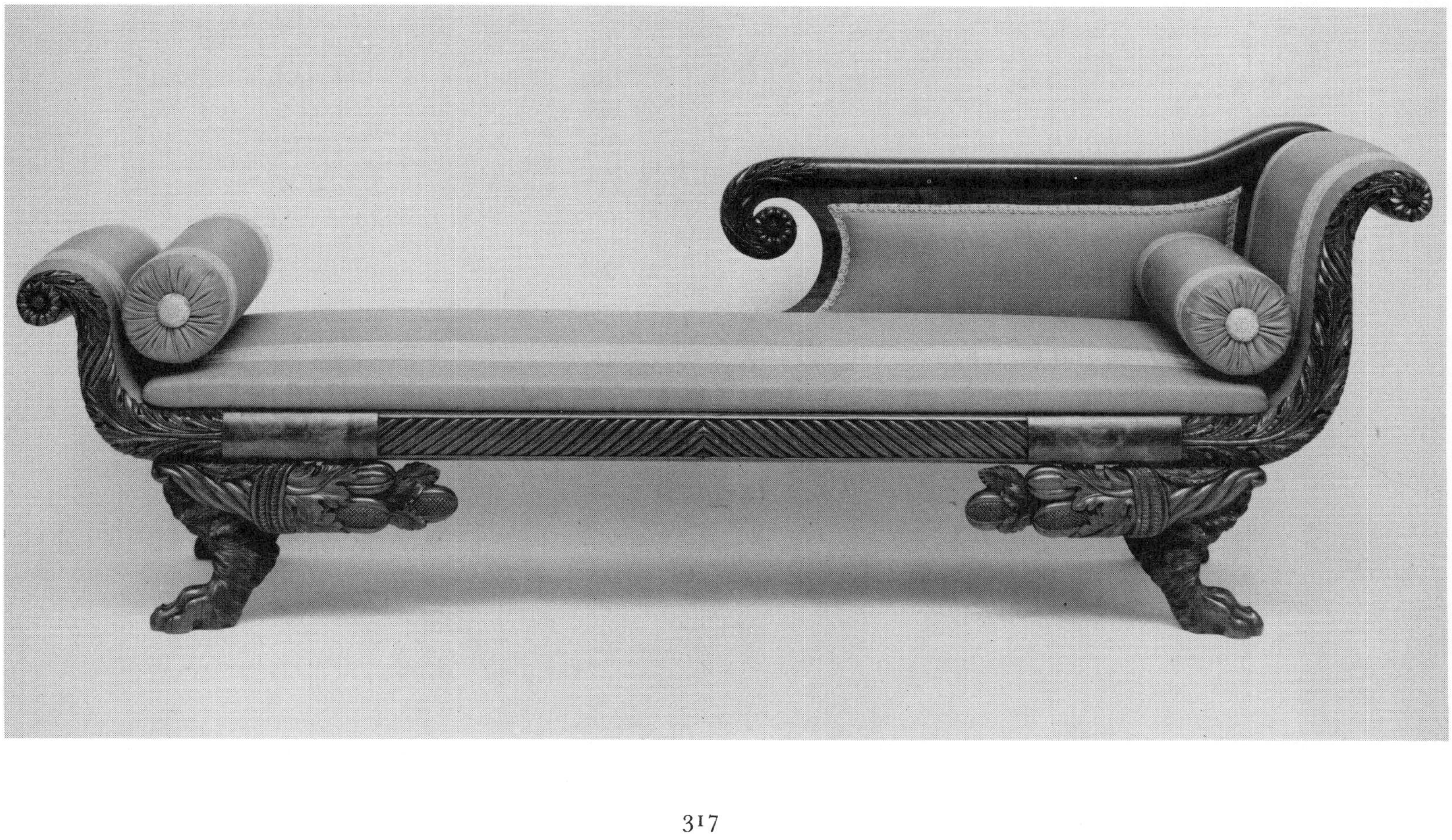

3 See Thomas Rawlin, *Familiar Architecture* (London, 1768), p. 57, as the source for one design of a plaited basket of fruit, as noted by Fales, *Samuel McIntire, A Bicentennial Symposium, 1757-1957*, pp. 55-67.

4 See the mantel from the Elias Hasket Derby Mansion in Downs, "Derby and McIntire," *Bulletin of the Metropolitan Museum of Art*, VI (October, 1947), 73-81.

5 Now in the Karolik Collection, Boston Museum of Fine Arts. McIntire's bill for carving is in the McIntire papers, Essex Institute. See fn. 2 above, Fales, p. 58.

6 In the collections of George A. Cluett, the Philadelphia Museum of Art, Benjamin Ginsberg (1964), and Joe Kindig, Jr. (1953). See Fiske Kimball, "Furniture Carvings by Samuel McIntire: II, Sofas", *Antiques*, XVIII (December, 1930), 498-502, Figs. 8 and 9, for illustrations of the first two sofas. The sofa in Winterthur's collection is illustrated in Fig. 7.

7 Joseph Downs noted that, among McIntire's sketches in the McIntire papers at the Essex Institute, there is a drawing for a carved basket of fruit in which the plaiting of the reeds matches the carving on this basket.

8 *Baltimore Furniture*, No. 94.

9 *Ibid.*, No. 96.

10 See Downs, *American Furniture*, Nos. 194, 233.

11 *The American Wing of the Metropolitan Museum of Art*, Special Issue of *Antiques*, L (October, 1956), 257, No. 22.

12 Manuscript in the Essex Institute, Salem, Massachusetts; cited in Swan, *Samuel McIntire, Carver, and The Sandersons, Early Salem Cabinet Makers*, frontispiece. This sofa and several others with carved baskets are illustrated in Fiske Kimball's article "Furniture Carvings by Samuel McIntire, II," *Antiques*, XVIII (December, 1930), 498-502.

13 In correspondence concerning Miss Hill's sofa, "Mr. Adams" of Salem is mentioned as the maker. He is thought to have been Nehemiah Adams. See Fiske Kimball's article, "Salem Furniture Makers: II, Nehemiah Adams," *Antiques*, XXIV (December, 1933), 218-220. Illustrated as Fig. 38, Dean A. Fales, Jr., "The Furniture of McIntire," *Samuel McIntire, a Bicentennial Symposium* (Salem: The Essex Institute, 1957). On pages 62 and 63 is a discussion of a bill for wedding furniture of Lucy Hill, Billerica.

For other sofas after the pattern illustrated Plate 35 of Sheraton's *Drawing Book* (1793), see the Catalogue of the *Girl Scouts Loan Exhibition*, No. 727; Hipkiss, op. cit., No. 121.

14 Now in the *Karolik Collection*, Boston Museum of Fine Arts. McIntire's bill for carving is in the McIntire papers, Essex Institute.

15 In addition to the obvious similarities, the back legs of both sofas are broad and flat instead of being square in section.

16 Information from letter of William H. Coburn to Dean A. Fales, Jr., April 29, 1955.

17 Sale Catalogue of the *Collection of the Late Philip Flayderman*, (New York: American Art Association Anderson Galleries, Inc., 1930), No. 408, pp. 134-135.

18 Stoneman, op. cit. For family connections, see pages 19-23, and for illustration of this sofa, see page 329.

19 *Ibid.*, pp. 205-206.

20 Phelps Warren, "Setting the Record Straight, Slover and Taylor, New York Cabinetmakers," *Antiques*, LXXX (October, 1961), 350-351.

21 For sofas with carved sunbursts and rosettes, though varying in detail, see fn. 24 and "The Almanac: Federal New York," *Antiques*, XXXVIII (November, 1940), 236.

22 Thomas Hamilton Ormsbee, "Autographed Duncan Phyfe Furniture," *American Collector*, XI (March, 1942), 5.

23 Edgar C. Miller, Jr., *American Antique Furniture* (New York: M. Barrows & Company, Inc., 1937), p. 292 and illustrations Nos. 522, 523, and 566.

24 *Classical America 1815-1845*. Loan Exhibition Catalogue (Newark, New Jersey; The Newark Museum, 1963), No. 28.

25 For example, similar motifs, though with less movement, are found in an English printed cotton textile dated 1792 in the Winterthur collection.

26 Another fine American couch in this style, owned by the Henry Ford Museum, is illustrated in "Elegant Furniture for a Grecian Parlor," *America's Arts and Skills* (New York: C. P. Dutton & Co., Inc., 1957), pp. 72-73.

27 Ethel Hall Bjerkoe, *The Cabinetmakers of America* (Garden City, New York: Doubleday and Company, 1957), p. 157.

28 Illustrated in Fiske Kimball's article "Furniture Carvings by Samuel McIntire: II," 502.

# Card Tables

Despite Thomas Sheraton's remark in his *Cabinet Dictionary* of 1803 that a card table is "a piece of furniture more often used than to good purpose," the playing of card games—whist, loo, faro, quadrille, and many others—was highly popular in England all through the eighteenth century. Many references indicate that the playing of cards was also popular in this country.

In 1830, Mrs. Trollope wrote:

> I was told that gambling is the favorite recreation of the gentleman, and that it is carried to a very considerable extent; but here, as elsewhere with-in the country, it is kept extremely well out of sight. I do not think I was present with a pack of cards a dozen times during more than three years that I remained in the country. Billiards are much played, though in most places the amusement is illegal. It often appeared to me that the old women of a state made the laws, and that the young men broke them.[1]

Almost fifty years earlier, on November 20, 1782, the Marquis de Chastelleux had written of an evening in Boston:

> For the first time since my arrival in America I was made to play whist. The cards were English, that is, much handsomer and dearer than ours, and we marked our points with either *louis* or *portugaises* [six-and-thirties]; when the party was finished, the loss was not difficult to settle; for the company was still faithful to that voluntary law established in society from the commencement of the troubles, which prohibited playing for money during the war. This law however, was not scrupulously observed in the clubs, and parties made by the men amongst themselves. The inhabitants of Boston are fond of high play, and it is fortunate, perhaps, that the war happened when it did, to moderate this passion which began to be attended with dangerous consequences.[2]

That gambling was not confined to the men is well demonstrated by the following note in a letter of Miss Mary Boardman Crowninshield written in February of 1816, when she was visiting in Washington. "Last eve I was at Mrs. Monroe's [the president's wife] our neighbor—quite a large party, but I was only invited to pass a sociable eve. We played loo and I won—I am afraid to say how much, but shall give it to the orphan asylum."[3]

Card tables were frequently made in pairs, and one notable set of four matching tables made by John Townsend of Newport has survived.[4] Basically there are four types: square (and variants thereof), circular tables, tripod tables, and pedestal tables. The following excerpt from *The Journeymen Cabinet and Chair-Makers Philadelphia Book of Prices* for 1795 clearly indicates one standard model and a few of the "extras" or variations which could be had by the purchaser.

A SQUARE CARD TABLE,

Three feet long, one fly foot, square edge to the top, plain Marlbro'
legs, all solid,                                                £. 1   0   0

| | | | |
|---|---|---|---|
| Each inch more or less in length, | 0 | 0 | 6 |
| A drawer in ditto, | 0 | 4 | 6 |
| An extra fly foot, | 0 | 1 | 10½ |
| Making a serpentine front to the above with straight end rails, | 0 | 10 | 0 |
| Sweeping the ends of the top serpentine, | 0 | 2 | 6 |
| Ditto the end rails half serpentine, | 0 | 8 | 6 |

Straight legs without beading or tapering are "plain marlboro legs." Tapering of the leg cost a penny for each side, and it may be observed that most legs were tapered only on three sides. In comparison to the one pound for the journeymen's wages quoted above for the making of a table, the selling price seems to have been about four pounds ten shillings. This was for a basic table with no extras such as inlay, veneers, or carved ornament. Similar specifications were given for making a "circular card table," "card table with ovalo corners," and "a hollow corner card table." (See pages 358 and 359 for an old illustration of various types of "Pier Table Tops" and their contemporary names. These apply to other table tops as well.) In all probability, card tables were much used as pier or side tables, standing against the wall when not in use. They are occasionally seen in this position in contemporary prints.

Mahogany veneers were widely used on table frames and leaves, but in New England extensive use was made of satinwood veneers on the frame—often with oval panels centered in the front. While tables with half-serpentine ends and serpentine or "elliptic" (bowed) fronts were the most popular in Boston and Salem, other shapes were also made in these cities. Particularly after 1800 the serpentine front was modified by the addition of an ovalo corner shaped to conform with the projection of the upper part of the turned front legs.

In New York, five-legged examples seem to have been very popular, and even card tables with six legs were made there and in Newport on occasion. *The New-York Book of Prices for Cabinet and Chair Work* of 1802 lists as the standard for square or circular card tables "four fast legs, and one fly leg." This seems to be a carry-over of earlier usage, for Chippendale card tables made in New York often had five legs. Five-legged tables of Philadelphia, Baltimore, or Massachusetts workmanship are occasionally seen, though less frequently than those of New York origin.

Since so many card tables are highly ornamented, and since more of them bear the label of the maker or shop in which they were made than any other American furniture form, card tables provide an excellent insight into the shapes of legs, carving, inlaid details, and veneers favored by individual cabinetmaking shops. Consequently they offer valuable clues to regional characteristics.

1 Mrs. Trollope, *Domestic Manners of the Americans* (London: Whittaker, Trencher and Co., 1832), II, p. 7.
2 Marquis de Chastelleux, *Travels in North America in the Years 1780, 1781, and 1782.* A revised translation by Howard C. Rice, Jr. (Chapel Hill, North Carolina: University of North Carolina Press, 1963), II, p. 507.
3 *Letters of Mary Boardman Crowninshield,* ed. Francis Boardman Crowninshield (New York: Riverside Press, 1905), p. 59.
4 Sold as two pairs in the sale of the collection of Philip Flayderman, Lots 470 and 471, held January, 1930, and now in the collection of the William Rockhill Nelson Gallery of Art, Atkins Museum of Fine Arts, and Mr. and Mrs. Stanley Stone, Milwaukee, Wisconsin.

## XXI North Alcove of the Billiard Room

*This highly ornamental circular card table (No. 284) was probably made in New York, and the pair of ladder-back side chairs in Philadelphia. Dice cups, bone dominoes, and backgammon board, as well as cards, suggest the variety of games for which card tables were used. The stylish Argand-type hanging lamp would have been the most up-to-date and effective source of illumination in the early nineteenth century. The wall hangings were painted by Michel Felice Corné about 1800.*

### 284  CIRCULAR CARD TABLE
*About 1800   New York City*

This brilliant achievement owes its success to the dramatization of the oval outline on a circular form. The spatial relationships are subtle and varied: oval to oval, oval to rectangle, oval to triangle, oval to diamond, oval within diamond, oval within rectangle. Dependent bellflowers of this type strung within intersecting ovals are found on sideboards and other furniture of New York and Albany origin. Five legs are standard for New York card tables.

Dimensions: height 29⅛; width 35¾; depth 17½.
Materials: mahogany and mahogany veneers; light and dark wood inlays; rails, white pine; flying rail, cherry; corner blocks, red gum.
Accession: 57.861                     see Inlay Fig. 110

### 285  CIRCULAR CARD TABLE
*About 1790   Philadelphia   Attributed to Jonathan Gostelowe (working 1768–1793)*

Jonathan Gostelowe died February 3, 1795. This table is believed to be one of a pair that he willed to his wife Elizabeth and which, by family tradition, was made by him.[1] It is believed never to have been out of the hands of Gostelowe descendants until acquired by the late Clarence Wilson Brazer, from whose estate it came to Winterthur.

On May 11, 1793, Jonathan Gostelowe advertised in the *Independent Gazetteer* that having "declined Business," he would sell at public auction "Work-benches, Tools, and the remaining Stock on hand" including a "Quantity of Mahogany and other Furniture"; among the listings are "Circular Card Tables."

In his published study of this table, Brazer called attention to the wages journeymen were to receive for their labor. In *The Journeymen Cabinet and Chair-*

**284**

**285**

*Makers Philadelphia Book of Prices* for 1795, these are listed as follows:

> A Circular Card Table. Three feet long, the rail veneer'd, one fly foot, a square edge to the top, plain marlbro' legs,    £1-8- 1 ½

Among "extras" listed therein and found here are:

> An extra fly foot,
> [both back legs swing]    0-1-10 ½
> An astragal or hollow and two
> beads on edge of top,    0-3- 7
> Working a hollow on the edge
> of the under top,    0-1- 0
> A cock-bead round the bottom
> of rail when straight,    0-1- 6

Omitted here but listed under a "Square Card Table" are brackets at seven pence each. However, brackets are believed to have been going out of style by 1795, and this fine table of rather heavy proportions may date from the 1780's. Unusual for Philadelphia, but common to Baltimore practice is the brace running from the front of the frame to the back rail. Short blocky spade feet like these are occasionally found on Philadelphia chairs.

Dimensions: height 29½; width 36¼; depth 17¾.
Materials: mahogany; rear rail, hard pine; flying rails, white oak; front rail, tulip.
Provenance: Clarence Wilson Brazer.
Accession: 58.46.6

## 286   CIRCULAR CARD TABLE
*1790–1800   New York City*

Rich veneers, careful workmanship, and fine proportions give this simple table the appearance of strength and dignity. The dark-figured mahogany veneers of the top are repeated vertically on the square edges of the leaves and on the unbroken surface of the rounded frame finished at the bottom with a bold astragal molding. Remnants of the original green baize are still to be seen on the playing surface. The sturdy effect of the legs is lightened by "scratch" beading on their front edges, and the transition from leg to frame is broadened by the use of six pierced brackets—a carry-over from the Chippendale style. Two are replacements.

It is difficult to say by whom or where this table was made. Although in character, but not in detail, it resembles a four-legged circular table made and stamped by Stephen Badlam,[2] of Dorchester, Massachusetts, the presence of an "extra fly foot" and cherry flying rails suggests New York City as its place of origin.

Dimensions: height 28¾; width 35½; depth 17½.
Materials: mahogany; side rails, front rails, and corner blocks, white pine; back and flying rails, cherry.
Accession: 57.1023

**287** CIRCULAR CARD TABLE

*About 1800   Charlestown, Massachusetts   Label of Jacob Forster (working 1786–1838)*

Without exotic woods or extraordinary craftsmanship, this table bearing the label of Jacob Forster is outstanding as a forthright accomplishment. Unsophisticated inlays of curving stems ending in a petalled flower of three pointed ovals and paired leaves of the same sort (see also No. 32) are seen on many labeled Forster pieces and may possibly be regarded as his signature. Thomas Howard, Jr., of Providence and several cabinetmakers in the South and Pittsburgh used related inlays, but the individual character of this work is quite different. Similar highly effective black-and-white, checkerlike "stringing" also occurs on other Forster work.

Dimensions: height 29⅛; width 35⅝; depth 17½.

Materials: mahogany; holly and dark wood inlays; front rail, corner block, white pine; flying rail, birch.

Provenance: Museum Purchase, 1957.

Accession: 57.103.2          see Inlay Figs. 31, 32, 92

**289**

**288**

**288** CIRCULAR CARD TABLE

*1790–1800   Newport, Rhode Island   Label of John Townsend (working 1764–1809)*

Several labels of John Townsend, famous for his furniture in the block-front style as well as that in the neoclassical taste, are numbered. This one is inscribed 1796 which may be the date the table was made.

The entry "Inlaid Flutes in Friezes, [on] Table Legs and Pillasters" in *The New-York Book of Prices for Cabinet and Chair Work* for 1802 (p. 60) properly identifies what have been called "book inlays" for a long time. The prices varied if "straight way, taper'd or diminish'd" or if "shaded." Elsewhere in the same book sunbursts and bellflowers such as seen here are identified as "patries [paterae] and husks." This particular flaring variety of husk is seen occasionally on Newport furniture often (as here) with veining of black lines. Originally such veining was called engraving. Both back legs swing.

Dimensions: height 28⅝; width 35⅝; depth 17½.

Materials: mahogany; light and dark wood inlays; front rail, white pine; rear rail, a soft maple.

Provenance: Guy W. Walker, Jr.

Accession: 58.135.3          see Inlay Fig. 95

**289** CIRCULAR CARD TABLE

*About 1800   Baltimore*

This circular card table, with rather deeper-than-usual frame (4¾ inches), has many features that

relate to fine furniture with Baltimore histories of ownership: satinwood teardrop-shaped panels, stained green and inlaid with elongated three-part husks on the legs; a satinwood oval with lilies of the valley inset on the upper part of each leg where it projects from the frame as a pilaster; and the large spread eagle in a half circle of green-stained satinwood inlaid on the upper leaf. The band of double line inlay variegated with pairs of oblongs of different colored woods edging the frame is another feature common to much Baltimore furniture. There is no medial brace, a feature often found on tables attributed to Baltimore.

Dimensions: height 30; width 36¼; depth 18.

Materials: mahogany; light and dark wood inlays; front rail and corner blocks, tulip; rear rail, white pine; flying rail, oak.

Accession: 57.778                        see Inlay Fig. 127

## 290  CIRCULAR CARD TABLE
*About 1800   Probably Baltimore*

Furniture inlaid with the American eagle is rare. But this eagle (similar to Inlay Fig. 119) is found more often than any other—usually on Baltimore and sometimes on Philadelphia pieces. It gives distinction to a plain table—though one with several "extras" which included: the making and "sinking" of the eagle inlaid ovals; the stringing on the edges of the top, the lower edge of the frame, the legs, and around the panels; and the inlaid cuffs on

the legs. The flying rail is white oak, a wood commonly used in Baltimore and Philadelphia tables.

Dimensions: height 29; width 36; depth 17¼.

Materials: mahogany; light wood inlay; rails, white pine; flying rail, white oak; corner blocks, tulip.

Accession: 57.932

## 291  CIRCULAR CARD TABLE
*About 1800   Baltimore*

A comparison of this southern table with those from Massachusetts will illustrate regional differences. In both areas, the vocabulary of neoclassical ornament is approximately the same, and the juxtaposition of curvilinear and rectangular panels of "string" outline or crotch veneers plays a vital part in the aesthetic theme. But Massachusetts cabinetmakers more often employed contrasts of golden-figured birch against the dark colors of mahogany or rosewood. In Baltimore work, the over-all impression is usually achieved through shading rather than contrast. Rich tonal effects of figured woods enlivened with intricate stained satinwood or other light-colored inset ovals or half circles are common. Seldom does one find large stained floral medallions inlaid in American table tops, as here, except in Baltimore examples. The clever hand of the Baltimore cabinetmaker is also evident in chevron-patterned veneers which cover the legs on their two front surfaces.

Dimensions: height 29¾; width 35¾; depth 17.

**292**

Materials: mahogany and mahogany veneers; light wood veneers and inlay; back rail, hard pine; flying rail, oak; medial brace, mahogany.
Accession: 57.777                    see Inlay Fig. 80

**292** CIRCULAR CARD TABLE (one of a pair)
*About 1800    Baltimore*

Although there are fewer inlays than usual on this table, the shaded vases of flowers, the edging on the frame, and the double string panels on the legs are intricate and effective. For the ends of such panels, *The New-York Book of Prices for Cabinet and Chair Work* of 1802 lists in "Table No. II" (p. 5) under the heading "Panelling with strings on Pillasters, Legs, Stump Feet, Table Claws, Etc...." that each "Gothic hollow corner or astragal end" cost five and one half pence for a double string—almost double the cost of each "hollow or round diamond or octagon end." There is a medial stretcher from the front to back of the frame.

Dimensions: height 31; width 36; depth 17¾.
Materials: mahogany; light and dark wood inlays; flying rails, oak; other rails and medial brace, white pine; corner blocks, hard pine.
Provenance: Roger A. Van de Straeten.
Accession: 57.618               see Inlay Figs. 74, 122

**293**

**293** SQUARE CARD TABLE with round corners and hollow front
*About 1800    Baltimore*

Highly sophisticated in form, decoration, and workmanship, this is one of the most distinguished examples of Maryland cabinetmaking. The overall effect is one of richness and rhythm. The outlines of fanciful satinwood string panels with "hollow," "double hollow," and "rounded ends" echo and repeat one another in close harmony. Fine veneers surround and enhance the effect of beautifully wrought and stained inlaid flowers in ovals above the tassels on the legs. (See also No. 351.) The delightful four-petal blossoms which serve as cuffs also occur on two or three other pieces of Baltimore furniture[3] and on one card table believed to have been made by Jacob Wayne in Philadelphia.[4]

Dimensions: height 29½; width 38¾; depth 17½.
Materials: mahogany; light wood veneers and "stringing"; front, back, end rails, and medial brace, white pine; flying rail, oak.
Accession: 57.697                    see Inlay Fig. 84

**294** SQUARE CARD TABLE with ovolo
corners

*About 1800    Newburyport, Massachusetts    Label of
Joseph Short[5] (working late eighteenth and early nineteenth centuries)*

A card table with "sash plan corners" was Sheraton's name for an example with this shape of top.
Twice in 1803 Jacob Sanderson paid Thomas
Hodgkins (of Salem) $8 for "making 2 sash cornard
Card tables."[6] Equally specific are the references
in price books, where such tables are listed as
"square card tables with Ovalo corners."

A rich though conservative effect is achieved
through the use of brilliant repeating mahogany
veneers on the skirt edged with a "black diamond"
band of inlay from which the "stringing" runs
down the legs to the floor.

Dimensions: height 28⅜; width 34⅛; depth 16¾.

Materials: mahogany; light and dark wood inlays; rear
corner blocks, rear rail, front rounded parts of rail,
white pine; front rail, soft maple (American).

Provenance: Museum Purchase, 1959.

Accession: 59.63                     see Inlay Fig. 52

**295** SQUARE CARD TABLE with ovolo
corners

*About 1810    Springfield, Massachusetts, Connecticut, or
Rhode Island*

Although most price books include a quotation for
a drawer in card tables as an "extra," drawers are
seldom found in high-style American examples of
the Federal period. Indeed, this is the only one with
a drawer in the Winterthur collection. "Icicle," or
segmented triangle, inlays, such as those on the
outer surfaces of the legs, are found on documented
Connecticut and Rhode Island furniture and often
on the work of William Lloyd of Springfield, Massachusetts.[7]

Dimensions: height 29½; width 36; depth 17¾.

Materials: mahogany and mahogany veneers; light wood,
walnut, and dark wood inlays; left medial brace, rails,
and drawer front, white pine.

Accession: 57.663                     see Inlay Figs. 63, 107

**296** SQUARE CARD TABLE with ovolo
corners

*About 1800    Providence, Rhode Island    Label of Joseph
Rawson (working about 1790–1835)*

Although several of the pieces labeled by Joseph
Rawson are quite plain and with little ornament,
this table, along with the famous secretary-desk

bearing the label of Webb and Scott,[8] reveals the high level attained on occasion by the cabinetmakers of Providence.

All too little is known of the fine furniture produced in this shipping center, which came into prominence after the Revolution. But on this outstanding example by Rawson are some features that may be typical of the finest Providence furniture of the Federal period: extensive use of restrained ornament with emphasis on contrasts of color and shape, as seen in the use of ovals within or in juxtaposition to rectangles; the bold division of individual elements, for example, the mitered center tablet and upper parts of the legs standing in relief to the frame; and the clear division of the tapered leg by the use of applied cuffs. "Stringing" is used to emphasize outline; but, as is clear on the legs, it is not always shaped into panels. Dart inlay, as on the edges of the leaves, appears on other Rawson work (No. 191).

Dimensions: height 28⅜; width 35¾; depth 17¾.

Materials: mahogany; mahogany and light wood inlays with "stringing"; blocks, front and rear rails, white pine; flying rail, maple.

Provenance: Mrs. Ruth L. Howard.

Accession: 62.113

**296**

### 297 SQUARE CARD TABLE with ovolo corners

*About 1800  Probably New York City*

A clue to the date of this brilliant piece is found in the words "Jefferson" and "Burr" painted on the shield of the gilt eagle featured on the glass center panel. In the presidential election of 1800—the last election without a specific place on the ticket for the vice president—Aaron Burr ran second to Jefferson and was named vice president. Presumably this table, which commemorates their administration, was made soon after the election.

Painted and gilt glass panels are more often found on furniture made in Baltimore than elsewhere, but their frequent occurrence on New York looking glasses indicates that the technique was also popular there. Five legs were the standard for New York card tables, and triple strings of black (ebony or light woods stained black) and white (holly or other light woods including satinwood) are often found on New York furniture. Less frequently found is ornamentation in the shape of "a flute formed by three strings to be the same as a shaded flute" as listed on page 60, table no. 7 in the 1802 edition of *The New-York Book of Prices for Cabinet and Chair Work*.

**297**

**298**

Dimensions: height 29 3/16; width 36; depth 17 1/8.

Materials: mahogany; light and dark wood stringing; rails and rear corner blocks, white pine; flying rail, walnut; glass tablet ornamented with gold leaf and painted decoration.

Accession: 61.144          see Inlay Figs. 67, 68

**298** SQUARE CARD TABLE with ovolo corners (one of a pair)

*About 1800   Baltimore*

Typical of the ornament found on much Baltimore furniture are bandings of two light wood squares separated by mahogany squares or rectangles set between string inlay, three-part husk (bellflower) inlay with elongated center petal, and painted glass panels inset as tablets (some of these have been broken and replaced). A medial brace runs from the front to the back rails.

Dimensions: height 29 3/4; width 35 1/2; depth 17 1/4.

Materials: mahogany and mahogany veneers; light and dark wood inlays; rails and blocks, tulip; flying rail, oak.

Accession: 57.659.1, 2

**299** SQUARE CARD TABLE with elliptic front

*About 1810   Salem   Attributed to Mark Pitman (working early nineteenth century)*

The shop where this table was made can now be identified with some certainty, following the recent discovery of a table bearing the label of Mark Pitman of Salem, Massachusetts. The Pitman table is identical to this one in form, construction, secondary wood, and types of inlay used.[9] On the labeled example, however, the same dart inlay frames the rectangular mitered panel instead of edging the skirt, and the legs have a straight taper instead of the pointing seen here.

Dimensions: height 27 1/2; width 36; depth 17 1/2.

Materials: mahogany and mahogany veneers; light and dark wood stringing; flying rail and front rail, white pine.

Provenance: Gift of Charles K. Davis, 1955.

Accession: G 55.51.4

**300** SQUARE CARD TABLE with half-serpentine ends and elliptic front

*About 1800   Salem   Painted with initials I + S, possibly those of Jacob Sanderson (working about 1790 to 1810)*

Similar in shape to the following table (No. 301), this handsome example is a study in harmonies as revealed in the contours of curved and straight lines, the interplay of oval and rectangle, and the rich contrast of rosewood, figured birch (center oval and panels at top of legs), and curly-grained satinwood veeners (skirting).

Inasmuch as Elijah Sanderson noted specifically that all his furniture in a particular shipment was "marked with a brand E S on the back of each piece,"[10] there may be reason to think that his brother Jacob Sanderson may also have marked with his initials those pieces consigned to ship captains as venture cargo.

Dimensions: height 29¾; width 35½; depth 16¼.
Materials: mahogany; satinwood, figured birch and rosewood veneers with light and dark wood stringing; rails and rear blocks, white pine; flying rail, birch; front blocks, mahogany and white pine.
Accession: 57.1012

**301** SQUARE CARD TABLE with half-serpentine ends and elliptic front
*About 1800   Salem   Possibly made by Jacob Sanderson (working about 1790 to 1810)*

Although here the ends are more squared, the inlay treatment slightly less effective (in the absence of

301

300

rectangular panels at the top of the legs), and the underside of the top hollowed, this table may be by the same hand as the preceding one. The skirt is veneered with figured birch and edged with rosewood, and a satinwood oval is set within a rosewood veneered tablet in the center.

Dimensions: height 29½; width 35¾; depth 16¾.
Materials: mahogany; satinwood, figured birch, rosewood, and ebony veneers with light and dark wood stringing; rails and corner blocks, white pine; flying rail, birch.
Accession: 57.649

**302** SQUARE CARD TABLE with half-serpentine ends and elliptic front
*About 1810   Boston   Label of Elisha Tucker (working as early as 1809 to 1827)*

Many variants are to be found in the New England interpretations of card tables of this shape. The figured birch oval within a mitered rosewood rectangular panel is a popular motif; but, despite the increased detail of inlaid edgings on the top, skirt, and panel, there is less drama in the over-all effect of this example than in some of those preceding. Labeled by Elisha Tucker of Boston, this table offers proof of the use there of the familiar dart inlay also found in Salem (No. 299) and Providence (No. 296) cabinetwork. Here the darts are framed by dentilled bands.

Dimensions: height 29 5/16; width 36; top (closed) 16 7/8; top (open) 33 3/4.

Materials: mahogany; figured birch and rosewood veneers with patterned stringing; corner blocks, front rail, and flying rail, white pine.

Provenance: Museum Purchase, 1960.

Accession: 60.332

**303** SQUARE CARD TABLE with half-serpentine ends and elliptic front

*About 1800    Massachusetts*

Although five-legged card tables were the norm in New York,[11] at least one and sometimes both rear legs on those tables were fly or swing legs. On this table with five legs, the center leg in the back pulls out on a slide to support the leaf.

The dart inlay along the square-edged top, the zig-zag inlay around the skirt, and the presence of white pine as a secondary wood suggest Rhode Island or Massachusetts as the place of origin of

this handsome table. Inlaid eagles on an oval within a mitered satinwood panel are found on Massachusetts, New York, and New Jersey furniture; but those with ruffed necks such as this one have been seen by the writer on several examples that show strong Bay State character.

Dimensions: height 28 3/4; width 36; depth 17 1/2.

Materials: mahogany; satinwood inlays; rails, sliding rail, and blocks, white pine.

Accession: 57.662         see Inlay Figs. 30, 49, 56, 96, 99

**304** SQUARE CARD TABLE with half-serpentine ends and elliptic front

*About 1800    Probably Massachusetts*

This table is similar to the preceding ones, but it lacks the sharply tapering foot and stringing on the legs that appear on some of them. Satinwood banding is used to outline a panel on the frame and bring attention to the richness of the mahogany veneers.

Sheraton referred to the problem of warping of card table tops as follows:

In the manufacturing of them, there is frequently much trouble to make them stand

302

303

to the United States after the French Revolution. Normally he seems to have followed the French practice of stamping or labeling his work, with the result that more than fifty pieces have been identified as the product of the shop he maintained during his sixteen years in New York.

With this table,[13] stamped with Lannuier's name, a new element appears in our study of american furniture of the Federal period—the influence of the French Louis XVI style. Ingeniously constructed of mahogany throughout, the back legs, which frame a drawer, pull out to support the extended top. The playing surface, except for round hollows at each corner for candlesticks, is covered in wine-colored felt and edged in leather stamped in gilt with a Greek-key fret. With its top closed, the table is an elegant interpretation of the French neoclassical style, reminiscent of the work of the great Parisian *ébéniste*, Jean-Henri Riesener.

The slender proportions, fluted legs, brass French feet, characteristic brass moldings outlining the skirt, and three delicate *ormolu* mounts are hallmarks of what may well be Lannuier's earlier work (see also Nos. 306 and 347).

By tradition, this table was purchased at the sale of Dolly Madison's estate and once was part of the

**305**

true in the upper top; to effect which, various methods have been studied by cabinet makers.... No wood will stand so well for these tops, as hard, straight-grained mahogany, well seasoned, and jointed in 3½ inch widths; and to be careful not to have curled veneers, but well dried, to agree with the ground work; and being well sized with glue, it may be laid with the hammer with as much safety as in a caul, and sometimes more so; because as soon as they are laid in this way, the under side may be turned upwards, and the veneered side placed so as to exclude the air from it.[12]

Dimensions: height 29⅜; width 35⅞; depth 17¼.
Materials: mahogany; mahogany, rosewood, and satinwood veneers; corner block and front rail, white pine.
Provenance: Gift of Charles K. Davis, 1957.
Accession: G57.128.1

**305** SQUARE CARD TABLE
*About 1810    New York City    Label and stamp of Charles-Honoré Lannuier (working 1803 to 1819)*

Charles-Honoré Lannuier was among the most successful of several cabinetmakers who emigrated

White House furnishings. Some evidence for this history is to be found in the auction catalogue of her effects; the sale was held in Philadelphia, May 9, 1899. Item 185 in the sale was a "Mahogany Antique Folding-top Card-Table, fluted legs."[14]

Dimensions: height 30; width 35¼; depth 17½.
Materials: mahogany; brass trim and appliqués; top and leaf, white pine, veneered with mahogany.
Provenance: Mrs. Louis W. Bond.
Accession: 54.44

### 306  SQUARE CARD TABLE with canted corners (one of a pair)
*About 1810   New York City   Label of Charles-Honoré Lannuier (working 1803 to 1819)*

Although the preceding table (No. 305), also by Lannuier, had a distinctive air of the Louis XVI style, this pair of tables conforms more nearly to those of his New York competitors—especially in the contours of the turned and reeded legs such as appear on the labeled work of George Woodruff (No. 331), Michael Allison (No. 198), and others.[15]

The double top revolves on a center pivot to expose a hollow compartment lined with yellow

paper, on which is pasted an engraved label framed by a cheval glass on paw feet. The inclusion of a spread eagle, shield, arrows, and laurel on the pediment of the label's frame gives an American flavor. The castors and the green baize on the top are original.

Dimensions: height 29¾; width 36; depth 17¾.
Materials: mahogany; rails and top, white pine; well lining, tulip; strip inside well and medial brace, cherry.
Accession: 57.707.1, 2

### 307  CARD TABLE with canted and ovolo corners
*About 1810   Probably Boston*

The shape of the top of this *tour-de-force* may be unique, and the fine reeding on the engaged colonnettes and the outlines of the feet unusual,[16] but the shape and turnings of the legs are common to many pieces of Boston-made furniture. The prominent lunette inlays, so often called the hallmark of John and Thomas Seymour but now known to have been used by other cabinetmakers as well,[17] are larger in scale than usual.

Dimensions: height 29⅞; width 37⅞; depth 18⅞.
Materials: mahogany with figured birch veneers and

**306**

**307**

satinwood inlays; front rail and corner blocks, white pine; flying rail, birch.
Provenance: Bequest of Mrs. Francis B. Crowninshield.
Accession: 59.3411

## 308 SQUARE CARD TABLE with half-serpentine ends and elliptic front
*About 1810  Salem  Possibly made by Nehemiah Adams (working about 1790 to ?; died 1840)*

Fiske Kimball wrote the following in 1933, "A card table [this one or No. 309] and two work tables [Nos. 405 and ?] in the collection of Henry F. du Pont... may unhesitatingly be attributed to [Nehemiah] Adams, so definitely do they display characteristics... of documented pieces by that cabinetmaker." Mr. Kimball had discovered a group of furniture believed to have been the subject of a letter dated January 5, 1810, which read in part: "The furniture was all done according to agreement with Mr. Adams." Of that group three pieces—a dressing table, a work table, and a card table—had turned and reeded legs of the distinctive type seen here with "a long cylindrical neck marked at top and bottom by a pair of small beads" and elongated feet with "a very individual curvature." [18]

Mr. Kimball's attribution of these tables to

**309**

**308**

Adams' hand may be correct, but we can be less sure of it today than he was thirty years ago. Three premises are definitely involved in his attribution: (1) that the letter described the same furniture that had descended in the family, (2) that the "Mr. Adams" cited in the letter was Nehemiah Adams, and (3) that no other cabinetmaker in Salem or elsewhere was making legs of this type. Contrary to Mr. Kimball's assumption, we know today that turners in an urban center worked for more than one cabinetmaker and that many cabinetmakers may have used similar, if not identical, patterns.

Dimensions: height 29⅜; width 36; depth 17¾.
Materials: mahogany; figured-birch veneers and ebony stringing; rails, flying rail, corner blocks, white pine.
Accession: 57.860

## 309 SQUARE CARD TABLE with half-serpentine ends and elliptic front
*About 1810  Salem  Possibly made by Nehemiah Adams (working 1790 to ?; died 1840)*

This and the preceding table (No. 308) are so much alike both in form and construction that they may well be from the same shop—possibly that of Nehemiah Adams of Salem.

Price books offered many "extras" for each piece of furniture. Some of the options for subtleties of visual effect are revealed through a comparison of these two tables. On this one the upper leaf is edged with mahogany and satinwood, the under edge of the top hollowed, and the frame veneered with figured birch. On No. 308 the leaves are square edged of solid mahogany, the frame veneered with crotch mahogany centering a mitered tablet with an oval panel of figured birch, and the skirt finished with a cock bead instead of a black veneered band.

Dimensions: height 29¼; width 35⅝; depth 17½.

Materials: mahogany and mahogany veneers; figured birch veneers and satinwood and dark wood banding; rails and corner blocks, white pine.

Accession: 57.1022

### 310 SQUARE CARD TABLE with elliptic front and ovolo corners above three-quarter colonnettes

*1815   East Sudbury, Massachusetts   Label of Samuel S. Noyes inscribed "January 1, 1815" (working as early as 1810)*

How helpful it would be for collectors of American furniture if more cabinetmakers had followed the practice of Samuel S. Noyes, the maker of this table. He carefully penned the date, January 1,

1815, on the printed label pasted under the top. Since at least one other piece bearing his label also has a date penned on it,[19] this was apparently a habit of this East Sudbury cabinetmaker.

The table is more important as a document of the rural cabinetmaker than as a work of art. Despite its maker's familiarity with handsome inlays, his powers at achieving unity fall short. The borders of the center panel are so striking that the absence of one at the top is disturbing to the eye, and the rather long flat surfaces at the ends of the bowed front are awkward. Also inadequate are the dainty turned rings in the upper leg when contrasted with the boldness of the reeding.

Dimensions: height 30½; width 35⅝; depth 16⅛.

Materials: mahogany; satinwood and mahogany veneers and stringing; flying rail, soft maple; side rails, white pine.

Provenance: Museum Purchase, 1956.

Accession: 56.66.1                 see Inlay Figs. 10, 33, 46

### 311 SQUARE CARD TABLE with half-serpentine ends, serpentine front, and ovolo corners

*About 1810   Salem*

The lines of the top, the veneered treatment of the half-column corners, and the serpentine front of this table and the following (No. 312) are similar,

**310**

**311**

335

but here the deeper frame and elongated cylinder in the upper and lower parts of the leg give a feeling of "legginess" and attenuation which are unsatisfactory. For a discussion of this type of leg and its association with the name of Nehemiah Adams, see No. 308.

Dimensions: height 29; width 38; depth 18⅝.

Materials: mahogany; figured birch and mahogany veneers; light and dark wood stringing; rails and corner blocks, white pine; flying rail, birch.

Accession: 57.705                    see Inlay Fig. 24

### 312 SQUARE CARD TABLE with half-serpentine ends, serpentine front, and ovolo corners

*About 1805   Salem*

Basically, this and the following table (No. 313) are of the same design and provide a study in the harmony and relationship of elements. The "hollow and two beads" on the edge of the upper leaf of this one adds interest and relieves the appearance of thickness. The choice of fluting for the corners is meaningful in its contrast to the turned rings and the reeding below (here the rings are larger and in better scale than on those of No. 313).

The lower leg ring finishes the reeding naturally and prepares the eye for the transition to the foot. A pair of well-carved cornucopias bound together with a ribbon is set off by vertical beads and featured as the center of interest on the handsomely veneered skirt.

Dimensions: height 29⅝; width 36 depth 18⅛.

Materials: mahogany and mahogany veneers; rails and rear corner blocks, white pine; flying rail, birch; front corner blocks, mahogany.

Accession: 57.881

### 313 SQUARE CARD TABLE with half-serpentine ends, serpentine front, and ovolo corners

*About 1810   Salem*

The rich figure of the mahogany veneer forms a natural frame for the lush carved basket centered on the front of this ambitious Massachusetts table. Superficially, the water leaves carved on the half-round colonnettes at the front corners of the frame remind one of those on No. 343, but, actually, the carving on this table lacks the deftness and skill of the carving on that pair by William Haskell and of much other Salem work. Deficient also is the con-

**312**

**313**

| | | | |
|---|---|---|---|
| Double eliptic tops, extra* | 0 | 4 | 0 |
| Treble eliptic ditto, | 0 | 6 | 0 |
| An eliptic rail veneered, with four flush stumps,* a bead or band on the lower edge,* | 0 | 14 | 0 |
| Ditto double eliptic,* | 0 | 18 | 0 |
| Ditto treble eliptic, | 1 | 4 | 0 |
| When the stumps project either in front* or under the rail,* each projection | 0 | 0 | 2 |
| Drops under ditto,* each | 0 | 0 | 2½ |

N. B. When a rail* to the above tables, the under side of the top not considered veneered.*

Dimensions: height 28¾; top 35¾ × 17⅞.

Materials: mahogany and mahogany veneers; front and end rails, white pine; back rail and flying rails, mahogany.

Provenance: Louis Guerineau Myers.

Accession: 57.711

cept of the lower leg, where the reeding fades without articulation into an open space, before slumping into an awkward drum and weak foot.

Dimensions: height 29½; width 36½; depth 18.

Materials: mahogany and mahogany veneers; rails and rear corner blocks, white pine; flying rail, birch.

Accession: 57.880

### 314 TRIPOD, OR PILLAR AND CLAW, CARD TABLE with double elliptic top

*About 1810   New York*

Among the finest New York card tables is a highly distinctive type of tripod table such as this one and No. 315 with rear feet that turn backward when the flaps are pulled out to support the leaf.[20] These tables are often superbly carved and have been attributed for a long time to the shop of Duncan Phyfe. That these tables were not exclusively made by Phyfe is clearly shown by the following listing (for all New York cabinetmakers) in *The New-York Revised Prices for Manufacturing Cabinet and Chair Work* for 1810. Features found on this table are marked below with an asterisk.

A Solid Eliptic Pillar and Claw Card Table Three feet long, three claws, (as No. 1, in plate) two of ditto to turn out with the joint rail,*
£4 12 0

The veneered version of the same table cost 5.8.0 and the following extras were listed:

### 315 TRIPOD, OR PILLAR AND CLAW, CARD TABLE with treble elliptic top

*About 1810   New York City*

Although this table does not have a skirt, or "rail," under the top, the form and the mechanism of moving legs are essentially the same as those of No. 314. Stylized leaf carving with well-defined raised central spine and flaring raised ribs of the sort seen on this table and the preceding one is found on the legs of several of the finest New York tables.[21] As here, reeding frequently extends from the end of the leaf to a brass paw with which the legs are often finished. Occasionally, however, paws are carved out of the solid. A similar table in the Winterthur collection, with similar carving and also without skirt, has a more elongated urn like that on No. 314.

Dimensions: height 30; width 36; depth 17¾.

Materials: mahogany; no secondary woods.

Accession: 57.723

### 316 PEDESTAL-BASE CARD TABLE with double elliptic swivel top

*About 1810   Philadelphia   Possibly made by Ephraim Haines or Henry Connelly (working late eighteenth and early nineteenth centuries)*

This table, well balanced on a wide-spreading pedestal base to support four colonnettes, has features of both Henry Connelly's and Ephraim Haines' work. Both of these well-known craftsmen

worked for the great financier, Stephen Girard; a pair of card tables with dolphin supports which Connelly made for him has the same molded legs, cut-leaf carving, and the same shape of top.[22] When open, the top (of the swivel type) shows on its upper surface an eighteen-ray sunburst of figured mahogany like those on Girard's pair of tables.

Dimensions: height 30; width 35¾; depth 19¼.

Materials: mahogany and mahogany veneers; lining of frame, white cedar.

Accession: 57.710

**316**

### 317 SQUARE CARD TABLE with canted corners and lyre support
*About 1815   Philadelphia*

Typical of much early nineteenth-century Philadelphia carving on table legs is that seen on this table and No. 316. These leaves, more luxuriant than those found so often on New York furniture, are confined to the knees and cut square at the lower end. Normally, as here, from the lower tip of the carving to the paw, the upper surface of the leg is of molded contour in contrast to the reeding usually used in New York. The top swivels on its frame to reveal a well which is lined with red baize.

Dimensions: height 29½; width 36; depth 17⅝.

Materials: mahogany and mahogany veneers; rails, medial brace, well bottom, and capping block, white pine.

Accession: 57.1077

### 318 SQUARE CARD TABLE with canted corners and pedestal base
*About 1815   New York City   Label of Joseph Brauwers (working early nineteenth century)*

This example and another matching labeled card table (both recently discovered) are the first identified work of Joseph Brauwers. Although on his label he calls himself an "ebenist, from Paris," he seems to have been working very much in the current New York fashion except for the addition of "Richest Ornaments, just imported from France" noted on his label. The following description on page 37 of the 1817 edition of *The New-York Book of Prices for Manufacturing Cabinet and Chair Work* seems to fit his fine table almost exactly: "A Square, Swivel Top, Pillar and Claw Card Table...with canted corners...and made with octagon block and four columns...." The brass mounts, column bases and capitals, carved claws

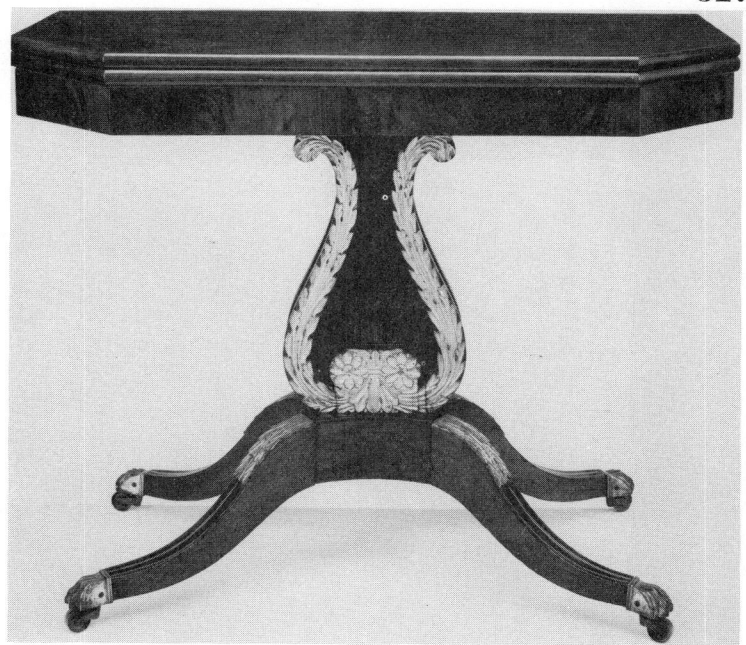

**317**

and castors would have been extras. But even the standard model quoted above cost about three times as much for labor as did the normal card table with five tapered legs. The playing surface originally "lipped" for cloth is now covered with leather which is a replacement.

Dimensions: height over-all 29; width 36; depth (closed) 18.
Materials: mahogany; bottom, tulip; block on which top turns, white pine; blocks at top of columns and bottom of base, mahogany.
Provenance: Gift of Mr. and Mrs. David Stockwell.
Accession: G 62.237

**319** SQUARE CARD TABLE with canted corners and lyre support
*About 1815    New York*

Basically this table is very much like the preceding one with the substitution of two carved lyres for the four columns.[23] Designs for lyres are illustrated in the 1817 edition of *The New-York Book of Prices for Manufacturing Cabinet and Chair Work.* Therein it is suggested that lyre strings may be of brass or ebony. These appear to be of iron. Brass moldings such as are found on much of Lannuier's work (No. 305) edge the frame and also the base which

supports the lyres. Leaf carving with a dominant spine and rippling edges extending rather far down the leg and ending in a point is seen on much of the finest New York cabinetwork (see No. 314).

Dimensions: height 29⅞; top 17¾ × 36 (closed).
Materials: mahogany; corner blocks and end rails, white pine; rear rail and medial braces, cherry; well bottom, tulip.
Provenance: Louis Guerineau Myers.
Accession: 57.1078

**320** SQUARE CARD TABLE with canted corners and lyre support
*About 1815    Possibly New York*

The molded legs and paneled pedestal base of this table are in accord with Philadelphia practice; but the carving on the lyres, the treatment of the square-edged top, and use of brass trim to outline the lower edge of the frame lead the writer to think that this table was made in New York. Almost identical detailed listings for lyre bases are given in the later price books for both New York and Philadelphia. The following notations are from table No. 32 of *The New-York Book of Prices for Manufacturing Cabinet and Chair Work* for 1817.

**318**

**319**

"Price of Lyres as in plate No. 5"
when No. 3 [lyre in plate] is made with eagle
head at top, deduct 2 d.

| | |
|---|---|
| Each brass string, extra | 0 0 3 |
| Each ebony ditto | 0 0 5 |
| When two lyres are crossed at right angles, the bridge and stretcher lapped together, extra | 0 2 6 |

All the above lyres considered with keys and
points, in the start.

Dimensions: height 30½; width 35¾; depth 18³/₁₆ (closed).

Materials: mahogany and mahogany veneers; brass edging and ebony strings; front and end rails, white pine; compartment bottom, tulip.

Accession: 61.1695

## FOOTNOTES

1 Clarence Wilson Brazer, "Jonathan Gostelowe: Philadelphia Cabinet and Chair Maker, Part II," *Antiques*, X (August, 1926), 125–132.

2 Swan, "A Revised Estimate of McIntire," *Antiques*, XX (December, 1931), 339.

3 *Baltimore Furniture*, Plate 17.

4 Hornor, "Documented Furniture by Jacob Wayne," *International Studio*, XCVI (June, 1930), 43.

5 Swan, "Newburyport Cabinetmakers," *Antiques*, XLVII (April, 1945), 222–225.

6 Swan, *Samuel McIntire, Carver, and The Sandersons, Early Salem Cabinet Makers*, p. 21.

7 Florence Thompson Howe, "The Decline and Fall of William Lloyd," *Antiques*, XVII (Febr., 1930), 117 to 121.

8 Sale Catalogue of the *Collection of the Late Philip Flayderman*, No. 431, p. 164.

9 Now in the collection of the writer.

10 Swan, *Samuel McIntire, Carver, and The Sandersons, Early Salem Cabinet Makers*, p. 9.

11 All start prices for card tables in *The New-York Book of Prices for Cabinet and Chair Work* for 1802 (pp. 21–22) are listed with four fast legs and one fly leg.

12 Sheraton, *The Cabinet Dictionary*, p. 129.

13 A virtually identical table also labeled and stamped by Lannuier is in the American Wing of the Metropolitan Museum. Illustrated in "The Almanac: Accessions to the American Wing," *Antiques*, XLIX (May, 1946), 312.

14 Lorraine Waxman Pearce, "Lannuier in the President's House," *Antiques*, LXXXI (January, 1962), 94–96.

15 A trictrac table with similar legs and stamped H. Lannuier is in the Benkard Memorial Room of the Museum of the City of New York. See Plate 173 of McClelland's *Duncan Phyfe and the English Regency*.

16 Feet of similar outline also occur on a sideboard owned by William McMahon and are illustrated on page 178 of Stoneman's *John and Thomas Seymour*.

17 Richard H. Randall, Jr., "Works of Boston Cabinetmakers, 1795–1825," *Antiques*, LXXXI (April, 1962), 412–415.

18 Fiske Kimball, "Salem Furniture Makers," *Antiques*, XXIV (December, 1933), 218–220.

19 Sale Catalogue of the *Collection of the Late Philip Flayderman*, No. 130, p. 34.

20 Catalogue of the *Girl Scouts Loan Exhibition*, No. 785.

21 In *Furniture Masterpieces of Duncan Phyfe*, Charles Over Cornelius illustrated a variety of carved motifs found on New York furniture. He called the kind seen here acanthus-leaf carving. Present-day botanists disagree with this identification and suggest it is simply stylized leaf carving. This idea is borne out by Sheraton who does not identify specifically most of the carved ornament shown in "An Accompaniment" to his *Drawing Book*.

22 These were exhibited in the spring of 1953 at an exhibition of the furniture of Henry Connelly and Ephraim Haines at the Philadelphia Museum of Art. The *Philadelphia Museum Bulletin*, Spring 1953, serves as a catalogue of the exhibition with a check list of the items shown and thirteen illustrations including one of the Girard card tables.

23 Catalogue of the *Girl Scouts Loan Exhibition*, No. 767.

# Drop-leaf and Dressing Tables

Among the tables included in this section are several innovations which became popular in the late eighteenth century. One of these was the three-part dining table. Drop-leaf, swing leg tables, commonly called gate-leg tables, had been made since the seventeenth century—first with turned legs, later with cabriole supports. About the middle of the eighteenth century, the vogue began to shift to straight marlboro legs which, after the Revolution, were often tapered and sometimes inlaid with lines and other decorative devices (see No. 321). However, during the Chippendale era and possibly earlier, a few rectangular tables with cabriole legs (though more frequently with straight legs) were made in sets of two or more to be placed end to end to accommodate larger numbers of diners. About the same time, sets of dining tables with half-round ends began to appear. Normally these circular ends stood against the wall as side or pier tables, but were available to extend the dining table when guests came. In the late 1700's and early 1800's, several inventions of extension dining tables were made; but the great innovation for dining comfort which became the rage of the early nineteenth century was the pedestal base table. Duncan Phyfe is known to have made many of these tables, and today they are often called Duncan Phyfe tables, paradoxically, even when made in England where the form originated.

With the smaller houses and dining rooms of today, it is all too easy to overlook and forget the great and splendid dinners given in earlier times. When Mary Boardman Crowninshield of Salem visited Washington in 1815, she wrote home:

> I think I told you we were to dine at Mrs. Monroe's[1] the day before yesterday. We had there the most stylish dinner I have been at. The table wider than we have, and in the middle a large, perhaps silver, waiter, with images like some Aunt Silsbee has, only more of them, and vases filled with flowers, which made very showy appearance as the candles were lighted when we went to table. The dishes were silver and set around this waiter. The plates were handsome china, the forks silver, and so heavy I could hardly lift them to my mouth, dessert knives silver, and spoons very heavy—you would call them clumsy things.[2]

Also introduced during the Chippendale era, but made in much greater numbers in the later styles, was the pembroke or breakfast table. About the size of a card table or a little smaller, these tables usually have two drop leaves with one or two wooden flaps or brackets hinged to the frame on either side, to be swung out to support the leaves when desired. Occasionally, sliding or rotating slats were also used as leaf supports. These take the place of the swing legs usually found on dining and card tables. Often made with a drawer in one end and a sham drawer face on the other, pembroke tables served many purposes—for breakfast, for tea, for cards, for writing, or on any other occasion for which a small table was required. Although made from Maine to South Carolina, and finished and ornamented in accord with local preferences (often with considerable inlay), pembroke tables were most popular in New York, New Jersey, and Connecticut. It is estimated that at least half the surviving examples were made in these three states.

Rarest of all American drop-leaf tables is the long narrow "sofa table" with the leaves at either end. Made to stand before sofas, all American examples known to the writer have pedestal bases and were made in New York.

Side tables about three feet wide with long legs and usually one or two long drawers in front have often been called "serving tables" in exhibition catalogues. They may have been used for this purpose on occasion, but they answer to the description given for "chamber tables" in cabinetmakers' price books. It seems reasonable to suppose that they were introduced to take the place of the lowboy as a dressing or toilet table. But despite the fact that chamber tables are listed in both the Philadelphia and New York price books, the writer can identify no examples from the Quaker City or Baltimore, and only a few from New York. More New England examples are known, but even there they seem to have been much less popular than the earlier lowboy which had so often been made to match high chests of drawers (highboys) of the Queen Anne and Chippendale eras.

Although tables with arched kneeholes and flanking drawers seem admirably designed for toilet purposes and were widely made in England, a New England example (No. 335) may be the unique American survival of the period. Perhaps the original cost was too great to compete with the plain pine half-round tables made to be hung with chintz or dimity in ruffles or pleats. Matching the window curtains and bed hangings, these dressing tables were the American favorites.

1 Mrs. James Monroe, wife of the then Secretary of State.
2 *Letters of Mary Boardman Crowninshield*, p. 19.

# Du Pont Dining Room

*Fine furniture from several cabinetmaking centers is shown in this room: two sideboards, one from Newport (No. 359) and a great eight-legged example (No. 360) probably made in New York; a Massachusetts secretary and bookcase (No. 182); a three-part eagle-inlaid dining table (No. 321); and a set of New York urn-back chairs that have been in the du Pont family since the early 1800's (No. 65). Similar chairs were used by Washington in the banquet hall at Mount Vernon where two are to be found today.*

*The oil sketch of the Americans who negotiated the Treaty of Paris to end the Revolution and assure formal recognition of the independence of the United States was painted by Benjamin West. The curtains of French silk are woven after designs by the great French textile designer, Phillippe de Lassalle.*

345

**321** DINING TABLE, three parts
*About 1800    Baltimore (?)*

In Plate XXII the three parts of this rare table with eagle inlay are shown assembled. In order that the reader may see the inlaid details to better advantage, only one of the two half-round ends made to accompany the drop-leaf center section is shown here.

The basic price for making a "Dining table" is given in the 1796 edition of *The Journeymen Cabinet and Chair Makers' New-York Book of Prices* as follows (p. 40): "Hung with rule or square joints, four plain legs, one fly foot on each side, the length and width added together, at per foot, £0-2-10."

Extras included inlays, shaping the legs, and sweeping the flaps (drop leaves) serpentine or circular, etc. "If two or more tables are made to join together with tongues, and mortises, each joint [cost] 0-1-5." "If with spring and staple fastenings on hinge and button, ditto, each spring, hinge or button 0-0-5."

Under the heading a "half round Dining Table," specifications and extras for a table like the ends of this one are given as follows:

| | |
|---|---|
| Four feet long, veneer'd rail, three plain legs, | £1-3-0 |
| Each inch more in length, | 0-0-5 |
| Each extra fix'd leg, | 0-2-0 |
| Each fly leg, | 0-2-10 |
| Each leaf to ditto hung with a rule joint | 0-7-6 |

From the above entries, it is clear that two or more drop-leaf tables to be joined together in

**321**

groups and sometimes with half-round ends with or without drop leaves were to be had for the ordering. However, today such combinations are rarely found. When extended, such tables are fragile and were barely equal to the burdens they were called upon to bear. Since repairs or damage on surviving examples is common, breakage may account for their rarity.

The assumption that the half-round tables were used as pier tables when needed for large parties is supported by Hepplewhite's comments on his "Plan of a Room" (his Plate 124). He observed that for a dining room "instead of the Pier tables [shown in his drawing room] should be a set of dining-tables, ..."

The account book entries of Daniel Trotter for October 13, 1796, for furniture supplied by him to Stephen Girard give us interesting comparative prices but no details of the objects involved.

| | |
|---|---|
| A mahogany Circular Beaurea | 11.5.0 |
| a Breakfast Table | 3.0.0 |
| a Large Dining Table & 2 Circular d° | 16.0.0 |

Dimensions: height 28¾; length 151; width 51¼.
Materials: mahogany and mahogany veneers; light and dark wood inlays; long rails of center and end sections, Spanish cedar; all blocks and curved rails of end sections, mahogany; short rails of center section and gates of swing legs, white oak.
Accession: 57.851.1–3                    see Inlay Fig. 82

**322**

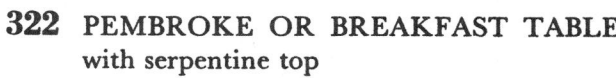

## 322 PEMBROKE OR BREAKFAST TABLE
with serpentine top

*About 1779–1800   Salem, Massachusetts   Four labels
of Elijah and Jacob Sanderson (working about 1779 to
1810)*

Essentially Chippendale in form with serpentine top and fluted straight legs, this breakfast table may nevertheless have been made as late as 1800. "Plain" or "plain marlbro" legs were cited as the standard in most price books up to that time. Though fluting or tapering was an extra, it seems that most city cabinetmakers paid the extra penny a leg to have them tapered after about 1795.

Every collector is in the debt of Mabel Munson Swan for her research and publications on American cabinetmakers. In *Samuel McIntire, Carver, and The Sandersons, Early Salem Cabinetmakers* (p. 1), she relates in detail the activities of the men whose labels this table bears. In her own words:

> Elijah and Jacob Sanderson were Salem's most prominent cabinetmakers. In 1779, in partnership with Josiah Austin, they instituted a cooperative business venture in which cabinetmakers, carvers, gilders, turners, upholsterers, and many other craftsmen contributed their respective parts in the making of furniture for exportation to the southern states, the East and West Indies, the Madeiras, South

America, and Africa,—wherever a cargo could be disposed of to the best advantage.

Elijah sailed from Salem as supercargo on the *Ruth* in December of 1788 for Charleston. There he disposed of 70 of the 166 pieces of furniture he had on board and on his return he brought 53 cedar logs.[2] It is, of course, unsafe to assume that the drawers of this table are lined with wood cut from those logs, but it may be true.

Dimensions: height 27¾; top 34×34⅞ (open).
Materials: mahogany; side rails, white pine; back, mahogany; flying rail, cherry; drawer back and bottom, red cedar.
Provenance: Guy W. Walker, Jr.
Accession: 58.135.5

## 323 PEMBROKE OR BREAKFAST TABLE
*1800–1815   Connecticut*

Of graceful but standard form, this table is remarkable for the prodigal amount of inlay lavished upon it; and, in this respect, as well as in the unusual nature of the inlays, it appears to be typical of many pieces of Connecticut furniture. The wide spacing of the descending husks, each with a clapper-like pendant and twelve black pellets, the sawtooth cuffs below them, and the oval paterae shaded in serpentine sectors at the corners of the frame are all arresting in their novelty. The last-

named feature, undoubtedly used by a number of Connecticut cabinetmakers, appears on a sideboard made by Silas E. Cheney at Litchfield, Connecticut, in 1800 for Tapping Reeve, founder of America's first law school in Litchfield. The alternating dark and light banding on the apron is another characteristic found on furniture made in Litchfield.[3] This and the use of cherry as the major wood support a Connecticut or Connecticut Valley attribution. The drawers, now as originally, are without pulls of any sort and are opened by grasping the drawer on the underside.

Dimensions: height 27¼; width 31⅜; length open 40¼.
Materials: cherry; light wood inlays; fly rail, rail above drawer, and drawer front, cherry; blocks, drawer supports, and drawer lining, white pine.

Accession: 53.91          see Inlay Figs. 61, 62, 100

### 324 PEMBROKE OR BREAKFAST TABLE
*1795–1815 New Brunswick, New Jersey   Attributed to Matthew Egerton, Sr. or Jr. (working after 1750 to 1836)*

A variety of inlays over the full length of the legs and the rich figure of the mahogany make this table a striking example. The inlaid flutes on the stiles, the drawer front with veneered and string-outlined panel, the overlapping drops, one-piece engraved husks and light wood cuffs on the legs, and the

brass casters are all a part of the repertoire of the New York cabinetmaker.

But as yet relationships between the products of New York, New Jersey, and certain southern New England cabinetmakers are not clear. Many pieces with Connecticut associations are enriched with large amounts of inlays. If made of cherry, this furniture usually has inlays of novel "offbeat" character (No. 323). For mahogany furniture, it seems either that New York inlays may have been imported into both Connecticut and New Jersey and there used in accord with local custom or that New York trained cabinetmakers working in these adjacent areas simply added more ornament to satisfy local taste. The pine-tree inlay at the bottom of the leg is unusual and unknown heretofore to the writer; but on two sideboards labeled by Matthew Egerton of New Brunswick, New Jersey, the legs are inlaid—on one are one-piece husks, on the other are overlapping drops as found at the top and middle respectively of the legs on this example. Identical structural features on this table and on one labeled by Egerton in the writer's collection indicate that both are from the same shop.

Dimensions: height 29¼; width 29¾; length open 40¼.
Materials: mahogany with mahogany veneers and light wood inlays; fly supports, soft maple; corner blocks, rails, drawer front, white pine; drawer bottom, tulip.
Provenance: Reginald Lewis.

Accession: 61.145          see Inlay Figs. 73, 113

**325** PEMBROKE OR BREAKFAST TABLE
*1795–1815   Rhode Island ( ? )*

Although this table may have been made in New York or Connecticut, the use of patterned stringing, as on the skirt, and black dots between plain one-piece husks strung beneath three leaves on a single inlaid line is not usual on the furniture of either area. The three-leaf inlay at the top of the legs is suggestive of the inlay used by Thomas Howard, Junior, in Providence.[4] Brilliant paterae are sometimes found on the stiles of Newport tables as are broad bands of light wood around drawers. "J D Eliot Dayton O" painted in black on the bottom of the drawer may be the name of an early owner.

Dimensions: height 29; width 31; length open 40⅞.
Materials: mahogany; drawer bottom, basswood; rear rail and drawer back, tulip; drawer front, white pine.
Provenance: Reginald Lewis.
Accession: 61.146                    see Inlay Fig. 90

**326** PEMBROKE OR BREAKFAST TABLE
(one of a pair)
*About 1795–1810   New York   Possibly made by John Dikeman*

In 1953, Joseph Downs wrote of this pair of tables as follows:

**327**

This handsome pair of breakfast tables has the kind of inlays employed by John Dikeman, a cabinetmaker listed in the New York directories in 1784 at Gold and Beekman Streets, and at 167 William Street a year later. He signed a pair of Pembroke tables similar to this one and a tall clock with a Poughkeepsie maker's signature, Van Bomell, on the painted dial. These pieces were privately owned a decade ago.

The husk pattern is unlike that from other cities, in its large scale and overlapping elements, sometimes shaded with hot sand. Bands of rosewood finish the skirt and cuffs.

Although the writer is unable to locate the tables and clock to which Mr. Downs referred, other instances of documented furniture with such inlays are known. In the Winterthur Library, there are photographs of three sideboards with inlaid overlapping husks closely related to those on this piece, two by Elbert Anderson of New York City and one by Matthew Egerton of New Brunswick, New Jersey.

Dimensions: height 27½; width 31; length open 37.
Materials: mahogany with light wood inlays and rosewood bandings; end rails, chestnut; outer side rails, beech; inner side rails, drawer front, sides, white pine; drawer bottom, ash.
Accession: 57.1001.1, 2

**327** PEMBROKE OR BREAKFAST TABLE
*1795–1810   New York ( ? )*

The heavy light wood stringing which runs along both edges of the top, as well as forming a concentric oval within the top, and the overlapping shaded drops falling on the sides of each leg are inlays often found on New York tables; the inlaid fans and paterae are motifs frequently employed on sideboards made in that city. The presence of these devices would seem to indicate that this table without drawer is a New York product, but the band of chevron-patterned stringing on the lower edge of the frame and the abnormal height of the broad cuffs make a New York attribution less certain. These same motifs were also used in Connecticut and New Jersey, as were tulip and cherry as secondary woods.

Dimensions: height 28¾; width 32; length open 38¾.
Materials: mahogany with mahogany veneers and light wood inlays; end rails, tulip; side rails and blocks, white pine; leaf supports, cherry.
Accession: 57.657                    see Inlay Figs. 72, 117

**328** PEMBROKE OR BREAKFAST TABLE
with ovolo corners
*1790–1800   Probably New York City*

This table, which is reserved in expression but masterful in craftsmanship, achieves precise neatness in part through geometric shapes and inlays which accentuate each structural element and in part through reduction of the scale of the top. The drop leaves, shallower and thinner than is customary in New York table design, give an effect of agreeable lightness too seldom found in pembroke tables.

The heavy line of satinwood outlining the drawer front, triple stringing of light and dark woods, and the presence of cherry and tulip as secondary woods suggest New York as the place of origin of this table; but it may have been made elsewhere, possibly in Providence. A ring handle with a stamped "basket of fruit" backplate serves as a pull on the long drawer which runs the length of the table. A sham drawer with similar pull appears on the opposite end.

Dimensions: height 28½; width 31; length open 38¼.
Materials: mahogany and mahogany veneers on white pine; light and dark wood stringing; drawer linings, tulip; rails, blocks, and drawer front, white pine; fly supports, cherry.
Accession: 57.1021

**329** PEMBROKE OR BREAKFAST TABLE
*1790–1800   Probably Charleston*

Constructed in part of yellow buckeye, a wood indigenous only to Maryland and more southerly regions, this table in its restrained geometrical inlays and carefully chosen woods appears to be of urban workmanship. Actually the whole skirt on one end is the face of a long drawer; but it is so patterned as to look like two small veneered drawer fronts of stained oak within a cross-banded frame on either side of a vertical panel that also appears to be a part of the frame. Above the stringing on the legs is a most unusual inverted bellflower which is treated in a manner found on many Charleston pieces. The cuffs may be replacements.

Dimensions: height 28⅜; width 31⅞; length open 40½.
Materials: mahogany with stained oak, satinwood, palisander, and mahogany veneers; drawer front, white pine veneered with mahogany; drawer lining, yellow buckeye; drawer runners and side rails, tulip; end rail, spruce.
Accession: 57.655

**330** PEMBROKE TABLE with only one leaf
*About 1800   Southern New England or New York*

A top with but one drop leaf distinguishes this table from other pembroke tables of the period. The

**328**

**329**

novel design seems to indicate that, as in the case of its extraordinarily rare counterparts in the Queen Anne and Chippendale styles, this table with its veneered back rail was intended for use at the end of a sofa or possibly against a wall rather than for dining or gaming. Of simple construction, its only ornament is a narrow veneered band across each end at the edge of the skirt. Birch and tulip, when used as secondary woods, are most often found together on furniture made in New York and southern New England.

Dimensions: height 29; width 29; depth open 23⅞.

Materials: mahogany; rear rail, white pine with mahogany veneer; fly support, birch; right rear corner block, tulip.

Accession: 57.617

### 331 PEMBROKE OR BREAKFAST TABLE
*1808–1810  New York City  Label of George Woodruff
(working 1808–1816)*

Pasted on the bottom of the drawer of this table is an engraved label illustrating a cut of a bow-front sideboard identical to that used two years later by Southwick and Pelsue (printers) on the title page of *The New-York Revised Prices for Manufacturing Cabinet and Chair Work* (1810).[5] The text of the label reads as follows:

GEORGE WOODRUFF
CABINET MAKER
NO.54 JOHN STREET
Informs his friends and the public, that he has commenced his business at the above place, where all orders, in the city or from the country, will be thankfully received and punctually attended to, both with respect to workmanship and dispatch.
New York, May, 1808.
    H.C. Southwick, Printer No. 2, Wall-street.

Where he was before or after these dates is unknown, but the New York City directories list George Woodruff, cabinetmaker, only from 1808 to 1816. Since he was located at 54 John Street only from 1808 to 1810, the table can be dated with some accuracy. The New York vocabulary employed on this table—double elliptic leaves, reeded legs with a concave neck and ring above, and long balloon-shaped feet—suggests that Woodruff was trained in New York and was perhaps a local journeyman who set up his own shop in 1808. Although the lines of the legs are crisp and delicate, the original purchaser of this table did not choose to pay for a mahogany top of fine-figured grain or for molding or inlaying its edges.

Dimensions: height 28⅝; width 35¾; length open 43⅜.

Materials: mahogany with mahogany veneers; rails, blocks, front, white pine; fly supports, walnut; drawer linings, tulip.

Accession: 57.731

**332**

## 332 PEMBROKE OR BREAKFAST TABLE
*About 1810–1820   New York*

Perhaps no furniture is so typical of New York cabinetmaking of the second decade of the nineteenth century as the pedestal form of tables with long, concaved legs and urn shaft made by Duncan Phyfe and his contemporaries.[6] This example and another which almost matches it are distinguished by crisp, undulating leaf carving that overlays the principal members of the base. A longer drawer occupies the space under the top; the beaded edge and molded brass knob are repeated on the simulated drawer front on the opposite side. The drops at the corners of the apron and the double elliptic leaves are usual features found not only on pedestal tables but other New York tables as well. Tables of this shape had a variety of uses and served as parlor and card tables, as well as for breakfast tables. The pendants at the corners appear to be vestiges of the legs found on earlier pembroke tables.

Dimensions: height 30⅞; width 35⅞; length open 44⅜.
Materials: mahogany with light wood and rosewood; drawer front and side rail, white pine; drawer bottom, tulip; main top support and leaf support, cherry.
Provenance: Louis Guerineau Myers.
Accession: 57.732.1, 2

## 333 SOFA TABLE
*About 1810–1820   New York*

Sofa tables, as described by Sheraton in 1803, are "...used before a sofa, and are generally made between 5 and 6 feet long, and from 22 [inches] to 2 feet broad; the frame is divided into two drawers.... The ladies chiefly occupy them to draw, write, or read upon...."[7] They occur infrequently in American furniture and most known examples appear to have been made in New York where the form is first listed in the price book of 1810. There a sofa table is detailed (on p. 24) as "two feet two inches long on the bed, and four feet six inches wide when open; two turned or square pillars, straight stretcher and four claws; (as in plate, No. 1)...." Extras offered there and included here are four drawers, two on either side, and a sweep stretcher.

A wealth of reeding, carved pointed leaves with dominant spines, and single, double, or treble elliptic tops are features often found on fine New York tables; but comparison of this reeding and carving with that normally encountered on the finest examples reveals significant differences in character. Here the carved leaves, instead of covering the urn as on Nos. 315 and 332, serve only as a collar on an urn that is reeded above, and the reeds on both the urn and legs are rounded at the ends in an uncommon fashion. Such subtleties as the roundness of a fat pendant at each end of the frame echoed in the arched top of a tombstone-shaped

**333**

crotch mahogany panel inset above it, and the bowed stretcher, which in its downward sweep creates the illusion of a tripod at either end, add tremendously to the grace of this rare table.

Dimensions: height 28¾; length 58; depth 24.

Materials: mahogany and mahogany veneers on white pine; rails and double fly on each end, maple; drawer linings, tulip.

Accession: 57.730

## 334 CHAMBER TABLE OR DRESSING TABLE

*1790–1810   Rhode Island or Connecticut*

The perfection of Rhode Island block and shell furniture is unchallenged as a major contribution of the eighteenth-century American cabinetmaker. Chests of drawers and perhaps other forms continued to be made there through the 1790's and possibly even later in Connecticut, where many variations with Chippendale style supports were introduced. Without precedent in design or price books, this chamber table, one of three or four known with blocked façade, is a major innovation of its time. The recessed center presents an invitation to sit before it for use as a dressing table. Lest the legs be thought inadequate for the frame, they are outlined as is the drawer by a heavy band of almost black mahogany inlay.

Whether made in Rhode Island or eastern Connecticut is uncertain, but the clean lines with mini-

mum ornament suggest Rhode Island, perhaps Providence. Although cherry furniture is most often found in Connecticut, it was also made in Rhode Island. Chestnut was used as a secondary wood in both eastern Connecticut and Rhode Island.

Dimensions: height 31½; width 27⅝; depth 19½.

Materials: cherry with mahogany inlays; rear rail and drawer sides, tulip; blocks, white pine; drawer bottom and inner strips, chestnut.

Provenance: Reginald Lewis.

Accession: 61.143

## 335 CHAMBER TABLE OR DRESSING TABLE

*1800–1810   Portsmouth, New Hampshire (?)*

The basic price for the simplest sort of chamber table in price books is for a plain table with straight legs, straight front, and a drawerless apron four inches deep. This example is made with a "sweep front," more often called a "circular front," with one long and two short drawers, a "plain arch in sweep front..." and in a rather larger size (six inches longer and with an apron eight inches deeper).[8] Thus transformed into an elegant dressing table with veneers and inlays, the final price for labor would probably have been in excess of three pounds instead of the eight to ten shillings which the simpler form would have cost.

Sharply tapered feet and the use of mahogany cross-banding to outline drawer openings and edge tops are features often found on furniture made by eastern Massachusetts and nearby cabinetmakers. But not known on furniture of that area are inlaid ebony or mock ebony leaves, depending in a curiously irregular fashion from light wood strings along the center line of the legs. However, narrow light wood cuffs and cross-banding (also narrow and light in color) such as used here to outline the drawer fronts are sometimes found on New Hampshire furniture. The high quality of the workmanship marks this as a product of an urban center which might well be Portsmouth.

Dimensions: height 32½; width 36; depth 20½.
Materials: mahogany and mahogany veneers with light wood and dark wood banding and inlays; drawers, blocks, and framing, white pine, except lower front rail of soft maple.
Accession: 57.526

### 336 CHAMBER TABLE with elliptic front
*1805–1815   Probably Salem, Massachusetts*

Small tables such as this one with two drawers have often been referred to as serving tables and may have been used for this purpose on occasion; but most earlier editions of the price books include a listing for a "Chamber Table" starting at two feet six inches long with straight, circular, elliptic, or serpentine front. "Each drawer the length of the frame veneer'd and cockbeaded" cost four shillings, six pence extra for labor in New York in 1802. This New England example, with reeded legs, turned and ringed where they are quarter-engaged to the

frame, has feet like many tables found in and around Salem.

Dimensions: height 34¼; width 38½; depth 18½.
Materials: mahogany with bird's-eye maple veneers on the white pine drawer fronts; drawer linings and framing, white pine.
Accession: 57.913

### 337 CHAMBER TABLE with serpentine front
*1805–1815   Massachusetts*

The serpentine form, the carved sheaves of wheat bound with a cord, the curved drawer fronts veneered with what is known as "plum-pudding" mahogany, the exceptionally thin top, and the cock-beading on the skirt mark this as a finer table than No. 336, although the reeded legs are less shapely than those of others such as No. 338. The brass knobs stamped with a thistle motif are contemporary with the table, as are the brass keyhole escutcheons.

Dimensions: height 32; width 31½; depth 15⅝.
Materials: mahogany; lining, white pine; front, white pine veneered with mahogany.
Accession: 57.569

### 338 CHAMBER TABLE with circular front[9]
*1800–1810   Boston   Possibly by John and/or Thomas Seymour*

Within the last few years, it has been conclusively shown and become well known that there were

**336**

**337**

inlay and stringing specialists such as John Dewhirst of Boston who supplied nearby cabinetmakers with a variety of ornaments for application to their cabinetwares. For a long time, shaded lunette edging on banding has been considered a hallmark of the work of John and/or Thomas Seymour; but it has also been conclusively proven that this distinctive edging was used by Adams and Todd and others in the Boston area and was not the exclusive monopoly of the Seymours[10] though it seems to have been a favorite in their shop.

The neat arrangement of the rings at the quarter engaged corners, the rosewood bandings outlining the drawers veneered with figured birch, and especially the character of the shapely reeded legs with pointed feet of rounded carrot outline suggest that this table is the product of a shop headed by a master of design. (Compare legs to those of No. 307.)

Dimensions: height 34⅜; width 37¾; depth 17½.
Materials: mahogany; mahogany and figured-birch veneers over white pine; drawer linings and framing, white pine.
Accession: 57.1007                     see Inlay Fig. 60

## 339  CHAMBER TABLE
*1810–1820   New York City*

The over-all cast of dark mahogany, with reliance upon reeding for ornament, the half rounding of the upper sections of the turned legs and "shaping top to ditto," a squared section in the legs to receive a shelf, and the shape of the turned feet with brass ball terminals are characteristics of much

New York furniture of the second decade of the nineteenth century. Though larger in scale, this table approximates the form of the table desk (No. 198) bearing the label of Michael Allison dated 1823; its ornamental treatment is almost identical to an earlier writing table in the collection of the writer with label of the same maker dated 1816. This rare table may have been made by Allison or any other of the many New York cabinetmakers working in that city during this period.

Listed among the "extras" for a chamber table in the New York price book of 1802 is a "plain shelf with a hollow front." When exhibited in the Girl Scouts Loan Exhibition in 1929 (No. 784) as a "Sheraton style Dressing-table by Phyfe," this table had such a shelf. It has been replaced in the intervening years.

Dimensions: height 36⅜; width 35⅛; depth 18⅛.
Materials: mahogany and mahogany veneers; drawer fronts and rails, white pine; drawer linings and blocks, tulip.
Provenance: Louis Guerineau Myers.
Accession: 57.1055

## 340  GENTLEMAN'S DRESSING TABLE
*1810–1820   New York City*

Variously termed a "Gentleman's Dressing Table," a "Dressing Table," and a "Shaving Table" in design and price books, such tables as this one were made to provide the facilities of the modern bathroom. English dressing tables with provisions

**338**

**339**

**340**

for a basin, bottles, bidet, and other toilet equipment are not uncommon today; but American examples are almost unknown. Inasmuch as the cost of making them (as listed in the price books) was fairly expensive—approximately as much as the serpentine-front sideboard which survives in considerable numbers—Americans apparently were willing to forsake "conveniences for dressing"[11] but were loath to have their "dining-room incomplete without a sideboard."[12]

This example incorporates elements of both the shaving and dressing table. In accord with designs for the former, in the top compartment under the "tea chest lid" are a looking glass frame "hing'd to a sliding piece" that may be lowered when not in use, spaces for a wash basin, five bottles, two glasses, and two brushes. Dressing tables are sometimes fitted with a night stool, but this one has a "pot cupboard" in the center with a "fiddle

shaped" blue Staffordshire bidet below, fitted in what appears to be a drawer but is actually a stool supported on four legs, turned in the characteristic New York profile.

Dimensions: height 36; width 29½; depth 23⅝.
Materials: mahogany and mahogany veneers on white pine; drawer linings, mahogany; framing and drawer bottoms, tulip.
Provenance: Museum Purchase, 1965.
Accession: 65.73

### FOOTNOTES

1 Helen Comstock, "Mount Vernon Centennial," *Antiques*, LXIV (July, 1953), 30. Such chairs were very popular in New York. In addition to the du Pont set of twelve chairs, there are twelve other chairs in the Winterthur collections, all variants of the same design although the carving on the urn splats varies. Some are carved with leaves, others with fan-shaped devices at the top. The du Pont family set has seventeen flutes, others sixteen, and some fourteen on the top rail. Most have beaded front legs and some have spade feet. At the time it was made, this was known as an "Urn Back Chair." The entry "An Urn Back Stay Rail Chair" (with three upright splats) which cost seventeen shillings, six pence for labor in the 1796 edition of *The Journeymen Cabinet and Chair Makers' New-York Book of Prices* (p. 78) is clarified by the longer entry for this kind of chair in the 1802 edition of the same book, already cited under No. 65.
2 Swan, *Samuel McIntire, Carver, and The Sandersons, Early Salem Cabinetmakers*, p. 6.
3 William Stuart Walcott, Jr., "Ten Important American Sideboards," *Antiques*, XIV (December, 1928), 516–522.
4 See Nos. 38 and 48, Catalogue of *The John Brown House Loan Exhibition of Rhode Island Furniture* (Providence: The Rhode Island Historical Society, 1965).
5 A copy of this price book, now in the Winterthur collection, bears the autograph of Duncan Phyfe.
6 A table of the same design with similar carving and bearing the label of Stephen and Moses Young, 79 Broad Street, New York, was illustrated in the *American Collector* for January of 1938 (p. 5). It helps to establish the date for this table, for the Youngs were in partnership at that address from 1810 to 1818.
7 Sheraton, *The Cabinet Dictionary*, p. 305.
8 *The Cabinet and Chair Makers' Book of Prices* (Norwich, England, 1801), p. 27.
9 Illustrated as No. 715 in the Catalogue of the *Girl Scouts Loan Exhibition*.
10 Randall, "Works of Boston Cabinetmakers, 1795–1825, Part II," *Antiques*, LXXI (April, 1962), 412–415.
11 Sheraton, op. cit., p. 202.
12 Hepplewhite, "Introduction," *The Cabinet-Maker and Upholsterer's Guide* (London, 1794).

# Pier and Side Tables and Sideboards

In drawing rooms and dining rooms, principal areas of entertainment, pier or side tables and sideboards were meant to give a splendid effect and at the same time to be useful for serving food and drink. Many side tables have marble tops, whose purpose is intimated by President Jefferson's entry, "an elegant Mahogany *drink Table* with a Marble Top," in his 1809 inventory of the furnishings of the White House.[1] Marble, practical as well as handsome, was impervious to alcohol and was used for the tops of the finest side tables throughout Europe and America during the eighteenth century.

After the introduction of the sideboard with cellerette or bottle drawer, about 1785, a few householders may have used side tables or sideboard tables in their dining rooms; but most Americans preferred the sideboard, agreeing with George Hepplewhite that "the great utility of this piece of furniture has procured it a very general reception; and the conveniencies it affords render a dining-room incomplete without a sideboard."[2] Many sideboards were made all up and down the Atlantic Coast. Some of the very finest, and most of those identified by makers' labels, are of New York provenance; but superb examples were unquestionably made in every major city. Comparison of the 1796 New York and 1795 Philadelphia price books reveals the same listings in each, differing only in size. The standard New York sideboard was longer and deeper, the norm being six feet long, two feet six inches wide, and twenty-one inches deep, compared to a length of five feet and a fifteen-inch depth in Philadelphia. Also listed in both books were specifications for six other specific shapes of sideboards—a "round-front celleret sideboard," a "serpentine-front celleret sideboard," a "circular celleret sideboard," a "celleret sideboard with ovalo corners," a "celleret sideboard with elliptic middle and elliptic hollow on each side," and a "celleret sideboard with elliptic middle and ogee on each side."

In Maryland, sideboard tables without drawers, or sideboards with a single row of drawers under the top, sometimes called huntboards, appear to have been a favorite. At least one of these is labeled by John Shaw and a number of others may have been made by him. The prevalence of these shallow sideboard tables in Maryland may account for the number of cellerettes found in that region since Hepplewhite comments that "cellerettes called also gardes de vin, are ... of general use where sideboards are without drawers...."[3]

Sheraton commented that "sideboard tables [and sideboards] ... are those that are used for a dining equipage, on which the silver plate is placed."[4] But Hepplewhite was more specific about the drawers and compartments:

> ...plate 29 shows the internal construction and conveniences of the drawers; the right hand drawer has partitions for nine bottles, ... behind this is a place for cloths or napkins the whole depth of the drawer.

The drawer on the left hand has two divisions, the hinder one lined with green cloth to hold plate [silver], etc. under a cover; the front one is lined with lead for the convenience of holding water to wash glasses, etc.—there must be a valve-cock or plug at the bottom, to let off the dirty water; and also in the other drawer, to change the water necessary to keep the wine etc. cool; or they may be made to take out. The long drawer in the middle is adapted for table linen, etc.[5]

Many, if not most, American sideboards are equipped with bottle drawers but few were lined with lead to permit the washing of glasses and china in the dining room. This English custom was less feasible in American homes with fewer servants.

Wine coolers and cellerettes without stands seem normally to have stood under the sideboard. In "The Dinner Party," painted in Boston by Henry Sargent about 1815–1820, a case of bottles appears under the end of the sideboard—where the wine cooler shown near the head of the table may also have stood when not in use. This also was English custom as is confirmed by the designs of Robert Adam and others.

In the early 1800's, according to Sarah Anna Emery, the practice in fashionable homes in Newburyport was as follows:

The dining or sitting room almost invariably held a large mahogany sideboard. Beneath generally stood an ornamental liquor case, and upon the top were some half dozen cut-glass decanters filled with wine, brandy and other liquors; these were flanked by trays of wine glasses and tumblers. The old fashioned silver tankard had become obsolete, but a display of silver tumblers was considered desirable.[6]

Sheraton, after defining a pier as "that part of a wall which is between the windows" concludes, "hence the term pier table, in cabinet work, which are made to fit in between the architraves of the windows, and rise above the surbase."[7]

Pier tables also show diversity of form and plan and are among the most richly ornamented pieces of furniture in the Winterthur collection, in accord with Hepplewhite's observation: "Pier Tables become an article of much fashion; and not being applied to such general use as other Tables, admit, with great propriety, of much elegance and ornament. Four designs for Pier Tables are shown, with their proper ornaments; and also four designs for tops, which show as many various plans."[8]

On the facing page an engraving which appeared in three editions of *The London Cabinet Makers' Union Book of Prices* (1811, 1824 and 1836) shows eleven different shapes of pier and pembroke table tops as well as corners for doors or panels, ends for panels, "pillasters," and French feet. Many of these are identified with names in the text of the book, where it is also pointed out that the dotted lines on the illustrations indicate the method of framing each kind of top. A and B are for a pier table with quarter-round ends; C is for a pier table with ovolo ends; D is also for a pier table with ovolo ends and "solid end rails"; E is for another pier table with ovolo ends, but this time with "two extra legs to show a break, either part or their whole thickness"; F is for a pier table with "hollow ends"; G is for a pier table with hollow ends and a small ovolo corner; H is for a pier table with "round corners," and I for a pier table with "round ends." The corners on the left end of the pembroke table top are "double round" corners (a slight variant from the "double elliptic" top) and those at the right are "double round with an internal square." These are the kind of descriptive terms used by cabinetmakers for all tables during the Federal period.

Equally descriptive were the names for shapes of panels formed either with moldings or stringing. The following are the names given in the text for the corners and the ends shown in the illustration: "diagonal break" or "canted corner" (1); "hollow round

# PLATE 1.

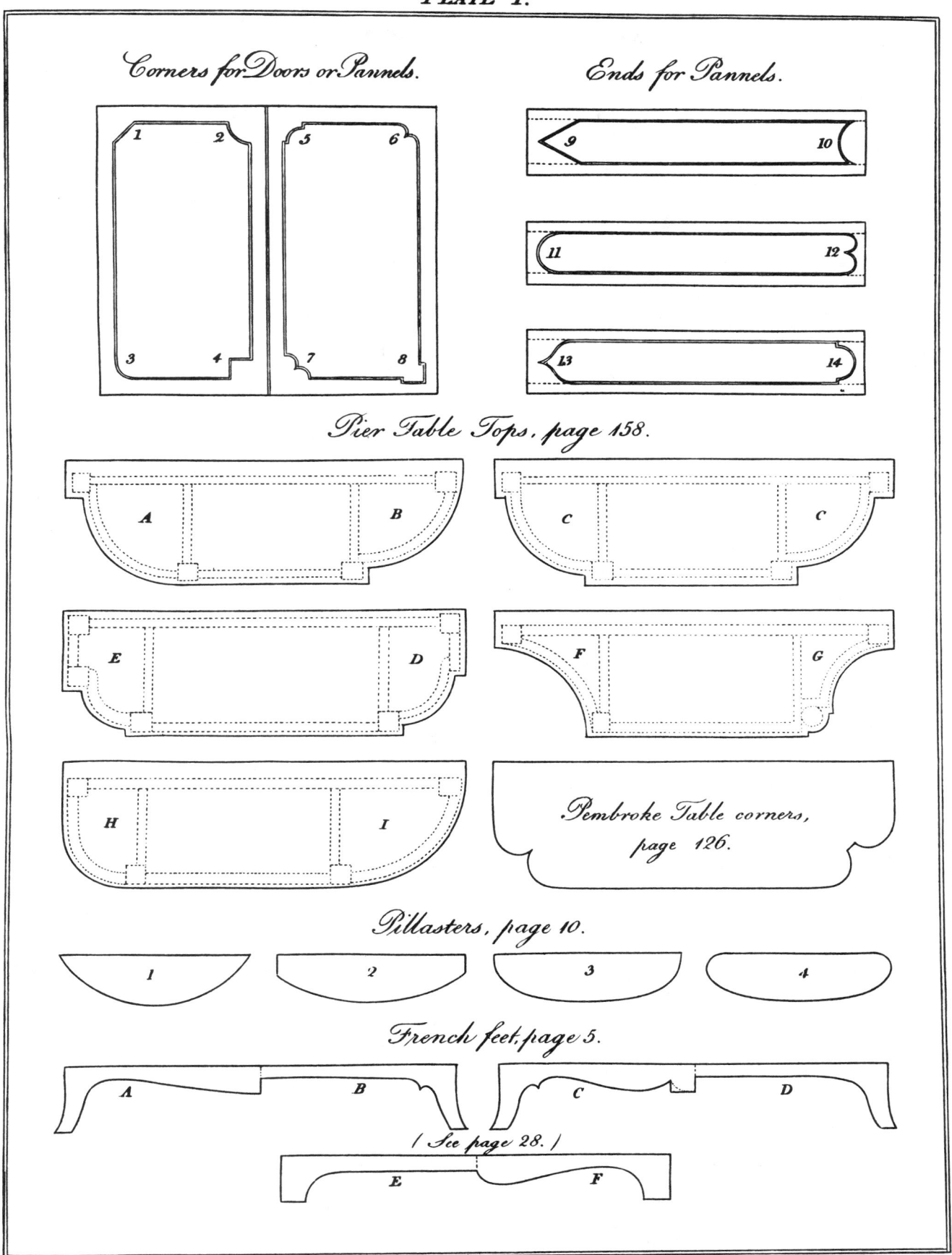

Corners for Doors or Pannels.

Ends for Pannels.

Pier Table Tops, page 158.

Pembroke Table corners, page 126.

Pillasters, page 10.

French feet, page 5.

( See page 28. )

corner" (2); "round corner" (3); "hollow square corner" (4); "ovalo corner" (5); "double round corner" (6); "double hollow corner" (7); corner with a "square break" (8); "diamond end" (9); "hollow end" (10); "round end" (11); "double round end" (12); "gothic end" or "a taper pointed panel" (13); "astragal" or "ovalo end" (14).

Shown at the bottom of the page of illustrations is a plinth frame for the front of a chest of drawers with "plain brackets" (bracket feet). E indicates the front scalloped with a "plain hollow" and F shows the front scalloped with a "double ogee." Unfortunately, no names are given for the scalloped outlines A, B, C and D shown under "French feet." But, A seems to be described by the phrase "French feet and drapery with plain sweep" listed as an extra in the 1810 New York price book (p.7). B and D appear to be fronts with a "plain hollow" and C is scalloped with a "double ogee" and a square or round (dotted lines) in the center. The latter shape of scalloping or drapery is one often found on Baltimore chests of drawers, whereas in New York a variant with a "round hollow" in the center was preferred by Michael Allison and others.

Cabinetmakers' price books also list the sizes for pier tables as from three feet to three feet six inches long and according to Hepplewhite: "The height of Pier Tables varies from the general rule, as they are now universally made to fit the pier, and rise level with or above the dado of the room, nearly touching the ornaments of the glass: if the latter, the top fits close to the wall."[9]

In contrast to the many pier glasses listed in the accounts of looking-glass makers, few pier tables appear in cabinetmakers' accounts; and surviving examples are much rarer than might be assumed from the number at Winterthur. Their scarcity may be accounted for by the supposition that card tables were often used in their stead, a supposition supported by another of Miss Emery's observations: "The heavy claw-footed furniture of a previous date had been followed by lighter, in the French style. Stiff looking, slender legged chairs and sofas were primly ranged round the room, with card table to match in the piers; these sometimes had marble tops. Above them hung large Dutch mirrors."[10]

Her reference to card tables with marble tops is interesting because the shape of each of the pair of marble-top pier tables, labeled by William Haskell of Salem, Massachusetts (No.339), is exactly that of many Salem card tables. The practical aspect of a table serving two purposes probably appealed to Americans.

Two small, free-standing, marble-top tables, here called mixing tables, believed to have served the same purposes as side tables, and two corner tables are included in this section, arranged in accord with the geographical provenance of the furniture—from North to South.

1 Marie G.Kimball, "The Original Furnishings of the White House, Part I," *Antiques*, XV (June, 1929), 486.
2 Hepplewhite, *The Cabinet-Maker and Upholsterer's Guide* (1794), p.3.
3 *Ibid.*
4 Thomas Sheraton, *The Cabinet Dictionary* (London, 1803), p.304.
5 Hepplewhite, *The Cabinet-Maker and Upholsterer's Guide* (1794), p.3.
6 Sarah Anna Emery, *Reminiscences of a Nonagenarian* (Newburyport: William H.Huse & Co., 1879), p.244.
7 Thomas Sheraton, *The Cabinet Dictionary* (London, 1803), p.284.
8 Hepplewhite, *The Cabinet-Maker and Upholsterer's Guide* (1794), p.2.
9 *Ibid.*
10 Sarah Anna Emery, *Reminiscences of a Nonagenarian*, p.244.

# XXIII Montmorenci Stair Hall

*Before paneled woodwork with motifs of classical inspiration stands a magnificent mahogany pier table (No. 347), a monument to the artistry of Charles-Honoré Lannuier. The table and the carved and inlaid armchair, both of very dark wood, were made in New York City. The pistol-handled urn and great gilt and sepia porcelain punch bowl were imported from China, the bejeweled candelabra from England, and the gilt looking glass from England or the Continent.*

### 341 MIXING TABLE
*1790–1810   New England*

A rare form—one of which few examples exist today—this so-called "mixing table" is unusual because of its lowness and because of the use of inset marble for its top. This example, which is probably a product of a north of Boston cabinetmaker or possibly one from Providence, has a thin band fo geometric two-color inlay around the base of the skirt and light wood stringing on the outer sides of the tapered legs which runs to the floor. The latter practice seems to be one favored by northern New England cabinetmakers. The handsome mottled gray, white, and tan marble slab provides a foil for the plain mahogany which surrounds it. The low height of this table may indicate that it was used beside a lolling chair for the service of alcoholic or hot beverages which would possibly damage a wooden top.

Dimensions: height 24¼; width 19³/₁₆; depth 13⁷/₈.

Materials: mahogany with light and dark wood stringing; supports for top and blocks, white pine; rails, birch; corner blocks, mahogany; top, marble.

Provenance: Museum Purchase, 1953.

Accession: 53.185.1

### 342 MIXING TABLE
*1790–1810   New England, probably Northeastern Massachusetts*

Rather higher and more ambitiously inlaid than No. 341, the legs of this table, with pink and gray marble top, are banded with patterned stringing to form cuffs, the stiles inlaid with dark wood diamonds, and the lower edge of the skirt bordered with dart-patterned stringing. Mahogany veneers on white pine, similarly patterned stringing, and diamond inlays are found on Providence and eastern Massachusetts furniture.

**341**

**342**

Dimensions: height 28 5/16; width 26 1/2; depth 20 1/2.
Materials: mahogany and mahogany veneers on white
  pine; light and dark wood patterned stringing; rails,
  blocks, and medial brace, white pine; top, marble.
Provenance: Museum Purchase, 1958.
Accession: 58.87

**343** SIDE TABLE (one of a pair)
*1815–1820  Salem, Massachusetts  Label of William
  Haskell (working about 1817–1859)*

Side tables of any size with marble tops are rare
and important pieces of furniture. This small pair
approximating the size and shape of New England
card tables, with serpentine front, ovolo corners,
and half-serpentine ends, may be the only pair
extant with the label of the maker. The shapely
reeded legs, carved where they project from the
frame with leaves or plumes on a snowflake-
punched ground, the vertically grained mahogany
veneer on the skirt edged with cock-beading, and
the black marble top veined and mottled with
mica and shaped to the table frame indicate that
William Haskell, who was trained under the
Sandersons,[1] was a workman of no mean ability.
Up to the present time, no other furniture bearing

the label of William Haskell has come to light.

The frame of the table under the veneers, like
much Massachusetts cabinetwork, is of white pine
as are the large quarter blocks (which brace the
front corners) and the thinner strips at the rear
angles. A double back rail separated by thin blocks
gives extra strength. Near the printed label on the
inner back rail "N1" is brushed in black paint.
"N2" appears on the companion table.

Dimensions: height 29; width 35 3/4; depth 17 1/2.
Materials: mahogany and mahogany veneers; frame and
  blocks, white pine; top, marble.
Accession: 57.1016.1, 2

**344** PIER TABLE[2]
*About 1800  Boston  Probably made by John and/or
  Thomas Seymour*

For nobility of proportion, exquisite workmanship,
and harmonious use of beautiful woods, no American pier table known to the writer matches this
one. With the grace and reasoned quality of fine
architecture, a cool gray and white marble top, set
within a rich brown molding of mahogany on a
frame veneered and finished on all four sides with
panels of golden-figured birch, is borne lightly like

**343**

**344**

**345**

a lintel upon piers. The leaf-carved brackets, suggestive of capitals, sweep outward from veneer-paneled legs to meet and support the frame and in so doing provide a transition from vertical to horizontal as do the carved solid brackets on so many other case pieces attributed to the Seymours. Again at the bottom of the supports, the transition is a curved line from the tapered legs to the spade-shaped brass cups above contemporary casters.

With the same history of ownership as the superb lady's secretary and bookcase (No. 186), there seems every likelihood that this pier table and that desk—with so many details associated with work attributed to the Seymours—were made by one or both of these outstanding Boston cabinetmakers.

Dimensions: height 30⅝; width 40⅛; depth 20¾.

Materials: mahogany with figured birch veneers and rosewood bandings on frame; maple veneer on legs; rails, cherry; medial brace and blocks, white pine; top, marble.

Provenance: Originally owned by Eben or Gorham Parsons of Boston and Byfield, Massachusetts; Gorham Parsons Sargent; Mary W. Sargent Hoffman; Schuyler Hoffman, Jr.

Accession: 57.689

## 345 SIDE TABLE
*1800–1810 Probably Boston*

The grandiose style which may be seen in numerous English houses designed and furnished by Robert Adam is not often found among extant American furniture of the Federal period. Outstanding for its rich materials and urbane pattern, the scale and elegance of this extraordinary table are comparable to those of furniture made abroad.

The top, richly veneered with crotch mahogany, is bordered on the curved front with a wide band of bird's-eye maple, and panels of the latter lighten the skirt. The ornament in relief is contrived of gilded composition work simulating the ormolu mounts sometimes applied to English and more often to French furniture. Such foliated borders and festoons as those on the frame of the table were familiar to the *fondeurs* of the Louis XVI epoch and are details found in metal on fine case pieces then made in France. Although this is the sole surviving American piece known to the writer with such ornament, John Doggett, a looking-glass maker of Boston, charged Harrison Gray Otis sixteen dollars for "gilding and painting 1 sofa" and two dollars for "composition [ornament] for ditto" in 1807.[3] Here red painted borders set off the gilded moldings around the panels and give color to the legs also ornamented in gilt.

The frame is constructed mostly of white pine—the back made with two separated boards similar to those of the pair of side tables (No. 343) labeled by William Haskell of Salem. The curved front is

**346**

built up of triple laminated strips. An old label pasted under the mahogany top is inscribed "C R Perkins," which is probably the name of an early owner.

Dimensions: height 34; width 52½; depth 26⅛.
Materials: mahogany with mahogany and bird's-eye-maple veneers; frame, white pine, except for lowest laminated strip of tilia; brackets, basswood; legs, elm.
Provenance: Museum Purchase, 1953.
Accession: 53.161

### 346 PIER TABLE
*About 1805    New York City    Stamp of Charles-Honoré Lannuier (working 1803 to 1819)*

If this table were not stamped "H. LANNUIER NEW-YORK" (twice on the top of drawer facing) and if the white pine and tulip secondary woods were not present, it would be readily assumed to have been made in France during the first years of the short-lived Consulate (1800–1804).[4] All the hallmarks of a "console en acajou" of the consular period are present: flaring brass-bound feet (called *toupie* by the French), cove with ring above reeded legs, a pierced brass gallery, and a brass-outlined shelf.

This pier table, which follows quite exactly designs published by La Mésangère in 1802, would have been au courant in Paris just before Lannuier

**347**

left there in 1803 and may be presumed to have been made soon after he arrived in New York where he advertised on July 15 of that year in the *New-York Evening Post:*

> Honoré Lannuier, Cabinet Maker, just arrived from France, and who has worked at his trade with the most celebrated Cabinet Makers of Europe, takes the liberty of informing the public, that he makes all kinds of Furniture, Beds, Chairs, &c., in the newest and latest French fashion; and that he has brought for that purpose gilt and brass frames, borders of ornaments, and handsome safe locks, as well as new patterns....[5]

Dimensions: height 36½; width 37; depth 14¾.
Materials: mahogany; rear rail and shelf, white pine; drawer bottom, tulip; moldings and gallery, brass; top, marble.
Accession: 61.1693

### 347 PIER TABLE[6]
*1805–1810    New York City    Label and stamp of Charles-Honoré Lannuier (working 1803–1819)*

Decorative motifs and elements found on both New York and French cabinetwork are evident in this splendid pier table which bears on its backboard a printed label with the announcement in both English and French that "Honoré Lanniuer, Cabinet Maker (from Paris) keeps his Ware-house and Manufactory and cabinet ware of Newest Fashion, at No. 60 Broad-Street."

In contrast to No. 346, the over-all form of this table is English rather than French. Current New York cabinetmaking usage in the early 1800's included astragal-ended panels of stringing or satinwood veneers, and paterae or other inlaid motifs on the stiles above the legs. Apparently derived from Lannuier's French training are the shape of the brass-rimmed peg-top feet, the fashioning of the legs (larger than those normally finished with such fine reeding in this country) with a coved neck and beading above, and the sheet brass moldings which edge the top and the cross stretchers. Although a carved mantle of leaves at the tops of legs was common French practice, the carving is in the New York manner. The old lion-head brass pulls are probably replacements.

Dimensions: height 37; width 49; depth 24½.
Materials: mahogany with satinwood and rosewood inlays; drawer linings, mahogany; rear rail and blocks, white pine; brass moldings.
Provenance: Louis Guerineau Myers.
Accession: 57.685

### 348 SIDE TABLE
*1815–1825 American (?)*

Although this side table might be attributed at first glance to Lannuier because of the brass ornament, the writer feels that such an attribution would be shortsighted. The workmanship on this table falls far below the high standards set by that skillful French émigré, and the brass stars and anthemions are inset instead of being appliquéd— his more usual practice. Their character, as well as that of the swelled, spiral-turned legs, is English rather than French. The place of manufacture is not obvious. The outline of the turnings at the tops of the legs and below the shelf are not typical of normally recognized New York work, the nearest parallel being a card table bearing the label dated 1817 of John Budd.[7] However, the swelling of the legs on that table occurs near the top instead of the center, as here, and those feet are typical of New York practice and these are not.

Dimensions: height 31; width 47; depth 21¾.

Materials: mahogany; corner blocks, replaced; medial braces and back rail, mahogany; stretcher and rails, white pine.

Accession: 57.714

### 349 PIER TABLE
*1810–1820 Philadelphia (?)*

Called a pier table only on the basis of height and general appearance, this article of furniture was most probably situated in a library or hall since its

**348**

interior compartment is fitted with a maze of geometrically divided trays possibly for curios, rough geological specimens, or, more probably, marbles or other stones cut to fit exactly into the small divisions. The entire top of the table, hinged at the back, is veneered with satinwood and mahogany. From a small mahogany semicircular disc at the back center, lines of mahogany run forward and outward to divide the top into fourteen rays of satinwood. A looking glass in conforming frame is fitted on the underside of the top.

The design is unique in the annals of furniture making in any country. Its grandiose character suggests that the table may have been designed originally for use in a very great house or as an accoutrement to a private subscription library or public institution. Lion's-paw monopodia were used in England for several years beginning about 1810, but these usually terminate in small lion heads instead of robust and skillfully carved eagles. The shape of the top, wider at the back and hollowed at the ends and front, is unusual and one not associated with card or standard pier tables.

Certain elements such as the contrasting mahogany ovals and mahogany banding of the panels against broad expanses of satinwood veneers and the execution of the acanthus leaves at the tops of the legs relate to characteristics seen in smaller scale Philadelphia furniture, notably the satinwood sewing tables attributed to Henry Connelly. (See No. 426.) The rayed top of satinwood with mahogany inset half circle reminds one not only of Connelly's work but also of a great pier table labeled by Joseph B. Barry,[8] also of Philadelphia.

Dimensions: height 39; width 49; depth 27.

Materials: mahogany; mahogany and satinwood veneers; rear rail, main vertical partitions, and tray sides, mahogany; eagles and bottoms of trays, tulip; front rail, white pine.

Accession: 57.945

## 350 PIER TABLE
*About 1790    Baltimore*

Lustrous pale mahogany, violet-toned brèche marble, alternating dark and light wood banding of the apron, and naturalistic inlaid lilies of the valley within faded green oval inlays comprise the restrained ornament of this rare table. The exceedingly thick marble top (one and one-eighth inches) is reduced visually by the chamfering of its lower edges.

Similar inlays and bandings, as well as hard pine and tulip, occur in many pieces of furniture with Maryland histories of ownership.

Dimensions: height 33¼; width 37¼; depth 19¼.

Materials: mahogany with light wood inlay; rails and blocks, hard pine; lowest lamination of rails, tulip.

Accession: 57.806

## 351 PIER TABLE with ovolo corners[9]
*1790–1800    Baltimore*

Hepplewhite, in the Introduction to the *Guide,* suggests that pier tables "became an article of much fashion and not being applied to such general use as other Tables, admit with great propriety, of much elegance and ornament." Each element of this outstanding table is highly ornamental. The top is framed with a veneered band. The finest of crotch mahogany veneers have been used for the panels on the frame, which is outlined with a chevron-like banding on the lower edge. The tapered legs are inlaid on two sides with panels of satinwood, framing bowknots with dependent cords and tassels ("engraved" and stained green), above string panels enclosing three inlaid husks and drops suspended from a loop. Below the cuffs formed of patterned stringing, the legs are stained black. For "a pier table with ovolo corners," "two extra legs" were offered as an option in *The Journeymen Cabinet and Chairmakers Philadelphia Book of Prices* for 1795. In electing this choice, as well as choosing as intricate and delicate inlays as are to be found on the supports of any piece of American furniture, the original purchaser and the maker provided us with a unique and an extraordinary piece of furniture.

**350**

**351**

Dimensions: height 39½; width 46½; depth 21¾.
Materials: mahogany with light and dark wood veneers and inlays; end rails, mahogany; front blocks, mahogany and tulip; backboard and rear blocks, white pine; front rail, hard pine.
Provenance: Mr. and Mrs. H. L. Duer.
Accession: 57.700                    see Inlay Fig. 123

however, are fans inlaid as these are at the tops of the legs.
Dimensions: height 38; width 40¾; depth 20.
Materials: mahogany and mahogany veneers; light wood inlays, stringing, and banding; rails and corner blocks, tulip.
Accession: 57.1028

### 352 CIRCULAR PIER TABLE
*1790–1800 Baltimore*

From the tip of its spade feet (formed with appliqués of dark mahogany) to the upper surface of its semicircular top veneered with sectors of crotch mahogany, this pier table is admirably conceived and exquisitely made. Light wood, patterned stringing, or banding outlines every edge. Effective but subtle diagonal and rayed patterns of little contrast, except for the figure of the wood, are found on the center panel of the skirt, in the herringbone veneers on the front and side faces of the legs, and on the upper surface of the top. There each sector is divided by light wood stringing, with a scallop on its outer end inset with a segment of darker wood.

Patterned stringing with emphatic squares (or circles) separated by three thin strings (as on the edge of the skirt), and light wood shaded husks with elongated center petals are thought to be hallmarks of Baltimore workmanship. Not often found,

### 353 PIER TABLE (one of a pair)
*1802–1810 Philadelphia or Baltimore Possibly the work of Joseph B. Barry*

The novel form of this table appears to be without precedent in published sources of design. The cupid's-bow façade of the top, apron, and shelf; the turned feet which almost repeat the outline of the façade; the turned and tapered legs, one-quarter engaged at the frame, blocked at the shelf, and seemingly divided into two parts by ring turning, are all uncommon features. Whether the maker was the creator of the completely new design for this pair of tables is unknown, but the scene in gilt on glass (blue background) at the center of the apron is taken detail for detail from Plate 11 of *The Accompaniment* to *The Cabinet-Maker and Upholsterer's Drawing Book* (1802) of Thomas Sheraton. At least three other pieces of furniture[10] are ornamented with glass panels copied from the same source, and it might seem logical to assume that these well-painted panels were probably imported from London. However, it appears likely that they were painted in this country since the gilt leaves on the stiles are also copied from the same plate. And, there were painters here who could fashion gilt pictures on glass as indicated by an advertisement in the *Maryland Journal* of October 28, 1791, which states that "Solomon Gotlip Binding...by trade a Painter and Glazier, lately arrived in the Ship Republican from Bremen...is naturally ingenious and can draw miniature pictures, with gold on glass...." [11]

Of this particular scene, Sheraton comments on page 22 of *The Accompaniment*:

> The subject is a faint moonlight scene, representing Diana in a visit to Endymion; who, as the story goes, having offended Juno, was condemned by Jupiter to a thirty-year sleep. It may not be improper to advertise some, that these, with a thousand other of the same kind of stories, are merely the fabrications of ancient poets and idolaters, forming to themselves innumerable gods, according to their vain imaginations, and which now, only serve to try the painters skill in decorating our walls. And in opposition to these vanities, I cannot well omit whispering into the ear of the reader, that "To us there is but one god, the Father, of whom are all things." One Cor. viii. 6.

A mate to the table illustrated, from the Marsden J. Perry collection[12] and now at Winterthur, has a glass tablet showing what is probably Orpheus with his lyre, one of the "thousand other of the same kind of stories...."

Philadelphia sofas with turned arm supports inlaid with light bands of vertical stringing are known, but turned legs enhanced in the same way have been seen by the writer only on these two tables and others like the matching pair of corner tables,[13] perhaps made en suite, which follow. All of these tables have Maryland histories of ownership as does a lady's writing table which is decorated with a glass panel of Diana and Endymion.[14] As will be developed under No. 354, there appears to be more than a possibility that these tables were made by Joseph B. Barry of Philadelphia and Baltimore.

Dimensions: height 36¾; width 45; depth 22.
Materials: mahogany with satinwood banding and light wood inlays; rear rails and two medial braces, white pine; front and end rails, tulip; top, marble.
Provenance: C. L. Pendleton (Providence, R. I.); Louis Guerineau Myers.[15]
Accession: 57.779.1, 2

**354** CORNER TABLE with marble top (one of two)

*1800–1810 Philadelphia or Baltimore*

Although not acquired together, these tables are so like the preceding pair as to appear to be from the same shop and possibly from the same set. Both have qualities of workmanship and inset gilt glass panels with blue backgrounds identical to that of No. 353. The form, like that of the pier tables, is a highly individual one. Two others like these with Maryland histories of ownership are known,[16] but except for this group, no other really high-style American corner tables have come to light. No other American corner tables match pairs of pier tables. Therefore, the following advertisement of Joseph B. Barry (Baltimore, 1803) assumes great importance in the identification of these tables.

> Elegant Furniture. THE subscriber takes this opportunity of informing the citizens of Baltimore, that he has imported and now opening, an elegant assortment of CABINET FURNITURE, of the newest London and French patterns,

**354**

...among which are the following articles, viz....Marble pier and corner tables....[17]

From Barry's statement that these tables were imported, one would assume they came from abroad. But Barry is careful to say "of the newest London and French patterns." The writer believes that the tables and other items listed were made in Barry's shop at 132 South Second Street in Philadelphia, and "imported" from there into Baltimore. On May 9, 1803, having moved from No. 130 Baltimore Street to No. 3 Light Street, Baltimore, Barry advertised more explicitly

> ...He has just received from Philadelphia, a few large hair mattrasses of the first quality, sophas with bolsters in satin and stripe hair cloth, large sets of Dining tables and biddets fitted up complete, with sundry other articles.... N.B. Persons wishing to become subscribers for his Elegant Tapestry, may have an opportunity of viewing it at his store, as a person will attend during his absence at Philadelphia. JOSEPH B. BARRY.[18]

Taking into consideration the fact that Barry was born in Ireland whence came a number of the richest Baltimoreans; that his Philadelphia trade card with furniture designs derived directly from Sheraton[19] is, with that of William Camp of Baltimore,[20] the most elaborate of American cabinetmakers' trade cards of the early nineteenth century; that a slightly later pier table with Barry's label is the most elaborate and highly finished piece of its period; that one of the pier tables shown on Barry's trade card has cupid-bow stretchers which relate to the façade of No. 353; and that Barry's advertisement citing both "marble pier and corner tables" is the only American reference known to pier and corner tables that presumably match, the likelihood seems great that these tables and No. 353 and its mate were made either in his Philadelphia or Baltimore shop.

Dimensions: height 36½; width 27⅝; depth 21.
Materials: mahogany with satinwood and ebony inlays; rails and diagonal braces, white pine; stretcher cleat, a replacement.
Accession: 57.651 (mate, 56.5)

## 355 CORNER TABLE
*1790–1810    Pennsylvania or Southern*

Corner tables are extremely rare today and apparently were never common. Presumably they were used as extra serving tables. This one, with light-colored inlaid cuffs and string-outlined ovals above the front legs, has a panel with most unusual

**355**

ends (formed by stringing) inlaid on the skirt, which is edged with a dentilled band. The combination of tulip and hard pine as secondary woods is seldom found on furniture made north of Philadelphia.

Dimensions: height 32⅜; width 32¾; depth 22⅞.
Materials: mahogany; light and dark wood stringing; rails, hard pine; blocks, tulip.
Provenance: Reginald Lewis.
Accession: 61.138

## 356 SIDE TABLE with serpentine front and rounded corners (one of a pair)
*About 1790–1810    South Carolina (?)*

The attribution of these tables to South Carolina is made on the basis of their having been found in that state,[21] although it is well known that much furniture was exported from a number of northern centers to southern ports. The presence of hard pine as a secondary wood points to a Philadelphia or more southerly origin as does the interlaced stringing with dependent flower on each front leg. Similar inlays are said to appear on several tables found in South Carolina.

The serpentine front, the particularly delicate inlays of the legs, the beautifully grained ovals and astragal-ended panels of Ceylon satinwood veneer, foiled by smaller ones of rosewood, lend variety and elegance to these side tables which in size and

very elegant with a marble top." [22] Figured woods, inlays, veneers, and contrast of color also signified elegance especially to less sophisticated cabinetmakers working in towns and smaller cities. Pattern books, rules of taste, and architectural principles which governed the work of the best urban cabinetmakers had less influence on country workmen, whose most ambitious pieces, often unique, may be naive, even bizarre, but are often highly imaginative and among the most interesting of all furniture.

The interior (stained red) behind the upper pair of doors is fitted to resemble the interior of a secretary drawer with open pigeonholes and a row of small drawers above and below. Although the interior does not pull forward, a writing surface is provided by a slider, like that on a dressing chest of drawers. The lower cupboards behind the two arched doors are painted blue, and each flanking drawer is divided for three bottles.

Dimensions: height 42⅛; width 51¾; depth 23.
Materials: mahogany; mahogany, bird's-eye-maple, and other light wood veneers; various patterned stringing

height resemble the "hunt boards" of Maryland, Virginia, and the Carolinas.

Dimensions: height 33¼; width 52¼; depth 25¼.
Materials: mahogany and mahogany veneers on white pine (the top, drawer front, and end rails); light wood stringing, Ceylon satinwood and rosewood inlays.
Accession: 57.852.1, 2

**357** SIDEBOARD TABLE with marble top and simulated secretary drawer

*About 1800     Newburyport, Massachusetts     Branded "Toppan" on back*

The character of this extraordinary piece of furniture, originally purchased in Newburyport by Israel Sack, lends credence to the identification of the "Toppan" branded on its back as Abner Toppan, working in that town as a cabinetmaker in the late eighteenth and early nineteenth century.

"A Straight Front Sideboard Table, four feet six inches long" is listed in early English cabinetmakers' price books and in the first editions to appear in this country. Among the many extras offered for this form, neither a secretary drawer, bottle drawers, nor marble tops are noted. But that marble tops denoted elegance is borne out by several contemporary references, among them the 1815 advertisement of the auctioneers, M. Poor and J. Hastings, for "two sideboards, one of which is

of light and dark woods; framing and drawer linings, white pine, except for some bottoms of basswood; top, gray marble.

Accession: 57.848          see Inlay Figs. 14, 21, 40, 48

### 358 ENCLOSED PIER TABLE with hollow ends

*1800–1810     Salem, Massachusetts     Label of Mark Pitman*

When the sequence of illustrations for this book was arranged, this unique table was thought to have been a serving table, and it may have been so used. However, in the earlier London and American price books an entry for an "Inclos'd" pier table follows each listing of a standard variety such as a pier table with a break, a round-front pier table, a pier table with ovolo corners, and a pier table with circular middle and hollow ends.

This table appears to be an enclosed but simplified version of a "Pier Table with Circular Middle and Hollow ends" listed as "Three feet six inches long one foot six inches wide, two doors in the middle part glued up and clamped, one sham ditto at each end, a fast shelf inside, the front veneer'd all flush, the edge of the top square, an astragal on the edge of the bottom, on taper stump feet..." A cock-beaded drawer is included as an extra. Hence, the form although unusual today was well known in the 1790's. The novel and ingenious part is the great arched opening in the front fitted with reeded

shutters to give access to the large cupboard space.

Most labeled Pitman pieces of furniture seen by the writer have been well made with a minimum of stringing or contrasting veneers. This cabinetmaker seems to have relied generally on rich figured mahogany veneers for decorative effects.

Dimensions: height 32; width 27¼ (front); 41⅜ (back); depth 17⅞.

Materials: mahogany; mahogany veneers on white pine; drawer linings and framing, white pine.

Provenance: Museum Purchase, 1959.

Accession: 59.8

### 359 SIDEBOARD

*1790–1800     Newport, Rhode Island*

Few forms in American furniture are more dramatic in contour than this sideboard with serpentine front, large ovolo corners, and hollow ends. No counterpart is to be found in design or price books, and few with such robust vigor of line are known. Skillfully contrived with deeply bowed doors opening into cupboards at either end and drawers in the serpentine front so shammed as to give the appearance of two tiers of narrow and shallow drawers, it actually has a long drawer over a slider of the same length above a single deep drawer on the right and two shallow drawers on the left. Figured mahogany veneers; cock-beading around drawers, doors, and panels; highly unusual brasses stamped in a triple paterae pattern with posts to match; and a minimum of inlay (restricted, except for fan-shaped light wood keyhole escutcheons, to the lower half of each leg) comprise the ornamental details.

Said by the late Israel Sack to have been found in Worcester, Massachusetts (he thought made in Newport), the provenance of this sideboard has provoked much discussion. Some have averred it was made in New York; others have insisted that it was made in eastern Massachusetts and that similar examples exist in Newburyport or Duxbury. The writer has been unable to find any of these, but the presence of tulip as a secondary wood seems to rule out the Massachusetts attribution. On the basis of the engraved husk inlays, which in their roundness and plumpness approximate those on a three-part dining table bearing the label of John Townsend of Newport,[23] this sideboard is here attributed to that center, an attribution that is supported by the presence of chestnut as a secondary wood and the statement on a sideboard of the same form that it "was presented to [Eliza Tennant Sweet] by her husband [Daniel Sweet of Newport] either upon their wedding day or soon afterward."[24]

Dimensions: height 40; width 66½; depth 26½.

Materials: mahogany; mahogany veneers on white pine; light wood stringing and inlays; drawer bottoms and sides, tulip; framing, white pine; drawer supports, chestnut.

Accession: 57.849

## 360 SIDEBOARD[25]
*1795–1805    New York*

The following statements of Robert Adam regarding architectural composition epitomize one aspect of his aesthetic theory which revolutionized English taste in the second half of the eighteenth century.

*Movement* is meant to express, the rise and fall, the advance and recess, with other diversity of form, in the different parts of a building, so as to add greatly to the picturesque of the composition. For the rising and falling, advancing and receding, with the convexity and concavity, and other forms of the great parts, have the same effect in architecture, that hill and dale, fore-ground and distance, swelling and sinking have in landscape: That is, they serve to produce an agreeable and diversified contour, that groups and contrasts like a picture, and creates a variety of light and shade, which gives great spirit, beauty, and effect to the composition.[26]

Few other pieces of American furniture show so

**360**

well such a variety of surface contours against a background of advancing and receding forms as does this great sideboard. Its conception is ceremonial, useful but not domestic.

Two years after a "Celleret Sideboard, with an Elliptic Middle and Ogee on each Side" was first listed and illustrated in the 1793 edition of *The Cabinet-Makers' London Book of Prices,* a similar entry appeared in a Philadelphia edition. A year later, it was included in the first New York issue with a basic price for the simplest version of nine pounds twelve shillings for labor—one of the higher quotations for making a piece of furniture. Although two extra legs cost but an additional seven shillings for labor, only a few eight-legged sideboards survive today and apparently few were made. But this sideboard, which is longer than the standard model of six feet, has many other extras. Inlaid ellipses; astragal-ended rectangles of satinwood; triple-string outlined panels of mahogany veneers on the body; inlaid "panels [of satinwood] with a gothic top, and a hollow bottom" on three sides of the front legs; inlaid flutes at the tops of the legs; extra drawers; and "a cupboard underneath the middle drawer with two doors, sweep [curved] front" and "stiles" on either side "worked round" would make this one of the most expensive pieces of American furniture to produce. Apparently, only a few, even of the most affluent, were willing to pay the price.

Although this sideboard might have been made in Connecticut where a few eight-legged sideboards with local histories of ownership are known, the character of the ornament and the presence of ash as a secondary wood seem to favor a New York attribution despite the fact that no known labeled New York sideboard, of which there are several, helps to identify this one. But on other furniture forms made in New York, triple-string outlined panels, inlaid flutes, and astragal-ended and elliptical inlaid satinwood panels are found.

Dimensions: height 41; width 79½; depth 28½.
Materials: mahogany; mahogany and satinwood veneers on white pine; and light and dark wood stringing; drawer linings, tulip; framing, white pine with ash strips under the top.
Accession: 57.850                    see Inlay Fig. 71

## FOOTNOTES

1 From the Elijah Sanderson manuscript records in The Essex Institute.

2 Illustrated and described in Stoneman, p. 292.

3 Entry under January 16, 1807 "John Doggett's [Day] Book, Roxbury [begun] December 4th 1802." DMMC 64 X 10.

4 An illustration of an identical table, entitled "console en Acajou à filets de Cuivre, placage en Ebène" (mahogany console with strips of brass and veneering of ebony), is shown on Plate 9, Number 2, of La Mésangère's *Collection de Meubles et Objets de goût,* issued on September 7, 1802. Most of the 755 plates known to have been issued by La Mésangère over a thirty-year period are in the collections of the Winterthur Library.

5 Gottesman, *The Arts and Crafts in New York 1800–1804,* p. 148, No. 355.

6 Illustrated and described as No. 709 in the Catalogue of the *Girl Scouts Loan Exhibition* and as No. 147 in the Exhibition Catalogue of *New York State Furniture.* See also Waxman, "The Lannuier Brothers, Cabinetmakers," *Antiques,* LXXII (August, 1957), 141–143; illus., p. 143.

7 McClelland, *Duncan Phyfe and the English Regency, 1795 to 1830,* p. 207, Plate 193.

8 Hornor, *Blue Book, Philadelphia Furniture,* Plates 433/434.

9 Illustrated as No. 34, *Baltimore Furniture 1760–1810,* p. 63, and as No. 1439, Edgar C. Miller, Jr., *American Antique Furniture,* p. 757.

10 See No. 78, *Baltimore Furniture 1760–1810,* p. 124; and No. 354 in this book.

11 *Maryland Journal* (Baltimore), October 28, 1791. Prime, II, p. 4.

12 Mr. Perry's collection was dispersed at auction in New York, April 3 and 4, 1936 (Catalogue 4246, American Art Association Anderson Galleries). This table (lot 112) has had its feet and shelf restored.

13 Illustrated as Nos. 31 and 32, *Baltimore Furniture 1760 to 1810,* pp. 60–61.

14 *Ibid.,* No. 78, pp. 124–125.

15 An old shipping label tacked to the frame reads "C. L. Pendleton 787 Westminster St. Providence, from J. A. Williar and Co. 711 Howard St. Baltimore." Both tables are said to have earlier belonged to E. D. Glass, whom the writer is, as yet, unable to identify.

16 Illustrated as Nos. 31 and 32, *Baltimore Furniture 1760 to 1810,* pp. 60–61.

17 *Federal Gazette & Baltimore Daily Advertiser,* February 9, 1803.

18 *Ibid.,* May 9, 1803.

19 Hornor, op. cit., Pl. 432.

20 Illustrated, *Baltimore Furniture 1760–1810,* p. 193.

21 Found in 1927 in Clinton, South Carolina, by Charles Navis, well-known Richmond, Virginia, antiques dealer.

22 *Federal Gazette & Baltimore Daily Advertiser,* August 29, 1815.

23 Illustrated in advertisement of Israel Sack, Inc., *Antiques,* LXXIX (June, 1961), inside front cover.

24 Quoted from an old statement of the early ownership of a sideboard of identical form but with different inlays on the legs. That sideboard is in the collection of George D. Crittenton, Glencoe, Illinois. The statement is pasted on the slider.

25 Illustrated as No. 716 in the Catalogue of the *Girl Scouts Loan Exhibition.*

26 Robert and James Adam, *The Works in Architecture of Robert and James Adam, Esquires,* No. I (London, 1773), p. 3.

# Small Tables
# and Stands

In this section are included several types of stands made for specific purposes, as indicated by their old names—"bason" stand, flower stand, globe stand, urn stand and other small multi-purpose tables usually referred to as stands or candlestands with a round or shaped top on a central pillar, or shaft, and with a tripod base. Those with four straight or slightly splayed legs will be grouped and discussed in the chapter on Work Tables. This separation of small tables into two divisions—stands and work tables—is an arbitrary one; but such a division seems more or less to follow the terminology established by the makers.

In the 1792 Hatfield list of prices for cabinetmakers and carpenters, a "Candlestand" with a diameter of seventeen inches is differentiated from a "Stand," which is described as three feet in diameter. These are also called "pillar and claw" tables in various price books, "claw" referring to a wide variety of legs and terminals. In most cases, "claw" as used at this time does not mean a claw-and-ball or rat's claw type of foot, a fact which is borne out by a variety of "claws" and "standards" for this kind of table illustrated in Plate 29, drawn by Hepplewhite, in the 1793 edition of *The Cabinet-Makers' London Book of Prices*. Such small tables were no doubt used as occasional tables for a candle, a tray, a book, or flowers—"flower stands" are specifically noted in the above price book.

In *The New York Book of Prices* for 1796 (p. 50) under the heading "Extras for A Pillar and Claw Table," the price given for making a "stand from 18 to 22 inches diameter, a solid block, the edge of the top square, with plain claws, as No. 2, in plate" [cabriole leg with snake feet] was £0.13.6 ($1.80). "If made to turn up," the cost was increased 0.2.6 ($.34) and to put on an iron "triangle on a pillar and claw table, or stand" (p. 74) cost five cents. Such an iron plate nailed on the underside of the legs at the bottom of the pillar greatly strengthens a table and prevents the legs breaking out of the dovetail-shaped slots into which they are fitted.

At first glance, many of these tables seem very much alike; but, in fact, they vary tremendously in materials used, shape, ornament, and workmanship. As with other furniture of this period, the finest examples are usually made of mahogany, frequently without a secondary wood. Consequently, one sometimes cannot be sure in exactly which American cabinetmaking center a specific example originated, nor is there always proof that certain examples were made in this country. There is endless variety in the round, oval, square, rectangular, and shaped tops; some are veneered or inlaid; others have molded or reeded edges; still others have strips applied on the edges to form a tray top. Some tops are hinged so as to turn up when not in use; a few are so contrived as to revolve on a "bird cage" (called a "box" in price books) as was normal in earlier tables.

Examination and comparison of the stems is rewarding. The turnings of some are harmonious and show great taste in the relationship of the various members. On others the proportions are awkward, and harmony is lacking.

Perhaps the most important single factor in establishing the quality of the entire composition is the shape of the legs and feet. The way they rise from the floor determines in large part the stance of a stand. They may give a sense of stability (Nos. 372 and 385), or they may seem literally to spring from the floor (Nos. 378 and 379), giving the stand a feeling of lightness and daintiness. The earliest support on stands of the Federal period in terms of form is the cabriole leg ending in a "snake" foot. This design carries over from Chippendale and earlier sources and was used concurrently with the leg ending in what is referred to today as the spade foot (Nos. 375, 378, etc.), called a "therm" in the price books, and with the concaved splay leg (Nos. 385, 386, 387) seen sometimes on finer tables. However, since all three types of legs were still being illustrated as late as 1834 in *The New-York Book of Prices for Manufacturing Cabinet and Chair Work,* it is clear that all continued in use over a long period of time.

In any consideration of the aesthetic quality of tilt-top stands, it is important to look at the stand with the top in both positions. Usually oval tops are more successful as tilt-top stands because, when turned up, this shape seems to harmonize with the base better than others.

Very different from the tripod stands discussed above are those articles of furniture also known as stands for basins, globes, plants, hot-water urns, and kettles. These are special types of three- or four-legged tables. In this day and age when almost every house in the United States has a bathroom, it may be hard to realize the impact of Sheraton's remarks on "Bason Stands" which he describes as a "piece of furniture much in use, and as generally known."[1] In more than two pages of fine print he describes the various types being made in 1803. Several are illustrated in the catalogue which follows.

1 Sheraton, *The Cabinet Dictionary* (1803), pp. 35–36.

# xxiv Counting Room

Small tradesmen and craftsmen often used the first floor of their houses as places of business. Even more frequently merchants devoted one room of their homes to use as an office or counting room.

Reminiscent of trade and the sea in this interior from the Red Lion Inn of Red Lion, Delaware, are a Pennsylvania bookshelf fitted for ledgers, a counting desk (No. 200) formerly owned by a Marblehead sea captain, a pipe box from Nantucket (decorated with a three-masted ship on its front), and a nineteenth-century model of an American naval vessel. As yet, it is impossible to say whether the two mahogany chairs, similar but not identical, were made in Rhode Island or Connecticut (see No. 41). The eagle-inlaid candlestand (No. 376) was probably made in Connecticut, where the remarkable tin-and-wire chandelier with twenty-four branches may once have hung in a tavern or church. A white pottery eagle, possibly from one of the Phoenixville, Pennsylvania, potteries, stands on the bookshelf with a bone or ivory birdcage beside it. On the floor is a New England hooked rug.

**362**

**361**

**361** CORNER BASIN STAND
*1790–1800    Charlestown, Massachusetts    Label of Jacob Forster (working 1786–1838?)*

This must be ranked as one of the most successful of American basin stands. Its form nears perfection in every detail; and, for this observer, no line could be changed nor anything added or taken away to improve it. "A Circular Corner Bason Stand" of this shape with a stretcher of the same sort and "one real and two sham drawers" but without the folding top and differing in other details is illustrated as Fig. 1, Plate 12 of *The London Cabinet-Makers' Book of Prices, and Designs of Cabinet Work* for 1788. Sheraton notes corner "bason-stands, with three legs" have "the two front ones to spring forward, to keep them from tumbling over."

Dimensions: height 34¾; width 23½; depth 16⅜.
Materials: mahogany; drawer lining, white pine.
Accession: 57.566

**362** CORNER BASIN STAND with serpentine
front
*1790–1800   New York or possibly Connecticut*

Although it lacks the "bason and two cupholes"
usually present in basin stands, there is little doubt
that this was made as a basin stand. In *The New-
York Revised Prices for Manufacturing Cabinet and Chair
Work* for 1810, an "extra" for a "Corner Bason
Stand" provides for "inclosing a stand between the
top and bottom rails, with two doors in front, or
one ditto, and a stile on each side, veneered and
cockbeaded, or with reed doors, the whole framing
one foot six inches deep or under, 1-0-0." This is in
addition to the "start price" of 1.14.0. The journeyman cabinetmaker would have received additional payment for fashioning the hollow-cornered
panels of stringing and for inlaying the unusual
vertebrae-shaped designs on the three front legs.
Related inlays are occasionally seen on furniture
attributed to New York, and sometimes cherry was
used there as a primary wood.

"Circular Inclosed Bason Stands" are listed in
both English and American price books and are
occasionally found today, but those with serpentine
façades are rare. Sheraton noted that the boards
at the top are "cut to a quarter round or ogee
shape. The design of these pieces is to prevent the
water from spraying the wall where they stand."[1]
The upper parts of those boards on this example
were at one time broken off and restored.

Dimensions: height 35½; width 23; depth 15½.
Materials: mahogany and cherry with light-colored inlays; door, cherry veneer over white pine; top rein-
   forcement, back paneling, and bottom, tulip.
Accession: 57.926

**363** ENCLOSED BASIN STAND
*1800–1810   New York*

This stand fits almost exactly the description given
in *The New-York Revised Prices for Manufacturing
Cabinet and Chair Work* for 1810 (page 46)—"one
foot four inches square, . . . a folding top, four inches
deep or under, a plain door, and one drawer
scratch beeded, a bason and two cup holes, a liping
on the top." This cost one pound, seventeen shillings, for labor. Here there is an extra sham
drawer and cock beading instead of scratch beading. The outline of these turned legs, without the
customary reeding, and especially the contour of
the foot, are characteristic of the work of Michael
Allison, George Woodruff, and other New Yorkers.

Dimensions: height 36; width 15⅞; depth 16.

Materials: mahogany; bottom of cupboard and basin compartment, and drawer linings, tulip; drawer front and rails, white pine; mahogany veneers and light wood stringing; brass mounts are replacements.
Accession: 57.1054

## 364 BASIN STAND
*1800–1810 Probably Northeastern Massachusetts*

This high-style and genteel piece of furniture may well be unique in American furniture. This interpretation of an almost identical form illustrated in Plate 42 in Sheraton's *Drawing Book* has been fitted with a pediment and modified to stand against a wall instead of in a corner. Of his design Sheraton

**364**

remarked at length in the following manner:

The bason-stand on the left has a rim round the top, and a tambour door to inclose the whole of the upper part, in which is a small cistern. The lower part has a shelf in the middle, on which stands a vessel to receive the dirty water conveyed by a pipe from the bason. These sort are made large, and the bason being brought close to the front, gives plenty of room. The advantage of this kind of bason-stand is, that they may stand in a genteel room without giving offence to the eye, their appearance being somewhat like a cabinet.

Sheraton's design also shows reeded pilasters flanking the tambour shutters, but the maker of this piece added a curved pediment, choosing not to include the finials normally found on furniture with pediments. The use of tambour shutters, the type of inlays, and the presence of only white pine as a secondary wood suggest Massachusetts as its place of origin.

Dimensions: height 60¾; width 30; depth 17½.
Materials: mahogany; light and dark wood patterned stringing; drawer fronts (veneered with mahogany) and lining, white pine; the brasses are old, but replacements.
Accession: 57.637       see Inlay Figs. 7, 45

## 365 BASIN STAND with marble top
*1800–1810 Boston*

Although this stand and similar ones have been called night tables, the writer believes they are properly termed basin stands, which, like "night tables," were commonly used before the advent of modern plumbing. Sheraton referred to a "Night Table, a useful piece of furniture for night occasions," and descriptions of this form in cabinetmakers' price books clearly include a stool or seat to be fitted with a chamber pot or pan.

With its gray marble top, flat tambour shutters, simulated pilasters, large brass side handles, and elliptical arches, this stand has many things in common with a similar stand attributed to John Seymour in the Karolik collection in the Boston Museum of Fine Arts.[2] This one has been linked also to other pieces attributed to the Seymours by a knowledgeable student of their work,[3] and it may well have been produced in their shop. The striped shutters, the simulated pilasters, the banding around the drawer, the contours of the legs, and the use of mahogany for the linings of small drawers are all in accord with practices found in

pieces attributed to the Seymours. But the use of strikingly patterned stringing to attain effects as precise as an architectural drawing seems not quite in character with the over-all output of the Seymours.

Dimensions: height 34¾; width 22; depth 13¼.

Materials: mahogany with light-and-dark-colored inlays; light tambour strips, maple; bottom panel, cherry; drawer bottom and top of frame (under marble), white pine; drawer sides, mahogany; top, marble.

Provenance: Museum Purchase, 1953.

Accession: 53.185.3                                  see Inlay Fig. 59

**366** ROUND TABLE with marble top and tambour shutters

*About 1798   Massachusetts*

For what purpose this unique table was made is unknown to the writer. No counterpart has been found in either cabinetmakers' design or price books. It may have been made as a small serving table, but the mahogany ring fastened to the shelf suggests that a basin and water bottle were intended to stand there and strengthens the possibility that this is a highly individual interpretation of a basin stand. The height corresponds to that of basin stands, but there are no splash boards, and white marble has been substituted for the normal mahogany tops with holes for basin and cup. During this period, cabinetmakers in many areas were using "rope" inlays and white pine as a secondary wood; but the delicate legs and the tambour shutters, both favored by Massachusetts cabinetmakers, suggest this state as the place of origin. Additional evidence, both of place and date, is afforded by a Boston newspaper of December 25, 1798, which is pasted on the back of the shutters.

Dimensions: height 34⅝; width 23⅛; depth 18⅞.

Materials: mahogany; all secondary woods, white pine; top, marble.
Provenance: Reginald Lewis.
Accession: 61.147

## 367 GLOBES AND STANDS
*About 1810   New York City*

In the 1793 and following editions of *The Cabinet-Makers' London Book of Prices, and Designs of Cabinet Work* are shown various "Standards for Tripod Flower-Stands." The concept of those stands and their standards, or supports, is related to the legs of this pair of globe stands. However, the creator of these highly imaginative stands gave a completely new twist to the design. He reversed the curves of the supports, terminating them in inturning reeded rosettes, and finished their outer edges with light-catching reeding. At the juncture of the stands, support, and pedestal, clear differentiation is achieved through the use of ornament. Reeding, channeling, and carved leafage separate and articulate the parts even as they relate the whole.

The old globes—probably then as now, terrestrial and celestial—were apparently replaced about 1851 with a then-modern pair. These bear the printed name of the firm, Merriam and Moore, Troy, New York. This partnership was in effect from January 15, 1851, to February 12, 1852.

Dimensions: height 33½; diam. at top 14.
Materials: mahogany; no secondary woods.
Accession: 54.108.1–2

## 368 URN OR KETTLE STAND
*About 1800   Probably Massachusetts*

This trim, dainty stand for kettle or urn with "a slider for the teapot to stand on"[4] is not only a great rarity, but is also an exquisite example of the cabinetmaker's art. It is reminiscent of several slightly larger tables of which No. 399 is typical. One's first inclination is to suggest Baltimore as its place of origin. However, the following features are most often found in furniture made in Massachusetts: figured-birch panels and chevron stringing,

**368**

ebony spade feet, and the use of maple and white pine as secondary woods.

Dimensions: height 28; width 13⅝; depth 10¼.

Materials: mahogany; figured birch veneers and light and dark wood stringing; rail, maple; blocks, mahogany and white pine.

Accession: 57.781         see Inlay Fig. 41

### 369  KETTLE STAND
*About 1810   American*

This unusual table, though simply made without the usual classic moldings or inlays, has a splayed frame, graduated drawers, and a marble top, which give it a quality of its own. The gray-and-white marble slab had a practical purpose. It was

not susceptible to damage from heat or liquids. Tulip and white pine were used as interior woods in southern New England, New York, and southward. Walnut was more commonly used south of New York.

Dimensions: height 30⅞; width 13; depth 11¼.

Materials: walnut with mahogany drawer fronts; bottom, tulip; back panel, front, rail, legs, walnut; lining, white pine; top, marble.

Accession: 57.639

### 370  PLANT STAND
*About 1810   New York*

Inasmuch as plant or flower stands were not included in price books for American cabinetmakers

**369**

**370**

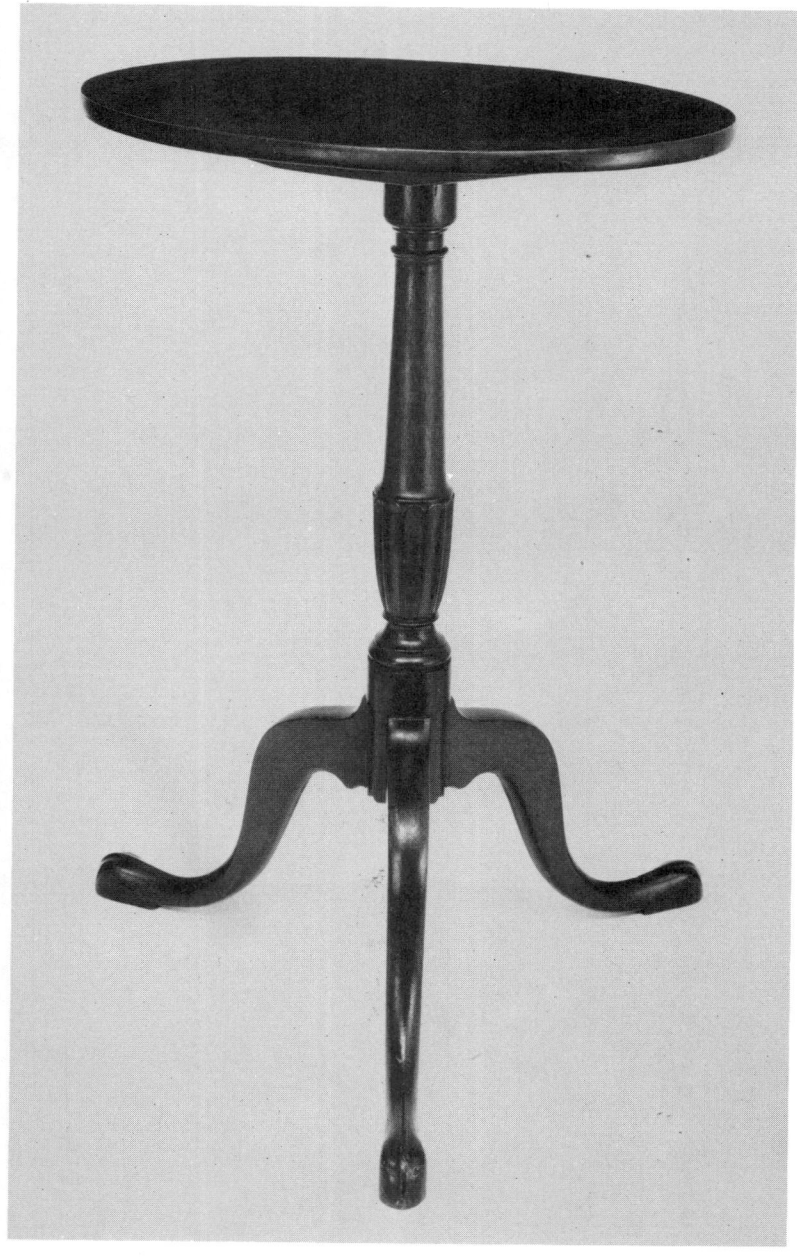

Dimensions: height 30¾; top 9×9.
Materials: mahogany; no secondary woods.
Provenance: Mrs. J. A. Haskell, whose name is burned on the underside of the lower section.
Accession: 57.724

**371** CANDLESTAND with oval tilt top
*About 1800    Newburyport, Massachusetts    Label of Joseph Short (working late eighteenth and early nineteenth centuries)*

Few candlestands show the harmony of proportion seen in this example with tilt top and handsomely turned stem. The distinctive urn on the latter is carved with ten fluted petals, whose upper outlines form a series of scallops. It is one of very few American candlestands whose source can be exactly identified. Of particular note is the sharp ridge which runs from the lower part of the leg over the toe. This is so distinctive that it may be an earmark of the work of Joseph Short of Newburyport, whose label, pasted to the underside of the top, reads:

WARRANTED
CABINET WORK
OF ALL KINDS, MADE AND SOLD BY,
JOSEPH SHORT,
At his Shop, Merrimack Street, between Market
Square and Brown's Wharf,
NEWBURYPORT.
All orders for Work will be gratefully
received and punctually executed.

A labeled card table (No. 294) also points to his abilities as a craftsman working in the neoclassical style. Attributed to his hand are equally successful chairs in the restrained Massachusetts style of Chippendale design.[5]

Dimensions: height 27; top 13½×18½.
Materials: mahogany; no secondary woods.
Accession: 52.62

and the writer has been unable to locate any other such high-style piece of American furniture, this may well be a unique piece in American cabinet-making. However, there can be little doubt as to its origin. Both the treatment of the reeding in the lower leg (ending in a hollow with ring at the top and a ring at the bottom) and the bulb-turned feet are characteristic of details found on New York-made tables and chairs. Although barely visible in the illustration, the reeding around the rim of the lower flowerpot container is repeated on the top of the upper box, providing a horizontal foil for the raked, reeded legs.

**372** CANDLESTAND with square tray top
*About 1795    Probably Rhode Island*

Earlier stands occasionally have tray, or dish, tops; but such tops are not often seen on late eighteenth-century examples. Other features which would indicate an early date are the rather heavy proportions of the baluster-turned stem, legs, and feet found on this stand. However, the fan inlays on the top and the segmental "icicle inlay" on the legs—sometimes seen on Rhode Island and Connecticut furniture—are not only unusual, but indicate a later date than might otherwise have been supposed, probably the end of the eighteenth century. The rather broad, snub-nosed feet on well-defined platforms resemble those found occasionally on tables with histories of Rhode Island ownership. One broken foot has been glued together, and a few pieces of inlay have been replaced in the top.

Dimensions: height 25; width 13⅞; depth 14⅛.

Materials: mahogany top; cherry legs and column; three iron strips with rose-headed nails brace the legs.

Accession: 56.44.1

## 373 CANDLESTAND with round tray, or dish, top
*About 1800    Probably Connecticut*

Although the dish top and the scalloping on its underside suggest an earlier date, the turning of the

**373**

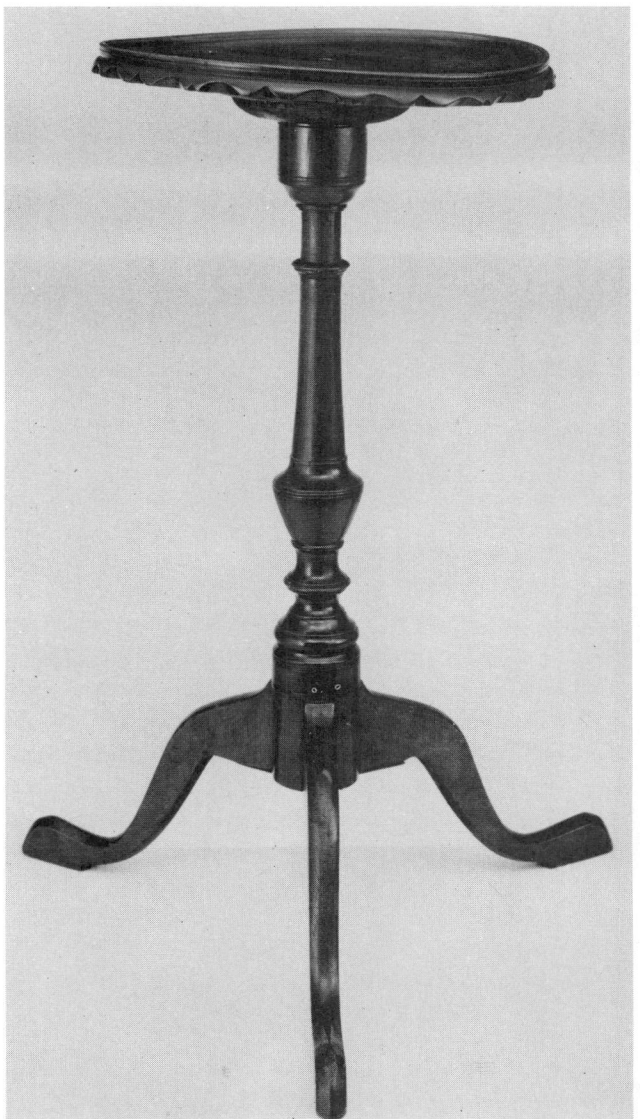

**372**

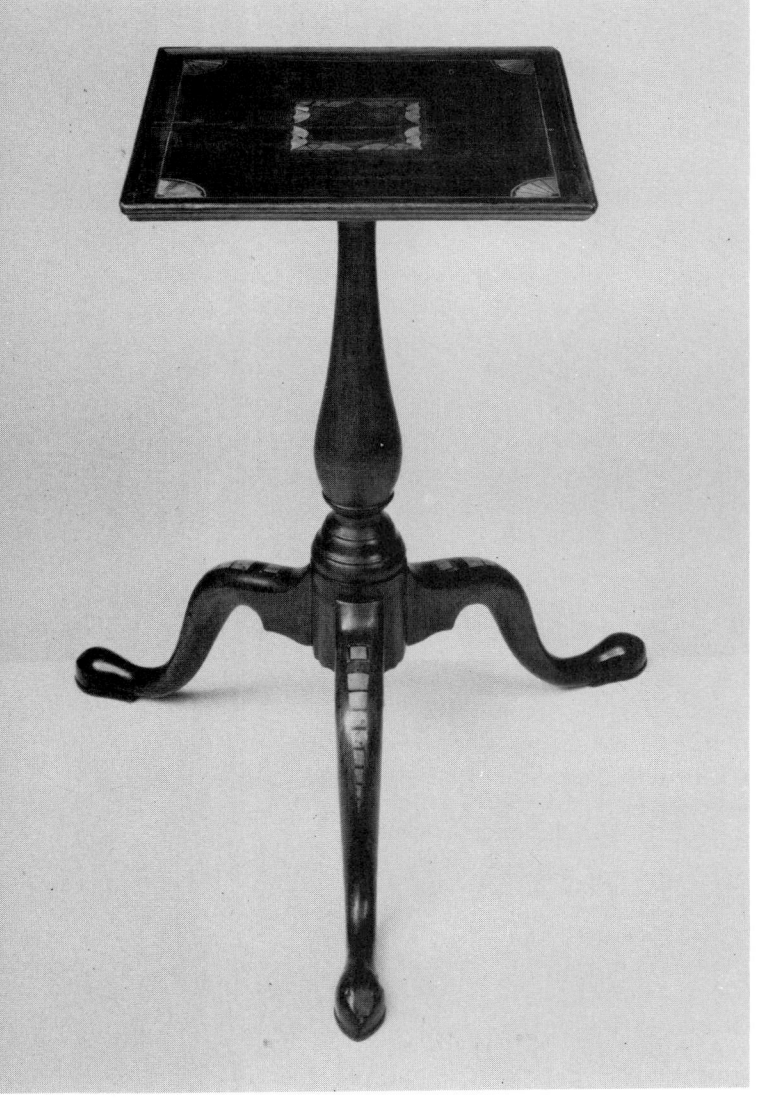

pillar places this stand in the Federal period. The scalloping and the use of cherry point to Connecticut as its place of origin. One would not expect to find the rather awkward sharp angle under the knee in the product of an urban cabinetmaker.

Dimensions: height 27½; diam. of top 13¼; width at base 19.

Materials: cherry.

Accession: 57.1083

## 374 CANDLESTAND with oval tilt top
*About 1800    Probably New York City*

In this sophisticated stand there are many harmonies to reward the inquiring eye. Surely the following relationships are not happenstance. The

incurves of the legs, echoed in the crotch grain of the top, lead naturally to the inlaid eagle, whose wings and tail feathers repeat the composition. The oval shape of the top is neatly emphasized by the triple string of inlay around its edge and is restated in the frame of the eagle. The outline of the shield forming the breast of the eagle is in turn repeated in the urn of the stem. Similar inlaid eagles are found on New York furniture. Each "snake foot" has a sharp rib on its upper surface and rests on a well-defined platform.

Dimensions: height 27¾; top 22 × 15½.
Materials: mahogany; light and dark wood inlays.
Accession: 57.999

**375** CANDLESTAND with oval tilt top
*About 1805 Probably Charleston*

A candlestand "made to turn-up" served as a fire screen or simply as decoration in a room when not in active use. For that reason, the surface of the top was often inlaid, and in this instance it allows one more occasion for the American eagle to proclaim the independence of the newly formed United States. A similar eagle appears on a cellarette (No. 434) with bald cypress as a secondary wood. On that account, this stand is attributed to Charleston. The upper surfaces of the legs, like the top, are edged with light stringing and finished with a wide, dark cuff above the floor line. One

vidual interpretations of American furniture styles with a wealth of ornament, as on this stand. Inlaid in the squarish top of serpentine outline are an eagle (related to the one on No. 378 but here more crudely executed and with two heads and two shields); a Masonic square and compass, as well as a level and plumb line; a quarter moon; a large star; and tulips. Inlaid segmented icicles in each corner serve as pointers to focus attention on the double eagle. A long drawer, which slides either way through the block to which the top is fastened, may have been used for candles. Such drawers are rarely found in candlestands.

The design for this highly unusual leg is to be found in various editions of *The New-York Book of Prices for Manufacturing Cabinet and Chair Work*, still shown as late as 1834. The top is made of two boards glued together and joined by "butter-fly keys." One broken leg has been glued back together.

broken leg has been glued together and strengthened by a screw.

Dimensions: height 29; top 15⅛ × 19¾.
Materials: mahogany; light wood inlays; pivot block, soft maple; no other secondary woods.
Accession: 57.958

**376** CANDLESTAND with square top of serpentine outline and round corners
*About 1800    Connecticut*

Frequently deviating widely from the popular norm of the urban center, Connecticut cabinetmakers produced some of the most highly indi-

**378**

are left plain. As shown, the left drawer is sham, the center one has a straight front, and the right one an angled front. The bold urn shape and large snake feet are typical of New York design. The drawers have tulip sides, and white pine bottoms, two woods often found in conjunction in the New York area. The original brasses serve the double purpose of escutcheons and drawer pulls.

Dimensions: height 28¼; width 26¾; depth 26½.
Materials: mahogany; drawer sides and back, tulip; drawer bottoms, white pine.
Accession: 57.919

**378** CANDLESTAND with oval tilt top
*About 1805    Probably Connecticut*

For stance, harmony of parts, and over-all composition, this stand has few peers. The feet and legs spring. The multiple reeding of the shaft is dazzling. The eagle soars. The whole effect is one of unity

**379**

Dimensions: height 28¼; width 16¾; depth 16½.
Materials: cherry; light wood and mahogany inlays; drawer bottom, white pine; a brass "triangle" is nailed with old sprigs at base of pillar to brace legs.
Accession: 57.1086

**377** CENTER TABLE
*1790–1800    New York*

This table is patterned on the so-called rent table made in England with numerous small drawers in the apron lettered alphabetically for the rent gatherer's convenience. Four sides of the octagonal revolving top are fitted with cock-beaded drawers. Two sides have false drawers for symmetry; two and grace. Similar eagles are found on other furniture thought to have been made in Connecticut, but Springfield, Massachusetts, or Providence, Rhode Island, are also possibilities. In both of these cabinetmaking centers, cherry wood was used, though perhaps less frequently than in Connecticut. For "therms for claws," that is, for the spade feet, the journeyman cabinetmaker received extra pay. One broken leg has been glued back together.

Dimensions: height 28¼; top 20⁷/₁₆×17¼.
Materials: cherry top; mahogany column and pivot block; red bay legs; light-colored wood and mahogany inlays; three iron strips with cut nails brace the legs.
Accession: 57.13

### 379 CANDLESTAND with oval tilt top
*About 1800    Boston or Salem*

Alternating rays of rich birch and mahogany ve-

neers on the top of this tilt-top stand give distinction to a flawless design executed by a cabinetmaker of great skill. Similar contrasting radiates and identical light and dark wood rope inlay are to be found in the famous semi-elliptical commode billed by Thomas Seymour to Mrs. Elizabeth Derby West in 1809[6] and also on a sideboard attributed to William Hook of Salem.[7]

Dimensions: height 29⅛; top 23⅞×15⅜.
Materials: mahogany; figured birch and light and dark wood inlays; block and cleat, birch; original "triangle" missing.
Provenance: Guy W. Walker, Jr.
Accession: 58.135.6                                    see Inlay Fig. 38

### 380 CANDLESTAND with square top and cloverleaf, or elliptic, outline
*About 1805    New England*

This and the following stands (Nos. 381, 382, 383,

**380**

**381**

384) are typical of those found along the Atlantic seaboard. Each has some distinctive feature, and most of them are above average in quality. Here distinctive flutelike paneling on the urn and upper base and the carved teardrop at the top of each knee are both very unusual, perhaps unique.

Dimensions: height 24⅞; top 17¼×17⅝.
Materials: cherry; brass "triangle" with cut nails braces the legs.
Accession: 58.2425

**381** CANDLESTAND with square top of serpentine outline and canted corners
*1810–1825  New England*

This stand is ambitious in terms of turned ornament but lacks unity. It was probably made in a rural area.

Dimensions: height 26; top 16¼×17.
Materials: maple top and column; birch legs and cleat; original "triangle" missing.
Accession: 57.876

**382** CANDLESTAND with square top and canted corners
*1800–1810  American*

Comparison with No. 383 quickly reveals the excellence of this stem. The gentle flow of the line upward from the bulb is more pleasing than the sharp break on the other stand. The tops on both stands are thinner than usual, adding to the appearance of daintiness in each.

Dimensions: height 26; top 11⅜×9.
Materials: mahogany top; cherry legs and column; cleat, soft maple.
Accession: 57.767

**383** CANDLESTAND
*1800–1810  American*

Dimensions: height 27⅞; diam. of top 13.
Materials: mahogany top; cherry legs and column; three strips of iron brace the legs.
Accession: 57.768

**384** CANDLESTAND with square top and canted corners
*1800–1810  Northern New England*

Patterned stringing on the upper surface of the top of this stand gives it distinction and identifies it as

being from northern New England. One broken leg has been glued back together.

Dimensions: height 28; top 16×22.
Materials: mahogany; satinwood inlays and stringing; three iron strips with cut nails brace the legs.
Accession: 57.930

**385** STAND OR OCCASIONAL TABLE with square tilt top and canted corners[8]
*About 1810  New York City*

Features on this and many related tables with New

**383**

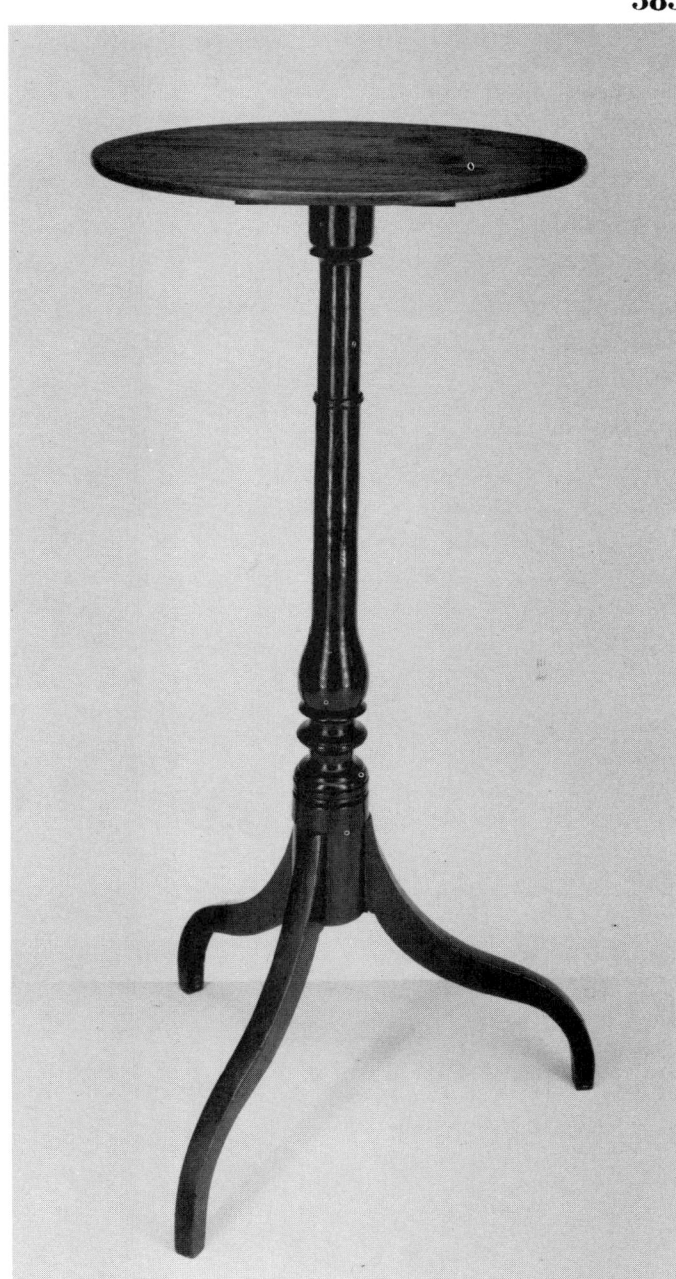

Materials: mahogany; no secondary woods; an iron "triangle," fastened with screws, braces the legs.
Provenance: Louis Guerineau Myers.
Accession: 57.654

**386** OCCASIONAL TABLE with twelve-sided tilt top

*About 1810   New York City*

The richness of the mahogany used in the twelve-sided top with reeded edges, the quality of the carving on the urn and upper surface of the legs, and the harmony of the proportions make this table one of the best of its kind. Here the New York type of carving on the legs is supplemented with reeding between the bottom of the leaf and the brass toe at the end of the leg. Concaved legs, or "claws," of this shape are first illustrated in Sheraton's *The Cabinet-Maker and Upholsterer's Drawing*

**384**

York histories of ownership are a shaped top handsomely veneered and bordered with cross-banding, a pedestal turned in a rather fat urn shape, and a tripod base with tapering concave legs, each carved on the upper surface with a special type of leaf featuring a raised spine, or vein, running the full length and pointed at the end. The legs end in carved paw feet. Such carving has long been associated with the name of Duncan Phyfe. Some of it may have been done in his shop, but probably many New York carvers were prepared to execute it.

Dimensions: height 28½; top 19¾×27¼.

*Book* in a plate dated 1792 showing an octagonal table with carving on its pedestal. The following year such a "claw" appears in *The Cabinet-Makers' London Book of Prices.*

Dimensions: height 28¼; top 24×24.
Materials: mahogany; no secondary woods; an iron "triangle," fastened with screws, braces the legs.
Accession: 57.728

### 387 OCCASIONAL TABLE with double-elliptic tilt top[9]
*About 1810 New York City*

In comparison with Nos. 385 and 386, this stand may seem simple. The edge of the double-elliptic, or clover-leaf, top (a shape favored in New York City) is unornamented and the urn is uncarved; but the neat reeding of the ends and upper edges of the claws and the clean precise lines of the turned details give a feeling of crispness not often seen in such furniture.

Dimensions: height 30; top 21½×25.
Materials: mahogany; no secondary woods.
Provenance: Louis Guerineau Myers.
Accession: 57.660

### 388 DRINKING STAND
*About 1810 American*

A stand fitted for bottles and glasses, somewhat reminiscent of this stand, is illustrated in the 1793 and later editions of *The Cabinet-Makers' London Book of Prices, and Designs of Cabinet Work* (Plate 22). Described as "a pillar and claw stand... made to turn around" and fitted to hold bottles, it is shown standing in the "hollow" of "A Gentlemen's Social Table" of horseshoe shape. At the top of the pillar is a hole just the right size for a measure or jigger. In the revolving drum are five large spaces for bottles and five smaller ones for glasses. The stand was found a few years ago in Salem, Massachusetts. It may have been made there. But neither the

**385**

**386**

shape of the legs nor the turnings of the pillar is related to Salem or any other identified cabinet-work known to the writer.

Dimensions: height 34⅛; diameter 16⅞.
Materials: mahogany; shaft, birch.
Provenance: Museum Purchase, 1957.
Accession: 57.66

**389** LARGE STAND with tambour shutters
*About 1810   New York City*

Within the drum, enclosed by fixed reeding and a reeded shutter which slides back about a quarter of the circumference, are two circular revolving shelves very much like the lower ones of No.390. As surmised for that one, this also may have been used in much the same way as an English dumb-waiter. If so, the sliding shutters would have made it possible to conceal unsightly and soiled glasses and dishes after use. Although it has no lock, it may also have been used as a cellerette.

**388**

**387**

Reeding was an extremely popular decorative device on New York cabinetwork. The finest tripod tables made there about 1810 were often fitted with leaf-carved and reeded legs and brass pawlike caps for the castors like those on this four-footed base. For the sake of harmony, this urn is reeded instead of being carved in the normal New York manner (see No.386).

Dimensions: height 34⅝; diameter of top 24⅞.
Materials: mahogany; shelves and struts, white pine; a vertical brace on tambour, cherry.
Provenance: Mrs. T. B. O'Toole.
Accession: 55.133.5

**390** THREE-TIERED STAND, dumb-waiter
*About 1810   American*

For some reason, dumb-waiters appear not to have been a popular furniture form in the United States and are not listed in the cabinetmakers' price books. This and No.388 are the only pieces of American furniture known to the writer which seem to approach the character of English dumb-waiters. Both are quite different from the common

English form, which normally has three or more trays of diminishing size fitted to an upright pillar supported on a tripod base. Sheraton noted in his *Cabinet Dictionary* (p. 203):

> Dumb-waiter, amongst cabinet-makers, is a useful piece of furniture, to serve in some respects the place of a waiter, whence it is so named. There are different kinds of these waiters, but they are all made of mahogany, and are intended for the use of the dining parlour, on which to place glasses of wine, and plates, both clean and such as have been used.

The shelves on this table will revolve, but not independently of each other, as on English examples.

Dimensions: height 31; diameter of top 19.
Materials: bottom shelf and leg, cherry; column, soft maple; framing and braces, tulip and maple; light

wood stringing is in this case boxwood.
Provenance: Museum Purchase, 1958.
Accession: 58.57.2

## 391 MUSIC STAND

*1800–1810    American, possibly New York*

As a young man, Thomas Jefferson wrote, "Music is the favorite passion of my soul, and fortune has cast my lot in a country where it is in a state of barbarism."[10] He said that until the time of the Revolution he played three hours or more a day and after 1785 often carried a violin with him on his travels. His own music stand, on display at Monticello, is somewhat earlier than this one or No. 392, but is designed on the same principle, with adjustable rack at the top.[11] On this one, the top is hinged to a block fastened to the pillar. Its inclination may be adjusted by means of brass ratchets.

A firm attribution of origin for this unique stand is impossible, but urns and claw feet of similar shape are found on New York candlestands, and four claw feet instead of the more normal three were the standard for work tables made in that city.

Dimensions: height 57; top 18×23.
Materials: all mahogany.
Accession: 57.633

## 392 MUSIC OR READING STAND
*1800–1810 New York (?)*

Music in the United States may still have been in "a state of barbarism" twenty-five years after Jefferson's remarks, but it is well known that it was popular; and sophisticated pieces of furniture like this one were apparently in some demand. Wages for their making are given in most price books from 1795 onward. The price listed in *The New-York Book of Prices for Cabinet and Chair Work* of 1802 for making "A Music or Reading Stand" is £1.6.6. It is described thus: "The top one foot eight inches long; one foot two inches wide; an astragal on the edge of ditto; a fram'd bottom fix'd to the pillar; a hollow on the edge of the framing; and a horse to support the top; three claws."

"Candle boards," which are assumed by the writer to be the supports for candlesticks seen here, cost one shilling two pence each. The frame for the rack is fixed to the vertical wooden stem by brass rings with steel springs like those used on firescreens. The very dark mahogany, the shape of the claws (legs), and the resemblance of the shaft to those on tripod stands made in New York lead the writer to

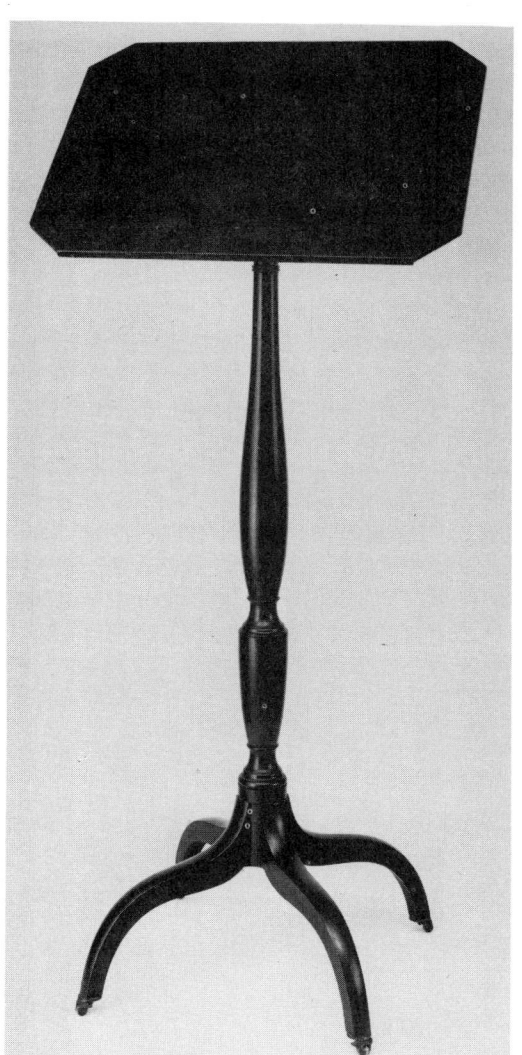

**391**

**392**

395

think this may have been made there also.

Dimensions: height 54½; top 20 × 19⅞ × 8.

Materials: all mahogany.

Accession: 57.752

## FOOTNOTES

1 Sheraton, *The Cabinet Dictionary*, p. 36.

2 Hipkiss, op. cit., pp. 73 and 132.

3 Stoneman, op. cit., pp. 286–287.

4 From the description of a "Square Urn Stand" in *The Journeymen Cabinet and Chair Makers' New-York Book of Prices*, 1796 and later editions.

5 Two such chairs are illustrated in Joseph Downs' *American Furniture* (58 and 153).

6 Original bill is in Boston Museum of Fine Arts. This table and that bill are illustrated (Pls. 159 and 202) in Stoneman. A mate to this table in the Boston Museum of Fine Arts is illustrated in Randall's *American Furniture*, No. 108.

7 Fiske Kimball, "Salem Furniture Makers. III. William Hook," *Antiques*, XXV (April, 1934), 144.

8 Illustrated as No. 783, Catalogue of the *Girl Scouts Loan Exhibition*, 1929.

9 *Ibid.*, No. 792.

10 Marie Kimball, "The Furnishing of Monticello," *Antiques*, XII (November, 1927), 380–385.

11 *Ibid.*, p. 381.

# Work Tables

What we know today as four-legged stands, candlestands, or occasional tables were all standard varieties of "work tables" in the Federal period. A work table as listed in the cabinetmakers' price books of the 1790's might be square, oval, or one with canted corners. In Philadelphia, the price books list the standard size for a "square work table" as "two feet long, one foot four inches wide." For an "oval work table" the size was smaller—"one foot six inches long, the rail two inches deep and veneer'd with a square edge to the top." Although turned legs with or without reeding could be had before 1800, an additional charge was made for them. The basic price included "plain marlbro" or "plain tapered legs" without drawer, shelf, or bag. About 1815, pedestal-base tables began to be advertised and soon thereafter they appeared in the price books.

Sometimes a work table included a writing drawer, a chessboard, a looking glass, or even a fire screen; and it is important to observe that what we know as a sewing table was one variant of such work tables. In 1803, in *The Cabinet Dictionary*, Sheraton described a "pouch" table as a "Table with a Bag, used by the Ladies to work at, in which bag they deposit their fancy needlework." Clearly this is what we know today as a sewing table, but the term "pouch table" was apparently little used in the United States, and it was not used in American price books. Instead, as an extra to the standard work table, one could have the top hinged "with a lock and a loose bottom prepared for a silk bag."

Other extras or options of the 1790's included: the corners of the top rounded; the top cut oval or serpentine; one or more drawers; a "plain shelf sweep'd and fix'd with stretcher plates"; a rim on each side of shelf; "the legs sprung at the bottom one way" (see No. 420).

The quoted labor cost for making work tables in New York and Philadelphia in 1795 ranged from a little more than a dollar for a square table to about two dollars and fifty cents for a table with astragal ends. But it must be remembered that these rates (quoted in the price books) were for work tables of the simplest sort (although of mahogany), without ornament, drawers, or silk bag, all of which might easily increase the journeyman's wages by three or four times. Multiplying the labor cost by a factor of three (or a little more) for material, shop overhead, and profit, one arrives at ten to twenty-five dollars as the selling price of work tables in the 1790's. According to the rates of the revised book of prices of 1811 for New York, wages had doubled by that time over those cited above; and the selling prices would then have been even more. In today's money, a work table would have cost from $100 to $250 and upwards, figures reached by using the factor of ten commonly employed by historians to convert the early nineteenth-century dollar to today's currency.

The commonest surviving work tables from New England are canted corner and square, with either tapered or round legs engaged at the corners to form a half-round (Nos. 405 and 412) or three-quarter-round break. These forms were also made in New York, where the canted corner was also popular, though not as common as the astragal-end form. In Philadelphia, astragal-end and oval tables seem to have been most often chosen. Oval and square tables were preferred in Baltimore. Massachusetts cabinetmakers, as in card tables and other forms, relied heavily upon patterned stringing and contrasting veneers of figured birch or satinwood for ornament. New Yorkers seem to have preferred rich, dark, figured mahogany, sometimes with light stringing for ornamental effect. Both mahogany and satinwood were used as primary woods in Philadelphia work tables. On those of satinwood, rosewood banding and ebony or other dark wood stringing are common. Light wood stringing for panels and drawer outlines is often found on both Philadelphia and Baltimore tables of mahogany.

Work tables were probably most used in bedrooms, parlors, and sitting rooms and are listed there in probate inventories. "The little table...with work" figures prominently in Margaret Quincy's revealing and intimate account of "preparations" for company.

> Mama and I were ready dressed, so descended to the parlour, opened windows, dropped blinds, placed the little table in the middle of the room with work, books, &, &, and seating ourselves on the sopha, Mama held some work, and I read aloud 'Red Gauntlet'. Our preparations were but just concluded, when the gentlemen drove up.[1]

1 M.A. De Wolfe Howe (ed.), *The Articulate Sisters* (Cambridge: Harvard University Press, 1946), p.66.

# XXV

# Sheraton Room

*More than a hundred years before women were given the right to vote in the United States, their interests were recognized, and furniture was designed to encourage their activities. Especially made for feminine use are the Massachusetts work table (No. 404), the desk and bookcase (No. 220), and the small easy chair (No. 133), shown in this view of the Sheraton Room. The wall clock (No. 156), signed on the dial by Simon Willard (Roxbury, Massachusetts), was as great a luxury in a world short of timepieces as were the creamware pottery, Sheffield plate oil lamp, and carved and gilt wall sconces from England.*

**393** SQUARE WORK TABLE

*About 1805   Massachusetts*

Highly ornamental and useful four-legged tables such as this one, with veneered drawer front and scalloped shelf below, show many of the earmarks of Boston and North Shore cabinetwork and often have Massachusetts histories of ownership. Characteristic features of this table and many other tables made in that area are the following: this particular shape of leg, reeded within turned rings; the highly individual vase turning at the top of the leg; figured birch panels; and "triangle inlay."

Dimensions: height 27⅞; width 16¾; depth 16½.

Materials: mahogany; mahogany and figured birch veneers and light wood stringing; secondary woods, white pine.

Accession: 57.922        see Inlay Figs. 25, 54

**394** SQUARE WORK TABLE

*1803–1810   New York City   Printed label of Charles-Honoré Lannuier (working 1803–1819)*

For four-square and clean uncluttered lines, this well-made table of satinwood is outstanding. Its blond color is unusual and exciting. The form is one seldom found in American furniture. As might be expected of the work of an émigré cabinetmaker who learned his craft in France in the late eighteenth century, it shows the influence of Louis XVI furniture design. The relationships of the delicate and precise straight-tapered legs, columnar supports, intervening blocks, and turnings are in the French fashion, rather than the English idiom which prevailed in New York in the early nineteenth century. Rosewood bandings and ebony string panels with hollow corners relate and frame the drawers, top, and shelf. Pasted on the underside of the frame is one of Lannuier's printed labels. This type is believed to have been superseded by his engraved label (see No. 342) about 1810.

Dimensions: height 31; width 17½; depth 12½.
Materials: satinwood with rosewood bandings; secondary woods, principally tulip, some cherry.
Accession: 53.67

## 395 SQUARE WORK TABLE with hollow front
### *1800–1810   New York*

The coved front on this table is indeed a rare treatment of the standard work-table form. However, a suggestion for it appears in the 1796 edition of *The Journeymen Cabinet and Chair Makers' New-York Book of Prices* (p. 62), where an extra for a "Canted Corner Work Table" includes not only a hollow front

but hollow ends as well. It reads, "Sweeping the front and end rails faint hollow, extra from strait, 0-5-6." The contours of the turned feet resemble those on much New York mahogany furniture and suggest that city as the place of origin. The old brass knobs, each with a die-stamped lion's head, are replacements.

Dimensions: height 32; width 19; depth 15.
Materials: curly maple; drawer bottoms and sides, tulip; front, maple veneered with curly maple.
Accession: 57.688

## 396 SQUARE WORK TABLE
### *About 1815   Rhode Island*

Few small pieces of furniture display such a wealth of inlaid detail as this "one of a kind" table. Quarter fans at the corners and a string-outlined, contrasting

**395**

**396**

ellipse (in the center) are inlaid in the top, whose four edges are highlighted with a band of alternating black-and-white diagonals. The outer surfaces of the tapered legs are also ornamented with unique inlays. There are what appear to be obelisks or candles in black holders at the top, and diving fish half-way down each leg.

Originally the table was owned by Ruth Gorham Holmes, the great-grandmother of Mrs. Henry Francis du Pont. Ruth Gorham married Dr. Jabez Holmes of Bristol, Rhode Island, in 1815.[1] The possibility that the table was made by an imaginative cabinetmaker in or near Bristol is suggested by the bold scale of the inlays. Rural rather than urban cabinetmakers tended to work in this fashion. The drawer appears to have been made as a secret drawer because the rail is so scooped out as to permit it to be opened without benefit of a knob. The old pull, stamped with an eagle's head, is probably an addition.

Dimensions: height 27¾; width 17½; depth 17¼.
Materials: cherry; light wood and mahogany inlay; corner blocks and drawer lining, basswood.
Provenance: Originally made for Ruth Gorham Holmes; Mrs. Henry Francis du Pont.
Accession: 57.1000

**397**

## 397 SQUARE WORK TABLE
*About 1790   Southern*

Not only are there more inlays on this small table than usual, but their character is ambitious and striking. On no other piece of furniture has the writer been able to find exact counterparts of the inset ovals with leaves (in the center of the top and flanking the drawer), the winged device on the center of the drawer, or the dependent flaring bell-flowers on the legs. The diamonds in the patterned stringing on the skirt and top are larger than was customary. Inlays of related character occur on cabinetwork found in North and South Carolina, and the presence of hard pine as a secondary wood also points to a southern origin.

Dimensions: height 28¼; width 24; depth 17¾.
Materials: mahogany with light wood inlays; lower front rail, drawer bottoms, hard pine; upper front rail, drawer sides, and frame blocks, white pine.
Accession: 57.1003

## 398 SQUARE WORK TABLE with serpentine sides
*About 1805   Connecticut or Rhode Island*

This table and another slightly less elaborate in ornamental detail are almost a pair. Both have the same serpentine-shaped top and frame, with one real and three sham drawers. Although the two tables seem to be from the same shop, certain details appear on this table that are not included on the other: stringing on the legs, a patterned string panel at the top of each leg, and inlaid fans in the corners of the top. Not only do other details of inlay relate the two tables closely, but the original brasses on both are identical and seem oversized for the height of the drawer. Similar black-and-white dart and dot-dash inlays are found on both Connecticut and Providence, Rhode Island, furniture. Cherry was also used in both places as a primary wood. As the measurements show, these tables are about four inches shorter than most small tables.

Dimensions: height 24⅞; width 21¾; depth 21¹/₁₆.
Materials: cherry; light and dark wood stringing; rails, drawer sides and bottoms, white pine.
Accession: 57.807

## 399 OVAL WORK TABLE
*About 1800   Newport or New York*

The notion that "small tables with perfectly oval tops..., if of American make are of Baltimore

origin"[2] is now accepted as erroneous. Oval work tables are listed in most American price books. In that for New York, 1796, the description (p. 60) reads, "One foot six inches long, the rail two inches deep, and veneer'd, square edge to the top, plain [marlboro] legs, £0-18-0." The fact that this price for the making is more than twice as much as the eight shillings listed in the same book for a square work table "Two feet long, one foot four inches wide" may account for the great rarity of oval tables of this kind. The top of this trim table is thicker and the overhang greater than usually seen on Baltimore tables. Birch is seldom found in Baltimore furniture but is found in that of Newport and New York, where white pine and tulip were also used as secondary woods. Excellent dark-figured mahogany veneers like those on the skirt of this table were also used by cabinetmakers in both cities.

Dimensions: height 28⅝; width 24¼; depth 18.
Materials: mahogany and mahogany veneers with light wood inlay; rail, birch; drawer front, white pine; drawer lining, tulip.
Accession: 57.780

### 400 OVAL WORK TABLE
*About 1802  Springfield, Massachusetts  Attributed to William Lloyd (working about 1802–1845)*

This cherry table, found near Poughkeepsie, was at first thought to have been made in that area, but an identical example owned by the Connecticut Valley Historical Society[3] (Springfield, Massachusetts) proves otherwise. That one, inscribed "William Lloyde, cabinetmaker of Springfield January 1802," identifies this piece as the work of a versatile craftsman by whom many labeled or inscribed examples are known. Inlaid hearts, fans, shaded icicles, and dotted band (around the skirt), though rather naive and slightly out of scale, lend great charm to this simple version of a sophisticated form. Some of Lloyd's furniture is of mahogany, the best

the frame, break the oval outline with a play of light and shade. The wide overhang of the top, the rather broad band of chevron inlay on the skirt, the crispness of the ring turnings, and the outset blocks suggest that the maker was one with a rather independent sense of design, probably working in a rural area—perhaps Connecticut.

Dimensions: height 27¾; width 20¼; depth 16½.
Materials: cherry; holly and mahogany inlays; no secondary woods.
Accession: 57.527

### 402  OVAL WORK TABLE
*About 1810  Philadelphia (?)*

This shapely table has many niceties of detail: the edge of the oval top is neatly rounded, the conforming oval framing is veneered with crotch mahog-

**401**

of it comparatively close to the high-style work of urban centers; but most of it, like that of his fellow townsman, Peletiah Bliss, is of cherry and is almost indistinguishable from the work of Hartford cabinetmakers and others who worked elsewhere in Connecticut.

Dimensions: height 27; width 24¼; depth 18¼.
Materials: cherry; rails, white pine.
Provenance: Museum Purchase, 1955.
Accession: 55.103.9                    see Inlay Fig. 105

### 401  OVAL WORK TABLE
*About 1810  Connecticut (?)*

The identification of this table must depend on its design alone, inasmuch as it has no secondary woods in it and the wild cherry of which it is made was a prevailing favorite both in the North and in the South. The legs are turned in unusual and pleasing contours. Their upper blocks, outset from

and Thomas Seymour. Severely rectangular lines and the use of solid brackets are common to many pieces associated with their names, as are rich bandings and lavish use of figured birch of contrasting and graded color effect. The mahogany legs are finished on three sides with figured mahogany veneers, and no effort has been spared to enrich this highly individual interpretation of what seems to have been a popular form.

As early as 1795, a "Canted Corner Work Table" was a standard item in the Philadelphia cabinet-making trade;[4] and a year later the entry for the same article in the New York book of prices was described as "One foot eight inches long, by sixteen inches wide, the rails veneer'd, plain taper legs." "Hinging the top with a lock, and a loose bottom prepared for a silk bag..." were options available. In this example, the top is hinged but the bag is fixed.

any finished at the bottom with a cock bead, and the legs project from the frame to form pilasters on the apron. Features of the legs similar in character to the work table (No. 423) signed by John Sailor of Philadelphia are multiple turned rings below a square, the smoothing of the top of the reeds below a hollow, and the thinness of the turned foot below the fat lower bulb.

Dimensions: height 28⅝; width 25¼; depth 18.
Materials: mahogany; rails, white pine.
Accession: 57.1019

**403** SQUARE WORK TABLE with canted
     corners
*About 1800   Boston   Possibly by John and/or Thomas
    Seymour*

One of the most beautiful American work or sewing tables, this may well come from the shop of John

and sides of the frame. These decorative elements and small drawers with mahogany (occasionally walnut) sides recur again and again on furniture attributed to the Seymours. The name "John Parker, Jr." stamped in ink on the underside of the top of this table is tantalizing. John Parker, who moved to Boston from Brookline before his marriage in 1779, was listed in the first Boston directory of 1789 as a merchant at 20 Long Wharf. A. Forbes and J. W. Green's pamphlet, *The Rich Men of Massachusetts* (Boston, 1851), states that John Parker "died a few years since, leaving one of the largest estates ever accumulated in New England." His son, John, Jr., was taken into partnership in 1806 and married Anna Sargent in 1809. In the probate inventory taken at John, Jr.'s death in 1844, his real estate was valued at $209,930 and his personal estate at $503,238. The total, $713,168! No inventory is known of his house in Colonnade Row, but that for the house on the Parker family farm in Roxbury included a mahogany "work table" in the dining room. Unfortunately, at present no link can be established between that table and this one, but it seems safe to say that he owned this table.

Dimensions: height 29¾; width 20¼; depth 15½.

Materials: mahogany with figured-birch veneers, rosewood bandings, and light wood inlays; drawer sides, walnut; inner structure, white pine; workbag, yellow-and-white-striped satin, embroidered in blue silk, late eighteenth century.

Accession: 57.915

**405** SQUARE WORK TABLE with canted corners

*1805–1815  Salem, Massachusetts*

Tops with what appear to be identical knurled or coarsely beaded edges are distinctive attributes of two pieces of furniture with a history of having been made by William Hook of Salem. But, as noted earlier (see No. 308), three tables with legs of the profile on this table have long been believed to be the work of Nehemiah Adams, also of Salem. However, it is now clear that identical turnings and similar decorative features may be found on the work of different cabinetmaking shops and that attributions based on stylistic features of a general nature are not firm.

This table with fine, figured-birch veneers and contrasting banding is indeed delicate and attractive, but it lacks the definition and integration of parts found in some other tables. The horizontal emphasis of the dark mahogany cross-banding which borders the lower edge but does not frame

Dimensions: height 28; width 18½; depth 13¾.

Materials: mahogany; mahogany, rosewood, figured birch, and ebony veneers; fixed trays in either end, white pine; bag, green silk taffeta.

Accession: 57.686

**404** SQUARE WORK TABLE with canted corners

*1800–1810  Boston    Possibly by John and/or Thomas Seymour*

This sewing table, among the finest of the New England group, has features of Seymour workmanship: the shape of the turned and reeded legs, almost exactly like those of No. 412 (with the exception of a single ogee turning at the tops of the legs), the border on the top of shaded lunettes, and the veneered panels of figured birch on the drawers

the skirt, and the tapered legs. The rectangular elements of the form are further emphasized by patterned stringing. Here the frame has been deepened to admit two drawers, the upper one with several small compartments—perhaps for ink bottle, pounce pot,[5] pincushion, and other accessories for a lady's amusement; the lower one, without a bottom, supports a silk workbag in which to stow sewing in progress. Of special note is the rather broad cross-banded edging on the top, finished on the outer edge with a veneered thumbnail molding.

the drawer, bag slide, or frame as in No. 404 and No. 412 and the square plinth above the plain drum in the upper part of each leg tend to emphasize the appearance of a box on stilts.

Dimensions: height 29; width 20¾; depth 16.

Materials: mahogany with figured-birch veneers; drawer frame and bottom, mahogany; front rail, a soft maple; rear rail, white pine; workbag, salmon-and-white-striped silk, brocaded with sprays of flowers and anchors, French, Louis XVI period.

Accession: 56.502        see Inlay Fig. 19

**406** SQUARE WORK TABLE with canted
      corners
*About 1800   Boston*

Handsome rectilinear patterns have been achieved in this work table through the use of contrasting cross-banding to outline the top, the drawer fronts,

Dimensions: height 30; width 20½; depth 15½.
Materials: mahogany with bird's-eye and figured-maple
and darker mahogany veneers; patterned stringing of
light and dark woods; white pine braces; bag, green
silk trimmed with green-and-pink fringe, about 1800.
Accession: 57.1068

**407** SQUARE WORK TABLE with canted
corners and writing compartment
*1813–1823  Saint John, New Brunswick    Label of
Thomas Nisbet*

There were many trade connections between the
thirteen original Colonies and Canada. Loyalists,
especially New Englanders, found a haven in the
English provinces to the north, notably Nova
Scotia. Many objects which they took with them
have been found in Canada. However, it is extremely difficult to differentiate between furniture
made within the present boundaries of the United
States and Canadian furniture made in the English
tradition. And, except for the surviving label of this
charming bird's-eye-maple sewing table with its
upper compartment fitted for writing, it surely
would be regarded as one made in the United
States. In *The London Cabinet Makers' Union Book of
Prices* (p. 223, 1824 edition), the unusual stretchers
on this table are described as: "Four elliptic hollow-
sided rails one-quarter and one-sixteenth inch
thick, framed into the legs, glued up in three thicknesses, not exceeding one inch and quarter deep
[wide]."

Thomas Nisbet arrived in Saint John in 1813 and
set up shop on Prince William Street. Ten years
later he moved his place of business to a new stand
in the same street, which he called his Cabinet and
Upholsterer Warehouse.[6] Today, Canadian-made
furniture of English inspiration, as well as that of
French derivation, is admired and appreciated.

Dimensions: height 30; width 20½; depth 16.
Materials: Bird's-eye maple; mahogany veneers; drawer
fronts, birch veneered with bird's-eye maple; drawer
sides and bottoms, white pine; bag, light-blue silk,
about 1800.
Accession: 57.534

**408** SQUARE WORK TABLE with canted
corners
*1810–1820  New York*

If one could spend but a day in the cabinetmaking
establishment of Duncan Phyfe as it was in 1810,
one could write with assurance on the dominant

forces which seem to have shaped New York furniture design in the early years of the nineteenth
century. Today we can only conjecture that Phyfe
prized two things above all others—fine mahogany
and fine craftsmanship. Considering the many
"hands" employed in his large shop as apprentices
or journeymen, many New York cabinetmakers
and carvers must have been influenced by his
standards and ideas. Of the highest quality, this
work table is worthy of Phyfe's shop; but, unfortunately, evidence is lacking on which to make a
firm attribution.

The New-York Book of Prices for Cabinet and Chair Work of 1817 (pp.53–55), under the heading for a "Canted Corner Work Table," includes wage schedules for most of the features.

| | | | |
|---|--|--|--|
| One foot ten inches long, one foot three inches wide, framing four inches deep or under, veneered; four plain legs, solid top, square edge to ditto, the cants on the frame veneered, and mitred on the corners; frame and top polished | 1 | 2 | 0 |
| Each inch more in length or width | 0 | 0 | 5 |
| Ditto when made with drawers | 0 | 0 | 8 |
| Ditto in depth of framing, to six inches | 0 | 0 | 10 |
| Ditto above six inches | 0 | 1 | 6 |
| Each outside drawer, slipped and veneered | 0 | 4 | 8 |
| When the corners are made to form small breaks, extra from start, each cant | 0 | 0 | 4 |
| A plain shelf shaped to the top, upper side polished, fixed with stretcher plates, square edge | 0 | 3 | 0 |
| Lower rails, extra from stretcher plates, each | 0 | 0 | 9 |
| In closing with reeds, ten inches deep or under | 1 | 1 | 0 |
| Each inch more in length or width when inclosed with reeds | 0 | 1 | 3 |
| Ditto in depth of reeds | 1 | 1 | 10 |
| Making the corners project to form small breaks, when inclosed with reeds, each cant | 0 | 1 | 0 |
| When framed through the bottom extra | 0 | 0 | 6 |
| A tambour door with a lock, a partition to cover ditto, extra | 0 | 4 | 9 |
| A pillar and four claws, as in plate No. 2, figure 1, extra from start | 0 | 14 | 0 |

Although the start price for labor for a canted-corner work table was 1.2.0 compared to the 1.18.0

for an astragal-end work table, there are so many extras on this example that it must have been one of the most expensive to produce. Superlative figured mahogany, paneling the canted corners, carving the legs, and fitting the fret with brass casters to match the carving would have added to the total cost of labor to bring it to five pounds or more (about $13 and at least two weeks' work). The selling price was probably forty or fifty dollars, that is to say, four or five hundred dollars in today's money.

Dimensions: height 30¼; width 24; depth 14⅛.

Materials: mahogany; secondary woods, tulip, except bottom case, which is white pine.

Provenance: Gift of Charles K. Davis.

Accession: G 57.129

### 409 SQUARE WORK TABLE
with canted corners

*About 1815   New York City   With label of Duncan Phyfe, "33 & 35, Partition-Street," his address from 1811 to 1816*

A drawer furnished with a baize-covered adjustable reading and writing flap and a compartment with sliding tray and storage space make this unique table adaptable to several uses. Its form may have been influenced by the illustrations of a canted-corner "sarcophogus wine cooler" and "sarcophogus knife case" illustrated in the 1805 *Supplement to the Cabinet-Makers' London Book of Prices.* The white marble top is serviceable and adds a touch of the monumental to the design. Although the novel shape of the upper section approximates that of a canted-corner work table with a wooden enclosure shaped like the more normal silk bag for sewing work, clues to the actual production of the form are offered in the 1817 edition of the *New-York Book of Prices for Manufacturing Cabinet and Chair-Work.* Under the heading a "Square Work Table" (pages 50–51) is listed:

> A plain tapered case to stand be-
> tween the legs of table, . . . a door
> in one end hinged to the back and
> locked; screwed to the shelf and
> blocked to the frame at the top;
> the front polished; all solid        1   6   6
> Canting the corners, when made as
> in preamble                                          0   0   6

The upper section of this table was constructed by fitting such a canted-corner tapered case (with a door in the front instead of the end) to a canted-corner work table with a drawer. It in turn was mounted on four pillars and an "octagon block"

with four claws (page 32, pillar-and-claw pembroke table), and the edges of the octagon block swept with "elliptic hollows" (Table 16, p. 126). Although brass trim is more common on the work of such cabinetmakers as Charles-Honoré Lannuier working in the French tradition, its use was common enough in the New York cabinetmaking trade for the price of "fixing on brass mouldings" to be included in the New York price book of 1810 and regularly thereafter. The 1802, 1807, and 1808 editions of *The London Chair-Makers' and Carvers' Book of Prices for Workmanship,* from which so many of Phyfe's designs are taken, include the price for carving "twisted flutes with fillets."

Dimensions: height 30⅞; width 22⅛; depth 15¾.

Materials: mahogany; drawer sides, mahogany; tray bottom, tulip; top medial brace, white pine; marble top and brass moldings.

Accession: 57.725

### 410 SQUARE WORK TABLE with writing drawer

*1800–1810   Massachusetts (?)*

Of excellent workmanship and materials, this table suffers, in the eyes of the writer, because of the lack of harmony of certain decorative elements. The severity of the fretwork band of stringing around the skirt and the straight lines of the legs are incompatible with the voluptuous ring turnings on engaged colonnettes. The top drawer contains a plush-covered flap, a pen tray, and five small compartments. The combination of mahogany, walnut, bird's-eye maple, birch, and white pine is found on some Massachusetts furniture, although walnut is not often used.

Dimensions: height 29¼; width 22; depth 18.

Materials: mahogany with light and dark wood stringing; drawer sides, walnut, bottoms, white pine; front, mahogany veneered with bird's-eye maple; front rails, birch.

Accession: 57.935

## 411 SQUARE WORK TABLE
### *About 1805 Salem, Massachusetts*

A rectangular top with circular projections at each corner was a shape favored by Thomas Sheraton and common to much furniture made in Massachusetts in the early 1800's. Also favored by Massachusetts cabinetmakers are the turned ribs (astragals and coves) on the upper part of the leg. On many Salem tables, variants of the elongated bulb foot seen here are found on examples attributed to Nehemiah Adams or William Hook[7] (see Nos. 308 and 311). However, the single ring at the upper part of this foot is very different from the multiple rings seen on examples attributed to Adams and Hook, just as the exquisite swelling of the leg and the ending of the reeds in an overhanging cove (at top) also differ from examples attributed to them. Though we cannot ascribe this table to a specific artisan, surely he worked in Massachusetts; and he must have had the eye of an artist to have achieved the harmony of contour and echoing motifs of reeding, ribbing, and shading. There is no indication that a sewing bag was ever fitted to the sliding frame, which pulls out on the right.

Dimensions: height 28¾; width 15; depth 19½.

Materials: mahogany with satinwood banding; lining, white pine.

Accession: 57.704

## 412 SERPENTINE WORK TABLE with ovolo corners and writing drawer
### *1800–1810 Boston Possibly John and/or Thomas Seymour*

For over-all beauty, harmony of elements, unity of form, rich materials, and fine craftsmanship, this work table has few rivals. Like No. 404, this table with serpentine top and ovolo corners is related to the Seymour school in the superb turnings of the legs and the rich veneers on all four sides of its serpentine frame—in this instance, of bird's-eye maple instead of satinwood or figured birch. The fluted corners are repeated on several sideboards and chests of drawers attributed to the Seymours' shop. Inside the upper mahogany-lined drawer is a reading-and-writing board covered with green baize, which may be raised on a ratchet, and to its right are covered boxes and a mahogany pen tray. The sewing bag pulls out from the right side.

There is great refinement of finish in every detail: the figures in the branch mahogany veneers converge from the four quarters at the center of the top; rosewood borders outlined with holly (or boxwood) frame each maple panel; the dovetails (seven-eighths inches long) at the drawer sides are extremely delicate.

**411**

Dimensions: height 28¾; width 20⅛; depth 16.
Materials: upper drawer bottom and writing panel, white pine; sides and lower drawer, mahogany; bag, green silk trimmed with green-and-white fringe. late eighteenth century.
Accession: 57.961

### 413 SERPENTINE WORK TABLE with ovolo corners
*About 1815    Salem, Massachusetts*

Rather larger than usual and with a full serpentine-curved body breaking out at the corners around richly carved half colonnettes of the upper legs, this is a sumptuous and lush stand.[8] Despite its ample proportions, it is not heavy because of the harmonious grouping of elements. A card table with similarly shaped legs, a canopy of carved acanthus leaves, and sharply projecting ring turnings with two beads on the feet, descended to the granddaughter of the Salem cabinetmaker, Natha-

niel Appleton, Jr.[9] On the basis of that table, the making of several such pieces has been attributed to Appleton and the carving to Samuel Field McIntire.[10] McIntire has a reputation as an outstanding carver, and this is worthy of his reputation; but the basis for such an attribution seems tenuous.

Dimensions: height 29; width 21¼; depth 19⅞.
Materials: mahogany and mahogany veneers; rails and drawer bottom, white pine; drawer back and sides, mahogany; drawer front, mahogany veneer over white pine.
Provenance: Museum Purchase, 1953.
Accession: 53.185.2

### 414 SQUARE WORK TABLE with ovolo corners
*About 1810    Rhode Island (?)*

Curly maple in a rich tiger stripe is used for the legs and body of this table. Veneered panels of

**413**

**414**

bird's-eye maple are fixed to the drawer fronts and sides. The ring-turned, tapered legs with ogee turnings at the top superficially resemble those on furniture made in the Boston and Salem area, but the presence of chestnut drawer linings suggests Rhode Island or contiguous areas of Massachusetts or Connecticut as the place of origin. Brass casters were commonly fitted to many tables in the neoclassical taste. The workbag slides forward on a narrow frame beneath the bottom drawer.

Dimensions: height 27⅞; width 17¾; depth 13¾.

Materials: curly maple; drawer back and sides, chestnut; drawer bottoms, white pine; front, birch veneered with bird's-eye maple; bag, blue silk taffeta with ball fringe, late eighteenth century.

Accession: 57.1069

**415** SQUARE WORK TABLE with ovolo corners

*About 1810   New York*

The practice of continuing the lines of a turned leg upward through the corner of a table, chest of drawers, or other piece of furniture became fairly common about 1800. The effect is that of an engaged column, or colonnette. One quarter of the column, or one half of it (as on the frame shown), or three quarters (as on the workbag) may be freestanding. Usually the curved outline of the top conforms to the surface of the leg, and occasionally the entire circumference of the leg is indicated with an applied boss, as on the top of No. 410. Although this practice is found most often in Massachusetts cabinetwork, it was used elsewhere and is succinctly described in *The New-York Book of Prices for Manufacturing Cabinet and Chair Work* of 1817 (p. 51). Options for "A Square Work Table" included

| | | | |
|---|---|---|---|
| When turned legs, quarter rounding the corners and shaping top to ditto, each leg | 0 | 0 | 6 |
| Ditto when half round, each leg | 0 | 1 | 6 |
| Three quarter ditto ditto | 0 | 2 | 6 |

This ambitious table, with a New York history of ownership, may have been made there. Of tigerstripe and bird's-eye maple and similar in form to No. 414, it nevertheless presents a very different appearance. The figure of the golden-colored woods is more striking. It is larger, and its boldness almost pugnacious. Although the workbag is of solid wood instead of fabric, it is not an unsophisticated table. The accents of ebony inlay around veneered bird's-eye-maple panels and the cast-brass lion-paw feet as a consistent echo of the lion-mask handles are a stroke of genius worthy of a

master cabinetmaker of the stature of Duncan Phyfe.

Dimensions: height 30¾; width 22¼; depth 15¾.

Materials: front, birch veneered with bird's-eye maple; top, mahogany veneered with striped maple; interior side rails, hickory; drawer sides and back, birch; bottom, white pine.

Provenance: James De Lancey Verplanck.

Accession: 52.130

**416** ASTRAGAL-END WORK TABLE with elliptic sweep ends

*1795–1810   New York (?)*

Webster defines astragal as "a small convex molding of rounded surface, generally from half to three quarters of a circle." In architectural usage, an astragal molding usually has a fillet, or "break," on one or both sides. Astragal-end work tables nor-

mally had breaks at both ends of the curve. Although the form was not popular enough in London to be included in cabinetmakers' price books published there, "An Astragal End Work Table" is first listed in *The New-York Revised Prices for Manufacturing Cabinet and Chair Work for 1810*. It appeared in the Philadelphia price book of 1811, but the form was probably being made in both cities by 1805 or earlier. As the examples on the following pages indicate, there is considerable variety in the way these tables are made. Some have shallow frames with or without silk bags; on others the frames are deeper, with drawers or reeding and tambour shutters. Most variants are included in the preamble and options given below from *The New-York Revised Prices for Manufacturing Cabinet and Chair Work* for 1810.

*An Astragal End Work Table*
Two feet long, one foot two inches

wide, the framing three inches deep, and veneered, a bead or band on the lower edge of framing, solid top, square edge, £1 15 0

| | | | |
|---|---|---|---|
| Each inch more in length or width, | 0 | 1 | 0 |
| Ditto in depth of framing, to six inches, | 0 | 1 | 0 |
| Ditto when above six inches, | 0 | 1 | 6 |
| Hinging the top, a lock to ditto, and preparing for a silk bag, | 0 | 4 | 9 |
| Banding the edge of the top, | 0 | 2 | 8 |
| A drawer prepared for forming a silk bag, and shelf under ditto, | 0 | 8 | 6 |
| Each extra plain drawer, | 0 | 3 | 2 |
| Elliptic sweep ends, extra | 0 | 4 | 2 |
| Inclosing with reeds, and reeding the square part of the legs to correspond, ten inches deep or under, | 1 | 4 | 0 |
| Each inch more in depth of reeds, extra | 0 | 1 | 8 |
| A pillar and four claws, (as in plate, No. 1) extra | 0 | 11 | 7 |
| A flap inside, square clamp'd, lip'd for cloth and a horse under ditto, | 0 | 6 | 0 |
| Lining ditto with cloth, | 0 | 0 | 7 |
| A half round lift cut in the end, two inches deep or under, | 0 | 4 | 6 |
| A glass-frame to run down at the back, and supported by a plain spring, | 0 | 5 | 6 |
| A square clamp'd door, and the reeds glewed on to ditto, or veneered, hinged and a lock, | 0 | 4 | 0 |
| Framing inner ends between the legs, or upright checks, when pillar and claw, fourteen inches deep or under, | 0 | 2 | 2 |
| Ditto when above fourteen inches deep, | 0 | 3 | 0 |
| *For drawers inside, see Counting House Book Case.* | | | |
| Each tray, | 0 | 2 | 6 |
| A tambour door, and pratition to cover ditto, | 0 | 3 | 0 |
| Ditto when the table is not inclosed with reeds, | 0 | 8 | 6 |

*For particulars, &c. see Furniture Drawer.*

This handsome and restrained table "with elliptic sweep ends" (flattened arcs instead of the more circular shape of the normal astragal end) originally had a fixed silk bag in the center section. By raising the hinged lid, there was ready access to it and the bowed compartments at either end. On the basis of the lavish use of satinwood and especially on account of the mahogany lozenges inlaid within hollow-cornered satinwood rectangles, the writer guesses that this table was made in New York.

Dimensions: height 29½; width 25¼; depth 17¼.
Materials: mahogany with satinwood and dark wood veneers and stringing; rails and corner blocks, white pine.
Accession: 57.1103

### 417 ASTRAGAL-END WORK TABLE
*1805–1815   Philadelphia*

Reeded legs with a plain or carved bulb at the top and with straight, tapered, or round spade feet are common to much Philadelphia furniture made just after 1800. The legs on this table recall those on the famous set of twelve ebony chairs and two settees made by Ephraim Haines for Stephen Girard in 1807.[11] But since the shape of the legs was determined by turners who worked for many different cabinetmakers, there is no knowing at present who made this fine little table.

The workbag is suspended on an open frame that slides from either end. There are three real drawers, one on each end and one at the front. The flanking drawers at the ends and the one on the back are sham. All are fitted with ivory knobs.

Dimensions: height 28½; width 25; depth 14⅛.
Materials: mahogany and mahogany veneers; drawer sides and bottom, tulip; bag frame and drawer front, white pine; bag, pink-and-tan striped silk, trimmed with lavender-and-yellow ball fringe, about 1800.
Accession: 57.1056

### 418 ASTRAGAL-END WORK TABLE[12]
*1800–1810   New York (?)*

When work tables are made without drawers, their tops are often hinged to give access to the interior, as in this example. Although the turnings on these legs are not usual on documented New York or Philadelphia cabinetwork, the satinwood-veneered frame and the large diamond inlaid in the top are reminiscent of other New York cabinetwork.

Dimensions: height 30⅛; width 23¾; depth 12½.

**417**

**418**

Materials: mahogany; satinwood veneers; bottom of fixed trays and end rails, tulip; lower section covered with green silk taffeta, edged with fringe.
Provenance: Louis Guerineau Myers.
Accession: 57.687

### 419 ASTRAGAL-END WORK TABLE [13]
*1805–1815  Philadelphia*

Cabinetmakers arrived at many solutions for enclosing a space to provide storage for sewing in progress. Wooden compartments are not uncommon. An ingenious solution, listed for "An Astragal End Work Table" in the New York and Philadelphia price books for 1810 and 1811, respectively, is "inclosing with reeds, and reeding the square part of the legs to correspond, ten inches deep or under." It added one pound, four shillings, to the "start" price of thirty-five shillings. There is a deep drawer at the front, and the hinged top opens to deep, half-round compartments on either end, a shallow tray in the center.

Although a table of this form bears the Partition Street label of Duncan Phyfe (used between 1806 and 1817), its character is quite different from this one, which is more closely related to a work table with two drawers instead of one—illustrated as Plate 381 in *The Blue Book of Philadelphia Furniture*. Another factor pointing to Philadelphia as its place of origin is the fact that the reeded legs are similar in outline to those on Philadelphia furniture.

Dimensions: height 29½; width 24½; depth 14½.
Materials: mahogany; drawer front and back, and bottom of upper compartment, white pine.
Accession: 57.622

### 420 ASTRAGAL-END WORK TABLE
*1805–1815  New York City*

With a reeded storage space as in Nos. 419 and 421, this simplified version lacks the large drawer of the former and the cupboard of the latter. A hinged top gives access to the interior where vertical dividers separate the space in the half-round end

**419**

**420**

sections from the center one, which is covered by a shallow removable tray of mahogany. Such unusual forward curving legs were offered as an "extra" for oval work tables in *The New-York Book of Prices for Cabinet and Chair Work* of 1802 (p.26). "When the legs are sprung at the bottom one way" meant an extra cost of two shillings.

Dimensions: height 31½; width 27; depth 14¾.
Materials: mahogany; secondary wood, tulip.
Accession: 63.732

## 421 ASTRAGAL-END WORK TABLE
*1805–1815 New York*

The supports of this sophisticated work table give it a very different over-all appearance from No.419. But to the maker, the chief difference lay in the pillar and four claws. "A pillar and four claws, (as

**421**

in plate, No.1,)" was listed in the 1810 New York revised edition of the book of prices as costing eleven shillings, seven pence, more than the standard plain or turned legs. This "extra" was also included in the Philadelphia edition of 1811. The "claw" (leg) No.1 in the plate is concave, exactly like those on this table; and "Reeding No.1,... with five reeds" (p.69) cost one shilling, six pence, for each claw on work tables. Reeding the edges of the top with three reeds cost four and a half pence a foot with an extra five pence for each "break" where the circular ends meet the long, or straight, edge of the front and back. The sham drawers on both front and back are mounted with beaded-edge brass pulls, and the space behind the reeded door is fitted for three sliding trays. The hinged lid lifts to reveal an adjustable writing flap, a pen tray, and other shallow compartments. Above the deep compartments at the ends are semicircular trays with radial partitions. The casters appear to be the original ones.

Dimensions: height 29⅛; width 25; depth 13¾.
Materials: mahogany; writing flap, tulip; bottom panel, mahogany; case-dividing panel, white pine.
Accession: 57.736

## 422 ANGULAR-END WORK TABLE
(one of a pair)
*1815–1830 New York or New Jersey (?)*

Perhaps to simplify his work, the maker of this pair of tables substituted angular contours for the curved lines of the astragal ends of the preceding tables, and in so doing gave them the appearance of chamfered panniers. An astragal molding around the skirt, cock-beading around the drawers, and the treatment of the lower drawer to give the effect of two are indicative of the work of a trained craftsman. But despite these details, the thick top and the lack of finesse of the turned legs with their awkward, elongated bulbs suggest that this interesting innovation was not made in an urban center, but by a country cabinetmaker with an acute sense of womankind. These tables have strength even in their precarious poise. Gumwood has been found in the inventories of Chester County, Pennsylvania, cabinetmakers, but was more frequently used in New York State and northern New Jersey. The pressed glass knobs held in place with brass bolts appear to be original.

Dimensions: height 27¼; width 24⅝; depth 13.
Materials: curly maple; drawer bottoms, supports, and compartments, red gum.
Accession: 57.1087.1, 2

**423** ASTRAGAL-END WORK TABLE
*1813 Philadelphia Inscribed in pencil "John Sailor Maker Phila July 11, 1813"*

The little-known John Sailor, who wrote his name on the bottom of the oblong removable tray under the hinged lid of this table, repeated the reeded pilasters and bulbous turned and reeded leg occasionally found on Philadelphia-made chests of drawers.[14] The curves of the top are approximated by the nine-sided ends of the frame. Large brass knobs embossed with compotes of fruit provide centers of interest for the ends of the table as well as the drawers.

Dimensions: height 28⅝; width 25½; depth 13.
Materials: mahogany and mahogany veneers; secondary wood, white pine.
Accession: 57.709

**424** ASTRAGAL-END WORK TABLE
*1810–1820 Philadelphia or New York*

Candle slides serve a dual purpose on this table. When pushed in, they provide covers for the end compartments of the table. When extended, they offer a place for a light that does not interfere with the opening of the hinged top. The stamped brass pull on the shallow drawer is ornamented with a lion mask. The key to the origin of the table may lie in the teardrop-shaped feet with ball terminals. At present, the writer cannot document the source of these pretty and unusual turnings; but this work-table form was made in both Philadelphia and New York. In both cities, tulip and white pine were employed as secondary woods, and the reeding of pilasters and the edges of tops was matched by multiple turned rings at the top of each leg.

**424**

**425**

Dimensions: height 29¾; width 25½; depth 14½.
Materials: mahogany; interior woods, tulip except for drawer front of white pine veneered with mahogany.
Accession: 57.931

Materials: mahogany; figured veneers of mahogany and satinwood on tulip, the only secondary wood used.
Accession: 57.1005

### 425 ASTRAGAL-END WORK TABLE
*1810–1820  Philadelphia (?)*

Repetition of a single motif in variant configuration, position, and color may unify the parts of a composition or form. In this work table, many variations of the ellipse are inlaid on the curved ends, drawer fronts, and pilasters. In the three-dimensional contours of the turned bulbs above the feet, ellipses become ellipsoids to stand as unrelated islands, so also do the satinwood and mahogany ellipses on the pilasters. The effect of both is bizarre and detrimental to the over-all unity. The top is hinged to give access to two deep end compartments and a shallow center tray behind the sham front of the top drawer.

Dimensions: height 27¼; width 27⅝; depth 14¹¹/₁₆.

### 426 KIDNEY-SHAPED WORK TABLE
*1805–1810  Philadelphia*

Exquisite, jewel-like, feminine—there are no superlatives adequate to describe the finesse and quality of this creation. No design or price book includes the formula for this lady's divertissement. Starting with the plan of an astragal-end work table, the maker reversed the curved lines of the ends to create drama and to introduce an inviting hollow front. The most exotic materials of the cabinetmaker's art, satinwood, rosewood, and ebony, are here combined in chaste harmonics for richest effect. One, or possibly more, Philadelphia cabinetmakers chose satinwood as the principal wood for several of the finest work tables, of which this one and another in the Garvan collection at Yale University are in the first rank. Both have

bulb feet and details of turning, reeding, and carving very similar to those found on the famous set of ebony furniture made by Ephraim Haines for Stephen Girard in 1806–1807.[15] Although the Garvan sewing table has additional carved bulbs just below the workbag, in both tables there is unending play of geometrical shapes; and, in both, rays and curved elliptical insets of ebony are used to create scalloped half fans at either end of the hinged top. Under it, half-round shallow mahogany trays are fixed in the ends.

Dimensions: height 28⅝; width 26; depth 13½.

Materials: satinwood with mahogany, rosewood, and ebony inlays and bandings; rails, white pine; bottom of bag, tulip covered with gold silk taffeta, edged with fringe.

Accession: 57.914  see Inlay Figs. 83, 120

## 427  KIDNEY-SHAPED WORK TABLE
*1805–1815  Philadelphia*

This excellent work table of satinwood, following the same design as No. 426, conceivably could have

**427**

been made in the same shop as that superb example; but it seems tame in comparison and lacks the drama and finesse of that *tour-de-force*.

Dimensions: height 27½; width 24½; depth 14½.

Materials: satinwood; mahogany and rosewood inlays and bandings; front rail, tray partition, and stretcher panel, white pine; tray bottom, tulip; stretcher rail, mahogany; bag covering, fluted green silk.

Accession: 57.529

## FOOTNOTES

1 The information that Dr. Jabez Holmes and Ruth Gorham were married in Bristol and lived there all their married life was kindly furnished by Clarkson A. Collins, 3rd, Librarian of the Rhode Island Historical Society.
2 *Baltimore Furniture, 1760–1810,* p. 54.
3 Florence Thompson Howe, "The Decline and Fall of William Lloyd," *Antiques,* XVII (February, 1930), 118.
4 *The Journeymen Cabinet and Chair-Makers Philadelphia Book of Prices* (2d ed., 1795), p. 63.
5 Pounce, a powder made from cuttlefish bone or of sandarac, was sprinkled over unsized paper, or spots where erasures had been made to prevent ink from spreading. It was kept in small vessels with perforated covers.
6 "Thomas Nisbet, Cabinet Maker of Saint John," *Art Bulletin of The New Brunswick Museum Art Department,* I (Fall, 1953), 1.
7 Fiske Kimball, "Salem Furniture Makers, III: William Hook," *Antiques,* XXV (April, 1934), 144–146.
8 Illustrated in Fales, *Samuel McIntire, A Bicentennial Symposium, 1757–1957,* Fig. 43.
9 Lockwood, *Colonial Furniture in America,* II, Fig. 780, p. 234.
10 Fiske Kimball, "Salem Furniture Makers: I, Nathaniel Appleton, Jr.," *Antiques,* XXIV (September, 1933), 90–91.
11 Marian S. Carson, "Sheraton's Influence in Philadelphia," *Antiques,* LXIII (April, 1953), 342–345.
12 Illustrated as No. 686 in the Catalogue of the *Girl Scouts Loan Exhibition.*
13 Illustrated as Frontispiece, *American Collector,* VIII (May, 1939).
14 John Sailor is not listed in the Philadelphia directories as a cabinetmaker, nor are other pieces known that can be documented as his work.
15 "Henry Connelly and Ephraim Haines, Philadelphia Furniture Makers," *The Philadelphia Museum Bulletin,* XLVIII (Spring, 1953), 42–43.

# Unusual and Specialized Furniture

No single trait of personality or character in a cabinetmaker, nor any single factor in the way he conducts his business, can be cited as the secret of success or failure of that business. In fact, one student of American furniture suggests that versatility is the keynote of the cabinetmaker's success.[1] Surveys of several cabinetmakers' account books reveal the many-sidedness of their undertaking. One might assume that the making of furniture was the principal occupation in a cabinetmaking shop. And so it was in some. But many cabinetmaking account books show that from twenty-five to fifty per cent of the entries relate to the repairs of furniture or other odd jobs of a service nature.

In some account books, coffins far outnumber other articles made in the shop. Over a thirty-year period, John Bachman of Lancaster, Pennsylvania, made 214 coffins.[2] In the 1780's and 1790's, a conservative estimate of the coffins made by David Evans of Philadelphia would probably number above two thousand.[3] The next most numerous item which he produced was venetian blinds, of which he made several hundred sets during the same period. Whereas the charges for these two items normally ran from one to ten pounds each, the charges for repairs often ranged from only two to five shillings.

However, repairs and odd jobs about the house were probably just as big a nuisance to the housewife of 150 years ago as today, and although the cabinetmaker may have made them to increase his income, pleasing his customers was unquestionably also in his mind. "To fixing sticks for window Curtings and putting them up and other work at his house" cost Gilbert Chase only seven shillings, six pence.[4] The charges were minimal and the returns small, but cabinetmakers set up beds and took them down, hung looking glasses and moved them about when required. "Putting up five bedsteads & hanging looking glasses" brought Job E. Townsend another seven shillings, six pence in 1791. In the same year, David Evans made a "memorandum of work done for Spanish Consul from October 10 to November 1." The charge for various repairs (cutting doors for carpets and fixing brasses) was only eight shillings, four pence; however, in the years which followed, the "Spanish Minister" became a good customer for new furniture.[5] Odd jobs were indeed a way to oblige old customers and often to gain new ones. In fact, some cabinetmakers, such as Karns and Hazlet of New York, advertised, "Old chairs repaired, painted, and made like new."[6]

A verse in a song sung in the Philadelphia Federal Procession of 1788 and attributed to Benjamin Franklin recognizes not only the astuteness of ladies as judges of workmanship but also indirectly the importance of pleasing them if a cabinetmaker was to have their custom:

Ye Cabinetmakers! brave workers in wood
As you work for the ladies, your work must be good.[7]

Unusual objects also fall into the category of pleasing the housewife or householder. The following, made on occasion but seldom repeated, are but a few of the many to be found in cabinetmakers' accounts from 1790 to 1805: "a squash squeezers," "to making a pair of lime squeezers," "to making a worl for a wooling wheel," "two crutches for walking with," "a pounder to pound clothes with," "2 washing tubbs," ironing boards, stocking boards, bread trays, "a carrying tray," a salt box, spinning boxes, "wooden scales," rulers, hanging shelves, cupboards, "a nest of sixteen large drawers," and small chests and cabinets in infinite variety. The latter cannot always be readily identified today. What, for instance, were the four goldsmith's cases made by Jonathan Kettell of Newburyport? On May 2, 1782, he made a "goldsmith's Case" for John Stickney for one pound, seven shillings. On June 2 of the same year, he made another for Joseph Moulton for one pound, four shillings. In June of 1790, he charged Jacob Pirkins two pounds, two shillings for a "large Goldsmith Case," and in November of the same year charged him five shillings for "one ditto to go within the large one." [8] Perhaps these cases were really cabinets and similar to No. 444, used in Winterthur today for the display of small gold and silver objects. In the accounts of Job E. Townsend are references to the making of hen coops, a pen for a cow and calf, a beehive, the building of pig sties, the mending of cellar doors, and on April 9, 1803, a charge of seven shillings, six pence, to John Taylor for "building a pigin house in his garret."

For fellow craftsmen, cabinetmakers also performed many small tasks, and some not so small. "To whitting a saw" for nine pence occurs hundreds of times, occasionally for "Stephen and John Townsend," in the accounts of Job E. Townsend. Sometimes the charge was increased to a shilling and six pence for "whitting and setting a very dull saw." Job Danforth,[9] cabinetmaker of Providence and relative of the pewtering Danforth dynasty of Connecticut, charged William Billings, Providence pewterer, three shillings, six pence in 1789 "for making a sine post and putting up your sine," but more remunerative was "fixing a tower hors vise, Bench and counter to your shop." This cost one pound, four shillings. Although Danforth made no charge for the first "teapot handle," soon he was turning them out two dozen at a time for nine shillings a dozen. When a wheelbarrow broke down (perhaps pewter was too heavy for it), Danforth charged Billings two shillings, three pence "for mending Sam Clarks whele barrow for you," and made what must have been a sturdy "pewter cart" for him at a cost of one pound, four shillings, six pence.

The friendships between craftsmen were often close and, while surprising, it is not unexpected to find in Danforth's books a charge "to boarding, finding wood, and washing for William Billings in the Hospital." Later when his son Ozias entered into partnership with Billings, the father made "a lathe to turn coars and clamps" for them. When they added brass founding to their pewter making, he made flasks for castings (repeatedly repairing them), several "patterns for handirons," "a pattern for a pump," and performed many other miscellaneous services. Such services were a part of the daily routine of the shop along with making "maple beureaus at 3–0–0," "low cases of drors at 2–0–0," "pembroke tables at 1–3–0," "black walnut chairs at 1–10–0," "a cetching table at 1–3–0," or "a cheretree clockcase at 6–0–0."

Cabinetmakers' newspaper advertisements give an excellent idea of the staples offered by a particular firm at a particular time and place. When they were "about to decline business" in 1812, Barrett & Ringold of No. 3 Great York Street, Baltimore, offered to "...dispose of their stock of furniture at cost prices for cash as follows."

| | |
|---|---|
| Pedestal Sideboards | Pillar & Claw tables |
| Elliptic Sideboards | Book Cases |
| Circular bureaus | Knife Cases |
| Eliptic     ,, | Ladies Worktables |
| Strait      ,, | Corner Bason stands |
| Elliptic Dining tables | Square Bason stands |
| Square    ,,    ,, | Candlestands |
| Double Eliptic Card tables | High Post Bedsteads |
| Single    ,,    ,,    ,, | Field  ,,      ,, |
| Pembroke tables | Low   ,,      ,, |
| | Easy Chairs [10] |

Presumably, such furniture was their regular stock in trade.

Gifford and Scotland of New York advertised, "Desk and bookcases, scrutoire do. chest of drawers, wardrobes, dining tables, pembrook do. card do. dressing do. night do. writing do. sofas and chairs both Plain and Inlaid. Also Compting-house desks, travelling do. clock cases, knife do. tambours, looking glass frames, picture frames shaving stands, bason do. spinning jennies, carding engines, with every other article in their way. Also Funeral Work performed." [11]

In the course of obtaining lumber supplies for their own needs, many of the larger cabinetmakers bought extra lumber which they offered for sale to their fellow work-men, and advertisements such as Gifford and Scotland's "Mahogany, in Logs, Planks and Boards and country wood for sale" are common. Very much in the same vein, they sold furniture hardware and brasses, and occasionally hair seating. Typical of a number of cabinetmakers, Charles Watts of New York and Charleston entered into mahogany ventures in which he imported, or bought after importation, logs which he had sawed up into veneers, planks, and material for bedsteads and other objects of furniture. Some of his shipments involved many thousands of feet of mahogany and sometimes $10,000 or $20,000 worth of lumber. [12]

Such analyses as those made by Morrison Heckscher and Anne Castrodale of the accounts of Samuel Ashton and Daniel Trotter, respectively, of Philadelphia have helped enormously to establish the main sources of cabinetmakers' incomes, the variety of services they rendered, and the staples of the cabinetmaking trade. [13] Although Ashton's accounts are far from complete for the twenty-five-year period he was in business (from about 1790 to 1815), an interesting picture emerges. Bureaus, cases of drawers, desks, tables, and coffins were produced regularly. Although occasionally produced, chairs were not a mainstay of his business; chairmaking was often a specialty of a shop and it did not happen to be one of Ashton's. This also was true of sofas and looking glasses. But over the twenty-five-year period, Ashton made a few sets of chairs, two sofas, three looking glasses, and many miscellaneous objects such as two knife boxes, three picture frames, one stool, four trays, four yardsticks, one ruler, one clothes press, and one large wardrobe. In her study, Miss Castrodale has pieced together a remarkable record of Daniel Trotter's activities. Although his account books are lost, she has brought together from miscellaneous sources every scrap of information presently known about this craftsman, including a corpus of bills and papers preserved in the family. She has analyzed these to show the nature of his business, the prices he charged for each article, and the number of each in surviving references. Bedsteads, bureaus, coffins, chairs, stands, and tables were his mainstays with an occasional "furr box," bread tray, ironing board, "walnut bookcase," and several hatters' baskets and bows. His records, like those of other cabinetmakers, include many repairs.

Music seems to have played an increasingly important part in the lives of Americans after about 1800. Eliza Bowne noted when she visited Bethlehem, Pennsylvania, in 1803, "There is scarcely a house in the place without a Piano-forte; the Post Master has an elegant grand Piano."[14] While it may be true that the Pennsylvania Germans were more musical than Americans of English ancestry, there are many newspaper notices in the seaboard cities offering musical instruments imported from Europe and made by émigré instrument makers working here. But the only evidence known to the writer as to the source of cases for the pianos, organs, melodions, and other American-made instruments advertised, is one entry in David Evans' account book dated November 3, 1781: "sold a frame for a spinit for cash 1–10–0." Although it is not known whether these cases were generally made in cabinetmaking shops or by cabinetmakers working in the shops of instrument makers, they conform closely to the prevailing cabinetmaking idiom for each regional center.

An interesting, final note to this brief discussion of unusual and specialized furniture is offered by two entries in the account book of David Evans. On December 31, 1790, he charged four pounds, ten shillings for "making a mace for the Senate of Pennsylvania for the Sergeant at Arms," and on the same day he charged Jonathan Germon eighteen shillings, nine pence, "To making a stick for a mace for the Sergeant at Arms of the United States of America."

1 Goyne, "Furniture Craftsmen in Philadelphia, 1760–1780."
2 In a leaflet, Bachman listed each coffin he made. It still remains in Bachman's account book owned by his descendants.
3 Account Book of David Evans (1796–1812), Historical Society of Pennsylvania. Microfilm copy M-305, DMMC.
4 Entry dated August 4, 1802, in Account Book of Job E. Townsend (1781–1808), Newport Historical Society, Newport, Rhode Island. Microfilm copy M-26, DMMC.
5 Account Book of David Evans (1796–1812).
6 *Weekly Museum*, January 5, 1799. Gottesman, *1777–1799*, p. 122, No. 381.
7 John F. Watson, *Annals of Philadelphia* (Philadelphia: Leary, Stuart Co., 1927), II, 346.
8 Account Book of Jonathan Kettell (1781 to about 1799), The Essex Institute, Salem, Massachusetts.
9 Most of these are from the account book of Job Danforth in the Rhode Island Historical Society. It was kindly brought to my attention by Mrs. Clifford P. Monahon who has done so much to bring to light the work of Providence cabinetmakers.
10 *Federal Gazette & Baltimore Daily Advertiser*, January 15, 1812.
11 *New-York Daily Gazette*, April 29, 1791. Gottesman, *1777–1799*, p. 119, No. 369.
12 From the account book and other papers of Charles Watts; these have been privately owned.
13 Heckscher, "The Organization and Practice of Philadelphia Cabinetmaking Establishments, 1790–1820." Castrodale, "Daniel Trotter, Philadelphia Cabinetmaker."
14 Eliza Southgate Bowne, *A Girl's Life Eighty Years Ago* (New York: Charles Scribner's Sons, 1887), p. 173.

# XXVI

# Billiard Room

*Americans have always enjoyed games of all kinds: games of chance, such as backgammon, cards, and dice; games of amusement and instruction, such as geography and ortho ("designed not only for amusement but instruction in the orthography of the English language"); and games of skill, such as battledore and shuttlecock, quoits, bowls, and billiards. Of all the unusual and specialized furniture made by the American cabinetmaker, none could better illustrate his ingenuity and the heights to which he rose on occasion than this great Maryland-made billiard table.*

*With the exception of the settee (No.268) from Massachusetts and the pair of gilt looking glasses which may be English, the furniture shown here was made in Philadelphia, Baltimore, or the South. The portrait of Mrs.Perez Morton of Philadelphia was painted by Gilbert Stuart.*

## 428 BILLIARD TABLE

*1790–1800   Annapolis   Attributed to John Shaw*

The game of billiards has been played in this country from the seventeenth century until the present time, but no other American-made billiard table dating before 1825 is now known.[1] Owned by the Lloyds of Wye House in Talbot County, Maryland, this one is believed to have stood on the second floor of their conservatory, known as the Orangerie, from the time it was made until it was acquired by Winterthur. It must be ranked not only as a unique survival but as one of the greatest pieces of cabinetwork of the Federal period. In all probability, its original cost and the number of man hours expended on its making exceed that of any other piece of furniture included in this book. Due to the large size and the problems of achieving a level bed that would not warp, a billiard table required special skills of craftsmanship. The bed of this table is ingeniously contrived. Comprised of forty-five hard pine square panels set within stiles and rails of the same, it is supported on a grid of two by three's and three by four's, mortised and tenoned within the frame of three by eight's. Further proof of the abilities of the maker is offered by the superb ornament—the finest of inlays, a wealth of cross-banding of satinwood and rosewood, and the remarkable matched mahogany veneers in each of the large satinwood ovals on the skirt.

A desk and bookcase and a chest with secretary drawer, each bearing the label of John Shaw, and two desks and bookcases with a strong attribution to his shop all have an extraordinary and unique feature—prospect doors with string-outlined cross-

banded arches each with contrasting keystone and imposts.[2] These pieces and others bearing Shaw's label are rich in ornamental cross-banding. The similarity of the arched heads on the cross-banded panels on the legs of the Lloyd family billiard table and the fact that Shaw made at least one of the secretary and bookcases cited above for Edward Lloyd IV[3] lends considerable support to the attribution of this table to John Shaw, master cabinet-maker of Annapolis.

Over the years, many of the veneers became loose or detached. To bring the table back to its original appearance, these have all been carefully reglued by the Winterthur cabinetmaker, Arthur Van Reeth, and facsimiles made of original elements to supply miscellaneous pieces of missing inlay and some of the large urns. The green baize covering and nets for the pockets were meticulously copied from surviving fragments.

Dimensions: height 38½; width 72¾; length 139½.

Materials: mahogany; inlays of various exotic woods including satinwood and rosewood; side and end rails, medial cross rails, tulip; paneled bed, a hard pine; the brass mounts are modern replacements copied from some of the period.

Provenance: Museum Purchase, 1958.

Accession: 58.58

428

## 429 BELLOWS

*1805–1810   Salem   Carving attributed to Samuel McIntire*

Few ornaments produced by the carvers' art more happily fill their allotted space than do the ribbon-

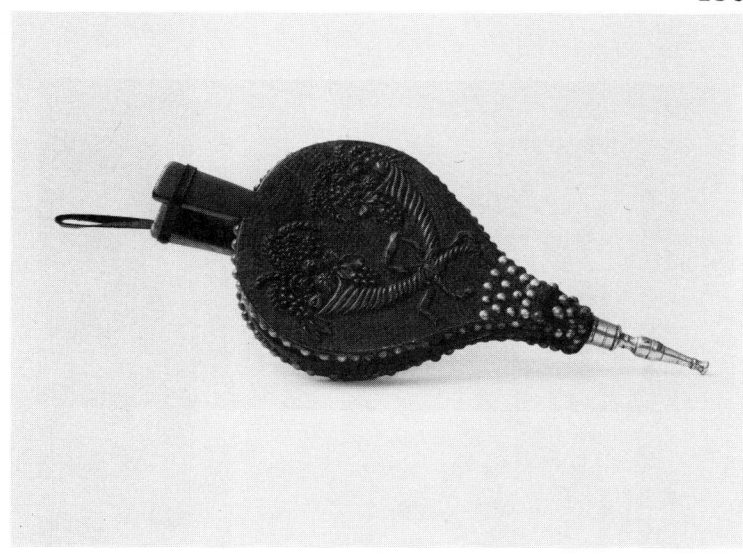

**430**

also working in Salem. Experts have not as yet managed to distinguish the work of these various carvers.

Dimensions: length 21⅞; width 8½.
Materials: front panel, mahogany; valve block, birch; back panel, walnut (American); leather and brass.
Accession: 57.787

## 431 CANTERBURY
*About 1790–1800    Probably Charleston*

In 1815 a writer for Ackerman's *Repository*, Londons' authoritative fashion magazine, commented as follows upon the general interest of women in music at that time: "The music room has not failed to experience the patronage of our fair country-women, who, in the choice of its furniture, have selected forms appropriate to its uses..."[4]

One of the new forms probably introduced in the 1780's was a special rack for music books, variously called a "Canterbury For Music Books"[5] and a "Canterbury Music Case,"[6] probably more often simply a canterbury. The one shown here, unusual for its large size and with a shelf—open at the back—instead of a drawer at the bottom, is the only American example of its kind that is known. With stringing and a veneered panel on all four sides, it is probably earlier than Nos. 432 and 433. Though rarely found today, these types seem to have been the standard forms after about 1815. Holly-outlined edges (latticework sides) and panels of stringing (on the scalloped sides and legs) are features found in the furniture of New York,

**431**

tied cornucopias on this pair of Salem-made bellows. And probably no other American form is more completely carved than this one attributed to either Samuel McIntire or his son. That over-all carving was the elder McIntire's practice is intimated in his charge of $4 to Jacob Sanderson, cabinetmaker of Salem, on "Nov^r 6 [1807] to Carving Bellows top" when on the same bill he charged only seventy-five cents each for "Reeding & Carving legs for a worktable and one dollar each for 'Carving and fluting 18 Chairs.'" The roundness and lushness of the carving suggest that these were carved late in the elder McIntire's career.

Dimensions: length 20; width 9.
Materials: front panel, mahogany; back panel, soft maple; leather and brass
Accession: 57.905

## 430 BELLOWS
*1805–1815    Salem*

Well-carved laurel leaves and berries, occasionally found on the cresting rail of square-back Salem sofas, and plaited baskets of fruit and flowers are a part of the vocabulary of ornament found in carving on furniture and interior woodwork associated with Samuel McIntire's name. But whether the carving on these bellows—a collector's prize—so carefully and closely framed within a notched outline and wreath of laurel is the work of Salem's master carver, his son, Samuel Field McIntire, or still another carver is impossible to determine at this time. After his father's death, the younger McIntire advertised the carving of "bellows tops," and there were other carvers of no mean ability

Philadelphia, Baltimore, and Charleston. But more conclusive for provenance are the ovals of branch mahogany inlaid in frames of mitered satinwood. Several sideboards believed to have been made in Charleston have this unusual decorative element.[7]

Dimensions: height 28; width 26¼; depth 18¼.

Materials: mahogany; mahogany and satinwood veneers and light wood stringing; lower shelf, tulip.

Accession: 57.1066

## 432 CANTERBURY

*About 1823   New York   Label of Michael Allison*

The 1823 label of Michael Allison pasted in the bottom of the drawer proves the New York origin for this canterbury. Despite the small size of this piece, the price of labor cited in the 1817 edition of the New York price book for a "Canterbury Music Case" of the simplest kind (pp. 98–99) is $6.40 compared to $8.80 for making a "Bureau" three feet six inches long. The swept back shape of the ends is similar to the treatment seen in contemporary New York window seats which were them-

selves closely related to chairs, and among the extras offered in the above publication were "sweeping legs above the drawer as [a] chair back leg" and "a scroll on top of legs…"[8]

While most canterburies are divided into "two or three hollow topped partitions" as recommended by Sheraton,[9] this example has one large undivided book rack which is enclosed on all sides by a balustered rail. The small turned legs which terminate in brass casters appear to be an elongated version of the feet found on Allison's table desk (No. 196) which bears the same label.

Dimensions: height 23¼; width 14¼; length 20.

Materials: mahogany; bottom of rack and bottom of drawer, tulip; framing, white pine.

Accession: 54.103

## 433 CANTERBURY

*1815–1825   New York City*

A smaller example than No. 432, this music rack, with its single drawer, slatted partition and sides, and curved upper rails, closely resembles and is apparently based on an illustration in the 1805

*Supplement to the Cabinet-Makers' London Book of Prices* (Pl. 2, Fig. 7). In basic structure, it conforms to the specifications listed in the 1817 New York price book (p. 98) with the exception of having only one interior partition instead of two. Extras listed in that publication include "scalloping partitions serpentine" and a "hand hole." This treatment adds an interesting crown to the central partition. The hand hold and the legs fitted with brass casters readily permit the canterbury, in Sheraton's words, to be "run in under the piano-forte."[10] The shape of the turned legs suggests a New York provenance.

Dimensions: height 20¼; width 16¹/₁₆; depth 12.
Materials: mahogany; lower left glued strip, white pine; rear glued strip, tulip.
Provenance: Museum Purchase, 1959.
Accession: 59.130

## 434 CELLARETTE
*1795–1805   South Carolina   Probably Charleston*

Most American sideboards have cellarette drawers, drawers so partitioned as to separate bottles of wine stored in them, but comparatively few American cellarettes are known. When found, they usually have Maryland or Southern associations, perhaps because the form was a popular one in Ireland and, as suggested by one writer, Maryland about 1800 was "the Ireland of America."[11] A similar piece of furniture with shorter legs and curved coffer-like cover appears repeatedly in the Gillow accounts after 1780 and is invariably termed a "Guard de vin" or "guardivine."

The identification of this fine cellarette on frame with its upper body divided into spaces for twelve bottles and the base fitted with a slider or mixing board would be guesswork, except for the presence of cypress as a secondary wood. On this account a provenance of South Carolina, perhaps Charleston, is suggested. The rather crude drawing of the large and unconventional eagle inlaid in a stained green oval is repeated in reverse in the inlay on No. 375.

Dimensions: height 40⅜; width 19⅞; depth 16.
Materials: mahogany and mahogany veneers with light wood inlays and stringing; slide, bald cypress.
Accession: 57.840                    see Inlay Fig. 118

## 435 WINE COOLER
*About 1790   The South   Charleston (?)*

Lined with copper and fitted with a lock, this piece of furniture was apparently intended to serve both as wine cooler and cellarette for the storage of wine.

Like cellarettes, most surviving American wine coolers or cisterns appear to be of Baltimore or southern origin. This oval one of highly sophisticated workmanship with encircling panels and bands of cross-banding, and coved and convex veneers offers no immediate clues as to provenance. The pointed patera on the cover and the wrap-around "pencilled" bellflowers on the legs are similar in character to many found on Charleston furniture.

Dimensions: height 28; width 26; depth 20½.
Materials: mahogany and mahogany veneers; base rail, mahogany veneer on maple; lid, mahogany veneer on walnut; brass ferules for casters.
Accession: 57.698

## 436 TEA CADDY
### *1790–1810   New York (?)*

Tea caddies, smaller versions of tea chests, are usually fitted with one or more wooden or tin (sometimes silver) canisters in which green, black, or both kinds of tea were stored under lock and key.[12] In the earliest New York and Philadelphia cabinetmakers' books of prices, "a plain veneered caddy 4½ inches long," "a plain double, ditto, 8½ inches long," and "oval" and "octagon" caddies are listed as special items under tea chests for which the basic price was quoted on one "ten inches long, all solid with two divisions inside" and without feet. In the 1796 Philadelphia price book, tea chests and tea caddies are listed separately, though the specifications are the same except that

the standard caddies were then listed as being five and one-half inches long and the double ones nine inches long.

Although caddies are listed in the early American price books, not many seem to have been made, since few survive today. English ones are common by comparison. This example, the only one known emblazoned with the arms of the United States (with red and white stripes on the shield), is doubly rare; and eventually the identity of the original owner whose initials "I McM" are engraved on the silver escutcheon may be discovered. A shell is inlaid on the top, and rope stringing outlines the corners. The lid is lined with orange paper, and the interior is fitted with a tin liner partitioned in the middle. Original green baize covers the bottom of the chest. The inlaid eagle matches one on a secretary in the Metropolitan Museum labeled by Michael Allison, who may have made a specialty of tea caddies (see Nos. 437 and 438).

Dimensions: height 5; width 8⅜; depth 5⅛.
Materials: mahogany and mahogany veneers; top of lid and bottom, tulip; sides of lid and body, white pine.
Provenance: Reginald Lewis.
Accession: 61.1690

## 437 TEA CHEST
### *1795–1805   New York or New Jersey*

Perhaps unique because of its serpentine form, this small chest is enriched with an extraordinary amount of inlay, cross-banding, and stringing. Excellent clues for the indentification of this chest,

**436**

**437**

which was originally lined with tin foil and divided into three parts, are offered by the unusual, hollow-centered, serpentine-scalloped skirt; French feet; and distinctive decorative motifs of rope-outlined, pointed oval and diamonds on the front. All except the rope stringing and patterned banding above the skirt are in accord with features found on larger pieces labeled by Michael Allison of New York and Matthew Egerton of New Brunswick, New Jersey, men whose work is closely allied.[13]

Dimensions: height 7; width 12½; depth 6 13/16.

Materials: mahogany and satinwood veneers; sides of top and chest, white pine; top and bottom, maple, light and dark wood stringing.

Provenance: Reginald Lewis.

Accession: 63.690

## 438 TEA CHEST
*1800–1815    New York or New Jersey*

With straight front but of essentially the same plan and with similar motifs as No. 437, this chest appears to have been made in the same shop, probably that of Michael Allison in New York City or Matthew Egerton of New Brunswick, New Jersey. Two thin white pine partitions from front to back divide the interior into sections for three rectangular canisters.

Dimensions: height 7 3/16; width 11⅛; depth 5¾.

Materials: mahogany; mahogany and satinwood veneers on white pine; light and dark wood stringing; small blocks on bottom, mahogany; ivory or bone escutcheon.

Accession: 64.977

## 439 SMALL CHEST
*1795–1805    Possibly Rhode Island*

A clue to the use and identity of this handsomely inlaid and veneered chest with "a cove top" and ogee bracket feet is offered in *The Edinburgh Book of Prices for Manufacturing Cabinet-Work* (1826).[14] Therein is listed a "Store Tea Chest, One foot six inches long, one foot wide, ten inches deep, lap-dove-tailed or veneered, divided for one large and two small cannisters, with lifting handles on ends." That a tea chest for a store was not thought of as one without ornament is indicated by such extras offered as "veneering the inside of the top, or lining ditto with velvet," and "corner stringing the chest."

White cedar is often found in Rhode Island, Philadelphia, Baltimore, and Southern furniture; but the character of the bellflowers and shape of the feet lead the writer to think this chest may have been made in Rhode Island.

Dimensions: height 11; width 20; depth 12⅛.

Materials: mahogany and satinwood veneers on tulip; blocks and bottom, white cedar.

Accession: 61.950

## 440 CHEST
*1790–1800    Northeastern Massachusetts*

Shaped like a trunk but much too handsome and fragile to be subjected to the rigors of travel, this large box draws attention to a significant and often overlooked change in custom. Clothes and bedding were commonly laid out flat in deep chests with lift-up tops in the seventeenth century. In the

**438**

**439**

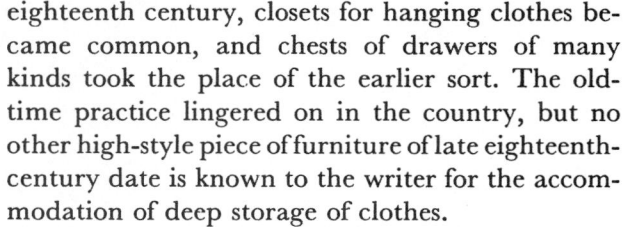

eighteenth century, closets for hanging clothes became common, and chests of drawers of many kinds took the place of the earlier sort. The old-time practice lingered on in the country, but no other high-style piece of furniture of late eighteenth-century date is known to the writer for the accommodation of deep storage of clothes.

Broad strips of flame-figured honey-colored veneers set within bands of mahogany cover all exposed sides of the chest. Microscopic analysis led to the discovery that these and other such veneers are figured birch and not satinwood as has long been supposed.

Dimensions: height 12½; width 26½; depth 13¾.
Materials: figured birch and mahogany veneers with light and dark wood stringing on white pine.
Accession: 54.63.1

## 441 CHEST OR CABINET
*1808–1818   Philadelphia   Label of Henry Connelly*

"This cabinet was presented by Henry Connelly to the Society for Alleviating the Miseries of Public Prisons" is inscribed in pen on the engraved label of Henry Connelly pasted on the inside of the lid of this small chest. Public indignation following the death of three persons from starvation in 1772 at Philadelphia's Market Street Prison lead to the founding, in 1776, of the "Society for the Relief of Distressed Prisoners." Members of the Society, equipped with wheelbarrows, went from door to door gathering food for unfortunate prisoners.[15] Disbanded during the British occupation of Philadelphia, the organization was revived in 1787 as the "Society for Alleviation of the Public Prisons." It undertook to reform the shocking conditions at the Walnut Street Jail.[16] Among its members were four physicians; one of them, Dr. Benjamin Rush, wrote in 1787 that "from the influence of the Prison Society, a reformation has lately taken place in the jail of this city in favor not only of humanity but of virtue in general."[17] Another supporter and later trustee of the Society was Henry Connelly, described as "of the City of Philadelphia aforesaid Cabinet Maker."[18]

The original purpose or intended use of Henry Connelly's "cabinet" is unknown. He apparently donated it for some use of the Society or to be disposed of for the Society's benefit. Perhaps it was used as a silver chest to rest on a sideboard or table. Old green baize to protect a polished surface still remains on the bottom.

Distinguished by cross-banding framing the base and encircling the great inlaid oval of crotch mahogany on the top, original brasses stamped with acorns and oak leaves, ivory escutcheons, and bold outlines of holly around real and sham drawers, this is one of two known pieces of furniture labeled by Connelly.[19]

Dimensions: height 13; width 24⅜; depth 18⅜.
Materials: mahogany and mahogany veneers; light wood stringing and satinwood crossbanding; drawer front, white pine; drawer sides and bottom, tulip; bottom, white pine.
Accession: 57.843

## 442 COAT OR HAT RACK
*1800–1810   Rhode Island (?)*

More useful than beautiful, not many coat racks survive today. Despite their present rarity, they seem to have been quite common at one time.

Moreau de Saint-Méry remarked while in Philadelphia (1798), "When one goes to an American home for dinner, one leaves his cane, hat and topcoat on a coat rack in the front hall." [20] Although at present no identified hat rack or tripod stand with identical base and turned urn is known to the writer, this one was found in Bristol, Rhode Island, and may have been made nearby.

Dimensions: height 82.
Materials: mahogany.
Provenance: Museum Purchase, 1957.
Accession: 57.102

## 443 COAT OR HAT RACK
*1810–1820    New England*

With sixteen long drumstick-like pegs, this rack would accommodate the coats and hats of many visitors or of a large family and consequently required a strong pole to support them. The rather coarse turned rings and the shape of the spritely legs suggest a slightly later date than for No. 443. The presence of birch and maple suggests New England as its source. When an inventory was taken in 1829 of the contents of John Andrews'

**442**

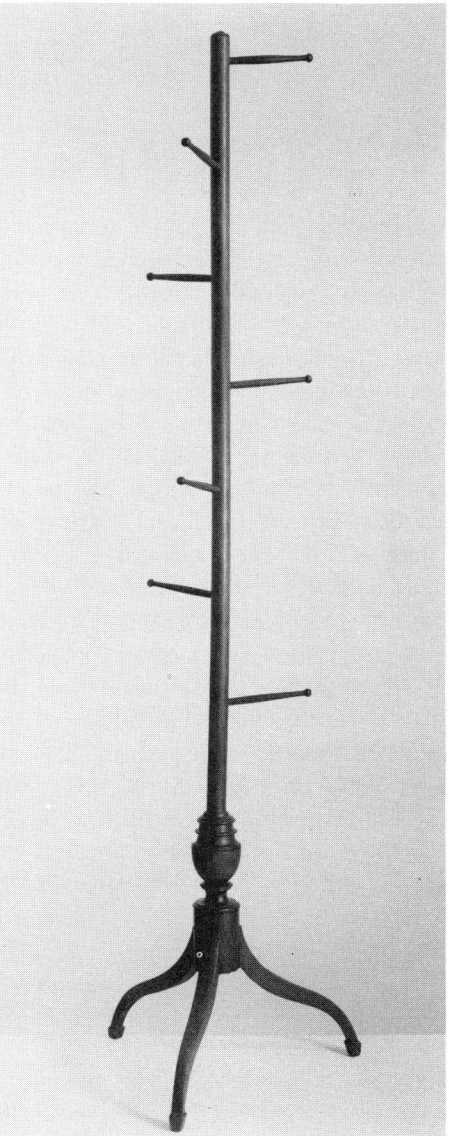

**443**

splendid brick house built in 1818 at 13 Washington Square, Salem, Massachusetts, "1 hat stand" at seventy-five cents and "1 lamp" at four dollars were listed as being in the front hall.

Dimensions: height 60¼.
Materials: legs, birch; pole, soft maple.
Accession: 57.1093

### 444 SMALL CUPBOARD OR CABINET [21]
*1790–1810 Baltimore*

Perhaps originally used for the display of a doll or other precious small objects, this cabinet now serves as a setting for Winterthur's collection of rare gold clasps, necklaces, sleeve links, and other pieces fashioned by American silversmiths. There

444

can be little doubt as to the provenance of this cabinet—a work of art in itself. Similar scalloped aprons occur on chests of drawers with histories of Baltimore ownership. Interlaced arcs forming a pattern of pointed ovals and diamonds are often found on tall clocks with Maryland-made movements; and chaste patterned stringing of this sort, especially squares separated by two thick lines flanking a thin center line, is almost a signature for Baltimore workmanship. The shelves have been tipped at an angle and covered with velvet for the present purpose of the cabinet.

Dimensions: height 31; width 17; depth 8¾.
Materials: mahogany and mahogany veneers with light and dark wood inlays; all other parts, tulip.
Provenance: Mrs. Breckinridge Long.
Accession: 59.110.4          see Inlay Figs. 76, 79, 121

### 445 CORNER CUPBOARD
*1795–1810 Philadelphia (?)*

Corner cupboards in the Colonial and Federal eras were common in American houses all along the Atlantic seaboard. But in Pennsylvania and to the south, many more were made as separate pieces of furniture than in the North, where they were most often built in as a part of the woodwork.

Although this cupboard may have been made in New York, it seems more likely that it was made in Philadelphia. The established retail price in Philadelphia in 1796 for a mahogany "corner cupboard in two parts, about 7 feet high and four feet wide, square head and straight panel or sash doors" was fifteen pounds ($40.00).[22] "Fret [as here] or eye dentil" was offered at one shilling six pence per foot and "Chinese doors (per pair)" were listed at three pounds ($8.00) extra. That doors of this type were called Chinese doors is proven by a drawing so titled in the Account Book of John Janvier.[23]

The white china in the cupboard is French, transfer printed in black with the likenesses of American naval heroes. The large green plates and a platter, all with gilt eagles, are Chinese export porcelain in the Fitzhugh pattern.

Dimensions: height 89½; width 50½; depth 25½.
Materials: mahogany; shelves behind glass doors, birch; all other parts, tulip.
Accession: 57.1017

### 446 BED STEPS
*1795–1810 New York or Philadelphia*

Once thought to have been library steps, there is now little question that these are bed steps. A similar set is illustrated in Thomas Webster's *Encyclopedia* and there described as "necessary to ascend some beds that are made very high and within is frequently placed a night convenience."[24] Beginning in 1810, bed steps are detailed in New York price books as "two feet three inches wide, two feet high, three steps, solid ends, back and front rail framed into four plain legs,... lipped and lined with carpet, fronts of ditto veneered." The treads on Winterthur's steps are outlined with cross-banding and now inset with leather instead of their original carpet. But among the options offered in the price books, two are found on these steps: "hinging the middle step, and a night stool to draw out" and "preparing and hinging the top for a pot cupboard."[25] The handsome veneers of light-colored

**445**

wood (maple?) inset with figured mahogany hollow-cornered panels suggest a New York or Philadelphia provenance.

Dimensions: height 27½; width 22½; depth 27¾.

Materials: mahogany; mahogany and light wood veneers; risers, blocks, and backboards, white pine; drawer lining, tulip; green leather on treads.

Accession: 60.338

### 447 CHAMBER OR BARREL ORGAN
*1790–1810 New York*

Notices offering "finger organs" for sale and inviting the public to hear one recently completed for a church are to be found in many New York newspapers between 1780 and 1810. "Bird Organs" and "Chamber Organs," the latter to be played with fingers or barrels, are also advertised. Their appeal is in part explained by the following 1797 advertisement.

> Organ.—For Sale, a new constructed and very Elegant Organ, with 4 Barrels, and plays 40 tunes; has a harp on the back that plays with or without the organ tunes; also a drum on the side of the organ, to keep time in Dancing. The musick of this piece is very fine and soft, and yet it is sufficient for 24 couples to dance by—There is a great variety of tunes— some of which are excellent Psalm tunes.[26]

When the crank on the front of this attractive chamber organ with handsome case is turned, a barrel with projecting brass pins and staples is made to rotate and a pair of bellows is pumped. The air pressure so created is released to sound notes as the slowly revolving pins open and close the valves of the pipes. By lifting a notch pin on the right end, the position of the barrel can be shifted to play ten different tunes. One extra barrel (with space for another) is stored inside the lower door and on the left end. It can be inserted into the mechanism behind the upper door. Beneath the hinged top are 108 wooden pipes of a different size for each note.

The intersecting husks on the legs, the flutes above them and on the frieze, and the quarter fans in the spandrels—all shaded light wood and inlaid—are typical of the finest New York ornament at the end of the eighteenth century, though inset reeded quarter columns as seen here are not often

found on cabinetwork of that city except on clocks.

Dimensions: height 67; width 33¼; depth 18¼.

Materials: mahogany and mahogany veneers; light and dark wood inlays; backboard of base, white pine; backboard of upper section, tulip; green wool velvet background for gilt pipes.

Accession: 57.869          see Inlay Figs. 109, 116

**447**

## 448 PIANO
*1804–1814   New York City   Inscribed "John Geib & Son Patent New-York"*

Music played an important part in the life of American citizens of the early Republic. "Organs, Harpsichords, Piano Fortes, Violencellos, Violins, German Flutes, Hautboys, Clarinets, Bassoons, French Horns [and] Fifes"[27] were offered for sale in New York by Thomas Dobbs in 1786. In 1792 Dodds and Claus of the same city noted in one of their many advertisements that "the Forte-Piano is become so exceedingly fashionable in Europe that few polite families are without it. This much esteemed instrument forms an agreeable accompaniment for the female voice, takes up but little room, may be moved with ease, and consequently kept in tune with little attention—so that it is on that account supperior to the harpsi-chord."[28] They also stressed that they had taken great pains "to prepare their wood to stand the effect of our Climatte, which imported instruments never do, but are sure to suffer not only from the agitation of the vessel, but the saline qualities of the seas"[29] and that they "make it an invariable rule to repair any instrument that may prove defective in the workmanship."[30]

Many English and European instrument makers came to this country as had Dodds, Claus, and Dobbs. Eminent among them was John Geib who came to New York from London in 1798 where he advertised that his company had produced "from eight to ten Piano Fortes every week, besides Church and Chamber Organs, the number of which are, Piano Fortes grand and small 4910, organized [pianofortes] about 400, church and chamber organs in proportion"[31] and that "for his improvement on Piano-Fortes he has at different times received two Patents from the King of England."[32] These patents were probably in connection with the "Grasshopper action" to provide faster, better, and more sensitive response from the touch on the keys.

In 1929 this piano was said to be "unquestionably the most fully decorated piece of New York furniture known to collectors."[33] The statement

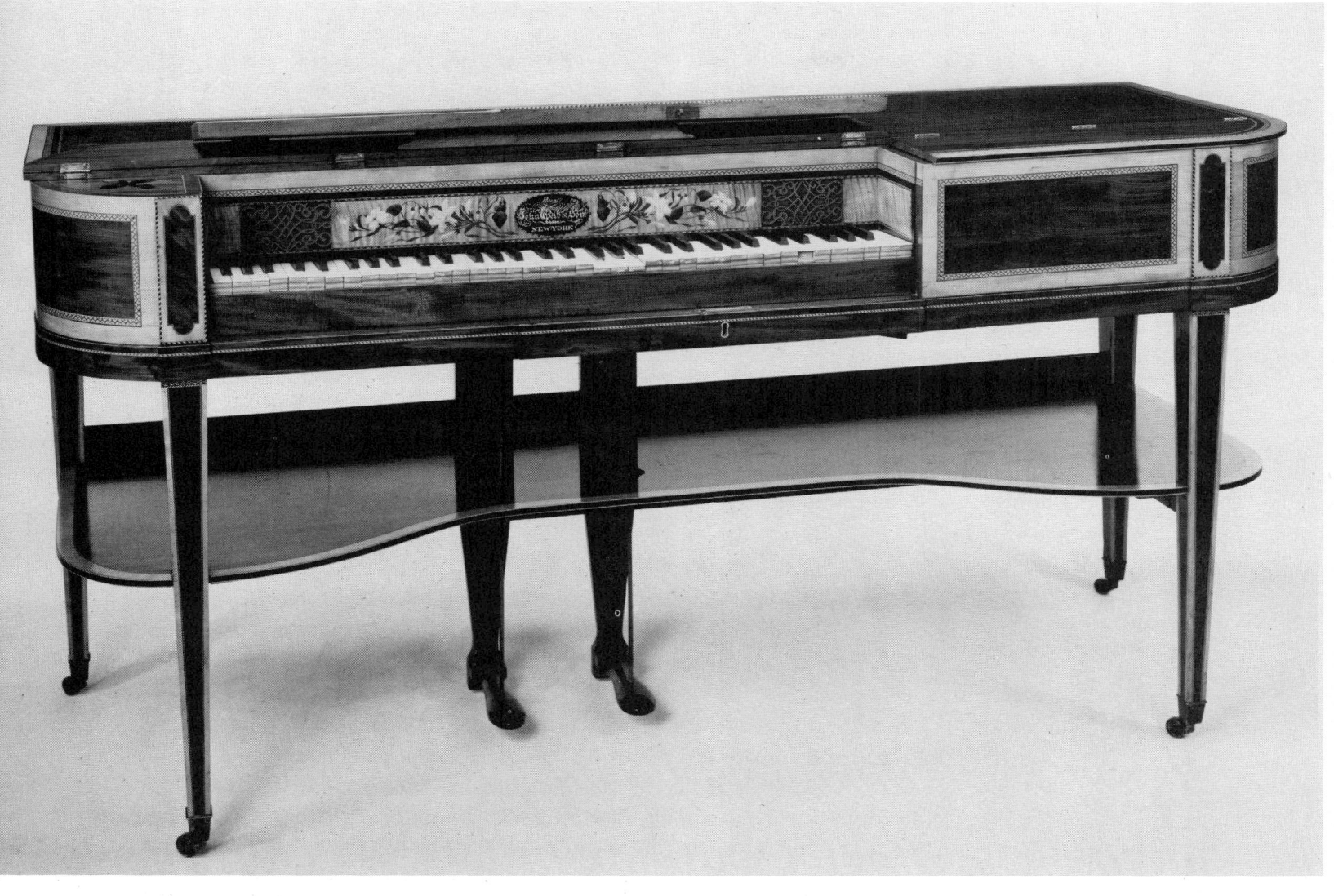

still holds true today for the era of 1804–1814 when John Geib and Son are listed in the New York directories. Whether the cases for Geib's pianos were made by his own workmen or by established cabinetmakers is not known. There is more patterned stringing and the broad bandings and bold displays of satinwood are more striking than usually found on New York cabinetwork, but astragal-ended rectangles of figured mahogany set within light wood panels are occasionally seen on work of that city. The name "John Geib and Son" is handsomely inscribed between trails of flowers exquisitely painted in color on the satinwood name board.

Dimensions: height 35½; width 69½; depth 24⅜.

Materials: mahogany; mahogany and satinwood veneers with colored floral inlays and patterned stringing of light and dark woods; rails under mahogany shelf, cherry; bottom of piano case, white pine; ivory and ebony keys; movement of piano, various woods and metals; pedals and pedal supports are replacements; filigree at right partially restored.

Provenance: Louis Guerineau Myers.

Accession: 57.803        see Inlay Fig. 69

### 449  PIANO STOOL
*1800–1810   American*

In 1810 a New York journeyman cabinetmaker was paid sixteen shillings ($2.14) for making a "Round Music Stool, the top and seat solid plank turned, a plain cross stretcher, and screw framed in, four plain legs to spread at the bottom."[34] Taking into account profit, overhead, and the cost of materials and upholstery, it is estimated that such a stool would have sold for about ten dollars retail. The turnings on this stool are unfamiliar ones, but the presence of tulip proves its American origin.

Dimensions: height 22; diameter 11½.
Materials: mahogany; seat base, tulip; screw post, hickory.
Accession: 57.805

## 450 PIANO

*1815–1819 New York City Inscribed "John Geib Jun! Patent New-York"*

As is to be expected, regional cabinetmaking preferences are usually closely reflected in piano cases. Among New York decorative motifs of the 1805 to 1820 period found on this case are brass inlaid stringing to outline dark mahogany panels, concaved legs carved with pointed leaves and fitted with brass paw feet, and abundant reeding as a foil for flat surfaces. Although used in other American centers, lyres were probably more generally used in New York than elsewhere. The one on the pedal post is backed with a mirror, and the small bronzed ones appear to be of composition work. Two shallow drawers at either end of the front are fitted with stamped brass backplates and ring pulls.

The last entry in the New York directories for John Geib and Son is in 1814. The writer has been unable to discover whether the elder Geib died or retired at that time; but John Geib, Jr., is listed as a pianoforte maker from 1816 to 1819.[35] In the interim, he advertised (1815) that he could be found at Duncan Phyfe's shop.[36] This suggests a close relationship between the two men, and earlier

writers have stated flatly that another piano case similar to this is Phyfe's work.[37] The attribution may be correct, but it is highly circumstantial. There were many able cabinetmakers working in New York at the time capable of making this splendid case and trestle, and one of them may have been working in Geib's own shop.

Dimensions: height 35¾; width 69; depth 25.
Materials: mahogany; mahogany veneers on white pine; brass stringing; patterned stringing of light and dark woods; name board, satinwood; framing and drawer fronts, white pine; drawer bottoms, tulip; drawer sides, mahogany; movement of piano, various woods and metals; keys, ivory and ebony.
Accession: 57.726                  see Inlay Fig. 70

## 451 MUSIC STOOL

*1815–1825 New York*

In 1939 Nancy McClelland in *Duncan Phyfe and the English Regency* (p. 182, Pl. 166) illustrated what appears to be an identical stool and stated that "only four of these dressing table chairs or piano stools are known." They may have been used at dressing tables; but the price of making "Music Stools" with backs, "plain top and stay rail" was included in *The Philadelphia Cabinet and Chair Maker's Union Book of Prices for Manufacturing Cabinet Ware* for 1828 (p. 26). Normally New York chair backs with lyres were framed in a different manner (see No. 73); but those known are of an earlier date than this stool with rather heavy reeded legs, and there seems little doubt from the character of the carving that this one was made in that city. The height of the stool may be raised or lowered by revolving the upholstered seat which is supported on a large screw threaded into the "fifth leg."

Dimensions: height 32½; diameter of seat 18.
Materials: mahogany; framing, white ash; upholstery, light-blue satin with stylized floral-and-leaf medallion in white and yellow, French, Empire style, early nineteenth century.
Accession: 57.727

## 452 WARDROBE OR CLOTHES PRESS

*1800–1815 New York Attributed to Michael Allison*

Sheraton and other English writers seem to have restricted the term wardrobe to those pieces of furniture which have rods, pegs, or hooks for hanging clothes and used the term clothes press for cupboards with sliding shelves behind doors. This is the usage followed in English cabinetmakers' price books. Hepplewhite, however, illustrated four designs with only drawers and sliding shelves (no compartments for hanging clothes) and called them wardrobes. American price books, following Hepplewhite's usage, termed such articles as this one—with four open-front sliding shelves behind cupboard doors—wardrobes.

Identical eagles inlaid against a black background in an oval set within a satinwood diamond and the same highly individual hollow-center serpentine outlined skirt with French feet are found on a number of chests of drawers and secretaries labeled by Michael Allison of New York.[38] Although none of those pieces have the ambitious scrolled pediment with lacy fretwork found on this distinguished wardrobe, further support for its attribution to Allison is given by the inlaid Prince-of-Wales feather on the plinth under the gilt brass eagle. Identical feathers are inlaid in a pembroke table labeled by Allison in the collection of the late Mrs. Andrew Varick Stout.[39]

The idea that the number of stars in the nimbus of the eagle may be equated with the number of states in the Union and hence used as a dating device is meaningless in this case. Three eagles have sixteen stars; one has eighteen.

Dimensions: height 100; width 51; depth 22.
Materials: mahogany and mahogany and satinwood veneers; light and dark wood stringing; sliding trays, drawer bottoms and some framing, tulip; drawer fronts, blocks, white pine.
Provenance: Louis Guerineau Myers.
Accession: 57.921                    see Inlay Figs. 111, 115

**450**

## 453 WARDROBE
*1805–1815 American*

"Wardrobes are far more convenient for keeping apparel than the chests of drawers formerly in general use."[40] So wrote Thomas Webster about 1840. He further noted:

> In wardrobes, the dresses are hung up, or laid on shelves which draw out, and are therefore not injured by folding; also, by unlocking one or two doors, the whole is exposed to view, or secured by locking them, without the trouble of employing the lock and key of each drawer. Wardrobes are made of various forms and sizes.

The Winterthur example is a small version of a winged wardrobe where dresses could be hung up in cupboards on either end, the upper center front section being fitted with sliding shelves where articles of clothing may be laid without folding. Webster's comments may seem old-fashioned to us today, but he felt it necessary to explain:

## 451

> ...the most perfect mode [for hanging dresses]... is to put the dresses on the apparatus [a coat hanger]... consisting of a handle and cross piece, something like a cross-bow. The cross piece goes into the arm holes of the dress, and several may be suspended on the same rod: by this means each dress may be easily seen and got at without disturbing the rest.[41]

The upper drawer in the front is fitted with three baize-covered writing surfaces, all hinged and the center one on a ratchet for adjusting its elevation. The use of white pine and tulip as the sole secondary woods and the rich dark expanses of figured veneers (giving an over-all sober appearance relieved only by thin string panels and a band of patterned stringing at the base and under the pediment) suggest a possible New York provenance. Plinths of satinwood are also occasionally found on furniture made there.

Dimensions: height 85⅝; width 61¾; depth 18¾.
Materials: mahogany and mahogany veneers on white pine; framing and drawer linings, tulip.
Accession: 57.1009

## FOOTNOTES

1 For an interesting study of the popularity of the game, despite legislation against it, and many documented references to it, see Louise C. Belden, "Billiards in America before 1830," *Antiques*, LXXXVII (January, 1965), 99–101.
2 Rosamond Randall Beirne and Eleanor Pinkerton Stewart, "John Shaw, Cabinetmaker," *Antiques*, LXXVIII (December, 1960), 554–558.
3 *Ibid.*, p. 558.
4 R. Ackerman, "Plate 7—Fashionable Furniture: Furniture for a Music Room," *The Repository of Arts, Literature, and Commerce, Manufactures, Fashions, and Politics*, IX (July, 1815), 107.
5 *The Prices of Cabinet Work with Tables and Designs Illustrating the Various Articles of Manufacture* (London, 1797), p. 245.
6 *The New-York Book of Prices for Manufacturing Cabinet and Chair Work* (1817), p. 98.
7 E. Milby Burton, *Charleston Furniture, 1700–1825.* See Figs. 51 and 62.
8 *The New-York Book of Prices for Manufacturing Cabinet and Chair Work* (1817), p. 99.
9 Thomas Sheraton, *The Cabinet Dictionary* (1803), p. 127.
10 *Ibid.*
11 R. L. Raley, "Irish Influences in Baltimore Decorative Arts, 1785–1815," *Antiques*, LXXIX (March, 1961), 276 to 279.

12 For an excellent history of tea chests and caddies, see Margaret Jourdain's article in *The Dictionary of English Furniture* (954, edited by Ralph Edwards), Vol. III, pp. 339 to 342.

13 In the Decorative Arts Photographic Collection at Winterthur are photographs of several chests of drawers and secretaries labeled by these two men which show the same scalloped skirt and French feet and reliance upon diamond motifs for decoration. The relationship, if there is one, between the Egertons (father and son) and Allison is yet to be established. Certain it is that many journeymen trained in New York set up shops in New Jersey. Fenwick Lyell, after working in New York for several years and producing various parts for New York cabinetmakers such as sideboard tops, established a shop in Middletown, New Jersey, a little before or after 1800.

14 A cove top was offered as an extra for tea chests in *The Journeymen Cabinet and Chairmakers Philadelphia Book of Prices* for 1796.

15 J. Thomas Scharf and Thompson Wescott, *History of Philadelphia 1609–1884*. 3 vols. (Philadelphia: L. H. Everts and Company, 1884), Vol. III, p. 1827.

16 *Ibid.*, p. 1829.

17 L. H. Butterfield (ed.), *Letters of Benjamin Rush*. 2 vols. (Princeton, New Jersey: Princeton University Press, 1951), p. 441.

18 W. M. Hornor, Jr., "Henry Connelly, Cabinet and Chairmaker," *International Studio*, XCIII (May, 1929), p. 46.

19 The other piece, a sideboard with quarter-round ends and serpentine front, is in the Philadelphia Museum of Art.

20 Kenneth L. Roberts (ed.), *Moreau de Saint-Méry's American Journey* (Garden City, New York: Doubleday and Company, 1947), p. 269.

21 Illustrated, *Baltimore Furniture, 1760–1810*, p. 142, No. 90, and *Accessions 1960*, The Henry Francis du Pont Winterthur Museum, No. 1, Fig. 8.

22 *The Philadelphia Cabinet and Chair-Makers' Book of Prices* (1794), p. 24.

23 See Leon de Valinger, Jr., "John Janvier, Delaware Cabinetmaker", *Antiques*, XLI (January, 1942), p. 38. John Janvier is now known to have worked in Philadelphia during the period 1794–1796.

24 Webster, *An Encyclopedia of Domestic Economy* (New York: Harper & Brothers, 1845), p. 299.

25 *The New-York Book of Prices for Manufacturing Cabinet and Chair Work* (1834), p. 128.

26 Gottesman, *1777–1799*, p. 377, No. 1256.

27 *Ibid.*, p. 360, No. 1202.

28 *Ibid.*, p. 361, No. 1203.

29 *Ibid.*

30 *Ibid.*

31 *Ibid.*, p. 328, No. 882.

32 *Ibid.*, p. 330, No. 883.

33 Catalogue of the *Girl Scouts Loan Exhibition*, No. 720.

34 *The New-York Revised Prices for Manufacturing Cabinet and Chair Work* (1810), p. 58.

35 In 1820 and 1821, a John Geib is listed in the New York directories without the "Jr." It is assumed that this is the same man and that the inventory of the estate of John Geib, dated October, 1821 (DMMC No. 54.67.95), is that of John Geib, Jr. In that manuscript, the amount of his interest in the firm of P. A. and W. Geib is listed at $6,700.

36 In *Duncan Phyfe and the English Regency, 1795–1830*, Nancy McClelland makes a statement on page 127: "In 1815, there was an advertisement in the New York Evening Post by John Geib, Jr., maker of piano actions, announcing that he could be found at Duncan Phyfe's shop."

37 McClelland, op. cit., p. 94.

38 Photographs of furniture by Allison with these features are included in the files of the Decorative Arts Photographic Collection at Winterthur.

39 For this information and a photograph of the table, the writer is indebted to Benjamin Ginsburg.

40 Webster, op. cit., p. 303.

41 *Ibid.*, p. 304.

# Fancy Furniture

The vogue for furniture with painted and gilt decoration grew out of the styles introduced by Robert Adam in England in the 1760's and 1770's. Painted furniture was high style for a few years in America following the 1790's (see Nos. 17, 18, 92) and swept the country after 1815. In 1788, Hepplewhite commented on the desirability of finishing chairs in this manner:

> For chairs, a new and very elegant fashion has arisen within these few years, of finishing them with painted or japanned work, which gives a rich and splendid appearance to the minuter parts of the ornaments, which are generally thrown in by the painter. Several of these designs are particularly adapted to this style, which allows a framework less massy than is requisite for mahogany; and by assorting the prevailing colour to the furniture and light of the room, affords opportunity, by the variety of grounds which may be introduced, to make the whole accord in harmony, with a pleasing and striking effect to the eye. Japanned chairs should have cane bottoms, with linen or cotton cases over cushions to accord with the general hue of the chair.[1]

The technique of ornamenting furniture with paint was not new. Both Englishmen and colonists of the late seventeenth and early eighteenth century were familiar with japanned furniture and japanning as an art through such works as Stalker's and Parker's *A Treatise of Japanning and Varnishing,* published in Oxford in 1688. However, toward the middle of the century japanning waned in popularity with the increased use of figured woods and carved ornament.

Throughout the eighteenth century, chests, cupboards, and tables were frequently exotically grained (particularly in northern New England) or ornamented with fanciful flowers and animals (Pennsylvania). However, this vernacular tradition had little in common with the high-style fancy furniture and represents a parallel but separate movement. Not so easily differentiated but always listed separately from fancy chairs in advertisements and apparently another distinct type are Windsor chairs. These turned chairs, produced in increasing numbers after 1750, seem invariably to have been painted—black, green, and yellow being the commonest colors. But painted scenes and ornamental devices are conspicuously absent from Windsor chairs; though occasionally on examples made after 1790, and usually on those with bamboo turnings, painted rings are found on spindles and other parts. Both Windsor and fancy chairs were advertised by the same shops; but, whereas Windsors were all-purpose chairs, used outdoors and inside, fancy chairs were as their name implies fit for the parlor and best rooms.

In *The Cabinet Dictionary,* Sheraton devotes a special section to the painting of furniture and points out that "as black chairs look well when ornamented with yellow lines, it may be proper to give some directions as to the mixture of the colour, and the manner of drawing these."[2] Directions are also given for "painting chairs with a green ground" and for compounding a "straw colour." From the following paragraph, an important inference can be drawn.

> The principal thing which constitutes this [the painting of furniture] a distinct branch of painting, is the general use of size and varnish colours, by which it is performed with much greater dispatch and effect. Yet the prices allowed in the country, at least in many parts of it, are so poor, that the painter can hardly distinguish furniture from common oil painting.[3]

"Varnish colours" as distinct from "common oil painting" was the finish employed on fancy furniture. Sheraton gives detailed directions for both the preparation and application of varnish colors which were to be applied over "grounds" of common oil paint.[4]

Cane seats are usually stipulated for the finest fancy chairs; rush-seated chairs, though often mentioned in advertisements and account books, are commonly listed separately. The rush seats of seventeenth- and eighteenth-century chairs seem mostly not to have been painted. The practice changed in the fancy chair era, and all rush-bottom seats were meant to be painted. Sheraton wrote:

> Rush-bottom chairs ought always to have their seats primed with common white lead, ground up in linseed oil, and diluted with spirits of turpentine. This first priming preserves the rushes, and hardens them; and, to make it come cheaper, the second coat of priming may have half Spanish white in it, if the price require it. The third coat should be ground up in spirits of turpentine only, and diluted with hard varnish, which will dry quick; but should not be applied till the priming be perfectly dry. Of this, probably the seats may require to have two lays, to make the work firm.[5]

He further pointed out:

> They who use any kind of water colour for rush bottoms, entirely deceive the purchaser, for it rots the rushes, and by the sudden push of the hand upon the seat, the colour will frequently fly off. All the other parts of chairs are primed with Spanish white, and glove leather size, as in any other mode of size painting. Sometimes once over may do, but when the work requires well finishing, three times, which should be rushed, or glass-papered down, for the beauty of the japan depends much upon the well-finished sizing; and it is better when the last coat of sizing is of white lead; upon such a ground, any colour may be laid with advantage, as it will always help the effect of the varnish colours, and particularly bright green and straws.[6]

The renaissance of high-style painted furniture in America during the 1790's can be ascribed to a number of causes. The neoclassical style, with its flat surfaces and its emphasis on two-dimensional decoration, provided a natural base for painted decoration. The *dernier cri* in English taste was, according to both Sheraton and Hepplewhite, painted furniture. American fancy-furniture makers quickly followed English practice. No figures are available on the vast numbers of fancy chairs produced in the United States, but their number was prodigious, and their popularity grew rapidly after 1800, continuing past the 1850's and 1860's. Their use after about 1820 was so common that they were cottage furniture rather than high style.

Finest in workmanship and most fanciful in design is the fancy furniture produced in Baltimore. There were many ornamental painters there as early as 1800, so that it is now impossible to identify who made what; but it is certain that John and Hugh Finlay, Irish born and trained, were in the forefront. Benjamin Latrobe is believed to have turned to them in 1809 to construct (after his designs) painted and ornamented Grecian chairs and couches for the White House—evidence enough of their reputation.[7] Their advertisements, beginning about 1803, tell us a great deal about the forms produced and the nature of their ornamental decoration. On January 31, they informed the public:

> ...they manufacture all kinds of Fancy Furniture, at their shop No. 3 south Frederick street, where furniture of the following kind may be seen, viz. TABLES Card, pier, tea, dressing, writing and shaving, of various colors and neatly gilt. CANE SEAT CHAIRS, Of various colors and of every description, painted and gilt in the most fanciful manner, with and without views adjacent to this city. RUSH BOTTOM And Windsor chairs, window and recess seats, wash and candle stands, fire and candle screens. Window cornices, bedsteads with cornices. &c.[8]

They ended their notice with "Coach and sign painting, japanning, gilding and ornamenting executed in the neatest manner."

The reader will note that although this furniture is "of various colors and neatly gilt" it is not described as being japanned. Whether this omission was inadvertent or not, the wording was changed on April 9 of the same year (1803), when they called attention to their "Elegant Fancy Furniture" and listed

> Japanned card, pier, tea, dressing, shaving and writing tables; cane seat, rush bottom and windsor chairs; fire and candle screens; wash, candle and workstands; bedsteads; bed and window cornices—all of various colors, ornamented and gilt in the most fanciful manner.[9]

On October 10, 1804, they informed "...ladies & gentlemen [that] they can supply them with views on their Chairs and Furniture which they alone can do, as they hold an exclusive right for that species of ornament.[10]

To know on what basis the Finlays claimed this right "to views on their chairs and furniture" and whether they actually had a monopoly of this kind of decoration would be of the greatest interest. If John and Hugh Finlay really had an exclusive right, then all Baltimore furniture so decorated while the "right" was in force could be assigned to them.

However, there is no uncertainty that John and Hugh Finlay's advertisements are more detailed than others' and that they explicitly list many other forms in addition to chairs. Other advertisers emphasize chairs and at most give a bare mention of other forms. Further, in a manner matched by no other American fancy-furniture advertiser, the Finlays spell out in detail the nature of the ornament used.

> CANE SEAT CHAIRS, SOFAS, RECESS, and WINDOW SEATS of every description and all colors, gilt, ornamented and varnished in a stile not equalled on the continent—with real Views, Fancy Landscapes, Flowers, Trophies of Music, War, Husbandry, Love, &c. &c. Also, A number of sets of new pattern Rush and Windsor Chairs and Settees; Card, Tea, Peir [sic], Writing and Dressing Tables, with Mahogany, Satin-Wood, Painted, Japanned and real Marble Top Sideboards; Ladies' Work Wash-Stand and Candle Stands; Horse Pole, Candle and Fire Screens; Bedsteads, Bed and Window Cornices, the centers enriched with Gold and Painted Fruit, Scroll and Flower Borders of entire new patterns, the mouldings in Japan, Oil and Burnish Gold, with Beads, Twists, Nelson Balls, &c. Likewise Brackets, Girondoles and Trypods; Ladies' Needle Work, Pictures and Looking Glasses Frames; old Frames Regilt; real Views taken on the spot to any dimension, in oil or watercolors; Coach, Flag and Masonic Painting; and particular attention paid to Gold Sign Lettering on Glass, Pannel or Metal. JOHN & HUGH FINLAY
> N.B. Orders for the West Indies, or any port of the continent, executed with dispatch.[11]

For these advertisements which so clearly define the character and extraordinary scope of the Finlays' work "not equalled on the continent," the writer is indebted to John H. Hill,[12] who discovered them during research for his master's thesis on

Baltimore cabinetmaking, 1790–1820. These newspaper notices and the catalogue of a great exhibition held at the Baltimore Museum of Art in 1947, *Baltimore Furniture, 1760–1810,* define fairly clearly the work of the Maryland fancy furniture school.

The following section is arranged geographically from South to North. Information presently available permits no more than sketchy characterization of the work of other areas. It is hoped that definition of the local idioms of each area can be more specifically spelled out at some future date. However, it is clear from such references as "most approved New York fashion" in the advertisement of Thomas West of New London, Connecticut (cited under No. 490) that there were styles associated with certain cities and that these styles were both exported to and imitated and produced in other centers. Another advertisement of West for "Fancy and Windsor Chairs" points to the complexity of the problem. It is but one of many such Connecticut advertisements emphasizing that he has "obtained from New-York a first rate workman at Gilding and Ornamenting."[13]

For the present, the most important facts to be observed are that fancy furniture was very popular and widely produced and that some of it was very high style and of remarkable quality. Probably most if not all that follows should be properly called japanned rather than painted; the colors were applied in varnishes over a painted ground.

1 *The Cabinet-Maker and Upholsterer's Guide* (1794), p. 1.
2 Sheraton, *The Cabinet Dictionary* (1803), p. 425.
3 *Ibid.,* p. 422.
4 *Ibid.,* pp. 415–432.
5 *Ibid.,* pp. 422–423.
6 *Ibid.,* p. 423.
7 Raley, "Interior Designs by Benjamin Henry Latrobe...," *Antiques,* LXXV (June, 1959), 568–571.
8 *Federal Gazette & Baltimore Daily Advertiser,* January 31, 1803.
9 *Ibid.,* April 9, 1803.
10 *American & Commercial Daily Advertiser* (Baltimore), October 10, 1804.
11 *Federal Gazette & Baltimore Daily Advertiser,* November 8, 1805.
12 Winterthur Fellow, Class of 1965.
13 This advertisement which appeared in the *Connecticut Gazette* (New London, Connecticut), July 24, 1816, is but one of more than two hundred given to me by Wendell Hilt of Simsbury, Connecticut. A generous and indefatigable researcher, his contribution to my knowledge and this book is immeasurable.

# XXVII

# Imlay Room

The wallpaper (now in this room) which John Imlay bought for his new house in Allentown, New Jersey, from William Poyntell of Philadelphia in 1794 may have been made by Poyntell. Also from Philadelphia and surely made there is the mantelpiece with portrait busts of Washington and Franklin in composition ornament. It comes from the Peter Breen House where Robert Wellford, who made a specialty of such ornament, lived for a number of years.

"Elegant fancy furniture, Tables of various colors and neatly gilt, Cane seat chairs," and "Window and recess seats, painted and gilt in the most fanciful manner, with and without views adjacent to this city." These phrases from the 1803 advertisements of John and Hugh Finlay of Baltimore seem as if written to describe the painted furniture in this room. Most if not all of it is believed to have been made in that city within a short time before or after the year 1805 which is the date woven into the black background of the Bessarabian carpet in the floor.

449

## 454 ARMCHAIR

*About 1814–1815    Baltimore    Attributed to Thomas S. Renshaw and John Barnhart*

There is little doubt as to the makers of this highly individual armchair. "Tho? S. Renshaw No. 37 S— Gay S? Balt? John Barnhart Ornamenter"[1] is inscribed in paint on the back of a settee of matching design now exhibited in the Baltimore Museum of Art. Although the settee and two side chairs from the same set are painted on a cream-colored ground and this on a deep red ground, the details of form and ornament are the same. The paintings on the backs in this set are said to be of local scenes, but they may be romantic conceptions. The ornate but insubstantial back is of a kind found to date only on Baltimore and English chairs.

Dimensions: height 34½; width 21; depth 17.

Materials: legs, a maple; seat rails and arm supports, a soft maple.
Accession: 57.1058

## 455 ARMCHAIR

*1805–1815    Baltimore*

Unique in American painted furniture of the early nineteenth century because of the use of chinoiserie scenes in color, this chair is ornamented in white and gold on a red background. Among the most elegant examples of painted furniture of its era, the crossed side stretchers, shapely back, and "crane neck arms" attached high in the back were then à la mode. Its long feet, icicle splats, and dentiledged panels are all a part of the Baltimore idiom of painted decoration.

Dimensions: height 38⅛; width 20½; depth 18.
Materials: right arm, cherry; left seat rail, soft maple (American); front stretcher, a soft maple.
Accession: 59.571

**456** SQUARE CARD TABLE with round corners and hollow front
*1800–1810 Baltimore*

A part of a set of fancy furniture of which three side chairs (No. 457), a settee (No. 458), and window stool (No. 459) are at Winterthur, this high-style Baltimore card table with hollow front and round corners displays the long round spade feet, legs striped to resemble inlay or reeding, and dentil-bordered panels characteristic of much painted Baltimore furniture. The background color is black, as is the top when closed. The top when open for playing reveals a surface handsomely veneered in mahogany.

If the large building depicted on the skirt is a "real view" such as advertised by John and Hugh Finlay, it must certainly have been a public building, for it is much larger than the country seats found on many pieces of Baltimore fancy furniture.[2] The statement that this set was made by Robert Fisher, maker of fancy furniture in Baltimore in the early 1800's, has twice appeared in print; but no reason or supporting evidence has been offered for the assertion.[3]

Dimensions: height 30⅞; width 38¾; depth 17½.

**456**

Materials: rails and medial brace, tulip; back rail of frame, hard pine; flying rail, oak.
Provenance: Mrs. Miles White, Jr.
Accession: 57.1071

**457** SIDE CHAIR (one of three)
*About 1800–1810 Baltimore*

Despite the sturdiness of its elements, the over-all effect of this chair is one of refinement, an effect created in large part by the grace of its painted decoration with such motifs as the paterae, dentil-edged panels, and trophies of musical instruments and torches. The icicle splats and the striped and stout columnar legs and back supports lend further dignity to the whole. This chair and its companions are part of a set with Nos. 456, 458, and 459, a set which originally may have included many other

**458**

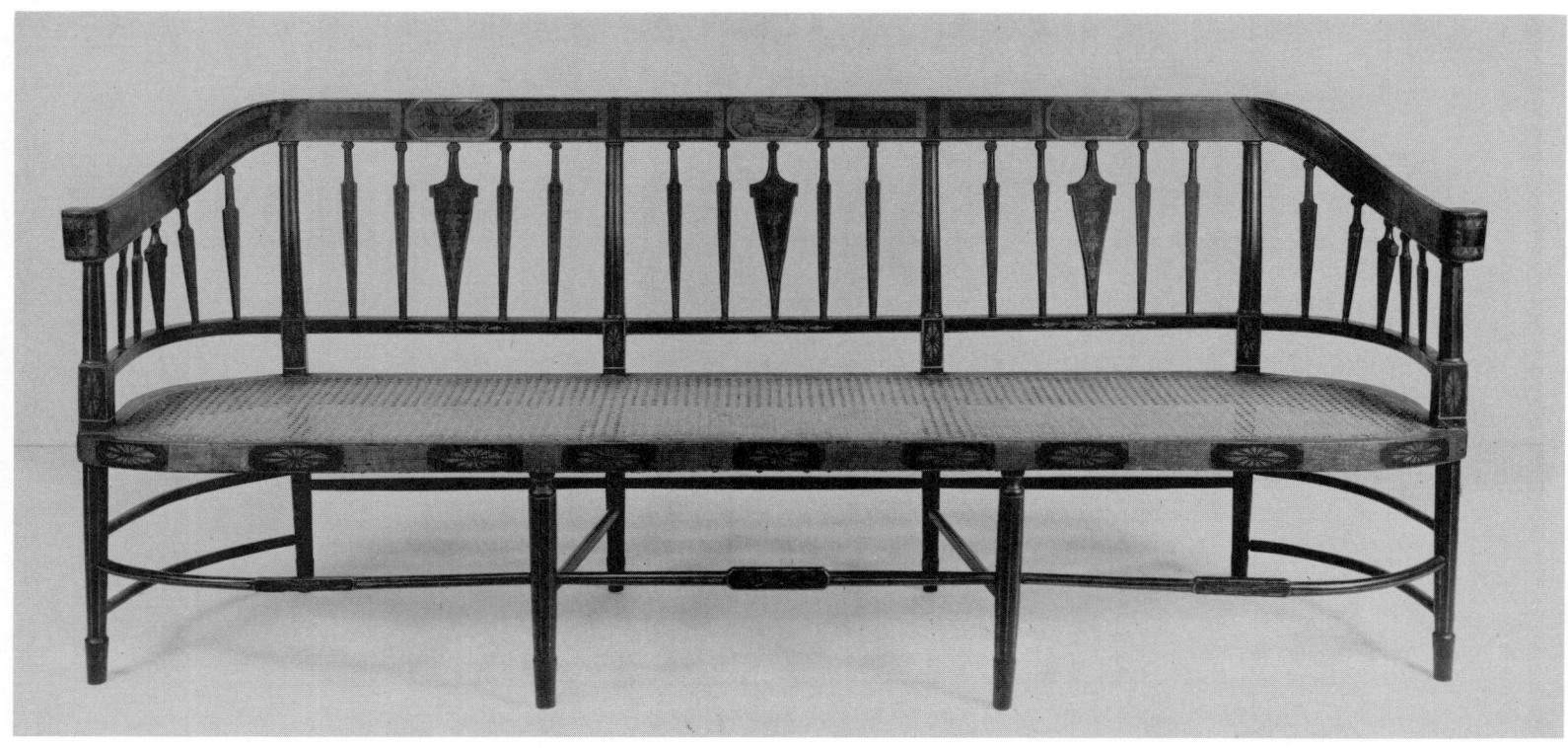

**459**

pieces of matching painted and decorated furniture.

Dimensions: height 33¾; width 19; depth 15.

Materials: legs, soft maple; seat frame, mahogany; seat rail, tulip.

Provenance: Mrs. Miles White, Jr.

Accession: 57.1060.1–3

### 458 SETTEE
*1800–1810   Maryland*

Exhibiting all of the characteristics of the matching side chairs (No. 457), this settee, in its bowed elements—front, corner rails, stretchers—and its outward curving, sloping arms supported by icicle splats of decreasing size, represents a peak in fancy seating furniture. The set (of which this is a part) of cane seat chairs, window seat, settee, and card table conforms in many ways to the "Elegant, Fancy Japanned Furniture" advertised by John and Hugh Finlay in "all colors, gilt, ornamented and varnished in a stile not equalled on the continent...with Flowers, Trophies of Music, War, Husbandry, Love &c &c...."[4]

Dimensions: height 32¾; width 79; depth 19¼.

Materials: maple and tulip; legs and stretchers, maple; rails and medial brace, tulip.

Provenance: Mrs. Miles White, Jr.

Accession: 57.1064

### 459 WINDOW SEAT
*1800–1810   Baltimore*

The Finlays offered japanned "window seats of every description and all colors."[5] This black one, matching Nos. 456, 457, and 458 in ornament, but with different feet, was evidently constructed to fit into a window recess of a particular size and to curve around the walls at the ends.

Dimensions: height 31½; width 50; depth 14.

Materials: legs, soft maple; rails, tulip; turned medial brace, a soft maple.

Provenance: Mrs. Miles White, Jr.

Accession: 57.1065

### 460 SIDE TABLE, circular
*1800   Baltimore (?)*

This semi-circular japanned side table has vertically striped legs such as are frequently found on Baltimore furniture, but the high-cuffed feet often associated with such legs are lacking. Three small scenes painted in octagonally framed panels against a rich green ground may be "ideal landscapes," or they may be "views adjacent to this city" such as John and Hugh Finlay advertised in Baltimore in 1803. On October 10, 1804, they called to the attention of "...ladies & gentlemen [that] they can supply them with views on their Chairs and Furniture which they alone can do, as they hold an exclusive right for that species of ornament...."[6] Today it is not known who gave them this exclusive right or how long they held it, if at all. Stencilled gilt sprays, grape leaves, and tendrils further ornament the apron.

Dimensions: height 31¼; width 41¾; depth 18½.
Materials: pine; front rail, back rail, and blocks, white pine; stiles, tulip.
Accession: 57.1070

### 461 BASIN STAND
*About 1800    Baltimore*

This japanned stand, the top of which is very much like that of a "corner Bason Stand" in Sheraton's

**463**

*The Cabinet-Maker and Upholsterer's Drawing-Book* (1793), Plate 42, has a dark-green background and ornament applied in red, yellow, brown, and gold. The striping of the legs lightens the effect of the supports and repeats the color of the musical instruments and vines. The musical trophies, the long round spade feet, and the striped legs support a firm Baltimore attribution.

Dimensions: height 42½; width 23; depth 16.
Materials: rails, legs, and drawer front, tulip; top cover, medial brace, and drawer bottom, white pine; drawer side, red gum.
Accession: 57.525

### 462 SIDE CHAIR
*1805–1815    New York or Baltimore*

The tablet top here ornamented with a gilt and sepia trophy of music on a pale-green ground, the intricate pierced back splat with Prince-of-Wales feathers, and the squared stretchers found on this black chair are not usual on fancy furniture made in Baltimore; but trophies of music, round spade feet, entwining motifs on legs and back supports, and grape leaves and tendrils are all elements often seen on seating furniture produced there.[7] Gum wood is most often found in New York furniture but was listed in the stock of woods owned at the time of death of some Baltimore cabinetmakers, among them William Camp.[8]

Dimensions: height 35; width 18½; depth 15¾.
Materials: skirt rail, red gum; legs, beech.
Accession: 57.975.1–3

**462**

are used to stripe the legs and band the panels.

Dimensions: height 29¼; width 36; depth 17¾.

Materials: back rail and blocks, white pine; end rails and top, tulip; flying rail, maple.

Accession: 57.1072.1, 2

## 465 SIDE CHAIR (one of five)
*1800–1810    Baltimore*

These chairs are simple yet sophisticated. The curves of the bowed seat frame, large panel, and paterae are a foil to the dominant flat surfaces and rectangular outlines of the upper rail, angular splat, and front stretcher. Broad stripes give the effect of chamfering on the front legs and back supports, further emphasizing the interplay of flatness versus roundness.[10]

Dimensions: height 33½; width 19; depth 16.

Materials: maple and butternut, painted light red and gold; rails, black walnut; legs, soft maple.

Accession: 57.1061.1–5

## 463 PIER TABLE
*1800–1810    Baltimore*

The top of this painted pier table with half-serpentine ends and elliptic front is similar in shape to those of Salem and Boston, but the character of the turned legs with painted stripes is quite different from those found on tables made in that area. The stylized trophies of love and music (in gold leaf and shaded with brown on a black ground) show the finesse of design and execution characteristic of fine Baltimore furniture.

Dimensions: height 34¼; width 53½; depth 24¼.

Materials: rear rail, front rail, and medial brace, white pine; rear corner braces and front corner block, tulip; rear leg, cherry; top, marble.

Accession: 57.699

## 464 CARD TABLE (one of a pair)
*1810–1820    Baltimore*

Long cuffed feet, bands of crosshatched decoration on the legs,[9] and decorative geometric panels are all Baltimore characteristics found on this square card table with serpentine front, half-serpentine ends, and ovolo corners. With the swing leaf closed (as illustrated), the top of this card table is of mahogany veneer. Opened, the playing surface is revealed to be vermillion like the rest of the table.

The fruit and flowers painted on the same ground are rather freer in style than most Baltimore furniture ornament and may point to a slightly later date than Nos. 456 and 460. Gilt, black, and white

## 466 SIDE CHAIR (one of a pair)
*1815–1825   New Jersey or Philadelphia*

With fulsome curves and exotic graining in red and black imitation of rosewood, this Grecian-style chair is boldly ornamented in gold leaf and yellow paint. The three-dimensional quality of the stencilled fruit-and-flower design contrasts with the flatness of the tulip-shaped stretcher and the large anthemion splat painted to give the effect of carving in low relief. Similar chairs have been found in New Jersey, adjacent to Philadelphia. These chairs may have been made in that area.

Dimensions: height 32¾; width 17¾; depth 15¾.
Materials: right front leg, hard maple; front rail, basswood; left front leg, soft maple.
Accession: 60.1145.1, 2

**466**

**467**

## 467 ARMCHAIR
*1805–1815   New York*

Painted vermillion, decorated in gilt, and fitted on the upper rail and splat with bronzed mounts, the set of eight chairs and a Grecian couch, of which this armchair and a matching side chair, also in the Winterthur collection, are a part, constitute one of the handsomest surviving groups of New York fancy furniture.[11] Similar scrolled backs and arms are found on much mahogany furniture made in New York, and bell-shaped rush seats trimmed with a thin tulip band and outflaring turned front feet were popular with the fancy chairmakers of that city. As on looking glasses of the same era, gilt balls are used as decorative motifs in the front double stretcher and latticework splat.

Dimensions: height 33½; width 20; depth 18½.
Materials: oak and maple; front legs, soft maple; rear legs, hickory; apron, tulip.
Accession: 56.580

**468** ARMCHAIR

*1810–1820   New York City   Possibly from the "Fancy Chair Store" of John K. Cowperthwaite*

Although the designs of the "angular splat" used here for arm braces and the lattice back are both derived from the 1802 edition of *The London Chair-Makers' and Carvers' Book of Prices for Workmanship* (Plate 3), the originality of the colored and shaded gilt decoration of drapery, tassels, and shells gives this white-painted armchair great charm. A cut of a side chair of identical form but different painted decoration appears on the bill head of the *Fancy Chair Store* of John K. Cowperthwaite, No. 4 Chatham-Square, New York City. Dated April 29, 1816, the bill of $12 to Mr. Stephen Wheeler for eight chairs was receipted for "Job Cowperthwaite [by] Thomas B. Parsils."[12]

Dimensions: height 35; width 20; depth 16.
Materials: legs, arms, top rail, soft maple; apron, tulip.
Accession: 57.973

**469** SIDE CHAIR (one of six)

*1815–1825   New York*

Of special interest for its reference to "landscape chairs" is the following advertisment which provides much information about fancy chairs offered in New York City in 1817.

> Wheaton & Davis, Fancy Chair Manufacturers, No. 153 Fulton-st. opposite St. Paul's Church, offer for sale an elegant assortment of Curl'd Maple, Plain Painted and Ornamented, Landscape, Conversation and Rocking Chairs, Settees, Sofas, Loungees, Music Stools, &c. all of the newest fashion.
> Old Chairs repaired, painted and ornamented.[13]

This "landscape chair," one of a set of six high styled fancy chairs with splayed and reeded front legs, is skillfully painted and artificially grained to simulate curled maple. All are ornamented with banding and striping in red-brown paint and

**470**

Hitchcock of Connecticut and his competitors beginning in the late 1820's, the curved seat frame, the turned and square tapered legs, and the nicely shaped and decorated center splat and front stretchers are evidence of an earlier origin. The scene painted on the splat (perhaps a version of the return of the prodigal son) may be by a different hand than the gilt panels on the legs, back supports, and seat rail, all of which are grained in imitation of rosewood. The New York attribution, based on the rounded bell-shaped seat frame and the "fancy" landscape view, is tentative.

Dimensions: height 33½; width 18½; depth 16¾.

Materials: seat rail and seat frame corner block, tulip; back stiles, ash; top rail, slat, front legs, and front stretcher, soft maple.

Accession: 57.614.1, 2

**471**

gold leaf. According to a member of the family this set was formerly in the Van Rensselaer Manor House at Albany, New York.[14] A New York provenance for the chairs seems likely not only on account of their history but because each of the six well-painted landscapes executed in rich natural colors appears to be a different view of the Hudson River and Valley. If as early as believed, these paintings must be placed in the very first years of the Hudson River School of landscape painting.

Dimensions: height 32¾; width 19; depth 16½.

Materials: front and rear legs, soft maple; seat framing, cherry; skirt rail, tulip, stretchers, hickory.

Provenance: Stephen Van Rensselaer; Mrs. James (Elizabeth Van Rensselaer) Frazer.

Accession: 57.1075.1–6

**470** SIDE CHAIR (one of a pair)
*1810–1820 Probably New York*

Although the cresting rail and back supports of this chair are reminiscent of those used by Lambert

**471** SIDE CHAIR (one of a pair)

*About 1815   Albany, New York   Attributed to William Buttre*

An "Eagle Fancy Chair" unmistakably like this highly unusual example was illustrated in a newspaper advertisement of William Buttre of Albany in 1815.[15] True, the head and neck of the eagle rising above the shield and the sunburst shown above the front rail in the newspaper cut were not included on Winterthur's chairs; but the unique shield back, supported on carved feathered legs, and every structural particular are the same—including the shape of the seat, the five balls below the stretcher, and the legs which are turned, squared, and tapered to end in ball feet. The original rush seat banded by a tulip strip is decorated with gilt

**472**

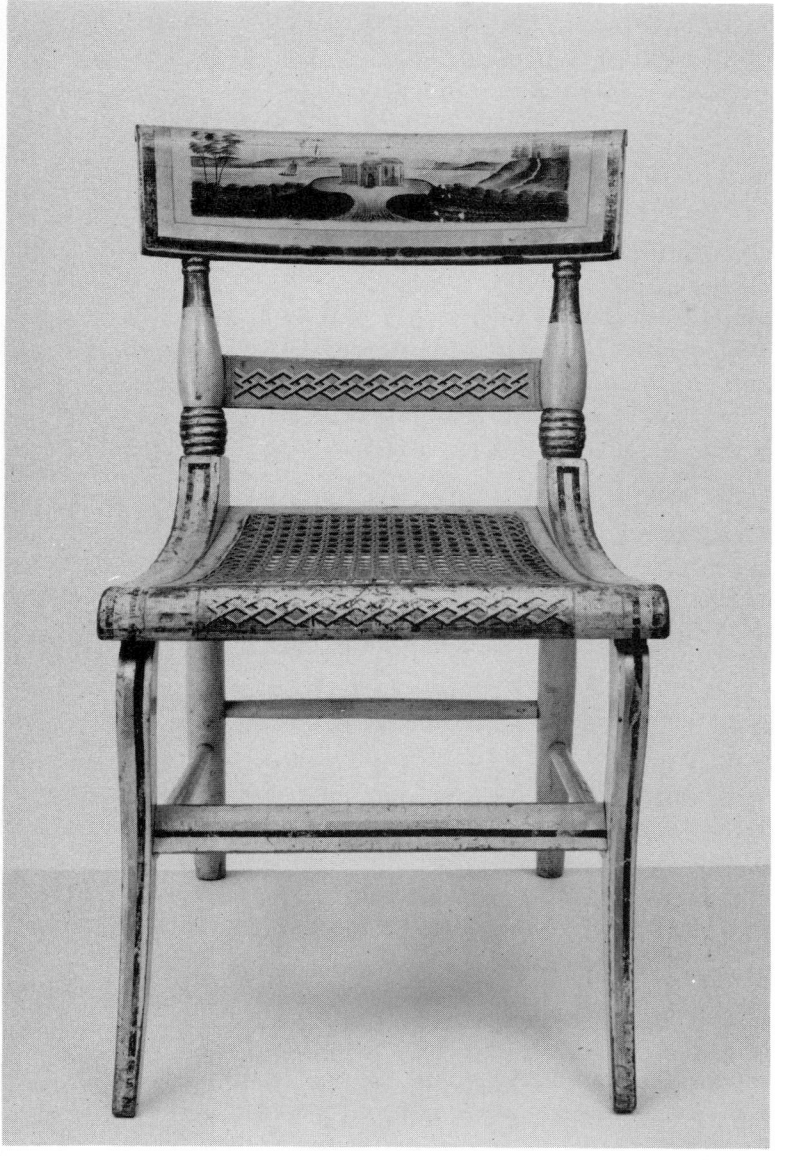

**473**

oak leaves over a deep bronze-brown with which the entire chair is painted. The gilt, running deer between foliated scrolls on the cresting rail may be a family crest. In his advertisement, Buttre stated that at his Fancy Chair Store he "has Constantly for sale a *large* assortment of elegant, well-made, and highly finished Black, White, Brown, Coquelico, Gold, and Eagle Fancy Chairs..." A chair of the same form but with different decoration is owned by the Metropolitan Museum of Art.

Dimensions: height 35; width 18; depth 16.

Materials: seat framing, ash; legs and back supports, beech; skirt rail, tulip.

Accession: 52.50.1, 2

**472** SIDE CHAIR

*About 1810   Probably New York*

The scene painted in black and gray on the top rail of this white chair and wall paintings found on the plaster of several central New York State houses

making.[16] In 1818 he established a shop in the village of Barkhamsted in western Connecticut for making chair parts which were shipped to the South. The business flourished. In 1825 he began making complete fancy chairs which were shipped all over the United States—Charleston, Detroit, and Chicago. He overexpanded, bankruptcy followed. He stayed on as manager and paid off his debts. In 1829 Arba Alford, Jr., was taken into partnership; Winterthur's pair of chairs with vigorous and skillful stencilled decoration on a black-and-red imitation rosewood ground are typical of those produced after this time when more than a hundred men, women, and children were employed producing chairs to be sold for about $1.50 each. The basket of fruit and flowers in shades of yellow, brown, and gold was a popular motif, though but one of many used by this factory.

Dimensions: height 35; width 17½; depth 15½.
Materials: right rear leg and right side seat rail, a birch; front right seat rail, beech (American).
Accession: 57.611.1, 2

indicate the popularity of landscape painting in that state in the 1820's and 1830's. One example of such wall painting, originally in a Springfield, New York, house and now at Winterthur, is signed "William Price" and dated by him 1831. In both the chair panel and Price's wall decoration are found spindly trees with high sponged foliage, sailing ships on an expanse of water, ruins, and tall buildings with classical elements.

To achieve a Grecian silhouette (with broad slat back) several changes in construction technique were necessary: both the turned back stiles and the turned and curved back legs were set into heavy outside seat rails. Inside these, smaller rails forming part of the seat frame are fastened. Gold leaf and yellow, brown, and black oil paint are also used to ornament the chair. On the back slat and front rail, the fretwork on gilt grounds echoes the pattern of the caned seat.

Dimensions: height 31½; width 17½; depth 15½.
Materials: top and seat rails, tulip; legs, red gum; stretchers and back posts, maple.
Accession: 57.1076

### 473   SIDE CHAIR (one of a pair)
*1829–1843   Connecticut   "Hitchcock, Alford Co. Hitchcocksville, Conn. Warranted" is stencilled on the back of the seat rail*

The story of Lambert Hitchcock and his chairs is one of the success stories of American cabinet-

### 474   CIRCULAR CARD TABLE
*1795–1810   Connecticut*

Painted yellow and heavily varnished, the surface of this round card table is ornamented with a rich variety of classical devices. Green and sepia rosettes, Adamesque urns, and a musical trophy decorate the skirt. The upper surface of the closed top bears a festoon of flowers bordered by a floral wreath, while the open top is revealed to be a uniform green edged with ivory. As this table was found in Middletown, Connecticut, and another said to be like it has been reported as having been originally owned in Hartford, it is not unlikely that the table originated in this state whose newspapers abounded in advertisements offering fancy furniture in the latest mode.

Dimensions: height 29; width 38; depth 18⅝.
Materials: maple; rails, white pine.
Accession: 52.164

### 475   HANGING SHELF
*1805–1815   Probably Northern New England*

Orrin G. Winchell advertised in the New Haven *Columbian Register* of December 5, 1820, that he had, in addition to "Fancy, Bamboo, and Windsor Chairs of every description ... Also a specimen of the much celebrated imitation of Rosewood, not claimed however, to be *superior* to the real Rosewood, but equal to any imitation of the kind in

which stands under a gilt framed looking glass, is covered with a finely worked muslin..." [17]

Found in Massachusetts, this table, painted white with gilt composition beading around the edges, is presumed to have been made there—an assumption supported by its thin delicate proportions, elliptic front, and attached dressing glass. These attributes appear again and again on Massachusetts furniture. On December 18, 1806, John Doggett, looking-glass maker and cabinetmaker of Roxbury, Massachusetts, charged Stillman Lothrop $30 for "6 toighlight tables and dressing boxes." One surviving example bearing Lothrop's label is painted white, ornamented with gilt looking-glass balls. [18]

Dimensions: height 34¼; width 36½; depth 19.
Materials: white pine; upholstery, festoons of green satin edged with fringe, French, late eighteenth century.
Accession: 57.959

New-York and not inferior to any before done in this city."

Although indeed painted to imitate rosewood, this hanging shelf which was found in Boston was probably made there or in another northern New England city rather than a Connecticut one. The bow front, suggestive of many Massachusetts chests of drawers, bears delicate stencilled heads of wheat tied with a bowknot; and the panels at each end of the drawer are ornamented with "trophies" composed of caducei, liberty caps, shields, and foliage. The turned baluster shelf supports, ornamented with gold leaf, are not relied upon completely to bear the entire weight since two L-shaped iron straps with eyes at their tops are fastened to the floor of the cabinet and to the back of each shelf.

Dimensions: height 37½; width 42; depth 11.
Materials: white pine.
Accession: 57.964

### 476  DRESSING TABLE
*1800–1810   Massachusetts*

"To accommodate a gentleman or lady with conveniencies for dressing," specialized tables of mahogany were sometimes made in the United States; but more often a pine frame hung with dimity, callico, or silk served the purpose. As early as 1793, Thomas Lee Shippen remarked of his chamber when visiting Westover "...my bottle and bason [are] of thick & beautiful china, and my toilet

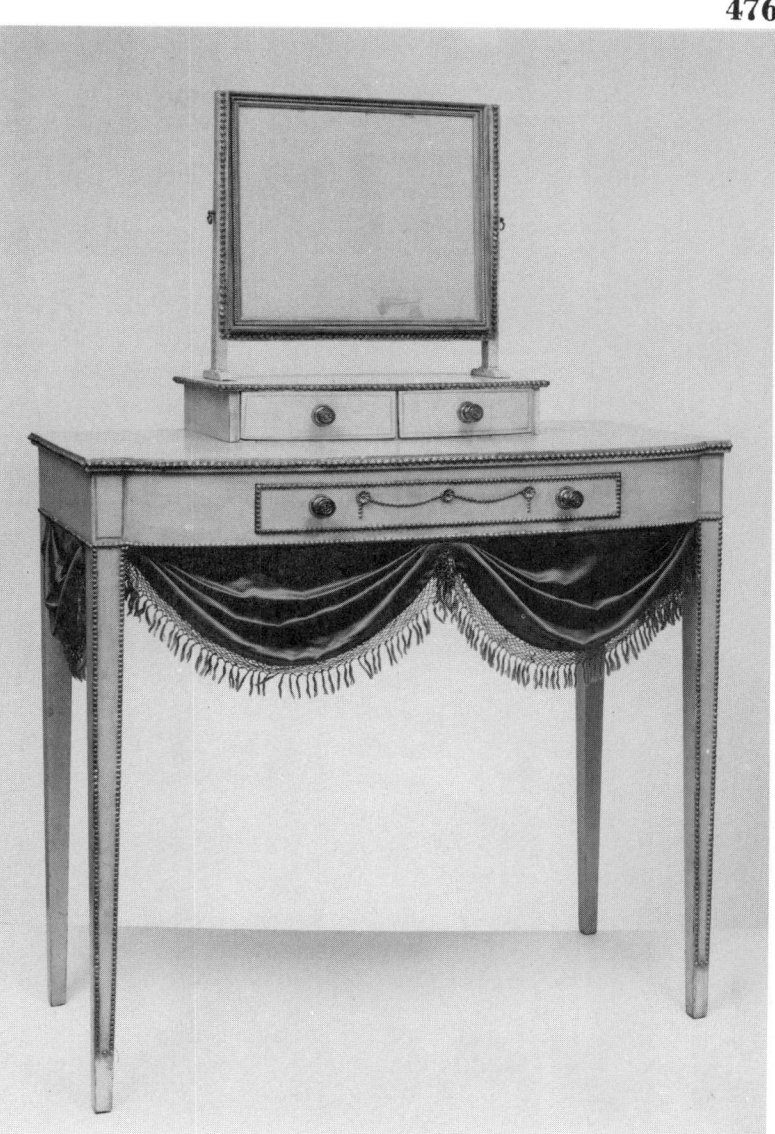

### 477 WORK TABLE with canted corners
*1808–1818   Boston   Inscribed "Vose and Coates" in ink on bottom of tray*

Unique among work tables, for design and decoration this one has no peer among American fancy furniture. Dainty and delicate, it stands secure on flaring legs held taut by curving stretchers. Seaweed, coral, and shells from far-off places are skillfully painted in their natural colors on all sides of the frame and the top against a background of varnished light wood. Bands of inlay outline the top and edge of the skirt. The top is hinged to give access to a removable compartmented tray, beneath which is the storage space of the silk bag.

Vose and Coates, listed in the Boston directories from 1809 to 1818, made purchases of John Doggett as early as November 21, 1808.[19] The woods used demonstrate the wide variety sometimes incorporated in the work of the American cabinetmaker and the complex nature of the problem facing the wood analyst.

Dimensions: height 29⅜; width 17; depth 13.

**477**

**478**

Materials: bottom of sewing bag, some tray partitions, and inner lamination of stretcher, basswood (tilia); middle lamination of curved stretcher and some inlays, nyssa; some tray partitions, pincushion boxes, and tray bottom, aspen; sewing bag, brown silk brocaded in a floral pattern, French, Louis XV.
Accession: 57.983

### 478 CHAMBER TABLE
*1816   Bath, Maine   Inscribed "Rachel H. Lombard, Bath, January 1816"*

A little before 1800, ornamental painting became a part of the curriculum in girls' schools in the United States; and as early as 1812 this was extended to include the painting of tables and work boxes. In the *Reminiscences of a Nonagenarian*, the author, writing of Newburyport, comments that in 1812 "Miss Mary Ann Colman was a good teacher of water color painting; the fruit and flower pieces executed at her school were natural and well done. She also taught painting on wood; several workboxes and work-stands, painted under her instruction, are still to be seen in the residences of some of our older citizens."[20]

This table, made by an unknown cabinetmaker

legs, quarter engaged at the corners. Although the drawer sides are rather thick and the dovetailing coarse, the proportions and conforming corners of the top make the form worthy of the sophistication of the painted fringe and tassels draping each leg. These and the large landscape on the top and the nosegay on the drawer are all on unpainted birch.

Dimensions: height 31¾; width 32; depth 17⅝.
Materials: birch; interior blocks and drawer lining, white pine.
Accession: 57.986

## 480 WORK TABLE
*About 1815 Bath, Maine, or other Northern New England area*

Decorated with vines, sprays of flowers, an antique landscape with ancient ruins, and a river scene, this table in both structure and style of decoration conforms to other examples of furniture from the coastal areas of northern New England.

Dimensions: height 28½; width 18; depth 18.

of some sensitivity and decorated, signed, and dated by "Rachel H. Lombard, Bath, [Maine] January 1816," is among the most "inspired" of such works. The top is ornamented with "Limerich Castle" (surrounded by birds and foliage), ode to Bunker Hill, and uplifting mottos such as "Wishing of all employments is the worst. Learn! Known thyself! All wisdom centers here." On the front are flowering vines and the signature, date, and a number of anagrams of names wherein Elizabeth is "Thelaziel" and Charlotte, "Telochart"! Among the views painted on the frame are a marine view, a rotunda in the Gardens of Stourhead, and Nutley Abbey.

Dimensions: height 32¾; width 32; depth 16¾.
Materials: birch and maple; top, upper front rail, and outer lamination, maple; backboard, birch; inner lamination of end, white pine.
Accession: 57.985

## 479 CHAMBER TABLE
*1815 Bath, Maine Inscribed "Executed By Wealthy P. S. Jones, Bath, March 6th, 1815."*

Similar in character to other inscribed Bath examples (See No. 478), this table also has ring-turned

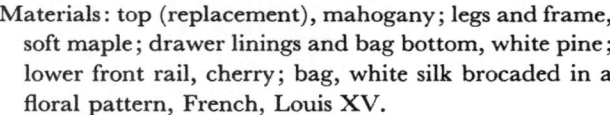

Materials: top (replacement), mahogany; legs and frame, soft maple; drawer linings and bag bottom, white pine; lower front rail, cherry; bag, white silk brocaded in a floral pattern, French, Louis XV.
Accession: 57.984

### 481 WORK TABLE
*1815–1825   Northeastern New England*

Voluptuous in the swelling curves of its serpentine body and vine-entwined legs, and romantically painted with scenes of ruins and rustic landscapes, this table must have been a schoolgirl's delight. The upper drawer with a baize-covered writing flap is fitted with pen and ink trays. A table reminiscent of this one is signed "Nancy Pearson Huse, Newbury, 1822."[21] As noted before (see No. 478), decoration of small tables and work boxes was a specialty of Miss Mary Ann Colman in a Newburyport girls' school. Although they may have been done elsewhere, most surviving examples seem to have originated in that area.

Dimensions: height 30½; width 17½; depth 17½.
Materials: basswood; drawer linings, white pine.
Accession: 57.987

### 482 WORK TABLE with canted corners
*1800–1810   Northern New England*

A bowl of fruit here framed in a wreath on the octagonal top of this table is similar to those in many theorem paintings on velvet that survive from the first quarter of the nineteenth century. The foliage on the drawer front and the vines on the legs remind one of those on others of this group of northern New England tables decorated by schoolgirls. Perhaps all are from a single school, but more likely they represent the product of several. The use of bird's-eye maple, the thinness of the top and the nicely tapered legs, and the continuation of the legs as pilasters through the canted corners indicate that the cabinetmaker was a sensitive artisan with ability.

Dimensions: height 29¾; width 15½; depth 14.

Materials: bird's-eye maple; drawer linings, white pine; bag frame, Scots or red pine; bag, pale-pink silk; Louis XVI period tassel.
Accession: 57.982

## 483 BASIN STAND
*1800–1810  New England*

Few pieces of furniture survive with their painted decoration in such pristine condition as this white washstand with legs and shelf outlined in dark red and top in sage green. Vines and sprays in the same colors frame three openings for glasses and wash bowl on the top and ornament the bowed surface of the drawer front and apron, which is deeper than usual but not deep enough to include the whole of the ornamentalist's pattern.

Following general designs shown in Sheraton's *The Cabinet-Maker and Upholsterer's Drawing-Book* (1793) and various editions of the London books of prices, the maker of this stand reduced the height, broadened its silhouette, and added scalloped backboards for the lower shelves.

Dimensions: height 35⅜; width 21; depth 13.
Materials: rails and legs, tilia (basswood); laminated drawer front, birch and tilia; shelves and blocking, white pine.
Accession: 51.61

## 484 CANDLESTAND
*1800–1815  New England*

Unorthodox legs that spell stability, a shaft of uncommon perfection, a top as thin as a pencil—these are the attributes that give uncommon grace to a conventional form to be found in every antiques shop. But form alone is not responsible for this extraordinary creation. Yellow ochre and earth-red paint applied in the rural vernacular, rather than in the fancy furniture mode, has transformed ordinary birch to exotic fantasy and gentle curves to figures of expression.

Dimensions: height 25½; top 14¼ × 14¾; width (at foot) 19.
Materials: birch.
Accession: 57.1101

**483**

**484**

**485** SETTEE
*1810–1820   New England (?)*

With thousands of parts being produced by turner specialists for hundreds of fancy chairmakers working all over the country, the identification of the maker or the center of manufacture of much of this delightful furniture is as yet impossible. Thought possibly to be of New England origin because of its thin lines and the presence of birch, this settee exhibits more classical detail than is usual in products of that region. The source of the gilt sunburst, paterae, and draped urns is to be found in the works of Sheraton and Hepplewhite; but the more freely executed leafy sprays and grape leaves and tendrils in brown, yellow, and gilt on the dark-green ground of the rails are a part of the vernacular of the American fancy painter. The arms, whose splats conform to the shape of the front stretchers and echo the curve of the back members, have turned contours resembling the pattern on No. 468.

Dimensions: height 34; width 66½; depth 19.
Materials: legs, soft maple; rails, mulberry; medial seat braces, ash; front stretchers, birch; medial stretchers, hickory.
Accession: 57.981

**486** SIDE CHAIR
*About 1810–1820   Southern New England or New York*

Representative of a multitude of "flag" or "common" fancy chairs of the early nineteenth century, this chair with turned spindles in the back adheres more closely than most to its seventeenth century prototype, the "Carver chair," with which the great tradition of the turned chair in America began—a tradition that continued through the slat-back chairs of the eighteenth and nineteenth centuries and still remains in those produced by mountain craftsmen and others today. Earlier chairs were heavier and usually left in natural wood or painted but one color. The black paint of this later example, typical of its fellows, is ornamented in red, yellows, and gold. Drapery and tassel motifs are found more often than shells. The presence of birch and tulip accounts for the attribution of this side chair to either southern New England or New York.

Dimensions: height 35; width 19; depth 15¾.
Materials: maple; stiles, birch; top rail, hard maple, skirt rail, tulip.
Accession: 57.613

**486**

**487**

**488**

**489**

**487** ARMCHAIR (one of a pair)
*1810–1820  Southern New England or New York*

Typical of many fancy chairs found in New England, this chair of pleasant form and proportions is ornamented with stylized vines, leaves, and shells in gilt, freely and gaily dispersed on the black legs, splats, arm and back supports, arms, and seat rail. A gilt eagle spreads his wings above banners and cannons on the cresting rail, and a rising sun peers over the edge of the stretcher. The use of tulip to edge the seat suggests an origin south of Massachusetts.

Dimensions: height 34¾; width 20¼; depth 15¾.
Materials: left rear leg, front seat rail, right arm support, soft maple; edging of seat, tulip; seat, rush.
Accession: 57.972.1, 2

**488** SIDE CHAIR (one of a pair)
*1810–1820  Southern New England or New York*

The variations of turning and ornament existing between this chair and No. 487 are so minor as to indicate that both came from the same factory. They may have been a part of the same set.

Dimensions: height 35½; width 17¾; depth 14¾.
Materials: right rear leg, a soft maple; outer edge of seat front, tulip; front seat rail, birch; seat, rush.
Accession: 57.977

**489** SIDE CHAIR  (a pair)
*1800–1820  American South of Massachusetts*

Indistinguishable in form, color, and its tightly composed decorative panels from many English fancy chairs, this rather sophisticated side chair with curved and hollowed back can be definitely called American only because of the presence of tulip wood. Painted in red, black, and gold on yellow ground, the decoration is composed of heavy stripes interspersed with floral panels. Unlike other fancy chairs at Winterthur, this one has no turned members, the severity of the square tapered legs being relieved only by their slight forward sweep.

Dimensions: height 34¼; width 18¼; depth 16.
Materials: legs, soft maple; side rails and apron strip, beech; front rail, tulip.
Accession: 57.634.1, 2

**490** SIDE CHAIR
*1800–1820  New England*

What was the style, shape, and decoration of the "Fancy chairs of the latest and most approved New York fashion" advertised by Thomas West of New London in 1810?[22] The writer can only guess, but key attributes of "the New York fashion" appear to be bell-shaped rush seats, bound with a thin outlining strip of wood, and a hollowed, back-curving top rail like those on scroll-back chairs (see No. 68) which were so popular in New York.

White paint ornamented with flowers, leaves, and stripes in red, green, and gold and the simplicity of the back with but three bent spindles make this a pretty chair, possibly one of a set for a parlor. An inset gilt composition mask on the cresting rail makes it unique. The thinness of the rush seat and the use of birch may be New England, possibly Massachusetts, attributes.

Dimensions: height 34½; width 17¾; depth 14⅞.
Materials: apron strip, rails, and back legs, birch; front legs, beech.
Accession: 57.976

light, thin curved elements are unequal to the stresses demanded of them and are found to be cracked or damaged.

That these were parlor chairs there can be little doubt. An exotic peacock plume, reminiscent of those on the ultra-stylish oval-back Derby chairs (see Nos. 17 and 18), is painted in vibrant colors as a focal point and crest against the over-all, pale-yellow ground. Stripes, sometimes subtly shaded as on the front rail, emphasize the free-flowing curves that meld limpid legs and hollowed seat into a concave, form-fitting back inviting the relaxed posture of early nineteenth-century high fashion.

At least three surviving sets of chairs branded by Gragg (one with matching armchairs and settee) testify to the popularity of this fancy furniture when made.[24] Half a century later, the ideas underlying its patented construction—that is, the exploitation of bent wood—reached their culmination in the tremendously popular bentwood furniture of Michael Thonet.

Dimensions: height 34⅜; width 18; depth 25⅛.
Materials: front seat rail, a birch; center seat strip, white oak (American); front leg, beech (American).
Provenance: Museum Purchase, 1961.
Accession: 61.321

## FOOTNOTES

1 Illustrated, Henry J. Berkley, "Early Maryland Furniture," *Antiques*, XVIII (September, 1930), 210.
2 See McClelland, pp. 238–239, for seven illustrations. See also *Baltimore Furniture, 1760–1810* (p. 156) for a list of the seventeen indentified country seats painted on a set in the Baltimore Museum of Art.
3 Luke Vincent Lockwood, *Colonial Furniture in America.* Card table, fig. xcix, p. 331; side chair, fig. xci, p. 310; settee, fig. xciv, p. 313; window seat, fig. xcvii, p. 315. Edgar G. Miller, Jr., *American Antique Furniture.* Volume I: side chair, No. 291, p. 209; settee, No. 516, p. 291; window seat, No. 536, p. 301. Volume II: card table, No. 1528, p. 793.
4 *Federal Gazette & Baltimore Daily Advertiser*, November 8, 1805.
5 *American & Commercial Daily Advertiser* [Baltimore], November 8, 1805.
6 *Ibid.*, October 10, 1804.
7 See *Baltimore Furniture, 1760–1810*, pp. 156–157.
8 His inventory is among those of Baltimore County, Maryland, at the Hall of Records, Annapolis, Maryland. DMMC, Microfilm No. 16.
9 See Plates 103 and 104, *Baltimore Furniture, 1760–1810.*
10 The design for the back is derived from Figs. 1 and 5, Plate 3, *The London Chair-Makers' and Carvers' Book of Prices for Workmanship* (1802).

## 491 SIDE CHAIR

*1808–1815 Boston Branded "S. [Samuel] Gragg Boston. Patent" (working 1808–1830)*

In daring, imagination, and exploitation of the plastic qualities of wood, few forms for the next fifty years were to match these incredible chairs[23] inspired by "Grecian forms" and anticipating the idea of the contour chair. By the mid 1700's, Windsor chairmakers used water and steam to master the bending of spindles, hoops, and backs for strong comfortable chairs. But in those chairs the curves were maintained after bending through ties or bracing of one kind or another; here the curves of the legs and back remain unfettered and free, but Samuel Gragg went almost too far. This chair is but one of a few to remain unbroken. Usually, the

11 Settee and four chairs in the Brooklyn Museum; two chairs in the Metropolitan Museum of Art.

12 The original bill is in DMMC (No. 61 × 92). In the *New York Evening Post* of July 28, 1817, a cut of the same chair was used in the advertisement of Wheaton and Davis, fancy chair manufacturers at 153 Fulton Street, New York City.

13 *New York Evening Post,* July 28, 1817.

14 A typewritten label pasted within the seat frame of two of the chairs reads: "Six American Chairs with scenes of the Hudson River. circa 1810. From the Van Rensselaer Manor House of Albany. [signed] Elizabeth Van Rensselaer Frazer."

15 *Albany Advertiser* [Albany, New York], February 16, 1815.

16 For much of this information, the writer is indebted to Ethel Hall Bjerkoe, *The Cabinetmakers of America* (Garden City, New York: Doubleday and Company, Inc., 1951), pp. 124–127.

17 Ethel Armes (ed.), *Nancy Shippen Her Journal Book* (Philadelphia: Lippincott Company, 1935), p. 305.

18 In the collection of the writer.

19 Daybook of John Doggett, p. 222. DMMC (64 × 10).

20 Sarah Anna Emery, *Reminiscences of a Nonagenarian* (Newburyport, Massachusetts: William H. Huse & Co., 1879), p. 223.

21 Dean A. Fales, Jr., *Essex County Furniture: Documented Treasures from Local Collections 1660–1860.* A Catalogue of a Loan Exhibition June 22 to October 12, 1965. (Salem, Massachusetts: The Essex Institute, 1965), No. 58.

22 *Connecticut Gazette* [New London, Connecticut], March 7, 1810. Since writing the above, the writer has seen in the Jeremiah Lee House, Marblehead, Massachusetts, four painted chairs and a curved five-chair-back settee that in design are very much like this chair including the lion mask on the splat. That set, with a local history of ownership, may have been made in Massachusetts but has turned feet like those on many New York mahogany chairs and tables.

23 Only one is at Winterthur; others are in the Museum of Fine Arts, Boston, and the private collection of Mr. and Mrs. Bertram K. Little.

24 Both are privately owned; one set, owned by the writer, has cabriole front legs with goat-hoof front feet.

# Carved details (PLATES XXVIII-XXXI)

*With catalogue number and probable place of origin.*

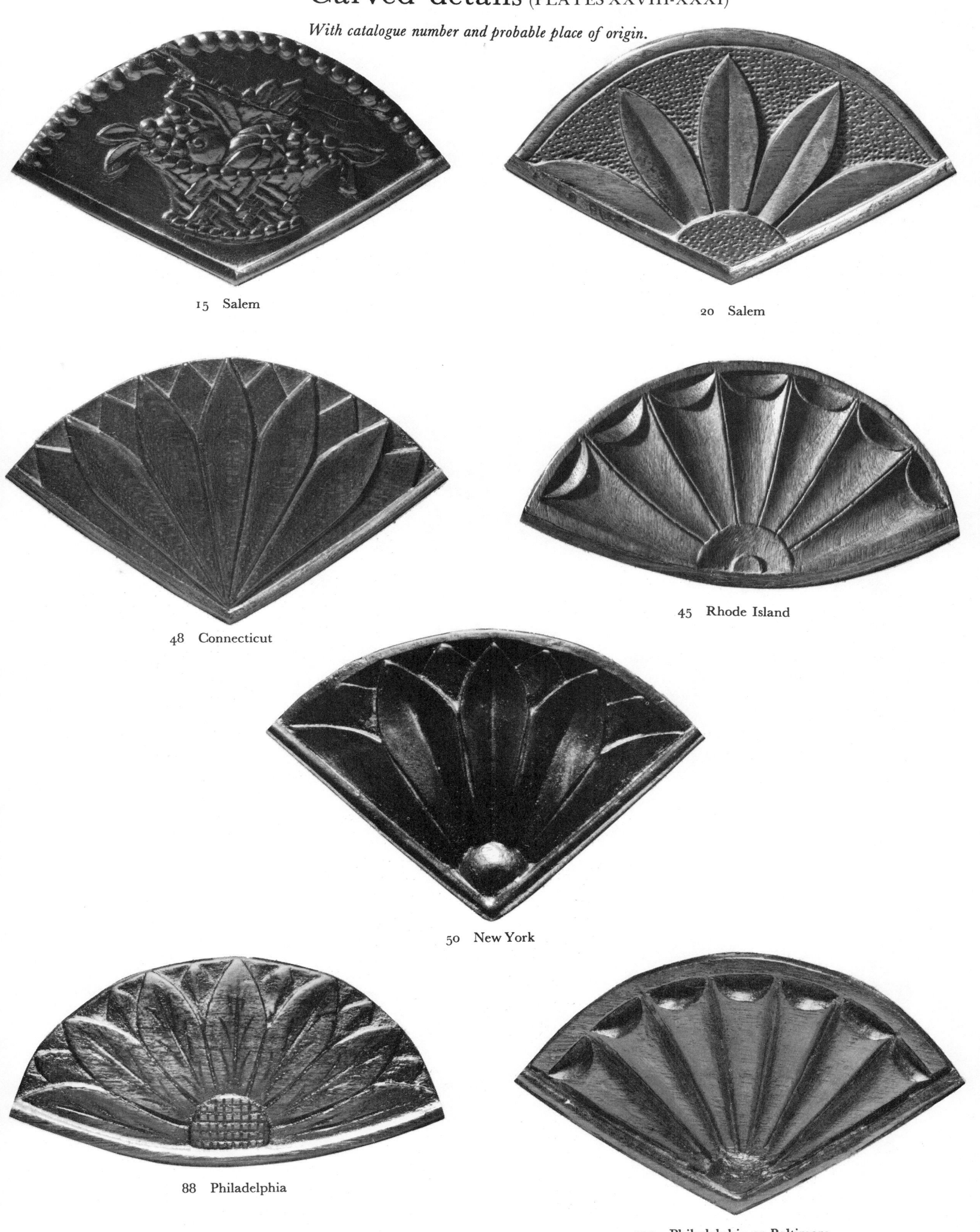

15 Salem

20 Salem

48 Connecticut

45 Rhode Island

50 New York

88 Philadelphia

101 Philadelphia or Baltimore

262 Salem

15 Salem

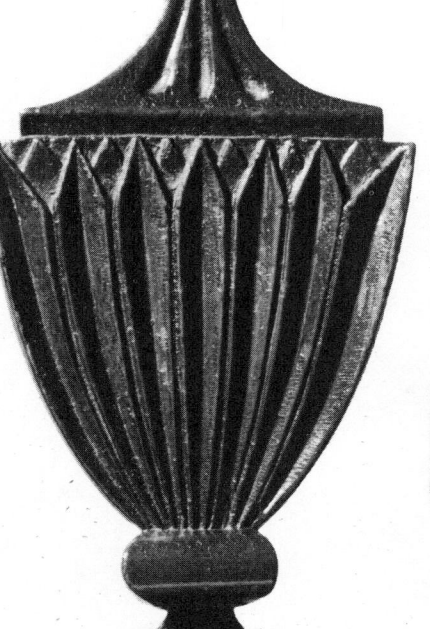

40 Connecticut

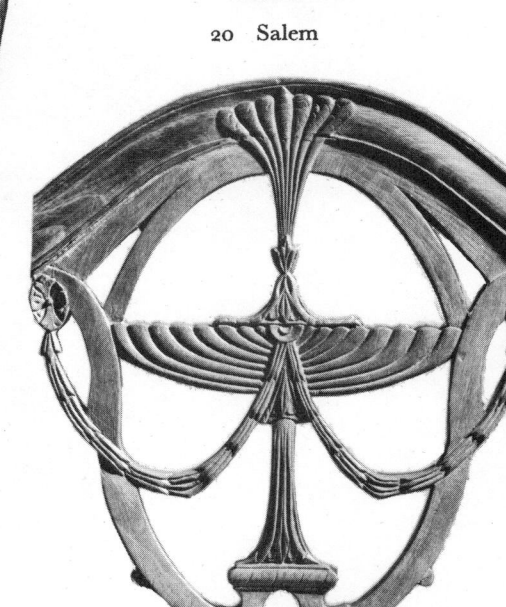

20 Salem

42 Rhode Island

58 New York

45 Rhode Island

99 Baltimore

99 Baltimore

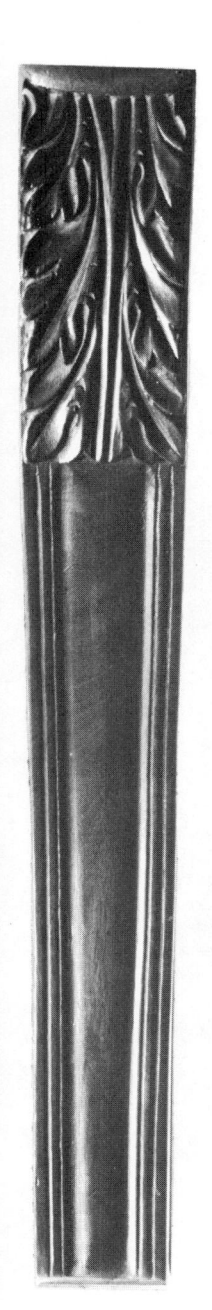

316 Philadelphia

29 Portsmouth

38 Boston

58 New York

72 New York

27 N. E. Massachusetts

93 Philadelphia

315 New York

82 Philadelphia

105 Maryland

99 Baltimore

91 Philadelphia

15 Salem

113 Philadelphia or South

91 Philadelphia

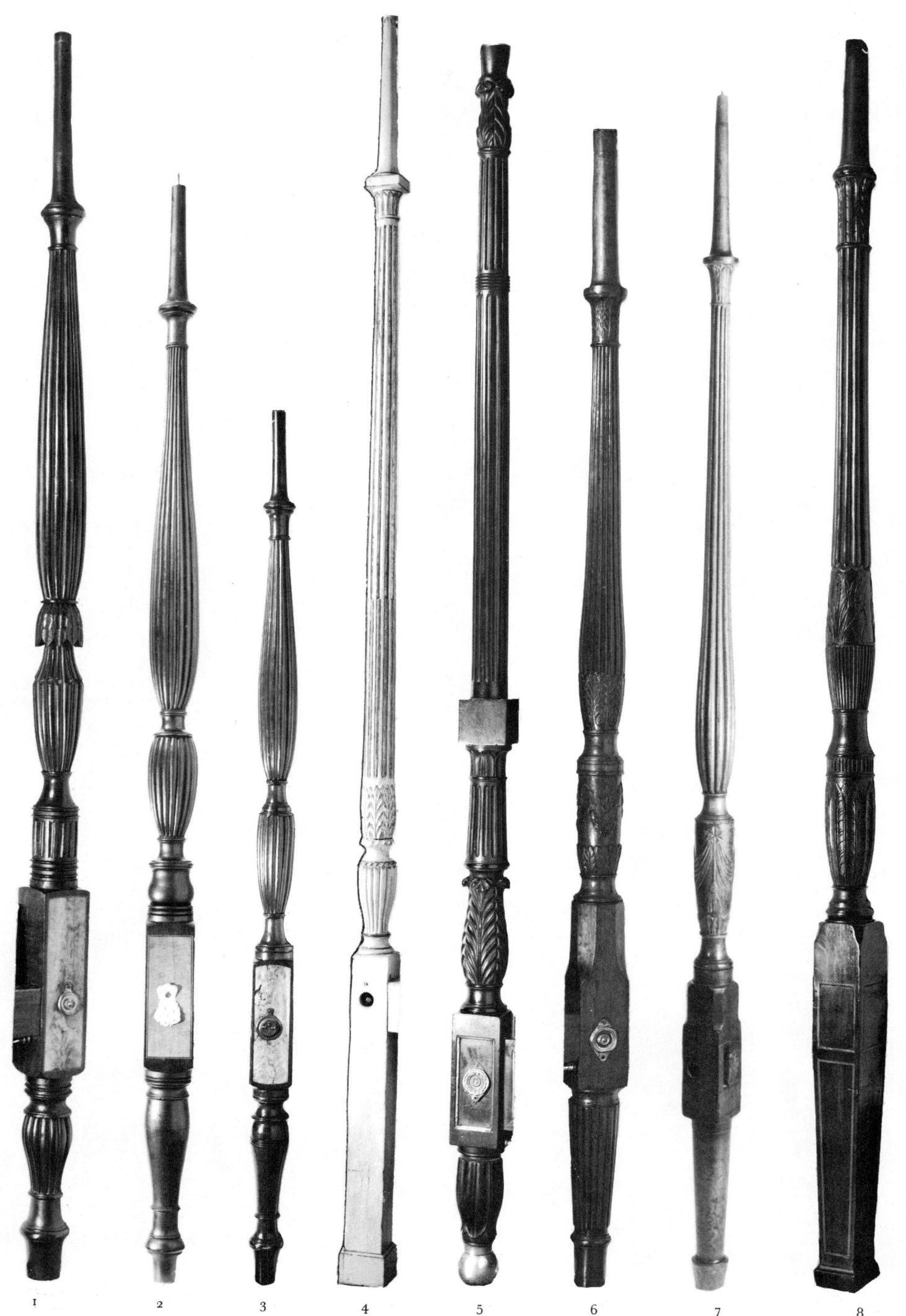

1          2          3          4          5          6          7          8

# Brands, Labels, Stamps, and Inscriptions (PLATES XXXII-XXXV)

*with catalogue numbers of the pieces on which they appear. The numbers of those pieces with similar identification are given in brackets [ ].*

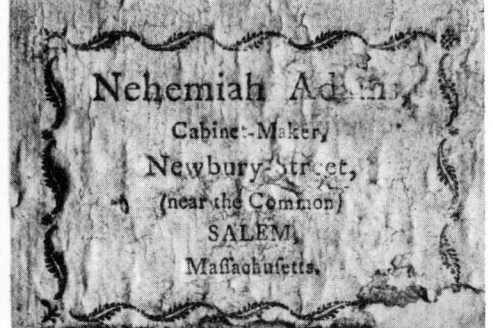

181

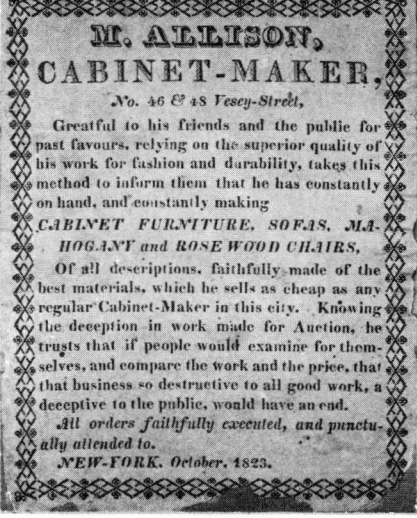

432 [198]

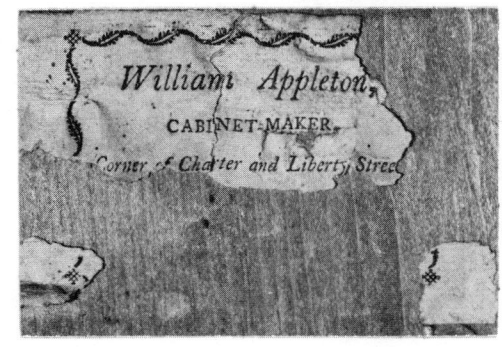

178

30 [110]

30 [110]

35

253

318

116

441

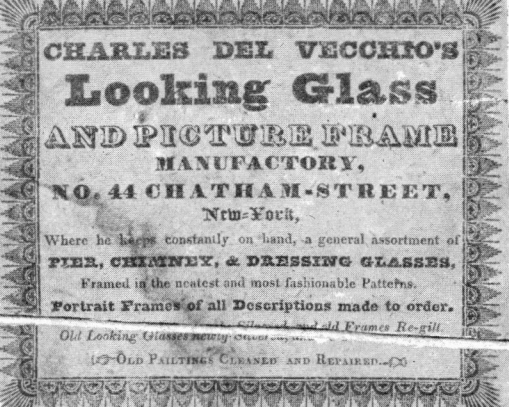

255

249

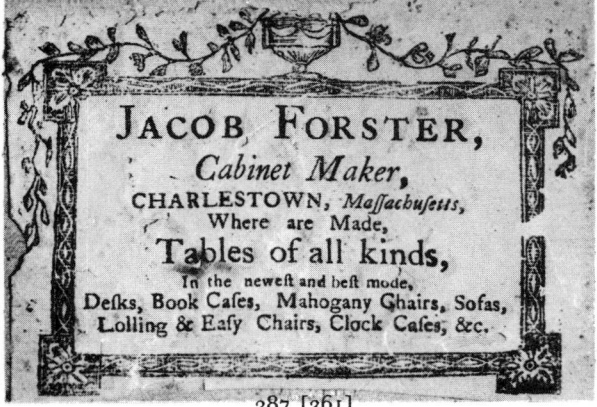

287 [361]

32

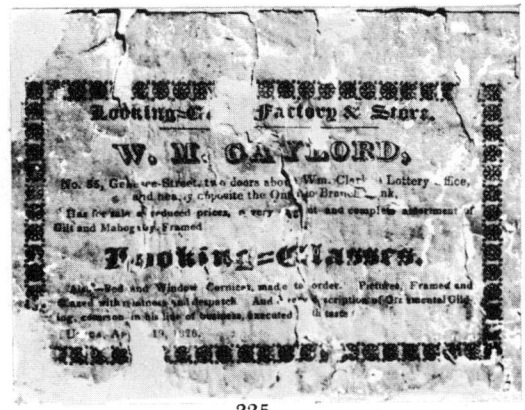

225

491

343

179

305 [346] [347]

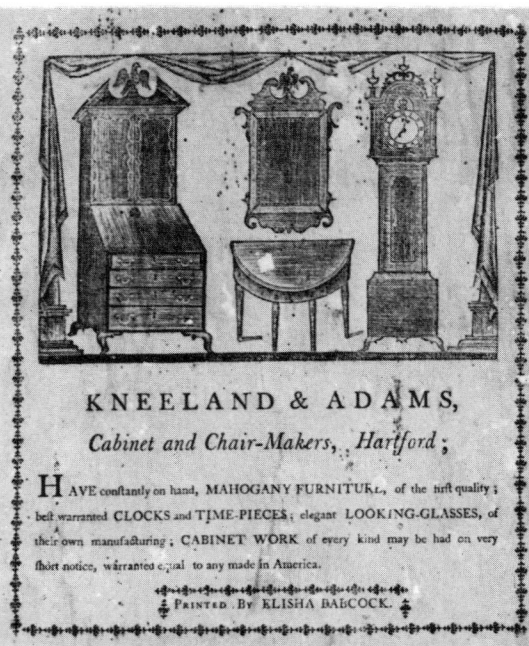

218

306

394

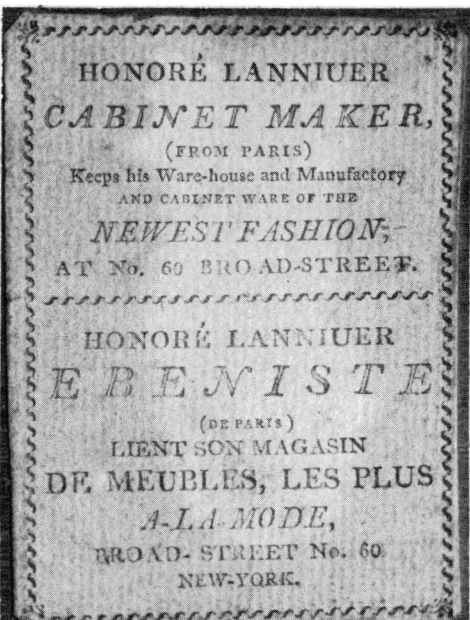

305 [347]

199 [282]

407

310

409

CABINET WORK,
OF ALL KINDS,
Made and warranted, by
*Mark Pitman*
ESSEX STREET, SALEM.
Nearly opposite to Cambridge Street.
Orders gratefully acknowledged, & promptly executed.

358

MADE
BY
Joseph Rawson,
PROVIDENCE.

296

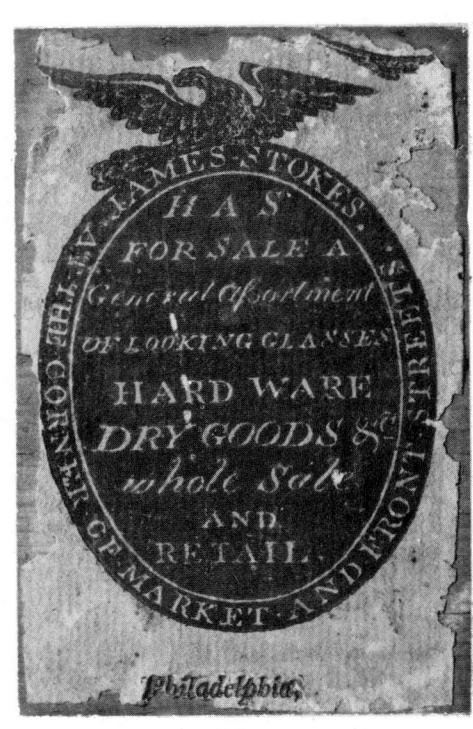

*Nathan Ruggles*
LOOKING-GLASS
*Manufacturer,*
Main-Street, Hartford;
*Connecticut.*
Embroidery & Pictures
Framed
Glass Silvered, Lettered, &c.
Looking Glass Plates, Silvered.

213

JOSEPH RAWSON & SON,
*Cabinet and Chair Makers,*
NEAR THE THEATRE...........SUGAR-LANE,
PROVIDENCE,
Rhode-Island.

191

LEVI RUGGLES,
CABINET MAKER.
No. 2
WINTER STREET—BOSTON.

144

I + S

300

MADE BY
*E & J. Sanderson,*
CABINET AND CHAIR-MAKERS
In Federal-Street,
SALEM,
MASSACHUSETTS.

322

JOHN SEYMOUR & SON,
CABINET MAKERS,
CREEK

184

JOHN S
CABINET MAKER,
ANNAPOLIS.

100

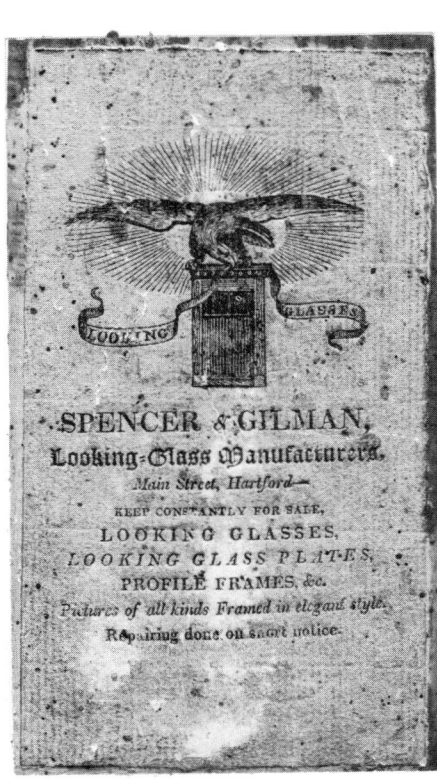

SPENCER & GILMAN,
Looking-Glass Manufacturers,
Main Street, Hartford—
KEEP CONSTANTLY FOR SALE,
LOOKING GLASSES,
LOOKING GLASS PLATES,
PROFILE FRAMES, &c.
Pictures of all kinds Framed in elegant style.
Repairing done on short notice.

244

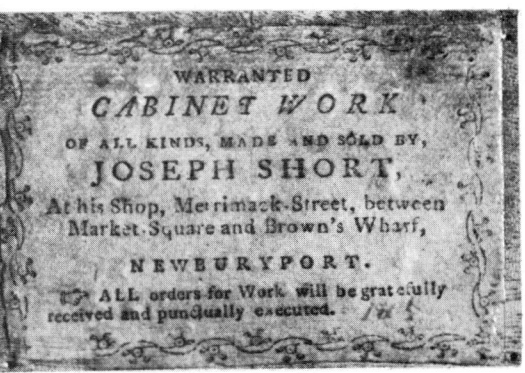

WARRANTED
CABINET WORK
OF ALL KINDS, MADE AND SOLD BY,
JOSEPH SHORT,
At his Shop, Merrimack-Street, between
Market Square and Brown's Wharf,
NEWBURYPORT.
☞ ALL orders for Work will be gratefully
received and punctually executed.

371 [294]

JAMES STOKES
HAS
FOR SALE A
General Assortment
OF LOOKING GLASSES
HARD WARE
DRY GOODS &c
whole Sale
AND
RETAIL
THE CORNER OF MARKET AND FRONT STREETS
Philadelphia.

221

147

31

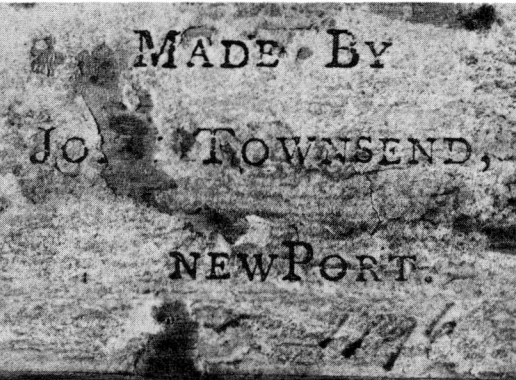

288

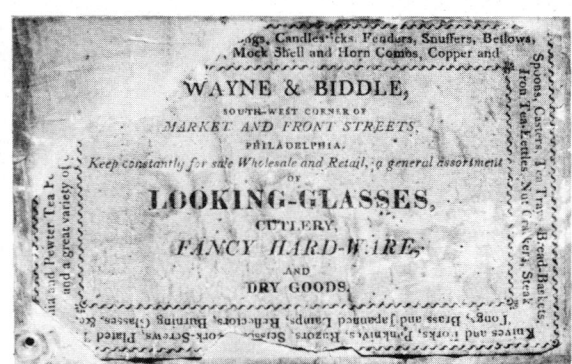

477

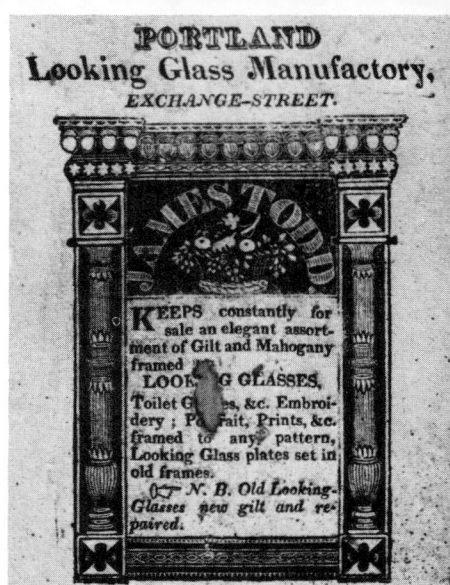

PORTLAND
Looking Glass Manufactory,
EXCHANGE-STREET.

JAMES TODD

KEEPS constantly for sale an elegant assortment of Gilt and Mahogany framed LOOKING GLASSES, Toilet Glasses, &c. Embroidery; Portrait, Prints, &c. framed to any pattern, Looking Glass plates set in old frames.

☞ N. B. No old Looking Glasses new gilt and repaired.

230

ELISHA TUCKER,
CABINET AND CHAIR MANUFACTURER

RESPECTFULLY informs his Friends and the he Manufactures and offers for Sale on reasonable terms 40, MIDDLE STREET....BOSTON, a general assortment CABINET FURNITURE and CHAIRS

Mahogany Looking-Glass Frames of all sizes, executed in the neatest manner and at the shortest

N. B. No exertions shall be spared which will satisfaction to those who may please to favor his demands.

223 [302]

WAYNE & BIDDLE,
SOUTH-WEST CORNER OF
MARKET AND FRONT STREETS,
PHILADELPHIA.
Keep constantly for sale Wholesale and Retail, a general assortment of
LOOKING-GLASSES,
CUTLERY,
FANCY HARD-WARE,
AND
DRY GOODS.

222 [245]

GEORGE WOODRUFF,
CABINET MAKER,
No. 54, JOHN-STREET,

New-York, May, 1818.

331

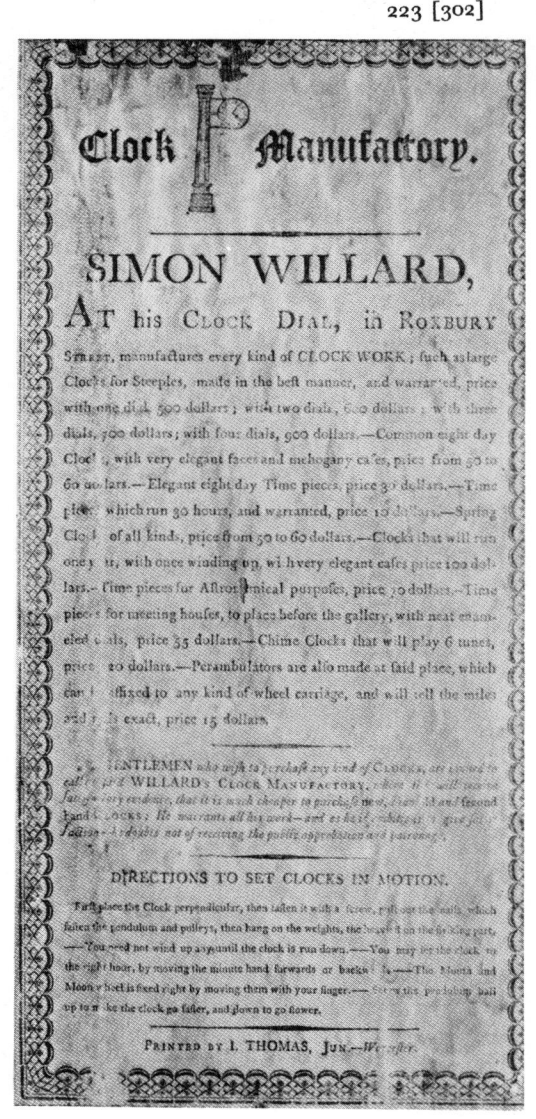

Clock Manufactory.

SIMON WILLARD,
AT his CLOCK DIAL, in ROXBURY

STREET, manufactures every kind of CLOCK WORK; such as large Clocks for Steeples, made in the best manner, and warranted, price with one dial 500 dollars; with two dials, 600 dollars; with three dials, 700 dollars; with four dials, 900 dollars.—Common eight day Clocks, with very elegant faces and mahogany cases, price from 50 to 60 dollars.—Elegant eight day Time pieces, price 30 dollars.—Time pieces which run 30 hours, and warranted, price 10 dollars.—Spring Clocks of all kinds, price from 50 to 60 dollars.—Clocks that will run one year, with once winding up, with very elegant cases price 100 dollars.—Time pieces for Astronomical purposes, price 70 dollars.—Time pieces for meeting houses, to place before the gallery, with neat enameled dials, price 55 dollars.—Chime Clocks that will play 6 tunes, price 20 dollars.—Perambulators are also made at said place, which can be affixed to any kind of wheel carriage, and will tell the miles and rods exact, price 15 dollars.

GENTLEMEN who wish to purchase any kind of CLOCKS, are invited to call at WILLARD's Clock Manufactory, where it will appear from very evidence, that it is much cheaper to purchase new, than old and second hand Clocks; He warrants all his work—and as he is ambitious to give satisfaction he doubts not of receiving the public approbation and patronage.

DIRECTIONS TO SET CLOCKS IN MOTION.

First place the Clock perpendicular, then fasten it with a screw, roll out the nails which fasten the pendulum and pulleys, then hang on the weights, the heaviest on the striking part.—You need not wind up at any until the clock is run down.—You may set the clock to the right hour, by moving the minute hand forwards or backwards.—The Moon and Moon wheel is fixed right by moving them with your finger.—Screw the pendulum ball up to make the clock go faster, and down to go slower.

PRINTED BY I. THOMAS, Jun.—Worcester.

148

# Cabinetmakers' Biographies

The work of the following American cabinetmakers and looking-glass makers and sellers is represented in the Winterthur collections by labeled or well-documented examples. For the most part, the information given here is restricted to working dates and shop locations, largely ascertained from city directories, newspaper advertisements, and the standard works. No attempt is made to include the wealth of biographical information to be found in such books as Ethel Hall Bjerkoe's *The Cabinetmakers of America* or Nancy McClelland's *Duncan Phyfe and the English Regency* or in individual studies which have appeared in numerous articles in *Antiques, American Collector,* and *The Antiquarian.* Under "Notes" new information is occasionally included. References will be found in the bibliography and footnotes to the more important articles on these men and their work. Transcriptions are given here (if complete labels are known) for those labels which are incomplete or which cannot be read in the preceding illustrations. Unless otherwise designated, the men listed are cabinet- or cabinet- and chairmakers.

*Adams, Nehemiah.* Salem. See 181
b. 1769; d. 1840
Working: c. 1790–1840
Location: Newbury and Williams Street, 1790–1804; shop burned, 1798; Brown Street, 1804, in partnership with Thomas Russell Williams.

*Allison, Michael.* N.Y.C. See 198 and 432
d. 1855
Working: 1800–1847
Loc.: 34 and 42 Vesey Street, 1801–1802; 40 Vesey Street, 1804–1805; 40 and 42 Vesey Street, 1806–1807; 42 and 44 Vesey Street, 1808–1815; 46 and 48 Vesey Street, 1816 to 1847.

*Appleton, William.* Salem. See 178
b. 1765; d. 1822
Working: c. 1794–c. 1805
Loc.: A few doors west of Sun Tavern, 1794; corner of Liberty and Charter Streets, 1795–1804.

*Badlam, Stephen.* Dorchester Lower Mills, Mass. See 30 and 110
b. 1751; d. 1815
Working: c. 1785–1815
Loc.: Corner of old Plymouth Road (now River Street), Dorchester Lower Mills.

*Badlam, Stephen, Jr.* Boston. See 253
b. 1779; d. 1847
Working: c. 1820
Loc.: 42 Cornhill, Boston; Old Court House, 1820; Jailer, office at Leveret, house adjoining City Court House, 1827 to 1833; (Res. 17 Warren Street, 1835–1838).

*Brauwers, Joseph.* N.Y.C. See 318
Working: By 1814

Loc.: 163 William Street, 1814; 305 Pearl Street, 1824.
Notes: Several cabinetmakers with various spellings of the name appear in New York directories by 1805; and, in 1814, a *John* Brauwer is listed at 163 William Street. According to Brauwers' label, he was an "ebenist from Paris" and imported ornaments from France.
Label: JOSEPH BRAUWERS
No. 163 William-Street, New-York
(EBENIST, FROM PARIS)
CABINET-MAKER
With the Richest Ornaments just imported from France.

*Buttre, William.* N.Y.C. and Albany. See 471
Working: 1805–after 1815
Loc.: 56 Beekman Street, N.Y.C., 1805; 4 Chatham Square, N.Y.C., 1807; 16 Bowery, N.Y.C., 1808; 17 Bowery, N.Y.C., 1809–1812; 17 Bowery and Crane Wharf, 1813 to 1814; 124 State Street, Albany, 1815.
Notes: Buttre was always listed as a chairmaker, and his advertisements for his Fancy Chair Store describe only various forms of painted seating furniture including rocking and windsor chairs.

*Cermenati (Paul) & Bernarda (John).* Looking-glass makers and sellers. Boston, Newburyport, and Salem. See 224
Working: 1807–1808
Loc.: 2 State Street, Boston, 1807.
Notes: In the 1803 Boston directory, John Bernarda's picture shop was listed at North Row, Fifth Street. On January 10, 1806, Paul Cermenati made purchases from John Doggett. From March 18, 1806, to January, 1807, Doggett's accounts list sales to Cermenati and Monfrino only. From January 8, 1807 to September 20, 1808, Cermenati and

Bernarda were buying glass, gold leaf, and gilt balls from Doggett. On October 31, 1808, Paul Cermenati began buying again in his own name. Barnard Cermenati: 10 State Street, Newburyport, 1807–1809; Essex Street, opposite Albert Gray's Hat Store, Salem, 1809–1812; Portsmouth, 1812; Boston, 1813. In the 1937 Lawton Sale (No. 347) was a looking glass with label of P. Cermenati & Co., 60 Cornhill, Boston. Mary Cermenati's looking-glass store (relation unknown) is listed at 6 Hanover Street in the 1818 Boston directory.

*Churchill, Lemuel.* Boston. See 116
Working: 1805–c. 1828
Loc.: Shop at 26 Orange Street (Res. 114 Orange Street), 1805; High Street, 1820; 33 Washington Street, 1821 to 1827; (Res. Castle Street, 1828).
Notes: Occasionally listed as carver instead of cabinetmaker.
Label: LEMUEL CHURCHILL, MAKES AND SELLS Cabinet Furniture and Chairs, of the NEWEST FASHIONS ALSO BEST OF WORK, AT...

*Connelly, Henry.* Philadelphia. See 441
b. 1770; d. 1826
Working: c. 1800–1824
Loc.: 16 Chestnut Street, c. 1800–1802; 44 Spruce Street, 1803–1807; 72 South Fourth Street, 1808–1818; 8 Library Street (now Sansom), 1819; 72 South Fourth Street, 1820 to 1822; 8 Library Street, 1823–1825.

*Del Vecchio, Charles.* Looking-class maker and seller. N.Y.C. See 255
d. c. 1847
Working: c. 1813–1844
Loc.: 136 Broadway (Looking Glass and Print Store), 1813; 2 Thames Street, 1821; 11 Park Street, 1822; 32 Frankfort Street, 1823; 172 Spring Street, 1824; 19 Nassau Street, 1825; 220 Broadway, 1826; 37 Nassau Street, 1827; 220 Broadway, 1829; 44 Chatham Street, 1830–1839; 220 Broadway (Charles Del Vecchio & Son), 172 Fulton Street, 1841–1842; 2 Chambers Street, 1844.
Notes: In 1837 and 1838, Del Vecchio was listed as an auctioneer and in 1839 and 1840 as fire commissioner. In 1835 through 1842, Joseph John Del Vecchio, probably Charles' son, was listed as making looking glasses at the same address as Charles; and, in 1844, Charles, Jr., is listed separately for the first time, but his home address is the same as Charles, Sr., and Joseph John. In 1847, James R. Del Vecchio is listed in the looking-glass business at 74 Fulton Street, but his home address is the same as the other Del Vecchios, 2 Chambers Street.

*Elliott, John, Jr.* Cabinetmaker and looking-glass seller. Philadelphia. See 249
b. 1739, England; d. 1810, Philadelphia
Working: c. 1762–1810
Loc.: Working with his father, John, Sr.: Walnut Street, 1762 to 1768; Second Street between Market and Arch Streets, or Walnut Street, probably the second Elliott Store ("Three Brushes"), 1768–1776; Market Street, after 1776–1784. Working independently: 60 South Front Street, 1784 to 1804. John Elliott [Jr.] & Sons (John and Daniel): 60 South Front Street, 1804–1810.
Notes: John Elliott, Jr., arrived in Philadelphia, May 27, 1753, with his parents and probably learned the looking-glass business in his father's store on Chestnut Street between 1753 and 1761. He was variously listed in city directories as looking-glass and medicine merchant and as looking-glass manufacturer and druggist. His will designated him as a druggist. The writer firmly believes that the looking glasses bearing the labels of both John Elliott, Sr. and Jr. were not made by them. Those by John, Sr., were mostly, if not all, imported; those by John, Jr., were advertised as of "American Manufacture" and wood analysis indicates them to be so.
Label: JOHN ELLIOTT,
    At No. 60, South Front Street, between Chestnut and

Walnut Streets,
PHILADELPHIA
Sells by Wholesale and Retail Looking Glasses. In neat Mahogany Frames of American Manufacture: Coach Glasses, Window Glass, Spectacles, Painters' Colours, Oil, Varnishes, &c.—And a general Assortment of Drugs and Medicines. N.B. Old Glass new quicksilvered and framed as usual, and new Glass supplied to People's old Frames.

*Forster, Jacob.* Charlestown, Mass. See 32, 287, 361
b. 1764; d. 1838
Working: 1786–c. 1810
Loc.: West corner of Main and Union Streets.

*Gaylord, Wills M.* Looking-glass maker. Utica, New York. See 225
Working: By 1826–1845
Loc.: 55 Genesee Street, nearly opposite the Ontario Branch Bank, 1826–1828; 87 Genesee Street, 1829; 59 Genesee Street, 1829–1834; 81 Genesee Street, 1834–1836; 55 Hotel Street, 1837–1838; 55 Hotel Street (W.M. & E. Gaylord, looking-glass and dry-goods store), 1839–1845.
Label: Looking-Glass Factory & Store W. M. GAYLORD No. 55, Genesee St., two doors above Wm. Clarkes Lottery Office and nearly opposite the Ontario Branch Bank.
    Has for sale at reduced prices, a very elegant and complete assortment of Gilt and Mahogany framed Looking-Glasses.
    Also—Bed and window Cornices made to order. Pictures, Framed and Glazed with neatness and despatch. And every description of Ornamental Gilding, common in his line of business, executed with taste. Utica, April 19, 1826

*Geib, John and Son.* Organ and piano makers. N.Y.C. See 448
Working: c. 1804–1814
Loc.: Bowery, 1804; Leonard, north of Broadway, 1805 to 1809; 95 Leonard, 1810; 36 Sugar-loaf and 95 Leonard, 1812–1813; 55 Sugar-loaf and Leonard, 1814.

*Geib, John, Jr.* Piano-forte maker. N.Y.C. See 450
Working: 1815–1822
Loc.: Franklin, corner of Church, 1816–1819; Carmine, north of Bedford, John Geib (no Jr.), 1820–1822.
Notes: Worked with father as the "son" in John Geib and Son from 1804 to 1814. John Geib, Jr., worked independently following the death of his father in 1814.

*Gostelowe, Jonathan.* Philadelphia. See 285
b. 1745; d. 1795
Working: c. 1768–1793
Loc.: Front Street, next to London Coffee House, before 1776; Church Alley, 1783–1789; 66–68 Market Street, 1790–May 10, 1793; Ridge Road, 1793–February 3, 1795.

*Gragg, Samuel.* Boston. See 491
Working: c. 1809–1837
Loc.: Common Street, house near 56 Newbury, 1809–1810; House on Southac Court, 1813; Tremont Street, house 6 N. Centre Street, 1818–1821; 64 Market Street, house 11 Cresent Court, 1826–1837.
Notes: A Samuel Gragg is listed in the 1803 directory as having a boarding house on Wilson's Lane; and, in 1807, Gragg & Hutchins are listed as chairmakers at 25 Hanover Street.

*Haskell, William.* Salem, Massachusetts. See 343
b. 1791; d. 1860
Working: Before 1817–after 1837.
Loc.: 379 Essex Street, Salem, 1837.

*Hitchcock [Lambert], Alford [Arba] & Co.* Hitchcocksville, Conn. See 473
b. 1795; d. 1852
Working (partnership): 1829–April 1, 1843.
Loc.: Hitchcocksville, Connecticut (now Riverton).
Notes: In 1818, Lambert Hitchcock established a shop for making chair parts on the Farmington River, near Bark-

hamstead, Connecticut. By 1825, he started constructing complete chairs, often stencilled "L. Hitchcock, Hitchcocksville, Connecticut. Warranted." In 1829, he took Arba Alford, Jr., into partnership, changing the firm's name to Hitchcock, Alford & Co.; and in the same year he was forced into bankruptcy with liabilities of $21,525.21. The business was transferred into the hands of four trustees, Hitchcock acting as its agent; but, by 1832, the state of the business had improved enough for him to be able to take it over again on his own account. Hitchcock moved to Unionville in 1843 to continue cabinetmaking, and Alford took his brother Alfred into the company, which continued as Alford and Company until 1846.

*Johnson, Edmund.* Salem, Massachusetts. See 179, 187
d. 1811
Working: c. 1793–1811
Loc.: River and Federal Streets, 1796–1800.
Notes: One of a long line of cabinetmakers, Edmund Johnson was actively involved with the Sandersons in the exportation of furniture, and there are many records of his part ownership of ships.
Label: ALL KINDS OF
       CABINET FURNITURE
       MADE & WARRANTED
       EDMUND JOHNSON,
       Federal Street, SALEM

*Kneeland & Adams.* Cabinet and looking-glass makers. Hartford, Conn. See 40, 218
Samuel Kneeland, b. 1755; d. 1828, Genesee, N.Y. Lemuel Adams, dates unknown
Working (partnership): September 10, 1792–March 9, 1795.
Notes: The firm employed workmen from New York and Boston. As early as 1786, Kneeland was advertising in Hartford, a few yards north of the Bridge; and, in 1798, he left Hartford to take over the shop of the deceased Thomas Bulkley, Farmington. His last advertisement was in the *Connecticut Courant,* August 5, 1799. In 1796, Adams made furniture for the Conn. State House and was listed as a cabinetmaker on the south side of Ferry Street in the 1799 Hartford directory. Nothing thereafter is known about him expect for the leasing of his property, June 1, 1808.

*Lannuier, Charles-Honoré.* N.Y.C. See 305, 306, 346, 347, 394
b. 1779, Chantilly, France; d. 1819, New York
Working: c. 1803–1819
Loc.: 60 Broad Street, 1804–1819.
Notes: After being trained in France, possibly under his brother, Nicholas-Louis-Cyrille Lannuier, *ébéniste* of Paris, Charles-Honoré came to New York in July of 1803. There for the next sixteen years, he made furniture in the French taste. Most of the more than fifty known documented pieces are of outstanding quality.

*McIntire, Samuel.* Carver, builder and architect. Salem. See 14, 15, 16, 23, 262, 263, 264, 269, 270, 429
b. 1757; d. 1811
Working: c. 1782–1811
Loc.: 29 Summer Street, Salem.
Notes: There seems little doubt that Samuel McIntire did not make furniture, but did carve it. No labeled pieces are known, and identification of his carving on furniture rests largely on pieces that have descended from Elias Hasket Derby, for whom he is known to have done carving.

*McIntire, Samuel Field.* Carver. Salem. See 413, 430
b. 1789; d. 1819
Working: c. 1800–1819
Loc.: 29 Summer Street, Salem.
Notes: Worked with his father until the latter's death in 1811, after which he was in business by himself on Summer Street. Although his later work is thought to be coarser than that of his father, it is impossible to differentiate their earlier work.

*Needham, Thomas.* Salem, Massachusetts. See 199, 282
b. 1780; d. 1858

Working: c. 1802–1841
Loc: Shop, Charter Street, Salem, 1802–?. In partnership with James Kimball, 1829–1841.
Notes: Inasmuch as there were at least three Thomas Needhams who were cabinetmakers in Salem and Boston at various times between 1750 and 1841, there has been some confusion as to their genealogy and identification. There were: Thomas, Sr. (b. 1728, d. ?); his son, Thomas, Jr. (b. 1755; d. 1787); and Thomas, Jr.'s son, Thomas (b. 1780; d. 1850). The inventory of the "Cabbinet Tools" and "Sundry Cabbinet" stock of one of these men (taken in Boston) is headed "Thomas Needham, Junʳ Cabbinet Maker late of Salem, July 12, 1787." It seems probable that he and his father, Thomas, Sr., went from Salem to Boston after the Revolution and that Thomas, Sr., continued working there after the death of his son and is the Thomas Needham listed in the Boston Directory of 1796. He is supposed to have returned to Salem and set up shop on Charter Street in 1802. This may be true, but it seems more likely that it was his grandson, then 22 years old (1780 to 1858), who started there at that time; and it is the writer's belief that the several known pieces of furniture labeled "Thomas Needham" were all made by the latter who had a distinguished career and served in many public offices. In 1829 he formed a partnership with James Kimball which lasted until 1841, when he retired from business. The last statement is based on Robert S. Rantoul's article, "A Notice of James Kimball," *Historical Collections of the Essex Institute,* XVIII (April, May, June, 1881), p. 145. wherein it is stated that James Kimball (b. Oct. 14, 1808, in Salem) left school April, 1822, "to become an apprentice with Thomas Needham of Salem in the trade of cabinet-making and with him, on reaching his majority, he formed a co-partnership. After twelve years as a partner with Mr. Needham, Mr. Kimball took the business [c. 1841] on his own account adding to it the manufacture of chairs...."

*Nisbet, Thomas.* St. John, New Brunswick, Nova Scotia. See 407
Working: 1813–1848
Loc.: Prince William Street, near the Treasurer's Office, 1813–1822; Prince William Street, next to Munson Jarvis, 1823–1848.
Notes: In 1834, Thomas Nisbet, Jr., became a partner, but died in 1845. Three years later Thomas Nisbet, Sr., turned over the business to another son, Robert.

*Noyes, Samuel S.* East Sudbury, Massachusetts. See 310
Working: Before 1810–1815 or later.
Loc.: Near the Causeway, East Sudbury.

*Phyfe, Duncan* N.Y.C. See 66, 67, 68, 277, 409
b. Loch Fannich, Scotland, 1768; d. New York, 1854
Working: c. 1792–1847
Loc.: (Duncan Fife) 2 Broad Street, 1792; (Duncan Phyfe), 3 Broad Street, 1794; 35 Partition Street, 1796–1805; 34–35 Partition Street, 1806–1810; 33–35 Partition Street, 1811–1815; Partition Street became Fulton Street and was renumbered 168–172 Fulton, 1816; 168–172 Fulton Street (Res. 169 Fulton), 1817–1827; 192–194 Fulton Street (Res. 193 Fulton), 1829–1836; 194 Fulton Street (Duncan Phyfe & Sons), 1837–1839; 194 Fulton Street (Duncan Phyfe & Son), 1840–1847.
Notes: Duncan Phyfe's widowed mother arrived in America in 1784 and settled in Albany, New York, with her children. There Duncan served his apprenticeship and possibly worked as a journeyman before coming to N.Y.C. about 1790 (possibly as late as 1792). Although much information is available about his later life and work, almost nothing is known of his early career.

*Pitman, Mark.* Salem. See 299 and 358
b. 1779; d. 1829
Working: c. 1800–c. 1827
Loc.: Essex Street, nearly opposite Cambridge Street, Salem.

Notes: Mark Pitman, Jr., was also a cabinetmaker. Mark Pitman, Sr., may have worked until the time of his death. However, the last record of him is Joseph True's bill for carving on October 18, 1827.

*Ruggles, Levi.* Boston. See 144
d. 1855
Working: c. 1810–1855
Loc.: 2½ Winter Street, 1813–1816; 51 Marlborough Street, 1817–1818; Rear 21 Marlborough Street, 1820–1821; 101 Charles Street, 1826–1855.
Notes: Ruggles' five sons also became cabinetmakers and worked with him.
Label: LEVI RUGGLES
    CABINET MAKER,
    No. 2
    WINTER STREET—BOSTON

*Ruggles, Nathan.* Looking-glass maker and seller. Hartford, Conn. See 213
b. 1774; d. 1835
Working: 1803–1835
Loc.: N. Ruggles & Co. (partnership with Charles Mather, Jr.), August 11, 1803–June 21, 1804; Ruggles & Dunbar (Azell), Main Street, near the bridge, July 5, 1804–April 1, 1806; Nathan Ruggles, same address, 1806–1819; Ruggles Eagle Looking-glass Manufactory, same address, 1819 to 1828; Nathan Ruggles & Son (partnership with Nathan, Jr.), 176 Main Street, 1828–1835.
Notes: It is not known when Ruggles began working, but he went bankrupt in Hartford as a merchant and chapman, March 3, 1803.
Label: Nathan Ruggles,
    LOOKING-GLASS
    Manufacturer,
    Main-Street, Hartford;
    Connecticut.
    Embroide[ry] & Pictures
    Fra[m]ed
    Glass-Si[lvered], Lettered, &c.
    Looking G[la]ss. Plates. Silvered.

*Sailor, John.* Philadelphia. See 423
Working: July, 1813
Notes: To date, no information has been found about John Sailor, cabinetmaker, in Philadelphia. However, there was a John Sailor listed in the directories as a tailor in the early 1800's and a John Sailor, brickmaker, in 1814.

*Sanderson, Elijah and Jacob.* Salem. See 300 and 322
Elijah: b. 1752, d. 1825. Jacob: b. 1757, d. 1810
Working (partnership): c. 1779–1810
Loc.: Federal Street, Salem.
Notes: The Sandersons were among the outstanding crafts-men of Salem, employing many apprentices and journey-men and directing a furniture cooperative export concern, which as early as 1788 was shipping Salem furniture to ports in the Southern states, East and West Indies, and South America, to be sold by the ship's captain to the best advantage possible.
Label: MADE BY
    E & J. Sanderson,
    CABINET AND CHAIR MAKERS,
    In Federal-Street,
    SALEM,
    MASSACHUSETTS

*Seymour, John & Son.* Boston. See 184, 185, 186
John: b. c. 1738; d. probably 1818. Thomas: b. 1771; d. 1848
Working (partnership): 1794–c. 1803
Loc.: John and Thomas, c. 1796–1803, Creek Square; Thomas alone, 1804–1843.
Notes: The Seymours arrived in Portland, Maine, from Axminster, County Devon, England, in 1785, where John Seymour had probably learned and practiced his trade. The family moved to Boston, 1794, and Thomas appears to have been taken in as a partner. After 1806, John lived

on Common Street, moving to Portland Street in 1813, but no occupation was listed. In 1805–1808, Thomas had a house and furniture warehouse on Common Street; in 1813 his warehouse was on Congress Street, and from 1815–1843 at various Washington Street addresses.

*Shaw, John.* Annapolis, Maryland. See 100
Working: 1773–prob. c. 1828, advertised until 1794.
Loc.: Church Street, 1775–1794.
Notes: The partnership of John Shaw and Archibald Chis-holm was first advertised in May, 1773, and notice of its dissolution was served November 13, 1776. However, at least once, in 1776, the firm advertised as Middleton, Shaw & Chisholm.

*Short, Joseph.* Newburyport, Massachusetts. See 294, 371
Working: Late 18th c.–early 19th c.
Loc.: Merrimack Street, between Market Square and Brown's Wharf.
Notes: One of a family of three generations of cabinetmakers, but Joseph was the only one known to have labeled his furniture.

*Spencer and Gilman.* Looking-glass makers and sellers. Hartford, Connecticut. See 244
Stephen Spencer: no dates known. Eli Gilman: b. 1787; d. 1842
Working (partnership): May 20, 1808–after January, 1825.
Loc.: Main Street, Hartford.
Notes: In May, 1806, Stephen Spencer and Elisha Smith removed their Looking Glass Manufactory from New Haven to Hartford. In January, 1800, Eli Gilman was taken into partnership under the new firm name, Spencer, Smith, and Company. When Smith left the partnership on May 20 of the same year, the firm name was changed to Spencer and Gilman. They continued to be listed in this way in the Hartford directories through 1825. But in the 1828 directory, the listing is Eli Gilman and Company. As late as 1842, the firm was still listed in this way. (For much of the above information, the writer is indebted to Thomas Harlow and Phylis Kihn of the Connecticut Historical Society.)

*Stedman, G.* Norwich, Vermont. See 147
Working: Early 19th c.
Notes: The only record of this craftsman is the inscription "Made by G. Stedman Norwich Vermont" pencilled on a drawer of Winterthur's bombé-front chest. The "Made by" unfortunately was not included in the photograph. To date the painstaking searches of Prof. Herbert Hill and members of the Vermont Historical Society has revealed not a trace of G. Stedman, who may have been an itinerant cabinet-maker possibly trained in Connecticut or Western Massa-chusetts. No greater success has rewarded the efforts of Houghton Bulkeley and Ada Chase in Connecticut.

*Stokes, James.* Looking-glass seller. Philadelphia See 221
Working: c. 1790–c. 1810
Loc.: Merchant, 2 South Front Street on southwest corner of Front and Market Streets, 1791–1798; Merchant, 16 South Market Street, 1801; Merchant, 2 South Front Street (Res. 1 North Eighth Street, 1802–1804); Gentlemen, 1 North Eighth Street, 1805–1809; Broker and commission merchant, 2 South Front Street, 1810.
Notes: Evidently, Stokes did not make looking glasses, but only sold them. In 1811, Wayne (Caleb P.) & Biddle (Charles, Jr.) became successors to Stokes at the same ad-dress. Biddle was Stokes' son-in-law.

*Stone & Alexander.* Boston
Working: 1792–1796
Notes: This partnership, in effect from about 1792 to 1796 at Prince and Back Streets, consisted of William Alexander and possibly Samuel Stone, listed as a cabinetmaker at Pitt's Lane in 1796.

*Todd, James.* Looking-glass maker. Portland, Maine. See 230
b. 1794; d. 1866
Working: 1820–1866

Loc.: Exchange Street, 1820–(?); Middle Street, (?)–1866.
Notes: Marion R. Small, Librarian of the Maine Historical Society, kindly supplied the following information from a clipping dated April 14, 1884, in a scrap book of Portland Obituaries (Vol. 9, page 67): Death of James Todd—born in Hingham, Mass., Jan. 8, 1794. He came to Portland in 1820 and commenced business on Exchange Street in the Preble block where he continued many years, subsequently removing to Middle Street under the firm name of Todd & Beckett and Jas. Todd & Son, until the great fire of 1866.
Label: PORTLAND
Looking Glass Manufactory,
EXCHANGE-STREET.
JAMES TODD
Keeps constantly for sale an elegant assortment of Gilt and Mahogany framed
LOOKING GLASSES,
Toilet Glasses, &c. Embroidery; Portrait, Prints, &c. framed to any pattern, Looking Glass plates set in old frames. N. B. Old Looking-Glasses new gilt and repaired.
*Toppan, Abner.* Newburyport, Mass. See 357
b. 1764; d. 1826
Working: 1790–1836
Loc.: High Street, 1798
*Townsend, John.* Newport, Rhode Island. See 288
b. 1732; d. 1809
Working: c. 1764–1809
Notes: Believed to have worked with his father, Christopher, until the latter's death in 1773, though extant bills indicate he was working "on his own" at least in part by 1764. More than a dozen labeled pieces attest to the high standards of workmanship of this Quaker cabinetmaker who worked in both the Chippendale and Federal styles. Houghton Bulkeley has dispelled the myth that he worked in Connecticut during the Revolution (*Bulletin*, Connecticut Historical Society, July, 1960, pp. 80–83).
*Trotter, Daniel.* Philadelphia. See 82
b. 1747; d. 1800
Working: 1769–1799
Notes: Completed apprenticeship under William Wayne, 1768. First known to have been working independently, August, 1769. Entered into partnership with John Webb, 1771. Dissolved partnership with John Webb, April, 1774. Opened shop on Water Street, c. 1774. Water Street between Front and Second, 1785. 61 N. Water, 1791. 100 N. Front, 1795. Entered into partnership with Ephraim Haines, his son-in-law, 1799.
*Tucker, Elisha.* Cabinet and looking-glass maker. Boston. See 223 and 302
d. 1827
Working: 1809–1827

Loc.: 40 Middle Street, 1809, 1810; Williams Court, 1826, 1827.
Label: ELISHA TUCKER,
CABINET AND CHAIR
MANUFACTURER,
RESPECTFULLY informs his Friends and the Publick, that he Manufactures and offers for Sale on reasonable terms, at No. 40 MIDDLE STREET... BOSTON, a general assortment of CABINET FURNITURE and CHAIRS. Mahogany Looking-Glass Frames of all sizes, executed in the neatest manner and at the shortest notice.
N. B. No exertions shall be spared which will serve to render satisfaction to those who may please to favor him with their comands.
*Vose and Coates.* Boston. See 477
Isaac Vose, c. 1823. Joshua Coates, d. 1818
Working (partnership): 1805–1818
Loc.: Washington Street, 1805–1818. (The firm name of Vose and Coates was changed to Vose, Coates and Company when Isaac Vose, Jr., was taken into the partnership in 1816.)
Notes: Isaac Vose, cabinetmaker, is listed at Orange Street, Boston, in 1789, and at Washington Street from 1800 to 1803.
*Wayne & Biddle.* Merchants. Philadelphia. See 222, 245. Caleb P. Wayne and Charles Biddle, Jr.
Working (partnership): 1811–1822
Loc.: Looking-glass and fancy store, southwest corner of Front and High (now Market) Streets.
Notes: In 1823, Wayne was listed as a merchant at the southwest corner of Fourth and Market Streets (130 Market), and Biddle retained the dry-goods and looking-glass store at Front and Market Streets. Although their label is incomplete, it shows that in addition to looking glasses they sold many articles of hardware as well as dry goods.
*Wilmerding, Christian William.* Looking-glass seller. N. Y. C. See 212
b. 1762, Brunswick, Germany; d. 1832
Notes: Came to N. Y. C., 1783. Advertised New-York Daily Gazette, Aug. 13 as importer, Broad Way and Dye Street. 46 Maiden Lane on label of looking glass sold May 5, 1791. He was abroad. His partner, Samuel Falkenhan, perhaps his brother-in-law, ran his shop in Maiden Lane, 1795 to 1798. Last listing in N. Y. directories as a merchant. Thereafter, listed as brewer. Retired from business to Moscow, N. Y., 1821.
*Woodruff, George.* New York. See 331
d. 1819
Working: c. 1808–1816
Loc.: 54 John Street, 1808–1810; 90 Beekman Street, 1811 to 1813; 57 Broad Street, 1814–1815; 57 & 59 Broad Street, 1816.

# Bibliography

## GENERAL

*America's Arts and Skills.* New York: E. P. Dutton & Company, Inc., 1957.

*The Antiques Treasury of Furniture and Other Decorative Arts.* Edited by Alice Winchester and the Staff of *Antiques Magazine.* New York: E. P. Dutton & Company, Inc., 1959.

Barr, Lockwood. "An 'Unique' Willard Timepiece," *Bulletin of the National Association of Clock Collectors,* Inc., IX (December, 1959), 16.

Bjerkoe, Ethel Hall. *The Cabinetmakers of America.* Garden City, New York: Doubleday and Company, 1957.

Brainard, Newton C. *The Hartford State House of 1796.* Hartford: The Connecticut Historical Society, 1964.

Brazer, Esther Stevens. *Early American Decoration.* Memorial edition. Springfield, Massachusetts: The Pond-Ekberg Company, 1947.

[Brazer], Esther Stevens Fraser. "Painted Furniture in America...," *Antiques,* V (June, 1924), 302–306; VI (September, 1924), 141–146; VII (January, 1925), 15–17.

Comstock, Helen. *American Furniture: Seventeenth, Eighteenth, and Nineteenth Century Styles.* New York: Viking Press, 1962.

—— (ed). *The Concise Encyclopedia of American Antiques.* 2 vols. New York: Hawthorn Books, Inc., [1958].

——. "Mount Vernon Centennial," *Antiques,* LXIV (July, 1953), 30–37.

——. "Sources of American Chair Design in the Federal Period," *American Collector,* XVI (February, 1947), 12–13, 20.

Davidson, Marshall B. *Life in America.* 2 vols. New York: Houghton Mifflin Company, 1951.

Downs, Joseph. *American Furniture, Queen Anne and Chippendale Periods.* New York: The Macmillan Company, 1952.

Drepperd, Carl William. *American Clocks and Clockmakers.* Boston: C. T. Branford Co., 1958.

Eckhardt, George H. *Pennsylvania Clocks and Clockmakers.* New York: Devin-Adair Co., 1955.

Gates, Winifred C. "Journal of a Cabinet Maker's Apprentice," *The Chronicle of Early American Industries Association, Inc.,* XV, No. 2 (June, 1962), 23–24; No. 3 (September, 1962), 35–36.

Groce, George C., and Wallace, David H. *The New-York Historical Society's Dictionary of Artists in America, 1564–1860.* New Haven: Yale University Press, 1957.

Hayward, Helena (ed.). *World Furniture.* New York: McGraw-Hill Book Company, 1965.

Hinckley, F. Lewis. *A Directory of Antique Furniture.* New York: Crown Publishers, Inc., 1953.

——. *Directory of the Historic Cabinet Woods.* New York: Crown Publishers, Inc., 1960.

Hoopes, Penrose R. *Connecticut Clockmakers of the Eighteenth Century.* Hartford, Conn.: Edwin Valentine Mitchell; New York: Dodd, Mead & Company, 1930.

——. *Shop Records of Daniel Burnap, Clockmaker.* [Hartford, Conn.]: The Connecticut Historical Society, 1958.

Hopkinson, Francis. *Account of the Grand Federal Procession, Philadelphia, 1788.* Edited by Whitfield J. Bell, Jr. Boston: The Old South Association, 1962.

Hummel, Charles F. "Samuel Rowland Fisher's Catalogue of English Hardware," *Winterthur Portfolio I.* Winterthur, Delaware: The Henry Francis du Pont Winterthur Museum, Inc., 1964, 188–197.

Kimball, Fiske. *The Creation of the Rococo.* Philadelphia: Philadelphia Museum of Art, 1943.

Kimball, Fiske, and Donnell, Edna. "The Creators of the Chippendale Style," *Metropolitan Museum Studies.* New York, 1928–1930.

Kimball, Marie G. *Furnishings of Monticello.* Charlottesville, Virginia: Thomas Jefferson Memorial Foundation, 1954.

——. "The Original Furnishings of the White House," *Antiques,* XV (June, 1929), 481–486.

Lea, Zilla Rider (ed.). *The Ornamented Chair, Its Development in America (1700–1890).* Rutland, Vermont: Charles E. Tuttle Company, 1960.

Lockwood, Luke Vincent. *Colonial Furniture in America.* 2 vols., 3rd ed. New York: Charles Scribner's Sons, 1926.

Lyon, Irving W. *The Colonial Furniture of New England.* Boston and New York: Houghton Mifflin Company, 1924.

Marsh, Moreton. *The Easy Expert in Collecting and Restoring American Antiques.* Philadelphia and New York: J. B. Lippincott Company, 1959.

Metropolitan Museum of Art. *Guide to the Collections, American Wing.* New York: The Metropolitan Museum of Art, 1961.

——. *A Handbook of the American Wing,* by R. T. H. Halsey and Charles Over Cornelius. 7th ed. revised by Joseph Downs. New York: The Metropolitan Museum of Art, 1942.

Miller, Edgar C., Jr. *American Antique Furniture.* New York: M. Barrows & Company, Inc., 1937.

Nagel, Charles. *American Furniture, 1650–1850.* New York: Chanticleer Press, 1949.

Nutting, Wallace. *Furniture Treasury.* 3 vols. Framingham, Massachusetts: Old America Co., 1928–1933; reprinted New York: The Macmillan Company, 1948, 1954.

Ormsbee, Thomas Hamilton. *Early American Furniture Makers.* New York: Tudor Publishing Company, 1930.

Otto, Celia Jackson. *American Furniture of the Nineteenth Century.* New York: The Viking Press, 1965.

Palmer, Brooks. *The Book of American Clocks.* New York: The Macmillan Company, 1950.

Pierson, William H., Jr. and Davidson, Martha (eds.). *Arts of the United States: A Pictorial Survey.* New York: McGraw-Hill Book Company, Inc., 1960.

Raley, Robert L. "Interior Designs by Benjamin Henry Latrobe for the President's House," *Antiques,* LXXV (June, 1959), 568–571.

Ralston, Ruth. "The Style Antique in Furniture, I: Its Sources and its Creators," *Antiques,* XLVII (May, 1945), 278–281.

——. "The Style Antique in Furniture, II: Its American Manifestations," *Antiques,* XLVIII (October, 1945), 208.

Randall, Richard H., Jr. *American Furniture in the Museum of Fine Arts, Boston.* Boston, Mass.: Museum of Fine Arts, 1965.

Rowell, Hugh Grant. "A Unique Willard Clock," *American*

Collector, XII (August, 1943), 5.

Sack, Albert. *Fine Points of Furniture: Early American*. New York: Crown Publishers, Inc., 1950.

Singleton, Esther. *The Furniture of Our Forefathers*. 2 vols. New York: Doubleday, Page & Co., 1906.

Swan, Mabel M. "The Man Who Made Brass Works for Willard Clocks," *Antiques*, XVII (June, 1930), 524–526.

Sweeney, John A. H. "The Cabinetmaker in America," *Antiques*, LXX (October, 1956), 366–369.

——. *Winterthur Illustrated*. [New York: Chanticleer Press], 1963.

Symonds, R.W. "The English Export Trade in Furniture to Colonial America, II," *Antiques*, XXVIII (October, 1935), 156–159.

United States. Department of Agriculture. *Woods, Colors and Kinds*. Washington, D.C., 1956.

Verlet, Pierre. *French Royal Furniture*. London: Barrie and Rockliff, 1963.

Walcott, William Stuart, Jr. "Ten Important American Sideboards," *Antiques*, XIV (December, 1928), 516–522.

Webster, Thomas. *An Encyclopaedia of Domestic Economy*. New York: Harper & Brothers, 1845.

## MONOGRAPHS AND STUDIES OF REGIONAL AMERICAN FURNITURE AND INDIVIDUAL CRAFTSMEN

"Account Book of Thomas Elfe, 1768–1775," *South Carolina Historical and Genealogical Magazine*, XXXV–XLII (1934 to 1941).

"All by Philadelphia Cabinetmakers," *American Collector*, III (April 18, 1935), 5.

Beirne, Rosamond Randall. "John Shaw, Cabinetmaker," *Antiques*, LXXVIII (December, 1960), 554–558.

Belknap, Henry Wyckoff. *Artists and Craftsmen of Essex County, Massachusetts*. Salem, Massachusetts: The Essex Institute, 1927.

——. "Furniture Exported by Cabinetmakers of Salem," *Essex Institute Historical Collections*, LXXXV (1949), 335 to 359.

Berkeley, Henry J. "Early Maryland Furniture," *Antiques*, XVIII (September, 1930), 208–211.

——. "A Register of the Cabinet Makers and Allied Trades in Maryland, as Shown by the Newspapers and Directories, 1746–1820," *Maryland Historical Magazine*, XXV (March, 1930), 1–27.

Bissell, Charles S. *Antique Furniture in Suffield, Connecticut, 1670 to 1835*. Hartford, Connecticut: Connecticut Historical Society and Suffield Historical Society, 1956.

Brazer, Clarence Wilson. "Jonathan Gostelowe, Philadelphia Cabinet and Chair Maker," Part 1, *Antiques*, IX (June, 1926), 385–392; Part 2, *Antiques*, X (August, 1926), 125 to 132.

Bulkeley, Houghton. "The Norwich Cabinetmakers," *The Connecticut Historical Society Bulletin*, XXIX (July, 1964), 76–85.

Burroughs, Paul H. *Southern Antiques*. Richmond: Garrett & Massie, Inc., 1931.

Burton, E. Milby. *Charleston Furniture, 1700–1825*. Charleston, South Carolina: The Charleston Museum, 1955.

——. "Thomas Elfe, Charleston Cabinet-Maker," *Museum Leaflet 25*. Charleston, South Carolina: The Charleston Museum, 1952.

Carpenter, Ralph E., Jr. *The Arts and Crafts of Newport, Rhode Island, 1640–1820*. Newport, Rhode Island: The Preservation Society of Newport County, 1954.

Carson, Marian S. "Henry Connelly and Ephraim Haines...," *Philadelphia Museum Bulletin*, XLVIII (Spring, 1953), 35–47.

——. "Sheraton's Influence in Philadelphia," *Antiques*, LXIII (April, 1953), 342–345.

——. "Washington Furniture at Mount Vernon," *American Collector*, XVI (July, 1947), 9–11, 22.

Castrodale, Anne. "Daniel Trotter, Philadelphia Cabinetmaker" (unpublished Master's Thesis, University of Delaware, 1962).

"A Chair Ascribed to the Seymours," *Antiques*, XL (September, 1941), 149.

Clark, Raymond B., Jr. "Jonathan Gostelowe (1744–1795): Philadelphia Cabinetmaker" (unpublished Master's Thesis, University of Delaware, 1956).

Comstock, Helen. "McIntire in Antiques," *Antiques*, LXXI (April, 1957), 338–341.

Cornelius, Charles Over. *Furniture Masterpieces of Duncan Phyfe*. Garden City, New York: Doubleday, Page, and Company for Metropolitan Museum of Art, 1922.

Decatur, Stephen. "Langley Boardman, Portsmouth Cabinetmaker," *American Collector*, VI (May, 1937), 4–5.

Dorman, Charles G. "Delaware Cabinetmakers and Allied Artisans, 1655–1855," *Delaware History*. Wilmington, Delaware, 1960.

Dow, George Francis. *The Arts and Crafts in New England, 1704–1775*. Topsfield, Massachusetts: The Wayside Press, 1927.

Downs, Joseph. "Derby and McIntire," *Bulletin of the Metropolitan Museum of Art*, VI (October, 1947), 73–81.

——. "Two Looking Glasses Made by W. Wilmerding," *Antiques*, XLIX (May, 1946), 299.

"The Editor's Attic: Forster of Charlestown," *Antiques*, XVI (December, 1929), 481.

Fales, Dean A., Jr. "The Furniture of McIntire," *Samuel McIntire, A Bicentennial Symposium, 1757–1957*. Salem: The Essex Institute, 1957.

"The Furnishing of Richmond Hill in 1797, The Home of Aaron Burr in New York City," *Quarterly Bulletin* of the New-York Historical Society, XI (April, 1927), 17.

Garrett, Wendell D. "The Newport Cabinetmakers: A Corrected Check List," *Antiques*, LXXIII (June, 1958), 558 to 561.

[Gottesman], Rita Susswein (comp.). *The Arts and Crafts in New York, 1726–1776*. New York: The New-York Historical Society, 1938.

Gottesman, Rita Susswein (comp.). *The Arts and Crafts in New York, 1777–1799*. New York: The New-York Historical Society, 1954.

——. *The Arts and Crafts in New York, 1800–1804*. New York: The New-York Historical Society, 1965.

Goyne, Nancy A. "Furniture Craftsmen in Philadelphia, 1760–1780: Their Role in a Mercantile Society (unpublished Master's Thesis, University of Delaware, 1963).

Heckscher, Morrison H. "The Organization and Practice of Philadelphia Cabinetmaking Establishments, 1790 to 1820" (unpublished Master's Thesis, University of Delaware, 1964).

"Henry Connelly and Ephraim Haines," *Philadelphia Museum Bulletin*, XLVIII (Spring, 1953).

Hornor, W.M., Jr. *Blue Book, Philadelphia Furniture, William Penn to George Washington*. Philadelphia, 1935.

——. "Documented Furniture by Jacob Wayne," *International Studio*, CXVI (June, 1930), 40–43, 82.

——. "George Whitelock of Wilmington," *The Antiquarian*, XIV (January, 1930), 30–31, 80.

——. "Henry Connelly, Cabinet and Chairmaker," *International Studio*, XCIII (May, 1929), 43–46.

——. "James McDowell, a Delaware Cabinetmaker," *The Antiquarian*, XV (November, 1930), 64–67.

——. "A New Estimation of Duncan Phyfe," *The Antiquarian*, XIV (March, 1930), 37–40, 96.

——. "Three Generations of Cabinet Makers. I. Matthew Egerton, 1739–1802," *Antiques*, XIV (September, 1928), 217–219.

——. "Three Generations of Cabinet Makers. II. Matthew

Egerton, Jr., and His Sons," *Antiques*, XIV (November, 1928), 417–421.

Howe, Florence Thompson. "The Decline and Fall of William Lloyd," *Antiques*, VII (February, 1930), 117–121.

Hummel, Charles F. "The Influence of English Design Books upon the Philadelphia Cabinetmakers, 1760–1820" (unpublished Master's Thesis, University of Delaware, 1955).

Hunter, Dard, Jr. "David Evans, Cabinetmaker; His Life and Work" (unpublished thesis, University of Delaware, 1954).

Ingerman, Elizabeth A. "Personal Experiences of an Old New York Cabinetmaker [Ernest Hagen]," *Antiques*, LXXXIV (November, 1963), 576–580.

Johnson, J. Stewart. "New York Cabinetmaking Prior to the Revolution" (unpublished Master's Thesis, University of Delaware, 1964).

Johnson, Marilynn A. "Clockmakers and Cabinetmakers of Elizabethtown, New Jersey, in the Federal Period" (unpublished Master's Thesis, University of Delaware, 1963).

Kihn, Phyllis. "Ruggles and Dunbar, Looking Glass Manufacturers," *Bulletin of the Connecticut Historical Society*, XXV (April, 1960), 56–60.

Kimball, Fiske. "Furniture Carvings by Samuel Field McIntire," *Antiques*, XXIII (February, 1933), 56–58.

——. "Furniture Carvings by Samuel McIntire, I–V," *Antiques*, XVIII (November, 1930), 388–392; XVIII (December, 1930), 498–502; XIX (January, 1931), 30–32; XIX (February, 1931), 116–119; XIX (March, 1931), 207–210.

——. "Salem Furniture Makers: I–III," *Antiques*, XXIV (September, 1933), 90–91 [Nathaniel Appleton, Jr.]; XXIV (December, 1933), 218–220 [Nehemiah Adams]; XXV (April, 1934), 144–146 [William Hook].

——. "Salem Secretaries and Their Makers," *Antiques*, XXIII (May, 1933), 168–170.

LaFond, Edward F., Jr. "The Henry Francis du Pont Winterthur Museum Collection of American Clocks: A Catalogue" (unpublished Master's Thesis, University of Delaware, 1964).

Leibundguth, Arthur W. "The Furniture-Making Crafts in Philadelphia, c. 1730–c. 1760" (unpublished Master's Thesis, University of Delaware, 1963).

Little, Nina Fletcher. "Carved Figures by Samuel McIntire and His Contemporaries," *Samuel McIntire, A Bicentennial Symposium, 1757–1957*. Salem: The Essex Institute, 1957.

McClelland, Nancy V. *Duncan Phyfe and the English Regency, 1795–1830*. New York: W. R. Scott, Inc., 1939.

Monahon, Eleanore Bradford. "Providence Cabinetmakers," *Rhode Island History*, XXIII (January, 1964), 1–22.

Montgomery, Charles F. "John Needles, Baltimore Cabinetmaker," *Antiques*, LXV (April, 1954), 292–295.

Naeve, Milo. "Daniel Trotter and His Ladder-Back Chairs," *Antiques*, LXXVI (November, 1959), 442–445.

Ormsbee, Thomas Hamilton. "Autographed Duncan Phyfe Furniture," *American Collector*, XI (March, 1942), 5.

——. "The Sandersons and Salem Furniture," *American Collector*, VIII (August, 1939), 6–7, 14; (September, 1939), 10–11, 14, 20.

Pearce, Lorraine Waxman. "Distinguishing Characteristics of Lannuier's Furniture," *Antiques*, LXXXVI (December, 1964), 712–717.

[Pearce], Lorraine Waxman. "French Influence on American Decorative Arts of the Early Nineteenth Century: The Work of Charles Honore Lannuier" (unpublished Master's Thesis, University of Delaware, 1958).

——. "The Lannuier Brothers, Cabinetmakers," *Antiques*, LXXII (August, 1957), 141–143.

Prime, Alfred Coxe (comp.). *The Arts and Crafts in Philadelphia, Maryland, and South Carolina, 1721–1785*. Vol. I. Topsfield, Massachusetts: Printed for the Walpole Society at The Wayside Press, 1929.

——. *The Arts and Crafts in Philadelphia, Maryland, and South Carolina, 1786–1800*. Vol. II. Topsfield, Massachusetts: Printed for the Walpole Society at The Wayside Press, 1932.

Quimby, Ian M. G. "Apprenticeship in Colonial Philadelphia" (unpublished Master's Thesis, University of Delaware, 1963).

Randall, Richard H., Jr. "George Bright, Cabinetmaker," *Art Quarterly*, XXVII (No. 2, 1964), 135–149.

——. "Seymour Furniture Problems," *Bulletin of the Boston Museum of Fine Arts*, LVII, No. 310 (1959), 102–113.

——. "Works of Boston Cabinetmakers, 1795–1825," *Antiques*, LXXI (February, 1962), 186–189; (April, 1962), 412–415.

Rippe, Peter M. "Daniel Clay of Greenfield, 'Cabinetmaker'" (unpublished Master's Thesis, University of Delaware, 1962).

Spinney, Frank O. "An Ingenious Yankee Craftsman," *Antiques*, XLIV (September, 1943), 116–119.

Stoneman, Vernon C. *John and Thomas Seymour, Cabinetmakers in Boston, 1794–1816*. Boston: Special Publications, 1959.

——. *A Supplement to John and Thomas Seymour, Cabinetmakers in Boston, 1794–1816*. Boston: Special Publications, 1966.

Swan, Mabel M. "Boston's Carvers and Joiners: II. Post-Revolutionary," *Antiques*, LIII (April, 1948), 281–285.

——. "Furnituremakers of Charlestown," *Antiques*, XLVI (October, 1944), 203–206.

——. "General Stephen Badlam—Cabinet and Looking Glass Maker," *Antiques*, LXV (May, 1954), 380–383.

——. "The Goddard and Townsend Joiners: I–II," *Antiques*, XLIX (April, 1946), 228–321; (May, 1946), 292 to 295.

——. "John Goddard's Sons," *Antiques*, LVII (June, 1950), 448–449.

——. "John Seymour and Son, Cabinetmakers," *Antiques*, XXXII (October, 1937), 176–179.

——. "Major Benjamin Frothingham, Cabinetmaker," *Antiques*, LXII (November, 1952), 392–395.

——. "The Man Who Made Simon Willard's Clock Cases: John Doggett of Roxbury," *Antiques*, XV (March, 1929), 196–200.

——. "McIntire: Check and Countercheck," *Antiques*, XXI (February, 1932), 86–87.

——. "McIntire Vindicated," *Antiques*, XXVI (October, 1934), 130–132.

——. "Newburyport Furnituremakers," *Antiques*, XLVII (April, 1945), 222–225.

——. "A Revised Estimate of McIntire," *Antiques*, XX (December, 1931), 338–343.

——. *Samuel McIntire, Carver, and The Sandersons, Early Salem Cabinet Makers*. Salem, Massachusetts: The Essex Institute, 1934.

——. "Where Elias Hasket Derby Bought His Furniture," *Antiques*, XX (November, 1931), 280–282.

"Thomas Nisbet, Cabinet Maker of Saint John," *Art Bulletin of the New Brunswick Museum* Art Department, I (Fall, 1953).

Warren, Phelps. "Setting the Record Straight: Slover and Taylor, New York Cabinetmakers," *Antiques*, LXXX (October, 1961), 350–351.

## CATALOGUES OF COLLECTIONS

*Antiques*. Special Issues.
*The American Wing of the Metropolitan Museum of Art*. October, 1946.
*[Colonial] Williamsburg*. March, 1953.
*Henry Ford Museum*. February, 1958.
*The Henry Francis du Pont Winterthur Museum*. November, 1951.
*[Old] Deerfield*. September, 1956.
*Old Sturbridge Village*. September, 1955.

*Connecticut Chairs in the Collection of the Connecticut Historical Society.* Hartford, Connecticut, 1956.

*Frederick K. and Margaret R. Barbour's Furniture Collection.* (Connecticut Furniture.) Hartford, Connecticut: The Connecticut Historical Society, 1963.

Hipkiss, Edwin J. *Eighteenth-Century American Arts. The M. and M. Karolik Collection...* Published for the Museum of Fine Arts, Boston, Massachusetts. Cambridge, Massachusetts: Harvard University Press, 1941.

*New York Furniture Before 1840 in the Collection of the Albany Institute of History and Art.* Albany, New York: Institute of History and Art, 1962.

*The White House, an Historic Guide to the White House.* Text by Lorraine Waxman Pearce. Washington, D.C.: White House Historical Association, 1962.

## CATALOGUES OF EXHIBITIONS

*Accessions 1960.* Winterthur, Delaware: The Henry Francis du Pont Winterthur Museum, Inc., 1960.

*Baltimore Furniture; the Work of Baltimore and Annapolis Cabinetmakers from 1760–1810.* Baltimore: Baltimore Museum of Art, 1947.

Biddle, James. *American Art from American Collections.* New York: The Metropolitan Museum of Art, 1963.

*Classical America 1815–1845.* Newark, New Jersey: The Newark Museum, 1963.

*The Decorative Arts of New Hampshire, 1725–1825.* Manchester, New Hampshire: The Currier Gallery of Art, 1964.

Downs, Joseph, and Ralston, Ruth. *A Loan Exhibition of New York State Furniture.* New York: Metropolitan Museum of Art, 1934.

*Early Furniture Made in New Jersey, 1690–1870.* Newark: The Newark Museum, 1958.

Fales, Dean A., Jr. *Essex County Furniture: Documented Treasures from Local Collections, 1660–1860.* Salem, Massachusetts: The Essex Institute, 1965.

*Girl Scouts Loan Exhibition Catalogue.* New York, 1929.

*The Hudson-Fulton Celebration, Catalogue of an Exhibition held in the Metropolitan Museum of Art.* Vol. II. New York, 1909.

*The John Brown House Loan Exhibition of Rhode Island Furniture.* Providence: The Rhode Island Historical Society, 1965.

Miller, V. Isabelle. *Furniture by New York Cabinetmakers, 1650 to 1860.* New York: Museum of the City of New York, 1956.

*Southern Furniture, 1640–1820.* (Virginia Museum of Fine Arts.) New York: Antiques Magazine, 1952.

*Three Centuries of Connecticut Furniture, 1635–1935.* Hartford: Tercentenary Commission of the State of Connecticut, 1935.

White, Margaret E. *Early Furniture Made in New Jersey, 1690 to 1870.* Newark: The Newark Museum, 1958.

## CATALOGUES OF SALES

*John F. Bernard Collection.* Albany, New York, September 14 to 15, 1938.

*Collection of Benjamin Flayderman.* New York: American Art Association, Anderson Galleries, Inc., April 17–18, 1931.

*Collection of the Late Philip Flayderman.* New York: American Art Association, Anderson Galleries, Inc., January 2–4, 1930.

*The Collection of Francis P. Garvan.* New York: American Art Association, Anderson Galleries, Inc., January 8–10, 1931.

*Property of Mr. and Mrs. Norvin H. Green.* New York: Parke-Bernet Galleries, November 29–30, December 1–2, 1950.

*Americana Collection of the Late Mrs. J. Amory Haskell.* Parts I–VI. New York: Parke-Bernet Galleries, Inc., 1944, 1945.

*Collection of Early American and English Furniture... formed by Louis Guerineau Myers.* New York: American Art Association, American Art Galleries, February 24–26, 1921.

*Colonial Furniture, the Superb Collection of the Late Howard Reifsnyder.* New York: American Art Association, Inc., American Art Galleries, April 24–27, 1929.

*Collection of Israel Sack.* New York: American Art Association, Anderson Galleries, Inc., November 7–9, 1929.

*One Hundred Important American Antiques. Collection of Israel Sack.* New York: American Art Association, Anderson Galleries, Inc., January 9, 1932.

*Roland V. Vaughn Private Collection.* New York: American Art Association, Anderson Galleries, Inc., November 14, 1931.

## DESIGN AND PATTERN SOURCES

Ackermann, Robert (ed.). *The Repository of Arts, Literature, Commerce, Manufacture, Fashions and Politics.* London, 1809 to 1828.

Adam, Robert. *The Works in Architecture of Robert and James Adam.* Vols. I–II. London, 1773.

Adam, Robert and James. *The Works in Architecture of Robert and James Adam.* Vol. III. London, 1822.

*The Cabinet-Maker and Upholsterer's Guide* [Hepplewhite's Guide]... *from Drawings by A. Hepplewhite and Co., Cabinet-Makers.* London: I. and J. Taylor, 1788; 2d ed., 1789; 3rd ed., 1794.

Carver, S. H. *Twelve New Designs of Frames for Looking Glasses.* London: I. Taylor, 1779.

Carver, Thomas Pether. *A Book of Ornaments Suitable for Beginners.* London, 1773.

Chippendale, Thomas. *The Gentleman and Cabinet-Maker's Director.* London, 1st ed., 1754; 2d ed., 1755; 3rd ed., 1762.

Gillingham, Harrold E. "Benjamin Lehman, A Germantown Cabinetmaker," *The Pennsylvania Magazine of History and Biography,* LIV (October, 1930), 289–306.

Hope, Thomas. *Household Furniture and Interior Decoration, Executed from Designs by Thomas Hope.* London: Longman, Hurst, Rees and Orme, 1807.

La Mésangère, Pierre (ed.). *Collection de Meubles et Objets de Goût.* Paris: Au Bureau de Journal des Dames, 1802 to 183[?].

Landi, Gaetano. *Architectural Decorations: A Periodical Work of Original Designs...* London, 1810.

Lock, Matthias. *A New Book of Pier-Frame's, Oval's, Gerandole's, Tables &c.* London, 1769.

Nicholson, Peter and Michael Angelo. *The Practical Cabinet Maker, Upholsterer and Complete Decorator.* London: Fisher, 1826.

Percier, Charles, and Fontaine, Pierre F. L. *Recueil de Décorations Intérieures...* Gidot L'aine, 1812.

*Practical Carpentry, Joinery, and Cabinet-Making.* London: Thomas Kelley, 1837.

Sheraton, Thomas. *The Cabinet Dictionary.* London: W. Smith, King Street, 1803.

——. *The Cabinet-Maker and Upholsterer's Drawing Book.* London, 1793; 3rd ed. revised, 1802.

——. *The Cabinet-Maker, Upholsterer and General Artist's Encyclopedia.* London, 1804–1806.

——. *Designs for Household Furniture.* London: J. Taylor, 1812.

Siddons, G. A. *The Cabinet-maker's Guide.* London: Knight and Lacy; Greenfield, Massachusetts: Ansel Phelps, 1825.

Smith, George. *The Cabinet-Maker and Upholsterer's Guide: Being a Complete Drawing Book.* London: Jones and Co., 1826.

——. *A Collection of Designs for Household Furniture and Interior Decoration.* London: J. Taylor, 1808.

——. *A Collection of Ornamental Designs after the Manner of the Antique.* London: J. Taylor, 1812.

Stokes, J. *The Complete Cabinet Maker and Upholsterer's Guide.* London: Dean & Monday, [1829].

Tatum, Charles Heathcote. *Examples of Ancient Ornamental Architecture.* London, 1799.

*Workwoman's Guide.* 2d ed. London and Birmingham, 1840.

## CABINETMAKERS' PRICE BOOKS, ENGLISH AND AMERICAN

### LONDON

*The Cabinet-Makers' London Book of Prices, and Designs of Cabinet Work* (also called *The London Cabinet Book of Prices*). 1788. Revised editions 1793, 1803.

*The Prices of Cabinet Work with Tables and Designs*, London, 1797.

*Supplement to the Cabinet-Makers' London Book of Prices, and Designs of Cabinet-Work*. 1805.

*The London Cabinet-Makers' Union Book of Prices*. 1811. Revised editions 1824, 1836, 1866.

*The London Cabinet-Makers' Union Book of Prices, for Work Not Provided in the Union Book; By a Committee*. 1831.

*The London Cabinet Makers' Book of Prices for Work Not Provided in the Union Book*. 1836.

*The London Cabinet-Makers' Book of Prices, for the Most Improved Extensible Dining Tables*. 1815. Other editions 1821, 1825, 1837, 1866.

*Designs of Ornaments for Cabinet Furniture with Prices*. 1811. Other editions 1821, 1826.

### LONDON (CHAIRMAKERS' PRICE BOOKS)

*The London Chair-Makers' and Carvers' Book of Prices for Workmanship*. 1802. Other editions 1807, 1823.

*Supplement to the London Chair-Makers' and Carvers' Book of Prices for Workmanship*. 1808.

*Second Supplement to the London Chair-Makers' and Carvers' Book of Prices for Workmanship*. 1811.

*Third Supplement to the London Chair-Makers' and Carvers' Book of Prices for Workmanship*. 1844.

### EDINBURGH, GLASGOW, MANCHESTER, NORWICH, NOTTINGHAM

*The Cabinet and Chair Makers' Norwich Book of Prices, 2nd ed.* 1801. Revised and corrected by a Committee of Journeyman Cabinet and Chair Makers.

*The Prices of Cabinetwork agreed by the Master Cabinet-Makers of Nottingham*. 1805.

*The Cabinet-Makers' Manchester Book of Prices*. 1810.

*The Cabinet-makers' Manchester Book of Prices Supplement*. 1825.

*The Glasgow Book of Prices for Manufacturing Cabinet-Work with Various Tables*. 1825.

*Supplement to the Cabinet-Makers Book of Prices. Edinburgh.* 1825.

*The Edinburgh Book of Prices for Manufacturing Cabinet-Work*. 1826.

### UNITED STATES (MISCELLANEOUS)

[Providence] *Rule and Price of Joyners Work—A Table of Joyners Worck*. Agreement of February 19, 1756. Revised Agreement of March 24, 1757.

*A Table of Prices for Cabinetwork in Hartford, Connecticut*. 1792.

*House Joiners and Cabinet Makers. Regulations, Ascertaining the Work and Wages of House Joiners and Cabinet Makers; Agreed Upon at Hatfield in the County of Hampshire, [Massachusetts]*. Printed by William Butler. 1796.

*Regulations Ascertaining the Work and Wages of House-Joiners and Cabinet Makers* (Hatfield, Mass.). Printed by Josiah Fay, Rutland. 1797.

*The Constitution, and Bye-Laws of the United Society of Journeymen, Cabinet and Chair Makers*, Baltimore. Printed by R. J. Matchett. 1817.

*The Cincinnati Cabinet-Makers' Book of Prices for Manufacturing Cabinet-Ware*. Printed for the Cabinet Makers by Whetsone and Buxton Rule. 1830.

*Cabinet Makers of Cincinnati, Book of Prices of the United Society of Journeymen Cabinet Makers of Cincinnati, for the Manufacture of Cabinet Ware*. Printed by N. S. Johnson. 1836.

*The Pittsburgh Cabinet Maker's Book of Prices*. Prepared by a committee appointed by the "Journeymen cabinet makers" of Pittsburgh. 1830.

*Buffalo Society of Journeyman Cabinet Makers. The Buffalo Book of Prices for Manufacturing Cherry and Black Walnut Cabinet Work*. Supplementary to the New-York Book of Prices of 1834. Printed by Steele. 1836.

*Price Book, Indianapolis, Catalogue and Price List for Furniture Manufactured by the Cabinet Makers' Union of Indianapolis, Indiana*. 1887.

### NEW YORK

*The Journeymen Cabinet and Chair Makers' New-York Book of Prices*. Printed by T. & J. Swords. 1796.

*Constitution and Bye Laws of the Mutual Society of Journeymen Cabinet Makers of the City of New York*. Printed by D. Denniston. 1800.

*The New-York Book of Prices for Cabinet & Chair Work agreed upon by the Employers*. Printed by Southwick and Crooker. 1802.

*Constitution and Bye Laws of the Mutual Society of Journeymen Cabinet Makers of the City of New York*. Agreed to January 17, 1804. Printed by W. W. Vermilye. 1804.

*The New-York Revised Prices for Manufacturing Cabinet and Chair Work*. Printed by Southwick and Pelsue. 1810.

*Revised Constitution and Rules of Order of the New-York Society of Cabinet Makers of the City of New York*. Printed by Southwick and Pelsue. 1810.

*Additional Prices Agreed Upon by the New-York Society of Journeymen Cabinet Makers*. 1815.

*Revised Constitution and Rules of Order of the Society of Cabinet Makers of the City of New-York*. Printed by Joseph Desnoues. 1816.

*The New-York Book of Prices for Manufacturing Cabinet and Chair Work*. Printed by J. Seymour. 1817.

*New York Revised Prices for Manufacturing Cabinet and Chair Work*. Printed by Daniel D. Smith. 1818.

*The New-York Book of Prices for Manufacturing Cabinet and Chair Work*. Printed by Harper & Brothers. 1834.

*The New-York Book of Prices for Manufacturing Piano-Fortes*. Printed by The Society. 1835.

### PHILADELPHIA

"Prices of Cabinet and Chair Work." Manuscript list of retail prices and wages to be paid journeymen. Inscribed "Binjamin Lehman, January 1786."

*The Philadelphia Cabinet and Chair-Makers' Book of Prices*. Copyright issued to John Lindsay. 1794.

*Federal Society of Cabinet and Chairmakers, The Philadelphia Cabinet and Chair-Makers' Book of Prices*. Copyright issued to Thomas Timmings, Christopher Appleton and John Gregory for Themselves and on behalf of the Federal Society of Cabinet and Chairmakers, as authors and proprietors, 30, April 1794. No copy known.

*The Journeymen Cabinet and Chair-Makers Philadelphia Book of Prices*. 1795. Second edition, corrected and enlarged.

*The Philadelphia Cabinet and Chair-Makers' Book of Prices*. Printed by Richard Folwell. 1796. Retail prices.

*The Cabinet-Makers Philadelphia and London Book of Prices*. From the Press of Snowden and McCorkle. 1796.

*The Journeymen Cabinet and Chair Makers' Pennsylvania Book of Prices*. Printed for the Society. 1811.

*The Philadelphia Cabinet and Chair Makers' Union Book of Prices for Manufacturing Cabinet Ware*. By a Committee of Employers and Journeymen. Printed for the Cabinet and Chair Makers' by William Stavely. 1828.

## ENGLISH BACKGROUND

Baillie, G. H., Clutton, C., and Ilbert, C. A. *Britten's Old Clocks and Watches and Their Makers*. 7th ed. London: E. F. N. Spon Ltd., 1956.

*The Book of Trades*. London, [after 1851].

*The Connoisseur Period Guides: Late Georgian, 1760–1810*. Edited by Ralph Edwards and L.G.G.Ramsey. New York: Reynal & Company, n.d.

*The Connoisseur Period Guides: Regency, 1810–1830.* Edited by Ralph Edwards and L.G.G.Ramsey. New York: Reynal & Company, 1958.

Edwards, Ralph. *The Dictionary of English Furniture.* 3 vols. London: Country Life, 1953.

——. *The Shorter Dictionary of English Furniture.* London: Country Life, 1964.

Edwards, Ralph, and Jourdain, Margaret. *Georgian Cabinetmakers, c.1700–1800.* London: Country Life, 1955.

Fastnedge, Ralph. *Sheraton Furniture.* London: Faber and Faber, 1962.

Gloag, John. *The English Tradition in Design.* London and New York: King Penguin Books, 1947.

——. *A Short Dictionary of Furniture.* New York: Holt, Rinehart and Winston, 1965.

Harris, Eileen. *The Furniture of Robert Adam.* London: Alec Tiranti, 1963.

Heal, Sir Ambrose. *The London Furniture Makers, From The Restoration to The Victorian Era, 1660–1840.* London: Batsford, 1953.

Jourdain, Margaret. *Regency Furniture 1795–1820.* London: Country Life, 1934.

Lees-Milne, James. *The Age of Adam.* London: Batsford, 1947.

Loudon, J.C. *An Encyclopaedia of Cottage, Farm, and Villa Architecture and Furniture.* London: Longman, Rees, Orme, & Co., 1833 and 1839.

Musgrave, Clifford. *Regency Furniture, 1800 to 1830.* London: Faber and Faber, 1961.

Swarbrick, John. *Robert Adam and His Brothers.* London: Batsford, 1915.

Ward-Jackson, Peter. *English Furniture Designs of the Eighteenth Century.* London: H.M.Stationery Office, 1958.

# *Index*

Caption numbers are in italics;
page numbers are in regular type;
footnotes are designated by the letter n.

Winchell, Orrin G., *fancy and windsor chairmaker, 475*
Wine cooler, 358, *435*
Wingate Family, *former owners, 138*
Wing chairs. *See* Chairs, easy
Wood, David, *clockmaker, 168, 169* clocks, *170* (att.), *171* (labeled)
Woodruff, George, *cabinetmaker,* pembroke table (labeled), *331*
Woods, 27–40
  banding, 33
  birch, 28; figured, 33, *139*
  buttonwood, 28
  charts, 37
  cherry, 28
  curly maple, *210*
  ebony, 33

gumwood, 36
holly, 33
identification of, 27–28
inlays, 32–40; color plates, 30, 31, 34, 35, 38, 39; imports of, 36; shaded, 33, 36; regional use, 30–31, 40
mahogany, 27, 28–29; Honduras, 28; San Domingo, 28
marquetry, 29
oak, 49
ornamental uses, 29–40
poplar. *See* tulip
primary woods, 28–29; table for regional use of, 37
rosewood, imitation of, 475
sales of, 29
satinwood, 29

secondary woods, 29; table, for regional use of, 37; white pine, 29; as regional identification aids, 29, 49
stringing, 29–31, 33–36; color plates 2, 3; patterned, 29; regional use, 36–40
tulip, 28, 29, 37
veneers, 29–33
walnut, 28
white pine, 49
whitewood. *See* tulip
Wool, 41

Yates, Gov. Joseph, *original owner, 4, 63, 64, 235*
Young, Stephen and Moses, *cabinetmakers,* 356 n. 6

WINTERTHUR

ENGRAVED BY CONZETT AND HUBER OF ZURICH—DESIGNED BY ULRICH RUCHTI